Black protest thought
in the twentieth century

Second edition of
Negro protest thought in the twentieth century

THE AMERICAN HERITAGE SERIES

The American Heritage Series

UNDER THE GENERAL EDITORSHIP OF
Leonard W. Levy and Alfred F. Young

Black protest thought in the twentieth century

SECOND EDITION

Edited by

AUGUST MEIER
Kent State University

ELLIOTT RUDWICK
Kent State University

FRANCIS L. BRODERICK
University of Massachusetts

Macmillan Publishing Company
New York
Collier Macmillan Publishers
London

Second Edition
Eleventh Printing — 1987

Library of Congress Catalog Card Number 79-119007
ISBN 0-02-380120-4

Foreword

This is an expanded and revised edition of an anthology that was the first of its kind when it originally appeared in 1965 under the title *Negro Protest Thought in the Twentieth Century.* In our opinion, it remains unique in at least three ways: First, it is a collection in which blacks speak for themselves; all the documents are by American Negroes. Second, the focus is on the organizations that have been the most important vehicles of twentieth-century protest. And third, the selections present programs and philosophy, rather than descriptions of conditions. The emphasis thus is less on "the way things are" than on "the way out."

The main purpose of this new edition is to add a lengthy new section, "The Era of Black Power," with a full array of the exponents and critics of the ideology that dominated the debate of 1965 to 1970. At the same time, about a dozen new documents have been added to earlier sections of the book which otherwise remain more or less intact.

Here, then, as before, one will find representative selections spanning the entire range of twentieth-century protest. Here is the thinking of the giants of the distant past: Booker T. Washington, W. E. B. Du Bois, and Marcus Garvey; of the recent past: Martin Luther King and Malcolm X; and of major, present-day spokesmen: Roy Wilkins, Whitney Young, James Farmer, A. Philip Randolph, Bayard Rustin, and Huey Newton. A large number of their well-known speeches and essays are here. But for them, as for the less famous, selections are also chosen from out-of-the-way material often lost to the historical record, such as convention declarations, pamphlets, interviews, and debates.

Whatever the purpose the reader brings to the book, the anthology conveys a remarkable sense of historical perspective. For any one period of the twentieth century, one can compare points of view on the entire spectrum of protest. Then, as one moves from period to period, one can trace the response to new challenges, often by the same men, sometimes by their ideological descendants. The result is a sense both of the continuity of ideologies—legalism, black nationalism, economic radicalism— as well as of the way in which the axis of debate has shifted to make yesterday's "radicals" today's "conservatives."

The first edition of this book was edited by Francis L. Broderick and August Meier, the second, by Meier with Elliott Rudwick. As scholars, they have been recognized by their colleagues, black and white, for their mastery of a wide range of subjects central to this book. Broderick and Rudwick each have written a biography of W. E. B. Du Bois: Broderick, a study of reconstruction and the Negro; Meier, a study of Negro thought in the age of Booker T. Washington; Rudwick, an analysis of the famous East Saint Louis riots; Meier and Rudwick together, a widely used interpretative history of the Negro.

Within the American Heritage Series, this volume takes its place alongside a number of volumes in print or in preparation, which together will give a comprehensive documentation of black history. These include volumes on slavery, anti-slavery thought, reconstruction, black thought in the nineteenth century, and black nationalism. Other volumes in the series— whether on the American Revolution, Abraham Lincoln, the New Deal, nonviolence, or the Supreme Court—give to black history the attention that has so often been missing in the general treatment of American history.

The series as a whole was created to provide the essential primary sources of the American experience, especially of American thought. It constitutes a documentary library of American history, filling a need long felt among scholars, students, libraries, and general readers for authoritative collections of original materials. Some volumes illuminate the thought of significant individuals, such as James Madison or John Marshall; some deal with movements, such as the Antifederalist or the

Populist; others are organized around special themes, such as Puritan political thought or American Catholic thought on social questions. Many volumes take up the large number of subjects traditionally studied in American history for which surprisingly there are no documentary anthologies; others pioneer in introducing new subjects of increasing importance to scholars and to the contemporary world. The series aspires to maintain the high standards demanded of contemporary editing, providing authentic texts, intelligently and unobtrusively edited. It also has the distinction of presenting pieces of substantial length which give the full character and flavor of the original. The series is, we believe, the most comprehensive and authoritative of its kind.

Alfred F. Young
Leonard W. Levy

Contents

PART ONE

from accommodation
to protest

PART TWO

the era of legalism

PART THREE

the era of nonviolent direct action

PART FOUR

the era of Black Power

Critiques of Black Power

Introduction

I.

Black protest in the United States extends back to the slave revolts and the activities of the free people of color in the generations before the Civil War. But the dramatic developments of the 1960s stem from the work of the organizations that arose in opposition to the ideology of accommodation to white supremacy, which was in the ascendancy among Negroes at the beginning of the twentieth century. The purpose of this volume is to assemble representative expressions of the major trends of this twentieth-century protest. Because this protest has been articulated primarily through organizations, our focus is on the philosophies, tactics, and strategies of the many groups involved in the protest movement.

Protest thought evolved against the background of the changing status of the blacks in twentieth-century society. For the black man, the century opened amid mounting oppression and discrimination, which had begun with the close of Reconstruction. For a quarter of a century after the founding of the NAACP in 1909, Afro-Americans were aided by a small but growing number of whites who displayed increasing interest in the Negro's civil rights. In the last generation, roughly since the days of the New Deal, Negroes and an increasing number of white supporters have stepped up the pace of improvement in the Negro's position in American society.

Demographic changes have also been an important part of the context in which twentieth-century black protest developed. It is noteworthy that the twentieth-century protest movement has been preeminently urban. At the opening of the century Negroes were 75 percent rural, and nine-tenths of them lived in the South. Nevertheless until mid-century the base of black protest lay principally in northern cities where Negroes enjoyed greater freedom of action. Beginning with World War I black people have moved in growing numbers to the North, and to the cities of both regions, so that today three-quarters of them are urban, and about one-half live outside of the old slave states. One concomitant of the migration has been the mounting strength of the black vote in the northern cities, which served as a vital element in drawing the federal government into defense of civil rights and making it more responsive to the needs of the black masses. As black protest rose in the South after the second World War, it was again centered principally in the cities. Today rural Negroes in the South still suffer from enormous disabilities because of their race, but the major unsolved problems now facing Negroes stem from discrimination embedded in urban patterns of housing, employment and education. And the urban ghetto, rather than the rural black belt of Alabama or Mississippi, is the base upon which the advocates of black power must work if their tactics are to prove successful.

Over the years the character of black protest has changed. Broadly speaking—and at the risk of oversimplification—one can detect certain major themes. What was once a liberal white and Negro upper-class movement has become a completely black-led and largely working-class movement. There have been shifts in strategy from verbal agitation, legislation and court litigation aimed at securing the black man's constitutional rights, to emphasis on direct-action techniques, and finally to mobilizing the potential power of the masses in the ghettos along political and economic lines. When, in the 1960s, the nation moved closer toward protecting the rights guaranteed by the Constitution, goals were redefined, and the Negro protest organizations went beyond constitutional rights to demand special efforts to overcome the poverty of the black masses.

Traditionally, and even now, the central thrust of black protest has always struck at discrimination and segregation; the central demand has always been for equal treatment with other citizens. Yet a salient characteristic of twentieth-century Negro protest has been an extraordinary amount of controversy within

the black community over the tactics and strategies to follow—
a nearly constant warring between "radicals" and "conservatives." Over the years, as conditions changed, definitions of
these two terms and the contents of the argument have naturally
shifted. Early in the century active propaganda, legal action,
and lobbying for legislation were considered radical techniques,
for they contrasted sharply with the soothing, soft words of the
accommodationists. Nowadays, agitation for racial equality has
so changed that these tactics are regarded as conservative. The
radical banner was taken over by the advocates of direct action
techniques such as sit-ins, picketing and boycotts, and, in the
mid-1960s by the advocates of "Black Power," militant separatism, and black revolution. This counterpoint of "radical" and
"conservative" has been so pervasive in the dialogue over Negro
strategies and tactics during the past two generations, that the
dynamic course of the twentieth-century protest can be understood only in terms of it. Yet "radical" is of course a relative
term; and indeed the central theme of black protest, aiming
at the inclusion of Negroes in American society on a basis of full
equality, rather than aiming at a radical transformation of that
society, is not truly radical at all.

Two other themes weave in and out of the blacks' protest:
economic radicalism and nationalist radicalism. Among economic radicals, Marxist and non-Marxist, only democratic socialists have been a consistently important force in the civil
rights movement since early in the century. Typically the economic radicals regard capitalism as the source of racial prejudice and discrimination, for they feel that white capitalists
play black workers against white workers in order to exploit
them both. Marxists go one step further: Only a socialized
economy can end the Negro's second-class citizenship. The contribution of democratic socialists in the whole movement has
tended to go unrecognized, because they have usually focused
on immediate steps forward rather than on the longer-range,
socialist goals.

Nationalist radicalism is vastly more complex, because its
roots are twisted in the gnarled ambivalence toward race and

nation that discrimination has produced in the attitudes of black Americans, and because it can function as an ideology either of protest or accommodation. Negroes wish to be accepted as Americans, yet they are forced into an ethnocentric loyalty to the black race. Blacks basically wish to participate in the American social structure, but alienation forces them to reject it. W. E. B. Du Bois, the most influential black voice of protest in our century, expressed this ethnic dualism most cogently:

> . . . One ever feels his two-ness—an American, a Negro; two souls, two thoughts, two unreconciled strivings; two warring ideals in one dark body. . . . The history of the American Negro is the history of this strife,—this longing to attain self-conscious manhood, to merge his double self into a better and truer self. He would not Africanize America, for America has too much to teach the world and Africa. He would not bleach his soul in a flood of white Americanism, for he knows that Negro blood has a message for the world. He simply wishes to make it possible for a man to be both a Negro and an American, without being cursed and spit upon by his fellows, without having the door of opportunity closed roughly in his face.[1]

In no case have black men, even those completely favoring integration and assimilation, been able to forget their connection with an oppressed group. From this very alienation came the thrust for separate institutions operated without white interference, such as the church and the mutual benefit society, calls for race pride and a cultural pluralism, and most recently the demands of the black power advocates. The gap between ideal and practice in American society has meant that Negroes not only wanted to be a part of that society, but that they also found it desirable to develop their own group life within it.

The blacks' sense of racial identity ranges widely in scope and intensity. Spokesmen for diverse views—from assimilation-

[1] W. E. B. Du Bois, *The Souls of Black Folk* (Chicago: A. C. McClurg and Co., 1903), pp. 3–4.

ists to separatists, from accommodationists to militants—believe
in stimulating the study of black history. Among those who
stress integration, some advocate cultural assimilation with
white American society and some support the maintenance of
separate but cooperating strands of white and black culture,
each enriching American culture in its own way (cultural
pluralism). The doctrine of self-help and racial solidarity, of Negroes elevating themselves and advancing their cause through
concerted group action, has been widely voiced in periods of
greatest frustration and discouragement. This doctrine, employed by both accommodators and militants, has been most
often associated with economic nationalism—the belief that
Negroes can solve their problems by supporting black business
and developing their own separate business institutions. It has
also characterized certain protest groups, ranging from the
Afro-American Council at the turn of the century, to the proponents of Black Power in the 1960s. Some political extremists,
seeing no future for Negroes in the United States, ask that territory within the United States be set aside for them; or they
advocate colonization in Latin America or, more commonly, in
Africa.

There are further complexities. Because of the ethnic ambivalence of American Negroes, race pride, economic nationalism,
self-help, and racial solidarity have usually been advocated as
leading toward ultimate acceptance of black men in American
society on a basis of equality—rather than leading toward permanent separation. These same ethnocentric sentiments have
been associated with philosophies for racial advancement which
in other respects are highly diverse. Thus the great antagonists
of the first part of the century, the conservative accommodator
Booker T. Washington and the radical protest leader W. E. B.
Du Bois, both advocated race pride, self-help, racial solidarity,
and black support of black business (or what Du Bois called the
development of a "group economy"). And the same things have
been advocated by extreme nationalists such as Marcus Garvey
and the Nation of Islam, who were disdainful of the goal of both

Washington and Du Bois—an integrated, racially egalitarian society.[2]

These principal themes—the demand for full rights as citizens, economic radicalism, and black nationalism—have been used in a bewildering variety of combinations. Yet they supply generally useful focuses for analyzing black protest.

II.

As the nineteenth century drew to a close, the Negro's position in American society was declining steadily. Disfranchisement, lynchings, jim crow laws, and farm tenancy were the Negroes' lot in the South. Throughout the country labor unions excluded them from the skilled trades. After 1900 race riots became a commonplace in both North and South, with Negroes as victims of what were essentially pogrom-like mob attacks upon the black minority. Under these conditions protest and agitation waned, and a philosophy of accommodation gained the upper hand. The most prominent representative of this trend was Booker T. Washington, principal of the Tuskegee Institute in Alabama. Between his famous Atlanta Exposition Address in 1895 and his death in 1915 Washington was the most prominent

[2] Gunnar Myrdal, noting the ethnic ambivalence and instability of black ideologies, described the situation perceptively. Observing that to a large degree Negroes are "denied identification with the nation," he continued: "to them social speculation, therefore, moves in a sphere of unreality and futility. Instead of organized popular theories or ideas, the observer finds in the Negro world, for the most part, only a *fluid and amorphous mass of all sorts of embryos of thoughts. Negroes seem to be held in a state of eternal preparedness for a great number of contradictory opinions*—ready to accept one type or another depending on how they are driven by pressures or where they see an opportunity. Under such circumstances, the masses of Negroes might, for example, rally around a violently anti-American, anti-Western, anti-White, black chauvinism of the Garvey type, centered around the idea of Africa as the mother country. But they might just as likely, if only a slight change of stimulus is provided, join in an all-out effort to fight for their native country . . . for the Western Civilization to which they belong, and for the tenets of democracy in the entire world. . . . Or they might develop a passive cynicism toward it all." From Gunnar Myrdal, *An American Dilemma* (New York: Harper and Row, 1944), p. 782.

black man in America. Though he covertly spent thousands of
dollars fighting disfranchisement and segregation laws, he publicly advocated a policy of conciliation and gradualism. Largely
blaming black people themselves for their condition, and describing the southern white man as the Negro's "best friend,"
he minimized the extent of racial prejudice and discrimination, accepted segregation and the separate-but-equal doctrine,
deprecated political activity, favored vocational training and
working with the hands at the expense of higher education and
the professions, and recommended economic accumulation and
the cultivation of Christian character as the best methods for
advancing the status of blacks in America. By helping themselves, by proving their usefulness to society through the
acquisition of wealth and morality, Negroes, he believed, would
earn the respect of the white man and thus eventually gain
recognition of their constitutional rights. Washington's ultimate
aims were stated so vaguely and ambiguously that southern
whites mistook his means for his ends. But his black supporters
understood that through tact and indirection he hoped to secure
the good will of white men and the ultimate recognition of the
blacks' citizenship rights (see Documents 1 and 2).

There was another side to the emphasis that Washington and
other accommodators placed upon Negroes helping themselves.
They advocated racial unity—or racial solidarity as it was called
at the time—especially in economic matters. They maintained
that it was essential for black people to support black business
in order to advance the race to the point where it would be respected by whites. While holding Negroes themselves largely
responsible for their lowly status, they advocated racial pride
and held that black people could shape their own destiny in
America. By helping themselves, and organizing to help each
other, they would advance the race and achieve equality in
American society. Thus their separatist ideology functioned
both as a mechanism of accommodation to American racism
and as a device for overcoming it (see Document 3).

Despite Washington's prominence, black protest, though
temporarily muted, did not completely disappear. The media

of mass communication, and the public at large, both black and
white, regarded the Montgomery, Alabama bus boycott of 1955–
1956 as a radical innovation. But at the opening of the century
Negroes conducted boycotts of trolley-car segregation in nearly
thirty southern cities, in protest against jim crow arrangements
then being introduced in state after state throughout the South.
Curiously, these boycotts were ordinarily led by some of the
most conservative members of the black community—businessmen and clerics who were often close friends of the accommodator Booker T. Washington. Trolley-car boycotts were a
"conservative" protest movement. They were "conservative" in
the generic sense that they attempted to preserve the status quo
against a radical change pushed by lower-class whites. They
were also "conservative" as a form of protest because they constituted a withdrawal, avoiding rather than precipitating a
confrontation with the racist whites. It is undoubtedly for these
reasons that this widespread protest movement, unsuccessful
though it was, occurred at all in a period of severe racial oppression and concomitant Negro accommodation in the South (see
Document 4).

After the turn of the century accommodation and separatism
were also challenged by a small band of militant black intellectuals. Led by the noted scholar and professor at Atlanta University, W. E. B. Du Bois, they formed in 1905 the all-black
Niagara Movement to oppose Washington's program, which
they denounced as a failure. On nearly every issue they stood
in direct contrast to Washington. In sharp language, the Niagara
group placed full responsibility for the race problem squarely
on the whites. They denounced the iniquities of segregation,
the separate-but-equal doctrine, and the disfranchisement laws.
They maintained that economic progress was not possible in a
democratic society without the protection afforded by the ballot, and insisted above all that Negroes could gain their rights
only by agitation and complaint. Partly because of Washington's
vigorous opposition, his critics in the Niagara Movement accomplished little. But these militant black integrationists were significant because they spoke out against accommodation and

black separatism at a time when nearly all influential whites and the most powerful among the Negro leaders endorsed these ideals as the appropriate solution for the race problem in America (see Documents 5, 6, 7, 9).

Ardent integrationists though they were, it should be noted that some of the black "radicals," as they were called in contrast to the "conservative" followers of Booker T. Washington, were themselves advocates of self-help and racial solidarity. This was particularly true of Du Bois. As early as the 1890s he had advocated "Pan-Negroism"—that sense of identity with Africa and black men everywhere that is today called "Pan-Africanism." He was a prominent leader in the first Pan-African Conference held in 1900 and in the five later Pan-African Congresses held between 1919 and 1945 (see Document 8). Moreover, like Washington he advocated black economic nationalism, or what he called the creation of a "group economy." Where Washington, however, spoke of developing "captains of industry," Du Bois's vision shifted from capitalism to the advocacy of a socialist system of producers' and consumers' cooperatives. In fact, Du Bois and several of the other radicals were strongly influenced by socialist doctrines (see Document 10).

Despite all of Washington's efforts to crush them, these black radicals carried the message of protest and the demand for integration to prominent white Progressives and Socialists. Together, in 1909–1910, they formed the National Association for the Advancement of Colored People, with the announced goal of fighting for the black man's constitutional rights and the undeclared aim of curbing Booker T. Washington's power (see Document 11). Though the founders of the NAACP regarded themselves as the spiritual heirs of the abolitionists, they really owed more to the reform impulse of the Progressive Movement, then at its height. The attitudes of Progressives on the subject of race ranged from profound prejudice to sincere equalitarianism, but an influential minority among them was deeply concerned that oppressed Negroes should be included in the program of reform. Given the context of the times, it was the wealth, prominence, and influence of this small band of concerned whites that made it possible for the radical Negroes to push their program with some degree of effectiveness. From the start the NAACP branches were typically black both in members and leaders; but at the national headquarters Du Bois, as editor of *The Crisis* (see Document 12) and director of research, was the only black executive until James Weldon Johnson became the association's secretary in 1921. The legal work was handled mainly by volunteer white attorneys until 1935 when Charles Houston became chief counsel. Today, all of the national staff but two are Negroes, as is the overwhelming majority of the national board of directors.

It is very difficult today, with the NAACP under attack as gradualist and conservative, to understand that in 1910 contemporaries regarded its position on the race question as exceedingly radical. Through propaganda and publicity, through litigation in the courts and lobbying in the legislatures, the NAACP hoped to topple the edifice of discrimination. Almost at the outset of its career, the NAACP convinced the Supreme Court to declare unconstitutional two discriminatory statutes. In 1915, the Court overruled the "grandfather clause," a provision in several southern state constitutions that, in effect, disfranchised Negroes by excluding from the vote those whose ancestors were ineligible to cast ballots in 1860. In 1917, the Court outlawed municipal residential segregation ordinances. Thus were taken the first legal steps in the lengthy struggle against disfranchisement and segregation.

Articulate Negroes in the era of Booker T. Washington vacillated and only gradually moved toward the "radical" camp. Gradualism, conciliation, cultivation of the middle-class virtues, racial solidarity, self-help, cultural pluralism, and sympathy for Washington tended to cluster together to form what at the time was regarded as a "conservative," Tuskegee point of view. Agitation for civil rights; advocacy of immediate and complete integration, even assimilation; interest in the labor movement and in socialism; and opposition to the Tuskegeean view tended to cluster together to form a "radical" NAACP outlook. The lines were never clear, however. Most articulate black people located themselves somewhere between the two extremes. Many changed their minds from time to time. Among the radicals only a few were interested in socialism or in labor solidarity across racial lines; most radicals stressed the frugal virtues and the importance of wealth, and some—most notably Du Bois himself—were cultural pluralists. Yet, for all the oscillation, the years recorded a steady drift toward the radicals. In 1916, soon after Booker T. Washington's death, the Amenia Conference, attended by representatives of all points of view, reached virtual unanimity on certain principles: the desirability of all types of education, the importance of the ballot, and the necessity of substituting mutual good faith for time-worn feuds (see Document 13). Then, in the very same year, the NAACP played an ironic masterstroke. It appointed the author and diplomat James Weldon Johnson, one of the most capable figures in Booker T. Washington's circle, its national organizer.

III.

Between the two World Wars, and well into the 1950s, the NAACP program (see Document 14) was in the ascendancy. The Association gained strength from the large numbers of southern Negroes who had migrated to northern cities, and from a small but growing black bourgeoisie of professionals and businessmen who served them. During the first World War the northward migration of southern black people reached major proportions. Disastrous floods and the spread of the boll weevil created economic misery in the rural South; at the same time war industries beckoned from the North. The North did not prove to be the promised land anticipated by the migrants, for the new urban slum dwellers faced frightfully overcrowded and deteriorated housing and, once the war ended, mass unemployment and a wave of race riots that swept the country from Washington, D.C. to Chicago. Still the Great Migration continued.

The growing black bourgeoisie, its income drawn chiefly from the ghettos developing in the northern urban centers, became increasingly militant, eschewed dependence on whites, and inculcated a sense of racial pride. The twenties were in fact the heyday of a militant economic nationalism, an ideology that gained all the greater force because of the decline of the older business and professional upper class that had depended mostly on white customers. Contemporaries spoke confidently of a "New Negro"—race-proud, self-reliant, militant, believing in racial cooperation and self-help and determined to fight for his constitutional rights. Writers and artists of the movement known as the "Harlem Renaissance" reflected this same spirit in their use of the Negro's own cultural tradition and experiences as materials for their works (see Documents 17, 18).

The NAACP depended on this new militancy; at the same time, it was in part responsible for it. The Association did extraordinary service, giving legal defense to victims of race riots and unjust judicial proceedings. It obtained the release of the soldiers who had received life sentences on charges of rioting against intolerable conditions in Houston in 1917. It successfully defended Negro sharecroppers in Elaine, Arkansas, who in 1919 had banded together to gain fairer treatment, had become the objects of a massive armed hunt by whites to put them "in their place," then faced charges of insurrection when they resisted. With the help of Clarence Darrow, it secured the acquittal of Dr. Ossian Sweet and his family who had moved into a white neighborhood in Detroit, shot at the mob attacking their home, killed a man, and eventually obtained the judgment of having committed the act in self-defense. A major effort of the NAACP during the 1920s was to secure passage of an anti-lynching bill. Though the law was not enacted, the NAACP rallied a great deal of public support, and the number of lynchings gradually declined in the nation.

In the long run the most important of the NAACP's activities was the litigation designed to secure the enforcement of the Fourteenth and Fifteenth Amendments. It continued the battle against disfranchisement and residential segregation. With the outlawing of municipal residential segregation ordinances in 1917, white property-owners and realtors retreated behind other subterfuges, particularly restrictive covenants, under which homeowners' associations excluded blacks through agreements among themselves. The decade of the 1920s saw the beginning of the lengthy legal battle against this form of jim crowism. At the same time the NAACP embarked upon the almost endless fight against the white primaries. The Association, despite its immediatist philosophy, was compelled to use an essentially gradualist approach, attacking one small aspect of discrimination at a time, hacking away piece by piece at the structure of discrimination. Though recognition of the Negroes' constitutional rights was still a long way off, the NAACP could at least point to a corpus of definite accomplishment. Less successful, however, were the attempts to prevent the development of school segregation in a number of northern cities. Gerrymanders of school boundaries and other devices initiated by boards of education were fought with written petitions, verbal protests to school officials, legal suits, and in several cities school boycotts. But in the end all proved to be of no avail.

The Association, regarded as radical during the ascendancy of Booker T. Washington, after World War I found itself in the curious position of being classed as a conservative organization by militant Marxists and nationalists. In the socialist *Messenger* magazine, A. Philip Randolph, its editor, even roasted Du Bois as a political opportunist and a "handkerchief head . . . hat-in-hand" Negro. *The Messenger* condemned the NAACP as basically a middle-class organization oblivious to pressing economic problems. Taking a Marxist position on the causes of prejudice and discrimination, Randolph called for a new and radical black man unafraid to demand his rights as a member of the working class. He advocated physical resistance to white mobs, and he believed that only united action of black and white workers against capitalists would achieve social justice (see Document 15).

Although Randolph addressed himself to the urban masses, few of them knew or understood the intellectual theories of *The Messenger*, which circulated chiefly among elite Negroes. The one man who really reached the frustrated and disillusioned residents in the northern ghettos was a Jamaican citizen, Marcus Garvey. Garvey, founder in 1914 of the Universal Negro Improvement Association, aimed to liberate both African and American Negroes from their oppressors. His utopian means of accomplishing both goals was the wholesale migration of American Negroes to Africa. He contended that whites would always be racist and insisted that the Negro must develop "a distinct racial type of civilization of his own and . . . work out his salvation in his motherland. . . ." On a more practical level he urged Negroes to support black businesses, and the UNIA itself organized a chain of groceries, restaurants, laundries, a hotel, and a printing plant. Thousands bought stock in the UNIA's Black Star Steamship Line, which proposed to establish a commercial link between the United States, the West Indies, and Africa. Garvey's followers proudly waved the association's flag (black for Negro skin, green for Negro hopes, and red for Negro blood) and sang the UNIA anthem, "Ethiopia, Thou Land of Our Fathers." Stressing race pride, Garvey gloried in the African past and taught that God and Christ were black.

Garvey condemned the light-skinned, integrationist, upper-class Negroes active in the NAACP for being ashamed of their black ancestry and desiring to amalgamate with the white race. He insisted that the UNIA was the only agency able to protect the darker-skinned Negro masses against the Du Bois-led "caste aristocracy" of college graduates. Thus while *The Messenger* denounced Du Bois as a cowardly, renegade socialist, Garvey charged him with preferring white men to black. In turn both *The Messenger* and *The Crisis* joined in denouncing Garvey. The established Negro leaders resented and feared the "provisional President of the African Republic" and several of them called the attention of the United States government to irregularities in the management of the Black Star Line. Once Garvey had been jailed and then deported on charges of using the mails to defraud, the movement collapsed. But Garvey dramatized as never before the bitterness and alienation of the black slum dwellers who, having come North to seek the Promised Land, found only overcrowded and deteriorated housing, mass unemployment, and race riots (see Document 16).

Regardless of Randolph's and Garvey's castigation of the NAACP, the true conservatives of the era between the two World Wars counseled gradualism and tactful moral suasion as the most expedient way to attain racial justice. This approach was best represented by the National Urban League, founded about the same time as the NAACP, by whites and blacks sympathetic toward Booker T. Washington. The League attained only modest success, even during the prosperous 1920s, in seeking jobs for black migrants to the cities. It used arguments that appealed to the white businessman's sense of economic self-interest as well as to his conscience.

IV.

Despite the contributions of the NAACP and the interest of philanthropic whites in the Urban League and Harlem Renaissance during the 1920s, it was only during the 1930s that a clear-cut reversal in the attitudes of white Americans started to become evident. The New Deal marked a turning point in American race relations, although its programs were not free of discrimination. Federal housing policies expanded urban ghettos; the Agricultural Adjustment Administration subsidized white landowners, while crop restrictions forced many Negro sharecroppers off the land. Nevertheless, black people shared in relief, jobs, and public housing, and black leaders, who felt the open sympathy of many highly placed New Dealers, held more prominent political positions than at any time since President Taft's administration. The concern of people like Eleanor Roosevelt and Secretary of Interior Harold Ickes was part of the larger humanitarian interest in the welfare of the underprivileged in American society. At the same time, the black vote had reached sizeable proportions in many northern cities, creating an additional motivation for the attention to Negro welfare among New Deal politicians. By 1936, Negroes had deserted their traditional allegiance to the Republican party. Finally, the emergence of the Congress of Industrial Organizations, which attempted to erase racial discrimination, gave some substance to the dream of an alliance of black and white workers for the first time since the decline of the Knights of Labor nearly a half century earlier.

The depression, the New Deal, and the CIO together produced in the black protest movement a greater concern with economic problems. For example, blacks staged "Don't Buy Where You Can't Work" campaigns in a number of cities, boycotting and picketing commercial establishments owned by whites that depended on the Negro market (see Document 19).

Various forms of economic radicalism had considerable vogue. Communist influence affected the thinking of many Negroes; its extent was difficult to measure, but in any case it converted only a handful (see Documents 20, 21, 27). More significantly, many intellectuals and labor leaders, aware of the overwhelming importance of economic problems and hopeful because of the CIO, argued anew that Negroes could hope to attain equality in American society only through an alliance with white labor (see Documents 22, 26, and 35).

Massive unemployment and the general radicalization of American thinking during the 1930s led to bitter attacks on the NAACP's program. Du Bois resigned as editor of *The Crisis* in 1934 largely because he became convinced that the NAACP was so identified with the black bourgeoisie that it would continue protesting disfranchisement and segregation without pursuing basic economic goals. Du Bois, furthermore, had never given up completely his belief in the value of collective racial economic endeavor. His ardent advocacy of a separate black cooperative economy as a solution to the problems posed by the depression led to a clash with those who backed the NAACP's traditional position of opposing any form of segregation, and resulted not only in his withdrawal from his position with the NAACP, but also, as a consequence, in his withdrawal from a position of effective leadership (see Document 23). Younger critics of the NAACP such as Abram L. Harris and Ralph

Bunche, then professors at Howard University, also assailed the Association for its gradualism and its blindness to the problems of the masses (see Documents 22, 26). Under these pressures, the organization not only spent much effort attacking discrimination in New Deal agencies, but by the end of the decade came out in full support of the new interracial industrial unions (see Documents 25, 28).

Moreover, in the favorable atmosphere of the 1930s the NAACP broadened the scope of its legal work (see Documents 24, 28). Despite a serious legal setback the NAACP continued its attack, begun in the 1930s, on the white primaries; ultimately (in 1944) the Supreme Court handed down a decision that ended southern subterfuge on that issue. But the core of NAACP legal strategy in the 1930s was the long-range battle against segregation. For tactical reasons the chief emphasis was placed upon educational discrimination. The strategy adopted was to attack the obvious inequities—the lower salaries paid black teachers and the absence of graduate and professional schools for Negroes in southern states. By this indirect attack the Association hoped that segregation would become so expensive and burdensome that it would fall of its own weight. Not until about 1950 did the Association decide to attack directly the principle of segregation in the schools, on the grounds that segregated facilities were inherently unequal.

V.

The changes in white attitudes that began with the New Deal accelerated during and after World War II. Thoughtful whites had been painfully aware of the contradiction in opposing Nazi racial philosophy while doing nothing about racism at home. The revolution against western imperialism in Asia and Africa brought new respect for the nonwhite peoples of the world. American racial attitudes liberalized in large part because new nonwhite nations emerged and took increasing responsibilities in international councils. Moreover, Negroes benefited from the Cold War, since the Russians raised the issue of American racism to embarrass the country in the eyes of the world.

While the NAACP was continuing its traditional legalism (see Documents 34 and 36), the early part of World War II witnessed two new movements that anticipated later developments: the March on Washington Movement and the Congress of Racial Equality (CORE). In 1941 A. Philip Randolph, president of the Brotherhood of Sleeping Car Porters, threatened a mass march on Washington unless President Roosevelt secured employment for blacks in the discriminatory defense industries. The President's Executive Order 8802 establishing a federal Fair Employment Practices Commission forestalled the demonstration. Even without enforcement powers, the FEPC set a precedent for treating fair employment practice as a civil right. The short-lived March on Washington Movement prefigured future trends as an explicitly all-black organization basing its strategy on mass action by the urban slum dwellers and concentrating on economic problems (see Document 29).

Randolph's approach was greatly influenced by the tactics of Gandhi's movement of nonviolent resistance in India, as was his postwar campaign against jim crow in the armed services (see Document 38). But it was CORE that was chiefly responsible for projecting the use of nonviolent direct action as a civil rights strategy. CORE's origins lie in the activities of the Fellowship of Reconciliation (FOR), a Christian pacifist organization founded during the first World War. Certain leaders of the FOR, interested in the use of nonviolent direct action to fight racial discrimination, founded CORE in 1942 with the hope of enlisting persons whose major concern was in race relations instead of pacifism. CORE combined Gandhi's techniques with the sit-in, derived from the sit-down strikes of the 1930s. Until about 1959, CORE's main activity was attacking discrimination in places of public accommodation in the cities of the northern and border states. A cornerstone of its philosophy was that American racism could be destroyed only through an interracial movement. It was thoroughly interracial, even "color-blind" in its internal operations; as late as 1961, two-thirds of its membership and the majority of its national officers were white. Although CORE affiliates employed direct-action techniques like the sit-in more than any other group, they were not alone. Certain NAACP college and youth groups used this tactic from time to time—one instance occurring as early as 1944 (see Documents 30–33).

In the new postwar contest, the campaign for black rights gained new strength. The political impact of the heavy black migration to northern and western cities now became evident. The growing black vote made civil rights a major issue in national elections, was a critical factor in the reelection of Truman in 1948 (see Document 37) and the subsequent desegregation of the armed forces, and ultimately led to the establishment of a federal Civil Rights Commission in 1957. The NAACP and other organizations campaigned successfully in a number of northern and western states for laws guaranteeing fair-employment practices, equal access to public accommodations, and nondiscriminatory housing. The NAACP, piling up victory after victory in the courts, successfully attacked racially restrictive covenants in housing, segregation in interstate transportation, and discrimination in publicly owned recreational facilities. *Brown v. Board of Education* in 1954 brought to a triumphant conclusion the legal campaign of NAACP against educational segregation in public schools of the South. Meanwhile, the Association's membership rolls filled with urban working-class Negroes and, in the rural South, with relatively poor black farmers and even sharecroppers. Its program broadened, although not as extensively as its membership. It conducted drives to register voters, and it established housing and labor departments. Basically, the NAACP was expanding its work along the legal and legislative lines it had employed in earlier years (see Document 39).

CORE, by mid-century, was embarking upon demonstrations in the border states. Public accommodations were still its major target. CORE also began experimenting with direct action, including the boycott, to open up opportunities for industrial employment. And as early as 1947, CORE, in cooperation with FOR, had conducted a "Journey of Reconciliation"—or what would later be called a "Freedom Ride"—in the upper South. Its purpose was to test compliance with the *Morgan v. Virginia* decision of the preceding year, in which the Supreme Court had declared segregation in interstate transportation unconstitutional. The riders met resistance in some areas, and the pacifist Bayard Rustin, who was to become a prominent civil rights leader in the 1960s, was one of those sentenced to a thirty-day term on a North Carolina road gang.

But what captured the imagination of the nation and of the black community in particular, and what was chiefly responsible for the growing use of direct-action techniques, was the Montgomery, Alabama bus boycott of 1955–1956, which catapulted into national prominence the Reverend Martin Luther King, Jr., the man who most nearly achieved charismatic leadership in the civil rights movement of the 1960s. Like the founders of CORE, but unlike the great majority of civil rights activists, King professed a Gandhian belief in the principles of nonviolence. For King, who spoke of the creation of a "beloved community," love was more powerful than hate, and civil rights demonstrators who were beaten and jailed by hostile whites educated and transformed their oppressors through the redemptive character of their unmerited suffering (see Document 40). King won in Montgomery when a judicial ruling desegregated the buses. Even before this victory, a similar boycott had started in Tallahassee, Florida, and afterward another got started in Birmingham, Alabama. At about the same time, the Tuskegee Civic Association undertook a three-year boycott of local merchants because the state legislature had enacted a gerrymandering statute that placed nearly all the black voters outside the town's limits; this boycott was crowned with success when the Supreme Court ruled the gerrymandering illegal.

These events in Montgomery, Tallahassee, Birmingham, and Tuskegee were widely heralded as indicating the emergence, especially in the South, of another "New Negro"—militant, no longer fearful of white hoodlums or police or jails, and ready to use his collective weight boldly. Seizing upon this new mood, King in 1957 established the Southern Christian Leadership Conference (SCLC). Permeated with the spirit of Gandhian nonviolence, SCLC's program included both direct-action demonstrations and voter-registration (see Document 41).

Martin Luther King's symbolic appeal did much to account for the current popularity of direct action (see Document 48). But the fact was that Negroes were ready for a new approach; the older techniques of legal and legislative action had revealed their limitations. Impressive as it was to cite the advances in the fifteen years after the end of World War II—advances that included state laws and Supreme Court decisions—something was clearly wrong. Though the number of blacks registered to vote in the Southern states rose from about 200,000 to well over a million in the decade following the outlawing of the white primary in 1944, millions more were still disfranchised, especially in the deep South. There, Supreme Court decisions desegregating transportation facilities were still largely ignored. After the 1954 decision against segregation in public schools, the South resisted with White Citizens' Councils' attempts to outlaw the NAACP, intimidation of civil rights leaders, "massive resistance" to the Court's decisions, and the forcible curtailment of black voter registration. Discrimination in employment and in housing abounded, even in northern states with model civil rights laws. Beginning in 1954, black unemployment grew constantly, as a result of recessions and automation.

At the very time that legalism was thus proving itself a limited instrument, Negroes were developing a new confidence in the future as they watched the rise of the new African nations, the success of King and others in nonviolent direct action in the South, the new laws and court decisions, the international situation, and the evident shift of white public opinion. In short, there had occurred what has appropriately been described as a revolution in expectations. Negroes no longer felt that they had to accept the humiliations of second-class citizenship, and consequently such humiliations—somewhat fewer though they now were—appeared to be more intolerable than ever. Paradoxically, it was the NAACP's very success in the legislatures and the courts, more than any other single factor, that led to this revolution in expectations and the resultant dissatisfaction with the limitations of the NAACP's program. This increasing black impatience and disillusionment accounted for the rising tempo of nonviolent direct action—including some by NAACP branches—in the late 1950s. It culminated in the student sit-ins of 1960 and the inauguration of what is popularly known as the "Civil Rights Revolution," or the "Negro Revolt."

VI.

The black protest movement would never be the same again. The southern college student sit-ins set in motion waves of events that shook the power structure of the black community, made direct action temporarily preeminent as a civil rights technique, ended NAACP hegemony in the civil rights movement, speeded up incalculably the whole process of social change in race relations, largely destroyed the barriers standing against the recognition of the blacks' constitutional rights, and ultimately turned the black protest organizations toward a deep concern with the economic and social problems of the masses. Involved was a steady radicalization of tactics and goals: from legalism to direct action and ultimately to Black Power; from participation by the middle and upper classes to mass action by all classes; from guaranteeing the protection of the Negro's constitutional rights to securing economic policies that would insure the welfare of the culturally deprived in a technologically changing society; from appeal to the white American's sense of fair play to demands based upon the power in the black ghetto.

First, direct action proved successful in a large-scale way in the South and won predominance over other tactics. The college student sit-in groups that suddenly flowered in the South formed the Student Nonviolent Coordinating Committee (SNCC) in April 1960 (see Documents 42, 43), and many local *ad hoc* direct-action groups also appeared. Furthermore, the thrust from the youth stimulated the established organizations and created competitive rivalry among civil rights groups. And the competition in turn encouraged widespread use of direct action. Old techniques, some of them radical in their day, now seemed conservative and slow-moving; many youthful sit-in demonstrators regarded the NAACP as hopelessly outmoded and cripplingly dominated by the middle class, which lacked any concern for the welfare of the masses (see Document 43). New personalities challenged the entrenched leaders. The older civil rights organizations reacted to the threat with renewed vigor. The NAACP met the challenge by making direct action a major rather than a peripheral activity (see Document 44), and a number of its leaders in local branches became enthusiastic proponents of this tactic. Though the NAACP had lost its preeminence, it chalked up more accomplishments than ever, and its program, ranging from litigation, through extraordinarily effective lobbying in Washington, to direct-action campaigns, was the most highly varied of all the civil rights organizations. By 1960, CORE appeared to have had its method appropriated by more lusty successors. But in the following year a renaissance of activity placed CORE in the front rank of race advancement organizations. Even the National Urban League, while not engaging in direct action, adopted a more militant spirit (see Document 45).

Negroes clearly established themselves as the leaders of the protest. CORE, which was still the most interracial of all the civil rights groups, became predominantly black in membership and staff. The influence of white liberals generally declined in the movement. Because they were wedded to compromise as a political device and were committed to many causes not related to the blacks, white liberals often lacked the single-minded militance that was now demanded for active participation in the movement. In fact, whites came increasingly under attack (see Document 51). What was true of middle-class liberals was even more true of labor leaders, even those heretofore closest to the civil rights movement. Even the industrial unions came under criticism for not according Negroes representation in the union hierarchies and not taking a stronger hand against discriminatory practices in their southern locals. The feeling was wide-spread that whites could now play only the roles of followers and foot soldiers.

Some civil rights leaders believed, however, that as an under-privileged minority Negroes could not gain their goals entirely on their own. These leaders insisted upon the importance of white allies: liberals, trade unionists, and such white moderates as the church leaders who became so active in behalf of civil rights in 1963. To some, especially democratic socialists like A. Philip Randolph and Bayard Rustin, the dream of a Negro-labor alliance was still a lively hope (see Documents 52, 57, and 58).

As the earlier goals (such as voting rights and desegregation of public accommodations) were gradually being won, civil rights organizations became more concerned with the kind of discrimination that particularly affected the masses: discrim-ination in employment opportunities and in the quality of education and housing (see Documents 56, 57 and 58). Blacks had always been mostly relegated to the low-paid, unskilled jobs. They consequently faced severe problems with the advance of automation.

All this led to a change in emphasis for the civil rights move-ment. Direct action, which since 1960 had been concentrated in the South, now reappeared in new forms in the North. There were school boycotts, rent strikes, and demonstrations against discriminatory employers and unions. Along with this change in emphasis came another change: more and more now, the masses of Negroes were themselves participating in civil rights activity. The tactics of direct action had made it possible for ordinary citizens to participate in the fight for their freedom. Leaders, although they still came mostly from the middle and upper classes, increasingly articulated the needs and frustrations of the masses (see Document 46).

Accompanying these changes was a growing belief that a long-run solution to the civil rights question required a solu-tion to the nation's economic problems. Fair-employment prac-tices would be meaningless for black workers without full employment. Mass unemployment lent urgency to the black protest at the same time that it made the attainment of civil rights a largely empty goal for the masses. Some civil rights leaders predicted an inevitable trend toward increasing socialization of the American economic system, and they suggested that the black protest movement, by compelling the nation's decision-makers to provide more jobs, could play an important role in eliminating poverty among whites as well as Negroes (see Document 57). Others, in the most militant sectors of the movement, went so far as to assert that American society as it stood was hardly worth integrating with, and only "fundamental social changes" arising out of a real confrontation with the "power structure" could eliminate racial inequities (see Document 49).

The competitive rivalry of the civil rights organizations, combined with the rising participation of the black masses, resulted in the Black Revolt becoming ever more militant, inclusive, and far-reaching in its demands, and immediatist in its attitude. There was a tendency toward erosion of the nonviolent principle (see Document 49). The growing participation of lower-class youth led to instances of spontaneous outbreaks of violence. And with the hardening resistance of the deep South and the difficulties inherent in attacking the deep-seated problems of employment, housing, and schools, there was discussion among militants about retaliating in self-defense against the brutality of police and white hoodlums. A tiny minority was already advocating the deliberate use of violence. Thus hope kindled by progress, and frustration created by obstacles, joined to make blacks more militant—and one extreme of their militancy was represented by violence (see Document 50).

Paradoxically, in the face of indubitable progress there were signs of increasing nationalist protest. This was the result of at least three forces. One force was the growing sense of confidence and self-respect emerging from the successes achieved. A second, was the disillusionment with the slow pace of change and the increasing brutality and white violence in the South (see Document 47)—which gave blacks a greater sense of isolation at the very time that white support for the cause of civil rights was actually increasing. A third, was the rising participation of lower-class Negroes, especially in some CORE chapters and in SNCC.[3] Among lower-class people, nationalist sentiments have always been more deeply rooted than among the middle and upper classes; the alienation of the lower classes was actually heightened because of the rise in unemployment. The aspirations of these people had been raised, but in vain. They soon found that the civil rights movement had, in effect, passed by the lower classes. They were in fact worse off than before.

It was among exactly such lower-class Negroes that the most important nationalist movement of the early 1960s flourished. The Nation of Islam, a sect established about 1930, did not grow rapidly until the recession of 1954. Then increasing unemployment, along with the revolution in expectations, created a climate in which the Black Muslims, as they were called, thrived. They preached an eschatological vision—the doom of the white devils and the coming dominance of the black man. They promised a utopian separate territory within the United States where black people could establish their own state. And they offered an immediate practical program of building up black business through hard work, thrift, and racial unity (see Document 53). Basically, like the integrationist civil rights organizations, the Black Muslims manifested both the Negroes' quest for recognition of their human dignity and the blacks' rejection of the philosophy of gradualism.

At its height the Nation of Islam was seriously weakened by a factional struggle between its top leader Elijah Muhammad and the minister of its Harlem temple, the dramatic spokesman

[3] Actually, in the absence of carefully collected empirical data, it is impossible to speak with precision about the sources of members and leaders in the various protest organizations. Individuals of middle- and upper-class background or attainments have predominated in the leadership of all of them; and the backbone of NAACP branch membership has been as much working class in origins as in any of them. Two key observations can be made: 1) that the different organizations tended to attract different types of personalities; and 2) that the direct-action organizations involved working-class people in their activities, while the NAACP was generally more geared to legal action and lobbying tactics that did not include participation of rank-and-file people.

Malcolm X. Early in 1964 Malcolm X left the movement and formed the Organization of Afro-American Unity (see Document 54). Malcolm X aimed at a less sectarian and more broadly based movement, but before he could get beyond setting forth the outlines of his program, he was assassinated. Yet, for many, the very manner of his death, combined with his fierce denunciation of white racism and his charismatic leadership, elevated him to the level of the sacred, and made him the single most influential symbol for the black nationalist impulses of the late 1960s.

Other nationalist tendencies also became prominent after 1960. The trials and successes of the movement gave Negroes a new sense of dignity, self-esteem, and power. This led to a burgeoning interest in black history; as Negroes gained pride and self-respect, they looked to the past in their search for an identity. Negroes were coming to feel that they could create changes in their environment through their own power, and this was reflected in the demand for black leadership within the movement. There was a revival of self-help ideologies as a solution for the economic problems of the masses. Politically, nationalist sentiment found expression in the proposal, which emerged in some northern cities during 1963, for an all-Negro "Freedom Now" party. Culturally, nationalist feelings were expressed most clearly by a group of intellectuals who indicated their alienation by rejecting the values of American society and championing a militant cultural pluralism that preserved the autonomy of Negro culture (see Document 55).

In the early 1960s, as in the age of Booker T. Washington, black racial ideologies tended to cluster into "conservative" and "radical" outlooks. A "conservative" approach centered on the use of the courts, lobbying in the state and national legislatures, and on nonpartisan registration campaigns to increase the voting power of Negroes and thus strengthen the likelihood of obtaining favorable laws and helpful executive action. A "radical" approach centered on direct action, and often included socialist or Marxist concepts. By the middle of the decade the most radical blacks showed increasing signs of a sharp aliena-

tion from American society, specifically with the American political system, and were urging independent black political
action. At the extreme fringes of radicalism, militant nationalism, Marxism, and the advocacy of violence coalesced into a
genuinely revolutionary ideology.

But black voices speak a complex message, and all analytical
categories are at best crude tools. Thus it would be dangerous
to oversimplify.

The "conservative" NAACP was no more led by whites than
was the "radical" SNCC. Voter-registration—a conservative
strategy of long standing—became, in the face of stubborn
white resistance in Alabama, Mississippi, and Louisiana, a form
of radical direct action. SNCC initiated the work of attempting
to register voters in the rural counties of the deep South; CORE,
some NAACP militants, and eventually SCLC followed. By the
middle of the 1960s SNCC and CORE leaders concluded that
direct action was not a panacea, and stressed independent political action. By this they meant the mobilization of the potential political power of the inarticulate masses into a bloc that
instead of automatically voting for Democratic politicians,
would elect genuine spokesmen of the lower-class community
to wage a vigorous fight for social change in the Black-Belt
counties of the rural South, and in the black ghettos of the cities
(see Document 59).

Within the NAACP, still denounced for its conservatism,
feelings on direct action ranged from disdain to enthusiastic
participation. The NAACP labor secretary initiated dramatic
direct-action demonstrations to gain improved employment opportunities from both unions and industry. And to win school
desegregation, the NAACP's education department enthusiastically supported militant tactics which were disapproved by
many white liberals and conservatives in the NAACP.

Concern with the employment problems of the urban masses
has been a hallmark of the "radicals" since Randolph founded
The Messenger; yet the conservative Urban League has made a
contribution in this area equal in importance to that of radical
CORE and SNCC (see Document 56).

Complexities blur the lines on other issues. Cultural pluralists and assimilationists could both be found along the entire spectrum of organizations. The Marxist critique of American society occurred both among the movement's dedicated pacifists and among its advocates of violence.

There were also shades of difference among the "radicals." Certain types of direct action—school boycotts, rent strikes, blocking street intersections, going limp in the hands of arresting officers (or even resisting arrest), staying in jail rather than putting up bail money—are more radical than others. In retrospect, the well-dressed student sit-inners of 1960 now appear to have engaged in a highly dignified, middle-class, relatively conservative kind of action. The eminent clergy who were arrested in direct-action demonstrations in 1963 in fact helped give respectability to nonviolent direct action. The character of the movement changed so much that those who insisted upon the older varieties of disciplined nonviolence, such as nonresistance to arrest and white brutality, by 1964 were sometimes called "Uncle Toms" by extreme militants.

VII.

At first the new militance of the 1960s tended to propel the more "conservative" black community leaders, whether prominent in the NAACP or not, into a more radical tactical position. In crisis situations engendered by mass arrests, especially where these were accompanied by blatant police brutality, temporary unity was achieved between organizations and classes generally on the militants' terms, as nonactivist-oriented individuals and groups rushed to the support of the demonstrators (see Document 46). Nonviolent direct action enjoyed an enormous vogue among all organizations. Even the National Urban League, while never utilizing this tactic, was able to take an increasingly militant stance toward the white business community because of the popularity and effectiveness of direct action.

Yet by 1965 direct action had passed its heyday. It had succeeded in desegregating public accommodations in the South, and in obtaining thousands of jobs in retail stores and consumer-oriented industries in the North. It had played a central—even essential—role in the passage of the Civil Rights law of 1964 and the Voting Rights law of 1965 (though the lobbying of the NAACP-oriented coalition known as the Civil Rights Leadership Conference was also of critical assistance). On the other rights workers in the deep South, while in the North direct action in the form of rent strikes, school boycotts, and demonstrations against discrimination in the building trades unions had failed. Indubitable progress had been made, but it had certainly not kept pace with rising expectations, and genuine equality appeared as distant as ever. As a consequence there was a loss of faith in nonviolent direct action.

Meanwhile, the tendency toward a unity of strategy, if not between personalities, that was emerging during 1963 was dissipated by mid-1964 and had disappeared by mid-1965. At the very time that white support for the movement was actually rising, its most militant members felt increasingly isolated from the American scene. Persons in this radical left wing of the civil rights movement were growing disdainful of American society and the middle-class way of life, cynical about liberals and the leaders of organized labor. Any compromise, even if a temporary tactical device, had become anathema to them. They talked more and more of the necessity for "revolutionary" changes in the social structure, even of violence. They became increasingly skeptical of the value of white participation in the movement, racially chauvinistic in their insistence that black power alone could compel concessions from the "power structure" of capitalists, politicians, and bureaucratic labor leaders. The black nationalist, Malcolm X, after his assassination in 1965, became the symbolic hero for the militants. At the extreme left wing of the movement Marxism and nationalism coalesced into a truly revolutionary ideology (see Document 50). In contrast, were those who, impressed by changes in public attitudes, came to view the role of the movement as exercising influence within established institutions rather than fighting them from the outside. Between the two poles of thought there existed a group who recognized the new willingness of the nation's decision-makers to move toward greater racial justice, but perceived also that powerful pressure would be needed to push them in that direction (see Documents 52, 58). While it would be a gross oversimplification to pigeonhole Negro protest leaders and organizations, broadly speaking it can be said that the militant left wing was composed of SNCC and many individuals in CORE; that the right wing consisted of Urban League officials and a substantial group in the NAACP; and that varieties of the centrist position, while found among many CORE and NAACP people, were best articulated by Bayard Rustin, A. Philip Randolph, and Martin Luther King.

For a period—roughly between 1964 and 1966—the theory that political action, based upon the potential of the united vote of the black masses, should be the principal strategy, enjoyed considerable vogue in all wings of the movement. Yet in applying this theory there were wide differences. The most radical advocated "independent" politics and the creation of black political organizations like the Black Panther party of Lowndes County, Alabama. It was evident, however, that the future of this tactic would necessarily lie with the urban ghettos; there the main emphasis was on organizing the masses to challenge the Democratic machines from within the party, and elect officials who really represented the interests of the poor. The right wing, impressed by the legislation of 1964 and 1965, and the selection of prominent protest leaders for high public office, viewed the Democratic party establishment and city machines not as enemies but as allies. The centrist group, on the basis of experience in obtaining the civil rights legislation of 1964 and 1965, developed a theory of "coalition politics." Under no illusions about alliances with the Democratic party leadership, they based their strategy on a coalition of Negroes with white liberals and sympathetic elements among the white clergy and organized labor (see Documents 58 and 59).

Between 1964 and 1966 the black protest movement was becoming increasingly fragmented and ineffective. Fundamentally this growing disunity was rooted in the frustration of radically heightened expectations and the extraordinary problems involved in achieving genuine equality for the black poor. Confronted with these circumstances, the various segments of the movement became increasingly divided on how to tackle the situation.

The 1964 Democratic Party Convention foreshadowed this trend. Events there, in the eyes of the militants, thoroughly discredited both the Democratic party establishment and the white liberal elements in the interracial coalition backing the national civil rights legislative program. A Mississippi coalition of CORE, NAACP, and SNCC known as the Council of Federated Organizations (COFO) had worked to register Negroes in that state against incredible odds, and had organized the Mississippi Freedom Democratic party (MFDP) because of the continued resistance to black political participation. MFDP challenged the legitimacy of the credentials of the regular Mississippi delegates of the convention, and offered its own candidates for the state's seats. The black militants believed that the party's compromise offer to the MFDP of two delegates-at-large was mere tokenism, proof of the insincerity of the Lyndon B. Johnson administration. Moreover, the growing distrust of white liberals became complete when many of them reluctantly accepted the compromise. Finally, the Negroes themselves were deeply divided, with SNCC and CORE refusing to approve the compromise, while NAACP elements in the Freedom Democratic party and men like King argued for its acceptance.

The Vietnam War exacerbated the growing cleavages. Some believed that it diverted funds from solving the country's leading domestic problems. Others charged that both the war and domestic racism involved the attempt of the American "white power structure" to keep a colored race in a colonial status. At the opposite pole were those who held that Vietnam was irrelevant to the black protest, and that to mix the two issues was tactically dangerous. While the Urban League and the NAACP refused to identify themselves with the Vietnam protest, King openly attacked United States policy in Vietnam, as did SNCC and CORE.

The 1964 anti-poverty act had several effects on the protest movement. It accelerated the shift from an emphasis on a national legislative program to grass-roots action by the poor themselves. The struggle over who would administer the community action programs exacerbated the polarization between the more moderate middle-class leaders, often identified with the NAACP and Urban League, and the more radical types. Finally, the anti-poverty program unintentionally increased the frustration and discontent among the black poor by further escalating expectations but delivering nothing substantial. Yet paradoxically, the War on Poverty, in stressing that government programs should be initiated and administered by the ghetto-dwellers themselves, failed to solve the problems of the poor but led to a heightened militance among them.

By the summer of 1966 the disillusionment with the national administration and the white liberals, the fragmentation of the Negro protest movement, the enormous difficulties that stood in the way of overcoming the problems of the black masses, and the riots that had erupted spontaneously in 1964 and 1965 as a consequence of the anger and frustration of the urban slum-dwellers, all set the stage for the dramatic appearance of the slogan "black power."

VIII.

"Black power" first articulated a mood rather than a program—disillusionment and alienation from white America, race pride, and self-respect, or "black consciousness." The precipitating occasion was James Meredith's march from Memphis to Jackson in the early summer of 1966, but the slogan expressed tendencies that had been present for a long time and had been gaining strength in the black community. Having become a household phrase, the term generated intense discussion of its real meaning, and a broad spectrum of ideologies and programatic proposals emerged.

In politics, "black power" meant independent action: Negro control of the political power of the black ghettos and its conscious use to better the slum dwellers' conditions. It could take the form of organizing a black political party or controlling the political machinery within the ghetto without the guidance or support of white politicians. Where predominantly black areas lacked Negroes in elective office, whether in the rural Black Belt of the South or in the urban centers, black power advocates sought the election of Negroes by voter registration campaigns, and by working to redraw electoral districts. The basic belief was that only a well-organized and cohesive bloc of black voters could provide for the needs of the black masses. Even some black politicians allied to the major political parties adopted the phrase "black power" to describe their interest in the Negro vote. In economic terms, black power meant creating independent, self-sufficient Negro business enterprise, not only by encouraging black entrepreneurs but also by forming black cooperatives in the ghettos and in the predominantly black rural counties of the South. In the field of education, black power called for local community control of the public schools in the black ghettos. Throughout, the emphasis was on self-help, racial unity, and, among the most militant, retaliatory violence, the latter ranging from the legal right of self-defense to attempts to justify looting and arson in ghetto riots, and to guerrilla warfare and armed rebellion.

Phrases like "black power," "black consciousness," and "black is beautiful" enjoyed an extensive currency in the Negro community, even within the NAACP and among relatively conservative politicians. Expressed in its most extreme form by small, often local, fringe groups, among the national organizations the black power ideology became most closely associated with SNCC and CORE.

Regarded as the most militant among the leading Negro protest organizations, CORE and SNCC had different interpretations of the black power doctrine. Though neither group was monolithic in its viewpoint, broadly speaking SNCC called for totally independent political action outside the established political parties, as with the Black Panther party in Lowndes County, Alabama; questioned the value of political alliance with other groups until Negroes themselves built a substantial base of independent political power; applauded the idea of guerrilla warfare; and regarded riots as rebellions (see Documents 60, 61). CORE, while not disapproving of the SNCC political strategy, advocated working within the Democratic party and forming alliances with other groups. It sought to justify riots as the natural explosion of an oppressed people against intolerable conditions, but it urged violence only in self-defense. While favorable toward cooperatives, it was more inclined toward job-training progams and developing a black entrepreneurial class based upon the market within the black ghetto. Others held similar views, and indeed such reformist interpretations of black power were far more widespread in the black community than were the revolutionary versions (see Document 66).

Actually SNCC and CORE both declined in size and influence. By 1969 SNCC practically disappeared as a functioning organization. CORE, although committed to the general principle of community organization, changed its principal emphasis to the encouragement of black capitalist enterprise. Other chiefly locally based groups took up the banner of black nationalism. There was a general surge of community organization, of a spirit of self-help and racial solidarity, of uniting ghetto residents for concerted action culturally, economically, and politically.

Far better known—because far more dramatic and far more extreme—were revolutionary separatist organizations, calling for armed resistance to white racism and rebellion in the streets. One version of the revolutionary ideology advocated both socialization and black leadership of the economic institutions in the black community, coupling this with a demand that the white churches pay reparations to Negroes because of the long history of race discrimination. Revolutionary ideology is also attached to two major forms of territorial separatism: complete black control of the central cities, advocated most notably by the Black Panthers; and the creation of a separate all-black sovereign state in the deep South, proposed by The Republic of New Africa (see Documents 62, 63, 65).

Nationalist tendencies are also evident in the black caucuses in predominantly white church denominations, learned societies, and teachers', policemen's, and social workers' organizations. There has been a rapid proliferation of Afro-American Societies and Black Student Unions on predominantly white university campuses, with their demands for greater black representation in the student body, on the faculty, and in the curriculum on the one hand, and for separate dormitories, recreational centers, and even separate colleges within the universities, on the other hand (see Document 64). Finally, there has been a revival of cultural nationalism, widespread in all sectors of the black community, whose manifestations range from the demands of the black student organizations for courses in black history and culture, to the many local black culture and black theater groups throughout the country. Interlacing all of these developments was a growing and outspoken emphasis upon pride in being black (see Document 67).

Black nationalism, black separatism, and black revolutionary rhetoric have seized the headlines. But striking and important as the popularity of various forms of black nationalism have been since 1966 when "black power" became a slogan, it must nonetheless be emphasized that full participation in American society on an integrated basis is still the goal of the vast majority of black Americans. Though nationalist thinking enjoys considerable currency in Negro middle-class circles in the North, as well as among ghetto youth, neither SCLC nor NAACP has adopted a nationalist program or ideology. The NAACP has counterattacked vigorously. Individuals like Kenneth Clark and Bayard Rustin, who were prominently associated with the earlier protest movement, have denounced the black separatists as segregationists and racists undermining the very things the black protest movement had sought for so many years to bring about. Martin Luther King's last months were spent in developing a major project intended to demonstrate the continuing viability of the nonviolent direct-action strategy (see Documents 68–71).

Paradoxically, the popularity of the phrase, "black power," and the vogue of separatist ideology in the late 1960s, represent both a sense of power produced by the earlier successes of the movement, and an escape into rhetoric caused by the powerless-ness to achieve continued rapid progress toward full equality. The slogan emerged when the Negro protest movement was slowing down, when it was finding increased resistance to its changed goals, when it discovered that nonviolent direct action was no more a panacea than legal action had been, when CORE and SNCC were declining in activity, membership, and financial support. Impotent to make any fundamental changes in the lives of the masses, the advocates of black power substituted an ideology of separatism for one of integration. Ironically, this occurred at the very time that black people were closer to the goal of integration than ever before. Where sixty years earlier the themes of racial unity and separatism had functioned pri-marily as part of an ideology of accommodation, while the black radicals had demanded integration, among the latest generation of black radicals it was fashionable to decry integration as a white man's strategy of tokenism aimed at holding Negroes in a subordinate position. Racial separatism had become part of a rhetoric of radicalism and militance, while the erstwhile radical program of integration was now denounced as conservative, and sometimes as downright racist.

Yet the situation is incredibly complex. Black separatism, considered militant and radical today, is associated with doc-trines ranging all the way from revolutionary neo-Marxism to black capitalism, and some of the advocates of the latter sup-ported Richard Nixon in the election of 1968. Integration, now viewed by many as accommodating and conservative, is an ideology popular among diverse groups ranging from Commu-nists through democratic socialists and liberals to economically conservative business and professional men. The NAACP, while adhering to its traditional ideology, has established a program to aid black businessmen. A heightened cultural nationalism has considerable vogue among integrationists as well as sep-aratists, and the demands of many of the reformist advocates of black power, most notably those in the black caucuses in the professions, are for greater integration of black people into American society.

In fact, it should be remembered that today, as traditionally, the main thrust of Negro protest has always been aimed at discrimination and segregation (the radicals of today distinguishing between voluntary separatism and enforced segregation); the central demand has always been for equal treatment with other citizens. The nationalist emphasis in militant black thought today is the latest expression of the ethnic ambivalence of American Negroes that is rooted in the contradictions of American society. Behind the revolutionary phrases of the black power militants is usually a profound desire for an equal share and an equal status in American society. And the mainstream of black protest has always been firmly embedded in the basic values of American society. It aims not at their destruction but their fulfillment.

August Meier
Elliott Rudwick

November 1969

Selected bibliography

The most provocative discussion of Negro thought is contained in two unpublished memoranda (available on microfilm from the New York Public Library) which Ralph Bunche wrote for the Carnegie Foundation–Gunnar Myrdal study of the Negro in America in 1940. Their titles are: "Programs, Ideologies, Tactics and Achievements of Negro Betterment and Interracial Organizations," and "Conceptions and Ideologies of the Negro Problem."

The best approach to Booker T. Washington is through a collection of articles edited by Hugh Hawkins, *Booker T. Washington and His Critics: The Problem of Negro Leadership* (Boston: D. C. Heath & Co., 1962). The most satisfactory biography thus far published is Samuel R. Spencer, Jr., *Booker T. Washington and the Negro's Place in American Life* (Boston: Little, Brown and Co., 1955).* Of Washington's autobiographical works, his *Story of My Life and Work* (Naperville, Ill.: Hertel, Jenkins and Co., 1900), is more revealing than the somewhat later *Up From Slavery* (New York: Doubleday, Page & Co., 1901). For an analysis of trends of thought during the period of Washington's prominence, see August Meier, *Negro Thought in America, 1880–1915* (Ann Arbor: The University of Michigan Press, 1963).

W. E. B. Du Bois's thought and career are treated in Francis L. Broderick, *W. E. B. Du Bois: Negro Leader in Time of Crisis* (Stanford: Stanford University Press, 1959), and Elliott Rudwick, *W. E. B. Du Bois: Propagandist of the Negro Protest* (revised edition, New York: Atheneum, 1968, and Philadelphia: University of Pennsylvania Press, 1969). Of Du Bois's two autobiographies, *Dusk of Dawn* (New York: Harcourt, Brace and

---

* An important contribution which appeared after this book was set in type is Louis R. Harlan, "Booker T. Washington in Biographical Perspective," *American Historical Review,* LXXV (October 1970) [Ed.].

Co., 1940), and the *Autobiography of W. E. B. Du Bois* (New York: International Publishers, 1968), the former is the more useful for tracing the evolution of his ideas. The career of Washington's other leading critic is described in Stephen R. Fox, *The Guardian of Boston: William Monroe Trotter* (New York: Atheneum, 1970).

A comprehensive history of the NAACP is yet to be published. Charles Flint Kellogg, *NAACP: A History of the National Association for the Advancement of Colored People, Volume I, 1909–1920* (Baltimore: Johns Hopkins University Press, 1967) covers the first decade in great detail. The best insights into the history of the organization down through the 1930s can be gained from Barbara Joyce Ross's unpublished doctoral dissertation, "Joel Elias Spingarn and the Rise of the N.A.A.C.P." (American University, 1969). Clement Vose, *Caucasians Only: The Supreme Court, the NAACP and the Restrictive Covenant Cases* (Berkeley: University of California Press, 1959), is an excellent case study of one NAACP legal campaign. Information of interest can also be gleaned from Robert L. Jack, *History of the National Association for the Advancement of Colored People* (Boston: Meador Publishing Company, 1943); from Langston Hughes, *Fight for Freedom: The Story of the NAACP* (New York: W. W. Norton & Co., 1962); from the Bunche memoranda cited above; and from the following autobiographies: James Weldon Johnson, *Along This Way* (New York: The Viking Press, 1933); Mary White Ovington, *The Walls Came Tumbling Down* (New York: Harcourt, Brace & Co., 1947); and Walter White, *A Man Called White* (New York: The Viking Press, 1948).

Arvarh E. Strickland's pioneering *History of the Chicago Urban League* (Urbana: University of Illinois Press, 1966), not only is a unique study of a local racial advancement organization, but it illuminates the whole history of the National Urban League. The cultural pluralism of the Harlem Renaissance is illuminated in *The New Negro*, edited by Alain Locke (New York: Albert and Charles Boni, 1925), and Robert Bone, *The Negro Novel in America* (New Haven: Yale University Press,

1958). Charles H. Loeb, *The Future is Yours: The History of the Future Outlook League, 1935–1946* (Cleveland: The Future Outlook League, Inc., 1947) describes the work of one of the most successful organizations involved in the "Don't-Buy-Where-You-Can't-Work" campaigns. Wilson Record, *The Negro and the Communist Party* (Chapel Hill: University of North Carolina Press, 1951), is a revealing analysis. Herbert Garfinkel, *When Negroes March* (Glencoe, Ill.: The Free Press, 1949), is a superb study of the World War II March on Washington Movement. Harold Cruse, *The Crisis of the Negro Intellectual* (New York: William Morrow, 1967), is an important commentary on black radical and nationalist movements in the twentieth century, while S. P. Fullinwider, *The Mind and Mood of Black America: 20th Century Thought* (Homewood, Ill.: The Dorsey Press, 1969), offers a novel interpretation, and Joanne Grant offers representative documents in *Black Protest: History, Documents and Analyses, 1619 to the present* (New York: Fawcett, 1968).

There is a growing literature on the history of black nationalism. Provocative surveys will be found in two essays by St. Clair Drake: "Hide My Face?—On Pan-Africanism and Negritude" in Herbert Hill, ed., *Soon, One Morning: New Writing by American Negroes, 1940–1962* (New York: Alfred A. Knopf, 1963); and "Negro Americans and the African Interest" in John P. Davis, ed., *American Negro Reference Book* (Englewood Cliffs, N.J.: Prentice-Hall, 1967). See also John H. Bracey, Jr., August Meier, and Elliott Rudwick, eds., *Black Nationalism in America* (Indianapolis: Bobbs-Merrill Co., 1970). Colonization movements of the early twentieth century are described in Edwin S. Redkey, *Black Exodus* (New Haven: Yale University Press, 1969), and in William Bittle and Gilbert Geis, *The Longest Way Home: Chief Alfred Sam's Back to Africa Movement* (Detroit: Wayne State University Press, 1964). The Garvey Movement is treated in E. David Cronon, *Black Moses: The Story of Marcus Garvey and the Universal Negro Improvement Association* (Madison, Wis.: The University of Wisconsin Press, 1955) and Amy Jacques-Garvey, *Garvey and Garveyism* (Kingston, Jamaica: United Printers, Ltd., 1963). On the Garvey-Du Bois controversy see Elliott Rudwick, "Du Bois vs. Garvey: Racial Propagandists at War," *Journal of Negro Education*, XXVII (Fall 1959). On the Black Muslims there are two perceptive studies: C. Eric Lincoln, *The Black Muslims in America* (Boston: Beacon Press, 1961), and E. U. Essien-Udom, *Black Nationalism: The Search for an Identity in America*. For the flavor of the Muslim rhetoric and ideology see Elijah Muhammad, *Message to the Blackman* (Chicago: Muhammad Mosque of Islam No. 2, 1965), and Louis Lomax, *When the Word is Given* (Cleveland: World Publishers, 1963). On Malcolm X see especially *Autobiography of Malcolm X* (New York: Grove Press, 1965), and George Breitman, *Malcolm X Speaks* (New York: Merit Publishers, 1965).

A provocative, if not always accurate, discussion of the civil rights revolution is found in Louis E. Lomax, *The Negro Revolt* (New York: Harper and Row, 1962). A very useful bibliographic survey of the literature on black protest in the 1960s is Ernest Kaiser, "Recent Literature on Black Liberation Struggles and the Ghetto Crisis," *Science and Society*, XXXIII (Spring 1969), pp. 168–196. The impact of African independence on black thought is given a suggestive treatment in Harold Isaacs, *The New World of Negro Americans* (New York: The John Day Co., 1963). The changes in black and white attitudes that paved the way for and accompanied the events of the 1960s are lucidly explained in Leonard Broom and Norval Glenn, *Transformation of the Negro American* (New York: Harper and Row, 1965), and Thomas F. Pettigrew, *A Profile of the Negro American* (Princeton: Van Nostrand, 1964). See also Lerone Bennett, Jr., *The Negro Mood* (Chicago: Johnson Publication Co., 1964). There is no history of CORE; sketchy accounts by active participants are given in James Peck, *Freedom Ride* (New York: Simon and Schuster, 1962), and James Farmer, *Freedom— When?* (New York: Random House, 1965). Inge Powell Bell, *CORE and the Strategy of Nonviolence* (New York: Random House, 1968) is an excellent case study of selected CORE chapters between 1961 and 1964. Howard Zinn, *SNCC: The New*

Abolitionists (Boston: Beacon Press, 1964) is by a scholar who worked closely with the student movement. King's views are best approached through his own works: *Stride Toward Freedom* (New York: Harper and Row, 1958), *Why We Can't Wait* (New York: Harper and Row, 1964), and *Where Do We Go From Here: Chaos or Community?* (New York: Harper & Row, 1967). The best biography of the SCLC leader thus far written is David Lewis, *King: A Critical Biography* (New York: Frederick A. Praeger, 1970). An anthology giving varied views and interpretations of King is C. Eric Lincoln, ed., *Martin Luther King* (New York: Hill and Wang, 1970). Important case studies of local protest movements are Charles V. Hamilton's description of the Tuskegee Civic Association, *Minority Politics in Black Belt Alabama* (New Brunswick: The Eagleton Institute, 1960); Jack L. Walker, *Sit-Ins in Atlanta: A Study in the Negro Revolt* (New Brunswick: Eagleton Institute, 1964); and William Ellis's analysis of a Chicago group, *White Ethics and Black Power: The Emergence of the West Side Organization* (Chicago: Aldine Publishing Co., 1969).

The leadership rivalries associated with the civil rights revolution of the early 1960s are described in Lomax, *The Negro Revolt;* August Meier, "New Currents in the Civil Rights Movement," *New Politics,* II (Summer 1963); Lewis M. Killian and Charles U. Smith, "Negro Protest Leaders in a Southern Community," *Social Forces,* XXXVIII (March 1960); Jack L. Walker, "The Functions of Disunity: Negro Leadership in a Southern City," *Journal of Negro Education,* XXXII (Summer 1963); and Gerald McWorter and Robert L. Crain, "Subcommunity Gladiatorial Competition: Civil Rights Leadership as a Competitive Process," *Social Forces,* XLVI (September 1967).

The voter-registration campaign of 1962–1964 is described in Pat Watters and Reese Cleghorn, *Climbing Jacob's Ladder: The Arrival of Negroes in Southern Politics* (New York: Harcourt, Brace & World, 1967). Economic concerns are described in Arthur M. Ross and Herbert Hill, eds., *Employment, Race and Poverty* (New York: Harcourt, Brace & World, 1965); Nat Hentoff, *The New Equality* (New York: The Viking Press,

1964); and in two books by Whitney Young, which also describe the changing program of the Urban League: *To Be Equal* (New York: McGraw-Hill Book Co., 1964); and *Beyond Racism* (New York: McGraw-Hill Book Co., 1969).

The changing role of whites in the movement is discussed in Bell, *CORE and the Strategy of Nonviolence;* Elizabeth Sutherland, ed., *Letters from Mississippi* (New York: McGraw-Hill Book Co., 1965); Alphonso Pinkney, *The Committed: White Activists in the Civil Rights Movement* (New Haven: College & University Press, 1968); Charles J. Levy, *Voluntary Servitude: Whites in the Negro Movement* (New York: Appleton-Century-Crofts, 1968); and two forthcoming articles in the *Journal of Social Issues*—one by Michael Aiken, Gerald Marwell, and N. J. Demerath III, on the experience of the white volunteers in SCLC's 1965 summer project, and the other by Gary T. Marx and Michael Useem, entitled, "Majority Involvement in Minority Movements: Civil Rights, Abolition, Untouchability."

The literature on black nationalism and black power since the middle 1960s is enormous. For precursors see the volumes on the Black Muslims and Malcolm X, above, and Robert F. Williams, *Negroes with Guns* (New York: Marzani and Munsell, 1962). The transition to black nationalism in the civil rights movement, as reflected in the history of CORE, is treated in Bell, *CORE and the Strategy of Nonviolence,* and Farmer, *Freedom— When?* Floyd Barbour, ed., *The Black Power Revolt* (Boston: Porter-Sargent, 1968) contains representative documents. Among other significant works are: Julius Lester, *Look Out Whitey! Black Power's Gon' Get Your Mama* (New York: Dial Press, 1968); Stokely Carmichael and Charles V. Hamilton, *Black Power: The Politics of Liberation* (New York: Random House, 1967); Nathan Wright, Jr., *Black Power and Urban Unrest: The Creative Possibilities* (New York: Hawthorn Books, 1967); Albert B. Cleage, Jr., *Black Messiah* (New York: Sheed, 1968); two books of essays by Eldridge Cleaver—*Soul on Ice* (New York: McGraw-Hill, 1968), and *Eldridge Cleaver: Post-prison Writings and Speeches* (New York: Random House, 1969); Lewis Killian, *The Impossible Revolution?* (New York:

Random House, 1968); Martin Duberman, "Black Power in America," *Partisan Review*, XXXV (Winter 1968); Joyce Ladner, "What 'Black Power' Means to Negroes in Mississippi," *Trans-Action*, V (November 1967); Martin L. Kilson, "Negro Separatism in the Colleges," *Harvard Today* (Spring 1968); the forthcoming article in the *American Political Science Review*, by Joel D. Aberbach and Jack L. Walker, entitled, "The Meanings of Black Power: A Comparison of White and Black Interpretations of a Political Slogan"; two special issues of *Negro Digest*, entitled "The Black University," XVII (March 1968), and "Toward a Black University," XVIII (March 1969); Leroi Jones (now Ameer Baraka) and Larry Neal, eds., *Black Fire: An Anthology of Afro-American Writing* (New York: William Morrow, 1968); William Couch, Jr., ed., *New Black Playwrights: An Anthology* (Baton Rouge: Louisiana State University Press, 1968); and Mercer Cook and Stephen E. Henderson, *The Militant Black Writer* (Madison: University of Wisconsin Press, 1969). The interested reader should also consult periodicals such as *Black World, Ebony, Liberator, Freedomways, The Black Scholar*, and the *Journal of Black Poetry*.

Gary T. Marx, *Protest and Prejudice: A Study of Belief in the Black Community* (revised edition, New York: Harper and Row, 1969), is an indispensable work, which, among other things, uses scientific polling techniques to ascertain the extent to which nationalist and separatist sentiments have replaced the ideology of integration among black men in the United States.

Editors' note and acknowledgments

The many selections included in this volume have been printed as in the original in each case, even with variant spellings and grammatical usages. However, it has been necessary to abridge some of them in order to present a wide spectrum of thought on this crucial American problem. Wherever this has occurred, ellipses mark the abridgment, but the reader may be sure that no passage has been pruned of its central thought.

The staff of the Schomburg Collection of the New York Public Library in numerous ways facilitated the gathering of many of the documents in this volume. In connection with the preparation of this second edition we are especially indebted to Professors B. Joyce Ross and John H. Bracey, Jr. for guiding us to certain inaccessible and fugitive documents. We acknowledge with gratitude the assistance of our student assistant Leonard Priebe, and of Mrs. Helen Peoples of the Kent State University Library. Our special thanks go to the Kent State University Center for Urban Regionalism, James G. Coke, director, for facilitating the preparation of the manuscript. Most of all, we wish to express our deepest appreciation to Alfred F. Young, general editor in charge of this volume, for his knowledgeable and painstaking criticism, his perceptive suggestions, and most of all for his warm encouragement at crucial moments.

A. M.
E. R.

from accommodation to protest

PART ONE

The philosophy of accommodation

1. BOOKER T. WASHINGTON'S
PLATFORM OF ACCOMMODATION

Booker T. Washington enunciated the strategy of accommodation that dominated black thought at the turn of the century. Though it was not original in content, his address at the Cotton States and International Exposition in Atlanta, Georgia, in September 1895, set the terms for the debate on Negro programs for the next two decades. The prestige that white acclaim gave to Washington, together with his shrewdness and his tireless capacity to organize and to travel, made him the foremost black spokesman in America.

Washington was founder and principal of Tuskegee Institute, a normal and industrial school in Alabama. Born in slavery, he had worked his way through Hampton Institute in Virginia, where General Samuel Chapman Armstrong, the principal, first set forth a program of agricultural and industrial training that would make the education of Negroes palatable to the dominant elements in the New South. It was Armstrong who taught Washington the doctrine of economic advancement combined with acceptance of disfranchisement and with conciliation of the white South—the doctrine that later became so closely identified in the public mind with the Tuskegeean. Washington taught at Hampton until 1881, when he was chosen to head a new school at Tuskegee. The Atlanta address fourteen years later catapulted him into national prominence, and for the next twenty years, until his death in 1915, no other Afro-American commanded a comparable influence among men of both races.

Booker T. Washington, "The Atlanta Exposition Address, September—1895" from UP FROM SLAVERY (New York: Doubleday, Page and Co., 1901), pp. 218–225.

This short speech summed up the changes that had occurred in black thought since Reconstruction—from rights to duties; from political action to economic progress; from demands for rapid integration to patient insistence on preliminary self-help. It epitomized the Negro's accommodation to the new order of white supremacy.

MR. PRESIDENT AND GENTLEMEN OF THE
BOARD OF DIRECTORS AND CITIZENS

One-third of the population of the South is of the Negro race. No enterprise seeking the material, civil, or moral welfare of this section can disregard this element of our population and reach the highest success. I but convey to you, Mr. President and Directors, the sentiment of the masses of my race when I say that in no way have the value and manhood of the American Negro been more fittingly and generously recognized than by the managers of this magnificent Exposition at every stage of its progress. It is a recognition that will do more to cement the friendship of the two races than any occurrence since the dawn of our freedom.

Not only this, but the opportunity here afforded will awaken among us a new era of industrial progress. Ignorant and inexperienced, it is not strange that in the first years of our new life we began at the top instead of at the bottom; that a seat in Congress or the state legislature was more sought than real estate or industrial skill; that the political convention or stump speaking had more attractions than starting a dairy farm or truck garden.

A ship lost at sea for many days suddenly sighted a friendly vessel. From the mast of the unfortunate vessel was seen a signal, "Water, water; we die of thirst!" The answer from the friendly vessel at once came back, "Cast down your bucket where you are." A second time the signal, "Water, water; send us water!" ran up from the distressed vessel, and was answered, "Cast down your bucket where you are." And a third and fourth signal for water was answered, "Cast down your bucket where you are." The captain of the distressed vessel, at last heeding the injunction, cast down his bucket, and it came up full of fresh,

sparkling water from the mouth of the Amazon River. To those
of my race who depend on bettering their condition in a foreign land or who underestimate the importance of cultivating
friendly relations with the Southern white man, who is their
next-door neighbour, I would say: "Cast down your bucket
where you are"—cast it down in making friends in every manly
way of the people of all races by whom we are surrounded.

Cast it down in agriculture, mechanics, in commerce, in domestic service, and in the professions. And in this connection it
is well to bear in mind that whatever other sins the South may
be called to bear, when it comes to business, pure and simple, it
is in the South that the Negro is given a man's chance in the
commercial world, and in nothing is this Exposition more eloquent than in emphasizing this chance. Our greatest danger is
that in the great leap from slavery to freedom we may overlook
the fact that the masses of us are to live by the productions of
our hands, and fail to keep in mind that we shall prosper in
proportion as we learn to dignify and glorify common labour and
put brains and skill into the common occupations of life; shall
prosper in proportion as we learn to draw the line between the
superficial and the substantial, the ornamental gewgaws of life
and the useful. No race can prosper till it learns that there is as
much dignity in tilling a field as in writing a poem. It is at the
bottom of life we must begin, and not at the top. Nor should we
permit our grievances to overshadow our opportunities.

To those of the white race who look to the incoming of those
of foreign birth and strange tongue and habits for the prosperity
of the South, were I permitted I would repeat what I say to my
own race, "Cast down your bucket where you are." Cast it down
among the eight millions of Negroes whose habits you know,
whose fidelity and love you have tested in days when to have
proved treacherous meant the ruins of your firesides. Cast down
your bucket among these people who have, without strikes and
labour wars, tilled your fields, cleared your forests, builded your
railroads and cities, and brought forth treasures from the bowels
of the earth, and helped make possible this magnificent representation of the progress of the South. Casting down your bucket

among my people, helping and encouraging them as you are doing on these grounds, and to education of head, hand, and heart, you will find that they will buy your surplus land, make blossom the waste places in your fields, and run your factories. While doing this, you can be sure in the future, as in the past, that you and your families will be surrounded by the most patient, faithful, law-abiding, and unresentful people that the world has seen. As we have proved our loyalty to you in the past, in nursing your children, watching by the sick-bed of your mothers and fathers, and often following them with tear-dimmed eyes to their graves, so in the future, in our humble way, we shall stand by you with a devotion that no foreigner can approach, ready to lay down our lives, if need be, in defence of yours, interlacing our industrial, commercial, civil, and religious life with yours in a way that shall make the interests of both races one. In all things that are purely social we can be as separate as the fingers, yet one as the hand in all things essential to mutual progress.

There is no defence or security for any of us except in the highest intelligence and development of all. If anywhere there are efforts tending to curtail the fullest growth of the Negro, let these efforts be turned into stimulating, encouraging, and making him the most useful and intelligent citizen. Effort or means so invested will pay a thousand per cent interest. These efforts will be twice blessed—"blessing him that gives and him that takes." . . .

Nearly sixteen millions of hands will aid you in pulling the load upward, or they will pull against you the load downward. We shall constitute one-third and more of the ignorance and crime of the South, or one-third its intelligence and progress; we shall contribute one-third to the business and industrial prosperity of the South, or we shall prove a veritable body of death, stagnating, depressing, retarding every effort to advance the body politic.

Gentlemen of the Exposition, as we present to you our humble effort at an exhibition of our progress, you must not expect overmuch. Starting thirty years ago with ownership here and there in a few quilts and pumpkins and chickens (gathered from miscellaneous sources), remember the path that has led from these to the inventions and production of agricultural implements, buggies, steam-engines, newspapers, books, statuary, carving, paintings, the management of drug-stores and banks, has not been trodden without contact with thorns and thistles. While we take pride in what we exhibit as a result of our independent efforts, we do not for a moment forget that our part in this exhibition would fall far short of your expectations but for the constant help that has come to our educational life, not only from the Southern states, but especially from Northern philanthropists, who have made their gifts a constant stream of blessing and encouragement.

The wisest among my race understand that the agitation of questions of social equality is the extremest folly, and that progress in the enjoyment of all the privileges that will come to us must be the result of severe and constant struggle rather than of artificial forcing. No race that has anything to contribute to the markets of the world is long in any degree ostracized. It is important and right that all privileges of the law be ours, but it is vastly more important that we be prepared for the exercises of these privileges. The opportunity to earn a dollar in a factory just now is worth infinitely more than the opportunity to spend a dollar in an opera-house.

In conclusion, may I repeat that nothing in thirty years has given us more hope and encouragement, and drawn us so near to you of the white race, as this opportunity offered by the Exposition; and here bending, as it were, over the altar that represents the results of the struggles of your race and mine, both starting practically empty-handed three decades ago, I pledge that in your effort to work out the great and intricate problem which God has laid at the doors of the South, you shall have at all times the patient, sympathetic help of my race; only let this be constantly in mind, that, while from representations in these buildings of the product of field, of forest, of mine, of factory, letters, and art, much good will come, yet far above and beyond material benefits will be that higher good, that, let us pray God, will

come, in a blotting out of sectional differences and racial ani-
mosities and suspicions, in a determination to administer absolute justice, in a willing obedience among all classes to the
mandates of law. This, this, coupled with our material prosperity, will bring into our beloved South a new heaven and a
new earth.

2. BOOKER T. WASHINGTON'S
PLAN TO ACHIEVE
THE RIGHTS OF CITIZENSHIP

The fullest statement of Booker T. Washington's philosophy appeared in *The Future of the American Negro,* a book that is cited
less frequently than it deserves to be. The volume is full of Washington's characteristically ambiguous phraseology and his unabashed
flattery of the white South. It also sets forth his essential belief that
by staying in the South, obtaining a useful education, holding a
useful job, and acquiring property the black man could ultimately
"earn" (the expression is Washington's) full citizenship rights.

Some have advised that the Negro leave the South and take
up his residence in the Northern States. I question whether this
would leave him any better off than he is in the South, when all
things are considered. It has been my privilege to study the
condition of our people in nearly every part of America; and
I say, without hesitation, that, with some exceptional cases, the
Negro is at his best in the Southern States. While he enjoys certain privileges in the North that he does not have in the South,
when it comes to the matter of securing property, enjoying business opportunities and employment, the South presents a far

Booker T. Washington, THE FUTURE OF THE AMERICAN NEGRO (Boston: Small, Maynard & Co., 1899), pp. 201–244.

better opportunity than the North. Few coloured men from the South are as yet able to stand up against the severe and increasing competition that exists in the North, to say nothing of the unfriendly influence of labour organisations, which in some way prevents black men in the North, as a rule, from securing employment in skilled labour occupations. . . .

. . . As a race, they do not want to leave the South, and the Southern white people do not want them to leave. We must therefore find some basis of settlement that will be constitutional, just, manly, that will be fair to both races in the South and to the whole country. This cannot be done in a day, a year, or any short period of time. We can, it seems to me, with the present light, decide upon a reasonably safe method of solving the problem, and turn our strength and effort in that direction. In doing this, I would not have the Negro deprived of any privilege guaranteed to him by the Constitution of the United States. It is not best for the Negro that he relinquish any of his constitutional rights. It is not best for the Southern white man that he should.

In order that we may, without loss of time or effort, concentrate our forces in a wise direction, I suggest what seems to me and many others the wisest policy to be pursued. . . . But I wish first to mention some elements of danger in the present situation, which all who desire the permanent welfare of both races in the South should carefully consider.

First.—There is danger that a certain class of impatient extremists among the Negroes, who have little knowledge of the actual conditions in the South, may do the entire race injury by attempting to advise their brethren in the South to resort to armed resistance or the use of the torch, in order to secure justice. All intelligent and well-considered discussion of any important question or condemnation of any wrong, both in the North and the South, from the public platform and through the press, is to be commended and encouraged; but ill-considered, incendiary utterances from black men in the North will tend to add to the burdens of our people in the South rather than relieve them.

Second.—Another danger in the South, which should be guarded against, is that the whole white South, including the wise, conservative, law-abiding element, may find itself represented before the bar of public opinion by the mob, or lawless element, which gives expression to its feelings and tendency in a manner that advertises the South throughout the world. Too often those who have no sympathy with such disregard of law are either silent or fail to speak in a sufficiently emphatic manner to offset, in any large degree, the unfortunate reputation which the lawless have too often made for many portions of the South.

Third.—No race or people ever got upon its feet without severe and constant struggle, often in the face of the greatest discouragement. While passing through the present trying period of its history, there is danger that a large and valuable element of the Negro race may become discouraged in the effort to better its condition. Every possible influence should be exerted to prevent this.

Fourth.—There is a possibility that harm may be done to the South and to the Negro by exaggerated newspaper articles which are written near the scene or in the midst of specially aggravating occurrences. Often these reports are written by newspaper men, who give the impression that there is a race conflict throughout the South, and that all Southern white people are opposed to the Negro's progress, overlooking the fact that, while in some sections there is trouble, in most parts of the South there is, nevertheless, a very large measure of peace, good will, and mutual helpfulness. . . .

Fifth.—Under the next head I would mention that, owing to the lack of school opportunities for the Negro in the rural districts of the South, there is danger that ignorance and idleness may increase to the extent of giving the Negro race a reputation for crime, and that immorality may eat its way into the moral fibre of the race, so as to retard its progress for many years. In judging the Negro in this regard, we must not be too harsh. We must remember that it has only been within the last thirty-four years that the black father and mother have had the responsibility, and consequently the experience, of training their own children. That they have not reached perfection in one generation, with the obstacles that the parents have been compelled to overcome, is not to be wondered at.

Sixth.—As a final source of danger to be guarded against, I would mention my fear that some of the white people of the South may be led to feel that the way to settle the race problem is to repress the aspirations of the Negro by legislation of a kind that confers certain legal or political privileges upon an ignorant and poor white man and withholds the same privileges from a black man in the same condition. Such legislation injures and retards the progress of both races. It is an injustice to the poor white man, because it takes from him incentive to secure education and property as prerequisites for voting. He feels that, because he is a white man, regardless of his possessions, a way will be found for him to vote. I would label all such measures, "Laws to keep the poor white man in ignorance and poverty." . . .

Such laws as have been made—as an example, in Mississippi —with the "understanding" clause hold out a temptation for the election officer to perjure and degrade himself by too often deciding that the ignorant white man does understand the Constitution when it is read to him and that the ignorant black man does not. By such a law the State not only commits a wrong against its black citizens; it injures the morals of its white citizens by conferring such a power upon any white man who may happen to be a judge of elections.

Such laws are hurtful, again, because they keep alive in the heart of the black man the feeling that the white man means to oppress him. The only safe way out is to set a high standard as a test of citizenship, and require blacks and whites alike to come up to it. When this is done, both will have a higher respect for the election laws and those who make them. I do not believe that, with his centuries of advantage over the Negro in the opportunity to acquire property and education as prerequisites for voting, the average white man in the South desires that any special law be passed to give him advantage over the Negro, who has had only a little more than thirty years in which to prepare himself for citizenship. In this relation another point of danger is that the Negro has been made to feel that it is his duty to oppose continually the Southern white man in politics, even in matters where no principle is involved, and that he is only loyal to his own race and acting in a manly way when he is opposing him. Such a policy has proved most hurtful to both races. Where it is a matter of principle, where a question of right or wrong is involved, I would advise the Negro to stand by principle at all hazards. A Southern white man has no respect for or confidence in a Negro who acts merely for policy's sake; but there are many cases—and the number is growing—where the Negro has nothing to gain and much to lose by opposing the Southern white man in many matters that relate to government. . . .

In the future, more than in the past, we want to impress upon the Negro the importance of identifying himself more closely with the interests of the South,—the importance of making himself part of the South and at home in it. Heretofore, for reasons which were natural and for which no one is especially to blame, the coloured people have been too much like a foreign nation residing in the midst of another nation. . . . The bed-rock upon which every individual rests his chances of success in life is securing the friendship, the confidence, the respect, of his next-door neighbour of the little community in which he lives. Almost the whole problem of the Negro in the South rests itself upon the fact as to whether the Negro can make himself of such indispensable service to his neighbour and the community that no one can fill his place better in the body politic. There is at present no other safe course for the black man to pursue. If the Negro in the South has a friend in his white neighbour and a still larger number of friends in his community, he has a protection and a guarantee of his rights that will be more potent and more lasting than any our Federal Congress or any outside power can confer.

We must admit the stern fact that at present the Negro, through no choice of his own, is living among another race which is far ahead of him in education, property, experience, and favourable condition; further, that the Negro's present condition makes him dependent upon the white people for most of the things necessary to sustain life, as well as for his common school education. In all history, those who have possessed the property and intelligence have exercised the greatest control in government, regardless of colour, race, or geographical location. This being the case, how can the black man in the South improve his present condition? And does the Southern white man want him to improve it?

The Negro in the South has it within his power, if he properly utilises the forces at hand, to make of himself such a valuable factor in the life of the South that he will not have to seek privileges, they will be freely conferred upon him. To bring this about, the Negro must begin at the bottom and lay a sure foundation, and not be lured by any temptation into trying to rise on a false foundation. While the Negro is laying this foundation he will need help, sympathy, and simple justice. Progress by any other method will be but temporary and superficial, and the latter end of it will be worse than the beginning. American slavery was a great curse to both races, and I would be the last to apologise for it; but, in the presence of God, I believe that slavery laid the foundation for the solution of the problem that is now before us in the South. During slavery the Negro was taught every trade, every industry, that constitutes the foundation for making a living. Now, if on this foundation—laid in rather a crude way, it is true, but a foundation, nevertheless—we can gradually build and improve, the future for us is bright. Let me be more specific. Agriculture is, or has been, the basic industry of nearly every race or nation that has succeeded. The Negro got a knowledge of this during slavery. Hence, in a large measure, he is in possession of this industry in the South to-day. The Negro can buy land in the South, as a rule, wherever the white man can buy it, and at very low prices. Now, since the bulk of our people already have a foundation in agriculture, they are at their best when living in the country, engaged in agricultural pursuits. Plainly, then, the best thing, the logical thing, is to turn the larger part of our strength in a direction that will make the Negro among the most skilled agricultural people in the world. The man who has learned to do something better than any one else, has learned to do a common thing in an uncommon manner, is the man who has a power and influence that no adverse circumstance can take from him. The Negro who can make himself so conspicuous as a successful farmer, a large tax-payer, a wise helper of his fellow-men, as to be placed in a position of trust and honour, whether the position be political or otherwise, by natural selection, is a hundred-fold more secure in that position than one placed there by mere outside force or pressure. . . .

Let us help the Negro by every means possible to acquire such an education in farming, dairying, stock-raising, horticulture, etc., as will enable him to become a model in these respects and place him near the top in these industries, and the race problem would in a large part be settled, or at least stripped of many of its most perplexing elements. This policy would also tend to keep the Negro in the country and smaller towns, where he succeeds best, and stop the influx into the large cities, where he does not succeed so well. The race, like the individual, that produces something of superior worth that has a common human interest, makes a permanent place for itself, and is bound to be recognised.

At a county fair in the South not long ago I saw a Negro awarded the first prize by a jury of white men, over white competitors, for the production of the best specimen of Indian corn. Every white man at this fair seemed to be pleased and proud of the achievement of this Negro, because it was apparent that he had done something that would add to the wealth and comfort of the people of both races in that county. . . . While race prejudice is strongly exhibited in many directions, in the matter of business, of commercial and industrial development, there is very little obstacle in the Negro's way. A Negro who produces or has for sale something that the community wants finds cus-

tomers among white people as well as black people. A Negro can
borrow money at the bank with equal security as readily as a
white man can. A bank in Birmingham, Alabama, that has now
existed ten years, is officered and controlled wholly by Negroes.
This bank has white borrowers and white depositors. A graduate
of the Tuskegee Institute keeps a well-appointed grocery store
in Tuskegee, and he tells me that he sells about as many goods
to the one race as to the other. What I have said of the opening
that awaits the Negro in the direction of agriculture is almost
equally true of mechanics, manufacturing, and all the domestic
arts. . . .

But it is asked, Would you confine the Negro to agriculture,
mechanics, and domestic arts, etc.? Not at all, but along the lines
that I have mentioned is where the stress should be laid just now
and for many years to come. We will need and must have many
teachers and ministers, some doctors and lawyers and statesmen;
but these professional men will have a constituency or a foundation from which to draw support just in proportion as the race
prospers along the economic lines that I have mentioned. During the first fifty or one hundred years of the life of any people
are not the economic occupations always given the greater attention? This is not only the historic, but, I think, the common-
sense view. If this generation will lay the material foundation,
it will be the quickest and surest way for the succeeding generation to succeed in the cultivation of the fine arts, and to surround
itself even with some of the luxuries of life, if desired. What the
race now most needs, in my opinion, is a whole army of men
and women well trained to lead and at the same time infuse
themselves into agriculture, mechanics, domestic employment,
and business. As to the mental training that these educated leaders should be equipped with, I should say, Give them all the
mental training and culture that the circumstances of individuals
will allow,—the more, the better. No race can permanently succeed until its mind is awakened and strengthened by the ripest
thought. But I would constantly have it kept in the thoughts
of those who are educated in books that a large proportion of

those who are educated should be so trained in hand that they can bring this mental strength and knowledge to bear upon the physical conditions in the South which I have tried to emphasise. . . .

To state in detail just what place the black man will occupy in the South as a citizen, when he has developed in the direction named, is beyond the wisdom of any one. Much will depend upon the sense of justice which can be kept alive in the breast of the American people. Almost as much will depend upon the good sense of the Negro himself. That question, I confess, does not give me the most concern just now. The important and pressing question is, Will the Negro with his own help and that of his friends take advantage of the opportunities that now surround him? When he has done this, I believe that, speaking of his future in general terms, he will be treated with justice, will be given the protection of the law, and will be given the recognition in a large measure which his usefulness and ability warrant. If, fifty years ago, any one had predicted that the Negro would have received the recognition and honour which individuals have already received, he would have been laughed at as an idle dreamer. Time, patience, and constant achievement are great factors in the rise of a race.

I do not believe that the world ever takes a race seriously, in its desire to enter into the control of the government of a nation in any large degree, until a large number of individuals, members of that race, have demonstrated, beyond question, their ability to control and develop individual business enterprises. When a number of Negroes rise to the point where they own and operate the most successful farms, are among the largest taxpayers in their county, are moral and intelligent, I do not believe that in many portions of the South such men need long be denied the right of saying by their votes how they prefer their property to be taxed and in choosing those who are to make and administer the laws. . . . But a short time ago I read letters from nearly every prominent white man in Birmingham, Alabama, asking that the Rev. W. R. Pettiford, a Negro, be appointed to a certain important federal office. What is the explanation of this?

Mr. Pettiford for nine years has been the president of the Negro bank in Birmingham to which I have alluded. During these nine years these white citizens have had the opportunity of seeing that Mr. Pettiford could manage successfully a private business, and that he had proven himself a conservative, thoughtful citizen; and they were willing to trust him in a public office. Such individual examples will have to be multiplied until they become the rule rather than the exception. While we are multiplying these examples, the Negro must keep a strong and courageous heart. He cannot improve his condition by any short-cut course or by artificial methods. Above all, he must not be deluded into the temptation of believing that his condition can be permanently improved by a mere battledore and shuttlecock of words or by any process of mere mental gymnastics or oratory alone. What is desired, along with a logical defence of his cause, are deeds, results,—multiplied results,—in the direction of building himself up, so as to leave no doubt in the minds of any one of his ability to succeed. . . .

My own feeling is that the South will gradually reach the point where it will see the wisdom and the justice of enacting an educational or property qualification, or both, for voting, that shall be made to apply honestly to both races. The industrial development of the Negro in connection with education and Christian character will help to hasten this end. When this is done, we shall have a foundation, in my opinion, upon which to build a government that is honest and that will be in a high degree satisfactory to both races. . . .

The problem is a large and serious one, and will require the patient help, sympathy, and advice of our most patriotic citizens, North and South, for years to come. But I believe that, if the principles which I have tried to indicate are followed, a solution of the question will come. So long as the Negro is permitted to get education, acquire property, and secure employment, and is treated with respect in the business or commercial world,—as is now true in the greater part of the South,—I shall have the greatest faith of his working out his own destiny in our Southern States. . . .

3. W. H. COUNCILL
UNITES BLACK NATIONALISM
WITH ACCOMMODATION
TO WHITE SUPREMACY

Today black nationalim is associated with black militance, but there is no necessary connection between the two. In fact at the turn of the century nationalist expressions were most often found as part of an accommodating ideology. In Booker T. Washington's conciliatory philosophy there was a strong emphasis on race pride, racial solidarity, and Negro support of Negro business.

An exceptionally good example of this use of black nationalism in an accommodating program is to be seen in the thinking of W. H. Councill. President of the State Normal School for black youth at Huntsville, Alabama, Councill was even more sycophantic toward the South than was Booker T. Washington.

American prejudice plays an important part in Negro opportunity. Never before in the history of any people has prejudice had such high valuation. Instead of seeking admission into places of amusement, pleasure and instruction run by white people for white people, let colored men open such places for their own accommodation and grow rich. Instead of knocking for admission into white circles, adorn, beautify, elevate, enlarge Negro circles and find scope for our broadest and most lofty ambition.

Every hotel which refuses a Negro a meal, every soda fountain which declines to serve him are voices telling him to go and open these places and make himself rich. That Negro is unwise who goes around asking for such accommodations among whites when the denial is only a friendly advice to open up this business for himself, place his own boys and girls in position and

From VOICE OF MISSIONS (Atlanta), December 1, 1900.

build up his own race by his own patronage. I want my race to find admission wherever honest service is wanted, and we will take care of the fun and pleasure places.

The Negro can grow only by being true to his own nature in his own sphere, as God intended. When he seeks to unrace himself—to run from his black skin, his flat nose, his thick lips and flat feet—then he will make himself despicable in the eyes of other races, and deserves the curse of God. We cannot make a white man a Negro, nor a Negro a white man. God has made the distinction, and set the bounds of each. Each will grow strong and great only as he is true to his own nature. I honor the white man because he honors himself. I honor him because he places his mother, sister, wife and daughter on a platform up among the stars, gets a thousand gatling guns, and decrees death to him who seeks to drag them down. I honor him because he throws his powerful arms around every little red-headed, freckle-faced, poor white girl and boy in the land and makes the way possible for them to rise in this world. I honor him because he does not go around whining and begging to be helped up, but by faith in his own muscle he cuts and carves out his own destiny. Let the Negro do likewise, according to his own nature, and in his own sphere, without prejudice to any, with love for all mankind, and he will succeed. Seize these opportunities, cultivate the most friendly relations with all men, feel a deep interest in our southland, and our deeds will count for something with man and God.

Political reverses

I shall not be surprised to see the Negro stripped of every privilege and right which were thrust upon him. People do not retain things for which they do not struggle. The Negro fought for his freedom. He won it. He is worthy of it. No man seeks to take it away. No earthly power can take it away. He did not struggle for the reins of southern state governments in 1866, when backed by northern bayonets; he stood upon the bosom of the white south prostrate in the dust of defeat. The white

south rose up, threw him off, and chased him from the legislatures and the national congress. The ballot was thrust upon him
without his knowledge of consent. He has lost it. He is being
stripped of all unpurchased rights. He stands naked and bare,
from which point all men must start, procure and secure the
things which are precious and sacred to them. Your race does
not enjoy a right for which it did not pour out its life blood
or toil and struggle. If the Negro is not willing to labor and
strive for rights, he is not worthy of them. When he wins them
by toil no man, in a free country, will dare seek to rob him of
them. He must stand upon a solid foundation, and then he will
recover through intelligence and merit what he now seems to be
losing through ignorance. Injustice will strengthen him. No
power outside of himself can harm him. When thus equipped
he will rise to the zenith in his own sphere as a Negro, and sink
to rest amid the golden splendors of usefulness, having cut out
his own way, and having carved his own history in the im-
perishable marble of time.

Salvation through Negro women

We complain too much of a lack of honor among our youth
when we do not exert ourselves to give them proper encouragement. We complain of the hardships of our women when we
never do one thing to relieve them. Our female element, under
mother influence, attends school and church, eschews the
brothels, stays at home, works, and to our shame is the backbone
of the Negro race today. Were it not for the Negro woman the
outlook would be dark. I am aware of the breadth of my speech
when I say that the world has never furnished a higher womanhood under like conditions than the Negro woman of the south
today. With strong appetites and passions, penniless, house-
less, working on "starvation wages," practically left to shift
alone, amid stumbling, falling, rising, fleeing—she goes on
washing, cooking, plowing, sowing, reaping—educating her
daughter, building the cottage, erecting churches and schools,
often supporting husband and son—this black woman deserves

the admiration of the gods. Every business man will say that a Negro woman's word is worth just what she values it at. Herein we see the nobility of white southern womanhood of long ago running through the black slave womanhood and lifting up her offspring of today—still lifting her up regardless of great drawbacks and weights.

Social separation—but justice

Can the strong Anglo-Saxon afford to be otherwise than just with the weak Negro in his midst? Treat the Negro fairly in the courts, in the common business transactions of life, in the labor markets of the south. I stand here, having affiliated for twenty-five years with the best white south in all that it considered its best welfare in politics and otherwise, and now with all the earnestness of my soul appeal for better treatment of the nurses, cooks and black mammies on the common carriers of the south. Separate the races in everything that looks like social intermingling, but in God's name treat us fairly. Do not subject us to treatment and to accommodation unworthy the gallantry and chivalry of the south. If the Negro girl is to be the servant girl of the south, then the white south is interested in making her refined and filling her with the tenderness, dignity, and virtue necessary for domestics in the best southern homes. Gentlemen, is there anything in the treatment of Negro women on the common carriers, and at the railroad stations to find them for service in good homes? You do not only run from social contact with the Negro, but you flee from the rough and riotous element in your own race. Help us to separate, as far as you can, from the unworthy of our race. The best blood of the south does not know that that nurse so well-beloved by their sunny haired children, that cook praised by the whole family, that "black mammy" the glory of many a southern heart are piled in a "jim crow" car, with dogs, convicts, train tools, roughs, their eyes, ears and noses insulted in a most ungodly manner, and forced with low men in the same dirty closets of waiting stations. As the white south honors its noble womanhood and precious childhood, it must throw around its servant class, everywhere, invironments of integrity and refinement.

Organic forces in the South

The few disturbances and outbreaks in the south show the wonderful organic forces in the south. We have here more than ten millions of Negroes and fifteen million whites, and yet we have probably in the whole south only one Negro and white man in ten thousand who clash. The other nine thousand nine hundred and ninety-nine rub against one another every hour of the day, in every walk of life, transact their business and go their way in perfect friendship. These peaceful relations of the 9,999 give a bolder prominence to the one exception which is held up by the enemies of the south as the general rule. The love and attachment between the races of the south are more than wonderful when we consider the untiring efforts of busy and meddlesome enemies—the politician, the newspaper, the magazine, and even the pulpit seeking to scatter seeds of discord and break up our peace. We 9,999 will stand firmly for good will and happiness of both races in the south. No enemy shall take that one sinner in ten thousand and disrupt and tear us asunder.

Lessons of the monuments

The world's monuments tell the story of human struggle. Where man has shed most tears and moistened the earth with his blood there the monuments have their foundations deepest. I have found that where man has toiled and struggled for man there the foundation of the monuments are broadest. I have found that where man has fought fiercest in the realm of mind there he has conquered most and there the monuments rear their heads highest. My race has built a monument in America which the hand of Time can not efface. As long as a man loves true liberty, as long as the spirit of justice finds lodgment in the human breast, as long as the virtues of fidelity and patience live among men, so long will the memory of the Negro race in

America live. All efforts to discount or wipe out our glorious
record of the past will only brighten it, and cause it to reflect
its refulgent glories far away across the ages to come.

Lesson from the Jews

Nothing is immortal but mind. Nothing survives but spirit.
Nothing triumphs but soul. The Jewish people are the fittest
people in the annals of man. They alone live. All others die. All
nations, whether ancient or modern, have been broken and shattered in proportion to the intensity with which they have thrown
themselves against this spiritual people. Oppress them, they increase. Persecute them, they flourish. Discriminate against them,
they grow rich. They go right on growing stronger by the cruelty
of their enemies. Babylon carried them into captivity. The Jew
is here. Where is Babylon? Egypt has beat him with many stripes
while he built her pyramids, her sphinx and her gigantic lake.
The Jew is here, the pyramids and sphinx which he built are
here. Where is Egypt? Rome whipped the Colosseum out of his
muscles. The Colosseum is here. The Jew is here. Where is
bloody Rome? Such will be the history of spiritual races unto
the end. The Negro is a spiritual race.

A coward; a brave man

Any coward can oppress a people—can be unfair—but it
takes a brave man to treat all men of whatever race and condition fairly and justly. Any other ideals, any other treatment
of men transmits to posterity a race of moral weaklings and
cowards. Teach every Negro boy and girl that the salvation of
life, the salvation of everything in the world is the glorious end
of education and duty. Then there could be no race conflict. I
would rather see every Negro, of the ten million in this country,
driven into the Gulf of Mexico and sink beneath its waters with
spotless souls, than continue to live with the blood of human
beings, with the blood of another race dropping from victorious
daggers in Negro hands.

Put up thy sword

Violence is the argument of cowards and unwise people. Shot guns correct nothing. Swords conquer nothing. Those who use the sword must perish by it. The Negro has the most powerful weapon known among men. It is the only convincing argument. It is the only weapon which brings lasting conquest. It is the sword of the spirit. It is faith in God. The Negro cannot hope to succeed with carnal armament. But with spirit forces there is no ocean which he cannot cross, no Alps which he cannot scale. Persecutions in time turn on the persecutor with a thousand fold more destructive malignity than were visited upon the persecuted. Wrongs are like the boomerang and return to the one who hurls them with more deadly results than they inflicted upon the intended victim. No people were ever persecuted down. They were always persecuted up. If we have been persecuted in this country, such persecution has more than doubled our population in thirty-five years and has increased our material wealth by a billion dollars in the same time.

His vivid imagination

It is not extravagant to say that a people so spiritual, so vivid in imagination, will yet put an interpretation upon the religion of Christ which will startle and refine more favored races. Such imagination, or spiritual insight, has never been more highly shown in any other people than in the Negro. He sees lights, dreams dreams, has visions, hears voices where other people can see or hear nothing, because until recently the Negro could exercise only his religious imagination, which was cultivated to the highest degree. The Negro fills all the air with heavenly music, or heavenly hosts to soothe, lead or protect the faithful servants of God. It is not extravagant to say that such vivid imagination when turned into the channels of art, will rival Phydias or Raphael; when turned toward science will discover and develop new worlds around about us and bring forth inventions for human salvation beyond the reach of materialistic races.

"No history"

It is said that we have no history. Blot out Egypt. Forget Hannibal. Do not remember noble Attucks. Wipe from history's page great Toussaint L'Ouverture or grand Douglass and still the Negro has done enough in the last forty years to give him creditable standing in the society of races, and to place his name in letters of gold across the azure blue above. Light up his wonderful imagination and emotion by the lamp of culture. Turn his imagination into mechanical and philosophical invention. Turn his deep emotion into music and poetry. Turn his constant stream of feeling into painting and sculptuary. Then the Negro, standing upon the shoulders of his Anglo-Saxon brother, will send wonder and amazement through the scientific and literary world. There are more inventions to be thought out, higher classes of forces yet undiscovered to be harnessed to appliances; more worlds to be discovered and dissected—more of God to be brought down to man. If the Negro is true to himself he will be God's instrument to bring it all about. God does not pay large prices for small things. Two millions of men did not meet forty years ago upon the battle field and redden the earth with their blood for nothing. God is helping the Negro to rise in the world.

Not solution—but evolution

We must train the hand to strike for man. Teach the heart to bear an injury, but never inflict one. All solutions of all human problems are simply evolutions. As man evolves out of selfishness into deep and broad sympathy, out of ignorance into light, out of sect, out of party into boundless humanity, then will racial conflict be diminished. There can be no racial solution, but amelioration of condition. Each individual must do his best at the black board of life, write plus, then go and "take his place in the silent halls of death." No three hundred years of human history have presented such wonderful evolutions as the three hundred years of Negro American history. Four millions of industrious Christians were evolved in the south from four million savages.

From four millions of penniless Negroes have evolved in thirty-five years ten millions of citizens worth a billion dollars, right here in the land of their bondage. From eight million white slave-holders have evolved fifteen million white tax payers who support churches and schools for their former slaves. Thus while all the outside world discusses solution, the glorious old south goes from one triumph to another in the process of evolution in thought and industry. This is our work in the south. By it the law of love shall reign supreme in all the land, and gentle peace shall come to abide forever in the Negro cabin, in the white man's mansion.

4. SUPPORT FOR A BOYCOTT
OF SEGREGATED STREET CARS
IN THE SOUTH

Even in the heyday of accommodation at the turn of the century, protest in the South did not entirely disappear. For example, between 1900 and 1906 blacks in more than twenty-five southern cities organized boycotts in response to the jim crow street car laws passed at the height of the wave of southern segregation legislation.

One wonders why a tactic that is part of the arsenal of militant, nonviolent direct action was employed in those repressive and discouraging years. For one thing, the street car boycotts were basically an attempt to preserve a status quo in the face of a radical innovation: the introduction of segregation on southern street cars. Secondly, as the social psychologist Thomas F. Pettigrew has written,[1] boycotts as a protest tactic have "the distinct psychological advantage" of appealing to all "three major types of responses human beings can make to oppression. . . . Such campaigns move toward the oppressor by seeking to achieve desegregation; they move against the oppressor by encouraging group unity and aggressively upsetting the white-controlled economy; and they move away from the oppressor by requesting the participators merely to avoid the scene of conflict."

This suggests why a widespread protest movement of this nature occurred in the South at a time when a philosophy of accommodation had achieved ascendancy in Negro thought and action. These

[1] Thomas F. Pettigrew, *A Profile of the Negro American* (Princeton, 1964), p. 200.

protests were in fact headed by black leaders known in their communities as impeccably respectable men rather than as radicals or firebrands. Some like Rev. R. H. Boyd of Nashville were close friends of Booker T. Washington. In many respects Boyd, general secretary of the National Baptist Publishing Board and president of the One Cent Savings Bank, was typical of the leadership. If anything, he was more conservative than most of the boycott leaders. Boyd once referred to racial discrimination as "only blessings in disguise. They stimulate and encourage rather than cower and humiliate the true, ambitious, self-determined Negro."[2]

In the document below, he expresses Negro resentment and protest in the tactful—even elliptical—manner of necessity often employed by southern Negro leaders. The selection shows that at first Nashville black leaders worked quietly against the street car segregation bill, then when it was passed, they sought to gain "advantages of the disadvantages" by urging the employment of black ticket-takers on separate street car trailers, and finally resorted to a boycott and the establishment of a black transportation company in 1905–1906.

To the Editor of the Banner.

Your paper has been very fair in discussing this common carrier automobile problem that now seems to be agitating the minds not only of the city of Nashville, but almost of every city in the South where they have street cars and "Jim Crow" street car laws. I have noticed that through the columns of your paper the negroes have never been criticised for their undertaking, but fair and impartially, as far as the paper could obtain it, the truth has been given. Therefore every promoter of this enterprise earnestly thanks you. We have endeavored to hide as much as possible every movement from the columns of the paper, for the reason that this is an untried venture, in its experimental stage, for two reasons—first, because the negroes themselves have never experimented in large financial ventures where united

R. H. Boyd, Letter to the Editor, from Nashville BANNER, September 27, 1905.

[2] *Report of the Fourth Annual Convention of the National Negro Business League* (Wilberforce, Ohio, 1903), p. 24.

financial skill and statesmanship were required, and, second, because automobiles, either as commercial machines or carriers, are almost wholly unknown in the South, thus making this venture a double experiment.

There is, however, one statement in your paper that we would beg to have stricken from your reports, and that is the statement that is constantly made that the negroes are boycotting or are attempting to boycott the street cars. This, to my personal knowledge, is not true. The negroes have never passed resolutions in their churches or mass-meetings to boycott the street car company. They have regretted the "Jim Crow" car law and believe it uncalled for. They regretted the active part taken in the making of this law by the street car management itself. So much did they regret this that a committee of negro business men called on the street car managers and begged them to refrain from taking such an active part, saying to them that the thirty or forty thousand negro citizens of Nashville and vicinity were liberal patrons of the railway and had refrained from giving them any trouble. They had patiently borne the unjust and abusive treatment given themselves and families by the street car conductors, hence we did not feel that we should be made an object for passing this law. But when assured by the street car management that, in their judgment, the law was a necessity, not on account of the negroes, but because of the discontent of the white people of the South, confusion, disturbance and possibly riots would arise, and to prevent the City Council from passing obnoxious and unreasonable laws against the interests of the company, the negroes withdrew their contention. They made no petition to the Legislature and registered no complaint, but when the law had been passed, such a law as they knew was formed by the street car company itself and pushed through the Legislature by the street car company's own representatives, and after being assured by the managers that they had the exact law they wanted, this committee, and I as spokesman of the committee, begged of the street car company that since the law was left absolutely in their hands, allowing them the right and privilege to appoint men with police power on all their cars, to make arrests, order and fine passengers at will, and since they had informed us that such a feeling existed among the white people that this law was necessary to keep down disputes and riots on the street cars, to attach trailers on the street car lines where there was the most negro travel and to place negro porters on these trailers to handle negro passengers. This proposition the street car company would not consider, and gave as their reason that this would not be satisfactory to their white street car conductors. Finding that our last and only petition was refused and denied even serious consideration, we felt that the street car company was in earnest in what they said—that the negroes were more trouble than profit, more damaging than of benefit to their revenue. So that we might not be a burden on the hands of these good people who are doing so much for the improvement and development of the city and are spending so much for this development and giving labor to so many of our unemployed, we decided to stay off the cars. Hence we feel that the street cars boycotted the negroes instead of the negroes boycotting the street cars. Thus it came about that the negroes of Nashville felt this was a good occasion for the raising and stimulating of the cause of the automobile as a common carrier.

We have every reason to believe that the enterprising and business-spirited people, both white and black, will encourage this movement in every laudable way. We expect, and have not been deceived, that some white people would take stock in this company and give us whatever aid and advice they can to make it a success. Should the negroes succeed in this laudable enterprise, it will be the solving of many of the problems of the South. First, it will stop agitation and feeling that is being carried on by the races on the street cars. Secondly, it will enable Southern people to launch, financier and manage their own enterprises, instead of going East and giving their valuable franchises into the hands of Eastern capitalists and syndicates. If the negroes of Nashville succeed in this enterprise with their five autos that they will place in the city of Nashville next week, they will increase them to twenty or fifty cars, and every city in the state will have a like number. Even the smaller cities that have no street car transportation will soon have these autos or motor cars running over their streets. The small or suburban town will not have to wait for the interurban railway to be built by Eastern syndicates and capitalists, but can have motor cars or wagonettes carrying passengers, mail and even freight between these interurban points. There need be then no discriminating laws, for the negroes can have their own transportation line, run by their own men, and everything will then move smoothly and nice.

We very much regret that there is talk of our city fathers attempting to legislate against this contemplated enterprise, and only hope that the powers that be will not cripple it in its infancy. The money in this enterprise has not been raised in the East, as has the money for the street cars. It is the hard earnings of the poor, hard-working negroes of the city of Nashville. It is expected that at least 2,000 negroes will take stock in this company at $10 per share, and that it will be a family affair rather than a corporation or syndicate. We regret being accused of being boycotters. The negroes are neither boycotters, strikers nor anarchists. The hard-working, industrious negroes are law-abiding citizens, and we are attempting to endure with patience whatever law or hardship is placed upon us until we can work out a remedy. As one of the promoters of this enterprise, I beg the hearty endorsement and approval of every reader of the Banner.

R. H. BOYD,
Purchasing Agent
Union Transportation Company.

5. MONROE TROTTER DENOUNCES
BOOKER T. WASHINGTON
AS A TRAITOR TO THE RACE

In 1901, when criticism of Washington had practically vanished, there appeared the most famous of all the anti-Tuskegee papers, the Boston *Guardian,* edited by William Monroe Trotter. The first Negro elected to Phi Beta Kappa at Harvard, Trotter was an uncompromising foe of all forms of segregation and discrimination. These two biting editorials in the *Guardian* best illustrate the temper of Trotter's attack on Washington as the agent of the forces of oppression.

A. "Why be silent?"

Under the caption, "Principal Washington Defines His Position," the *Tuskegee Student,* the official organ of Tuskegee, prints the institute letter in which Mr. Washington said: "We cannot elevate and make useful a race of people unless there is held out to them the hope of reward for right living. Every revised constitution throughout the southern states has put a premium upon intelligence, ownership of property, thrift and character." This little sheet begins by saying that the letter "appeared in all of the important papers of the country on Nov. 28. It has been unstintingly praised from one section of the country to the other for its clarity and forcefulness of statement, and for its ringing note of sincerity." Although such words are to be expected from the employes of the school they are for the most part only too true. It is true that, although the letter was sent to the *Age Herald* of Birmingham, Alabama, it appeared simultaneously "in all the important papers of the country."

Editorial, Boston GUARDIAN, December 20, 1902.

Then its effect must be admitted to have been greater than if any other Negro had written it, for admittedly no other Negro's letter could have obtained such wide publicity. If it had in it aught that was injurious to the Negro's welfare or to his manhood rights, therefore, such worked far more damage than if any other Negro or any other man, save the president himself, had written the words.

What man is there among us, whether friend or foe of the author of the letter, who was not astounded at the reference to the disfranchising constitutions quoted above. "Every revised constitution throughout the southern states has put a premium upon intelligence, ownership of property, thrift and character," and all the more so because Mr. Washington had not been accused by even the southerners of opposing these disfranchising constitutions. . . . If the statement is false, if it is misleading, if it is injurious to the Negro, all the more blamable and guilty is the author because the statement was gratuitous on his part.

Is it the truth? Do these constitutions encourage Negroes to be thrifty, to be better and more intelligent? For this sort of argument is the most effective in favor of them. . . . Where is the Negro who says the law was or is ever intended to be fairly applied? . . . If so, then every reputable Negro orator and writer, from Hon. A. H. Grimke on, have been mistaken. If so, every Negro clergyman of standing, who has spoken on the subject . . . have been misinformed. We happen to know of an undertaker who has an enormous establishment in Virginia, who now can't vote. Is that encouraging thrift? Two letter carriers, who have passed the civil service examinations, are now sueing because disfranchised. Is that encouraging intelligence? . . . Even a Republican candidate for governor in Virginia recently said Negro domination was to be feared if 10 Negroes could vote because they could have the balance of power. Mr. Washington's statement is shamefully false and deliberately so.

But even were it true, what man is a worse enemy to a race than a leader who looks with equanimity on the disfranchisement of his race in a country where other races have universal

suffrage by constitutions that make one rule for his race and
another for the dominant race, by constitutions made by conventions to which his race is not allowed to send its representatives,
by constitutions that his race although endowed with the franchise by law are not allowed to vote upon, and are, therefore,
doubly illegal, by constitutions in violation to the national constitution, because, forsooth, he thinks such disfranchising laws
will benefit the moral character of his people. Let our spiritual
advisers condemn this idea of reducing a people to serfdom to
make them good.

But what was the effect of Mr. Washington's letter on the
northern white people? . . .

No thinking Negro can fail to see that, with the influence
Mr. Washington yields [wields] in the North and the confidence
reposed in him by the white people on account of his school, a
fatal blow has been given to the Negro's political rights and
liberty by his statement. The benevolence idea makes it all the
more deadly in its effect. It comes very opportunely for the
Negro, too, just when Roosevelt declares the Negro shall hold
office, . . . when Congress is being asked to enforce the Negro's
constitutional rights, when these laws are being carried to the
Supreme Court. And here Mr. Washington, having gained sufficient influence through his doctrines, his school and his elevation by the President, makes all these efforts sure of failure by
killing public sentiment against the disfranchising constitutions.

And Mr. Washington's word is the more effective for, discred-
itable as it may seem, not five Negro papers even mention a
statement that belies all their editorials and that would have set
aflame the entire Negro press of the country, if a less wealthy
and less powerful Negro had made it. Nor will Negro orators nor
Negro preachers dare now to pick up the gauntlet thrown down
by the great "educator." Instead of being universally repudiated
by the Negro race his statement will be practically universally
endorsed by its silence because Washington said it, though it
sounds the death-knell of our liberty. The lips of our leading
politicians are sealed, because, before he said it, Mr. Washing-

ton, through the President, put them under obligation to himself. Nor is there that heroic quality now in our race that would lead men to throw off the shackles of fear, of obligation, of policy and denounce a traitor though he be a friend, or even a brother. It occurs to none that silence is tantamount to being virtually an accomplice in the treasonable act of this Benedict Arnold of the Negro race.

O, for a black Patrick Henry to save his people from this stigma of cowardice; to rouse them from their lethargy to a sense of danger; to score the tyrant and to inspire his people with the spirit of those immortal words: "Give Me Liberty or Give Me Death."

B. "Some real Tuskegee gems"

From Booker T. Washington's speech before the Twentieth Century Club at the Colonial Theatre last Saturday we have clipped some excerpts which, we feel, can properly be classed as "Tuskegee gems." . . .

Here is a gem of real value:

"Those are most truly free who have passed through the greatest discipline."

Then slavery was the best condition of society, for all admit it was the severest discipline yet experienced by man. Was it not wrong in Lincoln to deprive our race thus of the highest freedom?

Here are two more gems:

"My request to the white men of the north is that they bring more coolness, more calmness, more deliberations and more sense of justice to the Negro question."

"As soon as our race gets property in the form of real estate, of intelligence, of high Christian character, it will find that it is going to receive the recognition which it has not thus far received."

Editorial, Boston GUARDIAN, April 4, 1903.

The coolness is needed in the South, not in the North; this section needs to warm up a little in the interest of its former ideals.

As to the question of wealth and character, etc., winning one recognition, we see quite the contrary in the South. These things are damned there in Negroes. For proofs see the efforts made there to keep all Negroes from places of preferment. . . .

Gem No. 4 says:

"We have never disturbed the country by riots, strikes or lockouts; ours has been a peaceful, faithful, humble service."

Now, it is a doubtful compliment to have this said about us; for the reason that strikes and lockouts are sometimes necessary conditions in society, and people who brag that they do not resort to these necessities are not always to be commended. In fact, the Negro in any and all professions and callings is safest in doing just the same, and no different from his white brother.

Gem No. 5:

"One farm bought, one house built, one home sweetly and intelligently kept, one man who is the largest taxpayer or who has the largest banking account, one school or church maintained, one factory running successfully, one garden profitably cultivated, one patient cured by a Negro doctor, one sermon well preached, one life cleanly lived, will tell more in our favor than all the abstract eloquence that can be summoned to plead our cause."

All of this last is mere claptrap. All the wealth, skill and intelligence acquired and accumulated by Negroes before '61 did not do half so much toward freeing the slave as did the abstract eloquence of [Frederick] Douglass, [Samuel Ringgold] Ward,[1] [William Lloyd] Garrison and [Wendell] Phillips. . . . This habit of always belittling agitation on the part of Washington, that very thing which made him free, and by which he lives and prospers is one of his great faults if a man with such a blundering can have any degrees in stupidity.

---

[1] Samuel Ringgold Ward, escaped slave and Congregationalist minister, was a noted abolitionist, sometimes referred to as the "Black Daniel Webster" [Ed.].

6. W. E. B. DU BOIS
ATTACKS WASHINGTON'S POLICY OF
"ADJUSTMENT AND SUBMISSION"

The most influential dissent from Washington's policy came from W. E. B. Du Bois, a Massachusetts-born black whose family had been free from the stigma of slavery for over a hundred years. Du Bois was educated at Fisk University and then at Harvard; he won his Ph.D. in history at Harvard in 1895. Subsequently he became a professor of sociology at Atlanta University. There he devoted himself to training a generation of college-educated Negroes as racial leaders and to editing annual surveys of various aspects of Negro life.

At first friendly with Washington, Du Bois drifted away when Washington's emphasis on industrial education drew resources away from liberal arts colleges like Atlanta, and when the Tuskegeean's accommodating policies produced so little real gain for the race. Hints of dissent appeared in Du Bois's review of Washington's autobiography, *Up From Slavery*, in 1901. Then, two years later, Du Bois's most sensitive volume, *The Souls of Black Folk*, launched a full-scale attack that was reasoned, thoughtful, and unequivocal. With the publication of this book, Du Bois took the first rank in the struggle against Washington's program.

Easily the most striking thing in the history of the American Negro since 1876 is the ascendancy of Mr. Booker T. Washington. It began at the time when war memories and ideals were rapidly passing; a day of astonishing commercial development was dawning; a sense of doubt and hesitation overtook the freedmen's sons,—then it was that his leading began. Mr. Washington came, with a simple definite programme, at the psychological moment when the nation was a little ashamed of having bestowed so much sentiment on Negroes, and was concentrating

W. E. B. Du Bois, "Of Mr. Booker T. Washington and Others," THE SOULS OF BLACK FOLK (Chicago: A. C. McClurg & Co., 1903), pp. 41–53.

its energies on Dollars. His programme of industrial education, conciliation of the South, and submission and silence as to civil and political rights, was not wholly original; the Free Negroes from 1830 up to war-time had striven to build industrial schools, and the American Missionary Association had from the first taught various trades; and Price[1] and others had sought a way of honorable alliance with the best of the Southerners. But Mr. Washington first indissolubly linked these things; he put enthusiasm, unlimited energy, and perfect faith into this programme, and changed it from a by-path into a veritable Way of Life. And the tale of the methods by which he did this is a fascinating study of human life.

It startled the nation to hear a Negro advocating such a programme after many decades of bitter complaint; it startled and won the applause of the South, it interested and won the admiration of the North; and after a confused murmur of protest, it silenced if it did not convert the Negroes themselves.

To gain the sympathy and coöperation of the various elements comprising the white South was Mr. Washington's first task; and this, at the time Tuskegee was founded, seemed, for a black man, well-nigh impossible. And yet ten years later it was done in the word spoken at Atlanta: "In all things purely social we can be as separate as five fingers, and yet one as the hand in all things essential to mutual progress." This "Atlanta Compromise" is by all odds the most notable thing in Mr. Washington's career. The South interpreted it in different ways: the radicals received it as a complete surrender of the demand for civil and political equality; the conservatives, as a generously conceived working basis for mutual understanding. So both approved it, and to-day its author is certainly the most distinguished Southerner since Jefferson Davis, and the one with the largest personal following.

Next to this achievement comes Mr. Washington's work in gaining place and consideration in the North. Others less shrewd

[1] J. C. Price, founder and president of Livingstone College, Salisbury, N.C.; the first president of the Afro-American League, he was a renowned orator and conciliatory leader from about 1890 until his death in 1894 [Ed.].

and tactful had formerly essayed to sit on these two stools and had fallen between them; but as Mr. Washington knew the heart of the South from birth and training, so by singular insight he intuitively grasped the spirit of the age which was dominating the North. And so thoroughly did he learn the speech and thought of triumphant commercialism, and the ideals of material prosperity, that the picture of a lone black boy poring over a French grammar amid the weeds and dirt of a neglected home soon seemed to him the acme of absurdities. One wonders what Socrates and St. Francis of Assisi would say to this.

And yet this very singleness of vision and thorough oneness with his age is a mark of the successful man. It is as though Nature must needs make men narrow in order to give them force. So Mr. Washington's cult has gained unquestioning followers, his work has wonderfully prospered, his friends are legion, and his enemies are confounded. To-day he stands as the one recognized spokesman of his ten million fellows, and one of the most notable figures in a nation of seventy millions. One hesitates, therefore, to criticise a life which, beginning with so little, has done so much. And yet the time is come when one may speak in all sincerity and utter courtesy of the mistakes and shortcomings of Mr. Washington's career, as well as of his triumphs, without being thought captious or envious, and without forgetting that it is easier to do ill than well in the world.

The criticism that has hitherto met Mr. Washington has not always been of this broad character. In the south especially has he had to walk warily to avoid the harshest judgments,—and naturally so, for he is dealing with the one subject of deepest sensitiveness to that section. Twice—once when at the Chicago celebration of the Spanish-American War he alluded to the color-prejudice that is "eating away the vitals of the South," and once when he dined with President Roosevelt—has the resulting Southern criticism been violent enough to threaten seriously his popularity. In the North the feeling has several times forced itself into words, that Mr. Washington's counsels of submission overlooked certain elements of true manhood, and that his educational programme was unnecessarily narrow. Usually, however, such criticism has not found open expression, although, too, the spiritual sons of the Abolitionists have not been prepared to acknowledge that the schools founded before Tuskegee, by men of broad ideals and self-sacrificing spirit, were wholly failures or worthy of ridicule. While, then, criticism has not failed to follow Mr. Washington, yet the prevailing public opinion of the land has been but too willing to deliver the solution of a wearisome problem into his hands, and say, "If that is all you and your race ask, take it."

Among his own people, however, Mr. Washington has encountered the strongest and most lasting opposition, amounting at times to bitterness, and even to-day continuing strong and insistent even though largely silenced in outward expression by the public opinion of the nation. Some of this opposition is, of course, mere envy; the disappointment of displaced demagogues and the spite of narrow minds. But aside from this, there is among educated and thoughtful colored men in all parts of the land a feeling of deep regret, sorrow, and apprehension at the wide currency and ascendancy which some of Mr. Washington's theories have gained. These same men admire his sincerity of purpose, and are willing to forgive much to honest endeavor which is doing something worth the doing. They coöperate with Mr. Washington as far as they conscientiously can; and, indeed, it is no ordinary tribute to this man's tact and power that, steering as he must between so many diverse interests and opinions, he so largely retains the respect of all.

But the hushing of the criticism of honest opponents is a dangerous thing. It leads some of the best of the critics to unfortunate silence and paralysis of effort, and others to burst into speech so passionately and intemperately as to lose listeners. Honest and earnest criticism from those whose interests are most nearly touched,—criticism of writers by readers, of government by those governed, of leaders by those led,—this is the soul of democracy and the safeguard of modern society. If the best of the American Negroes receive by outer pressure a leader whom they had not recognized before, manifestly there is here a certain palpable gain. Yet there is also irreparable loss,—a loss of that peculiarly valuable education which a group receives when by search and criticism it finds and commissions its own leaders. The way in which this is done is at once the most elementary and the nicest problem of social growth. History is but the record of such group-leadership; and yet how infinitely changeful is its type and character! And of all types and kinds, what can be more instructive than the leadership of a group within a group? —that curious double movement where real progress may be negative and actual advance be relative retrogression. All this is the social student's inspiration and despair. . . .

Then came the Revolution of 1876, the suppression of the Negro votes, the changing and shifting of ideals, and the seeking of new lights in the great night. Douglass,[2] in his old age, still bravely stood for the ideals of his early manhood,—ultimate assimilation *through* self-assertion, and on no other terms. For a time Price arose as a new leader, destined, it seemed, not to give up, but to re-state the old ideals in a form less repugnant to the white South. But he passed away in his prime. Then came the new leader. Nearly all the former ones had become leaders by the silent suffrage of their fellows, had sought to lead their own people alone, and were usually, save Douglass, little known outside their race. But Booker T. Washington arose as essentially the leader not of one race but of two,—a compromiser between the South, the North, and the Negro. Naturally the Negroes resented, at first bitterly, signs of compromise which surrendered their civil and political rights, even though this was to be exchanged for larger chances of economic development. The rich and dominating North, however, was not only weary of the race problem, but was investing largely in Southern enterprises, and welcomed any method of peaceful coöperation. Thus, by national opinion, the Negroes began to recognize Mr. Washington's leadership; and the voice of criticism was hushed.

[2] The death of the renowned protest leader Frederick Douglass in 1895, the year of Washington's Atlanta address, has often been described as symbolizing the transition from the philosophy of protest to that of accommodation. But Douglass's leadership and point of view were in fact being eclipsed several years before his death [Ed.].

Mr. Washington represents in Negro thought the old attitude of adjustment and submission; but adjustment at such a peculiar time as to make his programme unique. This is an age of unusual economic development, and Mr. Washington's programme naturally takes an economic cast, becoming a gospel of Work and Money to such an extent as apparently almost completely to overshadow the higher aims of life. Moreover, this is an age when the more advanced races are coming in closer contact with the less developed races, and the race-feeling is therefore intensified; and Mr. Washington's programme practically accepts the alleged inferiority of the Negro races. Again, in our own land, the reaction from the sentiment of war time has given impetus to race-prejudice against Negroes, and Mr. Washington withdraws many of the high demands of Negroes as men and American citizens. In other periods of intensified prejudice all the Negro's tendency to self-assertion has been called forth; at this period a policy of submission is advocated. In the history of nearly all other races and peoples the doctrine preached at such crises has been that manly self-respect is worth more than lands and houses, and that a people who voluntarily surrender such respect, or cease striving for it, are not worth civilizing.

In answer to this, it has been claimed that the Negro can survive only through submission. Mr. Washington distinctly asks that black people give up, at least for the present, three things,—

First, political power,

Second, insistence on civil rights,

Third, higher education of Negro youth,—

and concentrate all their energies on industrial education, the accumulation of wealth, and the conciliation of the South. This policy has been courageously and insistently advocated for over fifteen years, and has been triumphant for perhaps ten years. As a result of this tender of the palm-branch, what has been the return? In these years there have occurred:

1. The disfranchisement of the Negro.

2. The legal creation of a distinct status of civil inferiority for the Negro.

3. The steady withdrawal of aid from institutions for the higher training of the Negro.

These movements are not, to be sure, direct results of Mr. Washington's teachings; but his propaganda has, without a shadow of doubt, helped their speedier accomplishment. The question then comes: Is it possible, and probable, that nine millions of men can make effective progress in economic lines if they are deprived of political rights, made a servile caste, and allowed only the most meagre chance for developing their exceptional men? If history and reason give any distinct answer to these questions, it is an emphatic *No*. And Mr. Washington thus faces the triple paradox of his career:

1. He is striving nobly to make Negro artisans business men and property-owners; but it is utterly impossible, under modern competitive methods, for workingmen and property-owners to defend their rights and exist without the right of suffrage.

2. He insists on thrift and self-respect, but at the same time counsels a silent submission to civic inferiority such as is bound to sap the manhood of any race in the long run.

3. He advocates common-school and industrial training, and depreciates institutions of higher learning; but neither the Negro common-schools, nor Tuskegee itself, could remain open a day were it not for teachers trained in Negro colleges, or trained by their graduates.

This triple paradox in Mr. Washington's position is the object of criticism by two classes of colored Americans. One class is spiritually descended from Toussaint the Savior, through Gabriel, Vesey, and Turner,[3] and they represent the attitude of revolt and revenge; they hate the white South blindly and distrust the white race generally, and so far as they agree on definite action, think that the Negro's only hope lies in emigration beyond the borders of the United States. And yet, by the irony of fate, nothing has more effectively made this programme seem hopeless than the recent course of the United States toward weaker and darker peoples in the West Indies, Hawaii, and the Philippines, —for where in the world may we go and be safe from lying and brute force?

---

[3] Gabriel Prosser, Denmark Vesey, and Nat Turner, leaders of the three most famous slave revolts in American history [Ed.].

The other class of Negroes who cannot agree with Mr. Washington has hitherto said little aloud. They deprecate the sight of scattered counsels, of internal disagreement; and especially they dislike making their just criticism of a useful and earnest man an excuse for a general discharge of venom from small-minded opponents. Nevertheless, the questions involved are so fundamental and serious that it is difficult to see how men like the Grimkes, Kelly Miller, J. W. E. Bowen,[4] and other representatives of this group, can much longer be silent. Such men feel in conscience bound to ask of this nation three things:

1. The right to vote.
2. Civic equality.
3. The education of youth according to ability.

They acknowledge Mr. Washington's invaluable service in counselling patience and courtesy in such demands; they do not ask that ignorant black men vote when ignorant whites are debarred, or that any reasonable restrictions in the suffrage should not be applied; they know that the low social level of the mass of the race is responsible for much discrimination against it, but they also know, and the nation knows, that relentless color-prejudice is more often a cause than a result of the Negro's degradation; they seek the abatement of this relic of barbarism, and not its systematic encouragement and pampering by all agencies of social power from the Associated Press to the Church of Christ. They advocate, with Mr. Washington, a broad system of Negro common schools supplemented by thorough industrial training; but they are surprised that a man of Mr. Washington's insight cannot see that no educational system ever has rested or can rest on any other basis than that of the well-equipped college and university, and they insist that there is a

[4] Archibald Grimké, Boston lawyer, consul in Santo Domingo, 1894–1898; Francis J. Grimké, minister of the 16th Street Presbyterian Church in Washington, D.C.; Kelly Miller, professor and later dean at the college of liberal arts at Howard University, and a noted essayist on racial affairs; J. W. E. Bowen, professor and later president at Gammon Theological Seminary, Atlanta, Ga. The Grimké brothers later joined the radicals; Bowen remained a conservative; Miller, known as a "straddler," attempted to synthesize both points of view [Ed.].

demand for a few such institutions throughout the South to train the best of the Negro youth as teachers, professional men, and leaders.

This group of men honor Mr. Washington for his attitude of conciliation toward the white South; they accept the "Atlanta Compromise" in its broadest interpretation; they recognize, with him, many signs of promise, many men of high purpose and fair judgment, in this section; they know that no easy task has been laid upon a region already tottering under heavy burdens. But, nevertheless, they insist that the way to truth and right lies in straightforward honesty, not in indiscriminate flattery; in praising those of the South who do well and criticising uncompromisingly those wo do ill; in taking advantage of the opportunities at hand and urging their fellows to do the same, but at the same time in remembering that only a firm adherence to their higher ideals and aspirations will ever keep those ideals within the realm of possibility. They do not expect that the free right to vote, to enjoy civic rights, and to be educated, will come in a moment; they do not expect to see the bias and prejudices of years disappear at the blast of a trumpet; but they are absolutely certain that the way for a people to gain their reasonable rights is not by voluntarily throwing them away and insisting that they do not want them; that the way for a people to gain respect is not by continually belittling and ridiculing themselves; that, on the contrary, Negroes must insist continually, in season and out of season, that voting is necessary to modern manhood, that color discrimination is barbarism, and that black boys need education as well as white boys. . . .

It would be unjust to Mr. Washington not to acknowledge that in several instances he has opposed movements in the South which were unjust to the Negro; he sent memorials [opposing disfranchisement of Negroes only, and proposing instead the application of identical literacy and property qualifications to whites and Negroes alike] to the Louisiana and Alabama constitutional conventions, he has spoken against lynching, and in other ways has openly or silently set his influence against sinister schemes and unfortunate happenings. Notwithstanding this, it is equally true to assert that on the whole the distinct impression left by Mr. Washington's propaganda is, first, that the South is justified in its present attitude toward the Negro because of the Negro's degradation; secondly, that the prime cause of the Negro's failure to rise more quickly is his wrong education in the past; and, thirdly, that his future rise depends primarily on his own efforts. Each of these propositions is a dangerous half-truth. The supplementary truths must never be lost sight of: first, slavery and race-prejudice are potent if not sufficient causes of the Negro's position; second, industrial and common-school training were necessarily slow in planting because they had to await the black teachers trained by higher institutions—it being extremely doubtful if any essentially different development was possible, and certainly a Tuskegee was unthinkable before 1880; and, third, while it is a great truth to say that the Negro must strive and strive mightily to help himself, it is equally true that unless his striving be not simply seconded, but rather aroused and encouraged, by the initiative of the richer and wiser environing group, he cannot hope for great success.

In his failure to realize and impress this last point, Mr. Washington is especially to be criticised. His doctrine has tended to make the whites, North and South, shift the burden of the Negro problem to the Negro's shoulders and stand aside as critical and rather pessimistic spectators; when in fact the burden belongs to the nation, and the hands of none of us are clean if we bend not our energies to righting these great wrongs.

The South ought to be led, by candid and honest criticism, to assert her better self and do her full duty to the race she has cruelly wronged and is still wronging. The North—her co-partner in guilt—cannot salve her conscience by plastering it with gold. We cannot settle this problem by diplomacy and suaveness, by "policy" alone. If worse come to worst, can the moral fibre of this country survive the slow throttling and murder of nine millions of men?

The black men of America have a duty to perform, a duty stern and delicate,—a forward movement to oppose a part of the work of their greatest leader. So far as Mr. Washington preaches

Thrift, Patience, and Industrial Training for the masses, we must hold up his hands and strive with him, rejoicing in his honors and glorying in the strength of this Joshua called of God and of man to lead the headless host. But so far as Mr. Washington apologizes for injustice, North or South, does not rightly value the privilege and duty of voting, belittles the emasculating effects of caste distinctions, and opposes the higher training and ambition of our brighter minds,—so far as he, the South, or the Nation, does this,—we must unceasingly and firmly oppose them. By every civilized and peaceful method we must strive for the rights which the world accords to men, clinging unwaveringly to those great words which the sons of the Fathers would fain forget: "We hold these truths to be self-evident: That all men are created equal; that they are endowed by their Creator with certain unalienable rights; that among these are life, liberty, and the pursuit of happiness."

7. W. E. B. DU BOIS ARGUES
FOR A COLLEGE-EDUCATED ELITE

A characteristic part of Du Bois's program appeared in a volume to which Booker T. Washington also contributed, *The Negro Problem*. Whereas Washington looked for progress from an economic base of successful Negro farmers, artisans, and businessmen, Du Bois looked to the college-educated intellectuals to advance the race and lift up the oppressed, lower-class blacks. Here was an elitist variant of the philosophy of self-help and racial solidarity that was not only widely prevalent at the time but was also the only doctrine shared by both Washington and Du Bois. But the followers of Tuskegee charged that Du Bois wanted a cadre of leaders with unskilled hands and airy

W. E. B. Du Bois, "The Talented Tenth," in Booker T. Washington and others, THE NEGRO PROBLEM: A SERIES OF ARTICLES BY REPRE-SENTATIVE NEGROES OF TO-DAY (New York: James Pott & Co., 1903), pp. 33–75, passim.

heads, while the radicals, for their part, claimed that Washington was training hewers of wood and drawers of water. In "The Talented Tenth," Du Bois made a full exposition of his ideas on the role of black intellectuals in racial self-elevation.

The Negro race, like all races, is going to be saved by its exceptional men. The problem of education, then, among Negroes must first of all deal with the Talented Tenth; it is the problem of developing the Best of this race that they may guide the Mass away from the contamination and death of the Worst, in their own and other races. Now the training of men is a difficult and intricate task. Its technique is a matter for educational experts, but its object is for the vision of seers. If we make money the object of man-training, we shall develop money-makers but not necessarily men; if we make technical skill the object of education, we may possess artisans but not, in nature, men. Men we shall have only as we make manhood the object of the work of the schools—intelligence, broad sympathy, knowledge of the world that was and is, and of the relation of men to it—this is the curriculum of that Higher Education which must underlie true life. On this foundation we may build bread winning, skill of hand and quickness of brain, with never a fear lest the child and man mistake the means of living for the object of life.

———————

If this be true—and who can deny it—three tasks lay before me; first to show from the past that the Talented Tenth as they have risen among American Negroes have been worthy of leadership; secondly, to show how these men may be educated and developed; and thirdly, to show their relation to the Negro problem.

———————

From the very first it has been the educated and intelligent of the Negro people that have led and elevated the mass, and the sole obstacles that nullified and retarded their efforts were slavery and race prejudice; . . .

And so we come to the present—a day of cowardice and vacillation, of strident wide-voiced wrong and faint hearted compromise; of double-faced dallying with Truth and Right. Who are to-day guiding the work of the Negro people? The "exceptions" of course. And yet so sure as this Talented Tenth is pointed out, the blind worshippers of the Average cry out in alarm: "These are exceptions, look here at death, disease and crime—these are the happy rule." Of course they are the rule, because a silly nation made them the rule: Because for three long centuries this people lynched Negroes who dared to be brave, raped black women who dared to be virtuous, crushed dark-hued youth who dared to be ambitious, and encouraged and made to flourish servility and lewdness and apathy. But not even this was able to crush all manhood and chastity and aspiration from black folk. A saving remnant continually survives and persists, continually aspires, continually shows itself in thrift and ability and character. Exceptional it is to be sure, but this is its chiefest promise; it shows the capability of Negro blood, the promise of black men. . . . Is it fair, is it decent, is it Christian to ignore these facts of the Negro problem, to belittle such aspiration, to nullify such leadership and seek to crush these people back into the mass out of which by toil and travail, they and their fathers have raised themselves?

Can the masses of the Negro people be in any possible way more quickly raised than by the effort and example of this aristocracy of talent and character? Was there ever a nation on God's fair earth civilized from the bottom upward? Never; it is, ever was and ever will be from the top downward that culture filters. The Talented Tenth rises and pulls all that are worth the saving up to their vantage ground. This is the history of human progress; . . .

How then shall the leaders of a struggling people be trained and the hands of the risen few strengthened? There can be but one answer: The best and most capable of their youth must be schooled in the colleges and universities of the land. . . .

All men cannot go to college but some men must; every isolated group or nation must have its yeast, must have for the talented few centers of training where men are not so mystified and befuddled by the hard and necessary toil of earning a living, as to have no aims higher than their bellies, and no God greater than Gold. This is true training, and thus in the beginning were the favored sons of the freedmen trained. Out of the colleges of the North came, after the blood of war, Ware, Cravath, Chase, Andrews, Bumstead and Spence* to build the foundations of knowledge and civilization in the black South. Where ought they to have begun to build? At the bottom, of course, quibbles the mole with his eyes in the earth. Aye! truly at the bottom, at the very bottom; at the bottom of knowledge, down in the very depths of knowledge there where the roots of justice strike into the lowest soil of Truth. And so they did begin; they founded colleges, and up from the colleges shot normal schools, and out from the normal schools went teachers, and around the normal teachers clustered other teachers to teach the public schools; the college trained in Greek and Latin and mathematics, 2,000 men; and these men trained full 50,000 others in morals and manners, and they in turn taught thrift and the alphabet to nine millions of men, who to-day hold $300,000,000 of property. It was a miracle—the most wonderful peace-battle of the 19th century, and yet to-day men smile at it, and in fine superiority tell us that it was all a strange mistake; that a proper way to found a system of education is first to gather the children and buy them spelling books and hoes; afterward men may look about for teachers, if haply they may find them; or again they would teach men Work, but as for Life—why, what has Work to do with Life, they ask vacantly. . . .

These figures illustrate vividly the function of the college-bred Negro. He is, as he ought to be, the group leader, the man who sets the ideals of the community where he lives, directs its thoughts and heads its social movements. It need hardly be argued that the Negro people need social leadership more than most groups; that they have no traditions to fall back upon, no long established customs, no strong family ties, no well defined

* Presidents of Negro colleges established by northern churches [Ed.].

social classes. All these things must be slowly and painfully evolved. The preacher was, even before the war, the group leader of the Negroes, and the church their greatest social institution. Naturally this preacher was ignorant and often immoral, and the problem of replacing the older type by better educated men has been a difficult one. Both by direct work and by direct influence on other preachers, and on congregations, the college-bred preacher has an opportunity for reformatory work and moral inspiration, the value of which cannot be overestimated.

It has, however, been in the furnishing of teachers that the Negro college has found its peculiar function. Few persons realize how vast a work, how mighty a revolution has been thus accomplished. To furnish five millions and more of ignorant people with teachers of their own race and blood, in one generation, was not only a very difficult undertaking, but a very important one, in that it placed before the eyes of almost every Negro child an attainable ideal. It brought the masses of the blacks in contact with modern civilization, made black men the leaders of their communities and trainers of the new generation. In this work college-bred Negroes were first teachers, and then teachers of teachers. And here it is that the broad culture of college work has been of peculiar value. Knowledge of life and its wider meaning, has been the point of the Negro's deepest ignorance, and the sending out of teachers whose training has not been simply for bread winning, but also for human culture, has been of inestimable value in the training of these men. . . .

The main question, so far as the Southern Negro is concerned, is: What under the present circumstance, must a system of education do in order to raise the Negro as quickly as possible in the scale of civilization? The answer to this question seems to me clear: It must strengthen the Negro's character, increase his knowledge and teach him to earn a living. Now it goes without saying, that it is hard to do all these things simultaneously or suddenly, and that at the same time it will not do to give all the attention to one and neglect the others; we could give black boys trades, but that alone will not civilize a race of ex-slaves; we might simply increase their knowledge of the world, but this would not necessarily make them wish to use this knowledge honestly; we might seek to strengthen character and purpose, but to what end if this people have nothing to eat or to wear? . . . If then we start out to train an ignorant and unskilled people with a heritage of bad habits, our system of training must set before itself two great aims—the one dealing with knowledge and character, the other part seeking to give the child the technical knowledge necessary for him to earn a living under the present circumstances. These objects are accomplished in part by the opening of the common schools on the one, and of the industrial schools on the other. But only in part, for there must also be trained those who are to teach these schools—men and women of knowledge and culture and technical skill who understand modern civilization, and have the training and aptitude to impart it to the children under them. There must be teachers, and teachers of teachers, and to attempt to establish any sort of a system of common and industrial school training, without *first* (and I say *first* advisedly) without *first* providing for the higher training of the very best teachers, is simply throwing your money to the winds. . . . Nothing, in these latter days, has so dampened the faith of thinking Negroes in recent educational movements, as the fact that such movements have been accompanied by ridicule and denouncement and decrying of those very institutions of higher training which made the Negro public school possible, and make Negro industrial schools thinkable. . . .

I would not deny, or for a moment seem to deny, the paramount necessity of teaching the Negro to work, and to work steadily and skillfully; or seem to depreciate in the slightest degree the important part industrial schools must play in the accomplishment of these ends, but I *do* say, and insist upon it, that it is industrialism drunk with its vision of success, to imagine that its own work can be accomplished without providing for the training of broadly cultured men and women to teach its own teachers, and to teach the teachers of the public schools.

But I have already said that human education is not simply a matter of schools; it is much more a matter of family and

group life—the training of one's home, of one's daily companions, of one's social class. Now the black boy of the South moves
in a black world—a world with its own leaders, its own thoughts,
its own ideals. In this world he gets by far the larger part of his
life training, and through the eyes of this dark world he peers
into the veiled world beyond. Who guides and determines the
education which he receives in his world? His teachers here are
the group-leaders of the Negro people—the physicians and
clergymen, the trained fathers and mothers, the influential and
forceful men about him of all kinds; here it is, if at all, that the
culture of the surrounding world trickles through and is handed
on by the graduates of the higher schools. Can such culture
training of group leaders be neglected? Can we afford to ignore
it? . . . You have no choice; either you must help furnish this
race from within its own ranks with thoughtful men of trained
leadership, or you must suffer the evil consequences of a headless misguided rabble.

I am an earnest advocate of manual training and trade teaching for black boys, and for white boys, too. I believe that next to
the founding of Negro colleges the most valuable addition to
Negro education since the war, has been industrial training for
black boys. Nevertheless, I insist that the object of all true education is not to make men carpenters, it is to make carpenters
men; there are two means of making the carpenter a man, each
equally important: the first is to give the group and community
in which he works, liberally trained teachers and leaders to
teach him and his family what life means; the second is to give
him sufficient intelligence and technical skill to make him an
efficient workman; the first object demands the Negro college
and college-bred men—not a quantity of such colleges, but a
few of excellent quality; not too many college-bred men, but
enough to leaven the lump, to inspire the masses, to raise the
Talented Tenth to leadership; the second object demands a good
system of common schools, well-taught, conveniently located
and properly equipped. . . .

Further than this, after being provided with group leaders of
civilization, and a foundation of intelligence in the public

schools, the carpenter, in order to be a man, needs technical skill. This calls for trade schools. . . .

Even at this point, however, the difficulties were not surmounted. In the first place modern industry has taken great strides since the war, and the teaching of trades is no longer a simple matter. Machinery and long processes of work have greatly changed the work of the carpenter, the ironworker and the shoemaker. A really efficient workman must be to-day an intelligent man who has had good technical training in addition to thorough common school, and perhaps even higher training. . . .

Thus, again, in the manning of trade schools and manual training schools we are thrown back upon the higher training as its source and chief support. There was a time when any aged and wornout carpenter could teach in a trade school. But not so to-day. Indeed the demand for college-bred men by a school like Tuskegee, ought to make Mr. Booker T. Washington the firmest friend of higher training. Here he has as helpers the son of a Negro senator, trained in Greek and the humanities, and graduated at Harvard; the son of a Negro congressman and lawyer, trained in Latin and mathematics, and graduated at Oberlin; he has as his wife, a woman who read Virgil and Homer in the same class room with me; he has as college chaplain, a classical graduate of Atlanta University; as teacher of science, a graduate of Fisk; as teacher of history, a graduate of Smith,— indeed some thirty of his chief teachers are college graduates, and instead of studying French grammars in the midst of weeds, or buying pianos for dirty cabins, they are at Mr. Washington's right hand helping him in a noble work. And yet one of the effects of Mr. Washington's propaganda has been to throw doubt upon the expediency of such training for Negroes, as these persons have had.

Men of America, the problem is plain before you. Here is a race transplanted through the criminal foolishness of your fathers. Whether you like it or not the millions are here, and here they will remain. If you do not lift them up, they will pull you down. Education and work are the levers to uplift a people.

Work alone will not do it unless inspired by the right ideals and guided by intelligence. Education must not simply teach work— it must teach Life. The Talented Tenth of the Negro race must be made leaders of thought and missionaries of culture among their people. No others can do this work and Negro colleges must train men for it. The Negro race, like all other races, is going to be saved by its exceptional men.

8. W. E. B. DU BOIS ON PAN-AFRICANISM: "THE PROBLEM OF THE TWENTIETH CENTURY IS THE PROBLEM OF THE COLOR-LINE . . ."

More than any other spokesman, Du Bois articulated the American Negroes' dual ethnic identification—with America on the one hand and with the black race on the other. Du Bois's critique of Booker T. Washington (see Document 6) and his Niagara Movement manifestos (see Document 9) exemplify his desire for integration into the larger American society. He also exhibited a strong sense of group pride, often advocated race unity and self help, and felt a profound identification with black men in other parts of the world. His concern for their problems reflected a passionate belief that blacks everywhere were victims of the color-line.

In the 1890s, Du Bois used the term "Pan-Negroism" to convey his hopes for racial solidarity among Africans and those of African descent. In 1900, he and a few other black Americans participated in a Pan-African conference in London, convened by H. Sylvester-Williams, a West Indian lawyer. Du Bois wrote the conclave's Address to the Nations of the World which, although conciliatory in tone, was a protest against white imperialism.

W. E. B. Du Bois, "To the Nations of the World," leaflet, 1900.

In the metropolis of the modern world, in this the closing year of the nineteenth century, there has been assembled a congress of men and women of African blood, to deliberate solemnly upon the present situation and outlook of the darker races of mankind. The problem of the twentieth century is the problem of the color-line, the question as to how far differences of race —which show themselves chiefly in the color of the skin and the texture of the hair—will hereafter be made the basis to denying to over half the world the right of sharing to their utmost ability the opportunities and privileges of modern civilization.

To be sure, the darker races are today the least advanced in culture according to European standards. This has not, however, always been the case in the past, and certainly the world's history, both ancient and modern, has given many instances of no despicable ability and capacity among the blackest races of men.

In any case, the modern world must remember that in this age when the ends of the world are being brought so near together the millions of black men in Africa, America, and the Islands of the Sea, not to speak of the brown and yellow myriads elsewhere, are bound to have a great influence upon the world in the future, by reason of sheer numbers and physical contact. If now the world of culture bends itself towards giving Negroes and other dark men the largest and broadest opportunity for education and self-development, then this contact and influence is bound to have a beneficial effect upon the world and hasten human progress. But if, by reason of carelessness, prejudice, greed and injustice, the black world is to be exploited and ravished and degraded, the results must be deplorable, if not fatal— not simply to them, but to the high ideals of justice, freedom and culture which a thousand years of Christian civilization have held before Europe.

And now, therefore, to these ideals of civilization, to the broader humanity of the followers of the Prince of Peace, we, the men and women of Africa in world congress assembled, do now solemnly appeal:

Let the world take no backward step in that slow but sure progress which has successively refused to let the spirit of class, of caste, of privilege, or of birth, debar from life, liberty and the pursuit of happiness a striving human soul.

Let not color of race be a feature of distinction between white and black men, regardless of worth or ability.

Let not the natives of Africa be sacrificed to the greed of gold, their liberties taken away, their family life debauched, their just aspirations repressed, and avenues of advancement and culture taken from them.

Let not the cloak of Christian missionary enterprise be allowed in the future, as so often in the past, to hide the ruthless economic exploitation and political downfall of less developed nations, whose chief fault has been reliance on the plighted faith of the Christian church.

Let the British nation, the first modern champion of Negro freedom, hasten to crown the work of Wilberforce, and Clarkson, and Buxton, and Sharpe, Bishop Colenso, and Livingstone, and give, as soon as practicable, the rights of responsible government to the black colonies of Africa and the West Indies.

Let not the spirit of Garrison, Phillips, and Douglass* wholly die out in America; may the conscience of a great nation rise and rebuke all dishonesty and unrighteous oppression toward the American Negro, and grant to him the right of franchise, security of person and property, and generous recognition of the great work he has accomplished in a generation toward raising nine millions of human beings from slavery to manhood.

Let the German Empire, and the French Republic, true to their great past, remember that the true worth of colonies lies in their prosperity and progress, and that justice, impartial alike to black and white, is the first element of prosperity.

Let the Congo Free State become a great central Negro State of the world, and let its prosperity be counted not simply in cash and commerce, but in the happiness and true advancement of its black people.

Let the nations of the World respect the integrity and inde-

* William Lloyd Garrison, Wendell Phillips, Frederick Douglass: Famous abolitionists and orators [Ed.].

pendence of the free Negro States of Abyssinia, Liberia, Haiti, and the rest, and let the inhabitants of these States, the independent tribes of Africa, the Negroes of the West Indies and America, and the black subjects of all nations take courage, strive ceaselessly, and fight bravely, that they may prove to the world their incontestible right to be counted among the great brotherhood of mankind.

Thus we appeal with boldness and confidence to the Great Powers of the civilized world, trusting in the wide spirit of humanity, and the deep sense of justice of our age, for a generous recognition of the righteousness of our cause.

ALEXANDER WALTERS (Bishop)
President Pan-African Association

HENRY B. BROWN
Vice-President

H. SYLVESTER-WILLIAMS
General Secretary

W. E. BURGHARDT DU BOIS
Chairman Committee on Address

9. THE NIAGARA MOVEMENT PLATFORM: "WE DO NOT HESITATE TO COMPLAIN . . . LOUDLY AND INSISTENTLY"

The Niagara Movement, founded in 1905, provided the "radicals" with an organized forum on the issue of racial justice. The Movement's name came from the location of the first meeting—the Canadian side of Niagara Falls. In the din of America, the weak voices of the radicals were lost. Although they were ignored and rather

"Declaration of Principles" (of the Niagara Movement), Washington, D.C., BEE, July 22, 1905.

helpless, radicals thus at least kept alive the tradition of virile protest.

Summoned initially by Du Bois, the Movement never gained a membership of more than four hundred, and it dissolved at the end of five years. Its members were, for the most part, Northern, urban, upper class, college graduates. Its program scorned submissiveness and ranged freely over the entire spectrum of grievances. The Movement's members came together once a year, exchanged views, published a declaration to America, and appointed committees to specialize in specific areas. Unlike the members of the Afro-American Council, they did not accommodate themselves to Booker T. Washington's views. And though they bowed to the traditional requirement of emphasizing the blacks' duties, a single paragraph in their Declaration of Principles, which follows, sufficed for this.

Some members of the Niagara Movement, most prominently Du Bois, threw in their lot with the biracial National Association for the Advancement of Colored People when it began to function in 1910. But some, like Trotter, held aloof because they feared white domination.

The members of the conference, known as the Niagara Movement, assembled in annual meeting at Buffalo, July 11th, 12th and 13th, 1905, congratulate the Negro-Americans on certain undoubted evidences of progress in the last decade, particularly the increase of intelligence, the buying of property, the checking of crime, and uplift in home life, the advance in literature and art, and the demonstration of constructive and executive ability in the conduct of great religious, economic and educational institutions.

At the same time, we believe that this class of American citizens should protest emphatically and continually against the curtailment of their political rights. We believe in manhood suffrage; we believe that no man is so good, intelligent or wealthy as to be entrusted wholly with the welfare of his neighbor.

We believe also in protest against the curtailment of our civil rights. All American citizens have the right to equal treatment in places of public accommodation according to their behavior and deserts.

We especially complain against the denial of equal opportunities to us in economic life; in the rural districts of the South this amounts to peonage and virtual slavery; all over the South it tends to crush labor and small business enterprises; and everywhere American prejudice, helped often by iniquitous laws, is making it more difficult for Negro-Americans to earn a decent living.

Common school education should be free to all American children and compulsory. High school training should be adequately provided for all, and college training should be the monopoly of no class or race in any section of our common country. We believe that, in defense of our own institutions, the United States should aid common school education, particularly in the South, and we especially recommend concerted agitation to this end. We urge an increase in public high school facilities in the South, where Negro-Americans are almost wholly without such provisions. We favor well-equipped trade and technical schools for the training of artisans, and the need of adequate and liberal endowment for a few institutions of higher education must be patent to sincere well-wishers of the race.

We demand upright judges in courts, juries selected without discrimination on account of color and the same measure of punishment and the same efforts at reformation for black as for white offenders. We need orphanages and farm schools for dependent children, juvenile reformatories for delinquents, and the abolition of the dehumanizing convict-lease system.

We note with alarm the evident retrogression in this land of sound public opinion on the subject of manhood rights, republican government and human brotherhood, and we pray God that this nation will not degenerate into a mob of boasters and oppressors, but rather will return to the faith of the fathers, that all men were created free and equal, with certain unalienable rights.

We plead for health—for an opportunity to live in decent houses and localities, for a chance to rear our children in physical and moral cleanliness.

We hold up for public execration the conduct of two opposite classes of men: The practice among employers of importing ignorant Negro-American laborers in emergencies, and then affording them neither protection nor permanent employment; and the practice of labor unions in proscribing and boycotting and oppressing thousands of their fellow-toilers, simply because they are black. These methods have accentuated and will accentuate the war of labor and capital, and they are disgraceful to both sides.

We refuse to allow the impression to remain that the Negro-American assents to inferiority, is submissive under oppression and apologetic before insults. Through helplessness we may submit, but the voice of protest of ten million Americans must never cease to assail the ears of their fellows, so long as America is unjust.

Any discrimination based simply on race or color is barbarous, we care not how hallowed it be by custom, expediency, or prejudice. Differences made on account of ignorance, immorality, or disease are legitimate methods of fighting evil, and against them we have no word of protest; but discrimination based simply and solely on physical peculiarities, place of birth, color of skin, are relics of that unreasoning human savagery of which the world is and ought to be thoroughly ashamed.

We protest against the "Jim Crow" car, since its effect is and must be, to make us pay first-class fare for third-class accommodations, render us open to insults and discomfort and to crucify wantonly our manhood, womanhood and self-respect.

We regret that this nation has never seen fit adequately to reward the black soldiers who, in its five wars, have defended their country with their blood, and yet have been systematically denied the promotions which their abilities deserve. And we regard as unjust, the exclusion of black boys from the military and navy training schools.

We urge upon Congress the enactment of appropriate legislation for securing the proper enforcement of those articles of freedom, the thirteenth, fourteenth and fifteenth amendments of the Constitution of the United States.

We repudiate the monstrous doctrine that the oppressor should be the sole authority as to the rights of the oppressed.

The Negro race in America, stolen, ravished and degraded, struggling up through difficulties and oppression, needs sympathy and receives criticism; needs help and is given hindrance, needs protection and is given mob-violence, needs justice and is given charity, needs leadership and is given cowardice and apology, needs bread and is given a stone. This nation will never stand justified before God until these things are changed.

Especially are we surprised and astonished at the recent attitude of the church of Christ—on the increase of a desire to bow to racial prejudice, to narrow the bounds of human brotherhood, and to segregate black men in some outer sanctuary. This is wrong, unchristian and disgraceful to the twentieth century civilization.

Of the above grievances we do not hesitate to complain, and to complain loudly and insistently. To ignore, overlook, or apologize for these wrongs is to prove ourselves unworthy of freedom. Persistent manly agitation is the way to liberty, and toward this goal the Niagara Movement has started and asks the co-operation of all men of all races.

At the same time we want to acknowledge with deep thankfulness the help of our fellowmen from the abolitionist down to those who to-day still stand for equal opportunity and who have given and still give of their wealth and of their poverty for our advancement.

And while we are demanding, and ought to demand, and will continue to demand the rights enumerated above, God forbid that we should ever forget to urge corresponding duties upon our people:

The duty to vote.
The duty to respect the rights of others.
The duty to work.
The duty to obey the laws.
The duty to be clean and orderly.
The duty to send our children to school.
The duty to respect ourselves, even as we respect others.

This statement, complaint and prayer we submit to the American people, and Almighty God.

10. W. E. B. DU BOIS
ESPOUSES SOCIALISM

At the very time that Du Bois was becoming the acknowledged leader of black protest, he was beginning to place the race question in a larger framework. He came to perceive a common cause and a common solution for the oppression faced not only by Negroes, but by white workers as well. Two years after he founded the Niagara Movement, Du Bois publicly declared his sympathy, though not his complete agreement, with the Socialists. In his noted article, "A Socialist of the Path," published in *Horizon* magazine, an unofficial organ for the Niagara Movement, he exhibited the mild type of non-Marxist Socialism that was characteristic of an influential minority among both the black and white founders of the NAACP.

From then on, for the rest of his life, Socialism and Marxism were important components of Du Bois's philosophy. But he was no doctrinaire Marxist. Basically Du Bois was an independent, not subject to the rigid ideologies of any particular party or left-wing sect. He was a member of the Socialist party for a brief period in 1912 and did not become a member of the Communist party until shortly before he moved to Ghana, a few years prior to his death in 1963.

Socialist of the path

I am a Socialist-of-the-Path. I do not believe in the complete socialization of the means of production—the entire abolition of private property in capital—but the Path of Progress and common sense certainly leads to a far greater ownership of the public wealth for the public good than is now the case. I do not believe that government can carry on private business as well as private concerns, but I do believe that most of the human business called private is no more private than God's blue sky, and that we are approaching a time when railroads, coal mines

W. E. B. Du Bois, "Socialist of the Path" and "Negro and Socialism," HORIZON, I, 2 (February 1907), 7–8.

and many factories can and ought to be run by the public for the public. This is the way, as I see it, that the path leads and I follow it gladly and hopefully.

Negro and Socialism

In the socialistic trend thus indicated lies the one great hope of the Negro American. We have been thrown by strange historic reasons into the hands of the capitalists hitherto. We have been objects of dole and charity, and despised accordingly. We have been made tools of oppression against the workingman's cause—the puppets and playthings of the idle rich. Fools! We must awake! Not in a renaissance among ourselves of the evils of Get and Grab—not in private hoarding, squeezing and cheating, lies our salvation, but rather in that larger ideal of human brotherhood, equality of opportunity and work not for wealth but for Weal—here lies our shining goal. This goal the Socialists with all their extravagance and occasional foolishness have more stoutly followed than any other class and thus far we must follow them. Our natural friends are not the rich but the poor, not the great but the masses, not the employers but the employees. Our good is not wealth, power, oppression and snobbishness, but helpfulness, efficiency, service and self-respect. Watch the Socialists. We may not follow them and agree with them in all things. I certainly do not. But in trend and ideal they are the salt of this present earth.

11. FOUNDERS OF NAACP "DEMAND . . . THAT THE CONSTITUTION BE STRICTLY ENFORCED"

The NAACP was a direct outgrowth of an interracial conference on the Negroes' status held in 1909. The participants were prominent black "Radicals" and white Progressives and Socialists, alarmed at

From PROCEEDINGS OF THE NATIONAL NEGRO CONFERENCE, 1909 (no imprint), pp. 222–224.

the deteriorating status of blacks in American society, and disillusioned with the ineffective program of Booker T. Washington. Among the most influential Negroes who were active in the affairs of the meeting were William Monroe Trotter, W. E. B. Du Bois, and the noted anti-lynching crusader, Mrs. Ida Wells-Barnett.

The discussions at the conference and the resolutions it adopted stressed securing the black man's constitutional rights. This "National Negro Conference" thus set the stage for the strategy followed for many years by the NAACP.

The Conference, after considerable discussion, then adopted the following resolutions:

"We denounce the ever-growing oppression of our 10,000,000 colored fellow citizens as the greatest menace that threatens the country. Often plundered of their just share of the public funds, robbed of nearly all part in the government, segregated by common carriers, some murdered with impunity, and all treated with open contempt by officials, they are held in some States in practical slavery to the white community. The systematic persecution of law-abiding citizens and their disfranchisement on account of their race alone is a crime that will ultimately drag down to an infamous end any nation that allows it to be practised, and it bears most heavily on those poor white farmers and laborers whose economic position is most similar to that of the persecuted race.

"The nearest hope lies in the immediate and patiently continued enlightenment of the people who have been inveigled into a campaign of oppression. The spoils of persecution should not go to enrich any class or classes of the population. Indeed persecution of organized workers, peonage, enslavement of prisoners, and even disfranchisement already threaten large bodies of whites in many Southern States.

"We agree fully with the prevailing opinion that the transformation of the unskilled colored laborers in industry and agriculture into skilled workers is of vital importance to that race and to the nation, but we demand for the Negroes, as for all others, a free and complete education, whether by city, State or nation, a grammar school and industrial training for all, and technical, professional, and academic education for the most gifted.

"But the public schools assigned to the Negro of whatever kind or grade will never receive a fair and equal treatment until he is given equal treatment in the Legislature and before the law. Nor will the practically educated Negro, no matter how valuable to the community he may prove, be given a fair return for his labor or encouraged to put forth his best efforts or given the chance to develop that efficiency that comes only outside the school until he is respected in his legal rights as a man and a citizen.

"We regard with grave concern the attempt manifest South and North to deny to black men the right to work and to enforce this demand by violence and bloodshed. Such a question is too fundamental and clear even to be submitted to arbitration. The late strike in Georgia is not simply a demand that Negroes be displaced, but that proven and efficient men be made to surrender their long followed means of livelihood to white competitors.

"As first and immediate steps toward remedying these national wrongs, so full of peril for the whites as well as the blacks of all sections, we demand of Congress and the Executive:

(1) That the Constitution be strictly enforced and the civil rights guaranteed under the Fourteenth Amendment be secured impartially to all.

(2) That there be equal educational opportunities for all and in all the States, and that public school expenditure be the same for the Negro and white child.

(3) That in accordance with the Fifteenth Amendment the right of the Negro to the ballot on the same terms as other citizens be recognized in every part of the country."

12. W. E. B. DU BOIS
CHARTS A STRATEGY OF ACTION

The NAACP gave Du Bois a forum in which to speak to a national audience. He had grown restive at Atlanta University: the administration had become weary and timid, support for his research had dwindled, and in any case the world outside had not responded to Du Bois's work. After 1905 the agitation connected with the Niagara Movement took more and more of his energy and money. In 1910, therefore, he welcomed the chance to join the staff of the NAACP as director of research and editor of the NAACP's magazine, *The Crisis.*

Du Bois, as editor of *The Crisis,* recorded, even supported, the NAACP's program—but his own program went far beyond. Still suspicious of white men, he wanted black men to control their own organizations, with their own ideals leading to their own identity. In his deep concern for the impoverished black masses, and in his sympathetic interest in socialism, he went beyond the NAACP's official program of seeking protection for the Negro's constitutional rights. This crack in the Association's unity, patched and plastered over for twenty-four years, eventually led to Du Bois's resignation.

In 1915 Du Bois put together a formal statement that indicated both his support of the NAACP and his unwillingness to be confined within it.

The immediate program of the American Negro means nothing unless it is mediate to his great ideal and the ultimate ends of his development. We need not waste time by seeking to deceive our enemies into thinking that we are going to be content with a half loaf, or by being willing to lull our friends into a false sense of our indifference and present satisfaction.

The American Negro demands equality—political equality, industrial equality and social equality; and he is never going to

W. E. B. Du Bois, "The Immediate Program of the American Negro," THE CRISIS, IX, 6 (April 1915), 310–312. Reprinted with the permission of THE CRISIS.

rest satisfied with anything less. He demands this in no spirit of braggadocio and with no obsequious envy of others, but as an absolute measure of self-defense and the only one that will assure to the darker races their ultimate survival on earth.

Only in a demand and a persistent demand for essential equality in the modern realm of human culture can any people show a real pride of race and a decent self-respect. For any group, nation or race to admit for a moment the present monstrous demand of the white race to be the inheritors of the earth, the arbiters of mankind and the sole owners of a heritage of culture which they did not create, nor even improve to any greater extent than the other great division of men—to admit such pretense for a moment is for the race to write itself down immediately as indisputably inferior in judgment, knowledge and common sense.

The equality in political, industrial and social life which modern men must have in order to live, is not to be confounded with sameness. On the contrary, in our case, it is rather insistence upon the right of diversity;—upon the right of a human being to be a man even if he does not wear the same cut of vest, the same curl of hair or the same color of skin. Human equality does not even entail, as is sometimes said, absolute equality of opportunity; for certainly the natural inequalities of inherent genius and varying gift make this a dubious phase [*phrase*]. But there is a more and more clearly recognized minimum of opportunity and maximum of freedom to be, to move and to think, which the modern world denies to no one being which it recognizes as a real man.

These involve both negative and positive sides. They call for freedom on the one hand and power on the other. The Negro must have political freedom; taxation without representation is tyranny. American Negroes of to-day are ruled by tyrants who take what they please in taxes and give what they please in law and administration, in justice and in injustice; and the great mass of black people must stand helpless and voiceless before a condition which has time and time again caused other peoples to fight and die.

The Negro must have industrial freedom. Between the peonage of the rural South, the oppression of shrewd capitalists and the jealousy of certain trade unions, the Negro laborer is the most exploited class in the country, giving more hard toil for less money than any other American, and . . . [has] less voice in the conditions of his labor.

In social intercourse every effort is being made to-day from the President of the United States and the so-called Church of Christ down to saloons and boot-blacks to segregate, strangle and spiritually starve Negroes so as to give them the least possible chance to know and share civilization.

These shackles must go. But that is but the beginning. The Negro must have power; the power of men, the right to do, to know, to feel and to express that knowledge, action and spiritual gift. He must not simply be free from the political tyranny of white folk, he must have the right to vote and to rule over the citizens, white and black, to the extent of his proven foresight and ability. He must have a voice in the new industrial democracy which is building and the power to see to it that his children are not in the next generation trained to be the mudsills of society. He must have the right to social intercourse with his fellows. There was a time in the atomic individualistic group when "social intercourse" meant merely calls and tea-parties; to-day social intercourse means theatres, lectures, organizations, churches, clubs, excursions, travel, hotels,—it means in short Life; to bar a group from such methods of thinking, living and doing is to bar them from the world and bid them create a new world;—a task to which no single group is today equal; it is to crucify them and taunt them with not being able to live.

What now are the practical steps which must be taken to accomplish these ends?

First of all before taking steps the wise man knows the object and end of his journey. There are those who would advise the black man to pay little or no attention to where he is going so long as he keeps moving. They assume that God or his vice-gerent the White Man will attend to the steering. This is arrant nonsense. The feet of those that aimlessly wander land as often in hell as in heaven. Conscious self-realization and self-direction is the watchword of modern man, and the first article in the program of any group that will survive must be the great aim, equality and power among men.

The practical steps to this are clear. First we must fight obstructions; by continual and increasing effort we must first make American courts either build up a body of decisions which will protect the plain legal rights of American citizens or else make them tear down the civil and political rights of all citizens in order to oppress a few. Either result will bring justice in the end. It is lots of fun and most ingenious just now for courts to twist law so as to say I shall not live here or vote there, or marry the woman who wishes to marry me. But when to-morrow these decisions throttle all freedom and overthrow the foundation of democracy and decency, there is going to be some judicial house cleaning.

We must *secondly* seek in legislature and congress remedial legislation; national aid to public school education, the removal of all legal discriminations based simply on race and color, and [of] those marriage laws passed to make the seduction of black girls easy and without legal penalty.

Third the human contact of human beings must be increased; the policy which brings into sympathetic touch and understanding, men and women, rich and poor, capitalist and laborer, Asiatic and European, must bring into closer contact and mutual knowledge the white and black people of this land. It is the most frightful indictment of a country which dares to call itself civilized that it has allowed itself to drift into a state of ignorance where ten million people are coming to believe that all white people are liars and thieves, and the whites in turn to believe that the chief industry of Negroes is raping white women.

Fourth only the publication of the truth repeatedly and incisively and uncompromisingly can secure that change in public opinion which will correct these awful lies. THE CRISIS, our record of the darker races, must have a circulation not of 35,000 chiefly among colored folk but of at least 250,000 among all men who believe in men. It must not be a namby-pamby box of salve, but a voice that thunders fact and is more anxious to be true than pleasing. There should be a campaign of tract distribution —short well written facts and arguments—rained over this land by millions of copies, particularly in the South, where the white people know less about the Negro than in any other part of the civilized world. The press should be utilized—the 400 Negro weeklies, the great dailies and eventually the magazines, when we get magazine editors who will lead public opinion instead of following afar with resonant brays. Lectures, lantern-slides and moving pictures, co-operating with a bureau of information and eventually becoming a Negro encyclopedia, all these are efforts along the line of making human beings realize that Negroes are human.

Such is the program of work against obstructions. Let us now turn to constructive effort. This may be summed up under (1) economic co-operation (2) a revival of art and literature (3) political action (4) education and (5) organization.

Under economic co-operation we must strive to spread the idea among colored people that the accumulation of wealth is for social rather than individual ends. We must avoid, in the advancement of the Negro race, the mistakes of ruthless exploitation which have marked modern economic history. To this end we must seek not simply home ownership, small landholding and saving accounts, but also all forms of co-operation, both in production and distribution, profit sharing, building and loan associations, systematic charity for definite, practical ends, systematic migration from mob rule and robbery, to freedom and enfranchisement, the emancipation of women and the abolition of child labor.

In art and literature we should try to loose the tremendous emotional wealth of the Negro and the dramatic strength of his problems through writing, the stage, pageantry and other forms of art. We should resurrect forgotten ancient Negro art and history, and we should set the black man before the world as both a creative artist and a strong subject for artistic treatment.

In political action we should organize the votes of Negroes in such congressional districts as have any number of Negro voters. We should systematically interrogate candidates on matters vital to Negro freedom and uplift. We should train colored voters to reject the bribe of office and accept only decent legal enactments both for their own uplift and for the uplift of laboring classes of all races and both sexes.

In education we must seek to give colored children free public school training. We must watch with grave suspicion the attempt of those who, under the guise of vocational training, would fasten ignorance and menial service on the Negro for another generation. Our children must not in large numbers, be forced into the servant class; for menial service is still, in the main, little more than an antiquated survival of impossible conditions. It has always been as statistics show, a main cause of bastardy and prostitution and despite its many marvelous exceptions it will never come to the light of decency and honor until the house servant becomes the Servant in the House. It is our duty then, not drastically but persistently, to seek out colored children of ability and genius, to open up to them broader, industrial opportunity and above all, to find that Talented Tenth and encourage it by the best and most exhaustive training in order to supply the Negro race and the world with leaders, thinkers and artists.

For the accomplishment of all these ends we must organize. Organization among us already has gone far but it must go much further and higher. Organization is sacrifice. It is sacrifice of opinions, of time, of work and of money, but it is, after all, the cheapest way of buying the most priceless of gifts—freedom and efficiency. I thank God that most of the money that supports the National Association for the Advancement of Colored People comes from black hands; a still larger proportion must so come, and we must not only support but control this and similar organizations and hold them unwaveringly to our objects, our aims and our ideals.

13. THE AMENIA CONFERENCE
ADOPTS A UNITY PLATFORM

The year after Booker T. Washington's death, Joel Spingarn, a prominent white leader of the NAACP, invited a number of distinguished blacks to a peace conference. With the great protagonist gone, there was less to fight about. Several dozen black leaders of all shades of opinions went to Spingarn's summer home at Amenia, New York, in August 1916, and there agreed upon a body of resolutions that defined the basic areas of agreement among all major Negro factions. General and conciliatory, the resolutions closed the era of Booker T. Washington and pointed hopefully toward cooperation in the years to come.

. . . The Amenia Conference believes that its members have arrived at a virtual unanimity of opinion in regard to certain principles and that a more or less definite result may be expected from its deliberations. These principles and this practical result may be summarized as follows:

(1) The conference believes that all forms of education are desirable for the Negro and that every form of education should be encouraged and advanced.

(2) It believes that the Negro, in common with all other races, cannot achieve its highest development without complete political freedom.

(3) It believes that this development and this freedom cannot be furthered without organization and without a practical working understanding among the leaders of the colored race.

(4) It believes that antiquated subjects of controversy, ancient suspicions and factional alignments must be eliminated and forgotten if this organization of the race and this practical working understanding of its leaders are to be achieved.

W. E. B. Du Bois, THE AMENIA CONFERENCE: AN HISTORIC NEGRO GATHERING (Amenia, N.Y.: Troutbeck Press, 1925), pp. 14–15.

(5) It realizes the peculiar difficulties which surround this problem in the South and the special need of understanding between leaders of the race who live in the South and those who live in the North. It has learned to understand and respect the good faith, methods and ideals of those who are working for the solution of this problem in various sections of the country.

(6) The conference pledges itself to the inviolable privacy of all its deliberations. These conclusions, however, and the amicable results of all the deliberations of the conference are fair subjects for discussion in the colored press and elsewhere.

(7) The conference feels that mutual understanding would be encouraged if the leaders of the race could meet annually for private and informal discussion under conditions similar to those which have prevailed at this conference.

the
era
of
legalism

PART TWO

The 1920s: the NAACP and its critics

14. THE NAACP CONFRONTS THE POST-WORLD WAR I CHALLENGE

During the First World War the NAACP had won its first two cases before the Supreme Court and had expanded its membership considerably. The Great Migration and the serious problems faced by the swelling number of urban dwellers presented organizations like the NAACP and the Urban League with ever greater responsibilities. Facing the postwar future, the NAACP made a new assessment of its task.

. . . First and foremost among the objectives for 1920 must be the continued strengthening of the Association's organization and resources. Its general program must be adapted to specific ends. Its chief aims have many times been stated:

1. A vote for every Negro man and woman on the same terms as for white men and women.

2. An equal chance to acquire the kind of an education that will enable the Negro everywhere wisely to use this vote.

3. A fair trial in the courts for all crimes of which he is accused, by judges in whose election he has participated without discrimination because of race.

TENTH ANNUAL REPORT OF THE NATIONAL ASSOCIATION FOR THE ADVANCEMENT OF COLORED PEOPLE, FOR THE YEAR 1919 (New York: NAACP, 1920), pp. 87–91.

4. A right to sit upon the jury which passes judgment upon him.

5. Defense against lynching and burning at the hands of mobs.

6. Equal service on railroad and other public carriers. This to mean sleeping car service, dining car service, Pullman service, at the same cost and upon the same terms as other passengers.

7. Equal right to the use of public parks, libraries and other community services for which he is taxed.

8. An equal chance for a livelihood in public and private employment.

9. The abolition of color-hyphenation and the substitution of "straight Americanism."

The Association seeks to overcome race prejudice but its objective may better be described as a fight against *caste*. Those who seek to separate the Negro from the rest of Americans are intent upon establishing a caste system in America and making of all black men an *inferior caste*. As America could not exist "half slave and half free" so it cannot exist with an upper caste of whites and a lower caste of Negroes. Let no one be deceived by those who would contend that they strive only to maintain "the purity of the white race" and that they wish to separate the races but to do no injustice to the black man. The appeal is to history which affords no example of any group or element of the population of any nation which was separated from the rest and at the same time treated with justice and consideration. Ask the Jew who was compelled to live in the proscribed Ghetto whether being held separate he was afforded the common rights of citizenship and the "equal protection of the laws?" To raise the question is to find the answer "leaping to the eyes," as the French say.

Nor should anyone be led astray by the tiresome talk about "social equality." Social equality is a private question which may well be left to individual decision. But, the prejudices of individuals cannot be accepted as the controlling policy of a state. The National Association for the Advancement of Colored

People is concerned primarily with *public equality*. America is a nation—not a private club. The privileges no less than the duties of citizenship belong of right to no *separate class* of the people but to *all* the people, and to them as *individuals*. The constitution and the laws are for the protection of the minority and of the unpopular, no less than for the favorites of fortune, or they are of no meaning as American instruments of government.

Such a program as has been outlined is worthy of the support of all Americans. The forces which seek to deny, and do deny, to the Negro his citizenship birthright, are powerful and intrenched. They hold the public offices. They administer the law. They say who may, and who may not, vote, in large measure. They control and edit, in many sections, the influential organs of public opinion. They dominate. To dislodge them by legal and constitutional means, as the N. A. A. C. P. proposes to endeavor to dislodge them, requires a strong organization and ample funds. These two things attained, victory is but a question of time, since justice will not forever be denied.

The lines along which the Association can best work are fairly clear. Its fight is of the brain and the soul and to the brain and the soul of America. *It seeks to reach the conscience of America.* America is a large and busy nation. It has many things to think of besides the Negro's welfare. In Congress and state legislatures and before the bar of public opinion, the Association must energetically and adequately defend the Negro's right to fair and equal treatment. To command the interest and hold the attention of the American people for *justice to the Negro* requires money to print and circulate literature which states the facts of the situation. And the appeal must be on the basis of the facts. It is easy to talk in general terms and abstractly. The presentation of concrete data necessitates ample funds.

Lynching must be stopped. Many Americans do not believe that such horrible things happen as do happen when Negroes are lynched and burned at the stake. Lynching can be stopped when we can reach the heart and conscience of the American people. Again, money is needed.

Legal work must be done. Defenseless Negroes are every day denied the "equal protection of the laws" because there is not money enough in the Association's treasury to defend them, either as individuals or as a race.

Legislation must be watched. Good laws must be promoted wherever that be possible and bad laws opposed and defeated, wherever possible. Once more money is essential.

The public must be kept informed. This means that our regular press service under the supervision of a trained newspaper man must be maintained and strengthened. Every opportunity must be sought out to place before the magazine and periodical reading public, constructive articles on every phase of Negro citizenship. . . . That colored people are contributing their fair share to the well-being of America must be made known. . . . That law-abiding colored people are denied the commonest citizenship rights, must be brought home to all Americans who love fair play. Once again, money is needed.

The facts must be gathered and assembled. This requires effort. Facts are not gotten out of one's imagination. Their gathering and interpretation is skilled work. Research workers of a practical experience are needed. Field investigations, in which domain the Association has already made some notable contributions, are essential to good work. More money.

The country must be thoroughly organized. The Association's more than 300 branches are a good beginning. An increased field staff is essential to the upbuilding of this important branch development. A very large percentage of the branch members are colored people. Colored people have less means, and less experience in public organization, than white people. But, they are developing rapidly habits of efficiency in organization. Money, again is needed.

But, not money alone is needed. Men and women are vital to success. Public opinion is the main force upon which the Association relies for a *victory of justice*. Particularly do we seek the active support of all white Americans who realize that a democracy cannot draw the color line in public relations without lasting injury to its best ideals.

15. A. PHILIP RANDOLPH
AND CHANDLER OWEN:
A SOCIALIST CRITIQUE IN THE MESSENGER

The program of the NAACP did not appeal to all groups, by any means. For many it was tame, its stress on constitutional rights irrelevant to the needs of the great mass of Negroes. No one voiced this criticism more explicitly and more literally than A. Philip Randolph and Chandler Owen, editors of the vigorous, brilliantly edited monthly, *The Messenger*—"The Only Radical Negro Magazine in America." Their editorials touched on many themes: the socialist critique of capitalism, the need for solidarity among black and white workers, the blacks' capacity to resist by violence and by boycott, and the poverty of their existing leadership. Randolph later achieved prominence as the organizer of the Brotherhood of Sleeping Car Porters in 1925, and as the initiator of the March on Washington movements of 1941 and 1963.

A. "Our reason for being"

First, as workers, black and white, we all have one common interest, viz., the getting of more wages, shorter hours, and better working conditions.

Black and white workers should combine for no other reason than that for which individual workers should combine, viz., to increase their bargaining power, which will enable them to get their demands.

Second, the history of the labor movement in America proves that the employing class recognize no race lines. They will exploit a white man as readily as a black man. They will exploit women as readily as men. They will even go to the extent of coining the labor, blood and suffering of children into dollars. The

"Our Reason for Being," Editorial, THE MESSENGER (August 1919), pp. 11–12.

introduction of women and children into the factories proves that capitalists are only concerned with profits and that they will exploit any race or class in order to make profits, whether they be black or white men, black or white women or black or white children.

Third, it is apparent that every Negro worker or non-union man is a potential scab upon white union men and black union men.

Fourth, self-interest is the only principle upon which individuals or groups will act if they are sane. Thus, it is idle and vain to hope or expect Negro workers, out of work and who receive less wages when at work than white workers, to refuse to scab upon white workers when an opportunity presents itself.

Men will always seek to improve their conditions. When colored workers, as scabs, accept the wages against which white workers strike, they (the Negro workers) have definitely improved their conditions.

That is the only reason why colored workers scab upon white workers or why non-union white men scab upon white union men.

Every member, which is a part of the industrial machinery, must be organized, if labor would win its demands. Organized labor cannot afford to ignore any labor factor of production which organized capital does not ignore.

Fifth, if the employers can keep the white and black dogs, on account of race prejudice, fighting over a bone; the yellow capitalist dog will get away with the bone—the bone of profits. No union man's standard of living is safe so long as there is a group of men or women who may be used as scabs and whose standard of living is lower.

The combination of black and white workers will be a powerful lesson to the capitalists of the solidarity of labor. It will show that labor, black and white, is conscious of its interests and power. This will prove that unions are not based upon race lines, but upon class lines. This will serve to convert a class of workers, which has been used by the capitalist class to defeat organized labor, into an ardent, class conscious, intelligent, militant group.

Sixth: The Industrial Workers of the World commonly termed the I. W. W. draw no race, creed, color or sex line in their organization. They are making a desperate effort to get the colored men into the One Big Union. The Negroes are at least giving them an ear, and the prospects point to their soon giving them a hand. With the Industrial Workers Organization already numbering 800,000, to augment it with a million and a half or two million Negroes, would make it fairly rival the American Federation of Labor. This may still be done anyhow and the reactionaries of this country, together with Samuel Gompers, the reactionary President of the American Federation of Labor, desire to hold back this trend of Negro labor radicalism. . . .

Eighth: The New York World, the mouth piece of the present administration, and also a plutocratic mouth piece, says in its issue of June 4, 1919, "The radical forces in New York City have recently embarked on a great new field of revolutionary endeavor, the education through agitation of the southern Negro into the mysteries and desirability of revolutionary Bolshevism. There are several different powerful forces in N. Y. City behind this move. The chief established propaganda is being distributed through *The Messenger,* which styles itself—"The only magazine of scientific radicalism in the world, published by Negroes." With the exception of *The Liberator,* it is the most radical journal printed in the U. S." . . .

The foregoing comments from such powerful organs as *The Providence Sunday Journal, The New York Sunday World, The National Civic Federation Review* and the Union League Club of New York, followed by action of the Legislature of the State of New York—demonstrates how powerful is the influence of a well written, logical publication, fighting for the interests of twelve million Negroes in particular and the working masses in general. These are the real reasons why the American Federation of Labor decided to lay aside its infamous color line. There is no change of heart on the part of the Federation, but it is acting under the influence of fear. There is a new leadership for Negro workers. It is a leadership of uncompromising manhood. It is not asking for a half loaf but for the whole loaf. It is insistent upon the Negro workers exacting justice, both from the white labor unions and from the capitalists or employers.

The Negroes who will benefit from this decision are indebted first to themselves and their organized power, which made them dangerous. Second, to the radical agitation carried on by *The Messenger;* and third, to the fine spirit of welcome shown by the Industrial Workers of the World, whose rapid growth and increasing power the American Federation of Labor fears. These old line Negro political fossils know nothing of the Labor Movement, do not believe in labor unions at all, and have never taken any active steps to encourage such organizations. We make this statement calmly, coolly and with a reasonable reserve. The very thing which they are fighting is one of the chief factors in securing for Negroes their rights. That is Bolshevism. The capitalists of this country are so afraid that Negroes will become Bolshevists that they are willing to offer them almost anything to hold them away from the radical movement. Nobody buys pebbles which may be picked up on the beach, but diamonds sell high. The old line Negro leaders have no power to bargain, because it is known that they are Republicans politically and job-hunting, me-too-boss-hat-in-hand-Negroes, industrially. Booker Washington and all of them have simply advocated that Negroes get more work. The editors of *The Messenger* are not interested in Negroes getting more work. Negroes have too much work already. What we want Negroes to get is less work and more wages, with more leisure for study and recreation.

Our type of agitation has really won for Negroes such concessions as were granted by the American Federation of Labor and we are by no means too sanguine over the possibilities of the sop which was granted. It may be like the Constitution of the United States—good in parts, but badly executed. We shall have to await the logic of events. In the meantime, we urge the Negro labor unions to increase their radicalism, to speed up their organization, to steer clear of the Negro leaders and to thank nobody but themselves for what they have gained. In organization there is strength; and whenever Negroes or anybody else make organized demands, their call will be heeded.

B. Capitalism as the cause of lynching

First, What is lynching?

Lynching, historically speaking, is a loose term applied to various forms of executing popular justice, or what is thought to be justice. It is punishment of offenders or supposed offenders by a summary procedure without due process of law. In short, the essence of lynching is that it is extra-légal.

What object does it achieve?

From the lyncher's point of view it avenges crime—and is calculated to prevent further crime.

During the Reconstruction period the Ku Klux Klan applied the lynch law to intimidate the newly enfranchised Negro voter; to prevent him from voting the Republican carpet-baggers, from the North, into control of the Southern State Governments. . . .

Today lynching is a practice which is used to foster and to engender race prejudice to prevent the lynchers and the lynched, the white and black workers from organizing on the industrial and voting on the political fields, to protect their labor-power. . . .

For clarity of exposition I shall divide the causes into two classes, and I shall treat them in the order of ultimate and immediate or occasion causes.

But, before proceeding to build our structure of the real causes of lynching, we shall do the excavation work by clearing away the debris of alleged but fallacious causes.

First, it is maintained by most superficial sociologists that "race prejudice" is the cause of lynching.

But the fallacy of this contention is immediately apparent in view of the fact that out of 3337 persons lynched between 1882 and 1903, there were 1192 white persons. . . .

Second, it is held by some that "rape of white women" is the real cause. Again this argument is untenable when it is known that out of the entire number of persons lynched, during the

A. Philip Randolph, "Lynching: Capitalism Its Cause; Socialism Its Cure,"
THE MESSENGER (March 1919), pp. 9–12.

above stated period, only 34 per cent can be ascribed to rape as the cause.

Third, still others contend that the "law's delay" is the controlling cause. This also is without force when the fact is known that men have had their day in court—taken out and lynched, despite the fact that they (the accused) were convicted or acquitted. . . .

We shall now consider the real and positive causes of this national evil.

As to the meaning of capitalism

Capitalism is a system under which a small class of private individuals make profits out of the labor of the masses by virtue of their ownership of the machinery and sources of production and exchange. . . . there is the crux of the problem. . . . It is to the interest of the employer to work the laborer as long hours and to pay as low wages as possible. . . . Hence, the conflict between the capitalists and the workers. The desire and the power to make profits of the owner of the means of wealth production, which labor must use in order to make wages with which to live, is at the basis of this conflict.

Let us see how it applies to our proposition in question.

We will now review its economic aspects. . . .

For 250 years the slave-owning class had the right, sanctioned by the government, to use a Negro as a horse, a machine. . . . Huge fortunes had been made and the slave-owners had lived in luxury, ease, comfort and splendor off the labor of Negroes.

When the end of this came, the industry of the South was paralyzed. There was a shortage of white labor-power. The Negroes had been freed and they distrusted and suspected their former masters. In short, intoxicated with the new wine of freedom, they were disinclined to work.

But cotton must be picked; lumber must be cut; turpentine must be dipped; railroads must be built. In fact, profits must be made. Negroes must work or be made to work, besides they must work cheaply.

How can this be done? This is how it was and is done:

Vagrancy laws are enacted which provided for the imprisonment of all Negroes who have no visible means of support. Of course, it is impossible for a Negro to show that he has any visible means of support. The result is that hordes of unemployed Negroes are hustled off to jail and the convict camps. Their fines are paid by employers of labor for lumber mills, cotton plantations, railroads, etc., they are assigned into their custody, put to work at a wage of 30 and 40 cents a day. They are also compelled to trade at the company's store, which sells its wares at 100 per cent higher than other stores. . . . And as a white planter himself tells the story: A planter can arrest a man upon the criminal charge of receiving money under false pretenses, which is equivalent to the charge of stealing; you get him convicted; he is fined, and being pennyless, in lieu of the money to pay the fine he goes to jail; then you pay the fine and the judge assigns him to you to work out the fine and you have him back on your plantation, backed up by the authority of the State. This is peonage. It is maintained for profits. This is capitalism. And this does not apply to Negroes only. It is the common fate of the servant class, black and white. But they must not understand that their interests are common. Hence race prejudice is cultivated. Lynching, jim-crowism segregation is used to widen the chasm between the races.

This profit system of capitalism also applies to the farmer through the crop-lien system. This is a system whereby a lien mortgage is taken upon the crops of the poor white and black farmers for a loan. . . .

The farmer's inability to meet his note results in the loss of his farm. He then becomes a farm tenant and works upon the metayer system or the plan of giving a part of the crop produced to the owner for the privilege of cultivating the land. This crop-lien system is profitable to the bankers of the South. Both white and black farmers are fleeced by this financial system. But white and black farmers won't combine against a common foe on account of race prejudice. Race antagonism, then, is profitable to those who own the farms, the mills, the railroads and the banks. This economic arrangement in the South is the fundamental cause of race prejudice, which is the fuse which causes the magazine of capitalism to explode into race conflicts—lynchings.

Prejudice is the chief weapon in the South which enables the capitalist to exploit both races. . . . The capitalists want profits, they don't care who makes them for them. In the South today over a million little white children are taken from school, put into factories and driven 10 and 12 hours a day until their little bodies are broken upon the wheels of industry; all because their labor is cheaper and more profits can be made out of them than out of grown-ups. They are competing with their fathers and brothers and they force the wage scale down by virtue of their increasing the labor supply.

This is how much the Southern white gentleman capitalists care about white children whom they prate [about] so much. Capitalism knows no color line. . . . So much for the economic aspects.

But this thing must be supported by laws. And this brings us to the political cause of lynching. How does it operate?

Vagrancy laws are enacted by politicians who are selected by political parties which are controlled by those who supply the campaign funds. These funds are contributed by the bankers, railroad directors, lumber mill and cotton plantation-owners whose large profits depend upon the low wages and long hours of work of the servant class. This has been the work of Vardaman, Tillman and the "Lily white" Republicans. The laws making the nonperformance of a labor contract a crime are placed on the statute books by certain anti-labor and incidentally anti-Negro politicians. Sheriffs into whose custody Negroes charged with criminal acts are placed are nominated, elected or appointed by parties, which are responsible to powerful financial agencies which profit by fostering race prejudice and lynching, etc. This is why sheriffs don't protect their prisoners and not because they are afraid of the mob. . . .

The ruling class of the South have, through disfranchisement and the poll-tax, deprived the working class of the power to protect their interests. The electorate there is small. It is easier for the capitalists to control or to corrupt a small electorate than a large one.

Politically race feeling is also capitalized by young, ambitious politicians who make their campaigns on the slogan of "Negro domination."

This is how politics fortifies and re-enforces lynch law in the South.

What are the social causes? There are three, the school, church and press.

An uneducated working class won't revolt, won't organize; hence, the meagre sums of $2.22 and $4.92 are appropriated for the education of the black and white child, respectively, per year.

The white church is paid to preach the Christianity of lynch law profits.

The press is owned and controlled by the employing class and it is used to influence the minds of the races; to foment race hatred; it gives wide circulation to that insidious doctrine of the Negroes being the hewers of wood and drawers of water for white men. It features in bold headlines such titles as "lynch the black brute," "young white girl raped by black burly fiend," etc.

This produces a psychology which expresses itself through the mob. Anything may occasion a community to burn a Negro. It might be a well-dressed Negro; a Negro who speaks good English or a Negro who talks back to a white man.

To sum up, capitalism is at the basis of the economic, political and social arrangements of the South and it is defended, supported, promoted and upheld by the Republican and Democratic parties of the North, South, East and West. Neither [the] Republican nor the Democratic party has ever condemned peonage or lynching. They can not. They are owned by the capitalists.

What then is the cure. I hold, maintain and aver that Socialism is the only cure. Why? . . .

How does this affect lynching?

Socialism would deprive individuals of the power to make fortunes out of the labor of other individuals by virtue of their ownership of the machinery which the worker must use in order to live. When an individual or class may make profits out of the labor of black and white workers, it is to his or to the interest of the class to use any means to keep them (the workers) from combining in order to raise wages; to lower their hours of work or to demand better working conditions. This is the only reason why prejudice is fostered in the South. Of course, it may not be possible to trace every lynching or act of prejudice to a direct economic cause, but the case may be explained by the law of habit. When social practices are once set they act or recur with a dangerous accuracy. So that it is now a social habit to lynch Negroes. But when the motive for promoting race prejudice is removed, viz., profits, by the social ownership, control and operation of the machinery and sources of production through the government, the government being controlled by the workers; the effects of prejudice, race riots, lynching, etc., will also be removed.

For instance, if railroads were owned and democratically managed by the government, its collective and social service function would not be prostituted to jim-crow cars in order to pander and cater to race prejudice. No individuals would be making profits out of them and consequently there would be no interest in promoting race antagonisms. Lynchings, the product of capitalism, would pass as the burning of heretics and the Spanish Inquisition, the product of religious intolerance, passed.

Besides Socialism would arm every man and woman with the ballot. Education would be compulsory and universal. The vagrancy law, child labor and peonage would no longer exist. Tenant-farming and the crop-lien system would be discarded. And every worker would receive the full product of his toil.

This is the goal of Socialism. This is why every Negro should be a Socialist.

In conclusion, workingmen and women of my race, don't allow Republican and Democratic leaders to deceive you. They are paid by Rockefeller, Morgan, Armour, Carnegie, owners of Southern railroads, coal mines, lumber mills, turpentine stills, cotton-plantations, etc., who make millions out of your labor. Don't be deceived by the small increase in wages which you are receiving; the capitalists are taking it back by increasing the cost of food, fuel, clothing and rent. Don't be deceived by any capitalist bill to abolish lynching; if it became a law, it would never be enforced. Have you not the Fourteenth Amendment which is supposed to protect your life, property, liberty and guarantee you the vote? Does it do it? No. Why? Because it is nullified through administration by capitalists, Republican and Democratic representatives, who profit from lynching; who want lynching to continue. Lynching will not stop until Socialism comes. You can strike a death blow to lynching by voting for Socialism.

Black and white workers unite. You have nothing to lose but your chains; you have the world to gain.

C. "Du Bois fails as a theorist"

Under the caption—"Leading Negroes Analyze Color Strategy," in the New York *Sun*, October 12th, William E. Burghardt Du Bois, Editor of *The Crisis*, discusses several salient points of the Negro problem. He begins by stating the problem, enumerating the different specific disabilities from which the Negro suffers. This, of course, is done splendidly. But the character and scope of the problem is not the unknown quantity in our social equation. This is known by every man in the street, and any school boy is not incompetent to state it. The only question that taxes the resources of sociologists, is the discovery of principles and the invention of methods that are calculated to effect a solution. It is here, where the Editor reveals his utter and lamentable incapacity to think fundamentally. For instance, he makes the following observations upon the group of Negroes known as "white folks niggers": "With the appearance of this Radical group (referring to the New Negro Radicals), comes the disappearance, practically, of another group of Negroes upon whom the white South has placed great dependence.

"Du Bois Fails As a Theorist," Editorial, THE MESSENGER (December 1919), pp. 7–8.

They were known among colored people as 'white folks nig-gers' and their business was to soothe the ruffled feelings of the colored people and to flatter the arrogance of the white people. Negroes were told that duties came before rights, and that they were asking for more than they deserved. Whites were assured that the Negroes wanted nothing but the right to work at such wages as the white people wished to give them." No unusual power of penetration is necessary to perceive that this statement is both fallacious and vicious. It is fallacious in that it is not true, and it is vicious in that it is misleading. Everybody knows that that hand-picked, me-too-boss, hat-in-hand, sycophant, lick-spittling group of Negroes, appropriately dubbed "white folks niggers," have not disappeared, for they are now the recognized leaders of the Negro. For, according to the definition of "white folks niggers" as presented by Du Bois himself, in the above named article: "as those that soothe the ruffled feelings of col-ored people and flatter the arrogance of white people, play up duties and soft-pedal rights and call for more work with any wages," fits the editor himself, since we have not known of any zealous efforts of his, in the interest of unionizing Negro workers to strike for more wages, shorter hours and better working con-ditions. On the contrary, he condemned and labelled as Pro-German the only labor organization in the country which did not discriminate against Negro workers, the Industrial Workers of the World. And the most credulous and generous would not contend that Moton and Emmett Scott, Terrell and George Haynes, Charles W. Anderson and W. H. Lewis, Roscoe Con-kling Simmons and Fred R. Moore* are not "dyed-in-the-wool

* Robert Russa Moton, Booker T. Washington's successor as principal of Tuskegee Institute; Emmett J. Scott, secretary of Howard University and formerly private secretary to Booker T. Washington; Robert H. Terrell, judge of Municipal Court in Washington, D.C.; George Edmund Haynes, National Urban League Executive; Charles W. Anderson, formerly Collec-tor of Internal Revenue for the Second District (including New York City), 1905–1915; W. H. Lewis, Boston attorney, and assistant attorney general of the United States, 1911–1913; Roscoe Conkling Simmons, newspaper editor and orator, and nephew of Booker T. Washington's third wife; and Fred R. Moore, editor of the New York *Age*. All, with the possible excep-tion of Haynes, had been close friends of the "Wizard" of Tuskegee [Ed.].

white-folks-niggers." They are certainly handy tools of the white political and industrial oligarchy of America. They have certainly preached the gospel of contentment and non-resistance to the Negro, of which the moneyed interests of the white folks are the beneficiaries. They are certainly paid by the capitalist white folks and we have yet to find the payee opposing the payer. Du Bois proceeds in his past-time of misrepresentation of the attitude of the rank and file of Negroes by pretending that the National Association for the Advancement of Colored People is the expression of the aims and strivings of the Negro. In this connection he states that, "The mass of thinking American Negroes are represented by the National Association for the Advancement of Colored People and they stand with white Americans, who have given thought and attention to the Negro problem." This is absolutely false. The National Association for the Advancement of Colored People is led, controlled and dominated by a group who are neither Negroes nor working people, which renders it utterly impossible to articulate the aims of a group that are the victims of certain social, political and economic evils as a race, and as a part of the great working people. Such a contention is equivalent to maintaining that an organization of Irishmen, whose officials are Jews, expresses the opinions of Irishmen on the question of Home Rule for Ireland! Or that an organization of Jews, whose policies and principles are formulated by Irishmen, can represent the thoughts and feelings of Jews on the question of pogroms in Poland. The point of discussion in the above named article, however, which interests us most and reveals Du Bois' ignorance of theory and his inability to advise the Negro in the most critical period of the world's history, is shown by his view of "revolution." He says "that they (the Negroes) are deeply in earnest concerning this race problem, but it is hardly necessary to say that they do not believe in violence, they do not believe in revolution, they do not believe in retaliation, they do believe in self defense."

Doubtless Du Bois is the only alleged leader of an oppressed group of people in the world today who condemns revolution. In other words, he would continue to defend and maintain the status quo, or things as they are: the exploitation of labor by capital, which breeds wars and engenders race strife, fosters lynchings and riots and perpetuates a mockery of democracy. He would reject and renounce the right of revolution, which is even vouchsafed in so conservative a political instrument as the Declaration of Independence. Of course, we realize that his attitude to the idea of revolution arises out of his ignorance of its history and its relation to social progress. Capitalism, the present social order which he would maintain, only came after a revolution which effected the overthrow of feudalism. The overthrow of the Inquisition, the "thought despot" of the Middle Ages, was the work of an intellectual revolution. The abolition of slavery, or the destruction of the rights of private property in human beings, was achieved through the mechanics of revolution. Our present industrial civilization, with its myriad labor saving devices and inventions for the utilization of the materials and forces of nature, was wrought in the laboratory of revolution. In short, every notable and worth-while advance in human history has been achieved by revolution, either intellectual, political or economic. The overthrow of the Czar of Russia and the deposition of the Kaiser of Germany and the House of Hapsburg of Austria-Hungary are instances in proof of the genius of revolution, fashioning a new world for mankind. And yet, Du Bois, the supposed leader of the most ruthlessly and mercilessly exploited and oppressed peoples of the world, would reject the only hope of the Negro, as well as of mankind—"revolution." It is because he thinks it means violence, blood shed, a reign of terror, whereas, on the contrary, it means the abolition of the causes of these things—the system of private property in the social resources and machinery of wealth production. Du Bois continues, "that the Negro puts his greatest dependence in the essential decency and sense of justice of the American nation." If this were true, it would simply indicate the utter hopelessness of the Negro, for who would depend upon the American sense of justice to abolish lynchings, riots, disfranchisement and the jim-crow car, when this alleged sense of justice has condoned, sanctioned and connived at these outrages for almost a half century. This is the policy of the Old Crowd Negro, and it has failed, and failed miserably, to save the life and property of Negroes in America. Du Bois ends with this piteous appeal: "If you, reader, were a black man, and a citizen of the United States, and if you saw your fellows being lynched without trial—two, three, and four a week; if you knew of the riots that are taking place and knew that not in a single case did Negroes start the riots; if you knew that you could not travel in large parts of this country without personal insult; that your children could not receive a decent education, and that you were deprived of the right to vote, let me ask you frankly, Would it be necessary for a man from Russia or from Kamchatka to incite you toward the doing of everything in your power to right these terrible wrongs?" This is offered in explanation of the supposed belief that the Negroes are giving ear to the doctrines of Bolshevism and I. W. W.'ism. This, of course, is the note of age, of fear, the supplication of the weak. Its psychology will escape no one. Du Bois is correct in one case, however, that is, when he says, "that we, who for twenty-five years have been called Radicals, were not in fact radicals at all." Indeed a belated admission but, nevertheless, he, like Karolyi of Hungary, the successor of the Hapsburgs who fell in the Revolution, is about to recognize that the times require leadership of the brand of what he once pretended to be, but of what he now finds he is not—radicalism.

D. "How to stop lynching"—by armed resistance

Lynching is our chiefest problem in America today. All Negroes are agreed, and some white people also, that it is the arch crime of America and that it ought to be stopped. The only difference is that of method. The question of How?

We are also pretty well agreed that the methods adopted by Negroes at the behest of Negro leaders, in the past, are futile and valueless.

"How to Stop Lynching," Editorial, THE MESSENGER (August 1919), pp. 8–10.

For instance, we have sent telegrams to Southern Governors only to be told in reply, that they have no power and oftentimes no inclination to stop what they are pleased to characterize as "an orderly lynching." Experience has taught us that appeal to "Big White Politicians" is simply ineffective. For even the President, Woodrow Wilson, made a pronouncement against lynching (Of course he was only interested in Robert Prager, a German who had been lynched, and especially in view of the fact that Germany had threatened to take revenge upon American citizens residing in Germany) with no visible effect upon the Southern mob.

The MESSENGER proposes an immediate program for Negroes. This program includes two methods. First, physical force and secondly, economic force.

Physical force

Anglo Saxon jurisprudence recognizes the law of self-defense. Our information also records that the right of self-defense is recognized in the laws of all countries. Not only is the right of self-defense recognized with respect to the person about to be injured, but it is recognized that the person about to be injured may summon others to assist him in repelling an attack. We are consequently urging Negroes and other oppressed groups confronted with lynching or mob violence to act upon the recognized and accepted law of self-defense. Always regard your own life as more important than the life of the person about to take yours, and if a choice has to be made between the sacrifice of your life and the loss of the lyncher's life, choose to preserve your own and to destroy that of the lynching mob. Recently we have had a few instances of the effect of organized self-assertion on the part of Negroes in the South. The NATION points out that on the 25th and 26th of May a mob in Memphis, Tenn., where Eli Persons was lynched a year ago, had settled upon a race riot. It was found out, however, that Negroes were well armed and organized to meet the attack with resistance. This having been learned, the Mayor of Memphis immediately called the Chief of Police, and both together promptly called off the riot. Just a few days ago, the Negroes of Long View, Texas, held up a mob which started out to lynch a Negro school teacher who had reported a lynching through the CHICAGO DEFENDER. Instead of leaving the Negro school teacher to himself, to make his own defense, a group of Negroes, well armed and well organized, fired upon the advancing mob, shooting down four members of the mob, whereupon its steps were taken backward rather than forward. The Governor of Texas, as a rule, has always claimed that he had no troops, and no power to stop the action of the mob but when the Negroes at Long View protected their lives with shot and shell and fire, the Governor of Texas sent militia and rangers and army planes to restore law and order in Long View. The MESSENGER wants to explain the reason why Negroes can stop lynching in the South with shot and shell and fire. All mobs act on the principle of pessimism. One hundred to fifteen thousand men usually take part in lynching one Negro, with the Negro handcuffed and arrested, unable to defend himself. The very numbers who engage in it are evidence of the cowardice of the mob. But when the mob knows that somebody is going to have to give his life, each man thinks that *he* may have to give *his* life. No one desires to make this sacrifice, and although it is perfectly certain that twenty millions of people can beat down eight millions, if the sacrifice to accomplish this is so great, it will deter the twenty million from its aim; and so with the mob. A mob of a thousand men knows it can beat down fifty Negroes, but when those fifty Negroes rain fire and shot and shell over the thousand, the whole group of cowards will be put to flight.

This may sound rather strange talk for the pacific editors of the MESSENGER, but we are pacific only on matters that can be settled peacefully. The appeal to the conscience of the South has been long and futile. Its soul has been petrified and permeated with wickedness, injustice and lawlessness. The black man has no rights which will be respected unless the black man enforces that respect. It is his business to decide that just as he went three thousand miles away to fight for alleged democracy in Europe and for others, that he can lay down his life, honorably and peacefully, for himself in the United States. In so doing, we do not assume any role of anarchy, nor any shadow of lawlessness. We are acting strictly within the pale of the law and in a manner recognized as law abiding by every civilized nation. We are trying to enforce the laws which American Huns are trampling in the dust, connived in and winked at by nearly all of the American officials, from the President of the United States down.

Economic force

Physical force is not the only weapon of the Negro. He has tremendous economic power. He constitutes one-seventh of the industrial population of the United States. In the South, his economic power is even greater. According to Professor Albert Bushnell Hart of Harvard, the Negroes in the South produce three-fifths of the wealth, that is, one-third of the population produces over one-half of the wealth. Now one of the best ways to strike a man is to strike him in the pocket-book. Cotton is the staple crop of the South. The Negroes are the chief producers of cotton. They also constitute a big factor in the South in the production of turpentine, tar, lumber, coal and iron, transportation facilities and all agricultural produce. They should be thoroughly organized into unions, whereupon they could make demands and withhold their labor from the transportation industry and also from personal and domestic service and the South will be paralyzed industrially and in commercial consternation. That state of affairs will attract the attention and interest of the whole world. Lynching will imediately be made a national and an international problem.

The problem will become *national* because the textile industries of the North and West are dependent upon the products of Negro labor. When Massachusetts, New Jersey and New York can no longer get cotton for the mills, the mills must close. Machinery stands idle. Men are unemployed. Discontent grows. Social unrest spreads. Revolution stares the government in the face. The building and lumber trades will also be at a standstill. Mechanics will be thrown out of work. Carpenters, masons, moulders, painters, plumbers, electricians, machinists, contrac-

tors and architects will have their work cut down. Something
will then have to be done. Both capitalists and workers will
become interested in abolition of lynching—the capitalists because their profits will be cut off, from the cessation of business,
and the workers because their wages will be cut off, from the
cessation of work. At this time, the whole of the United States
will for the first time, be interested in abolition of lynching, not
because they will love the Negro any more, but because it is
necessary for their own interests to stamp out this typical American injustice.

Lynching will then become an *international problem*, also.
During the Civil War, when the Southern Blockade was on, and
cotton could not be shipped to Europe, industrial paralysis was
thrown into Great Britain. In Manchester, Leeds, Liverpool and
London, the textile industries had to be closed. Work stopped
in those great industrial centers and every Englishman began
to inquire about American slavery. The Englishmen wanted
slavery abolished, because the fight over the institution was
striking them in the pocketbook. Slavery became an international problem because cotton could not be supplied. At that
time, however, only a few million bales of cotton were produced.
Today over a hundred million bales are being produced each
year, largely by Negroes. Now, if the hold up of a few million
bales made slavery an international problem, the hold up of
hundreds of millions of bales of cotton will make lynching an
international problem of prime importance. If Negroes withdraw their hands from the cotton fields, the cotton will rot on
the farms. The South will get on its knees, just as it was almost
on its knees over the migration during the war. It did not want
Negroes to leave there, not because they were hankering for
Negro company but because they wanted the Negro's work—his
labor power.

At the present time, these two forms of attack will suffice for
Negroes to enter upon. Whenever you hear talk of a lynching,
a few hundred of you must assemble rapidly and let the authorities know that you propose to have them abide by the law and
not violate it. Offer your services to the Mayor or the Governor,
pledging him that you can protect the life of any prisoner if the

State militia has no such power. Ask the Governor or the authorities to supply you with additional arms and under no circumstances should you Southern Negroes surrender your arms for lynching mobs to come in and have sway. To organize your work a little more effectively, get in touch with all of the Negroes who were in the draft. Form little voluntary companies which may quickly be assembled. Find Negro officers who will look after their direction. Be perfectly calm, poised, cool and self-contained. Do not get excited but face your work with cold resolution, determined to uphold the law and to protect the lives of your fellows at any cost. When this is done, nobody will have to sacrifice his life or that of anybody else, because nobody is going to be found who will try to overcome that force.

Industrially, let the farmers organize farmers' protective unions. Let the lumber workers, moulders, masons, plasterers and other Negro workers on railroads and in mines organize into unions, quietly and unostentatiously. Be prepared to walk out in concert, every man or woman who does any form of work. Let it be known that we are down to plain business, free from any foolishness or play.

Let every Negro in the South, begin to work on this program by agitating for it in the lodges, churches, schools, parlor and home conversation and while at work in factory or field. Write also to us about any detail in entering upon this work. If this program is pressed, a year from now, we can call out of the fields, the factories and the mines between a million and two million Negroes, who will initiate the true work of making America a real "land of the free and home of the brave."

16. MARCUS GARVEY:
THE CHALLENGE OF BLACK NATIONALISM

Randolph, Owen, and the *Messenger* group were middle-class intellectuals who voiced a deep concern about the welfare of the masses of the race. And though Randolph organized the Pullman porters into a union—against the opposition not only of the Pullman company but of a number of black leaders as well—their program went unheard among the slum-dwellers. Randolph and *The Messenger* spoke with fluent subtlety about capitalism and socialism, but it was Marcus Garvey who best articulated the alienation of the black masses. Perhaps as many as half a million of them, in thirty cities, joined his Universal Negro Improvement Association (UNIA). Garvey, a West Indian who came to the United States in 1916, exalted the Negro's black skin and assured the Negro that his glorious past history in Africa gave promise of a brilliant future there. His escapist ideology promised that blacks would return to Africa, leaving behind the America so riddled with white prejudice. To the urban Negroes, most of them wartime migrants from the South, the dream had potent appeal, for reality was bad housing, scarce jobs, and race riots. Garvey satisfied the yearnings of urban slum-dwellers by giving them a sense of racial identity and racial pride. A culture that made white the test of good was inverted; Garvey made black the standard of good, even deprecating the light-brown skins of people like Du Bois, who had mixed ancestry. On a more practical, immediate level, Garvey, like the Black Muslims later, espoused economic nationalism. He urged blacks to support black businesses. The UNIA itself undertook commercial enterprises, and in fact Garvey's downfall in 1925 came as a result of the inept and allegedly fraudulent practices of the ill-fated Black Star Steamship Line, which aimed to establish trade between Negroes in America and those in the West Indies and Africa.

The printed word does scant justice to Garvey, for it fails to recapture the characteristic personal force of his oratory.

A. "The true solution of the Negro problem"

As far as Negroes are concerned, in America we have the problem of lynching, peonage and dis-franchisement.

In the West Indies, South and Central America we have the problem of peonage, serfdom, industrial and political governmental inequality.

Marcus Garvey, "The True Solution of the Negro Problem" (1922), in PHILOSOPHY AND OPINIONS OF MARCUS GARVEY, ed. Amy Jacques-Garvey, I (New York: Universal Publishing House, 1923), pp. 52–53. Reprinted with permission of Amy Jacques-Garvey.

In Africa we have, not only peonage and serfdom, but outright slavery, racial exploitation and alien political monopoly.

We cannot allow a continuation of these crimes against our race. As four hundred million men, women and children, worthy of the existence given us by the Divine Creator, we are determined to solve our own problem, by redeeming our Motherland Africa from the hands of alien exploiters and found there a government, a nation of our own, strong enough to lend protection to the members of our race scattered all over the world, and to compel the respect of the nations and races of the earth.

Do they lynch Englishmen, Frenchmen, Germans or Japanese? No. And Why? Because these people are represented by great governments, mighty nations and empires, strongly organized. Yes, and ever ready to shed the last drop of blood and spend the last penny in the national treasury to protect the honor and integrity of a citizen outraged anywhere.

Until the Negro reaches this point of national independence, all he does as a race will count for naught, because the prejudice that will stand out against him even with his ballot in his hand, with his industrial progress to show, will be of such an overwhelming nature as to perpetuate mob violence and mob rule, from which he will suffer and which he will not be able to stop with his industrial wealth and with his ballot.

You may argue that he can use his industrial wealth and his ballot to force the government to recognize him, but he must understand that the government is the people. That the majority of the people dictate the policy of governments, and if the majority are against a measure, a thing, or a race, then the government is impotent to protect that measure, thing or race.

If the Negro were to live in this Western Hemisphere for another five hundred years he would still be outnumbered by other races who are prejudiced against him. He cannot resort to the government for protection for government will be in the hands of the majority of the people who are prejudiced against him, hence for the Negro to depend on the ballot and his industrial progress alone, will be hopeless as it does not help him when he is lynched, burned, jim-crowed and segregated. The future of the Negro therefore, outside of Africa, spells ruin and disaster.

B. The aims of the Universal Negro Improvement Association

Generally the public is kept misinformed of the truth surrounding new movements of reform. Very seldom, if ever, reformers get the truth told about them and their movements. Because of this natural attitude, the Universal Negro Improvement Association has been greatly handicapped in its work, causing thereby one of the most liberal and helpful human movements of the twentieth century to be held up to ridicule by those who take pride in poking fun at anything not already successfully established.

The white man of America has become the natural leader of the world. He, because of his exalted position, is called upon to help in all human efforts. From nations to individuals the appeal is made to him for aid in all things affecting humanity, so, naturally, there can be no great mass movement or change without first acquainting the leader on whose sympathy and advice the world moves.

It is because of this, and more so because of a desire to be Christian friends with the white race, why I explain the aims and objects of the Universal Negro Improvement Association.

The Universal Negro Improvement Association is an organization among Negroes that is seeking to improve the condition of the race, with the view of establishing a nation in Africa where Negroes will be given the opportunity to develop by themselves, without creating the hatred and animosity that now exist in countries of the white race through Negroes rivaling them for the highest and best positions in government, politics, society and industry. The organization believes in the rights of

Marcus Garvey, "Aims and Objects of Movement for Solution of Negro Problem (1923?), in PHILOSOPHY AND OPINIONS OF MARCUS GARVEY, ed. Amy Jacques-Garvey, II (New York: Universal Publishing House, 1925), pp. 37–43. Reprinted with permission of Amy Jacques-Garvey.

all men, yellow, white and black. To us, the white race has a right to the peaceful possession and occupation of countries of its own and in like manner the yellow and black races have their rights. It is only by an honest and liberal consideration of such rights can the world be blessed with the peace that is sought by Christian teachers and leaders.

The spiritual brotherhood of man

The following preamble to the constitution of the organization speaks for itself:

"The Universal Negro Improvement Association and African Communities' League is a social, friendly, humanitarian, charitable, educational, institutional, constructive, and expansive society, and is founded by persons, desiring to the utmost to work for the general uplift of the Negro peoples of the world. And the members pledge themselves to do all in their power to conserve the rights of their noble race and to respect the rights of all mankind, believing always in the Brotherhood of Man and the Fatherhood of God. The motto of the organization is: One God! One Aim! One Destiny! Therefore, let justice be done to all mankind, realizing that if the strong oppresses the weak confusion and discontent will ever mark the path of man, but with love, faith and charity toward all the reign of peace and plenty will be heralded into the world and the generation of men shall be called Blessed."

The declared objects of the association are:

"To establish a Universal Confraternity among the race; to promote the spirit of pride and love; to reclaim the fallen; to administer to and assist the needy; to assist in civilizing the backward tribes of Africa; to assist in the development of Independent Negro Nations and Communities; to establish a central nation for the race; to establish Commissaries or Agencies in the principal countries and cities of the world for the representation of all Negroes; to promote a conscientious Spiritual worship among the native tribes of Africa; to establish Universities, Colleges, Academies and Schools for the racial education and culture of the people; to work for better conditions among Negroes every-where."

Supplying a long-felt want

The organization of the Universal Negro Improvement Asso-ciation has supplied among Negroes a long-felt want. Hitherto the other Negro movements in America, with the exception of the Tuskegee effort of Booker T. Washington, sought to teach the Negro to aspire to social equality with the whites, meaning thereby the right to intermarry and fraternize in every social way. This has been the source of much trouble and still some Negro organizations continue to preach this dangerous "race de-stroying doctrine" added to a program of political agitation and aggression. The Universal Negro Improvement Association on the other hand believes in and teaches the pride and purity of race. We believe that the white race should uphold its racial pride and perpetuate itself, and that the black race should do likewise. We believe that there is room enough in the world for the various race groups to grow and develop by themselves without seeking to destroy the Creator's plan by the constant introduction of mongrel types.

The unfortunate condition of slavery as imposed upon the Negro, and which caused the mongrelization of the race, should not be legalized and continued now to the harm and detriment of both races.

The time has really come to give the Negro a chance to de-velop himself to a moral-standard-man, and it is for such an opportunity that the Universal Negro Improvement Association seeks in the creation of an African nation for Negroes, where the greatest latitude would be given to work out this racial ideal.

There are hundreds of thousands of colored people in America who desire race amalgamation and miscegenation as a solution of the race problem. These people are, therefore, opposed to the race pride ideas of black and white; but the thoughtful of both races will naturally ignore the ravings of such persons and hon-estly work for the solution of a problem that has been forced upon us.

Liberal white America and race loving Negroes are bound to think at this time and thus evolve a program or plan by which there can be a fair and amicable settlement of the question.

We cannot put off the consideration of the matter, for time is pressing on our hands. The educated Negro is making rightful constitutional demands. The great white majority will never grant them, and thus we march on to danger if we do not now stop and adjust the matter.

The time is opportune to regulate the relationship between both races. Let the Negro have a country of his own. Help him to return to his original home, Africa, and there give him the opportunity to climb from the lowest to the highest positions in a state of his own. If not, then the nation will have to hearken to the demand of the aggressive, "social equality" organization, known as the National Association for the Advancement of Colored People, of which W. E. B. Du Bois is leader, which declares vehemently for social and political equality, viz.: Negroes and whites in the same hotels, homes, residential districts, public and private places, a Negro as president, members of the Cabinet, Governors of States, Mayors of cities, and leaders of society in the United States. In this agitation, Du Bois is ably supported by the "Chicago Defender," a colored newspaper published in Chicago. This paper advocates Negroes in the Cabinet and Senate. All these, as everybody knows, are the Negroes' constitutional rights, but reason dictates that the masses of the white race will never stand by the ascendency of an opposite minority group to the favored positions in a government, society and industry that exist by the will of the majority, hence the demand of the Du Bois group of colored leaders will only lead, ultimately, to further disturbances in riots, lynching and mob rule. The only logical solution therefore, is to supply the Negro with opportunities and environments of his own, and there[by] point him to the fullness of his ambition.

Negroes who seek social equality

The Negro who seeks the White House in America could find ample play for his ambition in Africa. The Negro who seeks the office of Secretary of State in America would have a fair chance of demonstrating his diplomacy in Africa. The Negro who seeks a seat in the Senate or of being governor of a State in America, would be provided with a glorious chance for statesmanship in Africa.

The Negro has a claim on American white sympathy that cannot be denied. The Negro has labored for 300 years in contributing to America's greatness. White America will not be unmindful, therefore, of this consideration, but will treat him kindly. Yet it is realized that all human beings have a limit to their humanity. The humanity of white America, we realize, will seek self-protection and self-preservation, and that is why the thoughtful and reasonable Negro sees no hope in America for satisfying the aggressive program of the National Association for the Advancement of Colored People, but advances the reasonable plan of the Universal Negro Improvement Association, that of creating in Africa a nation and government for the Negro race.

This plan when properly undertaken and prosecuted will solve the race problem in America in fifty years. Africa affords a wonderful opportunity at the present time for colonization by the Negroes of the Western world. There is Liberia, already established as an independent Negro government. Let white America assist Afro-Americans to go there and help develop the country. Then, there are the late German colonies; let white sentiment force England and France to turn them over to the American and West Indian Negroes who fought for the Allies in the World's War. Then, France, England and Belgium owe America billions of dollars which they claim they cannot afford to repay immediately. Let them compromise by turning over Sierre Leone and the Ivory Coast on the West Coast of Africa and add them to Liberia and help make Liberia a state worthy of her history.

The Negroes of Africa and America are one in blood. They have sprung from the same common stock. They can work and live together and thus make their own racial contribution to the world.

Will deep thinking and liberal white America help? It is a considerate duty.

It is true that a large number of self-seeking colored agitators and so-called political leaders, who hanker after social equality and fight for the impossible in politics and governments, will rave, but remember that the slave-holder raved, but the North said, "Let the slaves go free"; the British Parliament raved when the Colonists said, "We want a free and American nation"; the Monarchists of France raved when the people declared for a more liberal form of government.

The masses of Negroes think differently from the self-appointed leaders of the race. The majority of Negro leaders are selfish, self-appointed and not elected by the people. The people desire freedom in a land of their own, while the colored politician desires office and social equality for himself in America, and that is why we are asking white America to help the masses to realize their objective. . . .

Help the Negro to return home

Surely the time has come for the Negro to look homeward. He has won civilization and Christianity at the price of slavery. The Negro who is thoughtful and serviceable, feels that God intended him to give to his brothers still in darkness, the light of his civilization. The very light element of Negroes do not want to go back to Africa. They believe that in time, through miscegenation, the American race will be of their type. This is a fallacy and in that respect the agitation of the mulatto leader, Dr. W. E. B. Du Bois and the National Association for the Advancement of Colored People is dangerous to both races.

The off-colored people, being children of the Negro race, should combine to re-establish the purity of their own race, rather than seek to perpetuate the abuse of both races. That is to say, all elements of the Negro race should be encouraged to get together and form themselves into a healthy whole, rather than seeking to lose their identities through miscegenation and social intercourse with the white race. These statements are made because we desire an honest solution of the problem and no flattery or deception will bring that about.

Let the white and Negro people settle down in all seriousness and in true sympathy and solve the problem. When that is done, a new day of peace and good will will be ushered in.

The natural opponents among Negroes to a program of this kind are that lazy element who believe always in following the line of least resistance, being of themselves void of initiative and the pioneering spirit to do for themselves. The professional Negro leader and the class who are agitating for social equality feel that it is too much work for them to settle down and build up a civilization of their own. They feel it is easier to seize on to the civilization of the white man and under the guise of constitutional rights fight for those things that the white man has created. Natural reason suggests that the white man will not yield them, hence such leaders are but fools for their pains. Teach the Negro to do for himself, help him the best way possible in that direction; but to encourage him into the belief that he is going to possess himself of the things that others have fought and died for, is to build up in his mind false hopes never to be realized. As for instance, Dr. W. E. B. Du Bois, who has been educated by white charity, is a brilliant scholar, but he is not a hard worker. He prefers to use his higher intellectual abilities to fight for a place among white men in society, industry and in politics, rather than use that ability to work and create for his own race that which the race could be able to take credit for. He would not think of repeating for his race the work of the Pilgrim Fathers or the Colonists who laid the foundation of America, but he prefers to fight and agitate for the privilege of dancing with a white lady at a ball at the Biltmore or at the Astoria hotels in New York. That kind of leadership will destroy the Negro in America and against which the Universal Negro Improvement Association is fighting.

The Universal Negro Improvement Association is composed of all shades of Negroes—blacks, mulattoes and yellows, who are all working honestly for the purification of their race, and for a sympathetic adjustment of the race problem.

The 1920s: cultural nationalism

17. LANGSTON HUGHES ON THE UNIQUE FEATURES OF NEGRO LIFE

During the 1920s, the race-proud intelligentsia of the New Negro literary movement known as the Harlem Renaissance wrestled with the problem of identity created by the ethnic dualism of black Americans. As the Rhodes Scholar, esthete, and Howard University professor Alain Locke put it:

> ". . . Each generation. . . will have its creed, and that of the present is belief in the efficacy of collective effort, in race cooperation. This deep feeling of race is at present the mainspring of Negro life. It seems to be the outcome of the reaction to proscription and prejudice; an attempt, fairly successful on the whole, to convert a defensive into an offensive position, a handicap into an incentive. . . . But this forced attempt to build his Americanism on race values is a unique social experiment, and its ultimate success is impossible except through the fullest sharing of American culture and institutions. . . . The racialism of the Negro is no limitation or reservation with respect to American life; it is only a constructive effort to build the obstructions in the stream of his progress into an efficient dam of social energy and power."[1]

A perceptive exploration of this problem was made by Langston Hughes, one of the luminaries of the Harlem Renaissance, who was

Langston Hughes, "The Negro Artist and the Racial Mountain," THE NATION, CXXII (June 23, 1926), 692–694.

[1] Alain Locke, ed., *The New Negro* (New York: Albert and Charles Boni, 1925), pp. 11–12.

then at the beginning of a notably productive career. Like many writers of the 1920s, Hughes throughout his life consistently drew inspiration for his work from the distinctive cultural milieu of the black masses. Writing for *The Nation* in 1926 he criticized middle-class blacks who were ashamed of their race, rejected the work of earlier Negro writers who had imitated prominent white authors, and urged black artists to proudly use themes and subject matter drawn from the life of the sharecroppers and slum-dwellers.

One of the most promising of the young Negro poets said to me once, "I want to be a poet—not a Negro poet," meaning, I believe, "I want to write like a white poet"; meaning subconsciously, "I would like to be a white poet"; meaning behind that, "I would like to be white." And I was sorry the young man said that, for no great poet has ever been afraid of being himself. And I doubted then that, with his desire to run away spiritually from his race, this boy would ever be a great poet. But this is the mountain standing in the way of any true Negro art in America—this urge within the race toward whiteness, the desire to pour racial individuality into the mold of American standardization, and to be as little Negro and as much American as possible.

But let us look at the immediate background of this young poet. His family is what I suppose one would call the Negro middle class: people who are by no means rich yet never uncomfortable nor hungry—smug, contented, respectable folk, members of the Baptist church. The father goes to work every morning. He is a chief steward at a large white club. The mother sometimes does fancy sewing or supervises parties for the rich families of the town. The children go to a mixed school. In the home they read white papers and magazines. And the mother often says "Don't be like niggers" when the children are bad. A frequent phrase from the father is, "Look how well a white man does things." And so the word white comes to be unconsciously a symbol of all the virtues. . . . One sees immediately how difficult it would be for an artist born in such a home to interest himself in interpreting the beauty of his own people. He is never taught to see that beauty. He is taught rather not to see it, or if he does, to be ashamed of it when it is not according to Caucasian patterns.

For racial culture the home of a self-styled "high-class" Negro has nothing better to offer. Instead there will perhaps be more aping of things white than in a less cultured or less wealthy home. The father is perhaps a doctor, lawyer, landowner, or politician. The mother may be a social worker, or a teacher, or she may do nothing and have a maid. Father is often dark but he has usually married the lightest woman he could find. The family attend a fashionable church where few really colored faces are to be found. And they themselves draw a color line. In the North they go to white theatres and white movies. And in the South they have at least two cars and a house "like white folks." Nordic manners, Nordic faces, Nordic hair, Nordic art (if any), and an Episcopal heaven. A very high mountain indeed for the would-be racial artist to climb in order to discover himself and his people.

But then there are the low-down folks, the so-called common element, and they are the majority—may the Lord be praised! The people who have their nip of gin on Saturday nights and are not too important to themselves or the community, or too well fed, or too learned to watch the lazy world go round. They live on Seventh Street in Washington or State Street in Chicago and they do not particularly care whether they are like white folks or anybody else. Their joy runs, bang! into ecstasy. Their religion soars to a shout. Work maybe a little today, rest a little tomorrow. Play awhile. Sing awhile. O, let's dance! These common people are not afraid of spirituals, as for a long time their more intellectual brethren were, and jazz is their child. They furnish a wealth of colorful, distinctive material for any artist because they still hold their own individuality in the face of American standardizations. And perhaps these common people will give to the world its truly great Negro artist, the one who is not afraid to be himself. . . . Certainly there is, for the American Negro artist who can escape the restrictions the more advanced among his own group would put upon him, a great field of unused material ready for his art. . . . But let us look again at the mountain.

A prominent Negro clubwoman in Philadelphia paid eleven

dollars to hear Raquel Meller sing Andalusian popular songs. But she told me a few weeks before she would not think of going to hear "that woman," Clara Smith, a great black artist, sing Negro folksongs. And many an upper-class Negro church, even now, would not dream of employing a spiritual in its services. The drab melodies in white folks' hymnbooks are much to be preferred. "We want to worship the Lord correctly and quietly. We don't believe in 'shouting.' Let's be dull like the Nordics," they say, in effect.

The road for the serious black artist, then, who would produce a racial art is most certainly rocky and the mountain is high. Until recently he received almost no encouragement for his work from either white or colored people. . . .

The Negro artist works against an undertow of sharp criticism and misunderstanding from his own group and unintentional bribes from the whites. "O, be respectable, write about nice people, show how good we are," say the Negroes. "Be stereotyped, don't go too far, don't shatter our illusions about you, don't amuse us too seriously. We will pay you," say the whites. Both would have told Jean Toomer not to write "Cane."[1] The colored people did not praise it. The white people did not buy it. Most of the colored people who did read "Cane" hate it. They are afraid of it. Although the critics gave it good reviews the public remained indifferent. Yet (excepting the work of Du Bois) "Cane" contains the finest prose written by a Negro in America. And like the singing of [Paul] Robeson, it is truly racial.

But in spite of the Nordicized Negro intelligentsia and the desires of some white editors we have an honest American Negro literature already with us. Now I await the rise of the Negro theater. Our folk music, having achieved world-wide fame, offers itself to the genius of the great individual American Negro composer who is to come. And within the next decade I expect to see the work of a growing school of colored artists who paint and model the beauty of dark faces and create with new tech-

[1] Jean Toomer, *Cane* (New York: Boni and Liveright, 1923), an avant-garde "novel," part prose, part poetry, much of it dealing with the southern Georgia lower-class or "folk Negro" [Ed.].

nique the expressions of their own soul-world. And the Negro dancers who will dance like flame and the singers who will continue to carry our songs to all who listen—they will be with us in even greater numbers tomorrow.

Most of my own poems are racial in theme and treatment, derived from the life I know. In many of them I try to grasp and hold some of the meanings and rhythms of jazz. I am sincere as I know how to be in these poems and yet after every reading I answer questions like these from my own people: Do you think Negroes should always write about Negroes? I wish you wouldn't read some of your poems to white folks. How do you find anything interesting in a place like a cabaret? Why do you write about black people? You aren't black. What makes you do so many jazz poems?

But jazz to me is one of the inherent expressions of Negro life in America: the eternal tom-tom beating in the Negro soul—the tom-tom of revolt against weariness in a white world, a world of subway trains, and work, work, work; the tom-tom of joy and laughter, and pain swallowed in a smile. Yet the Philadelphia clubwoman is ashamed to say that her race created it and she does not like me to write about it. The old subconscious "white is best" runs through her mind. Years of study under white teachers, a lifetime of white books, pictures, and papers, and white manners, morals, and Puritan standards made her dislike the spirituals. And now she turns up her nose at jazz and all its manifestations—likewise almost everything else distinctly racial. She doesn't care for the Winold Reiss portraits of Negroes because they are "too Negro." She does not want a true picture of herself from anybody. She wants the artist to flatter her, to make the white world believe that all Negroes are as smug and as near white in soul as she wants to be. But, to my mind, it is the duty of the younger Negro artist, if he accepts any duties at all from outsiders, to change through the force of his art that old whispering "I want to be white," hidden in the aspirations of his people, to "Why should I want to be white? I am a Negro— and beautiful!"

So I am ashamed for the black poet who says, "I want to be a poet, not a Negro poet," as though his own racial world were not as interesting as any other world. I am ashamed, too, for the colored artist who runs from the painting of Negro faces to the painting of sunsets after the manner of the academicians because he fears the strange un-whiteness of his own features. An artist must be free to choose what he does, certainly, but he must also never be afraid to do what he might choose.

Let the blare of Negro jazz bands and the bellowing voice of Bessie Smith singing Blues penetrate the closed ears of the colored near-intellectuals until they listen and perhaps understand. Let Paul Robeson singing Water Boy, and Rudolph Fisher writing about the streets of Harlem, and Jean Toomer holding the heart of Georgia in his hands, and Aaron Douglas drawing strange black fantasies cause the smug Negro middle class to turn from their white, respectable, ordinary books and papers to catch a glimmer of their own beauty. We younger Negro artists who create now intend to express our individual dark-skinned selves without fear or shame. If white people are pleased we are glad. If they are not, it doesn't matter. We know we are beautiful. And ugly too. The tom-tom cries and the tom-tom laughs. If colored people are pleased we are glad. If they are not, their displeasure doesn't matter either. We build our temples for tomorrow, strong as we know how, and we stand on top of the mountain, free within ourselves.

18. E. FRANKLIN FRAZIER
ON THE AMBIVALENCE
OF NEGRO INTELLECTUALS

A year after the appearance of Hughes's essay (Document 17), the young sociologist E. Franklin Frazier described with great lucidity the fundamental dualism in the black American's cultural tradition.

E. Franklin Frazier, "Racial Self-Expression," in Charles S. Johnson, ed., EBONY AND TOPAZ (New York: National Urban League, 1927), pp. 119–121. Reprinted with the permission of the National Urban League.

A professor at the Atlanta University School of Social Work at the time, Frazier subsequently taught at Fisk and Howard Universities, was the only Negro to serve as president of the American Sociological Association, and wrote the classic *The Negro Family in the United States* (1939).

Concurrent with the growing group consciousness among the colored people there has come into prominence two rather widely divergent opinions as to the principles which should govern the development of the group in America. The opinion represented by one group is that colored people should undertake to conform in every respect to the culture about them, while another group holds that they should develop their own unique culture. Although these two viewpoints can not be said to take this apparently mutually contradictory form in the minds of all leaders, they indicate to a large extent two emerging philosophies of racial development which are receiving emphasis by their respective protagonists. Moreover, it should be added that these two theories have been present since the Negro began to assert himself as a free man in this country, but have received new accentuation by the so-called renaissance of Negro artists and thinkers. The debate in the NATION between Langston Hughes and George Schuyler[1] was a skirmish in the clash between these two viewpoints. While the younger Negro artists are generally regarded as exponents of the opinion favoring a unique culture among the colored people, there is apparent disagreement among them. Countee Cullen's insistence that he wants to be a universal poet rather than a Negro poet is indicative of this lack of unanimity. . . . It is likely that both philosophies are rationalizations of tendencies which are observable in the different developments which are taking place in the experience of the colored group in America. In this essay, the writer hopes to contribute to the clarification of the issues involved and to evaluate the claims of the respective schools of

[1] George S. Schuyler, in the 1920's one of the radical editors of *The Messenger,* but today a conservative newspaper editor and columnist [Ed.].

opinion. As a first step in this analysis, the writer should say something about the relation between race and culture.

One of the first results of the general acceptance of the evolutionary hypothesis was the attempt to explain racial differences in terms of the evolutionary process. These á priori assumptions based upon superficial observations and favorable data have been totally discredited by the critical field studies of modern anthropologists. . . . The issue between the philosophies we are examining seems to resolve itself into the old issue of every nationalistic group. At first the group attempts to lose itself in the majority group, disdaining its own characteristics. When this is not possible there is a new valuation placed upon these very same characteristics and they are glorified in the eyes of the group. The same tendencies are observable in the case of the Negro group. There is, however, a conflict between the two tendencies noted above. On the one hand there is an attempt to efface Negroid characteristics and among the extremists of this group to dispense with the appellation, Negro; and on the other hand a glorification of things black. If the New Negro is turning within his group for new values and inspiration for group life, he is following the course of other nationalistic groups.

But to turn within the group experience for materials for artistic creation and group tradition is entirely different from seeking in the biological inheritance of the race for new values, attitudes and a different order of mentality. In the philosophy of those who stand for a unique culture among the Negroes there is generally the latter assumption. Moreover, while the group experience of the Negroes in America may be a fruitful source for the materials of art and to some extent a source of group tradition, it offers a very restricted source for building up a thorough-going group life in America. By the entrance of the Negro into America, he was practically stripped of his culture. His whole group experience in America has been directed towards taking over cultural forms about him. In spite of the isolation in which he has lived, the Negro has succeeded in doing this to a remarkable degree. From the beginning he has not been able to draw upon a group tradition outside of America. When he has been charged with imitation of white models, he has been forced to plead guilty because there were no others. . . . In this respect the Negro's position is different from any other nationalistic group in America. While they can maintain their group life by drawing upon the national tradition from the Old World, and participate only to a small degree in the American tradition, the Negro has no source to draw upon outside of America and only an inadequately assimilated American tradition from his past in this country.

It is quite possible that those who advocate a unique culture among Negroes would agree on the whole with the position taken above but would insist that the main point at issue is the difference in temperamental endowment. Therefore, as promised above, we shall turn to the consideration of this question. It has been pointed out by some that the facility with which the evangelical denominations spread among Negroes as well as the spirituals, and the seeming lack of strong economic motives, are indications of the peculiar racial temperament of the Negro. In the latter respect he is often contrasted with the Jew. But even here we cannot say dogmatically that racial temperament has been the decisive factor in the emphasis placed by the Negroes on certain elements of American culture. There are historical and social factors which are adequate reasons to account for the fact that the majority of Negroes are Baptists and Methodists as well as the predilection of the Jew for economic activities. In Africa the Negro has always been a trader and his markets are an outstanding feature of African cultures. Even in America we find a remarkable development of business enterprises and this type of activities has become for many of the younger Negroes the surest means for the group to acquire status.

Mr. James Weldon Johnson has indicated, it appears to the writer, in "God's Trombones"[2] the unique contribution of the Negro artists. In this unique work of art he has used the literary

[2] James Weldon Johnson, *God's Trombones: Some Negro Sermons in Verse* (London: G. Allen, 1929) [Ed.].

language of America to give artistic expression to the racial experience of the Negro in America. Whatever of racial temperament there is in these poems has been made articulate through cultural forms which were acquired by the artist in America. . . . As the Negro group becomes more differentiated we see developing the same social types that are found in the white majority. There is a growing group of black Babbitts who are indistinguishable in their mental attitudes from the white Babbitts. The racial temperament of the Negro will assert itself in the cultural traits which he takes over; but such an indeterminable factor can not become the norm for determining the lines along which the Negro should build his culture. But it may be asked if it is desirable for the Negro to acquire uncritically all the traits of American culture. The remainder of this essay will be directed to an attempt to give a brief answer to this question.

The very fact that the issue between these two philosophies of racial development has been raised indicates a sophistication that could never have developed in cultural isolation. Negro leaders have enjoyed a cosmopolitan experience that enables them to view objectively their racial experience, as well as American culture and cultural traits in general. This appears to be increasingly one of the chief functions of the Negro intellectual. His strategic position makes him a critic of values for his group. But it still remains an open question how far the Negro group can escape the adoption of the cultural forms of America. One example will suffice to show that even in the sphere of economic life some selection may be possible. The Negro must fit into the competitive industrial life about him either as a laborer or capitalist; but if the cooperative system of production and distribution offers superior spiritual values, then as far as practical he should develop in his economic life a cooperative economic technique.[3] This he should do rather than slavishly

[3] From time to time Du Bois and others had, since the early part of the century, advocated that Negroes organize themselves cooperatively along quasi-socialistic lines, even perhaps organizing themselves into cooperative communities. This type of economic co-operation is to be distinguished from the type advocated by Booker T. Washington and Negro businessmen —i.e., Negroes patronizing Negro entrepreneurs on the basis of racial self-help and racial solidarity. (See also Document 23.) [Ed.]

take over both the form and spirit of modern industrialism. If such a course finds support in the racial experience of the Negro in America or in his temperamental endowment, the task will be easier and will be a distinct contribution to the general fund of American culture. Likewise, if because of racial temperament there is a greater disposition on the part of Negroes to enjoy life than among the whites and this is recognized as a superior value, without sacrificing the efficiency of the group this trait should not be smothered by forcing the Negro's life into generally accepted molds.

Something should be said about another aspect of this question; namely, the building of a group tradition. It seems to the writer that any such effort should be encouraged only so far as it is compatible with a fuller participation in American culture. In this matter the experience of immigrant groups has a lesson for the Negro. Those immigrant groups which have maintained the greatest group efficiency have suffered the least amount of social mal-adjustment. The efficiency of their group organization has been the best means for fitting their members for participation in American life. One of the primary needs of the Negro in America where he is not treated as an individual is the development of group efficiency. The work of the Association for the Study of Negro Life and History under Dr. Carter G. Woodson is very rapidly creating a group tradition which is necessary for group morale. This is a socializing process through which the individual members of a group acquire status. This is a healthy sign among Negroes and need not be incompatible with their struggle for fuller participation in American culture so long as it does not increase their isolation.

This discussion has undertaken to evaluate the over-simplified assumption expressed and implied by those who are advocating a unique cultural development for the Negro, that our modern culture is the expression of certain special intellectual and temperamental traits and that the Negro should build a culture in harmony with his racial endowment. It was pointed out that the racial experience of the Negro was unique because of historical and social factors rather than of biological inheritance. Even those traits which are so universally ascribable to temperamental rather than intellectual differences were shown to have a possible explanation in social factors. While for the artist this unique experience was recognized as a fertile source, it was not deemed adequate for the building up of a thorough-going racial tradition which would afford maximum individual development. On the other hand, the utility of a group tradition built even upon African material for group efficiency was given due recognition. But finally it was shown that any nationalistic program that made the Negro seek compensations in a barren racial tradition and thereby escape competition with the white man which was an inevitable accompaniment of full participation in American culture, would lead to intellectual, spiritual and material impoverishment such as one finds among the Southern mountain whites.

The depression:
the search for economic solutions

19. NEGROES IN THE DEPRESSION: RALPH J. BUNCHE DESCRIBES A DIRECT-ACTION APPROACH TO JOBS

The early years of the depression spawned the Don't-Buy-Where-You-Can't-Work campaigns, a type of direct-action activity more commonly associated with the 1960s than with the 1930s. Groups specifically organized to do battle on this issue boycotted and picketed white-owned stores in black neighborhoods, chiefly in the North, that refused to employ black clerks. The NAACP was involved in some of these campaigns, one of them as far south as Richmond, Virginia.

In some cities these demonstrations were conducted by working-class people; in others they were sponsored by middle- and upper-class organizations. The New Negro Alliance of Washington, D.C., described by Ralph J. Bunche, at the time a professor of political science at Howard University, was of the latter type. Like many of the Don't-Buy-Where-You-Can't-Work campaigns, its activities were characterized by nationalist overtones.

The New Negro Alliance, Incorporated, of Washington, D. C., is an excellent example of the Negro boycott organizations. Its motto is "Buy Where You Work—Buy Where You Clerk."

Ralph J. Bunche, "The Programs, Ideologies, Tactics, and Achievements of Negro Betterment and Interracial Organizations" (unpublished memorandum prepared for the Carnegie-Myrdal Study of the Negro in America, 1940), pp. 380–392. Printed by permission of Ralph J. Bunche.

The factors giving rise to this organization are significant. Early in 1933 the management of a Hamburger Grill on "U" Street, N.W., in Washington, discharged its Negro employees and replaced them with white workers. This establishment was in the heart of the Negro belt of Northwest Washington and its entire trade was Negro. Several young Negroes happened to witness the discharge of the Negro employees and the injustice of the situation struck them with full force. They decided to organize a picket line in front of the grill and in a surprisingly short time the discharged Negro workers were back on their jobs. In setting up the picket line in front of the Grill, these young Negroes had perfected an organization. Inspired by their victory at the Grill, they decided to expand their organization and to make it a permanent force in the Negro community. It was named the New Negro Alliance, Incorporated. It was proposed as "an organization with a new vision, a new thought, and spirit, fearless in its undertakings, and willing to sacrifice and fight for its principles even if it meant being thrown in jail."[1]

From this beginning the organization went on to develop its policy of picketing stores in Negro districts which refused to employ Negro clerks. The Alliance tackled the Kaufman Department Store on upper Seventh Street, N. W. and caused it to lose the greater part of its Christmas trade. The Sanitary, the A. & P., and the High Ice Cream Company Stores were next tackled. The Kaufman, High and Sanitary Stores succeeded in getting injunctions against the Alliance. The injunction obtained by the Sanitary Stores went so far as to stipulate that in addition to no picketing, Alliance officials were enjoined from door to door campaigns—another weapon that had been employed effectively by the Alliance. While this litigation was pending and while the organization was thus deprived of its most effective weapon, the organization prepared a Civil Rights Bill for the District of Columbia, modeled after those in Pennsylvania and New York. This bill was introduced by Congressman Koppleman in the House of Representatives as HB No.

[1] *New Negro Alliance Yearbook* (1939), p. 15.

5333. In 1938 after four years of bitter court action, the Supreme Court of the United States dismissed the injunction. The opinion was handed down by Mr. Justice Roberts on March 28, 1938. The court ruled that the relationship of employer-employee is not essential in order to bring an organization such as the Alliance within the purview of the Norris-LaGuardia Act which permits peaceful picketing. Thus, the Alliance—striving to obtain employment for persons from employers who discriminated against them on account of race and color—was interpreted as a "person interested" in a labor dispute and so within the protection of the law prohibiting "interference."[2]

The New Negro Alliance is directed by regularly elected officers and maintains a number of committees and subcommittees. The officers and committee members work without remuneration. The Alliance claims to be non-political and non-sectarian.[3]

The program of the New Negro Alliance is set forth as follows: (1) the securing of positions which will increase the earning capacity of Negroes: (2) the securing of opportunities for advancement and promotion in positions secured; (3) the uniting of the purchasing power of the colored people to be used as a lever in securing economic advantages; (4) the creation of bigger and better Negro business through increased earning power of Negroes, through a better business outlook resulting from contact and experience with successful businesses of the other group, and through the stimulation of businesses now run by Negroes to higher levels of efficiency and service; (5) the concentrated support of all businesses which employ Negroes or in which Negro capital is invested[4]; (6) re-

[2] "The Supreme Court Speaks," by Leon A. Ransom, *New Negro Alliance Yearbook* (1939), p. 17.
[3] Cf. Article by John A. Davis, in *Opportunity* (August 1938), pp. 230–37.
[4] Though this is an official statement of the organization's program, this item is misleading. The Alliance does not give its support to "all businesses which employ Negroes," since this would embrace businesses such as the Peoples' Drug Stores, which it has vigorously picketed. The Alliance supports those businesses which employ Negro clerks and other white collar workers.

search and investigation which will discover and thoroughly analyze the possibility for Negro business and Negro labor in new fields.[5]

The tactics of the Alliance are those of a pressure group dependent largely upon the weight of the Negro consuming public. The proposal is to organize Negro consumers and to get them to support or withhold their support from designated stores and other business enterprises, and to persuade or force them to employ Negroes in proportion to Negro purchasing power. The Alliance essays a thorough survey of the trading area from which the store draws its patronage and definite efforts are made to determine the exact percentage of Negro business enjoyed by the store in question. Such statistics are presented by a committee representing the Alliance to officials of the store, and on the basis of such facts definite demands are made in proportion to the percentage of income from Negro trade. If no action has been taken upon these demands after a reasonable time has elapsed, a picket line is placed in front of the establishment. Negroes in this trading area are acquainted with the program of the organization and the reasons for the boycott through the distribution of circular letters from door to door.[6]

The support of the Alliance is through membership fees and voluntary contributions. Membership fees range from one to twelve dollars per year. For some time the Alliance published the "New Negro Opinion" as the official organ of the organization. This was a weekly set up in newspaper style.

The "New Negro Opinion" in its issue of February 3, 1934, presented a comparative study of the records of the New Negro Alliance under the heading "Figures Don't Lie" in order to demonstrate the profitable returns gotten for the Negro community on a very small investment through the efforts of the Alliance. These figures read as follows: Expenditures for office, stenographer, postage, etc.—$225; for printing, advertising

[5] *New Negro Alliance Yearbook* (1939), p. 11.
[6] *Ibid.*, p. 48.

signs, pickets, etc.—$175; total expenditures—$400. Returns—
A. & P.—18 clerks per year, $13,104; Hamburger Grill—four
clerks per year, $3,744; Sanitary—four clerks per year, $2,912;
others—nine clerks per year, $5,594; total returns—$25,354.[7]

The organization boasts a number of successes with local
employers and in two instances with large chain stores. However, in its attempt to compel the Peoples Drug Stores to
employ Negro clerks, it met with failure. The Peoples Drug
Stores is a chain of some 56 stores in Washington and nearby
states. The Alliance began its campaign against these stores
with a letter to the management requesting a conference on the
matter of the employment of Negro clerks and professional
workers in those stores in which the preponderance of trade
was Negro. After a second letter, a conference with the district
manager was obtained, and on June 21, 1938, a committee from
the Alliance met with the district manager. The Alliance Committee was told on behalf of the executive committee of the
Peoples Drug Stores Corporation that the definite policy of the
company was that Negroes be barred from clerical and professional positions and that they be refused service at soda
fountains. The committee was told that since the management
of the stores did not believe that colored people would stay out
of the stores because of such policy, no change was contemplated. On June 25, 1938, the New Negro Alliance placed a
picket in front of the Peoples Drug Store at Fourteenth and
U Streets, N.W., where a check had shown that approximately
75% of the trade was Negro. The signs carried by the pickets
urged all fair-minded people to stay out of the store and
circulars were distributed explaining the nature of the controversy. On July 15, 1938 a second picket line was begun in front
of the Peoples Drug Store at Seventh and M. Streets, N.W.,
where a check had shown that approximately 70% of the trade
was Negro. These picket lines were maintained for well over a
year and a half, yet, despite the claims of the Alliance that the

[7] Reprinted in the *New Negro Alliance Yearbook* (1939), p. 15.

number of Negro patrons entering the Fourteenth and U Streets store immediately dropped from approximately 1,000 per day to a little more than 100 a day, the management of the store remained adamant and ultimately the Alliance was compelled to abandon its struggle without any concession from the management.[8]

The membership of the Alliance is "ninety-nine and forty-four one hundred per cent pure Negro" with a "few unsolicited whites as members."[9] The organization has no affiliation with any other group—political or civic—and claims to be free from all restraining influence in its work.[10]

The main problem of the organization is that of financial support. Since membership fees are its sole source of revenue and since the number of members who pay dues within the course of the year does not exceed 1,500, the Alliance is hard pressed for funds to meet its normal expenditures. In its picketing campaigns it has found that it cannot recruit enough volunteer pickets and has been compelled to resort to paid pickets to carry on the work. During the picketing of the Peoples Drug Stores the monthly payroll was in the neighborhood of $150.[11]

The administrator of the organization states that the maintenance of the picket line before the two Peoples Drug Stores was chiefly a "symbol." He claims that the particular stores picketed became dead-weights and the firm was able to carry them only because of the chain character of the organization. Proof of the effectiveness of the picketing was claimed to be found in the fact that following its inception the clerical staff of the Fourteenth Street store was reduced by seven. Moreover it is contended that the maintenance of these lines proved invaluable because of its effect upon individual white enter-

[8] "We picket the Peoples Drug Stores," *New Negro Alliance Yearbook* (1939), p. 21.

[9] Interview with Eugene Davidson, Administrator of the New Negro Alliance, December, 1939. William Bryant's memo.

[10] *Ibid.*

[11] *Ibid.*

prises in the same neighborhood. The owners of such businesses were said to realize that they cannot keep their stores open on the strength of other holdings and have usually capitulated to the demands of the Alliance without struggle. It is claimed that Seventh Street from New York Avenue to Florida Avenue is an excellent example of the influence of the Alliance since there is now scarcely a store on upper Seventh Street which does not have at least one colored clerk.[12]

The organization is now proposing to train its sights on the public utilities in Washington, but appreciates the fact that considerable mass education of Negroes is a necessary prerequisite to such a move. The Alliance contemplates the employment of tactics similar to those used by Negroes in New York under the direction of the New York Coordinating Committee. This involves a closely knit organization of the Negro masses so that when the organization decides to have all of the Negroes in Washington turn off their electric lights on any particular night of the week, it would get impressive cooperation. The Alliance is also putting its active support behind the new proposed Civil Rights Bill of the District of Columbia.

It is stated that frequently the Alliance has run across the problem of union labor. In some cases employers have expressed a willingness to put on Negro employees, but are faced with the fact that the white employees are union men and that the unions will not accept Negro members. In the case of Heurich Brewers, for example, the company got around the difficulty with the union by employing Negroes as truck drivers and paying them union wages for their work. It was explained that, though the unions would not accept Negroes into their ranks, they did issue permits to the Negroes to drive the trucks for union wages. This was made necessary because of the fact that some fourteen Negro establishments had withdrawn their trade from the Heurich Company.[13]

12 *Ibid.*
13 *Ibid.*

In the statements of its aims, the New Negro Alliance points out that

> In our cities we find two types of businesses. First there is the 'neighborhood' store which caters to and relies upon the trade of the people living within a few blocks of the store. The other type of business whether a street railway company or a large department store, is one which serves the entire city. The neighborhood store owes to the community which supports it a fair return in the form of such employment as the store can give. The business which serves the entire city and makes a profit out of city-wide trade should give all persons in the community an opportunity to work as need arise and fitness can be shown. Where a neighborhood store is located in a colored neighborhood, its obligation to the neighborhood is an obligation to colored people. Where the neighborhood is one of white persons those are the persons who can rightly insist on a chance to work in neighborhood stores. . . . In each case the right is based not on race, but on the obligation of the neighborhood store to the neighborhood. . . .
>
> The New Negro Alliance does not sponsor jim-crow economy, but we must organize our purchasing power behind the demands for equal opportunity to work and also in support of those businesses in which Negroes can do work without discrimination. The support of businesses owned and operated by Negroes is, of course, an essential part of such a program.[14]

As to the effect of its policy upon the relations between Negro and white workers the Alliance explains that it has

> never fought to drive white workers into the streets. In every case the Alliance has sought to place Negroes it has taken the position that in any business of any size the normal course of replacements, displacements, and additions to personnel causes vacancies to arise from time to time. Moreover where Negroes represent the large part of the patronage of a store, the addi-

[14] *The New Negro Alliance Yearbook* (1939), p. 47.

tional cost of adding a few Negroes to the payroll is more than compensated for by the increase of business the establishment will receive.[15]

Despite its protestations to the contrary, it is clear that the New Negro Alliance pursues a narrowly racial policy—one that has no orientation in terms of labor unity or organization, and one that definitely opposes Negro against white workers.[16] Its membership is middle class and so is its ideology. Its efforts are devoted almost entirely to obtaining white collar jobs for Negroes and this is amply demonstrated by the claims made as to its successes.[17] Practically all of the jobs it has gotten for Negroes have been white collar jobs and these mainly clerks. It emphasizes the support of Negro business and says very little about the importance of organized labor to the Negro worker. Though employing the tactics and weapons of labor it is in no sense a labor organization. In terms of economic status it is quite clear that the ultimate results of the efforts of this organization will be of slight consequence to the Negro community.

Although both have been connected with the New Negro Alliance in an official capacity since its very beginning, Mr. Hastie and Mr. Fitzhugh have widely different conceptions of the organization's sympathizers. Mr. Fitzhugh places the membership at 1500 and the number of sympathizers at 5,000. Mr. Hastie, on the other hand places the membership at 1,000, but estimates 50,000 sympathizers.

Critique of the "don't buy where you can't work" organizations

The "Don't Buy Where You Can't Work" or "Buy Where You Can Work" movements are a logical corollary of the Negro

[15] *Ibid.*

[16] "The Why of the Alliance," by William H. Hastie, *The New Negro Alliance Yearbook* (1939), p. 14.

[17] See "Notes from Alliance Case Book," *New Negro Alliance Yearbook* (1939), pp. 24ff.

business philosophy. This credo has been expressed through organizations such as the New Negro Alliance, the League for Fair Play and the Afro-American Federation of Labor. The movement began in Chicago about 1931 and rapidly spread to the East and more recently to the South and West.

The organizations participating in this recent movement occasionally have employed the labor weapons of boycott and picketing against white stores in Negro districts which refuse to employ Negro white collar workers. This has undoubtedly been of educational value to the Negro in that it has given him some inkling of his latent economic power and an acquaintance with the recognized weapons of organized labor. The most violent manifestation of this movement was in the Harlem Riot of 1935 when thousands of Harlem Negroes vented their fury, born of poverty, against the small white—mostly Jewish—shopowners on Lennox and Seventh Avenues.

The philosophy of this movement is narrowly racial. If successful, it could only result in a vicious cycle of job displacement since it creates no new jobs but only struggles to displace white workers, and, since Negro communities do not offer sufficient economic activity to absorb even a small number of the Negroes now employed in white industry. Its appeal has been primarily in the interest of the Negro white collar worker and its support has come chiefly from Negro middle class professional and intellectual groups. It appears unable to realize that there is an economic system as well as a race problem in America and that when a Negro is unemployed, it is not just because he is a Negro but more seriously because of the defective operation of the economy under which we live—an economy that finds it impossible to provide an adequate number of jobs and economic security for the population. More seriously, still, this movement tends to widen the menacing gap between white and black workers by insisting that jobs be distributed on a racial basis. It is a philosophy which, like that of Negro business, offers only racialism with no significant hope for the mass Negro population.

20. ANGELO HERNDON:
A BLACK COMMUNIST
TELLS WHAT THE PARTY MEANT TO HIM

During the 1920s and early 1930s the Communist Party's platform in regard to the problems of American Negroes involved four major items: an attack upon all forms of racial oppression, denunciation of black intellectuals and *bourgeoisie* for allegedly supporting the interests of white capitalists against the interests of the race; a call for united revolutionary action upon the part of both white and black workers against the capitalist class; and "self-determination for the Black Belt," a proposal to carve an all-Negro "49th state" out of the heart of the Southern Black Belt. This last scheme was a mechanical adaptation of Stalin's plans for dealing with the ethnic minorities of the Soviet Union. It remained official Communist Party policy for years but played no role of importance, either in attracting Negroes to the Party or in shaping actual Party strategy in the area of race relations.

The Communist theoreticians held that the black population, as the most oppressed group in America, would be a likely source of recruits. But Communism made little progress among American Negroes. Negro intellectuals found it difficult to stay within the arbitrary disciplines of the Party, and for the masses the dialectics of official Party literature had little appeal.

Most of the pamphleteering by black Communists, such as the writings of James W. Ford, who several times ran as Communist Party candidate for Vice-President, was stale, cliché-ridden rehashes of whatever happened to be the Party line. But early in the 1930s appeared an autobiographical pamphlet by Angelo Herndon that reveals more vividly than any number of official ideological statements the secret of the Communist appeal for those working-class blacks who did join its ranks. Herndon, a Birmingham coal-miner, became one of the famous *causes célèbres* of the 1930s when

Angelo Herndon, "YOU CANNOT KILL THE WORKING CLASS" (New York: The International Labor Defense and the League of Struggle for Negro Rights, n.d. [ca. 1934]), pp. 5–16, 22–29.

he was sentenced to 18 to 20 years on the chain gang on charges of inciting to insurrection. Until he was freed by the Supreme Court, Herndon's case, because of its civil libertarian aspects, attracted wide support from diverse quarters, and provided an effective focus around which the Communists in the middle 1930s created a United Front. Whether or not Herndon actually wrote everything in the pamphlet that appeared under his name, it captures the essential spirit and outlook that animated many Negro Communists in the 1930s.

My father, Paul Herndon, and my mother, Hattie Herndon, lived for many years in Birmingham, and then came North. They settled down in Wyoming, Ohio, a little steel and mining town just outside of Cincinnati.

I was born there on May 6, 1913. My name was put down in the big family Bible as Eugene Angelo Braxton Herndon.

They say that once a miner, always a miner. I don't know if that's so, but I do know that my father never followed any other trade. His sons never doubted that they would go down into the mines as soon as they got old enough. The wail of the mine whistle morning and night, and the sight of my father coming home with his lunch-pail, grimy from the day's coating of coal-dust, seemed a natural and eternal part of our lives.

Almost every working-class family, especially in those days, nursed the idea that one of its members, anyway, would get out of the factory and wear clean clothes all the time and sit at a desk. My family was no exception. They hoped that I would be the one to leave the working-class. They were ready to make almost any sacrifices to send me through high-school and college. They were sure that if a fellow worked hard and had intelligence and grit, he wouldn't have to be a worker all his life.

I haven't seen my mother or most of my family for a long time—but I wonder what they think of that idea now!

My father died of miner's pneumonia when I was very small, and left my mother with a big family to care for. Besides myself, there were six other boys and two girls. We all did what we could. Mother went out to do housework for rich white folks. An older brother got a job in the steel mills. I did odd jobs, working in stores, running errands, for $2 and $3 a week. They still had the idea they could scrimp and save and send me through college. But when I was 13, we saw it wouldn't work.

So one fine morning in 1926, my brother Leo and I started off for Lexington, Ky. It was just across the border, and it had mines, and we were miner's kids.

A few miles outside of Lexington, we were taken on at a small mine owned by the powerful DeBardeleben Coal Corporation. There didn't seem to be any question in anyone's mind about a kid of 13 going to work, and I was given a job helping to load coal. . . .

. . . They weighed our coal and charged us for the slate in it. They cheated awfully on the slate. Then after they skinned us that way, they skinned us again on the weight. The check-weighman had been hired by the company. He had the scales all fixed beforehand, and the cars just slid over the scales. Everybody could see it was a gyp, but we weren't organized, and though we grumbled we couldn't get any satisfaction.

We lived in the company town. It was pretty bad. The houses were just shacks on unpaved streets. We seldom had anything to eat that was right. We had to buy everything from the company store, or we'd have lost our jobs. They kept our pay low and paid only every two weeks, so we had to have credit between times. We got advances in the form of clackers, which could be used only in the company store. Their prices were very high. I remember paying 30 cents a pound for pork-chops in the company store and then noticing that the butcher in town was selling them for 20 cents. The company store prices were just robbery without a pistol.

The safety conditions in the mine were rotten. The escape-ways were far from where we worked, and there was never enough timbering to keep the rocks from falling. There were some bad accidents while I was there. I took all the skin off my right hand pushing a car up into the facing. The cars didn't have enough grease and there were no cross-ties just behind me to brace my feet against. That was a bit of the company's economy.

The car slipped, the track turned over, and the next thing I knew I had lost all the skin and a lot of the flesh off my right hand. The scars are there to this day.

This DeBardeleben mine in Lexington was where the Jim-Crow system first hit me. The Negroes and whites very seldom came in contact with each other. Of course there were separate company patches for living quarters. But even in the mine the Negroes and the whites worked in different places. The Negroes worked on the North side of the mine and the whites on the South.

The Negroes never got a look-in on most of the better-paying jobs. They couldn't be section foremen, or electricians, or surveyors, or head bank boss, or checkweighman, or steel sharpeners, or engineers. They could only load the coal, run the motors, be mule-boys, pick the coal, muck the rock. In other words, they were only allowed to do the muscle work.

Besides that, the Negro miners got the worst places to work. We worked in the low coal, only 3 or 4 feet high. We had to wear knee pads, and work stretched flat on our bellies most of the time.

One day the company put up a notice that due to large overhead expenses, they would have to cut our pay from 42 to 31 cents a ton. We were sore as hell. But there wasn't any union in the mine, and practically none of us had any experience at organization, and though we grumbled plenty we didn't take any action. We were disgusted, and some of us quit. Whites and Negroes both.

I was one of those who quit. My contact with unions, and with organization, and the Communist Party, and unity between black and white miners—all that was still in the future. The pay-cut and the rotten conditions got my goat, and I walked off, because as yet I didn't know of anything else to do.

Well, my brother Leo and I set out for Birmingham, where there were relatives—and plenty more mines.

I finally got work at the Docena mine of the Tennessee Coal, Iron and Railroad Co.

I want to talk a little about that. When I sat in jail this spring and read that the workers of the Tennessee Coal and Iron Company had come out on strike, I knew that a new day had come in the South. The T.C.I. just about owns Alabama. It owns steel mills and coal-mines and a railroad and all sorts of subsidiary plants. It owns company patches and houses. It certainly owns most of the Alabama officials. It dictates the political life of the state. It has made Jim-Crowism a fine art. It has stool-pigeons in every corner. The T.C.I. is like some great, greedy brute that holds a whip over the whole state. Its shadow is everywhere— on factories, schools, judges' benches, even the pulpits of churches.

The Tennessee Coal and Iron Company has always been in the forefront of the fight against unions in the South. They had —and still have—a company-union scheme, which they make a great deal out of, but which doesn't fool any of the workers. I noticed that whatever checkweighman the company put up, would always be elected.

I started surface work at the Docena mine, helping to build transformation lines, cutting the right of way for wires. I was supposed to get $2.78 a day, but there were lots of deductions.

It was while I was on this job that I first got a hint of an idea that workers could get things by organizing and sticking together.

It happened this way: one of my buddies on the job was killed by a trolley wire. The shielding on that wire had been down two weeks, and the foreman had seen it down, and hadn't bothered with it. All of us surface men quit work for the day, when we saw our buddy lying burnt and still, tangled up in that wire.

The next week we were called before the superintendent to explain the accident. Of course we were expected to whitewash the foreman and the company, so they woudn't have to pay any insurance to the dead man's family. Something got into me, and I spoke up and said that the foreman and the whole company was to blame. The men backed me up. One of the foremen nudged me and told me to hush. He said: "Boy, you're talking too damn much." But I kept on. The foreman was removed and the dead man's family got some compensation from the T.C.I.

That was my first lesson in organization.

By this time the crisis had hit the United States. Mines and factories closed their doors, and businesses crashed, and workers who had never been out of jobs before began to tramp the streets. Those of us who still had jobs found our wages going down, down. The miners got one cut after another. Often, when we got our pay-envelopes, we'd find a blank strip. That meant that the company had taken all our wages for supplies and food advances.

The Jim-Crow system was in full force in the mines of the Tennessee Coal and Iron Company, and all over Birmingham. It had always burnt me up, but I didn't know how to set about fighting it. My parents and grand-parents were hard-boiled Republicans, and told me very often that Lincoln had freed the slaves, and that we'd have to look to the Republican Party for everything good. I began to wonder about that. Here I was, being Jim-Crowed and cheated. Every couple of weeks I read about a lynching somewhere in the South. Yet there sat a Republican government up in Washington, and they weren't doing a thing about it.

My people told me to have faith in God, and he would make everything come right. I read a lot of religious tracts, but I got so I didn't believe them. I figured that there was no use for a Negro to go to heaven, because if he went there it would only be to shine some white man's shoes.

I wish I could remember the exact date when I first attended a meeting of the Unemployment Council, and met up with a couple of members of the Communist Party. That date means a lot more to me than my birthday, or any other day of my life.

The workers in the South, mostly deprived of reading-matter, have developed a wonderful grapevine system for transmitting news. It was over this grapevine that we first heard that there were "reds" in town.

The foremen—when they talked about it—and the newspapers, and the big-shot Negroes in Birmingham, said that the "reds" were foreigners, and Yankees, and believed in killing people, and would get us in a lot of trouble. But out of all the talk I got a few ideas clear about the Reds. They believed in organizing and sticking together. They believed that we didn't have to have bosses on our backs. They believed that Negroes ought to have equal rights with whites. It all sounded O.K. to me. But I didn't meet any of the Reds for a long time.

One day in June, 1930, walking home from work, I came across some handbills put out by the Unemployment Council in Birmingham. They said: "Would you rather fight—or starve?" They called on the workers to come to a mass meeting at 3 o'clock.

Somehow I never thought of missing that meeting. I said to myself over and over: "It's war! It's war! And I might as well get into it right now!" I got to the meeting while a white fellow was speaking. I didn't get everything he said, but this much hit me and stuck with me: that the workers could only get things by fighting for them, and that the Negro and white workers had to stick together to get results. The speaker described the conditions of the Negroes in Birmingham, and I kept saying to myself: "That's it." Then a Negro spoke from the same platform, and somehow I knew that this was what I'd been looking for all my life.

At the end of the meeting I went up and gave my name. From that day to this, every minute of my life has been tied up with the workers' movement.

I joined the Unemployment Council, and some weeks later the Communist Party. I read all the literature of the movement that I could get my hands on, and began to see my way more clearly.

I had some mighty funny ideas at first, but I guess that was only natural. For instance, I thought that we ought to start by getting all the big Negro leaders like DePriest and Du Bois and Walter White into the Communist Party, and then we would have all the support we needed. I didn't know then that DePriest and the rest of the leaders of that type are on the side of the bosses, and fight as hard as they can against the workers. They don't believe in fighting against the system that produces Jim-

Crowism. They stand up for that system, and try to preserve it, and so they are really on the side of Jim-Crowism and inequality. I got rid of all these ideas after I heard Oscar Adams and others like him speak in Birmingham.

That happened this way:

Birmingham had just put on a Community Chest drive. The whites gave and the Negroes gave. Some gave willingly, thinking it was really going to help feed the unemployed, and the rest had it taken out of their wages. There was mighty little relief handed out to the workers, even when they did get on the rolls. The Negroes only got about half what the whites got. Some of the workers waiting at the relief station made up a take-off on an old prison song. I remember that the first two lines of it went:

> I've counted the beans, babe,
> I've counted the greens. . . .

The Unemployment Council opened a fight for cash relief, and aid for single men, and equal relief for Negro and white. They called for a meeting in Capitol Park, and we gathered about the Confederate Monument, about 500 of us, white and Negro, and then we marched on the Community Chest headquarters. There were about 100 cops there. The officials of the Community Chest spoke, and said that the best thing for the Negroes to do was to go back to the farms. They tried very hard to give the white workers there the idea that if the Negroes went back to the farms, the whites would get a lot more relief.

Of course our leaders pointed out that the small farmers and share-croppers and tenants on the cotton-lands around Birmingham were starving, and losing their land and stock, and hundreds were drifting into the city in the hope of getting work.

Then Oscar Adams spoke up. He was the editor of the *Birmingham Reporter,* a Negro paper. What he said opened my eyes —but not in the way he expected. He said we shouldn't be misled by the leaders of the Unemployment Council, that we should go politely to the white bosses and officials and ask them for what they wanted, and do as they said.

Adams said: "We Negroes don't want social equality." I was

furious. I said inside of myself: "Oscar Adams, we Negroes want social and every other kind of equality. There's no reason on God's green earth why we should be satisfied with anything less."

That was the end of any ideas I had that the big-shots among the recognised Negro leaders would fight for us, or really put up any struggle for equal rights. I knew that Oscar Adams and the people like him were among our worst enemies, especially dangerous because they work from inside our ranks and a lot of us get the idea that they are with us and of us.

I look back over what I've written about those days since I picked up the leaflet of the Unemployment Council, and wonder if I've really said what I mean. I don't know if I can get across to you the feeling that came over me whenever I went to a meeting of the Council, or of the Communist Party, and heard their speakers and read their leaflets. All my life I'd been sweated and stepped on and Jim-Crowed. I lay on my belly in the mines for a few dollars a week, and saw my pay stolen and slashed, and my buddies killed. I lived in the worst section of town, and rode behind the "Colored" signs on streetcars, as though there was something disgusting about me. I heard myself called "nigger" and "darky," and I had to say "Yes, sir" to every white man, whether he had my respect or not.

I had always detested it, but I had never known that anything could be done about it. And here, all of a sudden, I had found organizations in which Negroes and whites sat together, and worked together, and knew no difference of race or color. Here were organizations that weren't scared to come out for equality for the Negro people, and for the rights of the workers. The Jim-Crow system, the wage-slave system, weren't everlasting after all! It was like all of a sudden turning a corner on a dirty, old street and finding yourself facing a broad, shining highway.

The bosses, and the Negro misleaders like Oscar Adams, told us that these Reds were "foreigners" and "strangers" and that the Communist program wasn't acceptable to the workers in the South. I couldn't see that at all. The leaders of the Communist Party and the Unemployment Council seemed people very much like the ones I'd always been used to. They were workers, and they talked our language. Their talk sure sounded better to me than the talk of Oscar Adams, or the President of the Tennessee Coal, Iron and Railroad Co. who addressed us every once in a while. As for the program not being acceptable to us—I felt then, and I know now, that the Communist program is the only program that the Southern workers—whites and Negroes both —can possibly accept in the long run. It's the only program that does justice to the Southern worker's ideas that everybody ought to have an equal chance, and that every man has rights that must be respected. . . .

In June, 1930, I was elected a delegate to the National Unemployment Convention in Chicago. Up to this point I had been staying with relatives in Birmingham. They were under the influence of the Negro misleaders and preachers, and they told me that if I went to the convention I need never come to their house again. The very morning I was to leave, I found a leaflet on my doorstep, put there by the Ku Klux Klan.

I went to Chicago, riding the rods to get there.

In Chicago, I got my first broad view of the revolutionary workers' movement. I met workers from almost every state in the union, and I heard about the work of the same kind of organizations in other countries, and it first dawned on me how strong and powerful the working-class was. There wasn't only me and a few others in Birmingham. There were hundreds, thousands, millions of us!

My family had told me not to come back. What did I care? My real family was the organization. I'd found that I had brothers and sisters in every corner of the world, I knew that we were all fighting for one thing and that they'd stick by me. I never lost that feeling, in all the hard days to come, in Fulton Tower Prison with the threat of the electric chair and the chain-gang looming over me. . . .

. . . From the cradle onward, the Southern white boy and girl are told that they are better than Negroes. Their birth certificates are tagged "white"; they sit in white schools, play in white parks and live on white streets. They pray in white churches, and when they die they are buried in white cemeteries. Everywhere before them are signs: "For White." "For Colored." They are taught that Negroes are thieves, and murderers, and rapists.

I remember especially one white worker, a carpenter, who was one of the first people I talked to in Atlanta. He was very friendly to me. He came to me one day and said that he agreed with the program, but something was holding him back from joining the Unemployment Council.

"What's that, Jim?" I asked. Really, though, I didn't have to ask. I knew the South, and I could guess.

"Well, I just don't figure that white folks and Negroes should mix together," he said. "It won't never do to organize them in one body."

I said: "Look here, Jim. You know that the carpenters and all the other workers get a darn sight less pay for the same work in the South than they do in other parts. Did you ever figure out why?"

He hadn't.

"Well," I said, "I'll tell you why. It's because the bosses have got us all split up down here. We Southern workers are as good fighters as there are anywhere, and yet we haven't been able to get equal wages with the workers in other places, and we haven't got any rights to speak of. That's because we've been divided. When the whites go out on strike, the bosses call in the Negroes to scab. When the Negroes strike, the bosses call in the whites to scab.

"Did you ever figure out why the unions here are so weak? It's because the whites don't want to organize with the Negroes, and the Negroes don't trust the whites. . . .

. . . "We Southern workers are like a house that's divided against itself. We're like an army that goes out to fight the enemy and stops on the way because its men are all fighting each other.

"Take this relief business, now," I said. "The commissioners tell the whites that they can't give them any more relief because they have to feed so many Negroes, and the Negroes ought to be chased back to the farms. Then they turn around and tell the Negroes that white people have to come first on the relief, so there's nothing doing for colored folks. That way they put us off, and get us scrapping with each other.

"Now suppose the white unemployed, and the Negro unemployed, all go to the commissioners together and say: 'We're all starving. We're all in need. We've decided to get together into one strong, powerful organization to make you come across with relief.'

"Don't you think that'll bring results, Jim?" I asked him. "Don't you see how foolish it is to go into the fight with half an army when we could have a whole one? Don't you think that an empty belly is a pretty punk exchange for the honor of being called a 'superior' race? And can't you realize that as long as one foot is chained to the ground the other can't travel very far?"

Jim didn't say anything more that day. I guess he went home and thought it over. He came back about a week later and invited me to his house. It was the first time he'd ever had a Negro in the house as a friend and equal. When I got there I found two other Negro workers that Jim had brought into the Unemployment Council.

About a month later Jim beat up a rent collector who was boarding up the house of an evicted Negro worker. Then he went to work and organized a committee of whites and Negroes to see the mayor about the case. "Today it's the black worker across town; tomorrow it'll be me," Jim told the mayor.

There are a lot of Jims today, all over the South.

We organized a number of block committees of the Unemployment Councils, and got rent and relief for a large number of families. We agitated endlessly for unemployment insurance.

In the middle of June, 1932, the state closed down all the relief stations. A drive was organized to send all the jobless to the farms.

We gave out leaflets calling for a mass demonstration at the courthouse to demand that the relief be continued. About 1000 workers came, 600 of them white. We told the commissioners we didn't intend to starve. We reminded them that $800,000 had been collected in the Community Chest drive. The commissioners said there wasn't a cent to be had.

But the very next day the commission voted $6,000 for relief to the jobless!

On the night of July 11, I went to the Post Office to get my mail. I felt myself grabbed from behind and turned to see a police officer.

I was placed in a cell, and was shown a large electric chair, and told to spill everything I knew about the movement. I refused to talk, and was held incommunicado for eleven days. Finally I smuggled out a letter through another prisoner, and the International Labor Defense got on the job.

Assistant Solicitor John Hudson rigged up the charge against me. It was the charge of "inciting to insurrection." It was based on an old statute passed in 1861, when the Negro people were still chattel slaves, and the white masters needed a law to crush slave insurrection and kill those found giving aid to the slaves....

. . . Since the days of the Civil War that law had lain, unused and almost forgotten. Now the slaves of the new order—the white and black slaves of capitalism—were organizing. In the eyes of the Georgia masters, it was a crime punishable by death.

The trial was set for January 16, 1933. The state of Georgia displayed the literature that had been taken from my room, and read passages of it to the jury. They questioned me in great detail. Did I believe that the bosses and government ought to pay insurance to unemployed workers? That Negroes should have complete equality with white people? Did I believe in the demand for the self-determination of the Black Belt—that the Negro people should be allowed to rule the Black Belt territory, kicking out the white landlords and government officials? Did I feel that the working-class could run the mills and mines and government? That it wasn't necessary to have bosses at all?

I told them I believed all of that—and more.

The courtroom was packed to suffocation. The I.L.D. attorneys, Benjamin J. Davis, Jr., and John H. Geer, two young Negroes—and I myself—fought every step of the way. We were not really talking to that judge, nor to those prosecutors, whose questions we were answering. Over their heads we talked to the white and Negro workers who sat on the benches, watching, listening, learning. And beyond them we talked to the thousands and millions of workers all over the world to whom this case was a challenge.

We demanded that Negroes be placed on jury rolls. We demanded that the insulting terms, "nigger" and "darky," be dropped in that court. We asserted the right of the workers to organize, to strike, to make their demands, to nominate candidates of their choice. We asserted the right of the Negro people to have complete equality in every field.

The state held that my membership in the Communist Party, my possession of Communist literature, was enough to send me to the electric chair. They said to the jury: "Stamp this damnable thing out now with a conviction that will automatically carry with it a penalty of electrocution."

And the hand-picked lily-white jury responded:

"We, the jury, find the defendant guilty as charged, but recommend that mercy be shown and fix his sentence at from 18 to 20 years."

I had organized starving workers to demand bread, and I was sentenced to live out my years on the chain-gang for it. But I knew that the movement itself would not stop. I spoke to the court and said:

"They can hold this Angelo Herndon and hundreds of others, but it will never stop these demonstrations on the part of Negro and white workers who demand a decent place to live in and proper food for their kids to eat."

I said: "You may do what you will with Angelo Herndon. You may indict him. You may put him in jail. But there will come thousands of Angelo Herndons. If you really want to do anything about the case, you must go out and indict the social system. But this you will not do, for your role is to defend the system under which the toiling masses are robbed and oppressed.

"You may succeed in killing one, two, even a score of working-class organizers. But you cannot kill the working class."

Now began the long months in Fulton Tower Prison. . . .

But worse than anything was the way time dragged, dragged, till each separate minute became an eternity of torture. Time became my personal enemy—an enemy I had to fight with all my strength. The first hours became a day, and the first days became weeks, and then began the long succession of months— six of them, a year of them, seventeen, eighteen, nineteen. I lay on my filthy bunk, and studied the patterns on walls and ceilings, and learned to know every spot and crack. I watched the shadows of the jail bars on the floor shorten and lengthen again. I saw men come and go, and now and again return. Prisoners arrived with horrible stories of torture and brutality on the chain-gang for which I was headed. I said good-bye to ten men as they left the cell to go to the death-chair.

Meanwhile, beyond the walls, the working-class movement was fighting on. Sometimes I got a newspaper, torn and dirty, and lay on the floor piecing it together. Sometimes—very rarely —a friend was allowed to see me for a moment. In this way I learned what was going on. . . .

I wanted to be out in the struggle, taking my part in it, doing my share. But not for one minute did I doubt that the workers would make me free. Even the news that the Georgia Supreme Court had denied me a new trial did not dishearten me. From the letters I received, I knew that the workers everywhere were fighting for me. I wrote letters—never knowing if they would leave the jail or not—and I read what papers and books I had, and I waited. . . .

. . . One morning Joe Brodsky, the lawyer who'd also fought for the Scottsboro boys, came to my cell and said: "We're going, Angelo."

The working-class had determined on my release, and I was free. They had raised, penny by penny, the enormous sum of $15,000 to get a class brother out of jail.

I took the train for the North. All along the way I was greeted by my comrades. In Washington, in Baltimore, in Philadelphia and Newark, workers stood on the platform to watch the train come by, and they cheered me, and I cheered their spirit and their determination. I stepped out of the train at Pennsylvania Station, into the arms of 7,000 of my white and Negro class-brothers and class-sisters.

I am happy to be out. Now, for a time at least, I can take my place once more in the ranks of the working-class. Now I am back in the fight.

21. BLACK NEWSPAPER EDITORS
DISCUSS COMMUNISM

In the spring of 1932 *The Crisis* queried prominent Negro editors about Communism. These answers showed wide variety, naturally enough. Neither then nor later were any of these men Communist party members or Communist "fellow-travellers." But their common willingness to view Communism as a conceivable program for blacks, to weigh its advantages and disadvantages as a tactical device, reflected a widely prevalent mood among American Negroes. To some extent their statement mirrored the radical attitudes of many white American intellectuals during the 1930s. But even more, their viewpoint was a product of black alienation from American society and the Communists' militant stand for racial equality.

Carl Murphy, THE AFRO-AMERICAN, Maryland

The Communists appear to be the only party going our way. They are as radical as the N.A.A.C.P. were twenty years ago.

Since the abolitionists passed off the scene, no white group of national prominence has openly advocated the economic, political and social equality of black folks.

"Negro Editors on Communism: A Symposium of the American Negro Press," THE CRISIS, XXXIX, 4–5 (April-May 1932), 117–119, 154–156. Reprinted with the permission of THE CRISIS.

Mr. Clarence Darrow speaking in Washington recently declared that we should not care what political candidates think of prohibition, the League of Nations, the tariff or any other general issue. What we should demand, Mr. Darrow said, is candidates who are right on all questions affecting the colored people. I agree with him.

Communism would appeal to Mr. Darrow if he were in my place.

Communists in Maryland saved Orphan Jones from a legal lynching. They secured a change of venue from the mob-ridden Eastern Shore.

They fought the exclusion of colored men from the jury, and on that ground financed an appeal of the case to Maryland's highest court. They compelled estimable Judge Duncan of Towson, Maryland, to testify that he had never considered colored people in picking jurors in his court for twenty-six years.

The Communists are going our way, for which Allah be praised.

P. B. Young, NORFOLK JOURNAL AND GUIDE, Virginia

Because we recognize that throughout all ages new voices and new movements for the creation of a better social order have always been anathema to the "old guards" and the "stand-patters" of the period, it has been the policy of *The Journal and Guide* not to view Communism as a thoroughgoing, death-dealing evil but to regard it as just one of the factors in a growing world-wide ideal to improve the conditions of the underprivileged, to make government more the servant of all the people, to give the rank and file of those who labor a larger share in the fruits of production, and to afford to all men equality before the law, and equal opportunity to work and live.

The Communists in America have commendably contended for and have practiced equality of all races, and in their many activities, have accepted Negroes into their ranks in both high and lowly positions; more, they have dramatized the disadvantages of the Negro by walking in a body out of a jim-crow Pittsburgh hospital, by aiding ejected tenement dwellers, and in industrial strikes directed by them fighting against the practice of excluding Negroes from labor unions. All these accomplishments go to the credit side for the Communists.

To the debit side must go, however, the fact that they in their efforts to "sell" Communism, have not taken into full consideration the economic dependence of the Negro race, its minority position, and the traditional aversion of the rank and file of Americans to the "blood and thunder" appeals of "revolution" and "mass action." Forgetful, they have aroused such charged feelings in many sections which make it difficult for the best of both races to get together and study and correct problems in an orderly way. Besides, because the Negro is marked racially, he becomes a ready target for anti-Communist venom whenever that develops as at Camp Hill and in Chicago.

The Negro is patriotic and loyal, if he is anything, and Communism has gained adherents, and will continue to do so, only because traditional American conditions with their race prejudice, economic semi-enslavement, lack of equal opportunity, and discrimination of all sorts have made the Negro susceptible to any doctrine which promises a brighter future, where race and color will not be a penalty.

These barriers to the more abundant growth of the Negro must be removed, but despite the theories behind Communism, we do not think it offers the way out for the Negro which shall be most beneficial and lasting in the long run.

If the Negro masses are to be made Communism-proof, the disadvantages which have been raised against them by the white majority in power, must be voided by the union of the whites and Negroes of vision working together—fighting by all legal and sane means the proscriptions which are neither Christian, humane, or in the spirit of the fundamental laws of the land.

The treatment given the few thousand Negroes in Russia under the Soviet form of government is not, necessarily, the same treatment that would be accorded the twelve million Negroes in America should this propertyless white proletariat come into power; for it is this same ignorant white class in the North and

South which now fails to respond to just and intelligent appeals for racial and religious tolerance—the same ignorant white working class which forms the backbone of every lynching mob.

Communism in Russia has brought about revolutionary reforms affecting the welfare of that nation's hitherto subjugated masses; but these are for the most part white. And, white members of the party here have, almost without exception, revealed themselves as being without bias as to race or creed—we need have no fear as long as they are in control—but it is such a far cry from Ku Klux Klanism to Communism, and from the narrowminded, unwieldy white working-class in America to the unlettered, but wieldy, masses in Russia, the Negro can well afford to wait until he has more definite information as to how Communism in America would be practiced by those poor whites upon whose shoulders would ultimately fall the responsibilities of government.

Frank M. Davis, THE ATLANTA WORLD, Georgia

If, when the United States awoke some morning, it were suddenly discovered that everybody classed as a Negro had gone Red, it would cause an immediate change in race relations. There might be trouble for a day or so, but it would not long last. Whites, thoroughly aroused and afraid, would attempt to remove those injustices heaped upon Afro-America which cradled black Communists; for 12,000,000 souls, backed by the U. S. S. R. and possibly other jealous nations wishing secretly to wreck the United States, would be too big a group to deal with by force.

This is too remote and improbable, however, to merit serious consideration.

It is a fact that the Negro, getting the dirty end of the economic, social and political stick, finds in Communistic ideals those panaceas he seeks. Yet I believe that were our government adjusted according to Red standards, few members of this kaleidoscopic race would have sense enough to take advantage of it.

Actually, the Negro as a whole fears Communism—probably because white America has not accepted it. Some frankly believe Red promises would be forgotten were they in power, for aren't they white men too? Further: would the average, everyday white man be willing to forget his prejudices even if ruled by and imbued with Communistic ideals?

Small groups of Negroes in the South going Red have harmed themselves and others in the community. Violence and bloodshed have resulted. The defense that black Reds "started it" has been an A-1 excuse for police officials killing and wounding Negroes. Camp Hill bears this out and last year's sentiment in Alabama is proof of the damage done to race relations.

I have known personally of some racial brethren going Red purely because of the chance to mingle freely with white women in the movement. Then they need no longer ogle secretly or with their personal safety threatened. Talks . . . showed me that Communistic friendliness, pronouncements of social equality, the use of "Mr." and "Mrs." and their treatment in Dixie as men and women instead of Negroes was what got 'em.

But I have no fear of the rainbow brotherhood going Red in wholesale numbers—at least not until white America takes long steps in that direction. This race is slow to change. It would prefer keeping its present status, no matter how low, than fly to a system, no matter what its worth, that is constantly lambasted by press and radio. Too, the Negro considers himself too dependent upon white America to take any chance of losing the crusts now thrown him. Nor is the Communistic policy of crude and noisy militancy liked by this race, for every Negro knows that what he has obtained from white men has been through diplomacy or basically intellectual campaigning.

The past two years has been a mating season for Reds with blacks, yet few of the 12,000,000 have wed. If the Communists cannot make headway amid the disgust of Negroes with our economic order by which they lose their jobs in times of industrial illness, there is hardly any chance of success when the nation rides high.

If enough of us would go Red, Okeh; when we get that way in little bunches it breathes nothing but new trouble for an already over-burdened race.

Robert L. Vann, PITTSBURGH COURIER, Pennsylvania

. . . We have our serious doubts that the average American Negro understands communism. Communistic leaders are confused also. They think the radicalism of the present-day Negro fits him precisely for Communism. This is error. The radical Negro is nevertheless intelligent; he knows what he wants. He also knows he does not want Communism. It is significant to note that few intelligent Negroes are to be found in the Communistic movement. Almost all Negroes following Communism are being used chiefly to lend a semblance of democracy to the cause. The few intellectuals espousing the cause are no closer to the movement than the average ballyhoo man is to the circus he advertises. Communism will never make the Negro white, blue or green. In fact, as long as the Negro retains his present identity his absorption is next to impossible. If the cause of Communism ever rises in power to the point of assuming governmental control, the Negro will be treated by his Communistic leaders then just as the Negro is treated by the Republicans and Democrats now. The Negro's hope of escape lies in a concentrated production to balance the ledger of his present consumption. To teach him to do this simple thing, the Negro perhaps needs a club more than he needs communism.

We have no criticism of Negroes who desire to become Communists provided always they are thoroughly prepared to accept the ultimate consequences, whatever they may be.

Roscoe Dunjee, BLACK DISPATCH, Oklahoma

By far, the most perplexing problem I have faced during my adult years, rests in the determination of the attitude I should assume towards Communism. For the past seven years, I am frank to say, my mind has been in virtual chaos on this important subject. Today my orientation is not complete.

I always have argued that sooner or later the poor white man here in America must come to the realization that his economic problems are wrapt up with the interests of the Negro; that the ruling class whites have subtly kept the masses of the two races apart. During the past twenty years, I have stood on many platforms and proclaimed this doctrine to mixed audiences. The mental picture I have carried of the day when the two races would sit down side by side on a basis of equality and brotherhood, has always been my rainbow.

My consternation today, however, develops out of the fact that I have at my door a poor white man who talks, acts and preaches the kind and sort of equality about which across the years I have given sanction. He wants to fight about it; he calls meetings and stages parades. Boldly he carries banners through the streets of Dixie, with inscriptions which fairly scream and say all my previous demoted citizenship must vanish. Jim Crow, segregation and anti-marriage laws, yes, everything which has hitherto separated the white and the black here in America, is denounced by this poor white. . . .

This same white man, who preaches brotherhood and equality, has, however, his faults as well as his virtues. With one mighty arm he draws me into his embrace, while with the other he casts bombs at our existing governmental system. His economic nostrums are anti-individualistic. Fear grips me and says: Alliance with him may cause the seldom used Negro labor unit to be boycotted; alliance with him may destroy the black man's traditional record of loyalty towards the Stars and Stripes.

What the black man's attitude should be towards this complex situation is the burning issue. Here, standing at our door is the poor white, who heretofore has constituted the major portion of the mob; who hitherto has joined with the ruling class in denying us equality and opportunity. Shall we turn our back upon the Communist entirely, because of his political notions and economic theories, or, shall we join with him in wrecking the vicious social barriers, which he voluntarily expresses a desire to destroy?

Communism, as a political and economic theory, does not meet and join fully with my ideal notion of government. . . .

Regardless of the foregoing viewpoint, I believe some definite course should be charted by Negro leadership with reference to Communism. I believe we are today standing on the brink of revolutionary changes in our social and racial attitudes. . . .

Whatever the trend, Negro leadership should not overlook the chance to make the most of this moment.

The radical of today is the conservative of tomorrow. Ten years ago the N. A. A. C. P. was classified by many as dangerous to American institutions; so also were the Abolutionists, prior to the Civil War. In those days, motives and objectives were imputed to these two liberty loving organizations which were far from just and fair. The world has long since learned to accept and respect the brotherhood and justice in these two militant organizations. It is entirely possible that history may repeat itself. The Negro who fears the radicalism of Communism today may be classified by black leadership of another and future generation as traitors to the cause of liberty.

The important question for the Negro to decide is the method by which he may cement into lasting bonds of friendship this new relationship between the whites and blacks of America. We cannot afford to make a mistake.

Yonder stands the poor white with a bomb under his arm—yet love in his heart for me. What shall I do about it? Does that unsanitary looking human being hold within his grasp my rainbow of promise, and the power which I so sorely need? Is Communism the instrumentality through which I am to secure the racial opportunity which for years I have longed for and prayed?

22. THE SECOND AMENIA CONFERENCE URGES EMPHASIS ON ECONOMIC PROBLEMS

Over the years, younger black intellectuals had condemned the NAACP for ignoring the economic plight of the Negro masses while pursuing a program of civil libertarianism benefitting the black bour-

Recommendations of the Second Amenia Conference, August 18–21, 1933. NAACP Archives, Library of Congress, Washington, D.C. Printed with the permission of the NAACP.

geoisie. After the onset of the depression in 1929, such criticisms mounted and the NAACP became increasingly sensitive to them. In 1933, hoping that new directions for the race and the Association could be charted, Joel Spingarn, NAACP board chairman, invited a group of young black intellectuals to confer at his summer estate.

Like the first Amenia Conference seventeen years earlier (see Document 13), this gathering of race leaders with diverse points of view produced essential agreement on certain key issues. The conferees urged race leaders to surrender "artificial class differences," concern themselves with the problems of the black masses, and help form a new interracial labor organization to benefit all workers.

This conference was called to make a critical appraisal of the Negro's existing situation in American society and to consider underlying principles for future action. Such criticism at this stage does not involve the offering of concrete program for any organization for administrative guidance.

There has been no attempt to disparage the older type of leadership. We appreciate its importance and contributions, but we feel that in a period in which economic, political, and social values are rapidly shifting, and the very structure of organized society is being revamped, the leadership which is necessary is that which will integrate the special problems of the Negro within the larger issues facing the nation.

The primary problem is economic. Individual ownership expressing itself through the control and exploitation of natural resources and industrial machinery has failed in the past to equalize consumption with production.

As a result of this failure the whole system of private property and private profit is being called into question. The government is being forced to attempt an economic reorganization based upon a "co-partnership" between capital, labor and government itself. The government is attempting to augment consumptive power by increasing wages, shortening hours and controlling the labor and commodity markets. As a consumer the Negro has always had a low purchasing power as a result of his low wages coming from his inferior and restricted position in the labor market. If the government program fails to make full and equal provision for the Negro, it cannot be effective in restoring economic stability.

In the past there has been a greater exploitation of Negro labor than of any other section of the working class, manifesting itself particularly in lower wages, longer hours, excessive use of child labor and a higher proportion of women at work. Furthermore, there has been slight recognition by Negro labor or Negro leaders of the significance of this exploitation in the economic order. No technique or philosophy has been developed to change the historic status of Negro labor. Hence in the present governmental set-up there is grave danger that this historic status will be perpetuated. As a result the lower wages on the one hand will reduce the purchasing power of Negro labor and on the other be a constant threat to the standards and security of white labor.

The question then arises how far existing agencies working among and for Negroes are theoretically and structurally prepared to cope with this situation. It is the opinion of the conference that the welfare of white and black labor are one and inseparable and that the existing agencies working among and for Negroes have conspicuously failed in facing a necessary alignment of black and white labor.

It is impossible to make any permanent improvement in the status and the security of white labor without making an identical improvement in the status and the security of Negro labor. The Negro worker must be made conscious of his relation to white labor and the white worker must be made conscious that the purposes of labor, immediate or ultimate cannot be achieved, without full participation by the Negro worker.

The traditional labor movement, based upon craft autonomy and separatism, which is non-political in outlook and which centers its attention upon the control of jobs and wages for the minority of skilled white workers, is an ineffective agency for aligning white and black labor for the larger labor objectives.

These objectives can only be attained through a new labor movement. This movement must direct its immediate attention to the organizing of the great mass of workers both skilled and unskilled, white and black. Its activities must be political as well as economic for the purpose of effecting such social legislation as old age pensions, unemployment insurance, the regulation of child and female labor etc. These social reforms may go to the extent of change in the form of government itself. The conference sees three possibilities:

(1) Fascism

(2) Communism

(3) Reformed Democracy

The conference is opposed to Fascism because it would crystallize the Negro's position at the bottom of the social structure. Communism is impossible without a fundamental transformation in the psychology and the attitude of white workers on the race question and a change in the Negro's conception of himself as a worker. A Democracy that is attempting to reform itself is a fact which has to be reckoned with. In the process of reform, the interests of the Negro cannot be adequately safeguarded by white paternalism in government. It is absolutely indispensable that in this attempt of the government to control agriculture and industry, there be adequate Negro representations on all boards and field staffs.

While the accomplishment of these larger aims cannot be achieved except through the cooperation of white and black, the primary responsibility for the initiation, development and execution of this program rests upon the Negro himself. This is predicated upon the increased economic independence of the Negro. No matter what artificial class difference may seem to exist within the Negro group it must be recognized that all elements of the race must weld themselves together for the common welfare. This point of view must be indoctrinated through the churches, educational institutions and other agencies working in behalf of the Negro. The first steps toward the rapprochement between the educated Negro and the Negro mass must be taken by the educated Negro himself.

The Findings Committee recommends that the practical implications of this program be referred to a committee on continuation to be appointed by and at this conference.

23. W. E. B. DU BOIS AND
WALTER WHITE
DEBATE RACIAL SEPARATISM

With the onset of the depression, W. E. B. Du Bois grew disturbed over the fact that the NAACP did not modify its program to meet the challenge created by this new catastrophe. He had long been convinced that the solution to the Negro's economic problem lay in economic cooperation within the race. Early in the century he had discarded his faith in achieving racial advancement through the creation of a black business elite based on the economic support of the black masses. But he regarded the white workers as the Negroes' bitterest enemies, was contemptuous of the Socialists for their failure to espouse the cause of black workers, and suspected that the Communists were championing racial equality for ulterior motives.

Accordingly, taking a leaf from the nineteenth-century utopian socialists, he pushed with renewed vigor his proposal for the establishment of a Negro cooperative economy. When the NAACP did not adopt his program, he began to attack its policies openly in the pages of *The Crisis*. Though Du Bois was concerned basically with the plight of the masses, the ideological debate centered chiefly on the validity of endorsing segregation in any form. Du Bois pointed to instances when the NAACP had, for pragmatic reasons, accepted segregation, notably when it had fought for a segregated black officers' training camp during World War I, because that was the only way for blacks to obtain commissions in the army. Du Bois concluded that segregation did not necessarily mean discrimination, that the NAACP had traditionally been opposed not to separation but to discrimination, that "It has never denied the recurrent necessity of united separate action on the part of Negroes for self-defense and self-development."

The directors and other officials of the NAACP responded to Du Bois's criticism by a spirited defense of their position. *The Crisis* published statements from a few of them, including one by Walter

W. E. B. Du Bois, "Segregation," THE CRISIS, XLI, 1 (January 1934), 20. Reprinted with permission of THE CRISIS.

White, who had succeeded James Weldon Johnson as the organization's executive secretary. White reaffirmed the organization's traditional ideological opposition to racial separatism. Shortly after, amid a steadily worsening exchange of recriminations, Du Bois resigned from his post with the NAACP and returned to teaching at Atlanta University.

A. W. E. B. Du Bois

The thinking colored people of the United States must stop being stampeded by the word segregation. The opposition to racial segregation is not or should not be any distaste or unwillingness of colored people to work with each other, to cooperate with each other, to live with each other. The opposition to segregation is an opposition to discrimination. The experience in the United States has been that usually when there is racial segregation, there is also racial discrimination.

But the two things do not necessarily go together, and there should never be an opposition to segregation pure and simple unless that segregation does involve discrimination. Not only is there no objection to colored people living beside colored people if the surroundings and treatment involve no discrimination, if streets are well lighted, if there is water, sewerage and police protection, and if anybody of any color who wishes, can live in that neighborhood. The same way in schools, there is no objection to schools attended by colored pupils and taught by colored teachers. On the contrary, colored pupils can by our own contention be as fine human beings as any other sort of children, and we certainly know that there are no teachers better than trained colored teachers. But if the existence of such a school is made reason and cause for giving it worse housing, poorer facilities, poorer equipment and poorer teachers, then we do object, and the objection is not against the color of the pupils' or teachers' skins, but against the discrimination.

In the recent endeavor of the United States government to redistribute capital so that some of the disadvantaged groups may get a chance for development, the American Negro should voluntarily and insistently demand his share. Groups of communities and farms inhabited by colored folk should be voluntarily formed. In no case should there be any discrimination against white and blacks. But, at the same time, colored people should come forward, should organize and conduct enterprises, and their only insistence should be that the same provisions be made for the success of their enterprise that is being made for the success of any other enterprise. It must be remembered that in the last quarter of a century, the advance of the colored people has been mainly in the lines where they themselves working by and for themselves, have accomplished the greatest advance.

There is no doubt that numbers of white people, perhaps the majority of Americans, stand ready to take the most distinct advantage of voluntary segregation and cooperation among colored people. Just as soon as they get a group of black folk segregated, they use it as a point of attack and discrimination. Our counter attack should be, therefore, against this discrimination; against the refusal of the South to spend the same amount of money on the black child as on the white child for its education; against the inability of black groups to use public capital; against the monopoly of credit by white groups. But never in the world should our fight be against association with ourselves because by that very token we give up the whole argument that we are worth associating with.

Doubtless, and in the long run, the greatest human development is going to take place under experiences of widest individual contact. Nevertheless, today such individual contact is made difficult and almost impossible by petty prejudice, deliberate and almost criminal propaganda and various survivals from prehistoric heathenism. It is impossible, therefore, to wait for the millennium of free and normal intercourse before we unite, to cooperate among ourselves in groups of like-minded people and in groups of people suffering from the same disadvantages and the same hatreds.

It is the class-conscious working man uniting together who will eventually emancipate labor throughout the world. It is the race-conscious black man cooperating together in his own institutions and movements who will eventually emancipate the colored race, and the great step ahead today is for the American Negro to accomplish his economic emancipation through voluntary determined cooperative effort.

B. Walter White

Numerous requests have been made of the National Association for the Advancement of Colored People for a statement of the position of the Association on editorials by Dr. Du Bois on "Segregation" in the January and February issues of *The Crisis*. It is fitting and proper that the statement of the Secretary's position should first appear in *The Crisis*, the official organ of the Association.

Various interpretations have been placed upon Dr. Du Bois's editorial, a number of them erroneous and especially the one which interprets the editorial as a statement of the position of the N.A.A.C.P. The historic position of the N.A.A.C.P. has from the date of its foundation been opposed to segregation. Dr. Du Bois's editorial is merely a personal expression on his part that the whole question of segregation should be examined and discussed anew. There can be no objection to frank and free discussion on any subject and *The Crisis* is the last place where censorship or restriction of freedom of speech should be attempted. I wish to call attention to the fact that the N.A.A.C.P. has never officially budged in its general opposition to segregation. Since Dr. Du Bois has expressed his personal opinion why this attitude might possibly have to be altered I should like to give my personal opinion why I believe we should continue to maintain the same attitude we have for nearly a quarter of a century, but I repeat that what I am about to say is merely my personal opinion just as Dr. Du Bois's editorial expressed his personal opinion.

Let us put aside for the moment the ethical and moral princi-

Walter F. White, from "Segregation—a Symposium," THE CRISIS, XLI, 3 (March 1934), 80–81. Reprinted with permission of THE CRISIS.

ples involved. It is my firm conviction, based upon observation and experience, that the truest statement in the January editorial is:

> there is no doubt that numbers of white people, perhaps the majority of Americans, stand ready to take the most distinct advantage of voluntary segregation and cooperation among colored people. Just as soon as they get a group of black folk segregated, they use it as a point of attack and discrimination.

It is for this very reason that thoughtful colored people will be opposed to following the advice that "groups of communities and farms inhabited by colored folk should be voluntarily formed" where they involve government-financed and approved arrangements like the Homestead Subsistence projects.

It is unfortunate that Dr. Du Bois's editorial has been used, we learn, by certain government officials at Washington to hold up admission of Negroes to one of the government-financed relief projects. Protests have been made to Mrs. Roosevelt and others by the N.A.A.C.P. against such exclusion. Plans to admit Negroes as a result of the protest are being delayed with the editorial in question used as an excuse for such delay.

To accept the status of separateness, which almost invariably in the case of submerged, exploited and marginal groups means inferior accommodations and a distinctly inferior position in the national and communal life, means spiritual atrophy for the group segregated. When Negroes, Jews, Catholics or Nordic white Americans voluntarily choose to live or attend church or engage in social activity together, that is their affair and no one else's. But Negroes and all other groups must without compromise and without cessation oppose in every possible fashion any attempt to impose from without the establishment of pales and ghettoes. Arbitrary segregation of this sort means almost without exception that less money will be expended for adequate sewerage, water, police and fire protection and for the building of a healthful community. It is because of this that the N.A.A.C.P. has resolutely fought such segregation, as in the case of city ordinances and state laws in the Louisville, New Orleans and

Richmond segregation cases; has opposed restrictive covenants written into deeds of property, and all other forms, legal and illegal, to restrict the areas in which Negroes may buy or rent and occupy property.

This principle is especially vital where attempts are made to establish separate areas which are financed by moneys from the federal or state governments for which black people are taxed at the same rate as white. No self-respecting Negro can afford to accept without vigorous protest any such attempt to put the stamp of federal approval upon discrimination of this character. Though separate schools do exist in the South and though for the time being little can be done towards ending the expensive and wasteful dual educational system based upon caste and color prejudice, yet no Negro who respects himself and his race can accept these segregated systems without at least inward protest.

I cannot agree with the statement made by Dr. Du Bois in the February Crisis that the N.A.A.C.P. opposed the establishment of the Veterans' Hospital of Tuskegee "although it is doubtful if it would have opposed such a hospital in the North." The N.A.A.C.P. did oppose, and successfully, the recent attempt to establish a segregated Veterans' Hospital at Chester, Pennsylvania. It was the feeling of many of us then and to now that the fight should be made for the acceptance of Negro physicians, specialists and nurses on the basis of equality to the staffs of *all* Veterans' Hospitals rather than to ask for jim-crow hospitals.

Nor can I agree that the failure of the citizens of Philadelphia to resist more persistently, intelligently and militantly the establishment of a partial system of elementary Negro schools is necessarily approval of the segregation which has been established. This opening wedge will undoubtedly result in more segregation in schools and other public institutions unless aggressively fought. Like cancer, segregation grows and must be, in my opinion, resisted wherever it shows its head.

It is admittedly a longer and more difficult road to full and unrestricted admission to schools, hospitals and other public institutions, but the mere difficulty of the road should not and will not serve as a deterrent to either Negro or white people who are mindful not only of present conditions but of those to which we aspire. In a world where time and space are being demolished by science it is no longer possible to create or imagine separate racial, national or other compartments of human thought and endeavor. The Negro must, without yielding, continue the grim struggle *for* integration and *against* segregation for his own physical, moral and spiritual well-being and for that of white America and of the world at large.

24. JAMES WELDON JOHNSON ANALYZES IDEOLOGICAL ALTERNATIVES

The defense of the NAACP's traditional position fell to its executive secretaries, first James Weldon Johnson and later Walter White. Johnson had been a diplomat, poet, songwriter, and novelist before he became, in 1921, the first black executive secretary of the NAACP. In 1930 he retired from the NAACP to give full time to writing. In *Negro Americans, What Now?* he examined the major ideological alternatives espoused by various Negroes and concluded that the program of the NAACP was the only viable one. His essay eloquently restated familiar means and ends.

The world today is in a state of semi-chaos. We Negro Americans as a part of the world are affected by that state. We are affected by it still more vitally as a special group. We are not so sanguine about our course and our goal as we were a decade ago. We are floundering. We are casting about for ways of meeting the situation, both as Americans and as Negroes. In this casting about we have discovered and rediscovered a number of ways to which we have given more or less consideration. Let

James Weldon Johnson, NEGRO AMERICANS, WHAT NOW? Copyright 1934 by James Weldon Johnson, 1962 by Grace Nail Johnson. Reprinted by permission of the Viking Press, Inc. Pp. 3–18, 35–40, and 98–103.

us see if we cannot by elimination reduce confusion and narrow
down the limits of choice to what might be shown to be the one
sound and wise line to follow.

Exodus

Exodus has for generations been recurrently suggested as a
method for solving the race problem. . . .

A century and a quarter ago deportation of the free Negroes
might have been feasible; a half century later *that* was not a
practicable undertaking; today the deportation or exodus of the
Negro American population is an utter impossibility. Not within
a bounded period could twelve million people be transported;
and before that period was over the total number would be well
above twelve million. Nor is there any place to which to take
them. There are no more "vacant" places on earth; and no government in the world, with the barest possibility of Brazil as the
exception, would welcome even one-twelfth the whole number;
Liberia would no doubt be as reluctant as any. None of the
tribes of Colonial Africa would relish sharing their best lands
with us merely because we and they are of somewhat the same
complexion. The United States government might purchase territory somewhere and deport us. But that would involve a pretty
stiff political job and a financial expenditure that would make
the figures of the National Recovery program look small.

We may cross out exodus as a possible solution. We and the
white people may as well make up our minds definitely that we,
the same as they, are in this country to stay. We may be causing
white America some annoyance, but we ourselves are not passing the time in undisturbed comfort. White America will simply
have to sustain a situation that is of its own making, not ours.

Physical force

Our history in the United States records a half-dozen major
and a score of minor efforts at insurrection during the period of
slavery. This, if they heard it, would be news to that big ma-

jority of people who believe that we have gone through three centuries of oppression without once thinking in terms of rebellion or lifting a finger in revolt. Even now there come times when we think in terms of physical force.

We must condemn physical force and banish it from our minds. But I do not condemn it on any moral or pacific grounds. The resort to force remains and will doubtless always remain the rightful recourse of oppressed peoples. Our own country was established upon that right. I condemn physical force because I know that in our case it would be futile.

We would be justified in taking up arms or anything we could lay hands on and fighting for the common rights we are entitled to and denied, if we had a chance to win. But I know and we all know there is not a chance. It is, I believe, among the certainties that some day, perhaps not very far off, native blacks of Africa will, by physical force if necessary, compel the whites to yield their extra privileges and immunities. The increasing inability of the great powers to spare the strength and resources necessary for maintaining imperialism will hasten the certainty. The situation of the African natives is, however, on one point at least, the reverse of our own—on the point of comparative numerical strength.

Yet, there is a phase of physical force that we in the United States should consider. When we are confronted by the lawless, pitiless, brutish mob, and we know that life is forfeit, we should not give it up; we should, if we can, sell it, and at the dearest price we are able to put on it.

The revolution

Communism is coming to be regarded as the infallible solution by an increasing number of us. Those who look to the coming revolution (and why they should believe it is coming in the United States I see no good reason) seem to think it will work some instantaneous and magical transformation of our condition. It appears to me that this infinite faith in Communism indicates extreme *naïveté*. Those who hold this faith point to Soviet

Russia as a land in which there is absolutely no prejudice against Negroes. This is an unquestioned fact, but I can see no grounds on which to attribute it to Communism. There was no prejudice against Negroes in Tsarist Russia. Tsarist Russia was the country that could honor a black Hannibal; the country that could make a mulatto Pushkin its national poet; the country in which university students in St. Petersburg could unhitch the horses from the carriage of Ira Aldridge, the black American tragedian, after his performance of Othello, and themselves draw him back to his hotel. The simple truth is: the *Russian people* have no prejudice against Negroes.

In considering Communism with respect to the Negro, the question before us, of course, is not how it works in Russia, but how it would probably work in the United States. If the United States goes Communistic, where will the Communists come from? They certainly will not be imported from Russia. They will be made from the Americans here on hand. We might well pause and consider what variations Communism in the United States might undergo.

I hold no brief against Communism as a theory of government. I hope that the Soviet experiment will be completely successful. I know that it is having a strong influence on the principal nations of the world, including our own. I think it is a high sign of progress that Negro Americans have reached the point of holding independent opinions on political and social questions. What I am trying to do is sound a warning against childlike trust in the miraculous efficacy on our racial situation of any economic or social theory of government—Communism or Socialism or Fascism or Nazism or New Deals. The solving of our situation depends principally upon an evolutionary process along two parallel lines: our own development and the bringing about of a change in the national attitude toward us. That outcome will require our persevering effort under whatever form the government might take on.

It may be argued that although there is not and has not been any anti-Negro feeling in Russia, it is the country in which anti-Semitism was stronger than in any other, and that oppression and repression of the Jews have been greatly abated or entirely wiped out by Communism. Such an argument goes to prove the possibility that Communism in the United States would wipe out oppression and repression of Negro Americans and give them a status of equality. I grant the possibility—what though it may not be realized miraculously and suddenly. I grant that if America should turn truly Communistic (by which I mean— if it should adopt and practice Communism without reservations, and not adapt it as it has adapted democracy and Christianity so as to allow every degree of inequality and cruelty to be practiced under them); that if the capitalistic system should be abolished and the dictatorship of the proletariat established, with the Negro aligned, as he naturally ought to be, with the proletariat, race discriminations would be officially banned and the reasons and feelings back of them would finally disappear.

But except to a visionary there are no indications that the present or prospective strength of Communism is able or will be able to work such a change, either by persuasion or by military coup. In the situation as it now exists it would be positively foolhardy for us, as a group, to take up the cause of Communistic revolution and thereby bring upon ourselves all of the antagonisms that are directed against it in addition to those we already have to bear. It seems to me that the wholesale allegiance of the Negro to Communistic revolution would be second in futility only to his individual resort to physical force. . . .

Isolation or integration?

By this process of elimination we have reduced choices of a way out to two. There remain, on the one hand, the continuation of our efforts to achieve integration and, on the other hand, an acknowledgment of our isolation and the determination to accept and make the best of it.

Throughout our entire intellectual history there has been a division of opinion as to which of these two divergent courses the race should follow. From early times there have been sincere thinkers among us who were brought to the conclusion that our only salvation lies in the making of the race into a self-contained economic, social, and cultural unit; in a word, in the building of an *imperium in imperio.*

All along, however, majority opinion has held that the only salvation worth achieving lies in the making of the race into a component part of the nation, with all the common rights and privileges, as well as duties, of citizenship. This attitude has been basic in the general policy of the race—so far as it has had a general policy—for generations, the policy of striving zealously to gain full admission to citizenship and guarding jealously each single advance made.

But this question of direction, of goal, is not a settled one. There is in us all a stronger tendency toward isolation than we may be aware of. There come times when the most persistent integrationist becomes an isolationist, when he curses the White world and consigns it to hell. This tendency toward isolation is strong because it springs from a deep-seated, natural desire—a desire for respite from the unremitting, grueling struggle; for a place in which refuge might be taken. We are again and again confronted by this question. It is ever present, though often dormant. Recently it was emphatically brought forward by the utterances of so authoritative a voice as that of Dr. Du Bois.

The question is not one to be lightly brushed aside. Those who stand for making the race into a self-sufficient unit point out that after years of effort we are still Jim-Crowed, discriminated against, segregated, and lynched; that we are still shut out from industry, barred from the main avenues of business, and cut off from free participation in national life. They point out that in some sections of the country we have not even secured equal protection of life and property under the laws. They declare that entrance of the Negro into full citizenship is as distant as it was seventy years ago. And they ask: What is the Negro to do? Give himself over to wishful thinking? Stand shooting at the stars with a popgun? Is it not rather a duty and a necessity for him to face the facts of his condition and environment, to acknowledge them as facts, and to make the best use of them that he can? These are questions which the thinkers of the race should strive to sift clearly.

To this writer it seems that one of the first results of clear thinking is a realization of the truth that the making of the race into a self-sustaining unit, the creating of an *imperium in imperio,* does not offer an easier or more feasible task than does the task of achieving full citizenship. Such an *imperium* would have to rest upon a basis of separate group economic independence, and the trend of all present-day forces is against the building of any foundation of that sort.

After thoughtful consideration, I cannot see the slightest possibility of our being able to duplicate the economic and social machinery of the country. I do not believe that any other special group could do it. The isolationists declare that because of imposed segregation we have, to a large degree, already done it. But the situation they point to is more apparent than real. Our separate schools and some of our other race institutions, many of our race enterprises, the greater part of our employment, and most of our fundamental activities are contingent upon our interrelationship with the country as a whole.

Clear thinking reveals that the outcome of voluntary isolation would be a permanent secondary status, so acknowledged by the race. Such a status would, it is true, solve some phases of the race question. It would smooth away a good part of the friction and bring about a certain protection and security. The status of slavery carried some advantages of that sort. But I do not believe we shall ever be willing to pay such a price for security and peace.

If Negro Americans could do what reasonably appears to be impossible, and as a separate unit achieve self-sufficiency built upon group economic independence, does anyone suppose that that would abolish prejudice against them and allay opposition, or that the struggle to maintain their self-sufficiency would be in any degree less bitter than the present struggle to become an integral part of the nation? Taking into account human nature as it is, would not the achievement be more likely to arouse envy and bring on even more violent hatreds and persecutions?

Certainly, the isolationists are stating a truth when they contend that we should not, ostrich-like, hide our heads in the sand, making believe that prejudice is non-existent; but in so doing they are apostles of the obvious. Calling upon the race to realize that prejudice is an actuality is a needless effort; it is placing emphasis on what has never been questioned. The danger for us does not lie in a possible failure to acknowledge prejudice as a reality, but in acknowledging it too fully. We cannot ignore the fact that we are segregated, no matter how much we might wish to do so; and the smallest amount of common sense forces us to extract as much good from the situation as there is in it. Any degree of sagacity forces us at the same time to use all our powers to abolish imposed segregation; for it is an evil *per se* and the negation of equality either of opportunity or of awards. We should by all means make our schools and institutions as excellent as we can possibly make them—and by that very act we reduce the certainty that they will forever remain schools and institutions "for Negroes only." We should make our business enterprises and other strictly group undertakings as successful as we can possibly make them. We should gather all the strength and experience we can from imposed segregation. But any good we are able to derive from the system we should consider as a means, not an end. The strength and experience we gain from it should be applied to the objective of *entering into,* not *staying out of* the body politic.

Clear thinking shows, too, that, as bad as conditions are, they are not as bad as they are declared to be by discouraged and pessimistic isolationists. To say that in the past two generations or more Negro Americans have not advanced a single step toward a fuller share of the commonwealth becomes, in the light of easily ascertainable facts, an absurdity. Only the shortest view of the situation gives color of truth to such a statement; any reasonably long view proves it to be utterly false.

With our choice narrowed down to these two courses, wisdom and far-sightedness and possibility of achievement demand that we follow the line that leads to equal rights for us, based on the

common terms and conditions under which they are accorded
and guaranteed to the other groups that go into the making up
of our national family. It is not necessary for our advancement
that such an outcome should suddenly eradicate all prejudices.
It would not, of course, have the effect of suddenly doing away
with voluntary grouping in religious and secular organizations or
of abolishing group enterprise—for example, Negro newspapers.
The accordance of full civil and political rights has not in the
case of the greater number of groups in the nation had that
effect. Nevertheless, it would be an immeasurable step forward,
and would place us where we had a fair start with the other
American groups. More than that we do not need to ask. . . .

The correlation of all forces

A Super-Power

Now, these principal forces and resources that we have enumerated are far from negligible. Even at their weakest they are
assets. Their actual strength is great. Their potential powers
have not been estimated. . . .

How may we call these potential powers, these powers that
will prove effective, into being? The simplicity of the process
will probably throw doubt on the magnitude of the feat. It may
be done through the complete correlation of the existing forces.
The result will be not merely increased efficiency in all the various units and greater total strength; it will be the creation of an
entirely new power, a super-power, a power that will be a
fusion of all our energies. If we create this power and center its
force upon the walls that stand between us and the common
rights, guarantees, and privileges of citizenship, we can be confident of battering them down.

The practical method I suggest for the creation and utilization
of this power is to channel our forces so that they will function
through a central machine. I believe we have that machine at
hand in the National Association for the Advancement of Colored People. I believe we could get the desired results by mak-

ing that organization the nucleus, the synthesis, the clearing house, of our forces. It already has the experience, the skill, and, in good part, the machinery. It has proved itself honest, sincere, intelligent, and capable. For the purpose of achieving, maintaining, and safeguarding our citizenship rights, no other organization can be compared with it. Its policies and techniques have proved to be the most advantageous and effective that we have thus far been able to devise.

I know that this is not a wholly unanimous opinion. The statement I have made has been frequently put in the form of a question. I believe, however, that a study of the history and work of the association for the past twenty-five years and of the concurrent history of Negro Americans will furnish sufficient evidence to prove that the race has made positive gains through the efforts of the N.A.A.C.P. Its successful efforts to hold segregation within the limits of custom and prevent it from being put over into the realm of law; its leadership in the fight against lynching, and its keeping of that crime and other racial injustices before the conscience of the American people; and its half-dozen signal legal victories involving our constitutional rights are examples in point.

But there is another way of evaluating the work of the organization. When the N.A.A.C.P. was founded, the great danger facing us was that we should lose the vestiges of our rights by default. The organization checked that danger. It acted as a watchman on the wall, sounding the alarms that called us to defense. Its work would be of value if only for the reason that without it our status would be worse than it is. In cities where our numbers are large we still live grouped together in one or more "Negro sections." . . . in such cities Negro Americans by this time would all have been sentenced *by law* to live in black ghettos if the N.A.A.C.P. had not won the Louisville Segregation Case, in which the Supreme Court declared residential segregation on grounds of race to be unconstitutional. I am taking it for granted that no one will be so shallow as to ask if there is any difference between segregation by social conventions and segregation by legal enactment. I believe also that the National Association laid the foundation for the restoration of the ballot to Negro Americans in the South through its victories in the Texas Primary Cases. The Negro lost the right to vote conferred on him by the Fourteenth and Fifteenth Amendments because the Supreme Court through hair-splitting sophistry and astute evasion emasculated both amendments to the point of nullification. The signs are now that the right to vote will be re-established through the decisions of that same court. There is a school that holds that these legal victories are empty. They are not. At the very least, they provide the ground upon which we may make a stand for our rights. In the North we have a fair degree of civil rights and in the South we have the right to battle for those rights because the Fourteenth and Fifteenth Amendments are in the constitution. Let us suppose them not there, and we reach a quick realization of the material importance of legal enactments. Or note the effect of adverse laws.

If we correlate our numerical strength, the strength of our religious and fraternal organizations, such political and economic power as we have, and the power of our press in a way to make the National Association for the Advancement of Colored People the spearhead of our forces, in a way that will enable it to shift the emphasis more and more from protest to action and more fully to translate declarations into deeds, and to widen its field to include all the fundamental phases of life that affect us as citizens, there are Negro Americans now born who will live to see the race accorded the common rights of citizenship on the same terms upon which they are accorded to the other groups in the nation. . . .

Conclusion

In these few pages I have made no attempt at a general consideration of social problems; rather have I sought to limit the discussion to the peculiar and immediate problems that confront us as a special group. . . .

I have tried to show that the most logical, the most feasible and most worthwhile choice for us is to follow the course that leads to our becoming an integral part of the nation, with the same rights and guarantees that are accorded to other citizens, and on the same terms. I have pointed out that common sense compels us to get whatever and all the good we can out of the system of imposed segregation, to gather all the experience and strength that can be got from it; but that we should use that experience and strength steadily and as rapidly as possible to destroy the system. The seeming advantages of imposed segregation are too costly to keep. I have enumerated our principal forces and resources and set forth that none of these factors is a panacea; that we must correlate all our elements of strength to form a super-power to be centered on our main objective; that, knowing the rights we are entitled to, we must persistently use this power to defend those rights we hold, so that none may go by default, and to secure those we have not yet gained. I have stressed the vital need of plans and steps for uniting black and white workers. I have made plain the importance of interracial contact. I have pointed out the necessity of enlisting the energies of youth. I have shown that in addition to other factors there is an emotional factor to deal with. I have implied the fact that our policies should include an intelligent opportunism; by which I mean the alertness and ability to seize the advantage from every turn of circumstance whenever it can be done without sacrifice of principle. We require a sense of strategy as well as a spirit of determination.

To revolutionary elements it will no doubt appear that what I have outlined is too conservative. If it does, it is not because I am unconscious of the need of fundamental social change, but because I am considering the realities of the situation. Conservatism and radicalism are relative terms. It is as radical for a black American in Mississippi to claim his full rights under the Constitution and the law as it is for a white American in any state to advocate the overthrow of the existing national government. The black American in many instances puts his life in jeopardy, and anything more radical than that cannot reasonably be required.

I have suggested no quick or novel cure-all, for there is none. There is no one salient to be captured; our battle is along a wide front. What I have outlined is a plan for a long, hard campaign. A campaign that will demand courage, determination, and patience. Not, however, the patience to wait, but the patience to keep on working and fighting. This may seem far from a cheerful prospect; but why should we utter wails of despair? Our situation is luxuriously easy to what former generations have endured. We ought to gain fortitude from merely thinking of what they came through.

And we ought to gather inspiration from the fact that we are in the right. We are contending for only what we are entitled to under the organic law of the land, and by any high standard of civilization, of morality, or of decency. Black America is called upon to stand as the protagonist of tolerance, of fair play, of justice, and of good will. Until white America heeds, we shall never let its conscience sleep. For the responsibility for the outcome is not ours alone. White America cannot save itself if it prevents us from being saved. But, in the nature of things, white America is not going to yield what rightfully belongs to us without a struggle kept up by us. In that struggle our watchword needs to be, "Work, work, work!" and our rallying cry, "Fight, fight, fight!"

25. AN NAACP COMMITTEE CALLS FOR "A REFORMULATION OF THE ASSOCIATION'S ULTIMATE OBJECTIVES"

The worsening economic conditions in the depression and Du Bois's attacks on the Association during the segregated economy controversy of 1934 forced the NAACP to publicly reexamine its program.

From "Future Plan and Program of the N.A.A.C.P.," a report of the Committee on Future Plan and Program of the National Association for the Advancement of Colored People, 1935. NAACP Archives, Library of Congress. Printed with permission of the NAACP.

In July 1934, the board created a Committee on Future Plan and Program. As chairman, it appointed Abram L. Harris, an economics professor at Howard University and a member of the Second Amenia Conference (see Document 22). The Harris Committee report developed the ideas of the Second Amenia Conference, making specific suggestions for a program geared to the needs of the masses. In 1935 the NAACP board adopted a modified version of the report, but did little to implement it. Yet under its stimulus, the NAACP board had publicly agreed that its traditional emphasis on achieving civil and political equality for blacks required an economic program as well. And over the next half-dozen years the Association ultimately fashioned an alliance with labor unions of the new Congress of Industrial Organization.

I. Economic activities

1. Introductory statement

The work of the Association in the economic field has been conducted as an incidental phase of its civil liberty program. Its accomplishments have been important and cannot be easily dismissed. In addition to its persistent protests against discrimination and segregation of Negroes in industry and against the refusal of A.F. of L. unions to organize Negroes, it has the following outstanding accomplishments to its credit. In 1912 it assisted in the organization of southern Negro firemen and trainmen and caused the reinstatement of Negro firemen discharged as a result of contracts effected by organized white trainmen; in the same year, it waged a successful fight against the adoption of the famous "Full Crew Bill" by various state legislatures, especially Illinois; in 1913, it began its fight against the segregation and discrimination of Negro government employees opposing the Aswel-Edwards Bill designed to make this a national policy; in 1917, when the railroads were under Federal control it successfully fought the discrimination against Negro railway employees; in 1919–1920, it obtained, in cooperation with the Association of Colored Railroad Employees, increased pay for colored trainmen; in 1919, through its branches, it furthered the organization of Negro steel workers at Pueblo, Colorado; in

1920, it fought the Ku Klux Klan and its attempts to force Negro cotton pickers and domestics into accepting lower rates of pay in many southern states; in 1921, it caused the United States Department of Justice to protect Negro trainmen from the violence and intimidation of white trainmen in the South; and in very recent years its efforts to safeguard the rights of Negro workers in the Mississippi Flood Control area, at Boulder Dam, and in the various national, state and local emergency agencies, relief projects, and in the legislation of the present administration are well known and too numerous for detailed citation.

As significant as is the work typified in the foregoing accomplishments, it reveals the Association's primary objective as being that of securing for the Negro his rights as an American citizen under prevailing economic and social conditions. Belief in the possibility of securing these rights for the Negro grew out of the faith of the founders of the Association in the principles of the 18th century liberalism, a faith which stamped the Association as the spiritual descendant of the Abolitionist Movement, demanding equal citizenship rights and civil liberty, and linked it with the whole liberal reform movement of the late nineteenth and early twentieth centuries.

The principles which liberalism espoused were the guarantee of the individual's economic and political freedom. The individual's political freedom consisted in equality before the law, the right to free public expression and discussion, and to participation in government through untrammeled use of the ballot. The individual's economic freedom consisted in his right to state protection in the acquisition of property and in the employment of it for his private ends and profit. But democratic liberalism only guaranteed freedom in the use of property once it was acquired. It did not create the conditions which made the acquisition of property open to all members of society. In fact its principles were based upon a state of industry and economic relations which presupposed the great mass of men to be non-propertied workers whose chances for obtaining property became increasingly difficult and whose economic status was made increasingly precarious by technological and financial changes that resulted in periodic unemployment and loss of income. The full impact of these changes in finance and industry was offset in this country by the frontier and the opportunities which free land and unbounded natural resources afforded for private exploitation. As an escape from poverty, the frontier, always virtually closed to the Negro masses, prevented the crystallization of social classes and the development of radical class consciousness. For, long after the frontier and free land had fulfilled their historic mission, Americans continued to think and act in terms of the national creed they had created, a belief in the opportunity of every thrifty and energetic American to obtain economic independence. But with the passing of the frontier the economic freedom espoused by liberalism was one that more and more became a privilege of a fortunate few. While men continued to look upon each other as political equals, that is, as possessing legal equality, they were in fact unequal. Property, the substantial basis of their freedom and independence, was acquired with increasing difficulty, a difficulty created by the persistent growth of corporate wealth, consolidations, and monopoly in industry, commerce and transportation, and by the concentration of land-ownership and in the difficulty of obtaining credit and capital in agriculture. Although noticeable in the decade following the Civil War, these changes began to be strikingly manifest in the early 1880's and continued on down to our own time. In consequence, if at any time full citizenship rights and civil liberty had been acquired by the Negro, the real condition of the great mass of black men, who probably to a greater degree than the white masses, were unable to accumulate property or to enter the wealthy employing class, would have been unaltered in its essential features.

These features stamped the Negro as a landless proletariat in the country and as a propertyless wage-earner in the city, a reservoir of cheap labor which, because of its greater poverty and fewer opportunities for economic advancement, was more easily exploited than white labor. While the masses of white men did enjoy full political citizenship and freedom, the enjoyment of these rights did not prevent the growth of poverty, unemployment and real economic inequality among them. It is true that the industrial and agricultural changes of the nineteenth and twentieth centuries affected a proportionately greater number of Negroes and that the impact of these changes upon the Negro was greater than upon the white man. Yet, the tendency of the events was to reduce the white and black masses to a substantially identical economic position and to show that the plight of these black peasants and industrial workers was inextricably tied up with that of the white. Nothing proved this identity of interests and the bankruptcy of liberal reformism so convincingly as the depression of 1929 and subsequent events. The unemployment produced by the crisis of 1929 forced white and black workers to lower and lower levels of competition for jobs and income. Although the Negro suffered greater disadvantages from the competition, it enabled the employer to play white and black workingmen against each other to their mutual disadvantage. Similarly, the differential wages that were effected under N.R.A. codes was a further extension, if not crystallization of this state of affairs which enables employers to divide and rule. Moreover in southern agriculture, the concentration of the landlord's power and the displacement of white and black croppers and tenants show the reality of this identity of interests between white and black workers.

While the adoption of the economic program contemplated here should not necessarily mean a discontinuance of the Association's efforts to obtain economic justice for the Negro, it does call for a reformulation of the Association's ultimate objectives. Instead of continuing to oppose racial discrimination on the job and in pay and various manifestations of anti-Negro feeling among white workers, the Association would attempt to get Negroes to view their special grievances as a natural part of the larger issues of American labor as a whole. It would attempt to get white workers and black to view their lot as embracing a common cause rather than antithetical interests. Thus, on one hand, it would show the Negro that his special disadvantages are but the more extreme manifestations of the exploitation of labor; and, on the other hand, it would show white labor that the disadvantages suffered by Negro workmen and frequently supported by white labor not only perpetuate the historic hostility between white and black labor, but also place a reserve of cheap labor at the disposal of employers, serving as dead weight upon the effective unity and organization of labor. It would show that the world which labor would gain is not a white world, nor a black one, and that this world can only be gained through the solidarity of white and black labor.

To this end the following program is proposed for the Association's adoption:

A. It is recommended that the Association:

1. Conduct classes in workers' education designed to create among Negro working men a knowledge of their historic and present role in modern industry and a realization of their identity of interests with white labor; 2. Foster the building of a labor movement, industrial in character, which will unite all labor, white and black, skilled and unskilled, agricultural and industrial; 3. Lay the intellectual basis for united action between white and black workers in local, state and national politics for securing passage of adequate legislation on immediate problems, such as (a) old age pensions, (b) unemployment and sickness insurance, (c) widows' and orphans' pensions, (d) child and female labor, (e) lynching, (f) public discrimination and Jim Crowism; 4. Serve as a basis for national and regional labor conferences to discuss the problems of Negro industrial and agricultural workers and to formulate programs of legislative, political or propaganda activity to be carried out independently or in cooperation with other groups or agencies in sympathy with these objectives; 5. Serve as an opposition force to every manifestation and form of racial chauvinism in the labor movement and among workers everywhere, and to attempt to break down discrimination on the job and in pay, and Jim Crowism in the local and national trade union bodies, by showing the mutually disastrous effects of these conditions upon the interests of white and black labor; 6. Educate Negro industrial and agricultural workers into the practices of the Cooperative Movement in Denmark, Austria, Russia and England as a means of furthering immediate economic relief in employment, credit, housing and consumption on a nonprofit basis, but not as a solution of

the "Economic Problem" or as the basis of a separate Negro group economy, an ideal which the Association deems unsound; and, 7. Make its branches centers of education in the use of the ballot, and in local, state and national politics.

B. To faciliate this program of economic activity, it is recommended:

1. That the Association, in conjunction with the local branches, build up a literature adapted to the needs of workers in particular communities but designed to connect up their local interests with those of workers throughout the country (much of the existing literature on cooperation, the labor movement, white and black labor competition, and industrial and agricultural problems in general should be simplified in pamphlet form); 2. That the Association begin to conduct a more systematic type of research and investigations in industry and agriculture, the results of which are to be published from time to time in *The Crisis* and other periodicals, but more specifically in the form of books and pamphlets; (a) That the Association, as a basis of its agitation and investigation into economic conditions, cooperate with existing organizations in the field and seek the use of such records from their files as may be available; (b) as soon as its finances permit, that it procure the most efficient person available to direct these economic activities; and (c) that in launching this program, and to insure successful operation in its early stages, it be placed under the direction of the Board, with the advice of an Advisory Committee on Economic Activities, to be composed of not less than five members.

The execution of the above program will require the reorganization of the Association along regional lines as is proposed in the section dealing with structural reorganization. For this program to function it is imperative that the local branches become transformed from centers of sporadic agitation to permanent centers of economic and political education and agitation, conducting public lectures, forums, the dissemination of information on local conditions, and aiding in the formation of cooperative societies where desired. . . .

26. RALPH J. BUNCHE
PROBES THE LIMITATIONS
OF RACIAL ADVANCEMENT PROGRAMS

In Document 24 James Weldon Johnson described with his customary diplomacy and tact the major ideologies and programs for racial advancement, although he concluded by endorsing the program of the NAACP. For a searching and comprehensive criticism of the tactics and strategies of various organizations and ideologies, however, one must turn to the work of Ralph J. Bunche. Bunche is today Under Secretary of the United Nations, and is regarded by many militant activists as a conservative ally of the political establishment. But during the thirties, when he was chairman of the department of Political Science at Howard University, Bunche functioned as a militant young intellectual who criticized both the American social system and the established Negro leadership organizations.

Bunche, in his pessimistic attitude toward American society, especially American capitalism, shared the disillusionment exhibited at the time by many prominent intellectuals of both races. In an article that appeared in the *Journal of Negro Education* in 1935 he made a probing criticism of the programs of all the major racial advancement organizations, and argued persuasively that even the NAACP program was of limited value, because in effect it tended toward gradualism and conciliation. Instead Bunche argued in general terms for a reconstruction of American society through an alliance of the black and white workers.

J. S. Mill in his fine treatise on *Representative Government* expressed the belief that it is virtually impossible to build up a democracy out of the intermingling of racially differentiated groups of men. It may be that historical experience has indicated the error of Mill's thesis insofar as different "racial" groups

Ralph J. Bunche, "A Critical Analysis of the Tactics and Programs of Minority Groups," JOURNAL OF NEGRO EDUCATION, IV, 3 (July 1935), 308–320. Reprinted with the permission of the editors.

among the white peoples of the world are concerned, but there is apparently much evidence to substantiate it when related to the intermixture of white and black populations in the same society. Throughout the world today, wherever whites and blacks are present in any significant numbers in the same community, democracy becomes the tool of the dominant elements in the white population in their ruthless determination to keep the blacks suppressed. This is true, whether the blacks constitute the overwhelming majority of the population, as in South Africa and Algeria, or the minority, as in the United States.

The responsibility, however, rests not with the institution of democracy, *per se,* nor in the readily accepted belief that black and white simply cannot mix amicably on a common political and economic basis. Recent world history points out too clearly that modern democracy, conceived in the womb of middle-class revolutions, was early put to work in support of those ruling middle-class interests of capitalistic society which fathered it. It has remained their loyal child and has rendered profitable service for them. But when in modern European countries it came to be vigorously wooed by those mass interests of society whose lot under modern industrialism has been that of cruel oppression, democracy was quickly discredited and disowned, and fascism became the favored child of Big-Business-controlled governments. The significant fact is that democracy, while never offered in any large measure to the black populations of the world, has been extended to the great masses of the working-class population only so long as it was employed by them as a harmless device involving no real threat to the increasing control of the society by the ruling classes.

Minority populations, and particularly racial minorities, striving to exist in any theoretically democratic modern society, are compelled to struggle strenuously for even a moderate participation in the democratic game. Minority groups are always with us. They may be national minorities, *i.e.,* distinct ethnic groups with an individual nation and cultural character living within a state which is dominated by some other nationality, as in German and Polish Upper Silesia; or they may come under the

looser definition of minorities employed by the League of Nations, including any people in any state differing from the
majority population in either race, language or religion, such as
the Negro in the United States. But whatever the nature of the
minority group, its special problems may always be translated in
terms of political, economic, and social disadvantages. Group
antagonisms develop, which are fed by mythical beliefs and
attitudes of scorn, derision, hate and discrimination. These serve
as effective social barriers and fix the social, and hence, the political and economic status of the minority population. The mental images or verbal characterizations generally accepted as
descriptive of the members of the particular racial group,—the
"pictures in our heads" so aptly discussed by Walter Lippmann,
—give rise to stereotypes which are of the greatest significance
in race relations.[1] These race distinctions, along with similar
class and caste distinctions, are so thoroughly rooted in our social
consciousness as to command serious attention in any consideration of programs whose objective is equitable treatment for
minority racial groups.

Many are the non-scientific solutions for the problem of black-
white race relations that have been offered. Racial equality and
tolerance have been pled for far and wide. But these solutions
ignore the seemingly basic fact that whenever two groups of
peoples in daily contact with each other, and having readily
identifiable cultural or racial differentiations, are likewise forced
into economic competition, group antagonisms must inevitably
prevail.

The Negro as a minority group in the U.S.

The Negro group in the United States is characterized by the
conditions of easy racial identification and severe economic competition with the dominant white population. In addition, the
position of the Negro in this country is conditioned by the his-

---

[1] Walter Lippmann, *Public Opinion* (New York: Macmillan Co., 1922),
Ch. I, *passim.*

torical fact of his ancestral slavery. All of the present-day relations between the disadvantaged Negro group and the majority white group are influenced by this master-slave heritage, and the traditional competition between poor-white and Negro masses. The stamp of racial and social inferiority placed upon the Negro, the detached, condescending paternalism of the "better elements" of the Southern white population, the "missionary" enterprise of Northern philanthropy, the bitter antipathies between black and white laboring masses, "Uncle Tomism" in both its cruder and more polished modern forms, and the inferiority complex of the Negro group itself, may be directly traced to these historical roots.

The factors of race and the slavery tradition do not fully explain the perpetuation of the "race problem," however. Much of what is called prejudice against the Negro can be explained in economic terms, and in the peculiar culture of the Southern states, with their large "poor-white" populations. The determination of the ruling class of large land-holders in the South to perpetuate in law and custom the doctrine of the racial inferiority of the Negro was made possible only because this numerically preponderant poor-white population feared the economic competition and the social and political power of the large black population. The cultural, political and economic degradation of the Negro also gave the poor-whites their sole chance for "status."

Intelligent elements in the white Southern population have in recent years begun to admit that other factors than mere "race" are involved in many of the abusive practices employed to intimidate the Negro in the South. For example, Mr. Arthur Raper, in his excellent study, *The Tragedy of Lynching*, explains that the bases of the lynching of Negroes in the South reside in the determination of the white South to exploit the Negro, culturally, politically and economically. Such "social pressures," as he calls them, are exemplified, for instance, when a planter assures the outsider that the propertyless Negroes in his community are wholly satisfied with their small pay, their one-teacher schools and plantation-unit churches, and their chronic economic and political dependency. "The query," writes Raper, "but are they really satisfied?" is answered quickly and firmly: "Well, if they're not they'd better be!"[2] In other words the large white land-holding and industrial groups in the South are determined to keep the Negro in a servile condition and as a profitable and almost indispensable labor supply. In so doing, black workers have been aligned against white, from slavery days on, and bitter antagonisms have developed between these groups. The resulting "racial" situation has not been in any sense disadvantageous to the employing class, which is not insensitive to the merits of the policy of *divide et impera* in labor-employer relationships.

In reality the Negro population in the United States is a minority group only in the narrowly racial sense. In every other respect it is subject to the same divisive influences impinging upon the life of every other group in the nation. Economically, the Negro, in the vast majority, is identified with the peasant and proletarian classes of the country, which are certainly not in the minority. Politically, the Negro, until recent years under the spell of the "Lincolnian Legend," was almost completely identified with the Republican Party. He was aligned, therefore, with what constituted with monotonous regularity the majority political group. The Negro thus has been subjected to the same sectional, political and economic forces which have influenced the white population, with admitted additional aggravation due solely to the race equation.

Negro leadership, however, has traditionally put its stress on the element of race; it has attributed the plight of the Negro to a peculiar racial condition. Leaders and organizations alike have had but one end in view—the elimination of "discrimination against the race." This attitude has been reflected in the tactics which they have employed to correct abuses suffered by their group. They have not realized that so long as this basis conflict in the economic interests of the white and black groups persists,

[2] Arthur Raper, *The Tragedy of Lynching.* Chapel Hill: University of North Carolina Press, 1933, p. 48.

and it is a perfectly natural phenomenon in a modern industrial society, neither prayer, nor logic, nor emotional or legal appeal can make much headway against the stereotyped racial attitudes and beliefs of the masses of the dominant population. The significance of this to the programs of the corrective and reform organizations working on behalf of the group should be obvious. The most that such organizations can hope to do is to devote themselves to the correction of the more flagrant specific cases of abuse, which because of their extreme nature may exceed even a prejudiced popular approval; and to a campaign of public enlightenment concerning the merits of the group they represent and the necessity for the establishment of a general community of interest among all groups in the population.

Objectives sought by minority groups

In general, the objectives which minority groups traditionally struggle for are those tenets of social justice embraced by eighteenth-century liberalism, with its democratic creed of liberty, equality, and fraternity. This liberalism purported to guarantee the individual's economic and political freedom. Economic freedom for the individual assumed his right to the protection of the state in the acquisition and use of his property for his private benefit and profit. In fact, however, democratic liberalism did little to create those conditions which would facilitate the acquisition of property by any great numbers of the society. To the contrary, its principles were applied in countries whose economic structures were so ordered that the great masses of the population were presupposed to be non-property-holding workingmen, whose opportunities for obtaining property became progressively less easy, and whose economic status was increasingly less certain as a result of technological and financial developments within the economic structure—resulting in periodic unemployment, loss of income and dissipation of meager savings. In the United States the presence of the frontier, with the free land it offered and its rich natural resources, vitalized the American Dream that every energetic and thrifty American could win economic independence. The American frontier, however, was never widely open to the Negro population, and this was one of the factors that forestalled the development of class stratification, and a consciousness of it in the Negro population to the same degree as found in the white.

Political freedom for the individual assumed his right to equality before the law, the right to freedom of speech, press, religion, assemblage and movement, and to democratic participation in the government through the unabridged use of the ballot.

Tactics of minority groups

On this assumption that members of minority groups, like those of the majority populations in democratic countries, possess certain inalienable rights—political, social and economic—which they must struggle to preserve, leaders and organizations of minority groups map out programs and techniques of action designed to protect their people. Roughly, and rather arbitrarily, the tactics which such groups ordinarily employ in this struggle can be summarised as follows:

(1) *Violent*
   (a) Direct rebellion and secession by force.
   (b) Cooperation with other dissentient elements toward immediate or ultimate revolution.
(2) *Non-Violent*
   (a) Zionism and Garveyism, involving migration to new and foreign soil.
   (b) Economic, including passive resistance (the Gandhi movement) and economic separatism.
   (c) Conciliation, including interracial organizations.
   (d) Political, including a determined fight for the ballot and justice through laws, lobbying, picketing, mass demonstrations and the courts.

While each of these methods has been employed at one time or another by some minority group, those listed under the non-violent heading have been the tactics most seriously advocated by American Negro leadership in its efforts to free the group from political and economic inequality.

Violent tactics

Numerically, the American Negro is so overwhelmed by the white population, and in addition the members of the group are so scattered throughout this vast country, that serious consideration need not be afforded the tactic of direct secession and rebellion by force. Likewise, the Negro masses are so lacking in radical class consciousness; they are so conservative and deeply imbued with a peasant psychology and the lingering illusion of the American Dream, that any possibility of large-scale identification of the Negro population with revolutionary groups can be projected only in the future. The Communist Party has seriously proselyted among the Negro group but with only indifferent success. The immediate task of such movements in this country is to develop radical class-consciousness among the working-class masses of both white and Negro populations, with a view to the ultimate recognition of an identity of interest and consequent black and white solidarity in a militant labor movement.

Non-violent tactics

Racial Separatism. Because of the seeming hopelessness of the fight to win equal rights for many minority racial groups, some of the leadership of such groups has often espoused a "defeatist" philosophy, which takes the form of racial separatism. This defeatism in its most extreme form follows the general design of the Zionist movement. For the American Negro the Garvey program may be characterized as the black counterpart of the Zionist movement. Thousands of American Negroes came to believe that the racial barriers to equality in this country could never be surmounted, and they flocked to the support of the Garvey "back-to-Africa" movement which flourished after the last war. Like all programs of this character, Garveyism offered the Negro an emotional escape from oppresive conditions. Also like other such programs it was impractical, for attractive land for such venture was no longer available, due to the consuming greed and the inexorable demands of imperialist nations. The Garvey movement could offer only Liberia to the American Negro—one of the most backward and unhealthy territories of an altogether uninviting West Africa. Moreover, the Liberians themselves did not want the American Negroes.

Economic Passive Resistance. There are many variations of the nonviolent economic tactics, but the most significant are those which advocate economic passive resistance and economic separatism. Supporters of economic passive resistance usually look to Gandhi for their guidance. They see powerful weapons available to the oppressed group in the employment of the economic boycott and in fearless self-sacrifice. Through such tactics they propose to wring economic and political justice from the dominant group by striking at its most sensitive spot, its markets, and by shaming its Christian conscience. In the first place, the Ghandi movement has not succeeded in India, despite the fact that it was attempted in the one country offering it its greatest possibilities of success. The natives of India are overwhelmingly preponderant in the population and are capable of self-immolation on behalf of a cause to a degree unknown to Western peoples. Moreover, their country is not industrialized and their low standard of living is such that it cannot be materially affected by the inevitable reprisals of the controlling groups. Even so, however, the movement could not break down the military and financial buttresses of the relative handful of Englishmen allied with the native ruling interests which control the country.

In a highly industrialized country the possibilities from the employment of this method of resistance are much less. It means, of necessity, that the members of the group in the mass must be willing at the outset to accept an even lower standard of living than that which they already enjoy. But more important still is the fact that it is unlikely that any such movement could long withstand the unyielding and inevitable resistance which would be launched against it by the business rulers of the country. Presumably, in industrial societies this tactic would involve the organization of group cooperatives for the production of industrial and agricultural products. As soon as such a movement assumed threatening proportions, it would be obliged to withstand severe counter-boycotts which would deprive the members of the group of many necessary commodities which they could not produce themselves. Moreover, they would be denied essential credit and capital. The legal and police forces of the state would inevitably be aligned against them, and, in addition, they would be subjected to the characteristic gangster attacks which have recently proved so helpful to employers in labor disputes.

A mild version of this form of economic passive resistance has been from time to time advocated by Negro leaders in this country as one means of obtaining economic justice under the existing system. Particularly during the depression has this doctrine gained circulation in the guise of the "don't-buy-where-you-can't-work" movement. The fallacy of this method is obviously discovered in its assumption that it can offer any real relief to the great masses of Negroes. Its outlook is narrowly racial, and it fails to realize that it can create no new jobs but that it can only gain jobs for Negroes by displacement of whites. Since there is already a woefully inadequate number of jobs, whenever a Negro is thus forced into a job in a Negro community a white man is forced out and must seek employment elsewhere. And, since the Negro communities do not offer sufficient economic activity to absorb even the number of Negroes now employed, this can only mean that Negroes employed in white communities are endangered of losing their jobs in proportion to the success of the movement. At best, it could create only a vicious cycle of job displacement. Moreover, the proponents of the doctrine fail to grasp the fact that the Negro is not out of a job simply because he is a Negro, but, rather because the economic system finds itself incapable of affording an adequate number of jobs for all —in fact, its productive system is so organized that it must have a marginal labor supply. But the most serious defect in the rationalization of this tactic is in the fact that it widens still further the already deplorable gap between the white and black working-classes of the nation, by boldly placing the competition for jobs on a strictly racial basis. If the doctrine were carried out to its logical conclusion, it would necessarily advocate that Negro workers be organized as a great strike-breaking group.

Economic Separatism. As a result of the highly segregated life which racial minority groups are often compelled to live, there is a strong tendency for the doctrine of economic separatism to take root as a promising palliative for both political and economic oppression. This has been a particularly virulent creed among American Negroes, chiefly due to the impetus given the movement by Booker T. Washington and his successor, Major Moton. Negro businesses are almost entirely the product of segregation and can be characterized as "defensive enterprises." The promise of this hope of constructing an independent and segregated black economy within the walls of the white capitalist economy is excellently discussed by Spero and Harris in the following words:

> Yet how such an independent economy is to rise and function when the white world outside controls credit, basic industry, and the state is something which the sponsors of the movement prefer to ignore. If such an economy is to rise it will have to do so with the aid of white philanthropy and will have to live upon white sufferance. If the great white banks and insurance companies decide that they want Negro business it is hard to see how the little black institutions can compete successfully against them. The same holds for the chain stores and various retail establishments. They will be able to undersell their Negro competitors if they want to, and the Negro world will not continue indefinitely to pay higher prices for its goods merely out of pride of race. Basic industry will continue to remain in the hands of the white world, for even the most ardent supporters of an independent black economy will admit that there is no prospect of the Negro capitalists amassing enough wealth to establish steel mills, build railroads and pipe lines, and gain control of essential raw materials.[3]

[3] Sterling D. Spero and Abram L. Harris, *The Black Worker* (New York: Columbia University Press, 1931), p. 466.

Political Tactics: Civil Libertarianism. Perhaps the favorite method of struggle for rights employed by minority groups is the political. Through the use of the ballot and the courts strenuous efforts are put forth to gain social justice for the group. Extreme faith is placed in the ability of these instruments of democratic government to free the minority from social proscription and civic inequality. The inherent fallacy of this belief rests in the failure to appreciate the fact that the instruments of the state are merely the reflections of the political and economic ideology of the dominant group, that the political arm of the state cannot be divorced from its prevailing economic structure, whose servant it must inevitably be.

Leaders of the American Negro like Dr. Du Bois, and organizations such as the National Association for the Advancement of Colored People, which he helped to found in 1909, have conducted a militant fight under this illusory banner. They have demanded full equality for the Negro, involving the eradication of all social, legal, and political restrictions tending to draw a line of distinction between the black citizen and the white. The Negro, like the white American, is to quaff the full draught of eighteenth-century democratic liberalism. The Negro individual citizen must have every right boasted by the individual white citizen, including the franchise, freedom of economic opportunity (consisting chiefly of the right to employment without discrimination), the right to accommodations in public places and on common carriers, the right to voluntary choice of his place of residence without involuntary segregation, the right to jury service, and equal expenditures of public funds for education and other public services. In pursuing this struggle the Negro has been seriously handicapped, because he has never yet been able to win any large measure of participation in the franchise. It is estimated that today at least 90 per cent of the adult Negroes in the Southern states are excluded from the suffrage, and it is here that the great masses of the Negro population are concentrated. Consequently the group leadership has had to lean heavily upon sympathetic white supporters, lobbying, picketing, written and verbal protests, and appeals, mass demonstrations, and the courts.

The confidence of the proponents of the political method of alleviation is based on the protection which they feel is offered all groups in the society by that sacred document the Constitution. Particularly do they swear by the Bill of Rights and its three supplements, the Thirteenth, Fourteenth and Fifteenth amendments, as a special charter of the black man's liberties. The Constitution is thus detached from the political and economic realities of American life and becomes a sort of protective angel hovering above us and keeping a constant vigil over the rights of all America's children, black and white, rich and poor, employer and employee and, like impartial justice, blinded to their differences. This view ignores the quite significant fact that the Constitution is a very flexible instrument and that, in the nature of things, it cannot be anything more than the controlling elements in the American society wish it to be. In other words, this charter of the black man's liberties can never be more than our legislatures, and, in the final analysis, our courts, wish it to be. And, what these worthy institutions wish it to be can never be more than what American public opinion wishes it to be. Unfortunately, so much of American public opinion is seldom enlightened, sympathetic, tolerant or humanitarian. Too often it resembles mob violence.

Interracial Conciliation. It follows, therefore, that the policy of civil libertarianism is circumscribed by the dominant mores of the society. Its success, in the final analysis, must depend upon its ability to create a sympathetic response to its appeals among influential elements in the controlling population. In the long run its militancy must be softened and the inevitable tendency is for it to conform to the general pattern of the genteel programs of interracial conciliation, which attempt to cultivate the good will of the white upper classes. The churches, the young men's and young women's Christian associations, the interracial commissions, and social welfare agencies such as the Urban League, are the leading institutions among the Negro engaged in the dubiously valuable work of developing interracial fellow feeling.

It is not surpising, therefore, that assertedly militant civil-libertarian organizations like the N.A.A.C.P. should employ tactics which are progressively less militant. Such organizations, if they remain constant in their faith, are forced into a policy of conciliation with the enlightened, *i.e.*, the ruling interests, in the dominant group. They must rely upon sympathetic understanding and fair play in their campaigns for social justice, and they can scarcely expect to find these noble traits in the victimized and unenlightened masses. Consequently, the more "liberal" the better elements of the white South become, the less militant these associations can afford to be. They can be militant, but only politely so; they can attack, but not too harshly; they must entreat, bargain, compromise and capitulate in order to win even petty gains. They must politely play the game according to the rules even though they have no stakes. In other words, they play cricket.

The Courts. Such policies mere reflect the fact, established by the legal and political history of the group, that the Negro in the United States is a special ward of the Supreme Court. The Negro has had countless experiences which sufficiently establish the fact that he has rights only as this august tribunal allows them, and even these are, more often than not, illusory. It is only inadvertently that the courts, like the legislatures, fail to reflect the dominant mass opinion. It must be futile, then, to expect these agencies of government to afford the Negro protection for rights which are denied to him by the popular will. Moreover, even could we optimistically hope that the Supreme Court, in its theoretical legal detachment, would go counter to the popular will and wipe out the proscriptions imposed on the Negro, as it appeared to do in the Scottsboro cases, the condition of the group could not be greatly changed. In the first place, American experience affords too many proofs that laws and decisions contrary to the will of the majority cannot be enforced. In the second place, the Supreme Court can effect no revolutionary changes in the economic order, and yet the status of the Negro, as that of other groups in the society, is fundamentally fixed by the functioning and the demands of that order. The very attitudes of the majority group which fix the Negro in his disadvantaged position are part and parcel of the American economic and political order.

The peculiar position of the Negro as a ward of the judiciary is readily explained by his political history. The Civil War amendments were designed to give him a rather nebulous freedom and to protect him in his fundamental rights. The Thirteenth amendment guaranteed his physical freedom. The Fourteenth purported to protect his right of life, liberty and property, *i.e.*, to afford him the full privileges and immunities of citizenship, due process and equal protection of the laws. The Fifteenth amendment assured him that he would not be deprived of the suffrage because of his race, color, or previous servitude. These measures were realistic, they recognized that the newly-emancipated Negro citizen would be crushed by the Southern states unless special protection were afforded him. They were applied directly as limitations upon the states. But the Negro has never been accepted as a participating, legal member of his Southern state. There is perhaps a measure of government *for* the Negro in the South, but never *of* or *by* him. The Southern states recognize no duty to insure or extend his legal rights, and the Constitution imposes no such positive responsibility upon them. The state governments, being "democratic" governments, were keenly responsive to the popular will, and seriously devoted themselves to the task of preserving the inferior status of the Negro population. The issue is thus clearly drawn for the Negro. Against the subversive laws of the state legislatures and decisions of the state courts he opposes his "Constitutional rights." The burden of proof is always upon him. For the interpretation and realization of these rights he is forced to appeal to the Supreme Court.

Thus the Negro has been compelled to substitute the complicated, arduous and expensive processes of litigation for the ballot box. What other groups are able to do for themselves, the Negro hopes the judiciary to do for him. There is more than ample evidence in the decisions of the supreme tribunal of the land on questions involving the rights of the Negro to disprove the possibility of any general relief from this quarter.

The fight for the rights of the group before the courts directs itself to such impairments and deprivations of civil liberties as segregation, together with inferior accommodations and instruction in the public schools, unequal apportionment of school funds, segregation and inferior accommodations on common carriers, residential segregation, exclusion from jury service, disfranchisement, and peonage. These evils have all been attacked through litigation but with only indifferent success. In scores of decisions on these questions the highest courts of the land have amply demonstrated their willingness to acquiesce in the prevailing attitudes of the dominant population in respect to the Negro.

The legal theory behind such decisions is that race discrimination is contrary to the Constitution only when it involves inequality in rights or the possession by one race of rights which are denied to another solely because of its race. Race "distinctions," on the other hand, if based on substantial differences, do not constitute discrimination. Such permissible race distinctions in law are usually ascribed to one or more of the following motives: (1) the prevention of race conflicts; (2) the preservation of race purity by the prevention of intermarriage or of illicit sex relations; (3) the existence of race peculiarities which demand recognition in special legislation. It is well settled that statutes may be framed to attain any of these objectives which will not be objectionable to the protective clauses of the Fourteenth Amendment.

Thus, since the Fourteenth amendment is directed only against action by the states, a common carrier may, in the absence of federal legislation, provide for the separation of white and Negro passengers in interstate commerce.[4] Similarly, a restrictive covenant in a deed of conveyance of real estate, by which the grantee covenants that the property described shall never be used or occupied by, or sold, leased or given to, any Negro, has been held not to contravene the Fourteenth amendment.[5] Statutes requiring separate public schools for white and Negro children have long been sustained by the courts, as was a

[4] *Chiles* v. *Chesapeake and Ohio Ry.*, 218 U.S. 71 (1910).
[5] *Corrigan* v. *Buckley*, 271 U.S. 323 (1926).

statute of the state prohibiting the teaching of the two races in the same private school.[6] Likewise, a state is upheld in requiring Chinese pupils to attend the schools provided for Negro pupils.[7] Pursuing its racial theories to the extreme, the Court has admitted that fornication, when committed by persons of different races, may be punished more severely by the state than when committed by persons of the same race.[8]

The ability of the courts to hand down what appear to be legally sound opinions and still permit popular abuses of the Negro's rights to persist is largely due to the adroitness of the white legislators in the art of drawing up and administering their laws. These abuses generally occur under the protection of laws which are "fair on their face," and unless the court is disposed to look behind the face of the law to its administration the Negro can receive no relief. This is admirably illustrated by a comparison of the court's attitude in the case of *Yick Wo* v. *Hopkins*[9] and *Plessy* v. *Ferguson*.[10] In the *Yick Wo* case, involving the discriminatory administration of a law to the disadvantage of Chinese, the court, in deciding the case in favor of the appellants, said:

> Though the law itself be fair on its face and impartial in appearance, yet, if it is applied and administered by public authority with an evil eye and an unequal hand, so as practically to make unjust and illegal discriminations between persons in similar circumstances, material to their rights, the denial of equal justice is still within the prohibition of the Constitution.

Ten years later, however, in *Plessy* v. *Ferguson,* involving an attack by a Negro on a "separate-but-equal-accommodations" provision for common carriers in the law of the State of Louisiana, the court accepted the act at its face value and refused to admit the contention of violation of constitutional rights ad-

[6] *Berea College* v. *Kentucky,* 211 U.S. 45 (1908).
[7] *Gong Lum* v. *Rice,* 275 U.S. 78 (1927).
[8] *Pace* v. *Alabama,* 106 U.S. 583 (1883).
[9] 118 U.S. 356 (1886).
[10] 163 U.S. 537 (1896).

vanced by the plaintiff. The court, in fact, indorsed the provision, saying,

> . . . the case reduces itself to the question whether the statute of Louisiana is a reasonable regulation, and with respect to this there must necessarily be a large discretion on the part of the legislature. In determining the question of reasonableness it is at liberty to act with reference to the established usages, customs and traditions of the people, and with a view to the promotion of their comfort, and the preservation of the public peace and good order.

Perhaps no better example of the tendency of the Supreme Court to detach itself from political reality when questions involving Negro rights are concerned and to resort to legal fictions, can be afforded than the opinion of Justice Roberts in the recent Texas Primary case.[11] It is seemingly of no concern to the court in this unanimous decision that a party performs a vital political function, that the Democratic Primary in Texas is in fact the only significant election, and that exclusion from the primary robs the Negro of his franchise. The Court could only see that the prohibitions of the Constitution are prohibitions against the actions of the state, and that a political party is a private, voluntary association, presumably something akin to the Elks. It is significant to note that Chief Justice Hughes, in handing down an opinion in one of the celebrated Gold Clause cases, *Perry* v. *U.S.*,[12] while solemnly discussing the obligation of the government to keep faith with its contracts, said: ". . . the contractual obligation still exists and, despite infirmities of procedure, remains binding upon the *conscience of the sovereign*."[13] But Justice Roberts, in meeting the argument that if Negroes are refused admission to the Democratic Primary in Texas they are in fact altogether deprived of the suffrage, this sacred right of

[11] *Grovey* v. *Townsend,* No. 563, October Term (1934).
[12] No. 532, October Term (1934).
[13] Italics mine.

democratic government, failed to recognize that the sovereign
had any conscience at all, and sought refuge in the dialectical
stratosphere by admonishing that

> So to say is to confuse the privilege of membership in a party
> with the right to vote for one who is to hold a public office. With
> the former the state need have no concern, with the latter it is
> bound to concern itself, for the general election is a function of
> the state government and discrimination by the state as respects
> participation by negroes on account of their race or color is pro-
> hibited by the federal constitution.

Thus, although the Democratic Primary actually takes the place
of the general election in Texas (as in most other states below
the Mason and Dixon line), Mr. Roberts assures us that justice
is served, since the Negro may still go through the useless exercise of casting a shadow vote at the general election. The decision is especially ironical in view of the fact that the court
invoked the Fourteenth amendment—the most important section of the Negro's charter of liberty—as the sanction for thus
denying him the franchise.

The recent discouraging decision of the Supreme Court in
the Herndon case gives eloquent testimony to the ability of
the Court to avoid delicate issues by hiding behind legal
technicalities.

Such economic political tactics, while winning a minor and
too often illusory victory now and then, are essentially ineffica-
cious in the long run. They lead up blind alleys and are chiefly
programs of escape. No minority group should relent in the most
determined fight for its rights, but its leadership should recognize the limitations of opportunistic and socially blind policies.
The only realistic program for any minority group in modern
America is one which is based upon an intelligent analysis of the
problems of the group in terms of the broad social forces which
determine its condition. Certainly no program of opportunism
and no amount of idealism can overcome or control these forces.
The only hope for the improvement in the condition of the

masses of any American minority group is the hope that can be held out for the betterment of the masses of the dominant group. Their basic interests are identical and so must be their programs and tactics.

27. A. PHILIP RANDOLPH
CALLS FOR A UNITED FRONT

Angelo Herndon's Pamphlet (see Document 20) was written when Communist policy was to attack the Urban League and the NAACP as bourgeois organizations. By 1936, however, the Comintern had decided to join with bourgeois, liberal, and other radical groups in a United Front Against Fascism. The most notable Communist effort to form an alliance with black advancement organizations was the National Negro Congress (NNC). Organized in 1936, it was largely an outgrowth of the work of the Joint Committee on National Recovery (JCNR). This body, mainly financed by the NAACP, had been formed by some twenty black and interracial organizations to advance Negro interests with the New Deal agencies. Though Communist organizations were not invited to the early conferences of the JCNR, some of the leading delegates—including John P. Davis, who later became executive secretary of the NNC—were identified with the party or were sympathetic towards it.

The proposal for the Congress grew out of a conference at Howard University sponsored by the JCNR in 1935. The NAACP was aloof, but the sponsoring committee obtained the endorsement of such eminent non-Communists as Lester Granger, executive director of the Urban League and A. Philip Randolph, who became president. Although Ford was one of the principal speakers at the organizing meeting in Chicago the next year, the Congress adopted a broad racial-advancement platform, in which one cannot discern any truly

A. Philip Randolph, "The Crisis of the Negro and the Constitution," in OFFICIAL PROCEEDINGS, SECOND NATIONAL NEGRO CONGRESS, 1937. (No imprint, unpaged.)

Communist ideology. The organizations obtained the endorsement of many prominent blacks and the affiliation of a number of black fraternal and civic groups as well as some predominantly white left-wing unions. The speakers' list at the second conference read like a Who's Who of black leaders. One of the speakers, in fact, was the NAACP's executive secretary, Walter White, though the NAACP itself declined to affiliate with the Congress.

This kind of participation was achieved because the Communists had, for tactical reasons, temporarily shelved their revolutionary slogans and adopted a middle-of-the-road point of view. When the Communists moved to the right, their official position tended to coincide with that of liberals and socialists in an age marked by depression at home and the threat of Fascism abroad. Randolph, in addressing the 1937 conference, articulated brilliantly the broad range of Negro protest thinking at the beginning of Franklin D. Roosevelt's second administration.

Communist influence in the National Negro Congress grew markedly after the 1937 convention. The Congress did not hold conventions in 1938 and 1939, reportedly because the Communists feared that their domination would be exposed. By the time the third convention met, in 1940, the Russians had signed a non-aggression pact with Hitler and the Party line had shifted once more, this time away from a United Front. Flooding the convention with white pro-Communist union delegates, the Communists forced out A. Philip Randolph, president of the Congress, and other anti-Communists as well, and captured the Congress completely. The Congress now equated the black man's oppressors with those who favored United States entry into the second World War on the side of the Allies. Thus the Congress simply became a vehicle for Communist expression of the Party's "anti-imperialist-war" line.

After the Nazis attacked Russia in the spring of 1941, however, the Communist line changed again. For the next four years the erstwhile militant champions of black rights insisted that the campaign for equality should be soft-pedaled in order not to interfere with the war effort. The non-Communist black leaders of course saw no contradiction between the successful prosecution of the war and the attainment of Negro rights. On the contrary, it was their belief that in fighting a war to preserve democracy the United States should practice democracy, and that the efficient prosecution of the war demanded the recognition of the Negro's rights and the full utilization of his energies and talents without discrimination and segregation.

In this hour of crisis in the nation, in the whole wide world, in governments, in industry, in trade union movements and among oppressed minorities everywhere, the Second National Negro Congress, representing hundreds of thousands of Negroes in America, hails the Constitution on its 150th birthday. We hail it as a Magna Charta of human rights. The Negro people, oppressed and persecuted, especially look to the Constitution as an impregnable citadel of their liberties.

Caught between the powerful forces of the southern plantation economy, on the one hand, and the rising financial and industrial power of the north, on the other, the Constitution was a compromise on the question of slavery, but the 13th, 14th, and 15th Amendments sought to chart and establish the guarantees of their full citizenship rights of the Negro people.

Sinister tendencies toward the re-enslavement of the Freedmen manifested themselves soon after the Civil War had ended, and the uncompromising Sumner, and the valiant band of Abolitionists had lost their memorable fight to protect the newly emancipated slaves with federal troops in the south. This unhappy chapter in American history tells of the tragic loss of the liberty of an entire race following the breakdown of the great and inspiring experiment of Reconstruction, rendering the bourbon plantation owners and the former slave-masters free to use the shotgun, the tissue ballot and the Ku Klux Klan terror, to drive the Negro back into a semi-caste status. Indeed, the conditions calculated to achieve the full citizenship for the former slaves were never fulfilled by the Civil War, though the beginning was challenging. Verily, the Constitution, without the force of enlightened public opinion back of it, could not itself effect what a bourgeois revolution did not accomplish.

While the new South with its lumber, turpentine and cotton magnates, went out for cheap labor as its major interest, to pile up high profits, it also attacked the civil rights of the Negro with a view to breaking his hope and faith in the inner redemptive forces of the race so that they would undervalue their human worth and economic role in Southern industry and planting. This created the need and demand for the 14th and 15th Amendments to the Constitution. They were passed. But the due process clause has been employed more as a weapon for defending corporate wealth rather than the human rights of the Negro people.

Now, it has become a common-place that Black America is not only concerned with the 13th, 14th and 15th Amendments that grew out of the Civil War and the Reconstruction period, a period which though maligned, condemned and misrepresented by historians, with more of the Nordic bias than of the scientific spirit, will ever live as a glorious record of the capacity and genius of the Negro people for orderly, enlightened and the constructive administration of government, but Afro-Americans are, too, interested in the Bill of Rights of the Constitution which provides the framework and basis of civil and political liberties within and upon which alone as free people or rather may seek to secure and maintain their freedom, and build those institutions that help preserve freedom.

It is well nigh a truism that without the freedom of speech, of habeas corpus, of the freedom of worship, of the right to vote and be voted for, the basic institutions of modern society, such as the home, family, church, school, press, free business enterprise, trade union movements and associations seeking the liberation of all oppressed minority groups, could hardly exist and enjoy a healthy growth and development.

The Constitution stands as an imposing bulwark of these rights. But the Constitution is not an end in itself. Nor is it a perfect document. It possesses many grave limitations, and needs some fundamental and permanent change so as to make possible reforms for the protection and advancement of the workers. This worthy objective is now courageously sought by President Roosevelt, without the method of constitutional change, in his Supreme Court reorganization plan. Any such change through the method of legislation only, though desirable and timely, may not be so enduring as if wrought through change of the Constitution itself. But let us back the President's fight for judicial justice.

In very truth, the Constitution is a means to an end. The end is the attainment of an enlightened and humane government, and an economic order that will invest the people with the right and the power to live the good life, the more abundant life.

And today, in a world of storm and stress, of confusion and uncertainty, of arrogant cynicism and deadly pessimism, of war and Fascism, the American Constitution proudly reveals its deeper moorings of stability, assurance and hope for democracy.

While the Negro people, under the Constitution, because of nullification by the spirit of the Lost Cause, are still without the full measure of citizenship in the former Confederate States, the Constitution, at least, vouchsafes complete citizenship rights and provides the grounds of principle and promises to secure it.

Albeit, it is more and more becoming correctly understood that the task of realizing full citizenship for the Negro people is largely in the hands of the Negro people themselves. Assuring full citizenship rights to [the] Afro-American is the duty and responsibility of the State, but securing them is the task of the Negro; it is the task of Labor and the progressive and liberal forces of the nation. Freedom is never given; it is won. And the Negro people must win their freedom. They must achieve justice. This involves struggle, continuous struggle.

True liberation can be acquired and maintained only when the Negro people possess power; and power is the product and flower of organization—organization of the masses, the masses in the mills and mines, on the farms, in the factories, in churches, in fraternal organizations, in homes, colleges, women's clubs, student groups, trade unions, tenants' leagues, in cooperative guilds, political organizations and civil rights associations.

Organization is the purpose and aim of the Second National Negro Conference. While it does not seek, as its primary program, to organize the Negro People into trade unions and civil rights' movements, it does plan to integrate and coordinate the existing Negro organizations into one federated and collective agency so as to develop greater and more effective power. The Congress does not stress or espouse any political faith or religious creed, but seeks to formulate a minimum political, economic and social program which all Negro groups can endorse and for which they can work and fight.

The Congress supports the fight of the National Association for the Advancement of Colored People for a federal anti-lynching bill, for around this issue there is no basic difference of opinion among Negroes. All Negro people desire and seek fair opportunities for work and the right to join trade unions. No one can object to a proposal for more and better jobs, the abolition of Jim-crow labor unions, and for equal educational chances in public schools and universities.

It may not be amiss to add also, in this connection, that the Congress is not Communist or Republican, Democratic or Socialist. It is not Methodist, Baptist or Christian Scientist. It avoids control by any single religion or political party. It shuns the Scylla and Charybdis of the extreme left and the extreme right. But, in the true spirit of the united front, and in the pattern and purpose of integration and coordination, for mass strength, [it] embraces all sections of opinion among the Negro people. It does not seek to impose any issue of philosophy upon any organization or group, but rather to unite varying and various organizations, with various and varying philosophies, left, center, and right among the Negro people upon a simple, minimum program so as to mobilize and rally power and mass support behind vital issues affecting the life and destiny of the race.

Be it also known that the Congress does not seek to change the American form of government, but rather to implement it with new and rugged morals and spiritual sinews to make its democratic traditions, forms and ideals more permanent and abiding and a living force.

Startling changes, economic, political and social, have come upon the world. The empire of the Kaiser, apparently rock-ribbed and as steadfast as the sun, has been replaced by the totalitarian Third Reich. The Italian democratic state has given way to a corporate, fascist system. And of the Czar, of all the Russias, has been relegated to oblivion by the Soviets of the workers.

And even if the honored democracies of the United States, England and France, have not succumbed and capitulated to the drastic and dangerous pattern of the dictator, they are under constant, menacing stress and strain of tendencies toward the rule of fascist force. Deadlocked, withal, in a mighty struggle for supremacy are the governments by the rule of "The man on horseback" and governments by rule of a free people.

Add to our existing political disorder reflected in the amazing and rapid transformation of the structure and direction of modern governments, economic maladjustments as seen in world-wide chronic and permanent unemployment, monetary fluctuations and industrial instability, the ever rising threat of a widening sweep of the wave of war, then optimism and hope are shattered and replaced by pessimism and fear.

Already, large areas of the world are in the flames of war. The "little brown men" of militaristic Nippon are raining fire and destruction upon the land of Confucius, but the Chinese people, proud in their noble heritage, are defending their country with matchless courage and resolve, yielding no single inch of territory except under the imperative of superior force.

And when we turn our eyes to the West, to the Mediterranean, we witness the vile and vicious efforts of Mussolini and Hitler, in accordance with the terms of a Berlin-Rome axis seeking to encompass by open murder the destruction of democracy. Lulled and solaced in conscience by the non-intervention sham, the democratic nations, England, France and the United States, are observing defenseless women and children of the legitimate Loyalists government of Spain massacred in shocking barbarism by the hoards [hordes] of Franco, backed by the money and men in Italy and Germany. Whither doth it lead, comes the query?

It is well nigh accepted quite generally by the thoughtful peoples everywhere that if the dykes of democracy break in the land of the little Iberian peninsula, a world flood of fascism may not be far behind, and imperil free peoples everywhere.

This may be the tragic price that mankind must pay for its complacent and timid spirit before the brutal and ruthless aggression by Japan upon China in creating the puppet kingdom of Manchukuo, and the cruel and savage invasion of the ancient kingdom of Ethiopia by the fascist legions of Italy. The independence of Ethiopia has been sold down the river by the League of Nations, while winked at by England and France.

And when we return to our shores, we find closer at home that all is not well. Despite signs of some recovery from the depression, unemployment trenches hard upon eight million. Unemployment has taken on the picture of permanency. Production in certain industries increases while the workers decrease. The development of the machine, the refinements in management and the concentration and centralization of economic power in trusts and holding companies make this possible. With grave warning, President Roosevelt has declared that one-third of the population is in ill health, underfed, underhoused and underclothed. Relief needs have not appreciably lessened, for jobs are still scarce for the workers.

Civil rights, in industrial areas, where conflict between labor and capital is on, are arrogantly disregarded and broken down by pliant municipal representatives, and extra-governmental organizations such as the Ku Klux Klan, the Black Legion and other vigilante movements.

But not only are the rights of the workers assailed by vigilante mobs at the behest of the Liberty League and the organized open-shop business interests of America, but in State Legislatures and Congress, die-hard tories, such as Senator Vanderberg [Vandenberg] and others, are seeking to enact legislation, forcing upon trade unions and corporations, compulsory arbitration and the elmination of strikes.

And as we look to Labor we find its house divided. Thus it is obvious that the great problems of the workers in America today is the problem of unity. . . . Craft and industrial unionism can and must go side by side in the struggle of the workers for industrial democracy. These forms of organization must develop and function in one house of labor. Now, what of the Negro in relation to these problems?

The Negro people are an integral part of the American commonwealth. They, like our white brothers, bleed and die in war. They suffer and hunger in depression. Thus, theirs is the task of consolidating their interests with the interest of the progressive forces of the nation. Collective bargaining brings power to black as well as to white workers. The abolition of the company union frees the Negro workers from economic bondage and enables them to express their voice in the determination of wage rates, hours and working conditions the same as it does for white workers. Thus, the strengthening of the labor movement, the improvement of labor standards, brings comfort, health and decency to black as well as to white workers.

But there are other problems that the Negro people face. In the South there is a blight of Jim-crowism, segregation, disfranchisement through grandfather clauses and lily white primaries and the terror of the Ku Klux Klan.

Peonage, a form of involuntary servitude, in utter nullification of the 13th Amendment, holds the Negro in many Southern states in a condition of virtual slavery. Negro tenant farmers are browbeaten, persecuted and driven, when they evince any semblance of independence [,] out of their miserable and squalid shacks onto the highway. Civil and political rights for them are virtually unknown. Differentials in wages and hours of work are a common practice. Relief, though given by the Federal Government is administered by whim of Southern prejudice in the mood of arrogant superiority. What can be done about this? The answer is:

Let us build a united front of all Negro organizations, of varying strata, purpose and outlook. Let us build a united front in cooperation with the progressive and liberal agencies of the nation whose interests are common with Black America.

With the spirit and strategy of the United Front, the five remaining Scottsboro Boys can be released from their dark dungeon in Alabama. With it peonage in the South can be wiped out and the share cropper and tenant farmers, black and white, can organize and improve their economic status through collective bargaining. With it the horror of lynching in America may be eliminated and mob terror relegated to oblivion.

Thus, on the occasion of the 150th Anniversary of the American Constitution, and the Second Anniversary of the National Negro Congress, the Negro peoples face the future, with heads erect and souls uncurbed, resolved to march forward in the van of progress, with hope and faith in the creation of a new and better world. And the Congress shall help to guide them, to lead them on!

What now of the stewardship of the Congress since its memorable bow to black and white America?

Can more be said than that it has fought a good fight? It has kept the faith. It has worked and not grown weary for a happier humanity.

On the far-flung battle lines of steel, it marshalled militant black men to march in the van with the C. I. O. to chalk up an enviable record in bringing workers into the field of industrial organization. And it has worked with the American Federation of Labor. Our men did not fail or faint before blood or bullets—in South Chicago, Detroit, Michigan, Ohio and Pennsylvania.

The Congress has brought eager and aggressive black youth to grapple with the problem of the organization of the tobacco workers in Virginia. And these youth are winning their spurs.

To the laundry workers in Washington, D. C., the Congress is carrying the message of trade union organization. And it enlisted Negro organizers to join C. I. O. forces to organize the automobile industry.

On the civil and political rights' fronts, the Congress joined the fighting forces of the National Association for the Advancement of Colored People, to battle for the Wagner-Gavagan federal anti-lynching bill.

And to the rescue of Herndon and the Scottsboro Boys, the Congress has carried its unflagging fighting spirit.

But not only has it fought in the front for the defense of the rights of the Negro People, the Congress has also thrown its might with the progressive forces in the land to aid in the cause of Spanish Democracy, the independence of China from the domination of Japan, and the restoration of Hailie Selassie to an independent Kingdom of Ethiopia.

Yes it has joined the great demonstration of the nation against war and fascism. And, too, it is stirring the women and youth of the Negro people to join and struggle with the national and world agencies of their groups for a better world.

Therefore, with humble pride we cry out of the depths of our souls to mankind everywhere. Forward with the destruction of the imperialist domination and oppression of the great peoples of Africa! Forward to the abolition of the fascist rule of Italy over the noble independent, and unconquerable men of Ethiopia! Forward to the creation of a united, free and independent China! Forward to victory of the valiant loyalist armies over the fascist brigands of Franco! Long live the cause of World peace! Long live the spirit of world democracy! Long live the memory and love of the Black Revolution of the 18th Century, led by Denmark Vesey, Nat Turner, Gabriel, Harriet Tubman, Sojourner Truth, and Frederick Douglass! Long live the valor of those black regiments of slaves and freedom [freedmen] whose blood and courage made . . . Lincoln's Emancipation Proclamation a living reality!

Forward to the unity of the workers! Forward to democracy and freedom, progress and plenty! Forward with the torch of Education, the instrument of agitation, the weapon of organization to a day of peace on earth and toward men, good will!

28. WILLIAM H. HASTIE
SUMS UP THE EXPANDED NAACP PROGRAM

In 1939 the keynote address at the annual conference of the NAACP was given by William H. Hastie, dean of Howard University Law School, and a former judge in the Virgin Islands (who subsequently

William H. Hastie, "A Look at the NAACP," THE CRISIS, XLVI, 9 (September 1939), 236–264, 274. Reprinted with the permission of THE CRISIS.

had a varied career as a civilian aide to the Secretary of War, as Governor of the Virgin Islands, and as the first Negro appointed to a federal circuit court). Hastie, one of the group on the NAACP's national board who felt that the Association was remiss in failing to promote the economic interests of the masses, expressed the belief, widespread among intellectuals, that the advancement of the race lay in cooperation with underprivileged whites for fundamental social reform. His address also described the scope of the NAACP program during the 1930s, particularly its concern with the economic programs of the New Deal, the struggle for the ballot, and the beginnings of the litigation against southern school segregation. As this selection indicates, the NAACP, while broadening its activities to encompass economic issues, continued to emphasize the fight against disfranchisement and segregation.

It was in 1930 that the late Joel E. Spingarn became president of the National Association for the Advancement of Colored People. In that very year and through the agency of this Association, America was made to realize that, after a long lapse following the Reconstruction, the Negro again had become a powerful and an important figure in national politics. The dramatic occasion for that demonstration was the battle in the United States Senate against the confirmation of Judge John J. Parker, President Hoover's nominee to become a Justice of the Supreme Court. The National Association and the American Federation of Labor waged that fight against the full power of a national administration; and they won it. That victory and the subsequent defeat of Senators who had voted to confirm the Parker nomination probably impressed the nation more than any other thing accomplished by the American Negro during the 20th century. For years to come it will remain fresh and persuasive in the minds of politicians and all aspirants to Federal office.

Less sensational, but no less significant was the grant of a sum of money to the NAACP in 1930 for an offensive against specific types of discrimination.[1] That grant was followed by a decision

[1] The grant was made by the American Fund for Public Service, otherwise known as the Garland Fund [Ed.].

to devote a large part of the fund and an increasing portion of the energies of the national staff to a frontal assault upon discrimination in public education. This was the beginning of a campaign which already has made possible the epochal court decisions in the University of Maryland case and the University of Missouri case, and actively manifests itself today from Maryland and Virginia to Florida in the demands of Negro teachers that salary discriminations be abolished.

The year 1930 also marked another change in leadership. Walter White succeeded James Weldon Johnson as secretary....

Apart from the Parker fight, the beginning of the campaign against educational inequalities, and changes in leadership, the activities of the Association as it entered its third decade were such as already had come to be recognized as typical of the NAACP. The Association stood as a great watch dog, alert and ready to defend against particular instances of discrimination suffered by Negroes in the unpredictable course of human events. Unfair trials of Negroes in court, new residential restrictions, . . . serious racial affronts and insults of all kinds were the concern of the national office and local branches.

The program of the Association has expanded in one direction that was not anticipated in 1930. Since 1932 the Federal Government has entered into the economic life of the nation and has undertaken to perform social services to an extent and over an area much larger than could possibly have been foreseen. Federal policies could and can contribute largely to the improving of the disadvantaged status of labor generally and to the lessening of discrimination against Negro labor in particular. Racial attitudes reflected in Government-financed enterprises of various types are potentially significant for the modification of the pattern of American life.

In this situation the Association joined other national organizations in forming and supporting the Joint Committee on National Recovery to work in Washington and in the field for such objectives as have just been suggested. In addition the Association has worked from the beginning to remedy discriminatory practices in Government-financed enterprises. As early as 1932 the NAACP waged a successful fight to substitute reasonable wages, hours and living conditions for the semi-slavery of labor on the Mississippi Flood Control projects of the War Department. Since the beginning of the Roosevelt Administration the countless projects of PWA and WPA, large enterprises like TVA, such important legislation as the Wagner Labor Relations Act and the more recent Fair Labor Standards Act have presented problems of a variety and complexity that cannot even be outlined here. . . . the efforts of the NAACP have been effective in remedying abuses in particular cases and in influencing administrative policy to some degree. But limitations of time, money and personnel have prevented a continuing organized program in this field. . . . Until the Association is able to maintain a staff in Washington, working continuously upon such problems, feeding information to the branches, stimulating and assisting their local activities and in turn receiving their support when pressure is necessary on matters of general policy in Washington, much important work must remain undone.

Many persons believe that the struggle for the ballot is the most important phase of the Negro's effort to improve his status in America. Certainly, there is no more trenchant weapon than the ballot in such a nation as ours. During the 1930s the Association has scored notable victories in the campaign for the ballot. The conviction and fining of an election official in Wilkesboro, North Carolina, for refusing to register qualified Negro voters has influenced election officials in North Carolina and wherever else news of this conviction has spread.

The recent successful attack upon the Oklahoma registration law points the way to the removal of other obvious legislative devices for the disenfranchisement of the Negro. Within the last year in at least one large urban community Negroes have defied and overcome the cruder methods of terrorization and intimidation employed to keep them away from the polls. All of these lines of advance can and will lead to new victories in the years immediately ahead.

The most promising aspect of the picture is the increasing interest of particular communities in the ballot and the organized insistence of Negroes that they be permitted to vote. It is no secret that the working people of the South have long been un-represented and misrepresented by a great number of elected officials both at home and in Washington. If the drive of the Negro for the ballot can be allied with the growing interest of all southern toilers in the ballot and the interest of all can be focused upon the election of officials who represent working class interests, a fundamental solution of the suffrage problem will not be far off. . . .

Probably the struggle of the NAACP against educational dis-advantages in the South has attracted more attention during the past ten years than any phase of its activities. We have seen in-terest in the struggle increase and spread throughout the South. We have seen a few sensational victories in the courts.

Now we stand at a point where the South must take a fresh look at public education from the nursery school and the kinder-garten to the graduate school and the university, and determine whether it will move toward the abolition of discriminations all along the line, whether it will soberly take stock and realize that sooner or later the cost of separate education will become prohibitive. It will be sooner at the university and graduate level where the number of students is smaller and the corresponding waste of the dual system is greater.

In this connection it may well be asked why we should an-ticipate that anything substantial will be done after the excite-ment of a few sensational court cases has worn off. Almost all of the principles of law involved in the fight for equality in pub-lic education were announced by the Supreme Court fifty years ago. Yet, . . . the southern states have pursued a policy of in-creasing the disparity between white and Negro education, rather than decreasing it.

In such circumstances why should we anticipate at this late date a real effort to comply with the law of the land? And why should we believe that attempted evasions will be less successful in the future than they have been in the past?

There is developing in the South a body of public opinion which, although not often strong enough or bold enough to take the initiative against the order long established and entrenched behind inbred and traditional racial attitudes, is able to play a large part in achieving public acceptance of changes ordained by the courts or other public authority. The liberal press is urging the fairness of equalizing the salaries of white and colored teachers. College students are debating the question of admitting colored applicants to state universities. Such are the external evidences of the leaven that is working in the white south.

Thus, it is reasonable to anticipate that there will be an increasing number of cases in which state legislatures and educators will attempt in good faith to remove particular educational inequalities. In the majority of cases, however, Negroes will continue to be confronted with the attitude of the head of a southern state university who admitted that the law was clearly against him yet stated flatly that every application of a colored student for admission to his institution would have to be carried to the court of last resort before he would admit the applicant.

Against such resistance there will be arrayed the aggressiveness and militancy of more Negroes throughout the South than those who still hear the guns of Shiloh and see the spectre of the Reconstruction care to think about. It is symptomatic of a change rapidly taking place in the Negro community that while the state association of Negro teachers in North Carolina would not appropriate one penny out of its well-filled treasury to fight in the courts for equal salaries in 1933, five years later the colored teachers of Virginia not only appropriated money from their treasury for that purpose but also imposed a tax upon themselves to raise additional funds.

Another factor should serve to cause state school officials to hesitate before ignoring or defying plain requirements of law. A Federal statute makes the denial of rights guaranteed by the Constitution of the United States a criminal offense, punishable by fine and imprisonment. Prosecutions under that law are possible. A very small number of convictions and sentences would have substantial effect upon every public officer who should thereafter be called upon to grant the claim of a Negro to an educational privilege by the Constitution. . . .

The South is poor. Its educational facilities generally are woefully inadequate, not because of failure to spend a reasonable percentage of the public revenue upon public schools but because the total public income is so small. This situation is not improving. Hence, not only prejudice but poverty as well will continue to impede large scale improvements in education for Negroes. Yet, individual counties have found a way to equalize teachers' salaries. . . . But in the long run the south is bound to realize that it cannot afford the luxury of separate schools. The dual system is bound to break down. Its collapse will begin at the top, in the universities and graduate schools.

I have said nothing about the efforts of the Association to combat segregation and discrimination in public places and in access to miscellaneous public advantages, or its great struggle against lynching. During the past twenty or thirty years people in and out of the Association have come to regard such efforts as "NAACP work." By public agitation, political pressure and the advocacy of remedial legislation many new impositions have been blocked and some embrasures have been made in walls long standing. Power to discriminate against the Negro and to subject him to mob violence will continue to be vested in white America for an indefinite period. That power will be exercised so long as there is a strong community will to do so. Such ill will is bound to exist so long as the prevailing attitude toward the Negro is an amalgam of aversion with a belief that the Negro is innately inferior in ability and character. . . .

Thus, while we continue our efforts to arrest the manifestations of race prejudice in our communities, we must always strive toward the elimination of its causes. More and more people are becoming convinced that the most effective technic for dealing with prejudice is a diverting of minds to more important matters. Historically, we know that race prejudice has been a device serving to divert the attention of the South from its suffering. . . . Conversely, there is every reason to believe that the concentration of millions who suffer common disadvantages upon methods of bettering conditions under which all suffer will be the most effective way of subordinating race prejudice and ultimately causing men to realize how unimportant race really is. Labor exploitation, political misrepresentation, neglect of all types of responsibility of organized society for social services to its disadvantaged members—these are some of the evils which white and black may feel separately but not as unequally as we sometimes think.

Every time a branch of the NAACP can combine a demand of disadvantaged Negroes with a demand of disadvantaged whites, whether at the polls, or through labor organization, or through protest and demonstration, or through any other technic of joint action, that branch will have done something immediately useful and also significant in its implications for a future that will be significantly better than the present.

It should not be long before branches of the NAACP are reporting and emphasizing such achievements at their annual conferences. Indeed, while the defensive strategy of the Association nationally and locally, must still be directed largely at racial disadvantages, offensive strategy, the sustained and sustaining program of the organization, must increasingly emphasize and embody the recognition of common interests across the color line and the making of common cause by all working people. If to many branches this means reorientation as well as expansion of program, then such reorientation and such expansion should not be delayed.

World War II: tactics new and old

29. A. PHILIP RANDOLPH CALLS FOR A MARCH ON WASHINGTON

A. Philip Randolph, concerned about the discrimination against black workers in the expanding defense industries, proposed a mass march of Negroes to Washington in 1941 to petition for racial integration in the armed services and equal opportunities in employment. The white press ignored the proposal, and the leading black-advancement groups were at first skeptical. But enthusiastic support for the March on Washington Movement developed through publicity in the black press. President Franklin D. Roosevelt bowed to this pressure, and in June 1941 he issued an order creating a Fair Employment Practices Committee. Randolph called off the march but tried to keep the movement intact.

The Call for the March was a stirring document, urging a "thundering march on Washington" that would "shake up white America." Randolph's address to the conference of the March on Washington Movement in September 1942, proposed that nonviolent direct action be used to combat other forms of discrimination, and suggested the affinities between the movement's technique of mass action and Gandhi's nonviolent movement in India. This speech, in which Randolph set forth the ideology behind his organization, prefigured in many ways the direct-action movement of the 1960s.

Both documents exemplify Randolph's view that white participation in the March on Washington Movement was neither necessary nor desirable, that Negroes should take the lead in their fight for freedom, and that the black masses had the power to bring about their own liberation.

A. Call to the March

July 1, 1941

We call upon you to fight for jobs in National Defense.

We call upon you to struggle for the integration of Negroes in the armed forces, such as the Air Corps, Navy, Army and Marine Corps of the Nation.

We call upon you to demonstrate for the abolition of Jim-Crowism in all Government departments and defense employment.

This is an hour of crisis. It is a crisis of democracy. It is a crisis of minority groups. It is a crisis of Negro Americans.

What is this crisis?

To American Negroes, it is the denial of jobs in Government defense projects. It is racial discrimination in Government departments. It is widespread Jim-Crowism in the armed forces of the Nation.

While billions of the taxpayers' money are being spent for war weapons, Negro workers are being turned away from the gates of factories, mines and mills—being flatly told, "NOTHING DOING." Some employers refuse to give Negroes jobs when they are without "union cards," and some unions refuse Negro workers union cards when they are "without jobs."

What shall we do?

What a dilemma!

What a runaround!

What a disgrace!

What a blow below the belt!

'Though dark, doubtful and discouraging, all is not lost, all is not hopeless. 'Though battered and bruised, we are not beaten, broken or bewildered.

Verily, the Negroes' deepest disappointments and direst defeats, their tragic trials and outrageous oppressions in these

From THE BLACK WORKER, May 1941.

dreadful days of destruction and disaster to democracy and freedom, and the rights of minority peoples, and the dignity and independence of the human spirit, is the Negroes' greatest opportunity to rise to the highest heights of struggle for freedom and justice in Government, in industry, in labor unions, education, social service, religion and culture.

With faith and confidence of the Negro people in their own power for self-liberation, Negroes can break down the barriers of discrimination against employment in National Defense. Negroes can kill the deadly serpent of race hatred in the Army, Navy, Air and Marine Corps, and smash through and blast the Government, business and labor-union red tape to win the right to equal opportunity in vocational training and re-training in defense employment.

Most important and vital to all, Negroes, by the mobilization and coordination of their mass power, can cause PRESIDENT ROOSEVELT TO ISSUE AN EXECUTIVE ORDER ABOLISHING DISCRIMINATIONS IN ALL GOVERNMENT DEPARTMENTS, ARMY, NAVY, AIR CORPS AND NATIONAL DEFENSE JOBS.

Of course, the task is not easy. In very truth, it is big, tremendous and difficult.

It will cost money.

It will require sacrifice.

It will tax the Negroes' courage, determination and will to struggle. But we can, must and will triumph.

The Negroes' stake in national defense is big. It consists of jobs, thousands of jobs. It may represent millions, yes, hundreds of millions of dollars in wages. It consists of new industrial opportunities and hope. This is worth fighting for.

But to win our stakes, it will require an "all-out," bold and total effort and demonstration of colossal proportions.

Negroes can build a mammoth machine of mass action with a terrific and tremendous driving and striking power that can shatter and crush the evil fortress of race prejudice and hate, if they will only resolve to do so and never stop, until victory comes.

Dear fellow Negro Americans, be not dismayed in these terrible times. You possess power, great power. Our problem is to harness and hitch it up for action on the broadest, daring and most gigantic scale.

In this period of power politics, nothing counts but pressure, more pressure, and still more pressure, through the tactic and strategy of broad, organized, aggressive mass action behind the vital and important issues of the Negro. To this end, we propose that ten thousand Negroes MARCH ON WASHINGTON FOR JOBS IN NATIONAL DEFENSE AND EQUAL INTEGRATION IN THE FIGHTING FORCES OF THE UNITED STATES.

An "all-out" thundering march on Washington, ending in a monster and huge demonstration at Lincoln's Monument will shake up white America.

It will shake up official Washington.

It will give encouragement to our white friends to fight all the harder by our side, with us, for our righteous cause.

It will gain respect for the Negro people.

It will create a new sense of self-respect among Negroes.

But what of national unity?

We believe in national unity which recognizes equal opportunity of black and white citizens to jobs in national defense and the armed forces, and in all other institutions and endeavors in America. We condemn all dictatorships, Fascist, Nazi and Communist. We are loyal, patriotic Americans, all.

But, if American democracy will not defend its defenders; if American democracy will not protect its protectors; if American democracy will not give jobs to its toilers because of race or color; if American democracy will not insure equality of opportunity, freedom and justice to its citizens, black and white, it is a hollow mockery and belies the principles for which it is supposed to stand.

To the hard, difficult and trying problem of securing equal participation in national defense, we summon all Negro Americans to march on Washington. We summon Negro Americans to form committees in various cities to recruit and register marchers and raise funds through the sale of buttons and other legitimate means for the expenses of marchers to Washington by buses, train, private automobiles, trucks, and on foot.

We summon Negro Americans to stage marches on their City Halls and Councils in their respective cities and urge them to memorialize the President to issue an executive order to abolish discrimination in the Government and national defense.

However, we sternly counsel against violence and ill-considered and intemperate action and the abuse of power. Mass power, like physical power, when misdirected is more harmful than helpful.

We summon you to mass action that is orderly and lawful, but aggressive and militant, for justice, equality and freedom.

Crispus Attucks marched and died as a martyr for American independence. Nat Turner, Denmark Vesey, Gabriel Prosser, Harriet Tubman and Frederick Douglass fought, bled and died for the emancipation of Negro slaves and the preservation of American democracy.

Abraham Lincoln, in times of the grave emergency of the Civil War, issued the Proclamation of Emancipation for the freedom of Negro slaves and the preservation of American democracy.

Today, we call upon President Roosevelt, a great humanitarian and idealist, to follow in the footsteps of his noble and illustrious predecessor and take the second decisive step in this world and national emergency and free American Negro citizens of the stigma, humiliation and insult of discrimination and Jim-Crowism in Government departments and national defense.

The Federal Government cannot with clear conscience call upon private industry and labor unions to abolish discrimination based upon race and color as long as it practices discrimination itself against Negro Americans.

B. Address to the Policy Conference

Fellow Marchers and delegates to the Policy Conference of the March on Washington Movement and Friends:

A. Philip Randolph, "Keynote Address to the Policy Conference of the March on Washington Movement," in MARCH ON WASHINGTON MOVEMENT: PROCEEDINGS OF CONFERENCE HELD IN DETROIT, SEPTEMBER 26–27, 1942 (no imprint), pp. 4–11.

We have met at an hour when the sinister shadows of war are lengthening and becoming more threatening. As one of the sections of the oppressed darker races, and representing a part of the exploited millions of the workers of the world, we are deeply concerned that the totalitarian legions of Hitler, Hirohito, and Mussolini do not batter the last bastions of democracy. We know that our fate is tied up with the fate of the democratic way of life. And so, out of the depth of our hearts, a cry goes up for the triumph of the United Nations. But we would not be honest with ourselves were we to stop with a call for a victory of arms alone. We know that this is not enough. We fight that the democratic faiths, values, heritages and ideals may prevail.

Unless this war sounds the death knell to the old Anglo-American empire systems, the hapless story of which is one of exploitation for the profit and power of a monopoly capitalist economy, it will have been fought in vain. Our aim then must not only be to defeat nazism, fascism, and militarism on the battlefield but to win the peace, for democracy, for freedom and the Brotherhood of Man without regard to his pigmentation, land of his birth or the God of his fathers. . . .

When this war ends, the people want something more than the dispersal of equality and power among individual citizens in a liberal, political democratic system. They demand with striking comparability the dispersal of equality and power among the citizen-workers in an economic democracy that will make certain the assurance of the good life—the more abundant life—in a warless world.

But, withal this condition of freedom, equality and democracy is not the gift of the Gods. It is the task of men, yes, men, brave men, honest men, determined men. . . .

Thus our feet are set in the path toward [the long-range goal of] equality—economic, political and social and racial. Equality is the heart and essence of democracy, freedom and justice. Without equality of opportunity in industry, in labor unions, schools and colleges, government, politics and before the law, without equality in social relations and in all phases of human endeavor, the Negro is certain to be consigned to an inferior status. There must be no dual standards of justice, no dual rights privileges, duties or responsibilities of citizenship. No dual forms of freedom. . . .

But our nearer goals include the abolition of discrimination, segregation, and jim-crow in the Government, the Army, Navy, Air Corps, U. S. Marine Corps, Coast Guard, Women's Auxiliary Army Corps and the Waves, and defense industries; the elimination of discriminations in hotels, restaurants, on public transportation conveyances, in educational, recreational, cultural, and amusement and entertainment places such as theatres, beaches and so forth.

We want the full works of citizenship with no reservations. We will accept nothing less.

But goals must be achieved. They are not secured because it is just and right that they be possessed by Negro or white people. Slavery was not abolished because it was bad and unjust. It was abolished because men fought, bled and died on the battlefield.

Therefore, if Negroes secure their goals, immediate and remote, they must win them and to win them they must fight, sacrifice, suffer, go to jail and, if need be, die for them. These rights will not be given. They must be taken.

Democracy was fought for and taken from political royalists —the kings. Industrial democracy, the rights of the workers to organize and designate the representatives of their own choosing to bargain collectively is being won and taken from the economic royalists—big business.

Now the realization of goals and rights by a nation, race or class requires belief in and loyalty to principles and policies. . . . Policies rest upon principles. Concretely a policy sets forth one's position on vital public questions such as political affiliations, religious alliances. The March on Washington Movement must be opposed to partisan political commitments, religious or denominational alliances. We cannot sup with the Communists, for they rule or ruin any movement. This is their policy. Our policy must be to shun them. This does not mean that Negro Communists may not join the March on Washington Movement.

As to the composition of our movement. Our policy is that it be all-Negro, and pro-Negro but not anti-white, or anti-semitic or anti-labor, or anti-Catholic. The reason for this policy is that all oppressed people must assume the responsibility and take the initiative to free themselves. Jews must wage their battle to abolish anti-semitism. Catholics must wage their battle to abolish anti-catholicism. The workers must wage their battle to advance and protect their interests and rights.

But this does not mean that because Jews must take the responsibility and initiative to solve their own problems that they should not seek the cooperation and support of Gentiles, or that Catholics should not seek the support of Negroes, or that the workers should not attempt to enlist the backing of Jews, Catholics, and Negroes in their fight to win a strike; but the main reliance must be upon the workers themselves. By the same token because Negroes build an all-Negro movement such as the March, it does not follow that our movement should not call for the collaboration of Jews, Catholics, Trade unions and white liberals to help restore the President's Fair Employment Practice Committee to its original status of independence, with responsibility to the President. That was done. William Green, President of the A. F. of L. and Philip Murray, President of C. I. O. were called upon to send telegrams to the President to restore the Committee to its independence. Both responded. Their cooperation had its effects. Workers have formed citizens committees to back them while on strike, but this does not mean that they take those citizens into their unions as members. No, not at all.

And while the March on Washington Movement may find it advisable to form a citizens committee of friendly white citizens to give moral support to a fight against the Poll tax or white primaries, it does not imply that these white citizens or citizens of any racial group should be taken into the March on Washington Movement as members. The essential value of an all-Negro movement such as the March on Washington is that it helps to create faith by Negroes in Negroes. It develops a sense of self-reliance with Negroes depending on Negroes in vital matters. It helps to break down the slave psychology and inferiority-complex in Negroes which comes and is nourished with Negroes relying on white people for direction and support. This inevitably happens in mixed organizations that are supposed to be in the interest of the Negro. . . .

Therefore, while the March on Washington Movement is interested in the general problems of every community and will lend its aid to help solve them, it has as its major interest and task the liberation of the Negro people, and this is sound social economy. It is in conformity with the principle of the division of labor. No organization can do everything. Every organization can do something, and each organization is charged with the social responsibility to do that which it can do, it is built to do.

I have given quite some time to the discussion of this question of organizational structure and function and composition, because the March on Washington Movement is a mass movement of Negroes which is being built to achieve a definite objective, and is a departure from the usual pattern of Negro efforts and thinking. As a rule, Negroes do not choose to be to themselves in anything, they are only to themselves as a result of compulsive segregation. Negroes are together voluntarily for the same reason workers join voluntarily into a trade union. But because workers only join trade unions, does not mean that the very same workers may not join organizations composed of some non-workers, such as art museums or churches or fraternal lodges that have varying purposes. This same thing is true of Negroes. Because Negroes only can join the March on Washington Movement, does not indicate that Negroes in the M.O.W.M. may not join an inter-racial golf club or church or Elks Lodge or debating society or trade union.

No one would claim that a society of Filipinos is undemocratic because it does not take in Japanese members, or that Catholics are anti-Jewish because the Jesuits won't accept Jews as members or that trade unions are illiberal because they deny membership to employers. Neither is the March on Washington Movement undemocratic because it confines its members to Negroes. Now this reasoning would not apply to a public school or a Pullman Car because these agencies are public in nature and provide a service that is necessary to all of the people of a community.

Now, the question of policy which I have been discussing involves, for example, the March on Washington Movement's position on the war. We say that the Negro must fight for his democratic rights now for after the war it may be too late. This is our policy on the Negro and the war. But this policy raises the question of method, programs, strategy, and tactics; namely, how is this to be done. It is not sufficient to say that Negroes must fight for their rights now, during the war. Some methods must be devised, program set up, and strategy outlined.

This Policy Conference is designed to do this very thing. The first requirement to executing the policies of the March on Washington Movement is to have something to execute them with. This brings me to the consideration of organization. Organization supplies the power. The formulation of policies and the planning process furnish direction. Now there is organization and organization. Some people say, for instance, Negroes are already organized and they cite, The Sisters of the Mysterious Ten, The Sons and Daughters of I Will Arise, the Holy Rollers, the social clubs, and so forth. But these organizations are concerned about the individual interest of helping the sick and funeralizing the dead or providing amusement and recreation. They deal with no social or racial problem which concerns the entire people. The Negro people as a whole is not interested in whether Miss A. plays Contract Bridge on Friday or not, or whether the deacon of the Methodist Church has a 200 or 500 dollar casket when he dies. These are personal questions. But the Negro race is concerned about Negroes being refused jobs in defense plants, or whether a Negro can purchase a lower in a Pullman Car, or whether the U.S. Treasury segregates Negro girls. Thus, while it is true Negroes are highly organized, the organizations are not built to deal with and manipulate the mechanics of power. Nobody cares how many Whist Clubs or churches or secret lodges Negroes establish because they are not compulsive or coercive. They don't seek to transform the socio-economic racial milieu. They accept and do not challenge conditions with an action program.

Hence, it is apparent that the Negro needs more than organization. He needs mass organization with an action program, aggressive, bold and challenging in spirit. Such a movement is our March on Washington.

Our first job then is actually to organize millions of Negroes, and build them into block systems with captains so that they may be summoned to action over night and thrown into physical motion. Without this type of organization, Negroes will never develop mass power which is the most effective weapon a minority people can wield. Witness the strategy and maneuver of the people of India with mass civil disobedience and non-co-operation and the marches to the sea to make salt. It may be said that the Indian people have not won their freedom. This is so, but they will win it. The central principle of the struggle of oppressed minorities like the Negro, labor, Jews, and others is not only to develop mass demonstration maneuvers, but to repeat and continue them. The workers don't picket firms today and quit. They don't strike today and fold up. They practice the principle of repetition. . .

We must develop huge demonstrations because the world is used to big dramatic affairs. . . . Besides, the unusual attracts. We must develop a series of marches of Negroes at a given time in a hundred or more cities throughout the country, or stage a big march of a hundred thousand Negroes on Washington to put our cause into the main stream of public opinion and focus the attention of world interests. This is why India is in the news.

Therefore, our program is in part as follows:

1. A national conference for the integration and expression of the collective mind and will of the Negro masses.

2. The mobilization and proclamation of a nation-wide series of mass marches on the City-Halls and City Councils to awaken the Negro masses and center public attention upon the grievances and goals of the Negro people and serve as training and discipline of the Negro masses for the more strenuous struggle of a March on Washington, if, as, and when an affirmative decision is made thereon by the Negro masses of the country through our national conference.

3. A march on Washington as an evidence to white America

that black America is on the march for its rights and means business.

4. The picketing of the White House following the March on Washington and maintain the said picket line until the country and the world recognize the Negro has become of age and will sacrifice his all to be counted as men, free men.

This program is drastic and exacting. It will test our best mettle and stamina and courage. Let me warn you that in these times of storm and stress, this program will be opposed. Our Movement therefore must be well-knit together. It must have moral and spiritual vision, understanding, and wisdom.

How can we achieve this?

Our Movement must be blue-printed. Our forces must be marshalled with block captains to provide immediate and constant contact. Our block captains must hold periodic meetings for their blocks to develop initiative and the capacity to make decisions and move in relation to direction from the central organization of the Division.

Our educational program must be developed around the struggle of the Negro masses.

This can be done by developing mass plans to secure mass registration of the Negro people for the primaries and elections. Through this program the Negro masses can be given a practical and pragmatic view of the mechanics and function of our government and the significance of mass political pressure.

Plans should be mapped by the various divisions to fight for Negro integration in the public utilities as motormen and conductors. During the war women may be placed on these jobs. We must make a drive now to see to it that Negro men and women receive their appropriate consideration in every important field of American industry from which Negroes are now generally barred.

Our day to day exercise of our Civil rights is a constant challenge. In theatres, hotels, restaurants, amusement places, even in the North now there is discrimination against Negroes. This is true in every large city. Negroes have the moral obligation to demand the right to enjoy and make use of their civil and political privileges. If we don't, we will lose the will to fight for our citizenship rights, and the public will consider that we don't want them and should not have them. This fight to break down these barriers in every city should be carefully and painstakingly organized. By fighting for these civil rights the Negro masses will be disciplined in struggle. Some of us will be put in jail and court battles may ensue but this will give the Negro masses a sense of their importance and value as citizens and as fighters in the Negro liberation movement and the cause for democracy as a whole. It will make white people in high places and the ordinary white man understand that Negroes have rights that they are bound to respect.

The giant public protest meetings must continue. They are educative and give moral strength to our movement and the Negro masses.

For this task we need men and women who will dedicate and consecrate their life, spirit, mind, and soul to the great adventure of Negro freedom and justice.

Our divisions must serve as Negro mass parliaments where the entire community may debate the day to day issues such as police brutality, high rents, and other questions and make judgments and take action in the interest of the community. These divisions should hold meetings at least twice a month. In them every Negro should be made to feel his importance as a factor in the Negro liberation movement. We must have every Negro realize his leadership ability, the educated and uneducated, the poor and wealthy. In the March on Washington Movement the highest is as low as the lowest and the lowest is as high as the highest. Numbers in mass formation is our key, directed, of course, by the collective intelligence of the people.

Let us put our weight behind the fight to abolish the Poll tax. This will give the black and white workers of the South new hope. But the Negro people are not the only oppressed section of mankind. India is now waging a world shaking, history making fight for independence. India's fight is the Negro's fight.

Now, let us be unafraid. We are fighting for big stakes. Our stakes are liberty, justice, and democracy. Every Negro should hang his head in shame who fails to do his part now for freedom. This is the hour of the Negro. It is the hour of the common man. May we rise to the challenge to struggle for our rights. Come what will or may, let us never falter.

30. BAYARD RUSTIN:
". . . A WORKABLE AND CHRISTIAN TECHNIQUE FOR THE RIGHTING OF INJUSTICE"

The Congress of Racial Equality (CORE) was initiated in Chicago in the spring of 1942 by a small band of active members of the Fellowship of Reconciliation (FOR), a Christian pacifist organization established during World War I. They belonged to a wing within the Fellowship intensely interested in social action who wished to apply Gandhian techniques of nonviolent direct action to the resolution of racial and industrial conflict in the United States. The FOR was chiefly white, but it numbered several blacks among its officials, even in the South, and had clearly exhibited a concern about race relations.

One of the early CORE leaders was Bayard Rustin, an FOR youth secretary in 1942 when the selection below was written. As this essay indicates, for him and his associates, a massive nonviolent direct action campaign along Gandhian lines was the only alternative to futile Negro retaliatory violence on the one hand, and to the gradualist policies of the traditional racial advancement organizations—the NAACP and the Urban League—on the other.

Since the United States entered the war white-Negro tension has increased steadily. Even in normal times changes in the social and economic patterns cause fear and frustration, which in

Bayard Rustin, "The Negro and Non-Violence," FELLOWSHIP, VIII (October 1942), pp. 166–167.

turn lead to aggression. In time of war the general social condition is fertile soil for the development of hate and fear, and transference of these to minority groups is quite simple.

Organized violence is growing North and South. The Ku Klux Klan is "riding again," employing more subtle methods.

Negroes and whites in southern iron ore mines, as well as in Mobile, Alabama, shipyards, are going armed to work.

Negro soldiers often are forced to wait at Jim-Crow ticket windows, while whites are being served, until buses and trains have gone. Often bus drivers refuse to pick up any Negroes until all whites are seated, sometimes causing them hours' delay. Scores of Negroes have been beaten and arrested in Memphis, Tennessee; Beaumont, Texas; Columbia, Georgia; and Jackson, Mississippi, for insisting on transportation on buses overcrowded because of war conditions. Beaumont has threatened severe punishment for violation of Jim-Crow bus laws.

There have been numerous "wild cat" strikes both North and South where white employees refuse to work with Negroes. Several white and Negro C.I.O. officials have been attacked, and one twice assaulted by white workers for trying to get Negroes jobs.

There have been Negro soldiers and civilians killed by whites. On June 27, Walter Gunn, of Macon County, Alabama, wanted on a charge of drunkenness, was shot in the leg, stripped of his clothes, and beaten to death by a deputy sheriff in the presence of Gunn's wife and children. A similar police brutality occurred on the streets of New York City when a liquor-dazed young Negro was killed for refusing to remove his hand from his pocket.

A soldier was shot in the streets of Little Rock, Arkansas, because he refused to tip his hat to a local policeman and address him as "sir."

The world-famous singer, Roland Hayes, was beaten and jailed because his wife, who had taken a seat a "few yards forward" in a Georgia shoe store, insisted upon being served "where she was" or trading elsewhere.

On July 28 two Texas police, Clyde and Billy Brown, forced Charles Reco, a Negro soldier, into the back seat of a police car and shot him, once in the shoulder and once in the arm, during the ride to the police station because in a Beaumont bus he took a vacant seat reserved for a white.

Racial feeling has increased since June, 1942, when the Fair Employment Practices Committee began hearings on anti-Negro discrimination in Birmingham, Alabama. It has been fed by the anti-Negro propaganda stirred up by Governor Dixon of Alabama, Governor Talmadge of Georgia, and Representative John Rankin of Mississippi. This propaganda has encouraged such minor politicians as Horace C. Wilkinson, who has suggested developing a "League of White Supremacy" to make sure "that this menace to our national security and our local way of life will disappear rapidly."

Governor Dixon, in refusing to sign a Government war contract because it contained a non-discrimination clause, said: "I will not permit the citizens of Alabama to be subject to the whims of any Federal Committee and I will not permit the employees of the State to be placed in the position where they must abandon the principles of segregation or lose their jobs."

Following this letter, Alabama's Senator John Bankhead wrote General Marshall, Army Chief of Staff, demanding that no Negro soldiers be brought South for military training.

The effect on Negroes

These and other humiliations have had a very marked effect on great masses of Negroes, who are being told by the press "that equality of opportunity and social and political recognition will come *now or never*, violently or nonviolently." The Pittsburgh *Courier* and the *People's Voice*, typical of the general Negro press, initiators of the double victory campaign (victory at home and victory abroad), constantly remind the masses that greater economic and political democracy were supposed to have followed the last war. Instead, they pointed out, the

Negro found himself the scapegoat, "last hired and first fired," in a period of economic and social maladjustment that has lasted until the present time. Thus the average Negro is told "there can be no delay. What achievement there will be, must come now."

An increasingly militant group has in mind to demand now, with violence if necessary, the rights it has long been denied. "If we must die abroad for democracy we can't have," I heard a friend of mine say, "then we might as well die right here fighting for our rights."

This is a tragic statement. It is tragic also how isolated the average Negro feels in his struggle. The average Negro has largely lost faith in middle-class whites. In his hour of need he seeks not "talk" but dynamic action. He looks upon the middle-class idea of long-term educational and cultural changes with fear and mistrust. He is interested only in what can be achieved immediately by political pressure to get jobs, decent housing, and education for his children. He describes with disgust the efforts on his behalf by most middle-class Negro and white intellectuals as "pink tea methods—sometimes well-meanin' but gettin' us nowhere." It is for this reason, in part, that the March on Washington Movement, aiming to become a mass movement, has tended to "black nationalism." Its leadership, originally well-motivated, now rejects the idea of including whites in constituency or leadership. One local official said: "These are Negroes' problems and Negroes will have to work them out."

The March on Washington Movement is growing, but at best is only a partial answer to the present need. While the movement already exerts some real political pressure (President Roosevelt set up the F.E.P.C. at its request), it has no program, educational or otherwise, for meeting immediate conflict. To demand rights but not to see the potential danger in such a course, or the responsibility to develop a means of meeting that danger, seems tragic.

There are many Negroes who see mass violence coming. Having lived in a society in which church, school, and home problems have been handled in a violent way, the majority at this point are unable to conceive of a solution by reconciliation and non-violence. Thus, I have seen school boys in Arkansas laying away rusty guns for the time "when." I have heard many young men in the armed forces hope for a machine gun assignment "so I can turn it on the white folks." I have seen a white sailor beaten in Harlem because three Negroes had been "wantin' to get just one white . . ." before they died. I have heard hundreds of Negroes hope for a Japanese military victory since "it don't matter who you're a slave for."

Non-violence for the Negro

These statements come not only from bitterness but from frustration and fear as well. In many parts of America the Negro, in his despair, is willing to follow any leadership seemingly sincerely identified with his struggle if he is convinced that such leadership offers a workable method. Those of us who believe in the non-violent solution of conflict have in this crisis a duty and an opportunity. In all those places where we have a voice it is our high responsibility to indicate that the Negro can attain progress only if he uses, in his struggle, non-violent direct action—a technique consistent with the ends he desires. Especially in this time of tension we must point out the practical necessity of such a course.

Non-violence as a method has within it the demand for terrible sacrifice and long suffering, but, as Gandhi has said, "freedom does not drop from the sky." One has to struggle and be willing to die for it. J. Holmes Smith has indicated that he looks to the American Negro to assist in developing, along with the people of India, a new dynamic force for the solution of conflict that will not merely free these oppressed people, but will set an example that may be the first step in freeing the world.

Certainly the Negro possesses those qualities essential for non-violent direct action. He has long since learned to endure suffering. He can admit his own share of guilt and has to be pushed hard to become bitter. He has produced, and still sings, such songs as "It's Me, Oh Lord, Standin' in the Need of Prayer" and "Nobody Knows the Trouble I've Seen." He follows this last tragic phrase by a salute to God—"Oh! Glory, Hallelujah." He is creative and has learned to adjust himself to conditions easily. But, above all, he possesses a rich religious heritage and today finds the Church the center of his life.

Yet there are those who question the use of non-violent direct action by Negroes in protesting discrimination on the grounds that this method will kindle hitherto dormant racial feeling. But we must remember that too often conflict is already at hand, and that there is hence a greater danger: the inevitable use of force by persons embittered by injustice and unprepared for non-violence. It is a cause for shame that millions of people continue to live under conditions of injustice while we make no effective effort to remedy the situation.

Those who argue for an extended educational plan are not wrong, but there also must be a plan for facing *immediate* conflicts. Those of us who believe in non-violent resistance can do the greatest possible good for the Negro, for those who exploit him, for America, and for the world, by becoming a real part of the Negro community, thus being in a position to suggest method and to offer leadership when troubles come.

Identification with the Negro community demands considerable sacrifices, for the Negro is not to be won by words alone, but by an obvious consistency in words and deeds. The *identified* person is the one who fights side by side with him for justice. This demands being so integral a part of the Negro community in its day-to-day struggle, so close to it in similarity of work and so near its standard of living, that when problems arise, he who stands forth to judge, to plan, to suggest, or to lead, is really one with the Negro masses.

Our war resistance is justified only if we are going to see to it that an adequate alternative to violence is developed. Today, as the Gandhian forces in India face their critical test, we can add to world justice by placing in the hands of thirteen million black Americans a workable and Christian technique for the righting of injustice and the solution of conflict.

31. CORE:
THE PRINCIPLES OF NONVIOLENT
DIRECT ACTION

The original Chicago Committee of Racial Equality in 1942 drew up
a "Statement of Purpose" and an "Action Discipline," setting forth
the principles governing its direct-action demonstrations. When the
Congress of Racial Equality was created a year later, the federated
organization officially adopted both documents. The "Statement of
Purpose" sets forth in simple, terse phrases the founders' commitment
to interracial, nonviolent direct action. The "CORE Action Discipline," which reveals CORE's adaptations of Gandhian techniques
to the American scene, expressed the belief that direct action should
always be accompanied by a spirit of good will toward the discrim-
inator, a frame of mind calculated to change not only his racist behavior, but his attitudes as well. With minor revisions, the Action
Discipline remained the official statement of CORE's principles and
philosophy until the 1960s.

A. CORE statement of purpose

CORE has one purpose—to eliminate racial discrimination.
CORE has one method—inter-racial, non-violent direct
action.
CORE asks its members to commit themselves to work as
an integrated, disciplined group:

by abiding by all democratic group decisions and accepting CORE discipline for all projects in which the individual participates:

by renouncing overt violence in opposing racial discrimination and using the method of non-violent direct action:

Chicago Committee of Racial Equality, Statement of Purpose [1942]. Leaflet,
James Farmer Papers.

which refuses to cooperate with racial injustice;

which seeks to change existing practices by using such techniques as negotiation, mediation, demonstration, and picketing;

which develops a spirit of understanding rather than antagonism.

CORE members find a unique field of action:

in working against discrimination in public places such as schools, restaurants, churches, etc.

in attempting to attack the more basic social, economic, and political problems of discrimination as they are manifested in such forms as the restrictive covenant system.

CORE relates itself to other organizations and individuals on a basis of friendly cooperation with the possibility of mutual action on particular occasions. CORE welcomes the participation of individual members of other groups in specific projects, providing they accept the group discipline.

B. CORE action discipline

CORE and non-violence

The Congress of Racial Equality is a national federation of local interracial groups committed to the goal of erasing the color-line through methods of direct non-violent action. All groups affiliated with national CORE agree to follow to the best of their ability the non-violent procedure in all action which they sponsor. The discipline which is set forth here, and which has been approved by the national convention, is simply meant to make explicit what seems to be implicit in the non-violent method. This method consists of relatively un-

CORE Action Discipline. Version Adopted by the National Convention of the Congress of Racial Equality, June 1945. (A slightly amended version of original Discipline drawn up by the Chicago Committee of Racial Equality in 1942.) Leaflet, 1945, CORE Archives, State Historical Society of Wisconsin.

developed techniques for solving social conflicts, but it has great possibilities for good. It makes two assumptions. First of all, it assumes that social conflicts are not ultimately solved by the use of violence; that violence perpetuates itself, and serves to aggravate rather than resolve conflict. Moreover, it assumes that it is suicidal for a minority group to use violence since to use it would simply result in complete control and subjugation by the majority group. Secondly, the non-violent method assumes the possibility of creating a world in which non-violence will be used to a maximum degree. In working for this type of world, it confronts injustice without fear, without compromise, and without hate. The type of power which it uses in overcoming injustice is fourfold: (1) the power of active goodwill; (2) the power of public opinion against a wrong-doer; (3) the power of refusing to cooperate with injustice, such non-cooperation being illustrated by the boycott and the strike; and (4) the power of accepting punishment if necessary without striking back, by placing one's body in the way of injustice.

Below are listed some of the implications for action of the non-violent method.

Guarantees of the individual
to the group

1. A CORE member will investigate the facts carefully before determining whether or not racial injustice exists in a given situation.

2. A CORE member will seek at all times to understand the social situation which engendered the prejudiced attitude of the perpetrator of racial injustice.

3. A CORE member will seek to understand, without compromising his principles, the attitude of the person responsible for a policy of racial discrimination by discussing the problem through with him.

4. A CORE member will harbor no malice or hate toward any individual or group of individuals.

5. A CORE member will maintain an attitude of humility, and will be willing to admit his own inadequencies.

6. He will suffer the anger of any individual or group in the spirit of good-will and creative reconciliation.

7. In suffering such anger, he will submit to assault and never retaliate in kind, either by act or word. He will not submit out of personal fear of embarassment or punishment.

8. If a CORE member faces arrest, he will submit willingly to such arrest by a legally constituted official. He will not, however, voluntarily retreat before the threats of legal or non-legal personages. At the same time, he will never violate his pledge of non-violence.

9. The CORE member will never use malicious slogans or labels to discredit any opponent.

10. If in the course of non-violent action any person is violently assaulted, the CORE member will non-violently defend such person even at the risk of his own life.

11. A member will never patronize knowingly an institution which practises discrimination, where there is a choice of places to patronize, except in the event of learning facts, or of participating in action toward elimination of discrimination.

12. A member will never engage in any action in the name of the group except when authorized by the group or one of its action units.

13. When in an action project a CORE member will cheerfully obey the orders issued by the authorized leader or spokesman of the project, whether these orders please him or not. If he does not approve of such orders, he shall later refer the criticism back to the group or back to the committee which was the source of the project plan.

14. No member, after once accepting the discipline of the group for a particular action project, shall have the right of withdrawing from that discipline.

15. No person who is not a recognized member of the group or an accepted participant in a particular project shall be allowed to act as a participant in an action project.

16. No personal, family, or other consideration shall divert a member from his group discipline if he once agrees to a particular project.

Guarantees from the group
to the individual

17. Each member has the right to dissent from any group decision, and if dissenting, shall not participate in the specific action planned. A person who dissents, however, shall continue to have a voice in the discussion of the project.

18. Each member shall understand that all decisions on general policy shall be arrived at only through democratic group discussion.

19. If a member gets in trouble carrying out the work of CORE, he shall receive the uncompromising support of CORE, financially and otherwise, as he faces the difficulty.

32. THE EARLY SIT-INS

A. James Farmer describes CORE's first sit-in

In the civil rights movement the line between thought and action is a thin one. It therefore seems appropriate to illustrate CORE's activity by a selection from James Farmer's *Freedom—When?*, showing how the philosophy was applied in CORE's early years. Following Gandhian procedure, CORE members first tried to convert their opponents through careful, often lengthy negotiations. If this failed, CORE members successively moved on to more militant actions. Thus, agitation was employed to arouse public opinion. Finally, if this pressure did not succeed, direct action techniques such as picketing, boycotting, and sitting-in were used. Farmer's recollections reveal the slow, tedious efforts of these young people in trying to desegregate one restaurant or theater at a time, the long, drawn-out negotiations, and the idealistic efforts to "reach the heart" of discriminators.

From James Farmer, FREEDOM—WHEN? (New York: Random House, 1965), pp. 60–62. © Copyright 1965 by The Congress of Racial Equality. Reprinted by permission of Random House, Inc.

. . . One evening around this time [1942] James R. Robinson, one of the founders of CORE (later its executive secretary), and I, deep in a discussion of CORE, stopped for coffee at a little corner shop called the Jack Sprat, in a middle-class section near the university. The manager of the place served us with the greatest reluctance and then only after we reminded him that he would be violating state law if he refused. Even so, he tried at first to charge me twenty-five cents for a five-cent doughnut. A few days later our fledgling CORE chapter sent in a small interracial group. The manager had us served, but as we left he raked our money off the counter and threw it after us into the street, screaming, "Take your money and get out!"

At the meeting called to formulate a plan of action we turned down a proposal to parade through the Negro section with signs reading JACK SPRAT SERVES NEGROES FREE OF CHARGE, and, still being neophytes, mentally reviewed Shridharani to discover what our procedure ought to be. We had the facts. The next step: negotiation. Accordingly, we tried to telephone the manager, who hung up on us twice. Then we wrote him a letter, explaining our position and asking for a conference. When he did not reply, we wrote a second letter, which also was not answered. Then we sent four people into the restaurant to try to negotiate on the spot. A different manager was in charge this time; he too refused to talk with us. A few nights later we sent in another group. This time there was a third person in charge, a woman, who was somewhat more civil and who explained that they refused service to Negroes only because they feared the loss of white patrons. The CORE group, expressing considerably more sympathy with her point of view than a similar group would today, suggested several ways of proving to her that her fears were groundless, but she refused to try any of them.

We wrote the management one more letter, the "ultimatum" of Gandhi's outline, saying that if we did not hear from them after seven days, we would regretfully be compelled to go into other forms of action. On the eighth day we staged what I believe to have been the first civil rights sit-in. About twenty-five people, all pledged to the discipline of non-violence, entered the restaurant at dinner-time and quietly seated themselves at the counter and in the booths. Several of the white people were served without question; the Negroes were told that they would be served only in the basement. After a few minutes the manager realized that none of the white people had touched their food. They explained that they did not think it polite to eat until their friends had been served. Growing angry, the manager declared that she would not serve us if we sat there until midnight. Meanwhile, a number of the restaurant's regular patrons had come in, waited for a little while, and then, finding that no seats were becoming available, had walked out. Several other customers who had been served before we entered lingered over their dinners, curious to see the outcome of this novel performance. A girl at the counter near me caught on to the situation almost immediately, pushed aside her half-eaten dinner, and spontaneously joined the demonstration.

The manager, increasingly upset, announced that if the Negroes did not want to eat in the basement, she would seat them at the two rear booths, where they would be hidden from view, and have them served very nicely. We declined. Then she called the police, hoping to have us thrown out on a charge of disorderly conduct, but the two policemen who came in found no sign of disorder at all. In accordance with Gandhi's program, we had telephoned the police captain in advance, outlined the procedure we intended to follow, and even read him the state's civil rights law, with which he had apparently been unfamiliar. Consequently, when one of the officers phoned headquarters at the manager's insistence, he was told that nothing in the law allowed them to eject us. The police left. A short time later, the manager had us all served. The test groups sent in during the following weeks were all served promptly and courteously, without incident.

When I look back at that first sit-in, I am amazed at our patience and good faith. We have traveled a great distance since then. No action group today would prolong the attempts at negotiation for more than a month before finally deciding to demonstrate. No militant Negro today would dream of trying to persuade a manager to serve him on the grounds that Negro patronage would not be bad for business. We have grown too proud for that. But in those days we were childishly literal minded. We believed that people meant exactly what they said to us and heard exactly what we said to them. We regarded the sit-in as the successful culmination of a long campaign to reach the heart of the restaurant owner with the truth. What we took to be his conversion was as important to us as the fact that the restaurant had indeed been desegregated.

B. An early NAACP college chapter sit-in

In 1944 the Civil Rights Committee of Washington, D.C., sponsored by the Howard University NAACP, conducted a campaign against exclusionary restaurants. In April, the group held a sit-in at a restaurant of the Thompson chain. The leaflet below contains the first use of the words, "sitting in," which the editors have found. It is also significant because it reveals the middle-class orientation of most direct actionists of this period, in the insistence that a demonstrator "look my best," "refrain from any boisterous or offensive language," and "do or say nothing which will embarrass the Committee or the University."

(1) I conceive one of the most precious of all human rights to be the right of equal privileges in all places of public accommodation. I believe that any distinction, discrimination or exclusion from such places based solely upon race or color is undemocratic and is calculated to attach a badge of inferiority to the persons excluded. I oppose any discrimination of this kind, particularly where such exclusion is not sanctioned by

Leaflet circulated by Civil Rights Committee sponsored by the Howard University chapter of the NAACP, April 25, 1944. Mimeographed. Copy in CORE Archives, State Historical Society of Wisconsin.

laws, as contrary to the principles for which the present World War is being fought and because I believe it creates ill will and conflict between the races.

(2) I conceive the effort to eliminate discriminations against any person because of race or color to be a patriotic duty and an act of faith in the American boys who are fighting for the Four Freedoms in foreign lands, and who have every right to expect a fuller share of these freedoms when they return home.

(3) Because of these convictions, I pledge myself to give full and vigorous support to the present campaign of the Civil Rights Committee and the NAACP Howard Student Chapter to break down discrimination in restaurants, theatres, stores, and other places of public accommodation in Washington, D. C.

(4) I understand the aims of the Civil Rights campaign to be the opening up of places to Negroes through the art of persuasion and good will, and the developing of public opinion to extend the privilege of service to all members of the population. I understand further that there is no law enforcing segregation in Washington, D. C., and that I may enter any public place and remain there so long as I conduct myself in a lawful and proper manner.

(5) I therefore pledge myself to devote as much time as possible each week to the purposes of the Campaign; to be prompt at all meetings; to fulfill any obligation or assignment which I undertake in behalf of the Campaign, and to serve in whatever capacity I am best fitted—whether picketing, "sitting in" restaurants, making posters and signs, handing out leaflets, or speaking.

(6) I further pledge to abide by the rules and regulations of the Civil Rights Committee in carrying out this campaign; to do nothing to antagonize members of the public or the management of public places; to look my best whenever I act as a representative of the Committee, to use dignity and restraint at all times; to refrain from any boisterous or offensive language or conduct no matter what the provocation, and to do or say nothing which will embarrass the Committee or the University.

33. JAMES FARMER ON BLACK NATIONALISM: "WE CANNOT DESTROY SEGREGATION WITH A WEAPON OF SEGREGATION"

Since the goal of the early CORE leaders was to destroy segregation, they accepted only those means which were both nonviolent and interracial. Thus they had strong reservations about the avowedly all-black March on Washington Movement. Nevertheless, some of them supported it because of Randolph's charisma, militance, and use of direct-action tactics. In 1944 James Farmer, as editor of the FOR publication, *Equality,* in an oblique criticism of the March on Washington Movement for its "chauvinistic" tendencies, pointedly articulated the interracial emphasis of CORE ideology and condemned black nationalism.

Rapidly spreading in Negro culture, and likely to be pushed even more to the fore in post-war days, is the credo of chauvinism. Black nationalism or Negroism, as it is sometimes called, has developed naturally in Negro life as a reaction to segregation and prejudice.

Basically it is emotional, not rational; but when rationalized, the arguments are simple. "The white man shuts us out and hates us," the black man-in-the-street may argue; "therefore he can never be trusted, so we must shut him out and hate him."

The more erudite leaders are less virulent, more deliberate, in their explanations. "The problem of caste requires caste organization"; "The Negro must learn to stand on his own feet; when whites enter a movement they shove to the front and Negroes take a back seat"; and "Communist infiltration and control can be avoided best by excluding whites" are the not unreasonable arguments offered.

The anti-Negro forces in America which have produced this chauvinistic trend are likely to become more vocal following

[James Farmer] Editorial in EQUALITY, I (November 1944), 2.

the war, as we observed in EQUALITY last month. Black nationalism will thus, no doubt, make a stronger bid for control of
Negro life.

To attempt to refute the arguments tending toward nationalism would require more space than is available here. We must
be content here to point to the effects of such a philosophy, the
bankruptcy of such a policy toward solving the problem.

The stronger black nationalism becomes in Negro life in
America, the farther we are from a real solution to the problem
of color. The basic problem—if we may be trite for a moment—
is *to break down barriers* of segregation. Trying to break down
social and economic barriers of segregation while nurturing
mental barriers of segregation is fantastic. But that is precisely
what the nationalists are doing. We cannot destroy segregation
with a weapon of segregation.

Further, to be dealt with intelligently, the color problem
should not be seen in isolation. It must be seen as one part of
the larger problems of labor and the economic struggle, of
minorities in general, of civil liberties, etc.

We must join hands with our comrades in the larger struggles.
To do otherwise is to alienate our much needed allies of other
races who have as much at stake in winning the battle as we.

Garveyism, decades ago, had an appeal to Negro masses, for
it exalted their ego, and thus answered a need. Marcus Garvey,
with probable sincerity, exploited the situation skillfully. His
modern counterparts are seeking to exploit the same need by
similar means. By so doing, they are not liberating the Negro
people; they are further enslaving their minds under the yoke
of caste.

34. THURGOOD MARSHALL EXPLAINS
THE NAACP's LEGAL STRATEGY

Thurgood Marshall, the first Negro elevated to the United States Supreme Court (1967), was for nearly a quarter of a century special counsel to the NAACP and director of the NAACP Legal Defense and Educational Fund. Speaking at the NAACP Wartime Conference in 1944, he made a lucid exposition of the NAACP's legal approach and of the philosophy behind it. At the time of this speech, the continuing legal assault on discrimination was operating from a far narrower base of statutes and precedents than is now available to civil rights leaders.

On last night we heard a clear statement of some of the problems facing us today. My job tonight is to point out a part of the general program to secure full citizenship rights.

The struggle for full citizenship rights can be speeded by enforcement of existing statutory provisions protecting our civil rights. The attack on discrimination by use of legal machinery has only scratched the surface. An understanding of the existing statutes protecting our civil rights is necessary if we are to work toward enforcement of these statutes.

The titles "civil rights" and "civil liberties" have grown to include large numbers of subjects, some of which are properly included under these titles and others which should not be included. One legal treatise has defined the subject of civil rights as follows: "In its broadest sense, the term civil rights includes those rights which are the outgrowth of civilization, the existence and exercise of which necessarily follow from the rights that repose in the subjects of a country exercising self-government."

Thurgood Marshall, "The Legal Attack to Secure Civil Rights," an address delivered July 13, 1944 at the NAACP Wartime Conference. Reprinted with permission of Thurgood Marshall.

The Fourteenth and Fifteenth Amendments to the Constitution are prohibitions against action by the states and state officers violating civil rights. In addition to these provisions of the United States Constitution and a few others, there are several statutes of the United States which also attempt to protect the rights of individual citizens against private persons as well as public officers. Whether these provisions are included under the title of "civil rights" or "civil liberties" or any other subject is more or less unimportant as long as we bear in mind the provisions themselves.

All of the statutes, both federal and state, which protect the individual rights of Americans are important to Negroes as well as other citizens. Many of these provisions, however, are of peculiar significance to Negroes because of the fact that in many instances these statutes are the only protection to which Negroes can look for redress. It should also be pointed out that many officials of both state and federal governments are reluctant to protect the rights of Negroes. It is often difficult to enforce our rights when they are perfectly clear. It is practically impossible to secure enforcement of any of our rights if there is any doubt whatsoever as to whether or not a particular statute applies to the particular state of facts.

As to law enforcement itself, the rule as to most American citizens is that if there is any way possible to prosecute individuals who have willfully interfered with the rights of other individuals such prosecution is attempted. However, when the complaining party is a Negro, the rule is usually to look for any possible grounds for *not* prosecuting. It is therefore imperative that Negroes be thoroughly familiar with the rights guaranteed them by law in order that they may be in a position to insist that all of their fundamental rights as American citizens be protected.

The Thirteenth Amendment to the Constitution, abolishing slavery, the Fourteenth Amendment, prohibiting any action of state officials denying due process of the equal protection of its laws, and the Fifteenth Amendment, prohibiting discrimination by the states in voting are well-known to all of us. In addition to these provisions of the Constitution, there are the so-called Federal "Civil Rights Statutes" which include several Acts of Congress such as the Civil Rights Act and other statutes which have been amended from time to time and are now grouped together in several sections of the United States Code. The original Civil Rights Act was passed in Congress in 1866, but was vetoed by President Andrew Jackson the same year. It was, however, passed over the veto. It was reintroduced and passed in 1870 because there was some doubt as to its constitutionality, having been passed before the Fourteenth Amendment was ratified. The second bill has been construed several times and has been held constitutional by the United States Supreme Court, which in one case stated that "the plain objects of these statutes, as of the Constitution which authorized them, was to place the colored race, in respect to civil rights, upon a level with the whites. They made the rights and responsibilities, civil and criminal, of the two races exactly the same." (Virginia v. Rives, 100 U.S. 313 [1879])

The Thirteenth and Fourteenth and Fifteenth Amendments, along with the civil rights statutes protect the following rights:

1. Slavery is abolished and peonage is punishable as a federal crime. (13th amendment)

2. All persons born or naturalized in the U.S. are citizens and no state shall make or enforce any law abridging their privileges or immunities, or deny them equal protection of the law. (14th amendment)

3. The right of citizens to vote cannot be abridged by the United States or by any state on account of race or color. (15th amendment)

4. All persons within the jurisdiction of the United States shall have the same right to enforce contracts, or sue, be parties, give evidence, and to the full and equal benefit of all laws and proceedings as is enjoyed by white citizens.

5. All persons shall be subject to like punishment, pains, penalties, taxes, licenses, and extractions of every kind, and to no other.

6. All citizens shall have the same right in every state and territory, as is enjoyed by white citizens to inherit, purchase, lease, sell, hold and convey property.

7. Every person who, under color of statutes, custom or usage, subjects any citizen of the United States or person within the jurisdiction thereof to the deprivation of any rights, privileges, or immunities secured by the Constitution and laws is liable in an action at law, suit in equity, or other proper proceedings for redress.

8. Citizens possessing all other qualifications may not be disqualified from jury service in federal or state courts on account of race or color; any officer charged with the duty of selection or summoning of jurors who shall exclude citizens for reasons of race or color shall be guilty of a misdemeanor.

9. A conspiracy of two or more persons to deprive any person or class of persons of any rights guaranteed by constitution and laws is punishable as a crime and the conspirators are also liable in damages.

Most of these provisions only protect the citizen against wrong doing by public officials, although the peonage statutes and one or two others protect against wrongs by private persons.

Despite the purposes of these Acts which the United States Supreme Court insisted in 1879 "made the rights and responsibilities, civil and criminal, of the two races exactly the same," the experience of all of us points to the fact that this purpose has not as yet been accomplished. There are several reasons for this. In the first place, in certain sections of this country, especially in the deep south, judges, prosecutors and members of grand and petit juries, have simply refused to follow the letter or spirit of these provisions. Very often it happens that although the judge and prosecutor are anxious to enforce the laws, members of the jury are reluctant to protect the rights of Negroes. A third reason is that many Negroes themselves for one reason or another hesitate to avail themselves of the protection afforded by the United States Constitution and statutes.

These statutes protecting our civil rights in several instances provide for both criminal and civil redress. Some are criminal only and others are for civil action only. Criminal prosecution for violation of the federal statutes can be obtained only through the United States Department of Justice.

Up through and including the administration of Attorney General Homer S. Cummings, Negroes were unable to persuade the U.S. Department of Justice to enforce any of the civil rights statutes where Negroes were the complaining parties. The NAACP and its staff made repeated requests and in many instances filed detailed statements and briefs requesting prosecution for lynch mobs, persons guilty of peonage and other apparent violations of the federal statutes. It was not until the administration of Attorney General Frank Murphy that any substantial efforts were made to enforce the civil rights statutes as they apply to Negroes. Attorney General Murphy established a Civil Rights Section in the Department of Justice.

During the present administration of Attorney General Francis Biddle there have been several instances of prosecution of members of lynch mobs for the first time in the history of the United States Department of Justice. There have also been numerous successful prosecutions of persons guilty of peonage and slavery. However, other cases involving the question of the beating and killing of Negro soldiers by local police officers, the case involving the action of Sheriff Tip Hunter, of Brownsville, Tennessee who killed at least one Negro citizen and forced several others to leave town, the several cases of refusal to permit qualified Negroes to vote, as well as other cases, have received the attention of the Department of Justice only to the extent of "investigating." Our civil rights as guaranteed by the federal statutes will never become a reality until the U.S. Department of Justice decides that it represents the entire United States and is not required to fear offending any section of the country which believes that it has the God-given right to be above the laws of the United States and the United States Supreme Court.

One interesting example of the apparent failure to enforce the criminal statutes is that although the statute making it a crime to exclude persons from jury service because of race or color was declared unconstitutional by the U.S. Supreme Court in 1879, and is still on the statute books, there have been no prosecutions by the Department of Justice in recent years for the obvious violations of these statutes. The Department of Justice has most certainly on several occasions been put on notice as to these violations by the many cases carried to the Supreme Court by the NAACP and in which cases the Supreme Court has reversed the convictions on the ground that Negroes were systematically excluded from jury service. One whole-hearted prosecution of a judge or other official for excluding Negroes from jury service because of their race would do more to make this particular law a reality than dozens of other cases merely reversing the conviction of individual defendants.

There are, however, certain bright spots in the enforcement of the federal statutes. In addition to the lynching and peonage cases handled by the Washington office of the Department of Justice, there have been a few instances of courageous United States Attorneys in such places as Georgia who have vigorously prosecuted police officers who have used the power of their office as a cloak for beating up Negro citizens.

As a result of the recent decision in the Texas Primary Case, it is possible to use an example of criminal prosecution under the civil rights statutes by taking a typical case of the refusal to permit the Negroes to vote in the Democratic Primary elections. Let us see how a prosecution is started: In Waycross, Georgia, for example, we will suppose a Negro elector on July 4, 1944, went to the polls with his tax receipt and demanded to vote in the Democratic Primary. He should, of course, have witnesses with him. Let us also assume that the election officials refused to let him vote solely because of his race or color.

As a matter of law, the election officials violated a federal criminal law and are subject to fine and imprisonment. But how should the voter or the organized Negro citizens, or the local NAACP Branch go about trying to get the machinery of criminal justice in motion? Of course, the details of what happens must be put in writing and sworn to by the person who tried to vote and also by his witnesses. Then the matter must be placed before the United States Attorney. This is the *federal* district attorney.

I wonder how many of the delegates here know who is the United States Attorney for their district, or even where his office is. Every Branch should know the United States Attorney for that area, even if a delegation goes in just to get acquainted and let him know that we expect him to enforce the civil rights laws with the same vigor as used in enforcing other criminal statutes.

But back to the voting case. The affidavits must be presented to the United States Attorney with a demand that he investigate and place the evidence before the Federal Grand Jury. At the same time copies of the affidavits and statements in the case should be sent to the National Office. We will see that they get to the Attorney General in Washington. I wish that I could guarantee you that the Attorney General would put pressure on local United States Attorneys who seem reluctant to prosecute. At least we can assure you that we will give the Attorney General no rest unless he gets behind these reluctant United States attorneys throughout the south.

There is no reason why a hundred clear cases of this sort should not be placed before the United States Attorneys and the Attorney General every year until the election officials discover that it is both wiser and safer to follow the United States laws than to violate them. It is up to us to see that these officials of the Department of Justice are called upon to act again and again wherever there are violations of the civil rights statutes. Unfortunately, there are plenty of such cases. It is equally unfortunate that there are not enough individuals and groups presenting these cases and demanding action.

The responsibility for enforcement of the civil provisions of the civil rights statutes rests solely with the individual. In the past we have neglected to make full use of these studies. Although they have been on the books since 1870, there were very few cases under these statutes until recent years. Whereas in the field of general law there are many, many precedents for all other types of action, there are very few precedents for the protection of civil liberties.

The most important of the civil rights provisions is the one which provides that "every person who, under color of any statute, ordinance, regulation, custom or usage of any state or territory subjects or causes to be subjected any citizen of the United States or person within the jurisdiction thereof to the deprivation of any rights, privileges or immunities secured by the Constitution and laws shall be liable to the party injured in an action at law, suit in equity or other proper proceeding for redress." Under this statute any officer of a state, county or municipality who while acting in an official capacity, denies to any citizen or person within the state any of the rights guaranteed by the Constitution or laws is subject to a civil action. This statute has been used to equalize teachers' salaries and to obtain bus transportation for Negro school children. It can be used to attack *every* form of discrimination against Negroes by public school systems.

The statute has also been used to enjoin municipalities from refusing to permit Negroes to take certain civil service examinations and to attack segregation ordinances of municipalities. It can likewise be used to attack all types of discrimination against Negroes by municipalities as well as by states themselves.

This statute, along with other of the civil rights statutes, can be used to enforce the right to register and vote throughout the country. The threats of many of the bigots in the south to disregard the ruling of the Supreme Court of the United States in the recent Texas Primary decision has not intimidated a single person. The United States Supreme Court remains the highest court in this land. Election officials in states affected by this decision will either let Negroes vote in the Democratic Primaries, or they will be subjected to both criminal and civil prosecution under the civil rights statutes. In every state in the deep south Negroes have this year attempted to vote in the primary elections. Affidavits concerning the refusal to permit

them to vote in Alabama, Florida and Georgia have already
been sent to the United States Department of Justice. We will
insist that these election officials be prosecuted and will also
file civil suits against the guilty officials.

It can be seen from these examples that we have just begun
to scratch the surface in the fight for full enforcement of these
statutes. The NAACP can move no faster than the individuals
who have been discriminated against. We only take up cases
where we are requested to do so by persons who have been
discriminated against.

Another crucial problem is the ever-present problem of segregation. Whereas the principle has been established by cases
handled by the NAACP that neither states nor municipalities
can pass ordinances segregating residences by race, the growing problem today is the problem of segregation by means of
restrictive covenants, whereby private owners band together
to prevent Negro occupancy of particular neighborhoods. Although this problem is particularly acute in Chicago, it is at
the same time growing in intensity throughout the country. It
has the full support of the real estate boards in the several
cities, as well as most of the banks and other leading agencies.
The legal attack on this problem has met with spotty success.
In several instances restrictive covenants have been declared
invalid because the neighborhood has changed, or for other
reasons. Other cases have been lost. However, the NAACP is
in the process of preparing a detailed memorandum and will
establish procedure which will lead to an all-out legal attack
on restrictive covenants. Whether or not this attack will be successful cannot be determined at this time.

The National Housing Agency and the Federal Public Housing Authority have established a policy of segregation in federal
public housing projects. A test case has been filed in Detroit,
Mich., and is still pending in the local federal courts. The Detroit situation is the same as in other sections of the country.
Despite the fact that the Housing Authority and other agencies
insist that they will maintain separate but equal facilities, it
never develops that the separate facilities are equal in all re-

spects. In Detroit separate projects were built and it developed that by the first of this year every single white family in the area eligible for public housing had been accommodated and there were still some 800 "white" units vacant with "no takers." At the same time there were some 45,000 Negroes inadequately housed and with no units open to them. This is the inevitable result of "separate but equal" treatment.

I understand that in Chicago a public housing project to be principally occupied by Negroes is being opposed by other Negroes on the ground that it will depreciate their property. It is almost unbelievable that Negroes would oppose public housing for the same reason used by real estate boards and other interests who are determined to keep Negroes in slum areas so that they may be further exploited. The NAACP is in favor of public housing and works toward that end every day. It will continue to do so despite real estate boards and other selfish interests opposing public housing whether they be white or Negro. The NAACP is, of course, opposed to segregation in public housing and will continue to fight segregation in public housing.

We should also be mindful of the several so-called civil rights statutes in the several states. There are civil rights acts in at least 18 states, all of which are in the north and middle west. These statutes are in California, Colorado, Connecticut, Illinois, Indiana, Iowa, Kansas, Massachusetts, Michigan, Minnesota, Nebraska, New Jersey, New York, Ohio, Pennsylvania, Rhode Island and Washington. California provides only for civil action. Illinois, Kansas, Minnesota, New York and Ohio have both civil and criminal provisions. In New Jersey the only action is a criminal action, or an action for penalty in the name of the state, the amount of the penalty going to the state.

In those states not having civil rights statutes it is necessary that every effort be made to secure passage of one. In states having weak civil rights statutes efforts should be made to have them strengthened. In states with reasonably strong civil rights statutes, like Illinois and New York, it is necessary that every effort be made to enforce them.

The Chicago branch has the record of more successful prosecutions for violation of the local civil rights statute than any other Branch of the NAACP. In New York City resort to the enforcement of the criminal provisions has greatly lessened the number of cases. Outside of New York City there are very few successful cases against the civil rights statutes because of the fact that members of the jury are usually reluctant to enforce the statutes. I understand the same is true for Illinois. The only method of counteracting this vicious practice is by means of educating the general public, from which juries are chosen, to the plight of the Negro.

It should also be pointed out that many of our friends of other races are not as loud and vociferous as the enemies of our race. In northern and mid-western cities it repeatedly happens that a prejudiced southerner on entering a hotel or restaurant, seeing Negroes present makes an immediate and loud protest to the manager. It is very seldom that any of our friends go to the managers of places where Negroes are excluded and complain to them of this fact. Quite a job can be done if our friends of other races will only realize the importance of this problem and get up from their comfortable chairs and actually go to work on the problem.

Thus it seems clear that although it is necessary and vital to all of us that we continue our program for additional legislation to guarantee and enforce certain of our rights, at the same time we must continue with ever-increasing vigor to enforce those few statutes, both federal and state, which are now on the statute books. We must not be delayed by people who say "the time is not ripe," nor should we proceed with caution for fear of destroying the "status quo." Persons who deny to us our civil rights should be brought to justice now. Many people believe the time is always "ripe" to discriminate against Negroes. All right then—the time is always "ripe" to bring them to justice. The responsibility for the enforcement of these statutes rests with every American citizen regardless of race or color. However, the real job has to be done by the Negro population with whatever friends of the other races are willing to join in.

35. WILLARD S. TOWNSEND ADVOCATES
AN ALLIANCE
WITH THE INDUSTRIAL UNIONS

In the 1940s, Negro cooperation with the industrial unions reached its high point. Willard S. Townsend, president of the United Service Transport Employes of America (Red Caps), expressed especially well the vision of social justice through the alliance of blacks and the industrial unions.

Within the nature of our economy, labor, when constructively and aggressively organized, is the major productive force tending towards a complete eradication of all economic inequality, the pivot upon which our entire structure rests. Every effort should be made to understand the role of aggressive labor, for herein lies the key to the entire problem of common security and a democracy of equals in every sense of the word. Labor's aggressive historical role from the early days of unionization has been confined primarily to breaking down areas of inequality and a progressive extension of the democratic process. Universal suffrage, public schools, non-imprisonment for debt, minimum wages and social security are practical examples of the historical role of labor.

This is true despite the backwardness of certain sections of organized labor, whose inactive and defenseless position on industrial equality for Negroes is unsupportable and deserves the militant opposition of every worker in the country. However, it must be understood that discrimination against Negroes in the craft framework of certain sections of labor is used as a

Willard S. Townsend, "One American Problem and a Possible Solution," in Rayford W. Logan, ed., WHAT THE NEGRO WANTS (Chapel Hill, N.C.: University of North Carolina Press, 1944), pp. 175–177, 182–184. Reprinted with permission of the publisher.

defense mechanism to support a weak organizational structure and flows from existing community over-all social patterns perpetuated by the economy itself. The solution to this problem is through a rapid extension of the aggressive industrial union forms of organization as characterized by the Congress of Industrial Organizations, whose policies and program negate much of the social and organizational backwardness within the American Federation of Labor. . . .

To understand this kinship of common problems and the task of cementing the relationship of America's two great minorities in the struggle for a post-war future of hope, security and decency should engage the greater portion of our efforts today. To do so, we must understand the historical weaknesses and the present areas of strength in the joint struggle for security. . . .

The greatest degree of discrimination against Negro labor flourishes in the industrial backwoods of craft and semi-craft unionism. More than 20 international unions organized on a craft basis exclude Negroes from their organizations through constitutional provisions. Ten of these are affiliated with the American Federation of Labor. The others are independent unions and the operating railroad brotherhoods. These unions which exclude Negroes entirely through constitutional provisions are roughly estimated to have a membership of 1,200,000. At least 9 other unions with an approximate membership of 1 million exclude Negroes through various other means, the ritual oath being one of them. Close to one-third of the craft and semi-craft union membership of the AFL and the entire membership of the standard operating railroad brotherhoods are officially committed either through constitutional provisions or ritualistic oaths to the task of maintaining "white supremacy" in labor by accepting into their ranks only those who are "white, sober and of good moral character."

Even this does not give the whole picture of the extent of craft union exclusion of Negroes within the socially and industrially backward sections of organized American labor. There are close to 30 additional unions which do not use the crude constitutional provision or ritualistic oath, but experience has proved that it is as difficult for Negroes to obtain membership in these organizations as in the ones mentioned above. There are also some organizations which do not practise outright exclusion but permit Negroes to create separate Jim Crow locals or auxiliaries under the control of the nearest white local. To these second-class members little or no voice is given in the operation of the organization and all negotiations and grievances with management in their behalf are conducted by white union officials. . . .

In the formulation of these aims and purposes, the philosophy of craft unionism meekly accepted the inherent weaknesses and inequalities found in the economy of scarcity, rather than direct an open, courageous challenge to the growing inequities found in the new industrial order. The emergence of the factory system which quickly revolutionized manufacturing processes made it impossible for the weak craft structure of unions to exert a parallel degree of pressure in behalf of living standards. As a result, these organizations operated mainly as defense weapons against the rising tide of industrial combination and cartelization. Lacking the organizational structure to take the necessary offensive in meeting the problem of working standards, the proponents of craft unionism fell back upon the defense mechanism of creating an "aristocracy of skilled labor." To create this so-called aristocracy, membership exclusion was exercised against the large majority of unskilled workers, whose lack of skill was more or less used to enhance the prestige and to gain higher standards for the tightly organized skilled workers. In addition to the general exclusion of the unskilled, other types of restrictions were employed to maintain the standards of the skilled, such as rigid apprenticeship, high initiation fees and dues, and the placing of Negroes and other non-white racial groups upon the sacrificial altar of craft unionism. In the legislative field efforts were made to restrict immigration, and the passage of the Oriental Exclusion Act was one of the early demands of the craft unionists. (Incidentally, this support of the Oriental Exclusion Act was reaffirmed at the August, 1943, meeting of the Executive Council of the AFL in Chicago.) In this safe role as trusted defenders of the *status quo,* the craft unions settled down to a comfortable life of "business union-ism" and hardening of the arteries. . . .

Today the CIO stands as a national bulwark in the struggle to extend the democratic process into every phase of American life. Because of this, Negro labor today is perhaps the most articulate section of the Negro national community and is farther on the road to presenting a positive challenge to their problems as a race than any other section. Today more than 500,000 Ne-groes are estimated to be members of labor organizations. Ten years ago, Negro membership was less than 80,000. This great increase in organizational activity is due primarily to the ex-tensive campaigns of the CIO in our mass production industries.

On the question of race discrimination, President Philip Mur-ray of the CIO summarized the CIO's position in the following statement:

> Race discrimination is un-American. It is diametrically opposed to the guiding principles of the Congress of Industrial Organi-zations. It should be resisted immediately and effectively by our responsible organizations wherever it raises its vile head. Negroes and whites are today fighting side by side, shedding their blood on distant battle fields for the protection of those of us who remain at home. Let us demonstrate our American Democracy and the fraternal spirit of the CIO by extending the Negro workers their full rights in American industry.

The CIO did not stop with fine speeches. It has waged a con-sistent fight against the poll-tax, and for housing, education and full integration of Negroes into industry. Under the militant leadership of James B. Carey, secretary-treasurer of the CIO, it has established the Committee to Abolish Racial Discrimination which operates as an integral part of CIO machinery. In addi-tion, it has encouraged the development of a hard-hitting type of interracial local union leadership, which refuses to budge before the altars of race discrimination.

Today aggressive unionism becomes the major force for the extension of the rights and progress for the Negro race. It is the only segment of our society where Negroes and whites have been able to work together in common purpose. It has also become the political force through which civil rights acts may be enforced in states where they exist and efforts made to break down Jim Crow in states where it has a legal foundation.

36. BLACK LEADERS UNITE
ON A WARTIME PROTEST PLATFORM

Diversity of viewpoint notwithstanding, most Negro leaders agreed on the fundamentals. In 1944—an election year—Walter White, executive secretary of the NAACP, called a gathering of representatives of twenty national organizations. The representatives formulated a yardstick to measure candidates and political parties. "A Declaration by Negro Voters" set out the basic principles upon which the leading spokesmen of the race were agreed. Leaders of many groups signed the statement: officials of Greek-letter sororities and fraternities; NAACP officials William Hastie and Walter White; Mary McLeod Bethune, president of the National Council of Negro Women; such religious figures as Channing H. Tobias of the Social Action Committee of the Colored Methodist Church and Adam Clayton Powell (then on the eve of his political career); and such labor leaders as A. Philip Randolph, Ferdinand Smith of the National Maritime Union, and George L. P. Weaver, who was with the National CIO Committee to Abolish Racial Discrimination. Representing the Communist-front groups was Max Yergan of the National Negro Congress.

The Negro voter has not yet chosen sides for 1944.

His vote cannot be purchased by distributing money to and through party hacks. It cannot be won by pointing to jobs given

Walter White and others, "A Declaration by Negro Voters," THE CRISIS, LI, 1 (January 1944), 16–17. Reprinted with the permission of THE CRISIS.

to few individual Negroes, although the recognition of the Negro as an integral part of the body politic through the selection of qualified Negroes for appointive or elective offices is included among the Negro's demands. The Negro vote not longer can be won by meaningless generalities in party platforms which are promptly forgotten on election day.

Full citizenship demanded

The Negro voter will support a political party which by words and deeds shows its determination to work for full citizenship status for thirteen million American Negroes and to better the lot of all disadvantaged people in this country. The Negro knows that his voting strength in 17 or more states with 281 or more votes in the electoral college gives him the potential balance of power in any reasonably close national election and in many state and local elections. His vote no longer belongs to any one political party. Although the Negro has largely supported the Democratic Party in recent years, it is highly significant that in 1943 the Negro vote played an important part in the election of a Negro Communist to the New York City Council, a Negro Republican as Judge in the same community, a Democratic mayor in Cleveland and a Republican Governor in Kentucky with phenomenal manifestations of independent voting in many other important centers. Public officers who have not made a record of liberal and democratic action may expect the Negro to help remove them from office. If their successors are no better, they may expect the same fate at the next election. For if the Negro does not always find any satisfactory candidate to support, he can and will continue to help remove unsatisfactory officials until truly democratic forces shall come into power.

The undersigned are officers of church, fraternal, labor, civic and educational organizations with a total membership of more than 6,000,000. Though we speak as individuals, we shall recommend to the membership of our respective organizations that Negroes shall measure all appeals for their support made by political parties and by presidential and other candidates according to the following yardstick:

War chief issue

The Negro people, like all other Americans, recognize the war as the chief issue confronting our country. We demand of any political party desiring the support of Negroes a vigorous prosecution of the war. We are opposed to any negotiated peace as advocated by the Hitler-like forces within our country. Victory must crush Hitlerism both at home as well as abroad.

In evaluating the merits of parties and candidates we must include all issues—those touching the life of Negroes as a group as well as those affecting the entire country. The party or candidate who refuses to help control prices, or fails to support the extension of social security, or refuses to support a progressive public program for full post war employment, or opposes an enlarged and unsegregated program of government-financed housing, or seeks to destroy organized labor, is as much the enemy of the Negro as is he who would prevent the Negro from voting.

Franchise without restrictions

We insist upon the right to vote in every state, unrestricted by poll taxes, white democratic primaries, the gerrymandering of districts, or any other device designed to disfranchise the Negro and other voters. Any political party in power, or aspiring to power, must demonstrate its determination through legislation and through vigorous criminal prosecution by the Department of Justice to protect and secure voting as a fundamental right of citizenship.

The ever-serious evil of lynching and mob violence has become more critical as a result of unrestrained violence against Negroes in the armed services. No national administration can merit the support of the Negro unless it is committed to a legislative and administrative program for the elimination of this national disgrace.

Both parties remiss

Republican and Democratic members of the Senate alike have attempted to delude us by alleging that they favor anti-lynching, anti-poll tax, and other legislation against which filibusters by southern Democrats have been waged but on which these Republican and Democratic Senators, from states where Negroes vote, refuse to vote for cloture. We refuse to accept such subterfuges any longer. A vote against cloture or failure to vote for cloture will be construed by us as opposition to whatever legislation for the benefit of the Negro and other minorities against which a filibuster is waged. The Senate rule requiring a two-thirds majority to end debate, combined with the refusal of senators to vote for cloture, is one of the greatest obstacles to liberal legislation in general and to legislation for the betterment of the Negro's status in particular. Negroes insist that national parties and individual candidates for senator pledge in advance their support to the abolition of this two-thirds rule now required for cloture.

The program now being carried on through the Fair Employment Practice Committee to secure and protect the right to work without racial or religious discrimination must be continued and expanded during and after the war. No party or candidate for the Presidency or Congress can deserve the vote of the Negro without supporting a liberal appropriation for a Fair Employment Practice Committee when that issue shall be presented in the spring of 1944 and such legislation as is needed further to secure the right of minorities to work without discrimination.

The armed services

No injustice embitters Negroes more than continued segregation and discrimination in the armed forces. The policy of the present administration with reference to the Negro in the armed forces is bad in principle and has failed. Any party which hopes to win the support of Negroes must adopt a new and democratic program for their integration into the armed forces.

We are concerned that this war bring to an end imperialism and colonial exploitation. We believe that political and economic democracy must displace the present system of exploitation in Africa, the West Indies, India, and all other colonial areas. We insist that all parties and candidates formulate a foreign policy which will resolutely and unequivocally oppose either perpetuation or extension of exploitation based upon "white superiority" or economic or political advantage to "white" nations at the expense of the two-thirds of the people of the earth who are brown, yellow, or black of skin. The United States must point the way by including Negroes among its representatives at the peace conference or peace conferences and among its diplomatic, technical, and professional experts engaged in international post war reconstruction.

We hereby serve notice that if either major political party shall nominate for President or Vice-President a candidate of vacillating or reactionary character, or with an anti-Negro record, it will be vigorously opposed by the Negro vote.

We repudiate all venal politicians, Negro and white, who attempt for personal profit to "deliver the Negro vote." We hereby serve notice that the Negro has come of age politically.

This statement is designed both to make clear the Negro's present attitude of resentment against the shortcomings of both major political parties and to serve as a guide in measuring the future intentions of parties and candidates. . . . We call upon enlightened labor, church, farm, and other groups to oppose actively the current wave of reaction. We will combine on a minimum program with such enlightened groups. Together these groups constitute a majority of the electorate. Together we will beat back the tide of reaction and build a more decent world now and in the post war years which can insure a durable peace.

The post-war era:
politics, direct action,
and legalism

37. HENRY LEE MOON:
THE BALLOT AS
"THE INDISPENSABLE WEAPON"

During the postwar era, the NAACP increasingly emphasized the importance of Negroes' registering and voting. In 1944, *Smith* v. *All-wright*, outlawing the white primary, had opened the way for extensive registration of black voters. In Northeastern and Far Western cities, massive Negro populations already were in a position to wield considerable political power. The NAACP was non-partisan, but it believed that Afro-Americans should register and vote in large numbers, become knowledgeable about candidates' past performances, and try to bring about improvements in legislation and in the actions of elected officials.

The black vote in the South was responsible on a few occasions for the margin of victory of a moderate candidate. The NAACP and other liberal interest-groups worked in the North for laws to ban discrimination in public accommodations and in the sale and rental of public and private housing, and for equality of job opportunities through fair-employment-practice commissions. Hopefully, a larger black vote in both North and South could break the grip of the Southern Democrat-Republican coalition in Congress.

In Presidential elections in particular, the Negro's vote became

Henry Lee Moon, BALANCE OF POWER: THE NEGRO VOTE (Garden City, N.Y.: Doubleday & Co., Inc., 1948), pp. 9–11. Reprinted with permission of the author.

crucial. During the New Deal days blacks, hitherto wedded to the party of Lincoln, became overwhelmingly Democratic. The importance of the Negro vote for a Democratic Presidential candidate was revealed dramatically in 1948. After extremist Southerners bolted the Democratic convention to run their own candidates on the Dixiecrat ticket, Harry Truman, taking a forthright stand on civil rights, won the election without the Dixiecrats, but with overwhelming Negro support. Even before Truman's feat, NAACP strategists regarded the black vote as holding the "balance of power." This point of view was developed by the NAACP's public-relations director, Henry Lee Moon, in his book, *Balance of Power*.

. . . The ballot, while no longer conceived of as a magic key, is recognized as the indispensable weapon in a persistent fight for full citizenship, equal economic opportunity, unrestricted enjoyment of civil rights, freedom of residence, access to equal and unsegregated educational, health, and recreational facilities. In short, a tool to be used in the ultimate demolition of the whole outmoded structure of Jim Crow.

Already recognized as an important and sometimes decisive factor in a dozen northern states and in at least seventy-five non-southern congressional districts, the Negro is beginning to exert increasing political influence in the nation, although still not accorded the recognition his voting strength warrants. Meanwhile, he is again emerging as a positive political factor in the South, where for nearly two generations his suffrage rights have for all practical purposes been nullified.

The area of his political activities and influence, once confined largely to the great industrial cities in the East and North, has been expanded and extended by wartime migration into the Pacific coast states and into many of the smaller midwest and northeastern cities. The war stimulus, too, has generated a resurgence of political activity in the South following the invalidation of the "white primary" by the Supreme Court decision of April 3, 1944.

The maximum Negro voting strength is about seven and a quarter millions, which represents the total number of colored citizens over twenty-one years of age, according to the 1940 census. For the nation as a whole there are 91,600,000 citizens of voting age. These figures are, of course, far in excess of the total vote which under present conditions can be turned out. In 1940, the year of the greatest vote, there was a total turn-out of 49,815,000. In 1942, an off year, this figure dropped to 29,441,000, rising in 1944 to 48,025,000, and dropping again in 1946 to 35,000,000.

Two thirds of these potential Negro voters still reside in the South. Most of these, living as they do in inaccessible rural areas and small towns, probably will not become politically activized for a number of years, despite the truly significant increase in Negro voting strength in many southern cities.

By the end of 1946 there were 750,000 qualified Negro voters in the southern states, a significant increase over the 250,000 Ralph Bunche estimated in 1940. Meanwhile, this number has steadily increased despite efforts of some southern legislatures to circumvent the Constitution and Supreme Court decisions. Despite, also, intimidation and fraud. By November 1948, more than a million southern Negroes may well be qualified to vote. A total of 3,500,000 Negro voters in the 1948 elections is not only possible but likely.

Politicians of both major parties have long been aware of the strength of the Negro vote in the cities of such states as New York, Pennsylvania, New Jersey, Ohio, Indiana, Michigan, Illinois, and Missouri. And no one today seriously contemplates launching a third party without considering this vital vote along with other potentialities necessary for the success of such an undertaking. Southern and western politicians have now joined their eastern and northern colleagues in bidding for this vote.

The size, strategic distribution, and flexibility of the Negro vote lend it an importance which can no longer be overlooked. As significant as was this vote in the 1944 elections—and without it Franklin D. Roosevelt could hardly have been re-elected—it can, with wise and independent leadership, be even more important in the 1948 elections.

The importance of this vote is now generally conceded. What

is not usually recognized, and even less acknowledged, is that this vote is more decisive in presidential elections than that of the Solid South. In sixteen states with a total of 278 votes in the electoral college, the Negro, in a close election, may hold the balance of power; that is, in an election in which the non-Negro vote is about evenly divided. The eleven states of the old Confederacy comprising the Solid South have a total of 127 votes in the electoral college. And these votes, except on rare occasions, are precommitted to any candidate the Democratic party may nominate on whatever platform. Unlike the southern vote, the Negro vote today is tied to no political party. It cannot be counted in advance.

This development is of prime importance not only to the political future of the Negro, but also to that of the South and the nation. If the white politicians are unwilling to face the full implications of this historic shift of political power, the Negro leaders are fully aware of its significance and are prepared to press for fuller recognition of the race's just demands for first-class citizenship.

An alert, independent, and aggressive Negro electorate in collaboration with organized labor and other progressive forces may be an important factor in determining the political complexion of Congress. The growing Negro vote in the South, allied with white progressives, can bring about changes of far-reaching importance in that region. Indeed, the resurgence of Negro voting in Dixie presages the return of the two-party system. The passing of the "white primary," the imminent demise of the poll tax in the seven states which still retain it, the progressive militancy of Negro citizens, all tend toward broadening the base of suffrage in the South among both blacks and whites. This new electorate of both races threatens the continued domination of the courthouse gangs which have been the controlling factors in the Democratic party in the southern states. The success of such a coalition is limited only by the degree to which the white working class in the South can be liberated from the specious doctrine of "white supremacy" as preached by the Bilbos, the Rankins, and the Talmadges. . . .

38. A. PHILIP RANDOLPH URGES
CIVIL DISOBEDIENCE
AGAINST A JIM CROW ARMY

In 1948 the United States Congress considered the enactment of the first peacetime draft law in the nation's history. High-ranking government officials and leading generals favored the preservation of segregated armed forces. In testimony before the Senate Armed Services Committee, A. Philip Randolph, President of the Brotherhood of Sleeping Car Porters, who had become national treasurer of the Committee Against Jimcrow in Military Service and Training, solemnly warned the congressmen that if a draft law were passed without requiring desegregation, he would lead Negroes in a massive civil disobedience campaign and urge them to refuse to register and be conscripted in a jim crow army.

Randolph was the most influential black leader taking this position, and his stand was certainly one of the considerations that persuaded President Harry S Truman to issue a directive ending segregation in the armed forces. Thus was settled an issue about which Negroes had agitated constantly since Randolph listed it among the original demands of the proposed March on Washington of 1941.

Mr. Chairman:

Mr. Grant Reynolds, national chairman of the Committee Against Jimcrow in Military Service and Training, has prepared for you in his testimony today a summary of wartime injustices to Negro soldiers—injustices by the military authorities and injustices by bigoted segments of the police and civilian popu-

"Testimony of A. Philip Randolph, National Treasurer of the Committee Against Jimcrow in Military Service and Training and President of the Brotherhood of Sleeping Car Porters, AFL, Prepared for Delivery Before the Senate Armed Services Committee Wednesday, March 31, 1948." Mimeographed. Copy in CORE Archives, State Historical Society of Wisconsin.

lation. The fund of material on this issue is endless, and yet, three years after the end of the war, as another crisis approaches, large numbers of white Americans are blissfully unaware of the extent of physical and psychological aggression against and oppression of the Negro soldier.

Without taking time for a thorough probe into these relevant data—a probe which could enlighten the nation—Congress may now heed Mr. Truman's call for Universal Military Training and Selective Service, and in the weeks ahead enact a jimcrow conscription law and appropriate billions for the greatest segregation system of all time. In a campaign year, when both major parties are playing cynical politics with the issue of civil rights, Negroes are about to lose the fight against jimcrowism on a national level. Our hard-won local gains in education, fair employment, hospitalization, housing are in danger of being nullified—being swept aside, Mr. Chairman, after decades of work —by a federally enforced pattern of segregation. I am not beguiled by the Army's use of the word "temporary." Whatever may pass in the way of conscription legislation will become permanent, since the world trend is toward militarism. The Army knows this well. In such an eventuality, how could any permanent Fair Employment Practices Commission dare to criticize job discrimination in private industry if the federal government itself were simultaneously discriminating against Negro youth in military installations all over the world?

There can be no doubt of my facts. Quite bluntly, Chairman Walter G. Andrews of the House Armed Services Committee told a delegation from this organization that the War Department plans segregated white and Negro battalions if Congress passes a draft law. The *Newark Evening News* of March 26, 1948, confirmed this in a Washington dispatch based on official memoranda sent from Secretary Forrestal's office to the House Armed Services Committee. Nine days ago when we called this to the attention of the Commander-in-Chief in a White House conference, he indicated that he was aware of these plans for jimcrow battalions. This despite his Civil Rights message to Congress.

We have released all of this damaging information to the daily press, to leaders of both parties in Congress, and to supposedly liberal organizations. But with a relative handful of exceptions, we have found our white "friends" silent, indifferent, even hostile. Justice Roberts, who provided you last week with vigorous testimony in behalf of the President's draft recommendations, is a trustee of Lincoln University in Pennsylvania, a prominent Negro institution. Yet for nearly four months, Mr. Roberts has not shown us the courtesy to reply to letters asking his support for anti-segregation and civil rights safeguards in any draft law. Three days after the *Newark Sunday News* embarrassed Congressman Harry L. Towe in his home district by exposing his similar failure to acknowledge our correspondence, Mr. Towe, author of the UMT bill in the House, suddenly found time to answer letters which had been on his desk since December.

This situation—this conspiracy of silence, shall I say?—has naturally commanded wide publicity in the Negro press. I submit for the record a composite of newspaper clippings. In my travels around the country I have sounded out Negro public opinion and confirmed for myself the popular resentment as reflected by the Negro press. I can assure members of the Senate that Negroes *do* put civil rights above the high cost of living and above every other major issue of the day, as recently reported by the Fortune Opinion Poll, I believe. Even more significant is the bitter, angry mood of the Negro in his present determination to win those civil rights in a country that subjects him daily to so many insults and indignities.

With this background, gentlemen, I reported last week to President Truman that Negroes are in no mood to shoulder a gun for democracy abroad so long as they are denied democracy here at home. In particular, they resent the idea of fighting or being drafted into another jimcrow Army. I passed this information on to Mr. Truman not as threat, but rather as a frank, factual survey of Negro opinion.

Today I should like to make clear to the Senate Armed Services Committee and through you, to Congress and the American people that passage now of a jimcrow draft may only result in a mass civil disobedience movement along the lines of the magnificent struggles of the people of India against British imperialism. I must emphasize that the current agitation for civil rights is no longer a mere expression of hope on the part of Negroes. On the one hand, it is a positive, resolute outreaching for full manhood. On the other hand, it is an equally determined will to stop acquiescing in anything less. Negroes demand full, unqualified first-class citizenship.

In resorting to the principles of direct-action techniques of Gandhi, whose death was publicly mourned by many members of Congress and President Truman, Negroes will be serving a higher law than any passed by a national legislature in an era when racism spells our doom. They will be serving a law higher than any decree of the Supreme Court which in the famous Winfred Lynn case evaded ruling on the flagrantly illegal segregation practiced under the wartime Selective Service Act. In refusing to accept compulsory military segregation, Negro youth will be serving their fellow men throughout the world.

I feel qualified to make this claim because of a recent survey of American psychologists, sociologists and anthropologists. The survey revealed an overwhelming belief among these experts that enforced segregation on racial or religious lines has serious and detrimental psychological effects both on the segregated groups *and on those enforcing segregation.* Experts from the South, I should like to point out, gentlemen, were as positive as those from other sections of the country as to the harmful effects of segregation. The views of these social scientists were based on scientific research and on their own professional experience.

So long as the Armed Services propose to enforce such universally harmful segregation not only here at home but also overseas, Negro youth have a moral obligation not to lend themselves as world-wide carriers of an evil and hellish doctrine. Secretary of the Army Kenneth C. Royall clearly indicated in the New Jersey National Guard situation that the Armed Services *do* have every intention of prolonging their anthropologically hoary and untenable policies.

For 25 years now the myth has been carefully cultivated that

Soviet Russia has ended all discrimination and intolerance, while here at home the American Communists have skillfully posed as champions of minority groups. To the rank-and-file Negro in World War II, Hitler's racism posed a sufficient threat for him to submit to the jimcrow Army abuses. But this factor of minority group persecution in Russia is not present, as a popular issue, in the power struggle between Stalin and the United States. I can only repeat that this time Negroes will not take a jimcrow draft lying down. The conscience of the world will be shaken as by nothing else when thousands and thousands of us second-class Americans choose imprisonment in preference to permanent military slavery.

While I cannot with absolute certainty claim results at this hour, I personally will advise Negroes to refuse to fight as slaves for a democracy they cannot possess and cannot enjoy. Let me add that I am speaking only for myself, not even for the Committee Against Jimcrow in Military Service and Training, since I am not sure that all its members would follow my position. But Negro leaders in close touch with GI grievances would feel derelict in their duty if they did not support such a justified civil disobedience movement—especially those of us whose age would protect us from being drafted. Any other course would be a betrayal of those who place their trust in us. I personally pledge myself to openly counsel, aid and abet youth, both white and Negro, to *quarantine* any jimcrow conscription system, whether it bear the label of UMT or Selective Service.

I shall tell youth of all races not to be tricked by any euphonious election-year *registration* for a draft. This evasion, which the newspapers increasingly discuss as a convenient way out for Congress, would merely presage a synthetic "crisis" immediately after November 2nd when all talk of equality and civil rights would be branded unpatriotic while the induction machinery would move into high gear. On previous occasions I have seen the "national emergency" psychology mow down legitimate Negro demands.

From coast to coast in my travels I shall call upon all Negro veterans to join this civil disobedience movement and to recruit their younger brothers in an organized refusal to register and be drafted. Many veterans, bitter over Army jimcrow, have indicated that they will act spontaneously in this fashion, regardless of any organized movement. "Never again," they say with finality.

I shall appeal to the thousands of *white* youth in schools and colleges who are today vigorously shedding the prejudices of their parents and professors. I shall urge them to demonstrate their solidarity with Negro youth by ignoring the entire registration and induction machinery. And finally I shall appeal to Negro parents to lend their moral support to their sons—to stand behind them as they march with heads high to federal prisons as a telling demonstration to the world that Negroes have reached the limit of human endurance—that is, in the words of the spiritual, we'll be buried in our graves before we will be slaves.

May I, in conclusion, Mr. Chairman, point out that political maneuvers have made this drastic program our last resort. Your party, the party of Lincoln, solemnly pledged in its 1944 platform a full-fledged Congressional investigation of injustices to Negro soldiers. Instead of that long overdue probe, the Senate Armed Services Committee on this very day is finally hearing testimony from two or three Negro veterans for a period of 20 minutes each. The House Armed Services Committee and Chairman Andrews went one step further and arrogantly refused to hear any at all! Since we cannot obtain an adequate Congressional forum for our grievances, we have no other recourse but to tell our story to the peoples of the world by organized direct action. I don't believe that even a wartime censorship wall could be high enough to conceal news of a civil disobedience program. If we cannot win your support for your own Party commitments, if we cannot ring a bell in you by appealing to human decency, we shall command your respect and the respect of the world by our united refusal to cooperate with tyrannical injustice.

Since the military, with their Southern biases, intend to take over America and institute total encampment of the populace along jimcrow lines, Negroes will resist with the power of non-violence, with the weapons of moral principles, with the good-will weapons of the spirit, yes with the weapons that brought freedom to India. I feel morally obligated to disturb and keep disturbed the conscience of jimcrow America. In resisting the insult of jimcrowism to the soul of black America, we are helping to save the soul of America. And let me add that I am opposed to Russian totalitarian communism and all its works. I consider it a menace to freedom. I stand by democracy as expressing the Judean-Christian ethic. But democracy and Christianity must be boldly and courageously applied for all men regardless of race, color, creed or country.

We shall wage a relentless warfare against jimcrow without hate or revenge for the moral and spiritual progress and safety of our country, world peace and freedom.

Finally let me say that Negroes are just sick and tired of being pushed around and we just don't propose to take it, and we do not care what happens.

39. ROY WILKINS SUMS UP
NAACP STRATEGY
"AT THE BEGINNING OF A NEW ERA"

In an address delivered at the forty-sixth annual NAACP Convention, in 1955, Roy Wilkins, Walter White's successor as executive secretary of the NAACP, voiced both the hope raised by the Supreme Court's 1954 decision and the fear of complacency following a great victory. Wilkins emphasized voting and the NAACP's legislative program as major components in the organization's strategy, both in the preceding period and in the years that lay immediately ahead.

Last year at Dallas we had a celebration. The convention theme was victory, for we had just had the pronouncement of the

Roy Wilkins, THE CONSPIRACY TO DENY EQUALITY (New York: NAACP, 1955). Reprinted with permission of the author.

United States Supreme Court that segregation in the public schools was unconstitutional.

Most of us knew that the victory was sweet, not because it immediately desegregated the Jim Crow schools, but because it gave us the prize we had been seeking for fifty-eight years: the declaration by the nation's highest court that such segregation was now unlawful. Hitherto, we had had the moral conviction that these schools were wrong and contrary to the guarantees of American citizenship; we had had outrage and frustration as our companions while we went up and down the land seeking recruits to our army of moral and spiritual devotees.

But we had not had the law. We had no means of enforcing our moral convictions except through preachment and persuasion. We secured converts, but they—and we—were helpless without the law. On May 17, 1954, we got the law. On May 31, 1955, we got the decree as to how the law would have to be carried out.

With the May 31 opinion, it has become apparent that we have entered a new era, an era where racial discrimination and segregation are to be not merely morally wrong but contrary to the law and the Constitution. . . .

. . . Our great Association which has carried the fight thus far is faced with new challenges, new responsibilities, new and more pressing calls to duty, to devotion, intelligence and skill. Each and every officer and member, wherever he may be, shares the heavy burden of the transition. None may shirk his duty, for that would be to betray the ones who come after. Let no one in tomorrow's world be able to say that in the years of decision, when destiny was in our hands, we failed to measure up. The people of 1903 had no such challenge and opportunity; nor did those of 1923, or 1943. This great day is ours. Upon us depend the speed, the order and the completeness of the victory.

We have emerged from more than a half-century of the doctrine of "separate but equal" set forth in the now-famous *Plessy* v. *Ferguson* case of 1896. We Negroes always knew the Plessy doctrine to be wrong and we fervently believed it to be unconstitutional. But it was not until our attorneys carried to the

highest court the challenge to its legality that we finally shook off
the shackles that had hobbled our progress since the turn of
the century.

What did the Plessy era hold for us? To what kind of life were
we committed by it? Discrimination and segregation was our
lot. . . .

. . . We have been subject to the whims and fancies of white
persons, individually and collectively. We went to back doors
and were forced to live in hollows and alleys and back streets.
We stepped off sidewalks and removed our hats and said "Sir"
to all and sundry, if they were white. If schools were provided,
our children went to shanties and whites to schools. We rode in
the rear seats of buses and trolleys and in the dirty, dangerous
front end coaches of the trains. We could not vote. Our health
and our recreation were of little or no concern to the responsible
officials of government. In time of war we were called to serve,
but were insulted, degraded and mistreated even as we fought
to defend the flag that flew over every American. We were
beaten, shot, lynched and burned and no man was punished for
what he did to us.

Slowly in this fifty-eight years, we have lifted ourselves by our
own bootstraps. Step by halting step, we have beaten our way
back. It has been a long and tortuous road since the Dred Scott
decision of 1857 which branded us as non-citizens and which, by
the Plessy decision, gave the states and the nation as a whole the
green light to treat us as they pleased. . . .

We need only recall, not recount the victories along the way.
We wiped out lynching. We knocked out the strongest barriers to
voting, as well as the widely-used restrictive covenants on housing. We have clothed our fighting men with dignity. Travel is no
longer an ordeal of both the body and the spirit. The courts, in
the South as well as in the North, are becoming places where
color-blind justice is dispensed. Our men and women are working at more and better jobs and at better and better wages.

Now, our children, at long last, are to have equality in education. They are to have a chance in the race of life without being
penalized before they are born.

Truly, we are at the beginning of a new era. But just as the old order did not pass without prayer and struggle and sacrifice—even unto death—so the new order will not come into being unless we accomplish it by our own efforts. This is the beginning, not the end. This is a time for action, not for resting. Some have complained that they thought May 17 settled everything and that now they could retire and enjoy. Freedom never came to any people in that fashion.

We cannot be complacent as we see before our eyes the outlines of a conspiracy to deny, in 1955, the equality we have won for ourselves. For this school decision heralds the death of all inequality in citizenship based upon race. The Richmond, Virginia editor, Virginius Dabney, correctly stated in 1953 that public schools segregation was the keystone in the arch of segregation. It has been knocked out and the arch will fall.

The conspirators know this, hence the desperation of their tactics. To us who have known the refined as well as the brutal methods of persecution, the emerging pattern is not new.

First they are organizing. Here and there, dotting the South, organizations have sprung up overnight, some with fancy names like Virginia's Defenders of State Sovereignty and Individual Liberty and others like the White Citizens' Councils in Mississippi which frankly declare their anti-Negro purpose.

Terror and intimidation are the weapons being used. The Mississippi Councils—now spreading to Alabama—seek to freeze Negroes economically and frighten them bodily.

"We intend," said one organizer, "to see that no Negro who believes in equality has a job, gets credit, or is able to exist in our communities."

"Is able to exist"—that means agree and knuckle under, or flee, or die.

It is not strange that in such an atmosphere, Rev. George W. Lee was murdered by a shotgun blast on May 7 in his home town of Belzoni, Miss. Rev. Lee's "crime" was that he was the first Negro to register to vote in his county and he had refused orders from whites to remove his name from the voting list. The state headquarters of the White Citizens' Councils is a scant sixty miles from Belzoni, in Winona, Miss.

But naked terror alone will not do the job. Even murder will not guarantee victory to the conspirators.

They have a well-oiled system, rooted in politics, by which they hope to stave off defeat. All these years the system has worked. Today they are trying to use it still.

At the local and state levels they have enforced disfranchisement of Negroes which in turn has permitted the election of local and state officers wholly indifferent to the plight, wishes and demands of our citizens. No better illustration of the effectiveness of this technique at this level can be found than the actions of the South Carolina, Georgia, Louisiana and Mississippi legislators during the past year in passing legislation frankly and brazenly labelled as efforts to deny the Negro equality and to prevent him from voting.

This same disfranchisement has permitted the election of congressmen and senators to Washington who are pledged to block any executive or legislative moves which recognize the needs of Negroes as citizens. The southern congressmen and senators have used their committee posts to smother legislation and, in the Senate, the filibuster to kill legislation.

While ham-stringing Presidents and choking off legislation they have not had as much success in hampering the courts, although they have done their best through their power to confirm judicial appointees. With but few exceptions they are now in full cry against the courts and especially the Supreme Court. If they had a ghost of a chance they would emulate South Africa in making Supreme Court decrees subject to ratification by the Congress.

Thus we have had a two-pronged political operation, one prong bottling up the Negro vote in the South at the ballot box level, and the other nullifying the Negro vote in the North by the use of blackjack tactics in both Houses of the Congress.

This system has worked through the decades whether a Democratic or Republican president has been in office. The only

Chief Executive to buck it was Harry S. Truman who split his party rather than keep silent on his recommendations as to civil rights for Negro Americans.

The system has been aided by northern Democrats who seek "party unity" as they play poker politics with the civil rights of Negroes as the joker card.

The system is aided also by the Republicans who seek support for their program and who also continue to hope that they will be able to build a permanent party structure in the South. It might be added here that if they continue to talk like Dixiecrats, act like Dixiecrats, and vote like Dixiecrats, they will not have to infiltrate the South; it will have taken them over.

One of our principal objectives as an Association is the smashing of this iniquitous network of political strangulation which has its base in the choking off of Negro citizenship rights at the precinct or county level through denial of the ballot. During the past year we have stimulated increased registration by Negro citizens in many southern states. Intensive campaigns have been underway in Virginia, Alabama, North Carolina, and South Carolina. We expect to increase this activity in these and other states between now and the 1956 election.

Along with the effort to broaden the voting base in the South will go a campaign to use the northern Negro's voting strength to break the hold of the Dixiecrat system. Northern Democratic office holders may continue to receive Negro votes on the basis of their individual records, and many, like Senator Herbert Lehman of New York, have most excellent records. But increasingly, Negro voters—as far as the Democratic party is concerned—are demanding less unity with the system that disfranchises, insults, terrorizes, and generally creates an atmosphere in which violence can flourish. They want no unity with the White Councils of Mississippi; no unity with areas that murder men as Rev. Lee was murdered, for wanting to vote; no unity with the forces of slander, as exemplified by a nationwide radio talk of Senator Allen J. Ellender of Louisiana branding Negroes as ignorant, diseased, and crime-ridden; no unity with those who defy the law of the land as laid down by the Supreme Court, as exemplified by the recent television broadcast of Senator James O. Eastland of Mississippi.

On the other hand, the Republicans who hope and hope cannot expect substantial support as long as they "play footsie" with southern Democrats on civil rights. They wonder why the Negro vote does not return to the GOP fold. Well, thousands want to return because they are not comfortable in the party of Herman Talmadge, but they cannot see any percentage in changing as long as the Republicans play ball with the Dixiecrats.

These conspirators about whom I have been talking—the conscious as well as the unconscious ones—went so far as to enlist the prestige of the White House in their demands to maintain segregation and circumvent the national policy of no discrimination in the armed services. On June 8 the President in his press conference lashed out at those who seek anti-segregation amendments to pending legislation including the military reserves bill.

We who seek such amendments were accused of placing our special desires above the security of the nation. We want to say here plainly and unmistakably that it is not we who seek our own way at the expense of the country. It is the southern Democratic bloc which openly threatened to kill the military reserves bill unless it contained their provision for segregation. The President has every right to demand the legislation he deems necessary for the welfare of the nation, but in all fairness the blame for the delay on that legislation should be placed at the doorstep of those who are guilty.

We love our country. We have fought for it in the past and we will fight for it in the future, but we do not relish our patriotism being called into question because we demand our rights as American citizens.

We feel the same way about the anti-segregation amendment to the housing bill and to the bill which would provide aid to the states for the construction of public schools. We do not believe that housing which is provided out of the funds or the credit of all the people of the United States should be denied to any citizen because of his race or color. We do not believe that the tax funds of all the people of the United States should be given to any state or locality for the purpose of subsidizing these in defying the Supreme Court ruling on segregated schools.

Our legislative goals, of course, are not limited to amendments to pending bills. Although the President expressed the opinion in 1953 that the states should pass fair employment practice bills, only the states with Democratic administrations have so far complied, the latest being Minnesota and Michigan. Two state governments of the President's own party—Illinois and Pennsylvania—have defeated FEPC. Neither the 83rd or the 84th Congress has done anything on FEPC, nor has the President made any recommendation on this or any other civil rights bill.

Our Department of Justice will remain almost impotent in prosecuting civil rights crimes, such as the murders of Mr. and Mrs. Harry T. Moore of Florida, and Rev. Lee of Mississippi, until Congress passes a bill to strengthen the civil rights laws.

These and other bills to make secure the rights of all our citizens form the continuing objective of our members who will make their likes and dislikes known in the polling booths.

Yes, in fashioning the new era we shall use all the weapons at our disposal. Thurgood Marshall, our general counsel, has outlined how we will use the courts. We shall continue to use education and persuasion and moral pressure. Heartened by the support of millions of our white fellow citizens in all sections of the country, we welcome their participation in the crusade which is one not alone for us, but for our nation as a whole. And we shall use all the political power we can muster, for this is the most vital ingredient in a government of, by and for the people, not the white people, but all the people. . . .

We shall go upright. We shall go in faith, without hatred of any man, but with determination in the righteousness of our cause, armed with the weapons provided for us. We shall not— we cannot—fail. We shall, we will, be free men.

the
era
of
nonviolent
direct action

PART THREE

The philosophy
of Martin Luther King, Jr.

40. MARTIN LUTHER KING, JR.:
"OUR STRUGGLE" FOR
"AN INTERRACIAL SOCIETY
BASED ON FREEDOM FOR ALL"

The bus boycott in Montgomery, Alabama during 1955 and 1956 not only led to the desegregation of the city's buses but it also gave the nonviolent movement its greatest symbolic leader, Martin Luther King, Jr. King was one of those rare black activists who believed in nonviolence as a philosophy, rather than merely as a tactic. The selections reprinted here, written while the boycott was going on, describe the early months of the Montgomery Movement and King's own ideology of spiritual nonviolence and Christian love. Although King traced his intellectual antecedents to a number of philosophers and religious thinkers, his outlook was closely akin to, and largely derived from, that of the founders of CORE.

A. "We Negroes have replaced self-pity with self-respect and . . . with dignity"

The segregation of Negroes, with its inevitable discrimination, has thrived on elements of inferiority present in the masses of both white and Negro people. Through forced separation

Martin Luther King, Jr., OUR STRUGGLE: THE STORY OF MONTGOMERY (New York: Congress of Racial Equality, 1956).

from our African culture, through slavery, poverty, and deprivation, many black men lost self-respect.

In their relations with Negroes, white people discovered that
they had rejected the very center of their own ethical professions. They could not face the triumph of their lesser instincts
and simultaneously have peace within. And so, to gain it, they
rationalized—insisting that the unfortunate Negro, being less
than human, deserved and even enjoyed second class status.

They argued that his inferior social, economic and political
position was good for him. He was incapable of advancing beyond a fixed position and would therefore be happier if encouraged not to attempt the impossible. He is subjugated by a
superior people with an advanced way of life. The "master race"
will be able to civilize him to a limited degree, if only he will be
true to his inferior nature and stay in his place.

White men soon came to forget that the Southern social culture and all its institutions had been organized to perpetuate
this rationalization. They observed a caste system and quickly
were conditioned to believe that its social results, which they
had created, actually reflected the Negro's innate and true
nature.

In time many Negroes lost faith in themselves and came to
believe that perhaps they really were what they had been told
they were—something less than men. So long as they were prepared to accept this role, racial peace could be maintained. It
was an uneasy peace in which the Negro was forced to accept
patiently injustice, insult, injury and exploitation.

Gradually the Negro masses in the South began to re-evaluate
themselves—a process that was to change the nature of the Negro community and doom the social patterns of the South. We
discovered that we had never really smothered our self-respect
and that we could not be at one with ourselves without asserting
it. From this point on, the South's terrible peace was rapidly
undermined by the Negro's new and courageous thinking and
his ever-increasing readiness to organize and to act. Conflict and
violence were coming to the surface as the white South desperately clung to its old patterns. The extreme tension in race

relations in the South today is explained in part by the revolutionary change in the Negro's evaluation of himself and of his destiny and by his determination to struggle for justice. *We Negroes have replaced self-pity with self-respect and self-depreciation with dignity.*

When Mrs. Rosa Parks, the quiet seamstress whose arrest precipitated the non-violent protest in Montgomery, was asked why she had refused to move to the rear of a bus, she said: "It was a matter of dignity; I could not have faced myself and my people if I had moved."

Many of the Negroes who joined the protest did not expect it to succeed. When asked why, they usually gave one of three answers: "I didn't expect Negroes to stick to it," or, "I never thought we Negroes had the nerve," or, "I thought the pressure from the white folks would kill it before it got started."

In other words, our non-violent protest in Montgomery is important because it is demonstrating to the Negro, North and South, that many of the stereotypes he has held about himself and other Negroes are not valid. Montgomery has broken the spell and is ushering in concrete manifestations of the thinking and action of the new Negro.

We now know that:

We can stick together. In Montgomery, 42,000 of us have refused to ride the city's segregated buses since December 5. Some walk as many as fourteen miles a day.

Our leaders do not have to sell out. Many of us have been indicted, arrested, and "mugged." Every Monday and Thursday night we stand before the Negro population at the prayer meetings and repeat: "It is an honor to face jail for a just cause."

Threats and violence do not necessarily intimidate those who are sufficiently aroused and non-violent. The bombing of two of our homes has made us more resolute. When a handbill was circulated at a White Citizens Council meeting stating that Negroes should be "abolished" by "guns, bows and arrows, sling shots and knives," we responded with even greater determination.

Our church is becoming militant. Twenty-four ministers were arrested in Montgomery. Each has said publicly that he stands prepared to be arrested again. Even upper-class Negroes who reject the "come to Jesus" gospel are now convinced that the church has no alternative but to provide the non-violent dynamics for social change in the midst of conflict. The $30,000 used for the car pool, which transports over 20,000 Negro workers, school children and housewives, has been raised in the churches. The churches have become the dispatch centers where the people gather to wait for rides.

We believe in ourselves. In Montgomery we walk in a new way. We hold our heads in a new way. Even the Negro reporters who converged on Montgomery have a new attitude. One tired reporter, asked at a luncheon in Birmingham to say a few words about Montgomery, stood up, thought for a moment, and uttered one sentence: "Montgomery has made me proud to be a Negro."

Economics is part of our struggle. We are aware that Montgomery's white businessmen have tried to "talk sense" to the bus company and the city commissioners. We have observed that small Negro shops are thriving as Negroes find it inconvenient to walk downtown to the white stores. We have been getting more polite treatment in the white shops since the protest began. We have a new respect for the proper use of our dollar.

We have discovered a new and powerful weapon—non-violent resistance. Although law is an important factor in bringing about social change, there are certain conditions in which the very effort to adhere to new legal decisions creates tension and provokes violence. We had hoped to see demonstrated a method that would enable us to continue our struggle while coping with the violence it aroused. Now we see the answer: face violence if necessary, but refuse to return violence. If we respect those who oppose us, they may achieve a new understanding of the human relations involved.

We now know that the Southern Negro has become of age, politically and morally. Montgomery has demonstrated that we will not run from the struggle, and will support the battle for equality. The attitude of many young Negroes a few years ago was reflected in the common expression, "I'd rather be a lamp post in Harlem than Governor of Alabama." Now the idea expressed in our churches, schools, pool rooms, restaurants and homes is: "Brother, stay here and fight non-violently. 'Cause if you don't let them make you mad, you can win." The official slogan of the Montgomery Improvement Association is "Justice without Violence."

Modest demands rejected

The leaders of the old order in Montgomery are not prepared to negotiate a settlement. This is not because of the conditions we have set for returning to the buses. The basic question of segregation in intra-state travel is already before the courts. Meanwhile we ask only for what in Atlanta, Mobile, Charleston and most other cities of the South is considered the Southern pattern. We seek the right, under segregation, to seat ourselves from the rear forward on a first come, first served basis. In addition, we ask for courtesy and the hiring of some Negro bus drivers on predominantly Negro routes.

A prominent judge of Tuscaloosa was asked if he felt there was any connection between Autherine Lucy's effort to enter the University of Alabama and the Montgomery non-violent protest. He replied, "Autherine is just an unfortunate girl who doesn't know what she is doing, but in Montgomery it looks like all the niggers have gone crazy."

Later the judge is reported to have explained that "of course the good niggers had undoubtedly been riled up by outsiders, Communists and agitators." It is apparent that at this historic moment most of the elements of the white South are not prepared to believe that "our Negroes could of themselves act like this."

Because the mayor and city authorities cannot admit to themselves that we have changed, every move they have made has inadvertently increased the protest and united the Negro community.

Dec. 1—They arrested Mrs. Parks, one of the most respected Negro women in Montgomery.

Dec. 3—They attempted to intimidate the Negro population by publishing a report in the daily paper that certain Negroes were calling for a boycott of the buses. They thereby informed the 30,000 Negro readers of the planned protest.

Dec. 5—They found Mrs. Parks guilty and fined her $14. This action increased the number of those who joined the boycott.

Dec. 5—They arrested a Negro college student for "intimidating passengers." Actually, he was helping an elderly woman cross the street. This mistake solidified the college students' support of the protest.

Two policemen on motocycles followed each bus on its rounds through the Negro community. This attempt at psychological coercion further increased the number of Negroes who joined the protest.

In a news telecast at 6:00 p.m. a mass meeting planned for that evening was announced. Although we had expected only 500 people at the meeting, over 5,000 attended.

Dec. 6—They began to intimidate Negro taxi drivers. This led to the setting up of a car pool and a resolution to extend indefinitely our protest, which had originally been called for one day only.

Dec. 7—They began to harass Negro motorists. This encouraged the Negro middle class to join the struggle.

Dec. 8—The lawyer for the bus company said, "We have no intention of hiring Negro drivers now or in the foreseeable future." To us this meant never. The slogan then became, "Stay off the buses until we win."

Dec. 9—The mayor invited Negro leaders to a conference, presumably for negotiations. When we arrived, we discovered that some of the men in the room were white supremacists and members of the White Citizens Council. The mayor's attitude was made clear when he said, "Comes the first rainy day and the Negroes will be back in the buses." The next day it did rain, but the Negroes did not ride the buses.

At this point over 42,000 Montgomery Negroes had joined

the protest. After a period of uneasy quiet, elements in the white community turned to further police intimidation and to violence.

Jan. 26—I was arrested for travelling 30 miles per hour in a 25-mile zone. This arrest occurred just 2 hours before a mass meeting. So, we had to hold seven mass meetings to accommodate the people.

Jan. 30—My home was bombed.

Feb. 1—The home of E. D. Nixon, one of the protest leaders and former state president of the NAACP, was bombed. This brought moral and financial support from all over the state.

Feb. 22—Eighty-nine persons, including the 24 ministers, were arrested for participating in the non-violent protest.

The method of non-violence

Every attempt to end the protest by intimidation, by encouraging Negroes to inform, by force and violence, further cemented the Negro community and brought sympathy for our cause from men of good will all over the world. The great appeal for the world appears to lie in the fact that we in Montgomery have adopted the method of non-violence. In a world in which most men attempt to defend their highest values by the accumulation of weapons of destruction, it is morally refreshing to hear 5,000 Negroes in Montgomery shout "Amen" and "Halleluh" when they are exhorted to "pray for those who oppose you," or pray "Oh Lord, give us strength of body to keep walking for freedom," and conclude each mass meeting with: "Let us pray that God shall give us strength to remain non-violent though we may face death."

And death there may be. Many white men in the South see themselves as a fearful minority in an ocean of black men. They honestly believe with one side of their minds that Negroes are depraved and disease-ridden. They look upon any effort at equality as leading to "mongrelization." They are convinced that racial equality is a Communist idea and that those who ask for it are subversive. They believe that their caste system is the highest form of social organization.

The enlightened white Southerner, who for years has preached gradualism, now sees that even the slow approach finally has revolutionary implications. Placing straws on a camel's back, no matter how slowly, is dangerous. This realization has immobilized the liberals and most of the white church leaders. They have no answer for dealing with or absorbing violence. They end in begging for retreat, lest "things get out of hand and lead to violence."

Writing in *Life*, William Faulkner, Nobel prize-winning author from Mississippi, recently urged the NAACP to "stop now for a moment." That is to say, he encouraged Negroes to accept injustice, exploitation and indignity for a while longer. It is hardly a moral act to encourage others patiently to accept injustice which he himself does not endure.

In urging delay, which in this dynamic period is tantamount to retreat, Faulkner suggests that those of us who press for change now may not know that violence could break out. He says we are "dealing with a fact: the fact of emotional conditions of such fierce unanimity as to scorn the fact that it is a minority and which will go to any length and against any odds at the moment to justify and, if necessary, defend that condition and its right to it."

The answer to Faulkner

We Southern Negroes believe that it is essential to defend the right of equality now. From this position we will not and cannot retreat. Fortunately, we are increasingly aware that we must not try to defend our position by methods that contradict the aim of brotherhood. We in Montgomery believe that the only way to press on is by adopting the philosophy and practice of non-violent resistance.

This method permits a struggle to go on with dignity and without the need to retreat. It is a method that can absorb the violence that is inevitable in social change whenever deep-seated prejudices are challenged.

If, in pressing for justice and equality in Montgomery, we discover that those who reject equality are prepared to use violence, we must not despair, retreat, or fear. Before they make this crucial decision, they must remember: whatever they do, we will not use violence in return. We hope we can act in the struggle in such a way that they will see the error of their approach and will come to respect us. Then we can all live together in peace and equality.

The basic conflict is not really over the buses. Yet we believe that, if the method we use in dealing with equality in the buses can eliminate injustice within ourselves, we shall at the same time be attacking the basis of injustice—man's hostility to man. This can only be done when we challenge the white community to re-examine its assumptions as we are now prepared to re-examine ours.

We do not wish to triumph over the white community. That would only result in transferring those now on the bottom to the top. But, if we can live up to non-violence in thought and deed, there will emerge an interracial society based on freedom for all.

B. ". . . a nonviolent protest against injustice"

The present protest here in Montgomery on the part of the Negro citizens, grows out of many experiences—experiences that have often been humiliating and have led to deep resentment. The Negro citizens of Montgomery compose about 75% of the bus riders. In riding buses, they have confronted conditions which have made for a great deal of embarrassment, such as having to stand over empty seats, having to pay fares at the front door and going out to the back to get on, and then the very humiliating experience of being arrested for refusing to get up and give a seat to a person of another race.

These conditions and those experiences have now reached the point that the Negro citizens are tired, and this tiredness was expressed on December 5, when more than 99 percent of the Negro bus riders decided not to ride the buses, in a protest against these

Martin Luther King, Jr., "Walk for Freedom," FELLOWSHIP, XXII (May 1956), pp. 5–7.

unjust conditions. This protest has lasted now for many, many weeks and it is still in process.

From the beginning, we have insisted on nonviolence. This is a protest—a *nonviolent* protest against injustice. We are depending on moral and spiritual forces. To put it another way, this is a movement of passive resistance, and the great instrument is the instrument of love. We feel that this is our chief weapon, and that no matter how long we are involved in the protest, no matter how tragic the experiences are, no matter what sacrifices we have to make, we will not let anybody drag us so low as to hate them.

Love *must* be at the forefront of our movement if it is to be a successful movement. And when we speak of love, we speak of understanding, good will toward *all* men. We speak of a creative, a redemptive sort of love, so that as we look at the problem, we see that the real tension is not between the Negro citizens and the white citizens of Montgomery, but it is a conflict between justice and injustice, between the forces of light and the forces of darkness, and if there is a victory—and there *will* be a victory—the victory will not be merely for the Negro citizens and a defeat for the white citizens, but it will be a victory for justice and a defeat of injustice. It will be a victory for goodness in its long struggle with the forces of evil.

Violence is immoral

This is a spiritual movement, and we intend to keep these things in the forefront. We know that violence will defeat our purpose. We know that in our struggle in America and in our specific struggle here in Montgomery, violence will not only be impractical but immoral. We are outnumbered; we do not have access to the instruments of violence. Even more than that, not only is violence impractical, but it is *immoral;* for it is my firm conviction that to seek to retaliate with violence does nothing but intensify the existence of evil and hate in the universe.

Along the way of life, someone must have *sense* enough and morality enough to cut off the chain of hate and evil. The greatest way to do that is through love. I believe firmly that love is a transforming power that can lift a whole community to new horizons of fair play, good will and justice.

Love vs. bombs

Love is our great instrument and our great weapon, and that alone. On January my home was bombed. My wife and baby were there; I was attending a meeting. I first heard of the bombing at the meeting, when someone came to me and mentioned it, and I tried to accept it in a very calm manner. I first inquired about my wife and daughter; then after I found out that they were all right, I stopped in the midst of the meeting and spoke to the group, and urged them not to be panicky and not to do anything about it because that was not the way.

I immediately came home and, on entering the front of the house, I noticed there were some 500-1000 persons. I came in the house and looked it over and went back to see my wife and to see if the baby was all right, but as I stood in the back of the house, hundreds and hundreds of people were still gathering, and I saw there that violence was a possibility.

It was at that time that I went to the porch and tried to say to the people that we could not allow ourselves to be panicky. We could not allow ourselves to retaliate with any type of violence, but that we were still to confront the problem with *love*.

One statement that I made—and I believe it very firmly—was: "He who lives by the sword will perish by the sword." I urged the people to continue to manifest love, and to continue to carry on the struggle with the same dignity and with the same discipline that we had started out with. I think at that time the people did decide to go home, things did get quiet, and it ended up with a great deal of calmness and a great deal of discipline, which I think our community should be proud of and which I was very proud to see because our people were determined not to retaliate with violence.

"Stand up to the finish"

Some twenty-six of the ministers and almost one hundred of the citizens of the city were indicted in this boycott. But we realized in the beginning that we would confront experiences that make for great sacrifices, experiences that are not altogether pleasant. We decided among ourselves that we would stand up to the finish, and that is what we are determined to do. In the midst of the indictments, we still hold to this nonviolent attitude, and this primacy of love.

Pray for justice

Even though convicted, we will not retaliate with hate, but will still stand with love in our hearts, and stand resisting injustice, with the same determination with which we started out. We need a great deal of encouragement in this movement. Of course one thing that we are depending on, from not only other communities but from our own community, is prayer. We ask people everywhere to pray that God will guide us, pray that justice will be done and that righteousness will stand. And I think through these prayers we will be strengthened; it will make us feel the unity of the nation and the presence of Almighty God. For as we said all along, this is a spiritual movement.

41. THE SOUTHERN CHRISTIAN LEADERSHIP CONFERENCE: "THE ULTIMATE AIM IS THE 'BELOVED COMMUNITY' "

In 1957 Martin Luther King established the Southern Christian Leadership Conference (SCLC) to coordinate local nonviolent direct-action protest movements that were appearing in various parts of the South. The objectives, philosophy, and major activities of SCLC are set forth in *This Is SCLC*, a leaflet that has gone into several editions.

THIS IS SCLC (Leaflet: Southern Christian Leadership Conference, revised edition [1964?]). Reprinted with permission of Martin Luther King.

Aims and purposes of SCLC

The Southern Christian Leadership Conference has the basic aim of achieving full citizenship rights, equality, and the integration of the Negro in all aspects of American life. SCLC is a service agency to facilitate coordinated action of local community groups within the frame of their indigenous organizations and natural leadership. SCLC activity revolves around two main focal points: the use of nonviolent philosophy as a means of creative protest; and securing the right of the ballot for every citizen.

Philosophy of SCLC

The basic tenets of Hebraic-Christian tradition coupled with the Gandhian concept of *satyagraha*—truth force—is at the heart of SCLC's philosophy. Christian nonviolence actively resists evil in any form. It never seeks to humiliate the opponent, only to win him. Suffering is accepted without retaliation. Internal violence of the spirit is as much to be rejected as external physical violence. At the center of nonviolence is redemptive love. Creatively used, the philosophy of nonviolence can restore the broken community in America. SCLC is convinced that nonviolence is the most potent force available to an oppressed people in their struggle for freedom and dignity.

SCLC and nonviolent mass direct action

SCLC believes that the American dilemma in race relations can best and most quickly be resolved through the action of thousands of people, committed to the philosophy of nonviolence, who will physically identify themselves in a just and moral struggle. It is not enough to be intellectually dissatisfied with an evil system. The true nonviolent resister presents his physical body as an instrument to defeat the system. Through nonviolent mass direct action, the evil system is creatively dramatized in order that the conscience of the community may grapple with the rightness or wrongness of the issue at hand. . . .

SCLC and voter-registration

The right of the ballot is basic to the exercise of full citizenship rights. All across the South, subtle and flagrant obstacles confront the Negro when he seeks to register and vote. Poll taxes, long form questionnaires, harassment, economic reprisal, and sometimes death, meet those who dare to seek this exercise of the ballot. In areas where there is little or no attempt to block the voting attempts of the Negro, apathy generally is deeply etched upon the habits of the community. SCLC, with its specialized staff, works on both fronts: aiding local communities through every means available to secure the right to vote (e.g. filing complaints with the Civil Rights Commission) and arousing interest through voter-registration workshops to point up the importance of the ballot. Periodically, SCLC, upon invitation, conducts a voter-registration drive to enhance a community's opportunity to free itself from economic and political servitude. SCLC believes that the most important step the Negro can take is that short walk to the voting booth.

SCLC and civil disobedience

SCLC sees civil disobedience as a natural consequence of nonviolence when the resister is confronted by unjust and immoral laws. This does not imply that SCLC advocates either anarchy or lawlessness. The Conference firmly believes that all people have a moral responsibility to obey laws that are just. It recognizes, however, that there also are unjust laws. From a purely moral point of view, an unjust law is one that is out of harmony with the moral law of the universe, or, as the religionist would say, out of harmony with the Law of God. More concretely, an unjust law is one in which the minority is compelled to observe a code which is not binding on the majority. An unjust law is one in which people are required to obey a code that they had no part in making because they were denied the right to vote. In the face of such obvious inequality, where difference is made legal, the nonviolent resister has no alternative but to disobey the unjust law. In disobeying such a law, he does so peacefully, openly and nonviolently. Most important, he *willingly* accepts the penalty for breaking the law. This distinguishes SCLC's position on civil disobedience from the "uncivil disobedience" of the racist opposition in the South. In the face of laws they consider unjust, they seek to defy, evade, and circumvent the law, BUT they are *un-willing* to accept the penalty for breaking the law. The end result of their defiance is anarchy and disrespect for the law. SCLC, on the other hand, believes that civil disobedience involves the highest respect for the law. He who openly disobeys a law that conscience tells him is unjust and willingly accepts the penalty is giving evidence that he so respects the law that he belongs in jail until it is changed. . . .

SCLC and segregation

SCLC is firmly opposed to segregation in any form that it takes and pledges itself to work unrelentingly to rid every vestige of its scars from our nation through nonviolent means. Segregation is an evil and its presence in our nation has blighted our larger destiny as a leader in world affairs. Segregation does as much harm to the *segregator* as it does to the *segregated*. The *segregated* develops a false sense of inferiority and the *segregator* develops a false sense of superiority, both contrary to the American ideal of democracy. America must rid herself of segregation not alone because it is politically expedient, but because it is morally right!

SCLC and constructive program

SCLC's basic program fosters nonviolent resistance to all forms of racial injustice, including state and local laws and practices, even when this means going to jail; and imaginative, bold constructive action to end the demoralization caused by the legacy of slavery and segregation—inferior schools, slums, and second-class citizenship. Thus, the Conference works on two fronts. On the one hand, it resists continuously the system of segregation which is the basic cause of lagging standards; on the other hand, it works constructively to improve the standards themselves. There MUST be a balance between attacking the causes and healing the effects of segregation.

SCLC and the beloved community

The ultimate aim of SCLC is to foster and create the "beloved community" in America where brotherhood is a reality. It rejects any doctrine of black supremacy for this merely substitutes one kind of tyranny for another. The Conference does not foster moving the Negro from a position of disadvantage to one of advantage for this would thereby subvert justice. SCLC works for integration. Our ultimate goal is genuine intergroup and interpersonal living—*integration*. Only through nonviolence can reconciliation and the creation of the beloved community be effected. The international focus on America and her internal problems against the dread prospect of a hot war, demand our seeking this end.

The new student movement

42. THE STUDENT NONVIOLENT COORDINATING COMMITTEE: "NONVIOLENCE IS THE FOUNDATION"

When the college student sit-in demonstrators of 1960 formed their Student Nonviolent Coordinating Committee (SNCC) it was to Martin Luther King and his philosophy that they at first looked. Later, for reasons of personality and tactics, SNCC and SCLC drifted apart. But the statement of purpose adopted at SNCC's founding convention, with its spirit of moral idealism and emphasis on love and conscience, is a statement clearly based on the lofty principles expressed by Martin Luther King, Jr.

Statement of purpose

We affirm the philosophical or religious ideal of nonviolence as the foundation of our purpose, the presupposition of our faith, and the manner of our action. Nonviolence as it grows from Judaic-Christian traditions seeks a social order of justice permeated by love. Integration of human endeavor represents the crucial first step towards such a society.

Through nonviolence, courage displaces fear; love transforms hate. Acceptance dissipates prejudice; hope ends despair. Peace dominates war; faith reconciles doubt. Mutual regard cancels

"Statement of Purpose" adopted at the first general conference of the Student Nonviolent Coordinating Committee, Raleigh, N.C., April 17, 1960. Printed with permission of SNCC.

enmity. Justice for all overthrows injustice. The redemptive community supersedes systems of gross social immorality.

Love is the central motif of nonviolence. Love is the force by which God binds man to Himself and man to man. Such love goes to the extreme; it remains loving and forgiving even in the midst of hostility. It matches the capacity of evil to inflict suffering with an even more enduring capacity to absorb evil, all the while persisting in love.

By appealing to conscience and standing on the moral nature of human existence, nonviolence nurtures the atmosphere in which reconciliation and justice become actual possibilities.

43. JAMES M. LAWSON, JR.: "WE ARE TRYING TO RAISE THE 'MORAL ISSUE'"

For the group that founded SNCC in 1960, James M. Lawson, Jr. was as much an inspiration as was Martin Luther King himself. Lawson, a student expelled from the Vanderbilt University Divinity School in Nashville, Tennessee, for civil rights activities, was largely responsible for the moral fervor, philosophical sophistication, and exemplary courage that made the Nashville group the most dynamic student movement between 1960 and 1962. In his address to SNCC's founding convention, Lawson publicly articulated the dissatisfaction many youths were feeling with the old-guard leaders, especially in the NAACP. Lawson is now pastor of a Methodist church in Memphis.

These are exciting moments in which to live.

Reflect how over the last few weeks, the "sit-in" movement has leaped from campus to campus, until today hardly any

James M. Lawson, Jr., "From a Lunch-Counter Stool," address at SNCC conference, Raleigh, N.C., April 1960. Printed with permission of the author.

campus remains unaffected. At the beginning of this decade, the student generation was "silent," "uncommitted," or "beatnik." But after only four months, these analogies largely used by adults appear as hasty cliches which should not have been used in the first place. The rapidity and drive of the movement indicates that all the while American students were simply waiting in suspension; waiting for that cause, that ideal, that event, that "actualizing of their faith" which would catapult their right to speak powerfully to their nation and world.

The witness of enthusiastic, but mature young men and women, audacious enough to dare the intimidations and violence of racial injustice, a witness not to be matched by any social effort either in the history of the Negro or in the history of the nation, has caused this impact upon us. In his own time, God has brought this to pass.

But as so frequently happens, these are also enigmatic moments. Enigmatic, for like man in every age who cannot read the signs of the times, many of us are not able to see what appears before us, or hear what is spoken from lunch-counter stools, or understand what has been cried by jail cell bars.

Already the paralysis of talk, the disobedience of piety, the frustration of false ambition, and the insensitiveness of an affluent society yearn to diffuse the meaning and flatten the thrust of America's first major non-violent campaign.

One great university equates the movement to simply another student fad similar to a panty raid, or long black stockings. Many merchants zealously smothering their Negro customers with courtesy for normal services, anticipated an early end to the unprecedented binge. Certainly no southern white person and few Negroes expected the collegiates to face the hoses, jails, mobs and tear gas with such dignity, fearlessness, and non-violence. In fact, under any normal conditions, the mere threat of the law was sufficient to send the Negro scurrying into his ghetto. Even astute race reporters accentuate the protest element as the major factor.

Amid this welter of irrelevant and superficial reactions, the primary motifs of the movement, the essential message, the crucial issue raised are often completely missed. So the Christian student who has not yet given his support or mind to the movement might well want to know what the issue is all about. It is just a lot of nonsense over a hamburger? Or is it far more?

To begin, let us note what the issue is not. Many people of good-will, especially Methodists and Nashvillians, have considered my expulsion from Vanderbilt University and the self-righteousness of the press attack as the focus of attention. But nothing could be further from the truth. The expulsion, three months before the completion of the Bachelor of Divinity degree, drastically alters certain immediate personal plans. The press attack tended to make me a symbol of the movement. But such incidents illustrate an ancient way of escaping an existential moment. Call him "the son of the devil," or one of the "men who turn the world upside down," and there are always the gullible who will "swallow the camel."

Police partiality is not the issue. Nashville has been considered one of those "good" cities where racial violence has not been tolerated. Yet, on a Saturday in February, the mystique of yet another popular myth vanished. For only police permissiveness invited young white men to take over store after store in an effort to further intimidate or crush the "sit-in." Law enforcement agents accustomed to viewing crime, were able to mark well-dressed students waiting to make purchases, as loitering on the lunch-counter stools, but they were unable even to suspect and certainly not to see assault and battery. Thus potential customers, quietly asking for service, are disorderly, breaching the peace, inciting riots, while swaggering, vilifying, violent, defiant white young teenagers are law-abiding. The police of the nation have always reeked [wreaked] brutality upon minority groups. So our Nashville experience is nothing new, or even unexpected. We hold nothing against these hard-pressed officers. Such partiality, however, is symptomatic of the diagnosis only—an inevitable by-product—another means of avoiding the encounter. But the "sit-in" does not intend to make such partiality the issue.

Already many well-meaning and notable voices are seeking

to define the problem in purely legal terms. But if the students wanted a legal case, they had only to initiate a suit. But not a single city began in this fashion. No one planned to be arrested or desired such. The legal battles which will be fought as a consequence of many arrests never once touch on the matter of eating where you normally shop, or on segregation *per se*.

The apparent misuse of local laws requires new legal definitions which can only be made in the courts, under the judgment of the Constitution of the United States. Old laws and ordinances originally written to hamper labor have been revived to stop or crush the sit-in; disorderly conduct codes which could be used against almost every conceivable peaceful demonstration; conspiracy to block trade charges. Obviously these have no relation to the Bill of Rights and are but gimmicks designed to impede civil liberty.

Let us admit readily that some of the major victories gained for social justice have come through the courts, especially the Supreme Court, while other branches of government were often neglecting their primary function to sustain the American experiment. The Negro has been a law-abiding citizen as he has struggled for justice against many unlawful elements.

But the major defeats have occurred when we have been unable to convince the nation to support or implement the Constitution, when a court decision is ignored or nullified by local and state action. A democratic structure of law remains democratic, remains lawful only as the people are continuously persuaded to be democratic. Law is always nullified by practice and disdain unless the minds and hearts of a people sustain law.

When elements of good-will called for law and order during the crisis in Little Rock, their pleas fell on deaf ears. In many sections of the country where law no longer sustains and enforces segregation, the segregation persists because it is etched upon the habits of mind and emotions of both Negro and white. Separate but equal in transportation has by the Supreme Court been judged as impossible and unconstitutional. Yet in many cities like Nashville the buses more or less remain segregated.

Both Negro and white sustain the custom because their basic inner attitudes and fears remain unchanged. Eventually our society must abide by the Constitution and not permit any local law or custom to hinder freedom or justice. But such a society lives by more than law. In the same respect the sit-in movement is not trying to create a legal battle, but points to that which is more than law.

Finally, the issue is not integration. This is particularly true for the Christian oriented person. Certainly the students are asking in behalf of the entire Negro community and the nation that these eating counters become places of service for all persons. But it would be extremely short-sighted to assume that integration is the problem or the word of the "sit-in." To the extent to which the movement reflects deep Christian impulses, desegregation is a necessary next step. But it cannot be the end. If progress has not been at a genuine pace, it is often because the major groups seeking equal rights tactically made desegregation the end and not the means.

The Christian favors the breaking down of racial barriers because the redeemed community of which he is already a citizen recognizes no barriers dividing humanity. The Kingdom of God, as in heaven so on earth, is the distant goal of the Christian. That Kingdom is far more than the immediate need for integration.

Having tried to dispel the many smokescreens spewed to camouflage the purpose and intent of the "sit-in," let me now try as carefully as possible to describe the message of our movement. There are two facets to that message.

In the first instance, we who are demonstrators are trying to raise what we call the "moral issue." That is, we are pointing to the viciousness of racial segregation and prejudice and calling it evil or sin. The matter is not legal, sociological or racial, it is moral and spiritual. Until America (South and North) honestly accepts the sinful nature of racism, this cancerous disease will continue to rape all of us.

For many years Negroes and white have pretended that all was well. "We have good race relations." A city like Nashville has acquired national fame about its progress in desegregation. Yet when the "sit-ins" began, the underlying hatred and sin burst to the surface. A police department with a good reputation for impartiality swiftly became the tool of the disease always there. A mayor, elected with overwhelming Negro support, made the decisions which permitted mob rule. If Nashville had "good race relations," why did such violence explode? The fact is that we were playing make-believe that we were good. All the while Negro and white by pretension, deliberate cooperation and conscious attitudes shared in such a deluded world.

The South and the entire nation are implicated in the same manner. True, there has been progress. For example, lynching has virtually disappeared (although there are many signs that even it might break forth again with unprecedented fury); but the real lynching continues unabated—the lynching of souls, persons (white and Negro) violating its victims absolutely, stripping them of human traits. This actual lynching goes on every day even while we make-believe that lynching is a phenomenon of the past. What's more, the masses of people, including most moderates of both "races," are glibly unaware of the lynching.

The non-violent movement would convict us all of sin. We assert, "Segregation (racial pride) is sin. God tolerates no breach of his judgment. We are an unhealthy people who contrive every escape from ourselves." Thus a simple act of neatly dressed, non-violent students with purchases in their pockets, precipitated anger and frustration. Many "good" people (white and Negro) said, "This is not the way. We are already making adequate progress." Nonsense! No progress is adequate so long as any man, woman or child of any ethnic group is still a lynch victim.

That the non-violent effort has convicted us of sin, and thus appealed to consciences is attested by the new found unity and direction now established in Negro communities in places like Durham and Nashville. Witness further the many white people who say, "I never thought the problem was so serious. I feel so ashamed." Many of these people now support the movement.

In the second instance, the non-violent movement is asserting, "get moving. The pace of social change is too slow. At this rate it will be at least another generation before the major forms of segregation disappear. All of Africa will be free before the American Negro attains first-class citizenship. Most of us will be grandparents before we can live normal human lives."

The choice of the non-violent method, "the sit-in," symbolizes both judgment and promise. It is a judgment upon middle-class conventional, half-way efforts to deal with radical social evil. It is specifically a judgment upon contemporary civil rights attempts. As one high school student from Chattanooga exclaimed, "We started because we were tired of waiting for you adults to act."

The sum total of all our current efforts to end segregation is not enough to do so. After many court decisions, the deeper south we go, the more token integration (and that only in public schools) we achieve. *Crisis* magazine [published by the NAACP] becomes known as a "black bourgeois" club organ, rather than a forceful instrument for justice. Inter-racial agencies expect to end segregation with discussions and teas. Our best agency (the NAACP) accents fund-raising and court action rather than developing our greatest resource, a people no longer the victims of racial evil who can act in a disciplined manner to implement the constitution. The Negro church and minister function as in an earlier day and not as God's agents to redeem society.

But the sit-in is likewise a sign of promise: God's promise that if radically Christian methods are adopted the rate of change can be vastly increased. This is why non-violence dominates the movement's perspective. Under Christian non-violence, Negro students reject the hardship of disobedient passivity and fear, but embrace the hardship (violence and jail) of obedience. Such non-violence strips the segregationalist power structure of its major weapon: the manipulation of law or law-enforcement to keep the Negro in his place.

Furthermore, such an act attracts, strengthens and sensitizes the support of many white persons in the South and across the nation. (The numbers who openly identify themselves with the "sit-in" daily grow.)

Non-violence in the Negro's struggle gains a fresh maturity. And the Negro gains a new sense of his role in molding a redeemed society. The "word" from the lunch-counter stool demands a sharp re-assessment of our organized evil and a radical Christian obedience to transform that evil. Christian non-violence provides both that re-assessment and the faith of obedience. The extent to which the Negro joined by many others apprehends and incorporates non-violence determines the degree that the world will acknowledge fresh social insight from America.

The "conservative" response

44. ROY WILKINS:
FOR "SHOCK TROOPS"
AND "SOLID LEGAL MOVES"

Confronted with sharp criticism both nationally and locally for opposing or not supporting direct action, the NAACP officially endorsed
the student sit-in movement. Then in March 1960 the executive secretary, Roy Wilkins, addressed a memorandum to branch officers announcing an "expanded racial defense policy" of organizing boycotts
against the chain variety stores whose southern outlets refused to
serve black demonstrators at their lunch counters. Some of the Association's branches and youth councils had previously engaged in
direct action in northern and border states; now the NAACP deliberately speeded up the formation of youth councils and college chapters, especially in the South, with the specific purpose of engaging in
direct-action demonstrations. Many of the demonstrations of 1960
and 1961 were in fact carried on by NAACP youth councils and college chapters.

In May 1961 the Congress of Racial Equality dramatically came to
the attention of the general public with its famous "Freedom Ride,"
testing segregation in interstate bus travel in Alabama and Mississippi. Joined by SNCC youth and others, the CORE Freedom Riders,
like the college students who had conducted the lunch-counter sit-ins
before them, posed a challenge to the NAACP and its program.
Addressing a mass meeting in Jackson, Mississippi, in June 1961, Roy
Wilkins gave details of the NAACP's involvement in the direct-action

Roy Wilkins, remarks at a mass meeting of the Jackson, Miss., branch of the
NAACP, June 7, 1961. Printed with permission of Roy Wilkins.

movement, and also defended the continuing usefulness of the traditional NAACP legal and political strategy.

There has been considerable excitement since I visited here
last year, but in the main the situation on the Freedom Front
is developing in the way that many of us predicted.

Today we have student sit-ins, picket lines, selective buying
campaigns, and Freedom Riders. These activities all add up to
"no segregation."

They are the natural outcome of the successful battles of
past years through the NAACP, of its basic victories in the
courts in establishing the legal status and rights of Negro
citizens.

Today's exciting events follow as a matter of course from the
steady teaching of oncoming young people in past years. Once
the legal status and constitutional rights were established, the
battle to enjoy them follows as night the day.

The NAACP declared in 1955, after the Supreme Court's decree in the school cases, that segregation as a policy was dead.
We told white Americans that Negro citizens were sick of
segregation and wanted an end to it.

We asked our people to prepare petitions to school boards
requesting the drawing up of plans to desegregate the schools.
We offered to confer and to help work out mutually satisfactory plans.

You know what the answer was. Right here in Mississippi,
in Yazoo City, signers of such petitions were listed in a full-
page advertisement in the *Yazoo City Herald* of August 25,
1955, paid for by the White Citizens Council.

All the petitioners either lost their jobs or were forced to
remove their names from the petitions. Many had to leave town
and seek a living elsewhere.

(In the face of this and similar brutal squeeze plays in other
Southern states, the South has the nerve to accuse Negro freedom seekers of communism! The denial of the right of petition,

of dissent and of assembly are not only directly contrary to the guarantees in the American Constitution, but are hall marks of Soviet communism.)

Our opponents did not believe us when we said all Negroes (the silent ones and the noisy ones) wanted to abolish segregation. Not the few Uncle Toms, but the vast majority of Negro Americans.

Well, in the past year, just as we of the NAACP predicted, our people—especially our young people—have demonstrated beyond the shadow of a doubt that they want no more segregation.

The die-hard white people in the South are losing in this fight, not only for themselves, but for their states and region.

While striking at us in the name of a dead past, they are hurting their region and their country in today's changing and threatening world.

They are losing not only because they are being defeated wherever the constitutional issue is drawn in the courts, but because their own words and conduct are costing them support in the arena of public opinion.

One of the reasons for my coming here tonight is to join you in indicting the people in the South who are mistreating us and visiting violence upon us and trying in every desperate and despicable way to deny us the dignity and the rights that belong to every human being.

The Klan has played its part, and a dirty part it has been because it is laced through with racial and religious hatred and a belief in beating and killing. The Klan is a disgrace to the decent people of the South, white and black. The animal exhibition turned loose in Anniston, Birmingham and Montgomery did no credit to those people who brag that they are of the superior race.

And the so-called good white people of the South must share some of the blame for the Klan mobs, for they have brushed the K.K.K. under the rug and pretended it was not there. The Birmingham *News* wrote a shocked editorial after the riot of bloodshed and the do-nothing police action. It is time such newspapers were shocked. This ugly thing has been living right under the nose of the *News* for lo, these many years. . . .

The truth is that if the mobs are permitted today to run loose against Negroes and their allies, tomorrow they will run loose against anyone they do not like, white or black. If the police turn their backs today on an iron pipe beating of a Negro, they will turn their backs tomorrow on the beating of other people.

We might as well face, too, the fact that the South can no longer wave aside the charge that the treatment of the Negro is "the South's business" and is of no concern to the United States in the world of nations.

The continuing mistreatment of Negro citizens *is* hurting our country. It *is* handicapping our ambassadors and other foreign service personnel. It hurt our President on his delicate and important trip to Europe. It embarrassed him in his exchanges with Chairman Khrushchev, for how can Mr. Kennedy plead for democracy in Laos when at the very moment, Khrushchev is reading about discrimination, segregation and mob action in Alabama?

Our governmental system is on trial. Is this the land of the free, or only the land of the white free? If it is the latter, then we should prepare to join South Africa at the bottom of the list of nations, for there is no place of prestige or power in the world of the Sixties and Seventies for a Jim Crow nation.

The Klan has not been the only evil-doer. A certain type of Southern politician has done his share. . . .

Many, many Southern newspapers have also helped in the persecution by the type of their opposition and by their failure to educate and to guide their readers in a time of social change. They have catered unashamedly to the emotions. They have raked up discredited and discarded social, economic and political theories.

They have distorted the American theory of government and have misinterpreted the Constitution. Their basic sin has been the refusal to recognize the status of the Negro as a citizen, thus setting the stage for useless debate on Federal versus state powers.

The White Citizens Councils were started here in Mississippi, swearing by a new lay bible called "Black Monday," written by that great authority on race, blood and law, Judge Tom Brady of Brookhaven. It is not true, as some persons have asserted, that Judge Brady is the secret weapon of the NAACP. He just keeps doing the best he can preaching to the Councils on chimpanzees, cockroaches, jungles and miscegenation. He is definitely not going to have his daughter marry one.

But in spite of their control of government, in spite of their use of economic power as employers and creditors, in spite of their misuse of police power and their domination of the courts and in spite of their monopoly of the means of communication, the segregationists are losing the war.

They are losing because Negro citizens and their friends, no matter how many organizations may be at work, are united upon the goals to be achieved. Let there be no misunderstanding upon this by our opponents: *even though methods may differ here and there, and personalities may prance and snort a bit in calling upon their followers, there is basic agreement among Negro leaders and organizations on demands and targets.*

The objectives being announced today by this and that official are old objectives of the NAACP. In 1909, at the first meeting that gave birth to the NAACP, one of our founders announced the objective of non-segregated schools in the South.

NAACP young people have been jailed from one end of the South to the other in the sit-in and other campaigns, just as have the young people of other organizations, or of no organization. Our youth were arrested in the hundreds in Louisville, in the drive against segregation launched by Rev. Hodge, NAACP branch president.

More than 500 NAACP young people have been arrested in the state of South Carolina. Up the road a piece in Memphis, it was NAACP young people who sat down in the public library and succeeded in opening it up to all citizens.

Right here in Jackson, we take off our hats to the NAACP chapter members at Tougaloo and Jackson State Colleges who sat down in the public library and later challenged segregation on buses. We intend to carry their cases in the courts as far as is necessary in order to win.

If final victory is to be won, we must realize that no simple formula will do it. The problem is not simple. Methods will vary. But sneers are not in order. A newspaper last week quoted an Atlanta official as saying that the NAACP was not invited to a certain meeting "because we are activists and they are legalists."

Two days later these same people were chin-deep in court action, injunctions, fines, appeals, etc. We have offered our aid. No one knows better than we of the NAACP what action will accomplish. Out of our experience, we know that shock troops are necessary. We know that sacrifice is necessary. We know that testing and challenging are necessary.

We also know that solid, basic legal moves are necessary if there is to be a foundation for other action. Affirmative action by judicial, legislative and executive means is indispensable. This is still a nation of law. If we colored people hold the white people of the South to law and the Constitution, we cannot sneer among ourselves at the law and the legal processes.

By the same token, just because the NAACP does not agree down to the smallest detail with the plans and procedures of other organizations is no reason for us to throw roadblocks in their way.

For example, we believe the way to test a law is to set up a test case, carry it through the courts and get a determination. We do not believe you can test a law and get it thrown out by staying in jail. After one spends thirty or sixty or ninety days in jail, the law is still on the statute books and still constitutes a support for segregation.

But we of the NAACP do not sneer at those who choose to stay in jail, for they are thus registering a personal and powerful moral protest against injustice.

When the original Freedom Bus Ride was launched by James L. Farmer, national director of CORE, he conferred in our national office on the itinerary. It was their project, but we alerted NAACP units in every state and at every stop. The riders were greeted and offered assistance.

We could not do anything about Alabama because the NAACP is still under court order barring it from operating in that state—the only such in the nation. I must say for Mississippi that although it does not agree with us, the state has not thus far attempted to bar the Association from functioning, although certain localities have tried to harass colored people and either keep them from joining or make life miserable for them after they joined.

The Freedom Riders did not run into violence until they entered a state where there was no NAACP.

The work of the groups in this field must mesh. After all, increasing demands for Federal action can be made today because years ago the court battle was won that enlarged the vote of the Negro and made it important to Federal officials. The White Primary phase of that fight began with a brave Negro dentist and the NAACP in Texas 38 years ago.

It was that battle that doomed the chicken wire fence seen at the Democratic convention in Houston, that made possible the all-night fight for a civil rights plank and the Dixiecrat walkout in Philadelphia in 1948.

The growing Negro vote in and out of the South (not in Mississippi) and the use of it accounted for the enactment of the 1957 and 1960 civil rights bills on protection of the right to register and vote.

The point is that a telephone call about a Freedom Ride in 1961 is a powerful and persuasive act because long before that, men and women were hammering away at winning the right to vote and building it into such a power that a telephone call could not be ignored.

The lesson here is that all methods should be used and that history and experience should not be ignored. . . .

45. WHITNEY M. YOUNG, JR.:
FOR PROTEST PLUS "CORRECTIVE MEASURES"

The National Urban League, founded in 1911, has been chiefly a social-work agency concerned with opening new industrial opportunities for Negroes. Typically the Urban League, nationally and locally, aimed at an alliance with the white business community. Its staff was almost all black. Generally white businessmen and the more conservative blacks sat on the Urban League boards. The turn of events after mid-century, and especially after 1960, made a gradualist program anachronistic. The selection of Whitney M. Young, Jr., then dean of the Atlanta University School of Social Work, as executive director in 1961 coincided with a reversal in policy for the League. Young could afford to be—and was—far more outspoken than his predecessors. And just because through the years the League, by its very conservatism, had established close connections with economic decision-makers, it was now in a position to interpret the demands of the activist groups to them.

The Urban League is still regarded as the most conservative of the civil rights groups. But the fact is that it may now be classed as a protest organization. Whitney Young, in his address at the Urban League's 1963 national conference, made clear the changes in the group's underlying philosophy.

This year's National Conference of the Urban League convenes during a crucial period in America's race relations history. . . .

Every major city in the United States has felt some manifestation of the unrest and burning desire of its Negro citizens for equality—now! And hundreds of smaller communities have had reflected in their mirror the discontent that has spread like

Whitney M. Young, Jr., THE SOCIAL REVOLUTION: CHALLENGE TO THE NATION, ADDRESS AT THE 1963 NATIONAL CONFERENCE OF THE URBAN LEAGUE (New York: National Urban League, 1963). Reprinted with permission of the author.

wildfire and that has illuminated the land with the flames of a modern revolution the counterpart of which neither this nation or any nation has ever witnessed.

This revolution bears no similarity, however, to the American Revolution, or to the French Revolution, or to the Russian Revolution. There is no attempt here to overthrow a government. This is a revolution against historic injustice, against a way of life, against persons who maintain that the measure of achievement of man is determined by and related to the color of his skin. This is a revolution peculiarly characterized by a heroic drive and a courageous fight to gain the rights and respect that should be synonymous with the word "American." It is a revolution not by black people against white people, but by people who are right against those who are wrong.

This revolution is unlike any other also, because, after 300 years of deprivation, the deprived seek redress for their grievances in an expression of faith in a nation that has done very little to develop and nurture such faith. Their demands are simple and elemental, and those who would describe them as difficult and complicated do a disservice to America and to Americans.

This revolution is what I chose last year at our National Conference to call a "Revolution of Expectation." Today I would call it a "Revolution of Witnessing."

A review by me now of the events in this conflict as they have occurred since we met together last year is unnecessary. For there is not a person in this room tonight who cannot recall with his mind's eye, and with vividness and recurring horror, the photographs of brutality and barbarism. There is not a person in this room tonight who cannot remember with pride and humility the pictures of the bright-eyed children and courageous youth participants in the events of recent months.

For the Negro citizen, therefore, these are acts of bearing witness to his faith in democracy through peaceful non-violent demonstration, and by channelling in constructive ways justified resentments and pent-up frustrated emotions that have been born out of age-old abuses and contemptuous indignities.

For the white citizen these events mean bearing witness to the fact that democracy is more than a convenient institution through which privileges and material products flow to him.

For both, democracy is a way of life, an ideal in which all share its rewards, as well as its responsibilities. Indeed, without this concept, democracy has no meaning and certainly no permanence.

For the church and its membership, this is a time of witnessing that piety rests not in credal affirmation, but in the confirmation of deeds.

For the public official—whether city, state or federal—witnessing means greater concern for broad, democratic promises and human rights, rather than preoccupation with technical, constitutional details and states' rights.

For the private sector of our society—whether business, labor, or health and welfare—this is a time for witnessing that the free enterprise system works equally well for *all* American citizens.

For the Urban League this is a time to express willingness to witness that while our past contributions need no defense or apology, our future challenges and opportunities are greater and more demanding than any we have ever faced. These are times that call for us to be frank, not only with the perpetuators of injustice as to their responsibilities, but equally frank and forthright with the victims of injustice as to their responsibilities in this new day that is full with promise of a brighter destiny for those whom we are committed to serve.

It is not enough to remind white Americans that for 53 years the Urban League has warned them of this inevitable consequence of indifference; neither is it necessary to boast of League contributions that now help to make it possible for Negro Americans to express their grievances so courageously.

The past is prologue. Today the nation and its Negro citizens ask of the Urban League: "What have you done for me recently? What will you be doing for me tomorrow?"

We in the Urban League are in the position of being able to answer these questions in language and with machinery possessed by no other agency. Our job is clear. Our job is to give meaning and reality to the revolution to which we all now serve as witnesses.

As we win the battle for civil rights, we can, and might well lose the war for human rights.

In this age of automation and urbanization, the demands on Americans differ. The victories so courageously won in the streets can easily become an empty, hollow mockery if we do not simultaneously equip ourselves with the skills, the values, and the sense of community responsibility and participation which the future will demand.

At the risk of being misunderstood by the currently immature; by those who are merely seeking to remove the symbols that disturb their consciences; or even by the naive who believe that equality is a condition automatically arrived at through the lowering of overt barriers, the League hereby announces its intent to pursue what we know to be a necessary program.

We have this year shared our identity with all others who struggle for the goal of equality, and we will continue to do so. But while we applaud and respect the victories which they have won, by the use of methods different from those of the Urban League, we will continue to seek their understanding and mutual respect for the long-range and vitally necessary programs and methods of the Urban League—programs and methods which can only be achieved by a professionally-structured agency, devoting itself full time to this problem.

This we see not as competitive or in any way discrediting but rather as complementing and supplementing. To put it bluntly: We say that while there must be those who in the interest of justice and equality must walk the picket-line in front of restaurants, hotels, theatres, business establishments—these same persons, and others, with equal zest and determination, must walk to the libraries, to the adult education classes, and to the voting registrar's office. And they must take time to serve on policy-making bodies of agencies and institutions. For reality now dictates that we must recognize that those who would enter the new doors of opportunity must have the skills to qualify, the money to pay, and the confidence and security of knowing that they are, in fact, equal citizens.

I am not offering a substitute, or an either/or suggestion. Both are necessary—both must be done. The real test, therefore, of the sincerity and the maturity of all of us now participating in this struggle will be our willingness to labor in the vineyards where we are not televised and photographed, and in those places where our contributions may not be popular newscopy.

I feel very deeply that the increasing numbers of Negro women, as well as our allies among men and women of other racial groups, who are willing to volunteer a few hours a week to tutor youngsters who bear the scars of generations of deprivation, are making a lasting contribution to the struggle—a contribution as lasting as that made by the gallant heroes who go to jail, or those who lie in the streets.

The Urban League is challenged, therefore, to see that the barriers of yesterday—the barriers built by prejudice, fear and indifference which are now crumbling—are not replaced by new barriers of apathy, of underdeveloped skills, of lack of training. If this happens, our gains will be but temporary, our victories hollow.

Protest we must. Demonstrate if necessary. These are the time-tested weapons for correcting injustices and righting historic wrongs. But these alone are not enough. We will only have cleared the site. The next task is to build upon that site the new house of true democracy. This requires different skills—but equal commitment and equal energy. This we will do. This we must do. The same faith and determination that have been responsible for the Negro's survival in a hostile and cruel society will respond to the new challenge. That faith and determination will respond if given reasonable understanding and assistance from a total society more sympathetic and honest than heretofore. . . .

As George Bernard Shaw has said: "America has relegated the Negro citizen to be a bootblack, and now condemns him because his hands are dirty."

There is today great talk among our many new and self-appointed advisors about self-help and personal responsibility on the part of the Negro citizen himself. The curious, if not tragic aspect of this, is that this talk comes from so many white Americans who themselves have been passive participants in, or passive observers of the age-old denials responsible for the lacks which they now deplore.

If this is not done, then Negro America will have less need to be defensive, and its leadership will not run the risk of being misunderstood when it addresses itself to this aspect. Today nothing is more discouraging or inhibiting to responsible Negro leadership, and to discussion of self-help and self-responsibility, than the fact that this has become the chief theme-song of so many self-appointed advisors who would claim now to be our friends, but who for all these years have never raised their voices against the obvious racial injustices—those who even today say little about the real responsibilities of white Americans.

As President Kennedy noted recently—demonstrations would be minimized, if not eliminated, if there was as much concern and indignation about the injustices and the discrimination against Negro citizens to which these demonstrations are addressed, as there is to the demonstrations themselves.

The present and future test of the concern and sincerity of the responsible white leadership of America will be the degree to which they assume what seems to me clear-cut and obvious tasks. Let me indicate them.

1. White leadership must be honest about the fact that throughout the history of this country there has existed a special privileged class of citizens who have received special preferential treatment over other citizens purely on the basis of an accident of birth. The problems of social disorganization and racial unrest which we face today are the direct result of this fact. Honesty and decency should compel our mass media and responsible majority leadership to admit a long-established sociological fact—that the right ratio of dependency, crime and social disorganization among Negro citizens which so many of them deplore, actually occurs in the same degree among white

citizens of the same socio-economic class. Negro citizens representing the middle-income group have actually less social disorganization than white citizens in similar economic circumstances. These problems, therefore, are problems not of race, but of socio-economic conditions.

2. Responsible white leadership and the mass media must, with honesty and sincerity, promote and teach the idea that integration should and can be viewed as an opportunity for all Americans, rather than an irritating and uncomfortable problem —that integration can provide for all of us the creative experience that flows from inclusiveness, rather than the stagnating and damaging effects that accompany exclusiveness. . . . it is poignantly tragic that American citizens debate the rights of fellow-Americans to live in the same neighborhoods, attend the same schools, eat in the same restaurants, or attend the same houses of worship.

This is a time when great minds and great nations will reflect their true greatness by concentrating on the multitude of things we have in common. For the truth is, that today white Americans and black Americans are equally and mutually dependent upon each other.

3. Responsible white leadership in this nation can demonstrate the sincerity of its desire to accelerate constructive transition, by enthusiastic support of the Urban League's massive "domestic Marshall Plan," as the only fair and realistic way of closing the gap and correcting historic abuses. This is little indeed to ask of a great nation if it is to truly provide world leadership in the brief time allowed us by a fast-moving world society. . . .

In broad terms this plan calls for a transitional period of intensified special effort of corrective measures in education, in training and employment, in housing and in health and welfare. It calls for the same kind of expression of generosity and understanding which motivated this country to spend twelve billion dollars under the original Marshall Plan in a four-year period to rehabilitate war-torn Europe. It calls for the same kind of concern that has motivated our nation more recently to spend millions of dollars in providing special help for Hungarian and Cuban refugees fleeing oppression. Should this nation—can this nation do less for its own citizens whose blood, sweat and tears have gone into building and preserving this great country which is ours?

4. Responsible white leadership must provide support—unprecedented support—both morally and financially, to existing responsible Negro agencies and their leadership. As Winston Churchill said so forthrightly to America during the moment of England's gravest crisis in World War II: "Give us the tools and we will do the job."

For 53 years the Urban League has valiantly endeavored to provide America with responsible leadership. But the League was forced to do so with token financial support offered with the subtle inference that even such meagre support might be jeopardized if there was too close identification with the legitimate aspirations of the masses of Negro citizens for equality, dignity and first-class citizenship.

Today, however, there is strong evidence that a different and more mature point of view is now being adopted by corporations, government, labor and enlightened community funds. It is becoming clear now, that if the impatience and the heightened aspirations of the masses of Negro citizens are to be protected and to be channelled along constructive lines, then the Urban League must of necessity be involved in this feat of social engineering. To divorce ourselves from this would be an expression of irresponsibility; to isolate our organization from this activity would be to deny corporations, foundations and community funds a unique opportunity for representation and participation in a new era of social planning. The Urban League will be valueless to responsible institutions in our society if it does not maintain communication with and the respect of other responsible Negro organizations and the respect of the masses of Negro citizens.

The final aspirations of Negro citizens can never be realized unless they, too, respect the distinctive and vital role which the Urban League can play—a role which the Urban League is peculiarly and uniquely qualified for, and can perform. Only the Urban League has the professional equipment and the know-how for this role, and the contacts and machinery to implement. In this moment of grave racial crisis, the Urban League is gearing itself for accelerated activity in its traditional role; and girding itself to maintain identity with all other responsible groups in the struggle for human rights. In this process we will be enabled to understand motives and test the sincerity of our friends and supporters.

5. And finally: Responsible white leadership must not permit itself to be drawn into anxiety around an increasingly popular phrase "reverse reactions." For to do so is to suggest that there are still degrees of citizenship to which society is committed to grant Negro Americans.

Our expression must be loud and clear. Once and for all we must state it: Human rights and civil rights in America are not negotiable. There does not exist in the hands of any one group of citizens either the Divine Right or the Constitutional authority to give to or withhold from another, rights that are God-given and legally implemented.

Nonviolent direct action at high tide

46. BAYARD RUSTIN:
"THE GREAT LESSONS OF BIRMINGHAM"

The spring and summer of 1963 were momentous months. The
Negro revolt assumed a new urgency as "Freedom Now!" became
the slogan. The NAACP annual convention enthusiastically passed a
resolution calling for more direct action. For the first time, substantial
numbers of lower-class citizens were swept into direct action, as ever
and ever larger numbers of people "took to the streets" and went to
jail. At the same time small but significant numbers of upper-class
people became engaged in direct action and permitted themselves to
be arrested.

These tendencies had been evident in the demonstrations in Albany, Georgia, in 1961 and 1962. Then, in May 1963, the Birmingham demonstration led by Martin Luther King epitomized the
changed character of direct-action demonstrations in the South.

Bayard Rustin, a pacifist, formerly executive secretary of the War
Resisters League, and now executive director of the A. Philip Randolph Institute, has been a leading civil rights activist for over two
decades. Known for his ability at organizing large-scale demonstrations, he avoids identification with any one civil rights organization,
and operates in the interstices among them. A democratic socialist in
his political and economic philosophy, Rustin, like Randolph, believes
that black advancement lies largely in a Negro-Church-and-Labor
alliance for social justice.

In evaluating the significance of the Birmingham demonstration,
Rustin revealed his own activist philosophy of mass action and "crea-

Bayard Rustin, "The Meaning of Birmingham," LIBERATION, VIII, 4 (June
1963), 7–9, 31. Reprinted with permission of the author.

tive dislocation." Better than any other writer he has captured the
militant mood that caught fire among Southern blacks in the spring
of 1963.

Since the signing of the Emancipation Proclamation in 1863,
the struggle for justice by Afro-Americans has been carried out
by many dedicated individuals and militant organizations. Their
ultimate aim, sometimes stated, often not, has always been total
freedom. Many forms of strategy and tactics have been used.
Many partial victories have been won. Yet the gradual and token
"progress" that many white liberals pointed to with pride served
only to anger the black man and further frustrate him. That frustration has now given way to an open and publicly declared war
on segregation and racial discrimination throughout the nation.
The aim is simple. It is directed at all white Americans—the
President of the United States, his brother, Robert, the trade-
union movement, the power élite, and every living white soul
the Negro meets. The war cry is "unconditional surrender—end
all Jim Crow now." Not next week, not tomorrow—but *now*.

This is not to say that many have not felt this way for decades.
The slave revolts, the occasional resorts to violence in recent
times, the costly fifty-year struggle that the National Association
for the Advancement of Colored People has carried on in the
courts, the thousands arrested throughout the South since the
Montgomery bus boycott—all reveal an historic impatience and
a thirst for freedom. What *is* new springs from the white resistance in Birmingham, with its fire hoses, its dogs, its blatant disregard for black men as people, and from the Afro-American's
response to such treatment in "the year of our Lord" 1963.

For the black people of this nation, Birmingham became the
moment of truth. The struggle from now on will be fought in a
different context. Therefore, to understand the mood, tactics and
totality of the black people's relentless war on Jim Crow, we
must grasp fully what is taking place in this Southern industrial city.

For the first time, every black man, woman and child, regardless of station, has been brought into the struggle. Unlike the period of the Montgomery boycott, when the Southern Christian Leadership Conference had to be organized to stimulate similar action elsewhere, the response to Birmingham has been immediate and spontaneous. City after city has come into the fight, from Jackson, Mississippi, to Chesterton, Maryland. The militancy has spread to Philadelphia, where the "city fathers" and the trade-union movement have been forced to make reluctant concessions. It has reached the old and established freedom organizations. For example, Roy Wilkins, executive secretary of the N.A.A.C.P., who only a year ago, from a platform in Jackson, Mississippi, criticized the direct-action methods of the Freedom Riders, was arrested recently for leading a picket line in that very city, after hundreds of N.A.A.C.P. members had been arrested in a direct-action struggle.

Before Birmingham, the great struggles had been waged for specific, limited goals. The Freedom Rides sought to establish the right to eat while traveling; the sit-ins sought to win the right to eat in local restaurants; the Meredith case centered on a single Negro's right to enter a state university. The Montgomery boycott, although it involved fifty thousand people in a year-long sacrificial struggle, was limited to attaining the right to ride the city buses with dignity and respect. The black people now reject token, limited or gradual approaches.

The package deal is the new demand. The black community is not prepared to engage in a series of costly battles—first for jobs, then decent housing, then integrated schools, etc., etc. The fact that there is a power élite which makes the decisions is now clearly understood. The Negro has learned that, through economic and mass pressures, this élite can be made to submit step by step. Now he demands unconditional surrender.

It is significant that in city after city where the spirit of Birmingham has spread, the Negroes are demanding fundamental social, political and economic changes. One can predict with confidence that in the future the scope of these demands will be widened, not narrowed, and that if they are not met in the North as well as in the South, a very dangerous situation will develop.

Federal troops may well become a familiar sight in the North as well as the South, since the black community is determined to move vigorously and fearlessly and relentlessly ahead.

Gandhi used to say that the absence of fear was the prime ingredient of nonviolence: "To be afraid is to be a slave." A. J. Muste frequently says that to be afraid is to behave as if the truth were not true. It was the loss of all fear that produced the moment of truth in Birmingham: children as young as six paraded calmly when dogs, fire hoses and police billies were used against them. Women were knocked down to the ground and beaten mercilessly. Thousands of teen-agers stood by at churches throughout the whole country, waiting their turn to face the clubs of Bull Connor's police, who are known to be among the most brutal in the nation. Property was bombed. Day after day the brutality and arrests went on. And always, in the churches, hundreds of well-disciplined children eagerly awaited their turns.

While these youngsters, unlike Meredith, had the advantage of operating in groups, and while Meredith's ordeal must have been the most difficult borne by any freedom fighter short of death—the children of Birmingham, like no other person or group, inspired and shamed all Afro-Americans, and pulled them into a united struggle.

E. Franklin Frazier wrote in the past of the Negro bourgeoisie. He told of the efforts of the Negro upper classes to ape white people, of the exploitation of Negroes by wealthy members of their own race and of the absence of identity among Negroes. But had Frazier been alive to see Birmingham he would have discovered that the black community was welded into a classless revolt. A. G. Gaston, the Negro millionaire who with some ministers and other upper-class elements had publicly stated that the time was not ripe for such a broad protest, finally accommodated himself, as did the others, to the mass pressure from below and joined the struggle. Gaston owns much property, including a funeral parlor and the motel that eventually became the headquarters for the Birmingham campaign. The bombing of his motel was one cause of the outbreak of rioting on the part of elements that had not come into the non-violent struggle.

On the basis of the behavior of the black business community in the cities where protests have emerged since Birmingham, one can confidently predict that future struggles will find the Negro bourgeoisie playing a major role in social change and nonviolence. They know that unless they join in the struggle they will lose the business of their fellow Negroes, who are in no mood to tolerate Uncle Tom-ism.

Black people have waited a hundred years for the government to help them win their rights. President after President has made commitments before election and failed to use the executive power he possesses after election. Congress today, dominated by Southern Democrats, cannot pass any meaningful civil-rights legislation. The Supreme Court, from 1954 to 1963, took a gradualist approach, thereby putting its stamp of approval on "with all deliberate speed," which spells tokenism.

So the black people have looked elsewhere for allies, hoping to discover some major power group within American society which would join them not only in the struggle for Negro rights, but also in the struggle for a more democratic America. The trade-union movement and the churches have issued radical pronouncements but in fact have done precious little and on occasion have even blocked progress. Thus the black population has concluded that the future lies in casting not just a ballot, what Thoreau called "a piece of paper merely," but the *total* vote—the human person against injustice.

This is not to say that black people are not deeply appreciative of those few independent radicals, liberals and church people who have offered time, money and even their lives. They have nothing but admiration for people like Jim Peck, who was brutally beaten in Mississippi and Alabama during the Freedom Rides, Barbara Deming, who was arrested in Birmingham, Eric Weinberger, who fasted for a month in Alabama jails, and William Moore, the slain postman. One can be thankful that the number of such *individuals* is increasing. However, social change of such magnitude requires that major power groups in our society participate as meaningful allies.

The use of the "black body" against prejudice is necessary as a means of creating social disruption and dislocation precisely because the accepted democratic channels have been denied the Negro.

In practice, it works like this: having urged the social institutions to desegregate to no avail, having pleaded for justice to no avail, the black people see that the white community would rather yield to the threats of the segregationist (in the name of law and order) than change the social system. And so Negroes conclude that they must upset the social equilibrium more drastically than the opposition can. They place their bodies against an unjust law by sitting in a restaurant, or a library, playing in a park or swimming in a pool. The segregationists, frequently joined by the police, attack. Arrest and brutality follow. But the black people keep coming, wave after wave. The jails fill. The black population boycotts the stores. Businessmen begin to lose money.

At this point the white community splits into two groups. On one side are the political and law-enforcement agencies, supported by the arch-segregationists, who fearfully resort to indiscriminate violence as a stop-gap measure. Then the more enlightened sections of the community, including many business leaders, begin to act for the first time. They sense not only the rightness of the Negroes' demands but their inevitability. They realize that police violence may bring forth a violent response from unorganized elements of the black population and increased economic reprisals. Thus the business community, previously having sided with the forces of reaction, at first quietly and then openly sue for discussion and negotiation with the Negro community, an approach they had earlier dismissed when it was proposed by Negro leaders.

This method of massive nonviolence has many dangers. The greatest threat is that violence, which has been smoldering beneath the surface for generations, will inevitably manifest itself. But the creative genius of people in action is the only safeguard in this period and it can be trusted to bring about, ultimately, a better community, precisely because the tactic of mass action is accompanied by nonviolent resistance. The protesters pledge themselves to refrain from violence in word and deed, thereby confining whatever inevitable violence there may be in the situation to an irreducible minimum.

The genius of this method and philosophy lies in its ability to destroy an old unjust institution and simultaneously create a new one. For finally the white community is forced to choose between closing down the schools, restaurants, parks, buses, etc., and integrating them. Faced for the first time with a choice that can impose discomfort, inconvenience and economic turmoil on the white community—the community discovers that it would prefer integrated institutions to no public institutions at all.

It is therefore clear that we can now expect, following Birmingham, a more sympathetic ear from the power structure, in both the North *and* the South.

Loss of money to retail stores throughout the country, the reluctance of many industries to move to Little Rock during the school integration struggle, the fear of capitalists to invest in Mississippi and Alabama now, and the disrupting of the economy in Birmingham have caused big businesses, including steel, to take a second look at the "Negro problem."

The nation gives Robert Kennedy credit for the fact that the real rulers of Birmingham sat down with representatives of the black revolution. But knowledgeable people realize that it was the withdrawal of black purchasing power in a city which is almost half black, and the militant, unconditional surrender policies of the nonviolent struggle that turned the tide.

Again, Birmingham is a turning point in that all significant elements of the power structure have now acknowledged that the white community must recognize the true nature of the black revolution and its economic consequences.

Therefore, in city after city, following Birmingham, the real powers have moved to convince the politicians that they should negotiate. Chain store, moving picture, hotel and restaurant executives have recently sought out representatives of the black community to ask for negotiations leading to nation-wide desegregation. This is new. It is a consequence of the handwriting they see on the wall. They see it in police brutality and the bombed-out homes and business establishments. They see it in the eyes of Birmingham's children.

The tragedy is that the trade-union movement, the churches and educational institutions which lay claim to freedom and justice, reveal that they have learned nothing from the Battle of Birmingham. This is especially sad since the great battle lies ahead. And this battle the black population is now prepared to wage. This is going to be the battle for jobs.

Negroes are finally beginning to realize that the age of automation and industrialization presents them with peculiar problems. There is less and less of a market where the unskilled can sell his labor. Inadequate, segregated schools increase the problem. The negative attitude of the trade unions compounds it further. The Cold War economy, geared to armaments production (perhaps the most automated of all industries) is throwing millions out of work, but the minority groups are being hit hardest. For every white person unemployed, there are close to three Negroes without jobs.

In general, the unemployed, whether white or black, are not yet prepared to take radical action to demand jobs now. However, unemployed black people are prepared to move in conjunction with the rest of the black community and its many white supporters, within the context of the broad civil-rights upheaval. Since their most immediate ends are economic, their banner will be "Dignity of work with equal pay and equal opportunity." This agitation on the part of Negroes for jobs is bound to stimulate unemployed white workers to increased militancy. There will be sit-downs and other dislocating tactics. Nonviolent resistance will have to be directed against local and federal governments, the labor unions, against the A.F.L.-C.I.O. hierarchy and any construction plant or industry that refuses to grant jobs. Such mass disturbances will probably soon take place in the major industrial centers of the country and it is likely that they will be more vigorous in the North than they have been in the South. And they will have incalculable effects on the economic structure.

The great lesson of Birmingham is at once dangerous and creative; black people have moved to that level where they cannot be contained. They are not prepared to wait for courts, elections, votes, government officials, or even Negro leaders. As James Baldwin said in an interview published in the New York *Times* for June 3rd: "No man can claim to speak for the Negro people today. There is no one with whom the power structure can negotiate a deal that will bind the Negro people. There is, therefore, no possibility of a bargain." The black people *themselves* are united and determined to destroy all unjust laws and discriminatory practices, and they want total freedom, including equal economic opportunity and the right to marry whom they damned well please. They know that at a time when the Kennedy brothers were fighting hard to maintain an aura of leadership and control of the civil-rights movement, the children of Birmingham, using methods of nonviolent resistance, restored the leadership to the black community. This was, as reported in the June 6th issue of *Jet*, a "terrible licking" for the federal government. If *kids* can revitalize the civil rights movement in Birmingham, the least we can do is to act like men and women and fight now to provide them with a decent future.

The mood is one of anger and confidence of total victory. The victories to date have given added prestige to the method of nonviolent resistance. One can only hope that the white community will realize that the black community means what it says: *freedom now.*

47. RONNIE M. MOORE: "WE ARE CATCHING HELL DOWN HERE"

Martin Luther King and the sit-in students were the principal exponents of nonviolent direct action until CORE, under the leadership of James Farmer, its national director, initiated the famous "Freedom

Ronnie M. Moore, Memorandum to Richard Haley, Marvin Rich and Jim McCain, September 6, 1963 and "The Story of Plaquemine," n.d. [September 1963], typescript, CORE Archives, State Historical Society of Wisconsin. Printed with permission of Ronnie M. Moore.

Ride" to Alabama and Mississippi in 1961. Designed to test segregation in interstate bus travel, the Freedom Ride led to outbreaks of violence in Alabama and the jailing of hundreds who voluntarily undertook to "continue the ride" into Jackson, Mississippi. CORE thus became a major civil rights organization for the first time. CORE, which had heretofore been a northern organization, expanded into the deep South, thus joining the ranks of SNCC, SCLC, and NAACP, who were already active there. Though CORE had projects in several southern states, its most intensive work was done in Louisiana.

Ronnie M. Moore, a young field secretary who is today an official of the Scholarship, Education, and Defense Fund for Racial Equality, tells the dramatic story of CORE's nonviolent demonstrations in a parish seat of rural Louisiana. This document describes the climate of terrorism and the extraordinary spirit of courage and determination among civil rights workers and southern blacks that characterized the major direct-action campaigns from Danville, Virginia to Greenwood, Mississippi during the spring and summer of 1963.

September 6, 1963

MEMORANDUM
From: Ronnie M. Moore
To: Richard Haley
    Marvin Rich
    Jim McCain

"We are catching hell down here to say the least. I am sending the only copy of the Plaquemine Story. . . ."

THE STORY OF PLAQUEMINE

Since November 1962 the Congress of Racial Equality in conjunction with several local groups has been sponsoring an extensive voter registration drive in Iberville Parish. Headquarters has been at the Parish (County) seat, Plaquemine. In less than one year CORE has increased voter registration from 2,385 to a little over 3,000 with numerous bias complaints being filed with the United States Department of Justice.

During the past eight months, Mr. W. W. Harleaux, President

of the Iberville Voters League, Dr. Bertrand Tyson and Capt. Tolbert Harris acting as Volunteer Task Force workers for CORE have approached the Mayor and city council of Plaquemine and also the Sheriff and policy jury of Iberville Parish for the following objectives.

1. Bi-Racial Committee to take steps for equal job opportunities to off-set the parish unemployment problem; desegregation of public schools; desegregation of parish courthouse facilities; etc.

2. Incorporation of the unimproved Negro areas of Seymourville and Dupon Annex within the city limits of the town of Plaquemine.[1]

3. Negroes be involved in negotiating with city's committee for provisions under the ARA.[2]

These Negro leaders were ignored and threatened, but the struggle continued for a settlement without use of demonstrations.

However, on July 9, 1963 the Negroes of Plaquemine began picketing two local stores, namely West Brothers Department Store, and Food Town Supermarket for equal job opportunities. Over 100 persons took part in the daily picketing program.

After the second day of picketing, the city council met and adopted 25 ordinances limiting picketing to 2 persons at each store, outlawing peaceful assembly, protest marches, sit-in-demonstrations, and placing CORE activities under the banner of subversion with ordinances on conspiracy, and contributing to the delinquency of juveniles.

In hope of possible future negotiations, we voted to abide by the city ordinances by placing 2 picketers at each store and calling off all possible planned demonstrations for a limited period. After about 45 days, on August 19, 1963 about 10:30 P.M. about 1,500 Negro citizens led by James Farmer, Dr. Tyson, Rev.

---

[1] These Negro areas were gerrymandered outside of the town limits so that the town could avoid the expense of providing them with sewerage and other vital services. [Ed.]

[2] The Area Redevelopment Act, providing federal assistance to cities with high rates of unemployment and poverty-stricken rural areas. In the South blacks were usually excluded from the act's benefits. [Ed.]

Jetson W. Davis, and Mr. W. W. Harleaux marched to city hall in protest of the city's failure to adhere to [the] Negro protest.

As the group reached city hall, and began to sing, the leaders were placed under arrest and the group was dispersed with tear gas and Cop billies. From that night and in the following days through sit-in-demonstrations, the arrests jumped from four to 232.

With this number in jail for ten days the town of Plaquemine with a population of 8,500 was about broke with expenditures because prisoners had to be housed in the surrounding jails of Port Allen, Donaldsonville, and New Roads. Plus, a special stockade was rented to house prisoners in Plaquemine. To keep prisoners alone was costing Plaquemine at least $2.00 per prisoner a day.

However, the Chief of Police Dennis Songy got smart and went to the stockade and tricked the prisoners incarcerated into signing for release on their recognizance. 60 prisoners being released, believing on the basis of Songy's statement that Farmer and all others were going to be released, reduced our effectiveness. So, on August 28, 1963 all of us accepted bail on a property bond status.

This purpose was to regroup and plan our strategy, and return to jail.

Meanwhile, CORE once again was hit with a Federal restraining order by Kennedy appointee Judge E. Gordon West, outlawing the exercise of the right of free speech, redress of grievances, and public assembly by the Negro citizens of Iberville Parish. Our attorneys went to the 5th Circuit Court of Appeals and got a stay of the restraining order pending a hearing on the Iberville Parish's application for an injunction for September 9, 1963.

With the restraining order being set aside and after reorganizing our people, we started more sit-in-demonstrations on Saturday August 31, 1963. With 22 persons being arrested, we called a mass rally.

Near the end of the rally, we called for volunteers to march. Over 200 persons volunteered, mostly young people ranging from 14–22 in age. The group left the church to go to Sheriff

Griffon's home to protest the arrest of sit-in-demonstrators and to ask him to use his moral and political influence to bring about a settlement of the Negro grievances. As the kids marched near the Sheriff's house, they were stopped by "Hill-billy mounted police cowboys" on horses with electrical cattle prods and tear gas bombs. The persons were trampled by horses, being kicked in the heads, on the legs and breasts, also were forced into weeds by electrical cattle prods, and were molested in the usual manner with tear gas bombs.

Bruises, scratches, abrasions, lacerations, were too numerous to count. However, such incidents of police brutality, hospitalizing 3 persons and putting 12 persons under constant medical care brought the Negro community to its heels.

After putting the victims in ambulances officials of CORE summoned all the ministers to the home of Rev. Jetson Davis. As a result of the 3 hour meeting from 3 A.M. to 6 A.M. the ministers vowed to sponsor a mass rally and to lead the march on the next day September 1, 1963.

On the next night the rally began—over 1,000 persons in attendance with numerous spectators watching the overcrowded church. After prayers, freedom song singing, and liberty speeches about 500 persons left the church to march silently down Court Street to Railroad Street and then down Meriam Street to Federal Street and back to the Church. It was to be a silent protest march with no stops planned, then back to the church.

As the marchers left the church, several blocks away the ministers were stopped by U. S. Marshalls with the identical restraining order that was thrown out by the U. S. 5th Circuit [Court] reissued by Judge E. Gordon West. The ministers retreated but the march moved onward, and returned to the church.

Farmer and other CORE leaders were presented with restraining orders at the church minutes later.

The ministers returned and after getting legal advice on the constitutionality of the federal order asked for a second march. CORE agreed to sponsor a second march with over 800–1,000 persons participating. On this march, before the marchers got 6 blocks from the church, the ministers were arrested, and the crowd was dispersed with tear gas, fire hoses, cop billies, and electrical cattle prods injuring 28 persons.

The marchers who could returned to the church carrying the injured people. Farmer began demanding on the telephone for federal protection.

Other CORE leaders began calling for ambulances to carry the victims with cut heads, bruised knees, lacerated arms, bleeding babies and "torn flesh wounds" of numerous descriptions to the hospital.

Rudolph Lombard[3] and Ronnie Moore at this point, with over 28 persons definitely needing hospitalization and countless others being in need of medical care with Dr. Tyson, the only Negro physician being under arrest, urged the people to go home. The people refused.

While [we were] urging the people to go home and at the same time putting victims in ambulances, about 40 mounted cops (recruits including town councilmen, a state representative, and local businessmen) came riding down in front of the church shooting tear gas, forcing victims away from the ambulances and other persons back into the church and into the parsonage.

Plaquemine has only 11 full times cops. But at the church State Troopers and Plaquemine cop recruits with no law enforcement experience stampeded the church breaking the winlows with tear gas bombs, forcing over 700 persons to run out of two back doors and jump out of the windows taking for the weeds, private homes, graveyards, and local funeral home for shelter.

After tear gasing the church the cops used fire hoses and pumped water in the church, dragging victims out of the church and arresting everyone they could catch. Babies, teenagers, and adults fleed from the church. "Who could ever think that law enforcement officers would tear gas bomb and fire hose a church to break up a rally."

[3] CORE leader, originally from New Orleans and, at the time, national vice-chairman of CORE. [Ed.]

Then they began a house to house search for James Farmer, local leaders, and all CORE officials. When they would break into a home and couldn't find a leader, they would arrest all the residents present in the home.

For hours, the policemen rode down streets for blocks surrounding the church, searching homes, throwing tear gas in homes, molesting and arresting everyone who appeared to be a leader or a "Smart Nigger." All white CORE participants were automatically arrested, bringing total arrests to 400 for all demonstrations.

At one point during this night of terror, the three most wanted criminals (James Farmer, Ronnie Moore, and Rev. Jetson W. Davis), were trapped in a local funeral [home] awaiting at any minute an illegal police search. However, local people arranged for them to leave town to avoid an arrest by the mounted police mob.[4]

The night of horror ended with over 150 persons needing hospitalization, with the Plymouth (Freedom) Rock Baptist church being semi-totally demolished, and the church parsonage being unfit for habitation due to broken windows, furniture broken up, and damaged from the police search and vandalism.

48. MARTIN LUTHER KING, JR.:
"I HAVE A DREAM"

Despite the intimidation and terrorism that accompanied many of the southern direct-action demonstrations in 1963, they were pervaded by an optimistic, almost millennialistic faith that a racially equali-

Martin Luther King, Jr., Address at the March on Washington, 1963. From SCLC NEWSLETTER, I, 12 (September 1963), 5, 8. Reprinted with permission of Martin Luther King, Jr.

[4] Police searching for Farmer were heard saying that they intended to lynch him; he finally made his escape concealed in a hearse. [Ed.]

tarian America was in sight. Birmingham, in fact, the most famous of these demonstrations, became the great symbol of the heightened aspirations of black people in this country. Not only was there the wave of southern direct-action campaigns that spring and summer, but nonviolent direct action also crested in the North during the latter part of 1963 and the first months of 1964, taking the form of job campaigns, rent strikes and school boycotts.

No document expresses the hopes and vision of this period better than Martin Luther King's famous speech at the March on Washington in August 1963. Though only those who have heard the cadence of his voice can fully appreciate his effect upon his hearers, King's address carries its own drama, even on the printed page.

Five score years ago, a great American, in whose symbolic shadow we stand, signed the Emancipation Proclamation. This momentous decree came as a great beacon light of hope to millions of Negro slaves who had been seared in the flames of withering injustice. It came as a joyous daybreak to end the long night of captivity.

But one hundred years later, we must face the tragic fact that the Negro is still not free. One hundred years later, the life of the Negro is still sadly crippled by the manacles of segregation and the chains of discrimination. One hundred years later, the Negro lives on a lonely island of poverty in the midst of a vast ocean of material prosperity. One hundred years later the Negro is still languished in the corners of American society and finds himself an exile in his own land. So we have come here today to dramatize an appalling condition.

In a sense we have come to our nation's Capital to cash a check. When the architects of our republic wrote the magnificent words of the Constitution and the Declaration of Independence, they were signing a promissory note to which every American was to fall heir. This note was a promise that all men would be guaranteed the unalienable rights of life, liberty, and the pursuit of happiness.

It is obvious today that America has defaulted on this promissory note insofar as her citizens of color are concerned. Instead of honoring this sacred obligation, America has given the Negro people a bad check; a check which has come back marked "insufficient funds." But we refuse to believe that the bank of justice is bankrupt. We refuse to believe that there are insufficient funds in the great vaults of opportunity of this nation. So we have come to cash this check—a check that will give us upon demand the riches of freedom and the security of justice. We have also come to this hallowed spot to remind America of the fierce urgency of *now*. This is no time to engage in the luxury of cooling off or to take the tranquilizing drug of gradualism. *Now* is the time to make real the promises of Democracy. *Now* is the time to rise from the dark and desolate valley of segregation to the sunlit path of racial justice. *Now* is the time to open the doors of opportunity to all of God's children. *Now* is the time to lift our nation from the quicksands of racial injustice to the solid rock of brotherhood.

It would be fatal for the nation to overlook the urgency of the moment and to underestimate the determination of the Negro. This sweltering summer of the Negro's legitimate discontent will not pass until there is an invigorating autumn of freedom and equality. 1963 is not an end, but a beginning. Those who hope that the Negro needed to blow off steam and will now be content will have a rude awakening if the Nation returns to business as usual. There will be neither rest nor tranquility in America until the Negro is granted his citizenship rights. The whirlwinds of revolt will continue to shake the foundations of our Nation until the bright day of justice emerges.

But there is something that I must say to my people who stand on the warm threshold which leads into the palace of justice. In the process of gaining our rightful place we must not be guilty of wrongful deeds. Let us not seek to satisfy our thirst for freedom by drinking from the cup of bitterness and hatred. We must forever conduct our struggle on the high plane of dignity and discipline. We must not allow our creative protest to degenerate into physical violence. Again and again we must rise to the majestic heights of meeting physical force with soul force. The marvelous new militancy which has engulfed the Negro community must not lead us to a distrust of all white people, for many of our white brothers, as evidenced by their presence here today, have come to realize that their destiny is tied up with our destiny and their freedom is inextricably bound to our freedom. We cannot walk alone.

And as we walk, we must make the pledge that we shall march ahead. We cannot turn back. There are those who are asking the devotees of civil rights, "When will you be satisfied?" We can never be satisfied as long as the Negro is the victim of the unspeakable horrors of police brutality. We can never be satisfied as long as our bodies, heavy with the fatigue of travel, cannot gain lodging in the motels of the highways and the hotels of the cities. We cannot be satisfied as long as the Negro's basic mobility is from a smaller ghetto to a larger one. We can never be satisfied as long as a Negro in Mississippi cannot vote and a Negro in New York believes he has nothing for which to vote. No, no we are not satisfied, and we will not be satisfied until justice rolls down like waters and righteousness like a mighty stream.

I am not unmindful that some of you have come here out of great trials and tribulations. Some of you have come fresh from narrow jail cells. Some of you have come from areas where your quest for freedom left you battered by the storms of persecution and staggered by the winds of police brutality. You have been the veterans of creative suffering. Continue to work with the faith that unearned suffering is redemptive.

Go back to Mississippi, go back to Alabama, go back to South Carolina, go back to Georgia, go back to Louisiana, go back to the slums and ghettos of our modern cities, knowing that somehow this situation can and will be changed. Let us not wallow in the valley of despair.

I say to you today, my friends, that in spite of the difficulties and frustrations of the moment I still have a dream. It is a dream deeply rooted in the American dream.

I have a dream that one day this nation will rise up and live out the true meaning of its creed: "We hold these truths to be self-evident; that all men are created equal."

I have a dream that one day on the red hills of Georgia the sons of former slaves and the sons of former slaveowners will be able to sit down together at the table of brotherhood.

I have a dream that one day even the state of Mississippi, a desert state sweltering with the heat of injustice and oppression, will be transformed into an oasis of freedom and justice.

I have a dream that my four little children will one day live in a nation where they will not be judged by the color of their skin but by the content of their character.

I have a dream today.

I have a dream that one day the state of Alabama, whose governor's lips are presently dripping with the words of interposition and nullification, will be transformed into a situation where little black boys and black girls will be able to join hands with little white boys and white girls and walk together as sisters and brothers.

I have a dream today.

I have a dream that one day every valley shall be exalted, every hill and mountain shall be made low, the rough places will be made plain, and the crooked places will be made straight, and the glory of the Lord shall be revealed, and all flesh shall see it together.

This is our hope. This is the faith with which I return to the South. With this faith we will be able to hew out of the mountain of despair a stone of hope. With this faith we will be able to transform the jangling discords of our nation into a beautiful symphony of brotherhood. With this faith we will be able to work together, to pray together, to struggle together, to go to jail together, to stand up for freedom together, knowing that we will be free one day.

This will be the day when all of God's children will be able to sing with new meaning "My country 'tis of thee, sweet land of liberty, of thee I sing. Land where my fathers died, land of the pilgrim's pride, from every mountainside, let freedom ring."

And if America is to be a great nation this must become true. So let freedom ring from the prodigious hilltops of New Hampshire. Let freedom ring from the mighty mountains of New York.

Let freedom ring from the heightening Alleghenies of Pennsylvania!

Let freedom ring from the snowcapped Rockies of Colorado!

Let freedom ring from the curvacious peaks of California!

But not only that; let freedom ring from Stone Mountain of Georgia!

Let freedom ring from Lookout Mountain of Tennessee!

Let freedom ring from every hill and mole hill of Mississippi. From every mountainside, let freedom ring.

When we let freedom ring, when we let it ring from every village and every hamlet, from every state and every city, we will be able to speed up that day when all of God's children, black men and white men, Jews and Gentiles, Protestants and Catholics, will be able to join hands and sing in the words of the old Negro spiritual, "Free at last! free at last! thank God almighty, we are free at last!"

49. JOHN LEWIS:
"A TREND TOWARD AGGRESSIVE
NONVIOLENT ACTION"

In most parts of the South the real cutting edge of the nonviolent direct-action movement was the Student Nonviolent Coordinating Committee, the most militant of the major civil rights organizations.

The "revolutionary mystique" of SNCC militants, and the tendency in SNCC to depart from its original outlook, are revealed in an interview that the editor of a student publication at Cornell University had with John Lewis, chairman of SNCC from 1963 to 1966. Lewis's viewpoints were representative not only of many SNCC workers, but also of certain other groups especially in CORE. Noteworthy in this interview were Lewis's comments on the possibilities of violence, the manifestations of nationalism, the role of white activists, the growing concern with economic matters, and the necessity of federal intervention to protect black rights in the South. Running through Lewis's remarks was a certain disillusionment with the nonviolent direct-action technique that in 1960 and 1961 appeared to many to promise the millennium, and with the failure of the federal government to act more decisively in the deep South. Lewis himself remained committed to nonviolence and resigned from SNCC, in 1966, after it repudiated its original philosophy.

"An Interview with John Lewis: The Chairman of SNCC Discusses the Negro Revolt, Its Problems and Prospects," DIALOGUE MAGAZINE, IV, 2 (Spring 1964), 7–9. (DIALOGUE MAGAZINE was a student-edited intercollegiate journal published at Cornell University). Reprinted with permission of DIALOGUE MAGAZINE.

EDITOR: What differentiates the SNCC of today from the SNCC of two years ago?

LEWIS: A great deal. A few years ago SNCC was a more spontaneous, loosely organized group. Today it is still loosely organized, but in terms of the revolution, it is an organization with a sense of direction. I think there's a great sense of involvement on the part of both Negro and white students involved in SNCC, not only in terms of the question of Negro rights but on other basic questions. I think SNCC is becoming more liberal and open-minded.

EDITOR: What do you mean when you use the term "revolution"?

LEWIS: Well, I think we should call this a social revolution. That is, it's not a revolution that intends to destroy or overthrow a form of government, but rather to overthrow a racist political and economic structure. It's for a radical change across the board, not just in some areas.

EDITOR: Recently, Gloria Richardson of the Cambridge, Maryland movement announced that her group would no longer conduct demonstrations for public accommodations. Rather, she placed strong emphasis on jobs and food. Is this an indication of the direction SNCC is traveling?

LEWIS: I think it's a good example of the change in SNCC. Perhaps public accommodation is not the real heart of the matter, but it is an area in which we have rallied a lot of support. It is easier to dramatize the issues so that people know something is wrong. Under Gloria Richardson's leadership in Cambridge, SNCC picketed the welfare office for food. Fifteen were arrested when I was there—but they received the food last Saturday.

EDITOR: How do you think that having Negroes vote and perhaps having black people take the place of white people in jobs and government is going to radically change the economics of individuals?

LEWIS: I'm not suggesting that black people take the place of white people in jobs or government, but I am suggesting that individuals, whether they be black or white, take the place of people like Senator Eastland, Senator Talmadge, Senator Russell, and some of the others. When the Negroes and the poor whites of the South exercise their right—the right to vote—then we will move people like Senator Eastland and those others out of Congress. Eleven out of sixteen of the really powerful committees in the house are headed by guys from the South, and all of the Congressional representatives from the state of Mississippi have been in Congress for over 20 years except one, who's been there 16. These men have power, and we know that they keep any progressive, liberal legislation from getting out of the committees. When the Negro people get the right to vote, they're going to get rid of Eastland, and this action will help liberalize not only the South, but the political structure of this country and of Congress, so we can get some decent, honest, and good welfare legislation (if you want to call it that) passed.

EDITOR: How successful has SNCC been in getting Negroes to register to vote?

LEWIS: There has been very little progress in terms of getting a significant number of Negroes actually registered to vote. In some areas where we've been involved since the fall of '61, it's been like pressing against a stone wall.

EDITOR: What type of resistance do Southern whites put up?

LEWIS: In places like Mississippi and Alabama, there is constant harassment, intimidation, arrests of voter registration workers, fining of people, and forcing Negroes to move off plantations or their farms because they seek to register to vote. There have been cases, for example, in Canton [Miss.] two weeks ago, where people stood in line all day trying to register to vote and only seven were able to pass through the line. These seven must now wait thirty days to find out whether they even passed their literacy tests or not. Just two or three days ago, John Doar from the Justice Department was arguing a case in a federal court.

Judge Cox, who was appointed by President Kennedy, was supposed to hear the case today and make a ruling on it. He said in effect that "they're just a bunch of niggers"—a federal judge said this—the *New York Times* ran a story on it today or yesterday.

EDITOR: What do you think is going to happen before large numbers of Negroes will be able to participate in the voting process in the South?

LEWIS: In order for Negroes to become registered voters, there must be some type of confrontation between the federal government and the state government. The federal government and federal lawyers may literally have to take over a particular state or area, backed by court decrees, and federal marshals or troops, should be sent in, if necessary.

EDITOR: What's going to force that confrontation?

LEWIS: I'm not sure what will force the confrontation, but I do know that we must play it by ear and continue to dramatize the issue. The Negro people in the South—in the states of Mississippi and Alabama—have been denied the right to vote. They will have to demand, in increasing numbers, federal support for this demand. This is why SNCC is waging its "One Man—One Vote" campaign in the deep South.

EDITOR: It has been said by many, and Malcolm X was not the first, that if we're going to have a revolution it cannot be done unless some blood is spilled. Do you think those in power can be forced to give up their vested interests without violence?

LEWIS: I don't think the South and those in power are going to give up their interest without some form of struggle. They're just not going to hand it over. As Frederick Douglass said, "Without agitation there can be no progress." I believe in that. I think that somewhere in the history of Judeo-Christian tradition is the idea that there can be no salvation without the shedding of blood and there may be some truth in that. Personally, though, I now accept the philosophy of non-violence.

EDITOR: How does the shedding of blood fit into SNCC's framework?

LEWIS: The shedding of blood is not a part of our framework; it's not a part of our philosophy, but I think that when we accept non-violence, we don't say that it is the absence of violence. We say it is the present assumption—much more positive—that there might be the shedding of blood. You know what Ghandi says: "If I had the personal choice to make between no movement and a violent movement, I would choose a violent movement." In the past few days we have been involved in a study of our position. The thing we drew up back in 1960 was a type of creed, a philosophic and religious commitment. In SNCC now, there's a growing—and it's growing fast—trend toward "aggressive non-violent action." You no longer walk quietly to paddy-wagons and happily and willingly go to jail. There's another type of willingness, and personally, I don't see anything violent about it . . . I think it is good—very creative.

EDITOR: If SNCC continues to adhere to the philosophy of non-violence as a technique or as a philosophy of life, will it be able to control a growing resistance to this doctrine on the part of the masses?

LEWIS: I'm not so sure whether SNCC as an organization is ready and prepared to catch up with the masses. I think that in SNCC we may have been fooling ourselves. But we are not, as many people have called us, radical, militant and oppressive. But we *are* serving a purpose somewhere as a catalyst for the other civil rights organizations. Before the March on Washington, Martin King was considered by a lot of people, and the Southern press particularly, as an extremist. But right after the March he became the moderate of the South. Right now SNCC is considered by the Southern press as irresponsible, extremist, radical and militant. Even the Atlanta Constitution with Ralph McGill called us sick. He said drop the "N" out of SNCC and you have sick.

EDITOR: We read a great deal about Negro nationalism in the North. How much nationalist consciousness is there among Negroes in the South? Among people in the movement?

LEWIS: Something is happening to people in the Southern Negro community. They're identifying with people because of color. During the recent Panama crisis you heard Negroes on the streets saying, "Did you see what happened? Did you see those Americans shooting at those black people?" People in Mississippi, in the heart of the delta, have televisions. They're conscious of things that happen in Cuba, in Latin America, and in Africa. Even in SNCC, we talk about integration, about the beloved community, but there have been great changes going on. There's been a radical change in our people since 1960; the way they dress, the music they listen to, their natural hairdo's —all of them want to go to Africa.

EDITOR: Isn't this in a sense going to work against what you're after?

LEWIS: I don't think so. I think that they're saying, "We want integration, we want desegregation, but there is something we must hold on to, too. There is something we must keep. . . ." I think people are searching for a sense of identity, and they're finding it.

EDITOR: The late Dr. E. Franklin Frazier wrote an article in *Negro Digest* three years ago on Negro intellectuals. In effect, he said that Negroes, in their efforts to parrot white intellectuals, have turned out stale works, and that until Negroes rejoiced in their own contributions, the situation will remain the same. Has there been any change in the attitude of Negroes toward non-image intellectuals like Robeson and Du Bois?

LEWIS: I don't think we, as a whole, are ashamed of Du Bois and Paul Robeson. In a sense, the so-called Negro leaders who become part of the American structure, are ashamed, but not deep down within. In order to maintain an image, they must state publicly that Du Bois and Robeson are not the order of the day. But I think the masses and the Negro academic community really feel a great deal of understanding and love for people like Robeson and Du Bois.

EDITOR: What is your assessment of the NAACP's effectiveness over the years?

LEWIS: Some of my best friends are in the NAACP, but I'm not so sure I'd let one of them marry my daughter. . . . I think the NAACP is a very effective organization. . . . It has set the climate for the mass movements of today.

EDITOR: How do we get students, both white and black who are detached from the "revolution," to become conscious of it? What feelings do you have about student attitudes in general?

LEWIS: I think most of the students in the North, both Negro and white, feel they shouldn't get involved, that this isn't their problem: "Why should I be concerned? Why should I give money? This is not going to help me. . . . I should just go to school, get a good education, get a job, two cars, and a television, live a good, decent life and be free to live in an isolated world and forget that a revolution is going on." Rabbi Prinz made a point during the March on Washington that can be applied to college communities. He said that it is not so much the racists who are to blame but the "good people" who maintain an aura of complete silence, a nonchalant attitude toward injustice. . . . The students in this country could do a hell of a job in civil rights.

EDITOR: Much has been said about a mass saturation project which will include Negro and white college students this summer in Mississippi. What are SNCC's plans?

LEWIS: The program in Mississippi for the summer is under the banner of what we call COFO, the Council of Confederate Organizations. It will include CORE (The Congress of Racial Equality), SNCC, SCLC (Southern Christian Leadership Conference), and supposedly the NAACP although only their state and local branches will be involved. The National Council of Churches will also play a role in it. . . . The whole thing in Mississippi isn't just voter registration; it's the Delta program— Operation Delta. Resident freedom schools for gifted Negro students and day schools for basic learning and for dropouts will be established. We hope to get nurses and doctors to teach courses in such things as prenatal care. . . . It's a basic program across the state with the ultimate objective of the non-violent political overthrow of Mississippi.

EDITOR: Does this mark a departure from SNCC policy? Previously, the organization did not encourage white students to come to Mississippi because of the increased dangers to interracial teams.

LEWIS: It is not so much that SNCC doesn't encourage white students. In the organization, there's a great deal of independence and freedom and flexibility; you let staff people decide things and direct a project. Bob Moses, as the director of the Mississippi project, was very reluctant to let any white people in the state at all. Last summer, we convinced Bob that the time was right to integrate the project. The head of our project in eastern Arkansas is white and so is the director of the project in Greenville . . . that's tokenism.

EDITOR: The Northern Student Movement (NSM) has been trying to get white students to organize and effectively work with white people by organizing around similar issues and similar needs like housing, jobs, or education. I know that SNCC has a similar program in the South. NSM has found a great deal of reluctance on the part of a number of white students to get involved in a program in the North or even in the South among white people. What do you think can be done about this predicament?

LEWIS: For us, it's still in the planning stage. . . . There has been a great deal of discussion and dialogue about why so many white students are ready to come into the Negro community, even Southern white students. But getting these same people involved in the white community is a real problem we, and other civil rights organizations, have to face in the South.

50. ROBERT F. WILLIAMS: FOR "EFFECTIVE SELF DEFENSE"

Not until 1963, when spontaneous violence erupted from Negro onlookers or demonstrators in Birmingham, Alabama, Cambridge, Maryland, and Nashville, Tennessee, did the calculated use of violence become a subject for widespread discussion. The issue had been raised, in the rather unlikely state of North Carolina, as early as 1959. North Carolina has been one of the most progressive southern states, and indeed the nonviolent movement has probably been more successful there than anywhere else in Dixie. But some of the towns are as hostile toward Negroes as any city in the deep South. One such town is Monroe, North Carolina. Despairing and frustrated, Robert F. Williams, the NAACP's branch president there, made a speech declaring that blacks should meet violence with violence. He was denounced and suspended from office by the national board of the NAACP. In succeeding months he adopted the even more radical position that deliberate violence on the part of blacks would be needed to secure freedom. Permanently expelled from the NAACP, he organized a local movement. Subsequent events in Monroe led to his arrest, his release on bond, his flight to Cuba, and later to China. He returned to the United States in 1969.

In his book, *Negroes with Guns*, Williams set forth his philosophy of violence and his opposition to nonviolent direct action. From abroad Williams used the airwaves and the mails to urge Negroes to engage in violent retaliation against their white oppressors. As the

Robert F. Williams, "USA: The Potential of a Minority Revolution," THE CRUSADER MONTHLY NEWSLETTER ("Published in Cuba as a Private Publication, Robert F. Williams, Publisher in Exile") V, 4 (May–June 1964), 1–7.

selection that follows indicates, Williams not only advocates Marxian-style revolution in an abstract way but suggests the specific tactics to be employed.

When the brutally oppressed Afroamerican speaks of violent resistance to savage racial dehumanization, he reaps a whirlwind of reasons and causes why such a reaction supposedly is insane and suicidal. There is no end to the stereotyped polemics and heated opposition that beclouds a rational and objective discourse on the subject. From the camps of the rabid white supremacy power structure, the fellow traveling white liberal and the mercenary running dog Uncle Tom, any individual who raises such a question is labeled a bloodthirsty crackpot, not worthy of social acceptance in America's "democratic and Christian" society. Proponents of the peaceful transition philosophy are quick to evoke the Gandhian theory of appealing to the conscience of the brutal oppressor and conquering him with the power of nonviolence and love.

These Gandhian Fabians inadvertently extol the success of Gandhi's peaceful revolution. Gandhi's nonviolent revolution may have guaranteed the ruling powers immunity from the violence of the masses, but it most certainly left the masses exposed to the violence of the oppressors. It served to assure that only the blood of the oppressed would flow.

The disciples of the Gandhi theory of peaceful transition elect to omit the latter stage of the continuing revolution. Revolution is a continuing process. It is essential, in appraising the success of the Indian Revolution, to consider the fact that Nehru, a disciple of Gandhi, despaired of the love principle in extending liberation to Goa, Damao, and Diu. He refused to settle the Pakistan and the Chinese border questions peacefully as exemplified by the philosophy of nonviolence and love. Despite the Gandhian "power of love" theory's evolution to a "force of arms" theory, Afroamericans are still being drugged with the opium of the power of love and nonviolence.

The forces with a vested interest in the equilibrium of the

U.S. master-slave society and their agents of deceit are more than willing to point out to our miserably exploited and dehumanized masses that violent resistance and self-defense will mean total annihilation and extermination. This is in itself an unwitting admission of the beastly nature of the oppressor. If such an oppressor is conceded to be capable of such an act of genocide and history bears out his determination to maintain the status quo, where is the wisdom of the logic that he will tolerate the loss of his slave empire through peaceful means? The very essence of revolution is radical change. Revolution is necessitated by abusive and reactionary power. This abusive and oppressive power perpetuates itself through the medium of violence. In the outset the oppressive force commands the superior power, if it did not, violent revolution would not be necessary. If the oppressed controlled the means of power, a peaceful transition could possibly be executed by virtue of the will of the oppressed.

It is a universally known fact that the power structure of the racist USA is rabidly opposed to self-defense on the part of our oppressed people. They have a morbid fear of violent self-preservation on the part of U.S. freedom fighters. Is this because they love the dehumanized Negro? Is this because they are concerned with the welfare and well-being of our brutalized people? Is this because the American society is a pacifist society with an aversion for violence? No! A thousand times No! If the power structure had ever manifested any true concern for the welfare of our people (for whom it now professes great fear that we may commit suicide by fighting for the right to live as human beings) there would be no question of a violent liberation struggle. The question of peaceful persuasion, as a moral issue, is belied by its imperialist military actions against Cuba, South Vietnam, Cambodia, Laos and other liberated areas. Why is such a belligerently imperialist government not concerned about black Americans, and whites as well, being exterminated in a nuclear war? Was it not Kennedy, as the very head of the U.S. Government and white so-called liberal society, who said, ". . . We will live up to our commitments even if victory turns to ashes in our mouths?" Where were the panic preachers then, who express such great concern and alarm for the possibility of black Americans being exterminated in violently resisting racial oppression? Is not a black American just as dead when killed in an international war of conquest as in a national struggle for liberation?

Why are the liberals, Uncle Toms and the power structure so hysterical about the possibility of massive violence erupting on the national human rights scene?

The fact is that the racist oppressors of the Afroamerican realize the insecurity and vulnerability of the most powerful military complex in the world to a violent internal struggle, wherein its horrible and sophisticated weapons of war will be ineffective. The internal defense of the U.S. is a possibility that money cannot buy. Only a change in the moral and social structure of the system offers security against an enraged oppressed citizenry. The USA is either unwilling or morally incapable of bearing the cost of this type of internal security. The race question is her Achilles heel, her Maginot line.

The power structure, the liberals and Uncle Toms are in essence asking Afroamericans to cooperate with the very forces that are opposing them. How can oppressed people who seek liberation, afford to allow the enemy to dictate the method of struggle? How can a people, who are dead serious about their freedom, allow themselves to be duped into limiting themselves to the most ineffective method of struggle? It is not logical to accommodate the will of the oppressor, who has a vested interest in maintaining the status quo, and to wage a successful liberation struggle simultaneously.

The fact is that racist white America is not worried about the possibility of Negroes being exterminated. It is more worried about the loss of its privileged position in its racist caste society; its system of white supremacy and world domination. It is ironical that we note inherent inequality in the very method and tactics proposed to abolish the evil inequities of racism. The white barbaric racist is ceded a "white only" special privilege in the realm of all violence, both justified and unjustified.

The execution of human prerogative is again straddled with a limitation placed on brutally oppressed people whose miserable existence is the very personification of limited human endeavor. A democratic or equalitarian society is devoid of minority or majority distinctions based on race or class. An integrated society of racial equality in the United States is impossible if specific limitations are placed on black citizens, while excluding white ones. True equality must not only extend to the Afroamerican the right to full participation in virtuous endeavors but also the full right to the equal extent of the white nationalist class in some not so virtuous endeavors. Equality, total equality, must grant the black citizen the same right to be a devil or a god as the whites. It must grant him the same right of temper and the same right of self-defense as any other citizen. To limit the Afroamerican struggle to the narrow confines of non-violence, while the white oppressor class wages a violent struggle to maintain the status quo, is to invoke the principle of Jim Crow and its racial inequality. The power of non-violence and love is a farce. Socrates was nonviolent and he, too, stressed love. He died at the hands of violent men. Christ was nonviolent and he, too stressed love and nonviolence, he too, died a violent death. History is replete with examples of nonviolent men, as well as violent ones, who died from the power of violence either justified or unjustified. We have the case of millions of non-violent Jews, who found meekness to be greatly inadequate in the face of ruthless and intemperate Nazi violence. The evil force of Nazism was not crushed by nonviolence and love but a fighting spirit, backed up by force and violence. The Christians who were cast into the ancient lion pits were not saved by the power of nonviolence and love. Where is the example of the success of this power, of this nonviolence and love? The mystic principle of the power of nonviolence and love borders on the primitive poisonous snake-handling rituals of some religious cults.

The most noble of mankind must surely aspire for a human level of endeavor, wherein mankind can establish a utopian society divested of brute force and violence. The irony of this great dream is that if it is at all possible, it is possible only through the medium of violence. It is possible only through Revolution.

Many of the nonviolent preachers in North America tend to fuse Gandhism and Christianity. Their hybrid type of pacifism leans heavily on Christian teachings and on the bible, which threatens that the entire earth is to be destroyed by violent fire. Its watchword is the coming battle of Armageddon. Not a non-violent battle but the most ferociously violent one ever staged. These advocates of the Christian power of nonviolence and love omit that part of the Old Testament which describes the evil subversion attempted by the devil when peaceful coexistence degenerated in Heaven to a state of open conflict wherein the Christian's God, the highest ideal of peace and love, ordered the devil forcibly ejected from the heavenly society. In removing the devil and his evil from menacing the peace of the ideal community, it is significant to note that God did not see fit to relegate such an important task to the realm of nonviolence. Why is the mortal Afroamerican expected to be more peaceful and loving towards his enemy than his divine God?

From the very earliest event of the African's chained arrival in the New World, he has been subjected to every form of brute force, systematic demoralization and dehumanization conceivable. The insensate slave masters left no stone unturned in conditioning oppressed blacks to meekly accept their miserable lot. The black man's fate was presented as being inseparable from the will of the white man. He was deliberately conditioned to base the prospects of his fortune on the Christian charity or conscience of the good white folks. Our people have never been allowed to forget that all significant power is in the hands of and under the control of the all-powerful God chosen white man.

The lip agents, both black and white, of the white man's supremacy doctrine have been rapid and more than lavish in proclaiming the "white folks" as possessors of all the cannons, the bombs, the machine guns and the complete military establishment. This has been true and it is essentially true today, however, times have changed. These changes do not bear good tidings for the perennial and brutal oppressor dehumanizer and exploiter of our people.

Our people's freedom spirit has been ossified by the continuous harangue of "we cannot possibly win a violent struggle of liberation." It is impossible for a people to rise above their aspirations. If we think we cannot win, we most certainly cannot. Our greatest enemy is our defeatist attitude. Our oppressor's greatest weapon of repression is his psychological apparatus by which he impregnates our people with a defeatist complex. Are we to concede the fact that racial oppression and tyranny prevail invincible and unshakable? Are we to concede to the unchallenged all mighty power of our dehumanizer, that he is the supreme benefactor of our freedom? Are we destined to forever kneel beggingly at his feet seeking the alms of liberty and justice?

The sweetest fruits of liberty are plucked by those who readily display boldness and daring. The cringing and the reluctant constitute the hindmost part of a civilization in constant transition. The defeatist voice of cynicism is the inevitable scum that litters the shore before all daring world-shaking exploits of embarcation. What would civilization resemble if all revolutionaries, inventors, adventurers and scientists had heeded the inevitable voices of the doubting Thomases, who perennially admonish that every novel and daring exploit is predestined to fail? Ironically, the survival of the cynic and the conservative is assured by the dogged iconoclast.

Is it possible for a minority revolution to succeed in powerful America? The cynics, prophets of doom, and agents of the oppressive establishment maintain that to even raise such a question is insane. They energetically, with a clairvoyant air, assure us that violent self-defense or violent resistance to brutal racial oppression can lead only to suicide. How do they know? What is the basis of their logic? Are they any wiser than those cynics who brazenly stated that "man will never fly," that "it is impossible to cross the oceans," that "man can never reach the speed of a mile a minute and survive," and that "the American

Revolution can never succeed against the military might of the Crown?" How do they know that violent resistance on the part of our people will lead to suicide? Yes, they have been conditioned to accept America's racist tyranny as a condition bound to prevail until the tyrant himself elects to abandon the throne of tyranny. They are more than resigned to the premise that white supremacy might is the God of the fate and destiny of oppressed black humanity.

Yes, a minority revolution has as much, or more, chance of succeeding in the racist USA as any place else in the world. At the very outset, all revolutions are minority revolutions. In the early stages cynics think that all revolutions have a very remote chance of succeeding. Revolutionaries display a propensity to accomplish the impossible. Is the Afroamerican revolution to be an exception? Do we subscribe to the premise of white supremacy? Is it because the oppressor is white and the oppressed is black that most of the world accepts the premise that our struggle must be white-led and supported by the majority race or that it is insignificant and doomed to failure?

The fact of the matter is that the Afroamerican wants and has been seeking brotherhood with the white masses since his enslavement in the New World. A people as brutally oppressed as American Negroes cannot wait forever for the support of mythological and theoretical allies. Most white workers in the USA today have a vested interest in the status quo. The present system grants them special privileges in a jungle society. The cow of production may be lean and diseased but the Negro is the only herdsman limited to the cutlets of feet and tail. The vast majority of the whites have also been mentally poisoned with racism. It is asinine to expect them to recover from their race psychosis without a severe shock treatment.

The American society is a highly industrialized complex. A highly industrialized and mechanized system is also a very sensitive one. The more machinery required to serve a community, the greater the incidence of mechanical breakdown. The more dependent a community is on mechanization, the more important it is for the wheels of industry to perpetually turn smoothly. Social systems, like biological systems, tend to adjust to environmental conditions and requirements. The American society, over a long period of time, has adjusted itself to a high rate of productivity directly bearing on the relativity of consumption.

The physical conditioning of a society also manifests certain relative psychological traits. The American mind has been conditioned to think of great calamities, wars and revolutionary upheavals as taking place on distant soil. Because of the vast upper and middle classes in the USA, that have grown accustomed to comfortable living, the nation is not psychologically prepared for massive violence and a sudden disruption of the essential agencies of the affluent society. The soft society is highly susceptible to panic.

Afroamericans have long sought a peaceful solution to the race question. It is more than obvious that a people, who have manifested an unshakable faith in the vain hope that the government would eventually grant citizenship and justice, prefers a peaceful solution. Our people have dreamed and prayed for a peaceful transition from slavery to first class citizenship and human dignity. Peaceful evolution, through the mediums of legislation, law and negotiation are the methods that have been pursued for almost 200 years under the present government. The results are bitter and frustrating indeed. The orderly social process has been stymied by savage violence and brute force.

Instead of the majority race extending brotherhood and justice, it has resorted to a campaign of a massive drive aimed at extermination. The fascist elements are arming, not to liberate our brutally oppressed people but to liquidate us. It is becoming next to impossible for Negroes to conduct a "peaceful" demonstration in America. A Civil Rights Bill will have no more effect than the U.S. Constitution. What is integration when the law says yes, but the police and howling mobs say no? Our only logical and successful answer is to meet organized and massive violence with massive and organized violence. Our people must prepare to wage an urban guerrilla war of self-defense. Self-defense develops to the stage wherein the source of evil and terror must be eliminated.

In Monroe, North Carolina (the first instance wherein highly organized self-defense units supplemented nonviolent tactics and reduced the incidence of resulting terror) our force of defense was adequate in staving off local attacks. We had enough force and arms to reduce the entire city to ashes. The fault, however, lay in the fact that we had an isolated force without extensive outside forces to pin down, ambush and destroy the state reinforcements moving in to overpower us. Our self-defense forces had to remain purely static and defensive. The Monroe explosion came prematurely because of our shift in emphasis from self-defense to publicly overemphasizing nonviolence. The racists seized this time of weakness and confusion to launch an attack to annihilate our forces. A six year effective self-defense campaign terminated in ill-fated untimely experiment with nonviolence. The organization of external forces was just being conceived. A decision was made to spare the city thus avoiding an all-out confrontation prematurely. The town would have been destroyed but our defense forces would have been crushed by external power, and the state and white supremists would have used the example to intimidate other advocates of self-defense. The racist news media would have portrayed the entire operation as one conducted by psychotic extremists.

The lesson of Monroe teaches that effective self-defense, on the part of our brutally oppressed and terrorized people, requires massive organization with central coordination. External oppressive forces must not be allowed to relieve the beseiged racist terrorists. The forces of the state must be kept under pressure in many places simultaneously. The white supremacy masses must be forced to retreat to their homes in order to give security to their individual families.

The weapons of defense employed by Afroamerican freedom fighters must consist of a poor man's arsenal. Gasoline fire bombs (Molotov cocktails), lye or acid bombs (made by injecting lye or acid in the metal end of light bulbs) can be used extensively. During the night hours such weapons, thrown from roof tops, will make the streets impossible for racist cops to patrol. Hand grenades, bazookas, light mortars, rocket launchers, machine guns and ammunition can be bought clandestinely from servicemen, anxious to make a fast dollar. Freedom fighters in military camps can be contacted to give instructions on usage.

Extensive sabotage is possible. Gas tanks on public vehicles can be choked up with sand. Sugar is also highly effective in gasoline lines. Long nails driven through boards and tacks with large heads are effective to slow the movement of traffic on congested roads at night. This can cause havoc on turn-pikes. Derailing of trains causes panic. Explosive booby traps on police telephone boxes can be employed. High powered sniper rifles are readily available. Armor piercing bullets will penetrate oil storage tanks from a distance. Phosphorus matches (kitchen matches) placed in air conditioning systems will cause delayed explosions which will destroy expensive buildings. Flame throwers can be manufactured at home. Combat experienced ex-service men can easily solve that problem.

Techniques mentioned here are generalized and require a closer study, however, let the cynics take note that the mighty USA is not as snug and secure as it once was. Yes, a minority war of self-defense can succeed. The Afroamerican can win. We need not submit, passively to racist extermination and brutality. The race question is America's Achilles heel. America's great abundance is what makes America America, without it she would be a wretched land of chaos. Her economy is already under stress and her military might is spread out too thinly throughout the world.

The bourgeoisie has very little stomach for massive blood and violence. They love their property, the source of their power and wealth. They are highly susceptible to panic. The majority white supremacists do not command the loyalty of the entire race. There are a few John Brown type students and militants.

Afroamericans must remember that such a campaign of massive self-defense should not be based upon a lust for sadistical gratification. It cannot be a campaign for vengeance, however sweet and deserving vengeance may be. Such a campaign of self-defense and survival must be based on the righteous cause of justice. It must not be anti-white but anti-oppression and injustice. Uncle Toms should be as much a target as racist whites.

Like it or not, we cannot escape the trend of history. The hour is fast approaching when our people must make a decision to meekly submit to fascist forces of terror and extermination or surge forth to the battle to liberate ourselves, save America and liquidate its domestic enemies. If we truly seek freedom and human dignity we must be willing to pay for it in the fashion of the Algerians. Great multitudes of our people must be willing to fight and die in America's true cause and commitment to her Constitution, democratic principles and the rights of man, and for a victory that will not ". . . turn to ashes in our mouths," but to eternal freedom and happiness in our hearts. Such a victory would truly make the world safe for democracy. It would secure the world from extermination by hydrogen war. Not only is America's peace and security involved but also the peace and security of the whole world.

The horrible nightmare of massive violence need not fall upon the American scene. It can be staved off by the birth of a sincere spirit of humanity, dedicated to the proposition of brotherhood, peace and security.

When a brutally oppressed and dehumanized people are denied the peaceful channels through which to activate redress, and when their peaceful petitions are answered with ruthless violence, the only recourse left to them is to meet violence with violence.

We do not advocate the violent overthrow of the U.S. Government. We merely advocate self-defense for brutalized Afroamericans. If in the process of executing our Constitutional and God-given right of self-defense, the racist U.S. Government, which refuses to protect our people, is destroyed, the end result stems from certain historical factors of social relativity.

". . . This country, with its institutions, belongs to the people who inhabit it. Whenever they shall grow weary of the existing government they can exercise their Constitutional right of amending it, or their revolutionary right to dismember or overthrow it. . . . If by the mere force of numbers a majority should deprive a minority of any clearly written Constitutional right, it might, in any moral point of view, justify revolution . . . ," Abraham Lincoln, 1861.

The oppressor's heart is hard. The experience of history teaches that he only relents under violent pressure and force. There is very little hope that he will see the handwriting on the wall before it is too late. This year, 1964 is going to be a violent one, the storm will reach hurricane proportions by 1965 and the eye of the hurricane will hover over America by 1966. America is a house on fire—FREEDOM NOW!—or let it burn, let it burn. Praise the Lord and pass the ammunition!!!

New roles for whites

51. LOREN MILLER:
"FAREWELL TO LIBERALS"

The nationalistic Black Muslims (see Document 53) attacked white liberals as hypocrites trying to deceive blacks. White liberals also faced an attack from a more unexpected quarter. Rumblings of discontent about the lack of militancy among white liberals punctuated the civil rights movement during 1961 and 1962. Then in October 1962, Loren Miller published his now well-known article in *The Nation*. "Farewell to Liberals" is a critique of both labor leaders and old-line middle-class white participants in the civil rights movement. A vice-president of the NAACP at the time this article was written, the late Loren Miller was a newspaper publisher, noted civil rights attorney, and a municipal judge in Los Angeles.

Liberals who were shocked or surprised at James Baldwin's recent statement that Negroes "twenty years younger than I don't believe in liberals at all" haven't been doing their homework. Discontent with the liberal position in the area of race relations has been building up for the past several years. Of course there are liberals and liberals, ranging from Left to Right; still, there does exist a set of beliefs and attitudes, not easily defined but readily identified, constituting the liberal outlook on the race question. Simply stated, it contemplates the ultimate elimination of all racial distinctions in every phase

Loren Miller, "Farewell to Liberals: A Negro View," THE NATION (October 20, 1962), 235–238.

of American life through an orderly, step-by-step process adjusted to resistance and aimed at overcoming such resistance. In the field of constitutional law, the classic liberal position, exemplified in the Supreme Court's "all deliberate speed" formula of the school-segregation cases, requires and rationalizes Negro accommodation to, and acquiescence in, disabilities imposed because of race and in violation of the fundamental law.

On his part, the Negro has to put up with such practices, but he cannot admit that they have constitutional sanction; to do so would be to give away his case and knuckle under to the revisionist theory that the Civil War Amendments conferred less than complete equality under the law. The liberal sees "both sides" of the issue: the force of the Negro's constitutional argument and the existence of customs, sometimes jelled into law, that justify the gradualist approach. He is impatient with "extremists on both sides."

The Negro is outraged at being called an extremist. Since he takes the position that the Constitution confers complete equality on all citizens, he must rest his case on the proposition that there is only one side: his side, the constitutional side. That his attitude in that respect is firming up is evidenced by the fact that Negro spokesmen who once won applause by claiming that their activities made for progress in race relations are being elbowed aside by others whose catchword is Freedom Now. "We want our Freedom Here; we want it Now, not tomorrow; we want it All, not just a part of it," Martin Luther King tells receptive audiences. Whoever opposes, or even doubts, that doctrine is cast in the role of a foe, whether he calls himself conservative or liberal. The middle ground on which the traditional liberal has taken his stand is being cut from beneath him.

Every civil-rights victory adds to the Negro's intransigence; he becomes ever more impatient and demanding. To the extent that this attitude tends to precipitate racial conflict, a substantial number of liberals shy away. As they see it, their role is to ease, not heighten, racial tensions while they create a climate in which progress is possible. But the new militants don't want *progress;* they *demand* Freedom: "The courts take time and we want Freedom Now—Today," the Rev. Ralph Abernathy told cheering Georgians last month. Abernathy's cry, echoing King and the student leaders, underscores the strong trend away from dependence on legalistic methods and, equally important, implies rejection of the dogma that racial reforms must await a change in the hearts and minds of men—the so-called educational approach that once numbered many adherents.

The swing away from major reliance on legal methodology and the educational approach poses new problems for liberals. It was easy and comfortable to wait for the filing of civil-rights cases or proposals for anti-discriminatory legislation and then lend support to those causes, or an even greater mark of liberalism to initiate them. However, the persistence of discriminatory practices in the wake of the NAACP's sweeping court victories which have destroyed the legal base of the Southern segregation system, and in the face of an upsurge of civil-rights legislation in the North, has shaken the faith of the Negro in the efficacy of the law. It is significant that King abjures his followers to disobey "unjust laws" and ironic that some segregationists, harried by the direct actionists, now argue that racial issues should be left to the courts. The plea for civil disobedience flies in the face of liberal doctrine of respect for the law; direct action in the form of sit-ins or stand-ins is seen by many as raising grave questions as to infringements of personal and property rights.

The liberal dilemma does not spring solely from doubts as to the advisability of direct action or the disobedience doctrine. The hard core of the difficulty lies in the circumstance that in the eighty years since the failure of Reconstruction, racial discrimination has become deeply rooted and thoroughly institutionalized in governmental agencies (local, state and federal), in the civil service and in churches, labor unions, political parties, professional organizations, schools, trade associations, service groups and in that vast array of voluntary organizations which play such a vital role in our society. Racial discrimination can't be uprooted unless governmental agencies are administered with that purpose in mind and unless voluntary organizations exert constant and consistent pressure to that end on local, state and federal governments, and at the same time accord Negroes all of the privileges and benefits that accrue from membership in such organizations. Those requirements aren't being met. Negroes are dismayed as they observe that liberals, even when they are in apparent control, not only do not rally their organizations for an effective role in the fight against discrimination, but even tolerate a measure of racial discrimination in their own jurisdictions.

Again, the liberal is restrained by his historical choice of seeing "both sides" of the issue. He understands the justice of the Negro's claim, but he argues that as a responsible administrator, he must reckon with deep-seated resistance to quick change and with the breakdown that might follow precipitate disruption of institutionalized practices. He may vacillate, as the President has done in the case of the Executive housing order, in an attempt to coax a consensus favorable to a change in policy. In any event, he is not, he says, as free as the Negro thinks; he must gauge the situation and settle for progress in the face of Negro clamor for immediate action.

Take the case of a liberal administrator of a government agency. He may owe his eminence to a political victory insured by a four- or five-to-one vote cast by urban Negroes. He now finds himself head of an agency mired in civil service and hobbled by a heritage of discriminatory practices. His underlings are apt to be wedded to that past; they helped frame the rules. He is a new broom that can hardly sweep at all, let alone sweep clean. Ordinarily, he appoints a few Negroes and institutes such reforms as will not call down upon his head the wrath of Congress, the state legislature or the Chamber of Commerce. Not personal cowardice makes him fear that wrath, but concern lest the opposition—through a crippling withdrawal of funds from his agency, perhaps—might make *all* reform impossible.

He may have done the best he could, but he hasn't endeared himself to Negroes, who contrast performance to pre-election speeches and campaign promises.

Civil service is a trap for unwary Negroes who enter it and

find themselves frozen in its lower reaches. The United States Civil Rights Commission has found that, just as in private industry, there are "Negro" jobs and "white" jobs with Negroes at the bottom of the civil-service heap. The liberal who comes to head a civil service-staffed department of government is caught in a web of rules and regulations deliberately designed, in some instances, to institutionalize racial discrimination, or having that effect. Again there may be token appointments and token promotions, but the establishment yields slowly. The Negro looks for results and what he sees often makes him take the cynical position that the liberal differs no whit from his conservative predecessor.

Or take the situation in the AFL-CIO, where discrimination is rife in craft unions. The federation professes an inability to compel constituent unions to abandon time-honored racial practices. That is bad enough. What is worse is the stance of liberal-led industrial unions. The Steelworkers maintain Jim Crow locals in the South, where union halls double in brass as meeting places for White Citizens Councils. It is an open secret that Negroes have next to nothing to say in the policy-making bodies of unions, craft or industrial, on local, state or national levels. When the Pullman Porters' A. Philip Randolph, the only Negro member of the AFL-CIO Executive Board, urged reforms in federation, George Meany, described in labor circles as a liberal, shouted at him, "Who the hell gave you the right to speak for Negroes?" and accused him of attacking the labor movement. The Executive Board, at Meany's urging, then censured Randolph for anti-union activities—without a dissent from such liberals as Walter Reuther or David Dubinsky. Randolph's answer was the formation of a *Negro* labor council; he was denounced again by labor leaders of all shades of opinion on the ground that he was fathering "Jim Crow in reverse." Yet for many years, the AFL-CIO has thrown its official weight behind state and federal fair housing, fair employment and other civil-rights legislation and has assisted in tests of segregatory laws.

An examination of the practices of other voluntary organizations, including churches, would produce a similar yield of institutionalized discriminatory practices. In almost every case in which the leadership of such organizations is classified as liberal, there has been announced public support of civil-rights objectives. Everybody seems to want everybody else to practice what he preaches and nobody seems to be able, or willing, to practice what everybody else preaches.

It is very easy to charge hypocrisy in the situation, but what is really at play here is a cleavage between the burgeoning Freedom Now thinking of the Negro and the old progress concept to which liberals still cling. That conflict flares into the open when liberals exercise the prerogative, long held by them, of speaking *for* the Negro, and of espousing views which the Negro is abandoning. The liberal custom of speaking for the Negro is rooted in history; there was a time when the Negro needed spokesmen. Inevitably, a measure of paternalism and a father-knows-best attitude developed. But as the Negro becomes more articulate and discerning, he insists on voicing his own aspirations, particularly in the light of what he regards as the shortcomings of liberal leadership.

When the Negro insists on speaking for himself, the rebuffed liberal may shout as Meany did at Randolph that the dissenters are agitators or trouble makers (another replication, in a liberal context, of a familiar Southern cliché). Others take the tack popularized by John Fischer in *Harper's* and, transforming themselves into spokesmen for all whites, issue stern warnings that discrimination will prevail until all Negroes conform to middle-class standards of morality—a cozy variant of the theme that all Negroes are chargeable with the sins of every Negro. Negroes aren't dismayed at the opposition to their taking matters into their own hands. Detroit Negroes, led by unionists, revolted against the UAW's mayoralty endorsement in that city and turned the tide against the union's choice; the NAACP and the AFL-CIO are increasingly at odds over the treatment of Negroes in the labor movement; Roy Wilkins defended bloc voting by Negroes in his Atlanta keynote speech. Muslims are drawing substantial urban support by proposing to have done with all "white devils."

There is a growing cynicism about the current stress being laid on absolute fairness in public and private employment and in political appointments—beginning as of today. The Negro wants a little more than that. One hundred years of racial discrimination have produced a wide gap between him and white Americans. The Negro wants that gap closed in political appointments, in civil service, in schools and in private industry. He sees no way to close it unless he gets preferential treatment. Logic favors his position, but such a proposal runs into opposition from those who argue, correctly, that preferential treatment cannot be extended to a Negro without impinging on the personal rights of the white person over whom he will be preferred.

In truth, the impasse between liberals and Negroes is the end-product of a long historical process in which Americans of African, or partially African, descent have been treated as Negroes rather than as individuals, in legal lore as well as in popular concept. But constitutional protections run to persons—individuals—rather than to groups; American idealism exalts the individual and insists that group identification is an irrelevance. The liberal's historic concern is with individual rights and he seeks to apply that formula in the area of race relations. The Negro, whose ultimate ideal is the attainment of the right to be treated as an individual without reference to his racial identification, sees his immediate problem as that of raising the status of the group to which he has been consigned by popular attitude and action and by laws which permit racial classification. The liberal sees progress in the admission of a few select Negro children to a hitherto white school; the Negro wants all Negro children admitted and spurns the concession as mere tokenism.

The Negro's quarrel with liberal leadership does not portend his subscription to conservative or radical philosophies of race relations. Indeed, the Negro revolt, as Louis Lomax has pointed out, is a rebellion against white leadership, whether that leadership is asserted directly or filtered down through Negroes who accept it. There is a certain irony in the fact that liberals are the targets of Negro displeasure precisely because of their long association in the quest for equality. It is the ally, not the enemy, who gets the blame when the alliance fails to gain its objectives. Rejection of liberal leadership does not mean that Negroes do not want, and expect, continued liberal aid. But they want it on their own terms and they are too sophisticated to believe that liberals can resign a battle involving fundamental equalitarian issues out of pique at the rejection of their leadership.

It is against this background, and to some extent because of it, that the young Negro militants "don't believe in liberals at all." Profoundly influenced by the overthrow of white colonialism in Asia and Africa, they not only want Freedom Now, but insist on substituting a grand strategy for the liberal tactics of fighting one civil-rights battle at a time. They are determined to plot the strategy and dictate the tactics of the campaign. The details of the grand strategy haven't been blueprinted as yet, but in bold outline it calls for direct action by way of sit-ins, stand-ins, kneel-ins, boycotts, freedom rides, civil disobedience and as-yet-unheard-of techniques as the occasion demands, with resort to legal action when expedient—all under Negro leadership, all calculated to produce immediate results. Heavy stress is being laid on voter registration in the Deep South and it is significant that student leaders make no bones about the fact that *Negro* voting is seen as a device to elect *Negroes* to public office. The very choice of weapons, incidentally, requires action by Negroes. Only Negroes can desegregate a cafe or a hotel or an airport by a sit-in, or a beach by a wade-in, or a church by a kneel-in or withdraw Negro patronage through a boycott.

It would not be accurate to say that the direct actionists speak for all Negroes under all circumstances. It is fair to say that their philosophy is ascendant, that their influence is becoming pervasive and that their voices are heard with increasing respect and diminishing dissent in Negro communities. Those voices are harsh and strident, and jarring to the liberal ear. Their message is plain: To liberals a fond farewell, with thanks for services rendered, until you are ready to re-enlist as foot soldiers and subordinates in a Negro-led, Negro-officered army under the banner of Freedom Now.

52. BAYARD RUSTIN:
"THE NEGRO NEEDS WHITE ALLIES"

In 1963, at the suggestion of Bayard Rustin, A. Philip Randolph revived the March on Washington. Originally aimed at obtaining federal action to deal with rapidly mounting Negro unemployment, the
movement shifted its focus over the months. When events during
the spring, especially in Birmingham (see Document 46), compelled
the administration of John F. Kennedy to push for passage of a civil
rights bill, the movement's strategists reoriented their demands. As
in the case of the 1941 March on Washington Movement, some leaders were skeptical but unity finally emerged. And, this time, leaders of
several labor unions (most notably the United Automobile Workers)
and of the country's three major religious faiths actively supported
the endeavor. The result was a gigantic rally—a quarter million
people of both races—at the Lincoln Memorial in August of 1963.

The March symbolized two major developments of 1963. First,
employment and the problems arising from the poverty of the lower
classes were becoming the major concerns of the civil rights movement. Second, white moderates, led by white churchmen, were
beginning to take a serious interest in civil rights.

Bayard Rustin, the architect of the March of 1963, cogently set
forth, in the article that follows, the thesis that the civil rights movement needed allies among white labor and among white middle-class
moderates. He also argued the merits of creative nonviolent disrup-
tions, in opposition to those who talked of the necessity of violence.

1.) The March on Washington took place because the Negro
needed allies. One reason he needed allies was that the Negro
revolt had, quite properly, begun to become a revolution. The
struggle began with the problem of buses and lunch counters
and theaters—in a word, with the problem of dignity. But since
the roots of discrimination are economic, and since, in the long

Bayard Rustin, "The Meaning of the March on Washington," LIBERATION,
VIII, 8 (October 1963), 11–13. Reprinted with permission of LIBERATION.

run, the Negro, like everyone else, cannot achieve even dignity without a job, economic issues were bound to emerge, with far-reaching implications. Similarly, when the question of where Negro children go to school began to come to a head, deeper problems arose than when it was a question of a movie or a hamburger. When you touch the home and the job, you touch sensitive nerves. At the point where this happened, it became important for the Negro to have allies, for his own sake and for the sake of his white brothers as well.

Historically, the March on Washington broadened the base of the civil-rights movement. The March was not a Negro action; it was an action by Negroes and whites together. Not just the leaders of the Negro organizations, but leading Catholic, Protestant, and Jewish spokesmen called the people into the streets. And Catholics, Protestants, and Jews, white and black, responded. This response obviated the danger that the revolt would be an argument between Negroes and whites over a few jobs. It began the process of focussing attention where it belongs: on the problem of what kind of economic and political changes are required to make it possible for everyone to have jobs. The civil-rights movement alone cannot provide jobs for all. It cannot solve the problems raised by automation—and automation deprives more Negroes of jobs than any other single factor, including prejudice. Nor can it tackle alone the coalition of Dixiecrats and plutocrats which impairs the political and economic health of the country.

2.) The Birmingham demonstrations achieved a breakthrough in goals, the March in methods. Birmingham forced the nation to see that Negroes are no longer interested in merely integrating buses here and lunch counters or swimming pools there. It forced the liberals, both black and white, to see that over-all demands by the Negro were inevitable. For the first time it became clear that the Negro wanted everything in his life changed.

What Birmingham accomplished with respect to goals, the March achieved with respect to method. It forced people to see the necessity for masses in the street. It underlined the inevitability of nonviolent mass action. It pointed the way to massive civil disobedience, by both blacks and whites.

Most Americans are more interested in order than in law, more interested in law than in justice. This means that in the normal course of events they will line up behind the *status quo* rather than make the basic changes required to meet human needs. In practical terms, this means that it is better for the Negro to go on suffering for another hundred years than to cause a disturbance in Washington or embarrass Congress. That is why it was important to get thousands of white people into the streets in Washington. Until Birmingham, the objectives were on trial; until the successful completion of the March, the method was on trial. "Would 'they' not bring their guns and razors to Washington?" The March came off so beautifully that not only did it reassure our white allies, it also put our opponents on the spot. That some of them responded so cruelly, with the bombings in Birmingham (incited as they were, whether intentionally or not, by Governor Wallace and the "hold-the-line" Senators) and the subsequent shootings by Southern policemen, heightened the contrast between the nonviolent revolutionists and the *status quo* defenders of "law and order."

3.) The success of the March also put the Kennedy administration on the spot. Even newspapers which had opposed the March right up until the day it took place turned around afterwards and asked Kennedy to come through for us. But Kennedy cannot come through as easily as some people seem to think. For there is no way to satisfy the Negro and his allies under "politics as usual." Our demands cannot be met so long as the Dixiecrats maintain their political and economic power. And their power is maintained not only through the well-known coalition with Republicans, but through alliances and compromises with their fellow Democrats as well.

Kennedy is the smartest politician we have had in a long time. He calls the Negro leaders together and says in effect: "I want to help you get money so Negroes can vote." That's when he is bowing toward us. Then he turns and bows to the Dixiecrats and gives them Southern racist judges who make certain that the money the Negro gets will not achieve its purpose. On the one hand he blesses the march, and on the other hand he reassures the segregationists and sabotages the aims of the March by permitting his brother to launch suits against the civil-rights leaders in Albany, Georgia. The time has passed when the Negro can be fooled by such methods. Our demands are not only too urgent, but too all-encompassing to be trifled with in this manner.

4.) Inseparable from the problem of politics-as-usual is the problem of "business as usual." Historically, the significance of the March will be seen to have less to do with civil rights than with economic rights: the demand for jobs. The problem of how to get jobs for Negroes is really the problem of how to get jobs for people. And this brings us up against the whole power structure. The tentacles of the power structure reach all the way from Birmingham to New York and Pittsburgh and Chicago, even as they also reach from New York, Pittsburgh, and Chicago to Birmingham, Danville, and Jackson. We must put the total structure of the country under scrutiny, including the war economy. Not only does war industry fail to provide butter and schools, houses and hospitals, but it provides the least jobs per dollar spent of any sector of industry. It is the most highly automated part of the economy.

Under automation, we are faced with a new civil war situation all over again. Once again the union cannot endure only half free. It cannot survive if it is divided into those who receive high incomes and those who are unemployed and subsist on the dole. The white unemployed and the labor unions have not challenged this situation. The March did. The program was inadequate, but a crucial first step was made.

The difficulties we face were re-emphasized by the bombings in Birmingham. There have been 21 unsolved bombings in Birmingham alone since the war, 50 in the state of Alabama. But the bombings are only the most flagrant example of the counterrevolutionaries' strategy. All through the South, with the exception of a very few cities, an attempt is being made to crush the nonviolent movement by an excess of police violence, by beating and brutalizing the demonstrators. In Alabama, for instance when Negroes march, Al Lingo, State Director of "Public Safety," moves in with his head-beaters. Unfortunately, the Kennedy administration, with its ties to the Dixiecrats and its anachronistic foreign policy, is playing right into the hands of those who employ such tactics. In addition to the continuing appointment of racist judges, the abysmal failure of the F.B.I. to do its job, and the pressing of federal indictments in Albany, Georgia, President Kennedy called in the press, after the prominence given in the news media to the use of police dogs and fire hoses in Birmingham. He pointed out that the image of the United States was being sullied abroad, to its detriment in the Cold War. Now, although there is a lot in the papers about the civil-rights movement, the true picture is missing. The terrible daily brutality of the police goes for the most part unreported. The killing of six children in Birmingham could not go unreported, but Kennedy's only response was to send in two unenlightened representatives of the old order, the very order Negroes are trying to destroy in Birmingham.

The inevitable reaction of large numbers of concerned people is to demand an end to this hypocrisy and to call for federal troops to protect the Negroes against inhuman bombers and brutal Southern police. I wish that the problem could be solved by sending in federal troops, but unfortunately it cannot. Basically there is only one thing federal troops can do, and that is to defend the *status quo*. But if Negroes had accepted the *status quo* in the first place there would have been no bombings and considerably less police brutality. We need protection, but we need protection *and* progress. Troops will not break the power of the Southern oligarchy. We did not ask for troops on August 28th, and ten thousand were on hand. How can we expect that when we ask for them they will do what is needed?

The need of the civil rights movement is not to get someone else to manipulate power. They will not do it in our interests. Our need is to exert our own power, and the main power we have is the power of our black bodies, backed by the bodies of as many white people as will stand with us. We need to use these bodies to create a situation in which society cannot function without yielding to our just demands. We need to make things unworkable until Negroes have jobs, equality, and freedom.

There has been talk of violence, especially by those in the North. If violence could ever be justified, it would be justifiable now for the Negroes of Birmingham. But we are not interested in retaliation. We want our freedom. And we cannot get our freedom with guns. You cannot integrate a school or get a job with a machine gun. The only way we can do these things is to use our bodies in such a way that the school or the factory cannot operate successfully without integrating us. The same holds true for our pressing over-all demands. The civil-rights movement cannot go much further without taking on society. Until we do so there will be a continuation of the brutalization and serfdom that is the daily lot of the majority of Negroes and a large number of whites. We need to go into the streets all over the country and to make a mountain of creative social confusion until the power structure is altered. We need in every community a group of loving troublemakers, who will disrupt the ability of the government to operate until it finally turns its back on the Dixiecrats and embraces progress.

My words may seem extreme. But both the demands and the needs of the Negro people go so far beyond the present political possibilities that disruption is inevitable. The only question is whether it will be violent or nonviolent, creative or uncreative. In the present framework of Southern brutality, aided by the leaders of both major parties and abetted by the apathy and "patience" of the white masses, there is no longer any viability for a *minority* nonviolent movement. Furthermore, there is a moral deterioration that takes place if the individual must face the brutalization and murder of little children, the furious violence of the Southern police, and the hypocrisy of the Kennedy administration, without a big enough response. It is not a question of debating, in a vacuum, the morality of violence and nonviolence, on the one hand, or of "respect for law" *versus* civil disobedience, on the other. It is a question of program, of taking the offensive in an adequate way. For this, there must be masses in motion. There is no possibility of a practical program through violence. But unless those who organized and led the March on Washington hold together and give the people a program based on mass action, the whole situation will deteriorate and we will have violence, tragic self-defeating violence which will do immeasurable harm to whites and Negroes alike and will postpone indefinitely the day when all men will be free.

Toward black nationalism

53. MALCOLM X v. JAMES FARMER:
SEPARATION v. INTEGRATION

Thanks to flamboyant utterances, and to free publicity given by
the media of mass communication, the Black Muslims had become a
familiar conversation piece for white America by 1961. More significantly, however, the Muslims were a manifestation of the growing
alienation of the black masses in the midst of the civil rights revolution. The chief spokesman for this nationalistic group was the
well-known Malcolm X, who in addition to presiding over the organization's New York temple enjoyed numerous appearances on the
air and at leading colleges and universities.

On March 7, 1962, Malcolm X, the separatist, debated James
Farmer, the integrationist, at Cornell University. Malcolm X's position epitomized Negro alienation with American society, while Farmer's remarks provided a vivid example of the desire to be able to
participate in and identify with American society.

Malcolm X

In the name of Allah, the Beneficent, the Merciful, to whom all
praise is due whom we forever thank for giving America's 20
million so-called Negroes, the most honorable Elijah Muhammad as our leader and our teacher and our guide.

I would point out at the beginning that I wasn't born Malcolm

Malcolm X and James Farmer, "Separation or Integration: A Debate," DIA-
LOGUE MAGAZINE, II, 3 (May 1962), 14–18. Reprinted with permission of
DIALOGUE MAGAZINE.

Little. Little is the name of the slave master who owned one of my grandparents during slavery, a white man, and the name Little was handed down to my grandfather, to my father and on to me. But after hearing the teachings of the Honorable Elijah Muhammad and realizing that Little is an English name, and I'm not an Englishman, I gave the Englishman back his name; and since my own had been stripped from me, hidden from me, and I don't know it, I use X; and someday, as we are taught by the Honorable Elijah Muhammad, every black man, woman and child in America will get back the same name, the same language, and the same culture that he had before he was kidnaped and brought to this country and stripped of these things.

I would like to point out in a recent column by James Reston on the editorial page of the New York *Times,* December 15, 1961, writing from London, Mr. Reston, after interviewing several leading European statesmen, pointed out that the people of Europe, or the statesmen in Europe, don't feel that America or Europe have anything to worry about in Russia; that the people in Europe foresee the time when Russia, Europe, and America will have to unite together to ward off the threat of China and the non-white world. And if this same statement was made by a Muslim, or by the honorable Elijah Muhammad, it would be classified as racist; but Reston who is one of the leading correspondents in this country and writing for one of the most respected newspapers, points out that the holocaust that the West is facing is not something from Russia, but threats of the combined forces of the dark world against the white world.

Why do I mention this? Primarily because the most crucial problem facing the white world today is the race problem. And the most crucial problem facing white America today is the race problem. Mr. Farmer pointed out beautifully and quoted one writer actually as saying that the holocaust that America is facing is primarily still based upon race. This doesn't mean that when people point these things out that they are racist; this means that they are facing the facts of life that we are confronted with today. And one need only to look at the world troubles in its international context, national context, or local context, and one will always see the race problem right there, a problem that it is almost impossible to duck around.

It so happens that you and I were born at a time of great change, when changes are taking place. And if we can't react intelligently to these changes, then we are going to be destroyed. When you look into the United Nations set-up, the way it is, we see that there is a change of power taking place, a change of position, a change of influence, a change of control. Wherein, in the past, white people used to exercise unlimited control and authority over dark mankind, today they are losing their ability to dictate unilateral terms to dark mankind. Whereas, yesterday dark nations had no voice in their own affairs, today the voice that they exercise in their own affairs is increasing, which means in essence that the voice of the white man or the white world is becoming more quiet every day, and the voice of the non-white world is becoming more loud every day. These are the facts of life and these are the changes that you and I, this generation, have to face up to on an international level, a national level, or a local level before we can get a solution to the problems that confront not only the white man, but problems that confront also the black man, or the non-white man.

When we look at the United Nations and see how these dark nations get their independence—they can out-vote the western block or what is known as the white world—and to the point where up until last year the U.N. was controlled by the white powers, or Western powers, mainly Christian powers, and the secretaryship used to be in the hands of a white European Christian; but now when we look at the general structure of the United Nations we see a man from Asia, from Burma, who is occupying the position of Secretary, who is a Buddhist, by the way, and we find the man who is occupying the seat of President is a Moslem from Africa, namely Tunisia. Just in recent times all of these changes are taking place, and the white man has got to be able to face up to them, and the black man has to be able to face up to them, before we can get our problem solved, on an international level, a national level, as well as on the local level.

In terms of black and white, what this means is that the unlimited power and prestige of the white world is decreasing, while the power and prestige of the non-white world is increasing. And just as our African and Asian brothers wanted to have their own land, wanted to have their own country, wanted to exercise control over themselves and govern themselves—they didn't want to be governed by whites or Europeans or outsiders, they wanted control over something among the black masses here in America. I think it would be mighty naive on the part of the white man to see dark mankind all over the world stretching out to get a country of his own, a land of his own, an industry of his own, a society of his own, even a flag of his own, it would be mighty naive on the part of the white man to think that same feeling that is sweeping through the dark world is not going to leap 9000 miles across the ocean and come into the black people here in this country, who have been begging you for 400 years for something that they have yet to get.

In the areas of Asia and Africa where the whites gave freedom to the non-whites a transition took place, of friendliness and hospitality. In the areas where the non-whites had to exercise violence, today there is hostility between them and the white man. In this, we learn that the only way to solve a problem that is unjust, if you are wrong, is to take immediate action to correct it. But when the people against whom these actions have been directed have to take matters in their own hands, this creates hostility, and lack of friendliness and good relations between the two.

I emphasize these things to point up the fact that we are living in an era of great change; when dark mankind wants freedom, justice, and equality. It is not a case of wanting integration or separation, it is a case of wanting freedom, justice, and equality.

Now if certain groups think that through integration they are going to get freedom, justice, equality and human dignity, then well and good, we will go along with the integrationists. But if integration is not going to return human dignity to dark mankind, then integration is not the solution to the problem. And oft times we make the mistake of confusing the objective with the means by which the objective is to be obtained. It is not integration that Negroes in America want, it is human dignity. They want to be recognized as human beings. And if integration is going to bring us recognition as human beings, then we will integrate. But if integration is not going to bring us recognition as human beings, then integration "out the window," and we have to find another means or method and try that to get our objectives reached.

The same hand that has been writing on the wall in Africa and Asia is also writing on the wall right here in America. The same rebellion, the same impatience, the same anger that exists in the hearts of the dark people in Africa and Asia is existing in the hearts and minds of 20 million black people in this country who have been just as thoroughly colonized as the people in Africa and Asia. Only the black man in America has been colonized mentally, his mind has been destroyed. And today, even though he goes to college, he comes out and still doesn't even know he is a black man; he is ashamed of what he is, because his culture has been destroyed, his identity has been destroyed; he has been made to hate his black skin, he has been made to hate the texture of his hair, he has been made to hate the features that God gave him. Because the honorable Elijah Muhammad is coming along today and teaching us the truth about black people to make us love ourselves instead of realizing that it is you who taught us to hate ourselves and our own kind, you accuse the honorable Elijah Muhammad of being a hate teacher and accuse him of being a racist. He is only trying to undo the white supremacy that you have indoctrinated the entire world with.

I might point out that it makes America look ridiculous to stand up in world conferences and refer to herself as the leader of the free world. Here is a country, Uncle Sam, standing up and pointing a finger at the Portuguese, and at the French, and at other colonizers, and there are 20 million black people in this country who are still confined to second-class citizenship, 20 million black people in this country who are still segregated and Jim-Crowed, as my friend, Dr. Farmer has already pointed out. And despite the fact that 20 million black people here yet don't have freedom, justice and equality, Adlai Stevenson has the nerve enough to stand up in the United Nations and point the finger at South Africa, and at Portugal and at some of these other countries. All we say is that South Africa preaches what it practices and practices what it preaches; America preaches one thing and practices another. And we don't want to integrate with hypocrites who preach one thing and practice another.

The good point in all of this is that there is an awakening going on among whites in America today, and this awakening is manifested in this way: two years ago you didn't know that there were black people in this country who didn't want to integrate with you; two years ago the white public had been brainwashed into thinking that every black man in this country wanted to force his way into your community, force his way into your schools, or force his way into your factories; two years ago you thought that all you would have to do is give us a little token integration and the race problem would be solved. Why? Because the people in the black community who didn't want integration were never given a voice, were never given a platform, were never given an opportunity to shout out the fact that integration would never solve the problem. And it has only been during the past year that the white public has begun to realize that the problem will never be solved unless a solution is devised acceptable to the black masses, as well as the black bourgeoisie—the upper class or middle class Negro. And when the whites began to realize that these integration-minded Negroes were in the minority, rather than in the majority, they began to offer an open forum and give those who want separation an opportunity to speak their mind to.

We who are black in the black belt, or black community, or black neighborhood can easily see that our people who settle for integration are usually the middle-class so-called Negroes, who are in the minority. Why? Because they have confidence in the white man; they have absolute confidence that you will change. They believe that they can change you, they believe that there is still hope in the American dream. But what to them is an American dream to us is an American nightmare, and we don't think that it is possible for the American white man in sincerity to take the action necessary to correct the unjust conditions that 20 million black people here are made to suffer morning, noon, and night. And because we don't have any hope or confidence or faith in the American white man's ability to bring about a change in the injustices that exist, instead of asking or seeking to integrate into the American society we want to face the facts of the problem the way they are, and separate ourselves. And in separating ourselves this doesn't mean that we are anti-white or anti-America, or anti-anything. We feel, that if integration all these years hasn't solved the problem yet, then we want to try something new, something different and something that is in accord with the conditions as they actually exist.

The honorable Elijah Muhammad teaches us that there are over 725 million Moslems or Muslims on this earth. I use both words interchangeably. I use the word Moslem for those who can't undergo the change, and I use the word Muslim for those who can. He teaches us that the world of Islam stretches from the China Seas to the shores of West Africa and that the 20 million black people in this country are the lost-found members of the nation of Islam. He teaches us that before we were kidnaped by your grandfathers and brought to this country and put in chains, our religion was Islam, our culture was Islamic, we came from the Muslim world, we were kidnaped and brought here out of the Muslim world. And after being brought here we were stripped of our language, stripped of our ability to speak our mother tongue, and it's a crime today to have to admit that there are 20 million black people in this country who not only can't speak their mother tongue, but don't even know they ever had one. This points up the crime of how thoroughly and completely the black man in America has been robbed by the white man of his culture, of his identity, of his soul, of his self. And because he has been robbed of his self, he is trying to accept your self. Because he doesn't know who he is, now he wants to be who you are. Because he doesn't know what belongs to him, he is trying to lay claim to what belongs to you. You have brain-washed him and made him a monster. He is black on the outside, but you have made him white on the inside. Now he has a white heart and a white brain, and he's breathing down your throat and down your neck because he thinks he's a white man the same as you are. He thinks that he should have your house, that he should have your factory, he thinks that he should even have your school, and most of them even think that they should have your woman, and most of them are after your woman.

The honorable Elijah Muhammad teaches us that the black people in America, the so-called Negroes, are the people who are referred to in the Bible as the lost sheep, who are to be returned to their own in the last days. He says that we are also referred to in the Bible, symbolically, as the lost tribe. He teaches us in our religion, that we are those people whom the Bible refers to who would be lost until the end of time. Lost in a house that is not theirs, lost in a land that is not theirs; lost in a country that is not theirs, and who will be found in the last days by the Messiah who will awaken them and enlighten them, and teach them that which they had been stripped of, and then this would give them the desire to come together among their own kind and go back among their own kind.

And this, basically, is why we who are followers of the honorable Elijah Muhammad don't accept integration: we feel that we are living at the end of time, by this, we feel that we are living at the end of the world. Not the end of the earth, but the end of the world. He teaches us that there are many worlds. The planet is an earth, and there is only one earth, but there are many worlds on this earth, the Eastern World and the Western World. There is a dark world and a white world. There is the world of Christianity, and the world of Islam. All of these are worlds and he teaches us that when the book speaks of the end of time, it doesn't mean the end of the earth, but it means the end of time for certain segments of people, or a certain world that is on this earth. Today, we who are here in America who have awakened to the knowledge of ourselves; we believe that there is no God but Allah, and we believe that the religion of Islam is Allah's religion, and we believe that it is Allah's intention to spread his religion throughout the entire earth. We believe that the earth will become all Muslim, all Islam, and because we are in a Christian country we believe that this Christian country will have to accept Allah as God, accept the religion of Islam as God's religion, or otherwise God will come in and wipe it out. And we don't want to be wiped out with the American white man, we don't want to integrate with him, we want to separate from him.

The method by which the honorable Elijah Muhammad is straightening out our problem is not teaching us to force ourselves into your society, or force ourselves even into your political, economic or any phase of your society, but he teaches us that the best way to solve this problem is for complete separation. He says that since the black man here in America is actually the property that was stolen from the East by the American white man, since you have awakened today and realized that this is what we are, we should be separated from you, and your government should ship us back from where we came from, not at our expense, because we didn't pay to come here. We were brought here in chains. So the honorable Elijah Muhammad and the Muslims who follow him, we want to go back to our own people. We want to be returned to our own people.

But in teaching this among our people and the masses of black people in this country, we discover that the American government is the foremost agency in opposing any move by any large number of black people to leave here and go back among our own kind. The honorable Elijah Muhammad's words and work is harassed daily by the F.B.I. and every other government agency which use various tactics to make the so-called Negroes in every community think that we are all about to be rounded up, and they will be rounded up too if they will listen to Mr. Muhammad; but what the American government has failed to realize, the best way to open up a black man's head today and make him listen to another black man is to speak against that black man. But when you begin to pat a black man on the back, no black man in his right mind will trust that black man any longer. And it is because of this hostility on the part of the government toward our leaving here that the honorable Elijah Muhammad says then, if the American white man or the American government doesn't want us to leave, and the government has proven its inability to bring about integration or give us freedom, justice and equality on a basis, equally mixed up with white people, then what are we going to do? If the government doesn't want us to go back among our own people, or to our own people, and at the same time the government has proven its inability to give us justice, the honorable Elijah Muhammad says if you don't want us to go and we can't stay here and live in peace together, then the best solution is separation. And this is what he means when he says that some of the territory here should be set aside, and let our people go off to ourselves and try and solve our own problem.

Some of you may say, Well, why should you give us part of this country? The honorable Elijah Muhammad says that for 400 years we contributed our slave labor to make the country what it is. If you were to take the individual salary or allowances of each person in this audience it would amount to nothing individually, but when you take it collectively all in one pot you have a heavy load. Just the weekly wage. And if you realize that from anybody who could collect all of the wages from the persons in this audience right here for one month, why they would be so wealthy they couldn't walk. And if you see that, then you can imagine the result of millions of black people working for nothing for 310 years. And that is the contribution that we made to America. Not Jackie Robinson, not Marian Anderson, not George Washington Carver, that's not our contribution; our contribution to American society is 310 years of free slave labor for which we have not been paid one dime. We who are Muslims, followers of the honorable Elijah Muhammad, don't think that an integrated cup of coffee is sufficient payment for 310 years of slave labor.

James Farmer

When the Freedom Riders left from Montgomery, Alabama, to ride into the conscience of America and into Jackson, Mississippi, there were many persons who said to us, "Don't go into

Mississippi, go anyplace you like, go to the Union of South Africa, but stay out of Mississippi." They said, "What you found in Alabama will be nothing compared to what you will meet in Mississippi." I remember being told a story by one minister who urged us not to go. He said, "Once upon a time there was a Negro who had lived in Mississippi, lived for a long time running from county to county. Finally he left the state, and left it pretty fast, as Dick Gregory would put it, not by Greyhound, but by bloodhound, and he went to Illinois to live, in Chicago. And unable to find a job there, after several weeks of walking the street unemployed, he sat down and asked God what he should do. God said, "Go back to Mississippi." He said, "Lord you surely don't mean it, you're jesting. You don't mean for me to go back to Mississippi. There is segregation there!" The Lord said, "Go back to Mississippi." The man looked up and said, "Very well, Lord, if you insist, I will do it, I will go. But will you go with me?" The Lord said "As far as Cincinnati."

The Freedom Riders felt that they should go all the way because there is something wrong with our nation and we wanted to try to set it right. As one of the nation's scholars[1] wrote at the turn of the century, "The problem of the twentieth century will be the problem of the color-line, of the relations between the lighter and the darker peoples of the earth, Asia and Africa, in America, and in the islands of the sea." What prophetic words, indeed. We have seen the struggle for freedom all over the world. We have seen it in Asia; we have seen it in the island of the sea; we have seen it in Africa, and we are seeing it in America now. I think the racist theories of Count DeGobineau, Lothrop Stoddard and the others have set the pattern for a racism that exists within our country. There are theories that are held today, not only by those men and their followers and successors, but by Ross Barnett, John Patterson devotees and followers of the Klan and the White Citizens Councils, and Lincoln Rockwell of the American Nazi Party.

These vicious racist theories hold that Negroes are inferior and

[1] W. E. B. Du Bois [Ed.].

whites are superior innately. Ordained by God, so to speak. No more vicious theory has existed in the history of mankind. I would suggest to you that no theory has provided as much human misery throughout the centuries as the theory of races— The theories that say some people are innately inferior and that others are innately superior. Although we have some of those theories in our country, we also have a creed of freedom and of democracy. As Pearl Buck put it, "Many Americans suffer from a split personality. One side of that personality is believing in democracy and freedom, as much as it is possible for a man so to believe. The other side of this personality is refusing just as doggedly, to practice that democracy and that freedom, in which he believes." That was the split personality. Gunnar Myrdal, in his book, *The American Dilemma,* indicated that this was basically a moral problem, and that we have this credo which Americans hold to, of freedom, and democracy, and equality, but still we refuse to practice it. Gunnar Myrdal indicated that this is sorely troubling the American conscience.

All of us are a part of this system, *all* a part of it. We have all developed certain prejudices, I have mine, you have yours. It seems to me that it is extremely dangerous when any individual claims to be without prejudice, when he really does have it. I'm prejudiced against women drivers. I think they are a menace to civilization, and the sooner they are removed from the highways, the safer we will all be, but I know that's nothing but a prejudice. I have seen women drivers who are better drivers than I am, but does that destroy my prejudice? No. What I do then, is to separate her from the group of women drivers and say, "Why she is an exception." Or maybe I say she is driving very well because she feels guilty. She knows that other women in the past have had accidents, and so she drives cautiously.

I remember several years ago when I was a youth, attending a church youth conference, and a young fellow from Mississippi and I became very good friends. The last day of the conference as we walked along the road he put his arm on my shoulder and said, "Jim, I have no race prejudice." "No," said I. "Absolutely not," said he. I raised my eyebrows. "As a matter of fact," he went on, "I was thirteen years old before I knew I was any better than a Negro." Well sometimes a supposed absence of racial prejudice runs quite along those lines. Now prejudice is a damaging thing to Negroes. We have suffered under it tremendously. It damages the lives of little children. I remember when I first came into contact with segregation; it was when I was a child in Mississippi when my mother took me downtown, and on the way back this hot July day I wanted to stop and get a coke, and she told me I couldn't get a coke, I had to wait until I got home. "Well why can't I, there's a little boy going in," said I, "I bet he's going to get a coke." He was. "Well, why can't I go?" "Because he's white," she said, "and you're colored." It's not important what happened to me, the fact is that the same thing over and over again happens to every mother's child whose skin happens to be dark.

If the damage that is done to Negroes is obvious, the damage that is done to whites in America is equally obvious, for they're prejudiced. I lived in Texas a large part of my life; remember driving through the state, and after dusk had fallen being followed by cars of whites who forced me off the road and said to me, "Don't you know that your kind is not supposed to be in this town after sundown." I wondered what was happening to these people; how their minds were being twisted, as mine and others like me had had our minds twisted by this double-edged sword of prejudice. It is a disease indeed. It is an American disease. It is an American dilemma.

The damage to Negroes is psychological, it is also economic. Negroes occupying the bottom of the economic ladder, the poorest jobs, the lowest paying jobs. Last to be hired, and first to be fired, so that today the percentage of unemployed Negroes is twice as high as that of whites. There has been political damage as well. In the south we find that comparatively few Negroes are registered to vote. Many are apathetic even when they could register. The percentage who are registered in the north is almost equally as low. As a result, comparatively few Negroes are elected to political office. Thus, the damage to the Negroes, as a result of the disease of segregation has been psychological, economic, social, and political. I would suggest to you that the same damages have occurred to whites. Psychological damages are obvious. Economic—the nation itself suffers economically, as a result of denying the right of full development to one-tenth of its population. Skills, talents, and abilities, are crushed in their cradle, are not allowed to develop. Snuffed out. Thus, the nation's economy has suffered. People who could be producing are instead walking the streets. People who could be producing in better jobs and producing more are kept in the lower jobs, sweeping the floors and serving other persons. The whole nation has been damaged by segregation. Now, all of us share the guilt too. I myself am guilty. I am guilty because I spent half of my life in the South. During those years I participated in segregation, cooperated with it, and supported it.

We are all intricately involved in the system of segregation. We have not yet extricated ourselves. Negroes are involved, and guilty, and share the blame to the extent they themselves have, by their deeds and their acts, allowed segregation to go on for so long. I do not believe that guilt is a part of my genes or your genes. It hinges upon the deeds that you have done. If you have supported segregation, then you are guilty. If you continue to support it, then your guilt is multiplied. But that is your guilt, that is mine. We share the guilt for the disease of segregation, and its continued existence. All too long, Negro Americans have put up with the system of segregation, North and South. Incidentally, it is not a Southern problem, it is a Northern one as well. Segregation exists in housing and in jobs, and in schools. We have put up with it, have done nothing about it.

The day before the Freedom Riders left Washington, D. C. to ride into the South, I visited my father who was in the hospital on what proved to be his deathbed. I told him I was going on a freedom ride into the South. He wanted to know what it was and I told him. "Where are you going?" he asked, and I told him. He said, "Well, I'm glad that you're going, son, and I hope you survive. I realize you may not return, but," said he, "I'm glad you're going because when I was a child in South Carolina and

Georgia, we didn't like segregation either, but we thought that's the way things always had to be and the way they always would be, so we put up with it, took part in it, decided to exist and to stay alive. I am glad," said he, "that there are lots of people today who are no longer willing to put up with the evil of segregation, but want to do something about it and know that something can be done." How right he was indeed.

The masses of Negroes are through putting up with segregation; they are tired of it. They are tired of being pushed around in a democracy which fails to practice what it preaches. The Negro students of the South who have read the Constitution, and studied it, have read the amendments to the Constitution, and know the rights that are supposed to be theirs—they are coming to the point where they themselves want to do something about achieving these rights, not depend on somebody else. The time has passed when we can look for pie in the sky, when we can depend upon someone else on high to solve the problem for us. The Negro students want to solve the problem themselves. Masses of older Negroes want to join them in that. We can't wait for the law. The Supreme Court decision in 1954 banning segregated schools has had almost eight years of existence, yet, less than eight percent of the Negro kids are in integrated schools. That is far too slow. Now the people themselves want to get involved, and they are. I was talking with one of the student leaders of the South only last week; he said, "I myself desegregated a lunch counter, not somebody else, not some big man, some powerful man, but me, little me. I walked the picket line and I sat in and the walls of segregation toppled. Now all people can eat there." One young prize fighter was a cell-mate of mine in the prisons of Mississippi as a freedom rider; he had won his last fight and had a promising career. I saw him three weeks ago, and asked him, "How are you coming along?" He said, "Not very well, I lost the last fight and I am through with the prize ring, I have no more interest in it. The only fight I want now," said he, "is the freedom fight. Because I, a little man, can become involved in it, and can help to win freedom." So that's what's happening; you see, we are going to do something about freedom now, we are not waiting for other people to do it. The student sit-ins have shown it; we are winning. As a result of one year of the student sit-ins, the lunch counters were desegregated in more than 150 cities. The walls are tumbling down.

Who will say that lunch counters, which are scattered all over the country are not important? Are we not to travel? Picket lines and boycotts brought Woolworth's to its knees. In its annual report of last year, Woolworth's indicated that profits had dropped and one reason for the drop was the nationwide boycott in which many Northern students, including Cornellians participated. The picketing and the nationwide demonstrations are the reason that the walls came down in the south, because people were in motion with their own bodies marching with picket signs, sitting in, boycotting, withholding their patronage. In Savannah, Georgia, there was a boycott, in which ninety-nine percent of the Negroes participated. They stayed out of the stores. They registered to vote. The store owners then got together and said, "We want to sit down and talk; gentlemen, you have proved your point. You have proved that you can control Negroes' purchasing power and that you can control their votes. We need no more proof, we are ready to hire the people that you send." Negroes are hired in those stores now as a result of this community-wide campaign. In Lexington, Kentucky, the theatres were opened up by CORE as a result of picketing and boycotting. Some of the theatres refused to admit Negroes, others would let Negroes sit up in the balcony. They boycotted that one, picketed the others. In a short period of time, the theatre owners sat down to negotiate. All of the theatres there are open now. Using the same technique, they provided scores of jobs in department stores, grocery stores, and more recently as city bus drivers.

Then came the freedom rides. 325 people were jailed in Jackson, Mississippi, others beaten, fighting for freedom non-violently. They brought down many many barriers. They helped to create desegregation in cities throughout the South. The ICC order was forthcoming as a result of the freedom rides and a more recent Supreme Court ruling. CORE sent test teams throughout the South after the ICC order went into effect. The test teams found that in hundreds of cities throughout the South, where terminals had been previously segregated, they now were desegregated and Negroes were using them. Mississippi is an exception, except for two cities; Louisania is an exception, except for one pocket of the state; but by and large the Rides were successful. And then on Route 40. How many Negroes and interracial groups have driven route 40 to Washington or to New York and carried their sandwiches, knowing that they could not eat between Wilmington and Baltimore. The freedom rides there, and some Cornell students participated in those freedom rides, brought down the barriers in more than half of those restaurants and each weekend, rides are taking place aimed at the others. By Easter we will have our Easter dinner in any place we choose on Route 40. At least 53 out of the 80 are now desegregated. In voter registration projects, we have registered 17,000 Negroes in South Carolina, previously unregistered. The politicians, segregationists, it's true, now call up our leaders and say, "I would like to talk to you because I don't believe in segregation as much as my opponent," or, "We would like to sit down and talk," or, "Can you come by my house and let's talk about this thing." Because they are realizing that now they have to be responsible to the votes of Negroes as well as the handful of whites, these are the things that are being done by people themselves in motion. Not waiting for someone else to do it, not looking forward to pie in the sky at some later date, not expecting a power on high to solve the problem for them; but working to solve it themselves and winning.

What are our objectives; segregation, separation? Absolutely not! The disease and the evils that we have pointed to in our American culture have grown out of segregation and its partner, prejudice. We are for integration, which is the repudiation of the evil of segregation. It is a rejection of the racist theories of De-Gobineau, Lothrop Stoddard and all the others. It matters not whether they say that whites are superior to Negroes and Negroes are inferior, or if they reverse the coin and say that Negroes are superior and whites are inferior. The theory is just as wrong, just as much a defiance of history. We reject those theories. We are working for the right of Negroes to enter all fields of activity in American life. To enter business if they choose, to enter the professions, to enter the sciences, to enter the arts, to enter the academic world. To be workers, to be laborers if they choose. Our objective is to have each individual accepted on the basis of his individual merit and not on the basis of his color. On the basis of what he is worth himself.

This has given a new pride to a large number of people. A pride to the people in Mississippi, who themselves saw others, white and Negro, joining them in the fight for freedom; 41 local citizens went into the jails of Mississippi joining the freedom riders. They have come out now and they have started their own nonviolent Jackson movement for Freedom. They are sitting in. They are picketing, they are boycotting, and it is working. In Macomb, Mississippi, local citizens are now seeking to register to vote, some of them registering. In Huntsville, Alabama, as a result of CORE's campaign there (and we are now under injunction), for the past six weeks local Negro citizens have been sitting in every day at lunch counters. One of the white CORE leaders there in Huntsville was taken out of his house at gun point, undressed and sprayed with mustard oil. That's the kind of treatment they have faced, but they will not give up because they know they are right and they see the effects of their efforts; they see it in the crumbling walls in inter-state transportation and in other public facilities.

We are seeking an open society, an open society of freedom where people will be accepted for what they are worth, will be able to contribute fully to the total culture and the total life of the nation.

Now we know the disease, we know what is wrong with America, we know now that the CORE position is in trying to right it. We must do it in interracial groups because we do not think it is possible to fight against caste in a vehicle which in itself is a representative of caste. We know that the students are still sitting in, they are still fighting for freedom. What we want Mr. X, the representative of the Black Muslims and Elijah Muhammad, to tell us today, is what his program is, what he proposes to do about killing this disease. We know the disease, physician, what is your cure? What is your program and how do you hope to bring it into effect? How will you achieve it? It is not enough to tell us that it may be a program of a black state. The Communists had such a program in the thirties and part of the forties, and they dropped it before the fifties as being impractical. So we are not only interested in the terminology. We need to have it spelled out, if we are being asked to follow it, to believe in it, what does it mean? Is it a separate Negro society in each city? As a Harlem, a South Side Chicago? Is it a separate state in one part of the country? Is it a separate nation in Africa, or elsewhere? Then we need to know how is it to be achieved. I assume that before a large part of land could be granted to Negroes or to Jews or to anybody else in the country it would have to be approved by the Senate of the United States.

You must tell us, Mr. X, if you seriously think that the Senate of the United States which has refused or failed for all these years to pass a strong Civil Rights Bill, you must tell us if you really think that this Senate is going to give us, to give you, a black state. I am sure that Senator Eastland would so vote, but the land that he would give us would probably be in the bottom of the sea. After seeing Alabama and Mississippi, if the power were mine, I would give you those states, but the power is not mine, I do not vote in the Senate. Tell us how you expect to achieve this separate black state.

Now it is not enough for us to know that you believe in black businesses, all of us believe that all Americans who wish to go into business, should go into business. We must know, we need to know, if we are to appraise your program, the kind of businesses, how they are to be established; will we have a General Motors, a General Electric? Will I be able to manufacture a Farmer Special? Where I am going to get the capital from? You must tell us if we are going to have a separate interstate bus line to take the place of Greyhound and Trailways. You must tell us how this separate interstate bus line is going to operate throughout the country if all of us are confined within one separate state.

You must tell us these things, Mr. X, spell them out. You must tell us also what the relationship will be between the black businesses which you would develop and the total American economy. Will it be a competition? Will it be a rival economy, a dual economy or will there be cooperation between these two economies?

Our program is clear. We are going to achieve our goals of integration by non-violent direct action on an interracial level with whites and Negroes jointly cooperating to wipe out a disease which has afflicted and crippled all of them, white and black alike. The proof of the pudding is the eating. We have seen barriers fall as the result of using these techniques. We ask you, Mr. X, what is your program?

Rebuttal

James Farmer

I think that Mr. X's views are utterly impractical and that his so-called "black state" cannot be achieved. There is no chance of getting it unless it is to be given to us by Allah. We have waited for a long time for God to give us other things and we have found that the God in which most of us happen to believe helps those who help themselves. So we would like you to tell us, Mr. X, just what steps you plan to go through to get this black state. Is it one that is going to be gotten by violence, by force? Is it going to be given to us by the Federal government? Once a state is allocated, then are the white people who happen to live there to be moved out forcibly, or Negroes who don't want to go to your black state going to be moved in forcibly? And what does this do to their liberty and freedom?

Now Mr. X suggests that we Negroes or so-called Negroes, as he puts it, ought to go back where we came from. You know, this is a very interesting idea. I think the solution to many of the problems, including the economic problem of our country, would be for all of us to go back where we came from and leave the country to the American Indians. As a matter of fact, maybe the American Indian can go back to Asia, where I understand the anthropologists tell us he came from, and I don't know who preceded him there. But if we search back far enough I am sure that we can find some people to people or populate this nation. Now the overwhelming number of Negroes in this country consider it to be their country; their country more than Africa: I was in Africa three years ago, and while I admire and respect what is being done there, while there is certainly a definite sense of identification, and sympathy with what is going on there, the fact is that the cultures are so very different. Mr. X, I am sure that you have much more in common with me or with several people whom I see sitting here than you do with the Africans, than you do with Tom Mboya. Most of them could not understand you, or you they, because they speak Swahili or some other language and you would have to learn those languages.

I tell you that we are Americans. This is our country as much as it is white American. Negroes came as slaves, most of us did. Many white people came as indentured servants; indentured servants are not free. Don't forget it wasn't all of you who were on that ship, The Mayflower.

Now separation of course has been proposed as the answer to the problem, rather than integration. I am pleased however that Malcolm, oh pardon me, Mr. X, indicated that if integration works, and if it provides dignity, then we are for integration. Apparently he is almost agreeing with us there. He is sort of saying as King Agrippa said to St. Paul, "Almost Thou Persuadest Me." I hope that he will be able to come forth and make the additional step and join me at the integrationist side of this table. In saying that separation really is the answer and the most effective solution to this problem, he draws a distinction between separation and segregation, saying that segregation is forced ghettoism while separation is voluntary ghettoism. Well now, I would like to ask Mr. X whether it would be voluntary for Negroes to be segregated as long as we allow discrimination in housing throughout our country to exist. If you live in a black state and cannot get a house elsewhere, then are you voluntarily separated, or are you forcibly segregated?

Now Mr. X suggests that actually the Negroes in this country want the white man's women. Now this is a view, of course, which is quite familiar to you; I've heard it before, there are some Negroes who are married to white people, and I, just before I came up, was looking over a back issue of the paper of the Muslims, and saw in there an indication that I myself have a white wife. And it was suggested that therefore I have betrayed my people in marrying a white woman. Well you know I happen to have a great deal of faith in the virtues and the abilities and capacities of Negroes. Not only Negroes, but all of the people too. In fact, I have so much faith in the virtues of Negroes that I do not even think those virtues are so frail that they will be corrupted by contact with other people.

Mr. X also indicated that Negroes imitate whites. It is true, we do, he is right. We fix our hair and try to straighten it; I don't do mine, I haven't had a conk in my life, I think they call it a process now, etc. But this is a part of the culture of course. After the black culture was taken away from us, we had to adapt the culture that was here, adopt it, and adapt to it. But it is also true that white people try to imitate Negroes, with their jazz, with their hair curlers, you know, and their man-tans. I think, Mr. X, that perhaps the grass is always greener on the other side of the fence. Now when we create integration, perhaps it won't be so necessary for us to resort to these devices.

The black bourgeoisie—is it only the middle class that wants integration. Were the sit-in students black bourgeoisie? They didn't fit into the definition in E. Franklin Frazier's book on the black bourgeoisie. Quite to the contrary, these students were lower class people. Many of them were workers working to stay in school. In the Freedom Rides, were they black bourgeoisie? No, we didn't have exceptions there, we had some people who were unemployed. These are not the black bourgeoisie who want integration. Quite to the contrary, very frequently, the middle class developed a vested interest in the maintenance of segregation. Because if they have a store, and if segregation is eliminated, then I'll be in open competition with the white stores. And thus it is most often true as Frazier pointed out in his book, that the middle class tends to be opposed to desegregation. Now I would wonder also in the building of black businesses if we are not going to be building another black bourgeoisie? If Negroes may not perhaps be giving up one master for another, a white one for a black one? Are we going to build a new Negro middle class, and say that no matter how tyrannical it may prove to be it is my own and therefore, I like it?

Now we of course know that the Negro is sick, the white man is sick, we know that psychologically we have been twisted by all of these things; but still, Mr. X, you have not told us what the solution is except that it is separation, in your view. You have not spelled it out. Well, now, this sickness, as I tried to indicate in my first presentation, springs from segregation. It is segregation that produces prejudice, as much as prejudice produces segregation. In Detroit, at the time of the race riot, the only rioting, the only fighting, was in the all-Negro and all-white sections of the city, where separation was complete. In those several sections of the city where Negroes and whites lived together, next door to each other, there was no fighting because there the people were neighbors or friends. Now you propose separation as the solution to this problem, as the cure to the disease. Here we have a patient that is suffering from a disease caused by mosquitoes, and the physician proposes as a cure that the man go down and lie in a damp swamp and play with wiggletails.

Malcolm X

I hadn't thought, or intended anyway, to get personal with Mr. Farmer in mentioning his white wife; I thought that perhaps it would probably have been better left unsaid, but it's better for him to say than for me to say it, because then you would think I was picking on him. I think you will find if you were to have gone into Harlem a few years back you would have found on the juke boxes, records by Belafonte, Eartha Kitt, Pearl Bailey, all of these persons were very popular singers in the so-called Negro community a few years back. But since Belafonte divorced Marguerite and married a white woman it doesn't mean that Harlem is anti-white, but you can't find Belafonte's records there; or maybe he just hasn't produced a hit. All of these entertainers who have become involved in intermarriage, and I mean Lena Horne, Eartha Kitt, Sammy Davis,

Belafonte, they have a large white following, but you can't go into any Negro community across the nation and find records by these artists that are hits in the so-called Negro community. Because, sub-consciously, today the so-called Negro withdraws himself from the entertainers who have crossed the line. And if the masses of black people won't let a Negro who is involved in an inter-marriage play music for him, he can't speak for him.

The only way you can solve the race problem as it exists, is to take into consideration the feelings of the masses, not the minority; the majority not the minority. And it is proof that the masses of white people don't want Negroes forcing their way into their neighborhood and the masses of black people don't think it's any solution for us to force ourselves into the white neighborhood, so the only ones who want integration are the Negro minority, as I say, the bourgeoisie and the white minority, the so-called white liberals. And that same white liberal who professes to want integration whenever the Negro moves to his neighborhood, he is the first one to move out. And I was talking with one today who said he was a liberal and I asked him where did he live, and he lived in an all-white neighborhood and probably might for the rest of his life. This is conjecture, but I think it stands true. The Civil War was fought 100 years ago, supposedly to solve this problem. After the Civil War was fought, the problem still existed. Along behind that, the thirteenth and fourteenth Amendments were brought about in the Constitution supposedly to solve the problem; after the Amendments, the problem was still right here with us.

Most Negroes think that the Civil War was fought to make them citizens; they think that it was fought to free them from slavery because the real purpose of the Civil War are clothed in hypocrisy. The real purpose of the Amendments are clothed in hypocrisy. The real purpose behind the Supreme Court Desegregation decision was clothed in hypocrisy. And any time integrationists, NAACP, CORE, Urban League, or what you have, will stand up and tell me to spell out how we are going to bring about separation, and here they are integrationists, a philosophy which is supposed to have the support of the Senate, Congress, President, and the Supreme Court, and still with all of that support and hypocritical agreeing, eight years after the desegregation decision, you still don't have what the court decided on.

So we think this, that when whites talk integration they are being hypocrites, and we think that the Negroes who accept token integration are also being hypocrites, because they are the only ones who benefit from it, the handful of hand-picked high-class, middle-class Uncle Tom Negroes. They are hand-picked by whites and turned loose in a white community and they're satisfied. But if all of the black people went into the white community, over night you would have a race war. If four or five little black students going to school in New Orleans bring about the riots that we saw down there, what do you think would happen if all the black people tried to go to any school that they want, you would have a race war. So our approach to it, those of us who follow the honorable Elijah Muhammad, we feel that it is more sensible than running around here waiting for the whites to allow us inside their attic or inside their basement.

Every Negro group that we find in the Negro community that is integrated is controlled by the whites who belong to it, or it is led by the whites who belong to it. NAACP has had a white president for 53 years, it has been in existence for 53 years; Roy Wilkins is the Executive Secretary, but Spingarn, a white man has been the president for the past 23 years, and before him, his brother, another white man was president. They have never had a black president. Urban League, another so-called Negro organization, doesn't have a black president, it has a white president. Now this doesn't mean that that's racism, it only means that the same organizations that are accusing you of practicing discrimination, when it comes to the leadership they're practicing discrimination themselves.

The honorable Elijah Muhammad says, and points out to us that in this book ("Anti-Slavery") written by a professor from the University of Michigan, Dwight Lowell Dumond,* a person who is an authority on the race question or slave question,

---

* Dwight L. Dumond, *Anti-Slavery: The Crusade for Freedom in America* (Ann Arbor: University of Michigan Press, 1961) [Ed.].

his findings were used by Thurgood Marshall in winning the Supreme Court Desegregation decision. And in the preface of this book, it says that second-class citizenship is only a modified form of slavery. Now I'll tell you why I'm dwelling on this; everything that you have devised yourself to solve the race problem has been hypocrisy, because the scientists who delved into it teach us or tell us that second-class citizenship is only a modified form of slavery, which means the Civil War didn't end slavery and the Amendments didn't end slavery. They didn't do it because we still have to wrestle the Supreme Court and the Congress and the Senate to correct the hypocrisy that's been practiced against us by whites for the past umteen years.

And because this was done, the American white man today subconsciously still regards that black man as something below himself. And you will never get the American white man to accept the so-called Negro as an integrated part of his society until the image of the Negro the white man has is changed, and until the image that the Negro has of himself is also changed.

54. MALCOLM X
FOUNDS THE ORGANIZATION
OF AFRO-AMERICAN UNITY

Malcolm X broke with the Nation of Islam in March 1964. He then traveled extensively abroad to Mecca and Africa. These trips affected his political ideas about race and revolution. He spoke of "the importance of having a working unity among all peoples, black as well as white, but the only way this is going to be brought about is that

"Statement of the Basic Aims and Objectives of the Organization of Afro-American Unity," June 28, 1964. Reprinted from George Breitman, THE LAST YEAR OF MALCOLM X: THE EVOLUTION OF A REVOLUTIONARY (New York: Merit Publishers, 1967), pp. 105–111, with permission of Pathfinder Press, Inc.

the black ones have to be in unity first. . . . The black man has to be
shown how to free himself, and the white one who is sincerely
interested has to back whatever that black group decides upon to
do. . . ."[1] Thus in June 1964, Malcolm X founded the Organization of
Afro-American Unity, open for membership to all persons of "African
descent."

The document, "Statement of Basic Aims and Objectives of the
Organization of Afro-American Unity," reprinted here, summarizes
his nationalist program for American Negroes in the last year of his
life. It should be emphasized that Malcolm X called for a close alliance of Africans with Afro-Americans; as he said shortly before his
assassination, "The time is past due for us to internationalize the problems of Afro-Americans. We have been too slow in recognizing the
link in the fate of Africans with the fate of Afro-Americans. We have
been too unknowing to understand and too misdirected to ask our African brothers and sisters to help us mend the chain of our heritage."[2]

The Organization of Afro-American Unity, organized and struc-
tured by a cross-section of the Afro-American people living in
the U.S.A., has been patterned after the letter and spirit of the
Organization of African Unity established at Addis Ababa,
Ethiopia, May, 1963.

We, the members of the Organization of Afro-American
Unity gathered together in Harlem, New York:

Convinced that it is the inalienable right of all people to control their own destiny;

Conscious of the fact that freedom, equality, justice and dignity are essential objectives for the achievement of the legitimate aspirations of the people of African descent here in the
Western Hemisphere, we will endeavor to build a bridge of
understanding and create the basis for Afro-American unity;

Conscious of our responsibility to harness the natural and

[1] *Malcolm X Speaks: Selected Speeches and Statements,* George Breitman, Ed. (New York: Merit Publishers, 1965), p. 70.
[2] "Basic Unity Program, Organization of Afro-American Unity," printed in
George Breitman, *The Last Year of Malcolm X: The Evolution of a Revolutionary* (New York: Merit Publishers, 1967), pp. 122–23.

human resources of our people for their total advancement in all spheres of human endeavor;

Inspired by a common determination to promote understanding among our people and co-operation in all matters pertaining to their survival and advancement, we will support the aspirations of our people for brotherhood and solidarity in a larger unity transcending all organizational differences;

Convinced that, in order to translate this determination into a dynamic force in the cause of human progress, conditions of peace and security must be established and maintained;

Determined to unify the Americans of African descent in their fight for human rights and dignity, and being fully aware that this is not possible in the present atmosphere and condition of oppression, we dedicate ourselves to the building of a political, economic, and social system of justice and peace;

Dedicated to the unification of all people of African descent in this hemisphere and to the utilization of that unity to bring into being the organizational structure that will project the black people's contributions to the world;

Persuaded that the Charter of the United Nations, the Universal Declaration of Human Rights, the Constitution of the U.S.A. and the Bill of Rights are the principles in which we believe and these documents if put into practice represent the essence of mankind's hopes and good intentions;

Desirous that all Afro-American people and organizations should henceforth unite so that the welfare and well-being of our people will be assured;

Resolved to reinforce the common bond of purpose between our people by submerging all of our differences and establishing a non-religious and non-sectarian constructive program for human rights;

Do hereby present this charter.

I. Establishment

The Organization of Afro-American Unity shall include all people of African descent in the Western Hemisphere, as well as our brothers and sisters on the African Continent.

II. Self-defense

Since self-preservation is the first law of nature, we assert the Afro-American's right of self-defense.

The Constitution of the U.S.A. clearly affirms the right of every American citizen to bear arms. And as Americans, we will not give up a single right guaranteed under the Constitution. The history of the unpublished violence against our people clearly indicates that we must be prepared to defend ourselves or we will continue to be a defenseless people at the mercy of a ruthless and violent racist mob.

We assert that in those areas where the government is either unable or unwilling to protect the lives and property of our people, that our people are within their rights to protect themselves by whatever means necessary. A man with a rifle or club can only be stopped by a person who defends himself with a rifle or club.

Tactics based solely on morality can only succeed when you are dealing with basically moral people or a moral system. A man or system which oppresses a man because of his color is not moral. It is the duty of every Afro-American and every Afro-American community throughout this country to protect its people against mass murderers, bombers, lynchers, floggers, brutalizers and exploiters.

III. Education

Education is an important element in the struggle for human rights. It is the means to help our children and people rediscover their identity and thereby increase self-respect. Education is our passport to the future, for tomorrow belongs to the people who prepare for it today.

Our children are being criminally shortchanged in the public school system of America. The Afro-American schools are the poorest run schools in New York City. Principals and teachers fail to understand the nature of the problems with which they work and as a result they cannot do the job of teaching our children. The textbooks tell our children nothing about the great contributions of Afro-Americans to the growth and development of this country. The Board of Education's integration program is expensive and unworkable; and the organization of principals and supervisors in the New York City school system has refused to support the Board's plan to integrate the schools, thus dooming it to failure.

The Board of Education has said that even with its plan there are ten per cent of the schools in the Harlem-Bedford-Stuyvesant community they cannot improve. This means that the Organization of Afro-American Unity must make the Afro-American community a more potent force for educational self-improvement.

A first step in the program to end the existing system of racist education is to demand that the ten per cent of the schools the Board of Education will not include in its plan be turned over to and run by the Afro-American community. We want Afro-American principals to head these schools. We want Afro-American teachers in these schools. We want textbooks written by Afro-Americans that are acceptable to us to be used in these schools.

The Organization of Afro-American Unity will select and recommend people to serve on local school boards where school policy is made and passed on to the Board of Education.

Through these steps we will make the ten per cent of schools we take over educational showplaces that will attract the attention of people all over the nation.

If these proposals are not met, we will ask Afro-American parents to keep their children out of the present inferior schools they attend. When these schools in our neighborhood are controlled by Afro-Americans, we will return to them.

The Organization of Afro-American Unity recognizes the tremendous importance of the complete involvement of Afro-American parents in every phase of school life. Afro-American parents must be willing and able to go into the schools and see that the job of educating our children is done properly.

We call on all Afro-Americans around the nation to be aware that the conditions that exist in the New York City public school system are as deplorable in their cities as they are here. We must unite our effort and spread our program of self-improvement through education to every Afro-American community in America.

We must establish all over the country schools of our own to train our children to become scientists and mathematicians. We must realize the need for adult education and for job retraining programs that will emphasize a changing society in which automation plays the key role. We intend to use the tools of education to help raise our people to an unprecedented level of excellence and self-respect through their own efforts.

IV. Politics—economics

Basically, there are two kinds of power that count in America: economic and political, with social power deriving from the two. In order for the Afro-Americans to control their destiny, they must be able to control and affect the decisions which control their destiny: economic, political and social. This can only be done through organization.

The Organization of Afro-American Unity will organize the Afro-American community block by block to make the community aware of its power and potential; we will start immediately a voter-registration drive to make every unregistered voter in the Afro-American community an independent voter; we propose to support and/or organize political clubs, to run independent candidates for office, and to support any Afro-American already in office who answers to and is responsible to the Afro-American community.

Economic exploitation in the Afro-American community is the most vicious form practiced on any people in America; twice as much rent for rat-infested, roach-crawling, rotting tenements; the Afro-American pays more for foods, clothing, insurance rates and so forth. The Organization of Afro-American Unity will wage an unrelenting struggle against these evils in our community. There shall be organizers to work with the people to solve these problems, and start a housing self-improvement program.

We propose to support rent strikes and other activities designed to better the community.

V. Social

This organization is responsible only to the Afro-American people and community and will function only with their support, both financially and numerically. We believe that our communities must be the sources of their own strength politically, economically, intellectually and culturally in the struggle for human rights and dignity.

The community must reinforce its moral responsibility to rid itself of the effects of years of exploitation, neglect and apathy, and wage an unrelenting struggle against police brutality.

The Afro-American community must accept the responsibility for regaining our people who have lost their place in society. We must declare an all-out war on organized crime in our community; a vice that is controlled by policemen who accept bribes and graft, and who must be exposed. We must establish a clinic, whereby one can get aid and cure for drug addiction; and create meaningful, creative, useful activities for those who were led astray down the avenues of vice.

The people of the Afro-American community must be prepared to help each other in all ways possible; we must establish a place where unwed mothers can get help and advice; a home for the aged in Harlem and an orphanage in Harlem.

We must set up a guardian system that will help our youth who get into trouble and also provide constructive activities for our children. We must set a good example for our children and must teach them to always be ready to accept the responsibilities that are necessary for building good communities and nations. We must teach them that their greatest responsibilities are to themselves, to their families and to their communities.

The Organization of Afro-American Unity believes that the Afro-American community must endeavor to do the major part of all charity work from within the community. Charity, however, does not mean that to which we are legally entitled in the form of government benefits. The Afro-American veteran must be made aware of all the benefits due him and the procedure for obtaining them. These veterans must be encouraged to go into business together, using G.I. loans, etc.

Afro-Americans must unite and work together. We must take pride in the Afro-American community, for it is home and it is power.

What we do here in regaining our self-respect, manhood, dignity and freedom helps all people everywhere who are fighting against oppression.

VI. Culture

"A race of people is like an individual man; until it uses its own talent, takes pride in its own history, expresses its own culture, affirms its own selfhood, it can never fulfill itself."

Our history and our culture were completely destroyed when we were forcibly brought to America in chains. And now it is important for us to know that our history did not begin with slavery's scars. We come from Africa, a great continent and a proud and varied people, a land which is the new world and was the cradle of civilization. Our culture and our history are as old as man himself and yet we know almost nothing of it. We must recapture our heritage and our identity if we are ever to liberate ourselves from the bonds of white supremacy. We must launch a cultural revolution to unbrainwash an entire people.

Our cultural revolution must be the means of bringing us closer to our African brothers and sisters. It must begin in the community and be based on community participation. Afro-Americans will be free to create only when they can depend on the Afro-American community for support and Afro-American artists must realize that they depend on the Afro-American for inspiration. We must work toward the establishment of a cultural center in Harlem, which will include people of all ages, and will conduct workshops in all the arts, such as film, creative writing, painting, theater, music, Afro-American history, etc.

This cultural revolution will be the journey to our rediscovery of ourselves. History is a people's memory, and without a memory man is demoted to the lower animals.

Armed with the knowledge of the past, we can with confidence charter a course for our future. Culture is an indispensable weapon in the freedom struggle. We must take hold of it and forge the future with the past.

When the battle is won, let history be able to say to each one of us: "He was a dedicated patriot: *Dignity* was his country, *Manhood* was his government, and *Freedom* was his land." (from *And Then We Heard the Thunder*, by John Oliver Killens)

55. JOHN O. KILLENS:
"WE REFUSE TO LOOK AT OURSELVES
THROUGH THE EYES OF WHITE AMERICA"

Pride in being black and alienation from the values of white middle-class America may take the form of growing identification with Africa —as expressed by John Lewis (see Document 49)—or they may take the form of a conscious cultivation of cultural pluralism. In an illuminating article in 1964 the novelist John O. Killens, author of *Youngblood* and *And Then We Heard the Thunder*, cogently set forth this theme.

His statement should be compared with Langston Hughes's essay in *The Nation* in 1926 (see Document 17). Hughes admired the unique aspects of Negro life and made a plea that they not be de-

John O. Killens, "Explanation of the 'Black Psyche,' " The New York TIMES (MAGAZINE), June 7, 1964, pp. 37–38, 42, and 47–48. © 1964 by The New York Times Company and John Oliver Killens. Reprinted by permission of The New York Times Company and International Famous Agency.

spised and ignored. Killens went further, not only asserting his pride in the black way of life but denouncing certain aspects of white culture as inferior and objectionable. The difference between the two statements suggests the distance that the Negro protest movement has traveled in the last generation.

When I was a boy in Macon, Ga., one of the greatest compliments a benevolent white man could give a Negro was usually found in the obituary column of the local newspaper: "He was a black man, but he had a white heart." And the burden of every black man was supposedly just a little easier to bear that day. It was a time when many of us black folk laughed at the antics of Amos 'n' Andy and wept copious tears at a ridiculous movie, very aptly titled "Imitation of Life." Most of us looked at life through the eyes of white America.

The great fictional and filmic masterpieces on the American racial theme usually fell into two categories. One theme dealt with the utter heartbreak of the mulatto, who rejected his black blood and was in turn rejected by his white blood. A variation of this theme was the shattering experience of "passing." The other theme was the "Uncle Tom," or what I like to call the "Gunga Din," theme. This one also had many variations, but over all there was the image created by that great apologist for colonialism, Rudyard Kipling, of a man who—

> . . . For all 'is dirty 'ide
> 'E was white, clear white, inside
> When 'e went to tend the wounded
>   under fire!

With some "additional dialogue" by Hollywood, dear old "white inside" Gunga was a marvelous figment of Western man's wistful imagination, the personification of his wish fulfillment. Gunga was a water boy for the British regiment and, in the movie, finally blew the bugle against his own people. And how "whiter" inside could a "noble savage" be?

I am waging a quiet little campaign at the moment to substitute the term "Gunga Din" for that much maligned character "Uncle Tom," in designating the contemporary water boys who still blow the bugles for ol' Massa, better known these days as "Mister Charlie." For, although Mrs. Stowe's beloved "Uncle Tom" was indeed an Uncle Tom, as we understand the term today, he, nevertheless, in the final confrontation, chose death rather than blow the bugle against his people.

Variations of the Gunga Din theme were seen in a rash of movie epics like "Gone With the Wind" and "Virginia" and "Kentucky," etc., ad infinitum, ad nauseam, always played magnificently with tongue in cheek by such stalwarts as Hattie McDaniel and Louise Beavers. In the great emotional scene the black mammy was usually in the big house, weeping and moaning over little pure-white-as-the-driven-snow Missy Anne, who had just sneezed, while mammy's own young 'un was dying of double pneumonia, unattended down in the cabins. All in all, the slaves were presented as carefree and contented in their idyllic degradation. If the black man *really* believed in this romantic version of American slavery, he would have long since wasted away, pining for those good old happy-go-lucky days of bondage.

Last year I did considerable research on that bygone utopian era, and I got a very different picture, slightly less romantic. I found that the slaves were so happy that most of the plantation owners could not afford the astronomical rates of fire insurance. Those rapturous slaves were setting fire to the cotton patches, burning down the plantations, every day the good Lord sent them. They organized countless insurrections, killed their masters, poisoned their mistresses, put spiders in the big-house soup. They demonstrated their contentment in most peculiar ways.

I shall never forget an evening I spent in a movie house in Hollywood, watching a closed-circuit television broadcast of the first Patterson-Johansson fight, and the great shame I felt for my white countrymen that night, as they began to smell a possible victory for the white foreigner over the black American. Forgotten entirely was the fact that soft-hearted Floyd Patterson was a fellow-countryman. Color superseded patriotism. As I sat there hearing shouted exhortations like, "Kill the nigger!", I felt that Patterson and I were aliens in a strange and hostile country, and Ingemar was home amongst his people.

In fairness to my countrymen in the closed circuits of America that night, their reactions were not intellectual, not even willful. They were spontaneous, not unlike a conditioned reflex. This ecstasy at the sudden emergence of a new white hope came from the metaphoric guts of them; from their hearts, their souls, their bellies. This was their white insides reacting.

It has been rationalized to me that this incident had no racial implications at all, that these rabid Johansson fans were merely in the Old American tradition of rooting for the underdog. Well, I was also rooting for the underdog, and I knew that, win or lose, the underdog in America was Floyd Patterson, Harry Belafonte, Emmett Till, Rosa Parks, Meredith, Poitier, the black American *me*. The words, "Kill the nigger" could not possibly have come screaming from my throat, subconsciously, unconsciously or otherwise.

Just as surely as East is East and West is West, there is a "black" psyche in America and there is a "white" one, and the sooner we face up to this social and cultural reality, the sooner the twain shall meet. Our emotional chemistry is different from yours in many instances. Your joy is very often our anger and your despair our fervent hope. Most of us came here in chains and most of you came here to escape your chains. Your freedom was our slavery, and therein lies the bitter difference in the way we look at life.

You created the myth of the faithful slave, but we know that the "loyal slave" is a contradiction in terms. We understand, though, that the master must always make himself believe in the undying love of his slave. That is why white America put words in the black man's mouth and bade him sing—improbable lyrics like

> All de darkeys am a-weepin'
> Massa's in de cold, cold ground.

But my great-grandmother told me differently. "We wept all right, honey! Great God Almighty! We cried for joy and shouted hallelujah," when old master got the cold, cold ground that was coming to him.

In order to justify slavery in a courageous new world which was spouting slogans of freedom and equality and brotherhood, the enslavers, through their propagandists, had to create the fiction that the enslaved people were subhuman and undeserving of human rights and sympathies. The first job was to convince the outside world of the inherent inferiority of the enslaved. The second job was to convince the American people. And the third job, which was the cruelest hoax of all, was to convince the slaves themselves that they deserved to be slaves.

The propagandists for American slavery (the creative writers of the time) tackled these tasks with alacrity and a great measure of success, the effects of which still remain with us today, a hundred years after the Emancipation Proclamation, almost 200 years after the Declaration of Independence. Thus, the Negro was invented and the American Revolution thwarted. Knock on any door in Harlem. Ask any black man or woman in Alabama or Mississippi: Was 1776 for real?

Ironically enough, the fathers of our magnificent Revolution, Washington and Jefferson, themselves owned hundreds of human chattels and even though the great Thomas Jefferson made many speeches against the peculiar institution, he was never able to convince himself to the extent of manumitting his own slaves during his own lifetime.

Surely the great irony of the situation did not escape my ancestors back in the days of the Revolution. And now, today, it does not escape their great-great-grandchildren. When we black folk hear one of our white leaders use the phrase, "the free world," even though the same white leader may very well be the Governor of the state of Mississippi or Alabama, or any other state, for that matter, we—as the slaves of Washington and Jefferson must have done—stare at him incredulously and cannot believe our ears. And we wonder how this word "freedom" can have such vastly different meanings, such conflicting connotations.

But the time has come for you (white America) and me (black America) to work this thing out once and for all, to examine and evaluate the differences between us and the differences inside of us. Time is swiftly running out, and a new dialogue is indispensable. It is so long overdue it is almost half past midnight.

My fight is not to be a white man in a black skin, but to inject some black blood, some black intelligence into the pallid main stream of American life, culturally, socially, psychologically, philosophically. This is the truer deeper meaning of the Negro revolt, which is not yet a revolution—to get America ready for the middle of the 20th century, which is already magnificently here.

This new epoch has caught our country (yours and mine) napping in a sweet nostalgia of the good old days. Our country slumbers in a world of yesteryears, before Africa and Asia got up off their knees and threw off the black man's burden; the good old days when you threw pennies to the "natives" and there were gunboats in the China Sea and Big Stick Policies and Monroe Doctrines and "Old Coasters" from the U.K. sipped their gin-and-tonics in Accra and Lagos and talked about the "natives," as they basked in their roles of Great White Fathers in that best of all possible worlds.

That world is gone forever, and black and brown men everywhere are glad, deep in their hearts, but most Western men are chagrined, which is the understatement of the century. This is why the world is becoming much too much for Western men, even for most of you liberal Western men, even you radical Western men, whoever you are, and wherever.

But the world is becoming more and more to my liking, to my taste and in my image. It gladdens my heart to see black and brown men and women come with dignity to the United Nations in affirmation of the manhood and the selfhood of the entire human race.

The American Negro, then, is an Anglo-Saxon invention, a role the Anglo-Saxon gentlemen invented for the black man to play in this drama known euphemistically as the American Way of Life. It began as an economic expedient, frankly, because you wanted somebody to work for nothing. It is still that, but now it is much more than that. It has become a way of life within a way of life, socially, economically, psychologically, philosophically.

But now, in the middle of the 20th century, I, the Negro, am refusing to be your "nigrah" any longer. Even some of us "favored," "talented," "unusual" ones are refusing to be your educated, sophisticated, split-leveled "nigrahs" any longer. We refuse to look at ourselves through the eyes of white America.

We are not fighting for the right to be like you. We respect ourselves too much for that. When we fight for freedom, we mean freedom for us to be black, or brown, and you to be white and yet live together in a free and equal society. This is the only way that integration can mean dignity for both of us.

I, for one, am growing weary of those well-meaning white liberals who are forever telling me they don't know what color I am. The very fact that they single me out at the cocktail party and gratuitously make me the beneficiary of their blessed assurances gives the lie to their pronouncements.

My fight is not *for* racial sameness but for racial equality and *against* racial prejudice and discrimination. I work for the day when my people will be free of the racist pressures to be *white like you;* a day when "good hair" and "high yaller" and bleaching cream and hair-straighteners will be obsolete. What a tiresome place America would be if freedom meant we all had to think alike and be the same color and wear the same gray flannel suit!

If relationships are to improve between us Americans, black and white and otherwise, if the country is to be saved, we will have to face up to the fact that differences do exist between us. All men react to life through man-made symbols. Even our symbolic reactions are different from yours. To give a few examples:

In the center of a little Southern town near the border of Mississippi, there is a water tower atop which is a large white cross, illumined at night with a lovely (awesome to Negroes) neoned brightness. It can be seen for many miles away. To most white Americans who see it for the first time it is a beacon light that symbolizes the Cross upon which Jesus died, and it gives them a warm feeling in the face and shoulders. But the same view puts an angry knot in the black man's belly. To him it symbolizes the very, very "Christian" K.K.K.

To the average white man, a courthouse, even in Mississippi, is a place where justice is dispensed. To me, the black man, it is a place where justice is dispensed—with.

Even our white hero symbols are different from yours. You give us moody Abraham Lincoln, but many of us prefer John Brown, whom most of you hold in contempt and regard as a fanatic; meaning, of course, that the firm dedication of any white man to the freedom of the black man is *prima facie* evidence of perversion and insanity.

You look upon these times as the Atomic Age, the Space Age, the Cold War era. But I believe that when the history of these times is written, it will not be so important who reached the moon first or who made the largest bomb. I believe the great significance will be that this was the century when most of mankind achieved freedom and human dignity. For me, this is the Freedom Century.

So now it is time for you to understand us, because it is becoming increasingly hazardous for you not to. Dangerous for both of us. As Richard Wright said in his "Twelve Million Black Voices," voices you chose not to heed: "Each day when you see us black folk upon the dusty land of your farms or upon the hard pavement of your city streets, you usually take us for granted and think you know us, but our history is far stranger than you suspect, and we are not what we seem."

The Rev. Ralph Abernathy of Montgomery placed the question humorously when he said that the new Negro of Montgomery had stopped laughing when he wasn't tickled and scratching when he didn't itch.

In a word we are bringing down the curtain on this role you cast us in, and we will no longer be a party to our own degradation. We have become unbelievers, no longer believing in the absolute superiority of the white man's juju. You have never practiced what you preached. Why would we want to be like

you? We have caught you in too many lies. You proud defenders of the chastity of womanhood, you champions of racial
purity, you are, if I may coin a phrase, "the last of the great
miscegenators."

Yes, we are different from you and we are not invisible men,
Ralph Ellison notwithstanding. We are the most visible of Americans. We are both Americans and Negroes. Other Americans,
for the most part, excepting Puerto Ricans and Mexicans, are
just Americans. But we are more than just Americans, not because of our color but because of how America exploited our
color. We are different, not because we willed it, but because
America set us apart from the rest of the community for special
exploitation. And so we are special, with extraspecial insights.

In the summer and fall of 1961 I traveled in a Land Rover
12,000 miles through Africa. I talked to people in the cities, on
the farms, in the villages. I talked with workers, farmers, artists,
market women, ministers of state, politicians, teachers, and the
same question was asked me everywhere I went with variations:
"How can we believe your country's professions of goodwill to
us, with whom they have not lived, when they deny human dignity to you who come from us and have lived with them for
centuries and helped to build their great civilization?"

It is a question America has to answer to the entire New World
of Africa and Asia. The only way we Americans, black and white,
can answer this question affirmatively is to make freedom and
democracy work *here* and *now*. Just as most Negroes still believe
that the ultimate solution for us is in America, I am firmly convinced that the ultimate salvation of America is in the Negro.

The Negro loves America enough to criticize her fundamentally. Most of white America simply can't be bothered. Ironically
enough, in the middle of the 20th century, the Negro is the new
white hope. To live castrated in a great white harem and yet
somehow maintain his black manhood and his humanity—this is
the essence of the new man created out of the Negro Invention.
History may render the verdict that this was the greatest legacy
handed to the New World by the West.

Western man wrote *his* history as if it were the history of the entire human race. I hope that colored men all over the world have watched Western man too long to commit the fatal folly of writing history with a colored pencil. For there is great wisdom in the old Ghana proverb, which says "No one rules forever on the throne of time."

We black folk have learned many lessons during our sojourn in this place. One of them is the truth of another Ghana proverb that says: "Only a fool points to his heritage with his left hand." We are becoming prouder and prouder of our heritage in America and Africa. And we know the profound difference between pride and arrogance; the difference, if you will, between James Meredith and Ross Barnett, both of Mississippi. . . . Yes, we black people stand ready, eager, willing and able to make our contribution to the culture of the world. Our dialogue will not be protest but *affirmation* of the human dignity of all people everywhere.

I know there are white folk who want America to be the land of the free and the home of the brave, but there are far too few of them, and most of them are seldom brave. And I, too, cherish old John Brown and Garrison and William Moore. Let the winter patriots increase their ranks. Let those who truly love America join the valiant Negro Revolt and save the beloved country.

Toward economic solutions

56. WHITNEY M. YOUNG, JR.:
FOR A FEDERAL "WAR ON POVERTY"

By 1963, people in all segments of the movement for civil rights perceived the problems of jobs, housing, and education as their major future areas of activity. The recognition of the Negro's constitutional rights would not by itself eliminate black poverty and would not therefore bring about full equality for blacks in American society. An especially notable statement of this feeling was given by Whitney Young, Jr., of the Urban League, testifying at Congressional hearings on President Lyndon B. Johnson's proposal for a "War on Poverty."

I would like to depart from my testimony because of the question of time and talk very frankly with you about this problem since it is something that is so very close to the Urban League and it is something around which Negro citizens in particular have a great deal of real concern.

This testimony is here for the record and to some extent in what I have to say extemporaneously I will be following this. For the benefit of reporters and other members of the committee it may not all be the printed statement, however. Let me say that the Urban League endorses whole heartedly all of the

"Statement of Whitney M. Young, Jr., Executive Director, National Urban League, Inc.," in TRANSCRIPT OF HEARING, AD HOC SUBCOMMITTEE ON THE WAR ON POVERTY PROGRAM, Committee on Education and Labor, House of Representatives, April 14, 1964, pp. 2–7 (mimeographed). Printed with permission of Whitney M. Young, Jr.

titles of this legislation. We support the Poverty package. We feel, however, that it is a minimum package in light of the massive problems that we are facing, in the light of the massive problems of unemployment particularly that the Negro citizen faces, and the problem of undereducation and inferior education and inferior vocational education, housing and what-have-you. We have for some 54 years been working on this problem of raising the standards of Negro citizens in this country.

We have recently expanded and retooled our organization for the purpose of taking advantage of the Poverty program, of providing to the Federal Government and local governments, machinery by which the Poverty measures may in fact reach the mass of Negro citizens.

We have in the historical past been aware of where well meaning bills have been passed in Washington but by the time, if ever, they got to Joe Smith, a Negro who lived in Memphis, Tennessee, there was little similarity between the intent of the measure and what the benefits were to that particular person.

So we are particularly delighted that this bill makes provision for the utilization of responsible non-profit, private organizations like the Urban League, that have at the local level the contacts and the relationships to actually implement these programs. I would hope that in this case that you would make every effort to see that for maybe the first time in history, we would be involved at the level of policy making, planning and implementation, Negroes at all levels.

This is a way of shoring up responsible Negro leadership in the community and putting in charge of these programs people who have sometimes the greatest stake. We have been somewhat concerned by some of the statements which I understand have been made around the country and probably discussed in the committee to the effect that this program is largely a program which will benefit Negro citizens.

Not only does this ignore the fact that only 20 percent of the nation's poor happen to be Negro; it also implies, and this to me is a very dangerous thing, the inference that if such were the case in fact, if the Poverty Program only addressed itself to

Negroes, then it would be something around which the government would have less concern or less sense of urgency.

This would in fact simply be a confirmation of the predictions
since made by the Communists and certainly more currently
made by the Black Muslims, that the American white man is
congenitally incapable of giving up a privilege or being concerned about the Negro or the white person is morally bankrupt
as he relates to the Negro.

I am sure this is not what anybody intends to imply by this
suggestion that if the Poverty Program in fact helps Negroes;
then it is something that we should have a minimum concern
about. The National Urban League is concerned about all of the
poor, but we are particularly concerned about the Negro and
we think that the facts would reveal that we have every reason
not only to be concerned but that all America should be very
much concerned.

The problem that the Negro citizen faces in this country, and
it is a problem around which the whole thrust for first class citizenship is based—is not merely an attempt to remove one's
self from a mild inconvenience.

It is not simply a thrust for social status and for acceptance.
The conditions that Negro citizens find themselves in today is
not a mere recession. It is not even a depression. Let me cite you
some facts.

The Bureau of Labor Statistics will tell you that fifteen percent
of the unemployed happen to be Negro. They are referring only
to those people who are currently seeking employment, people
who walked into the employment offices the last two or three
weeks. They are not referring to what Dr. Killingsworth of
Michigan State University has called the chronic unemployed,
the person who long since despaired of finding work, who in an
attempt to find work found it was too expensive and a hopeless
task, and so resigned himself sometime ago to a life of chronic
dependency.

This represents 10 to 11 percent. So what we are talking about
when we talk about Negro unemployed is that one out of every
four Negro workers happens to be unemployed in this country.

We are talking about a group of people whose family income happens to be exactly 53 percent of that of the average white family's income.

That figure, Gentlemen, is worse than in 1952 when it was 57 percent. The gap is getting wider.

We are talking about a group of people 60 percent of whom have a family income under $3,000, 75 percent have a family income under $4,000. We are talking about a group of people who have 50 percent of this nation's youngsters between the ages of 16 and 21 who are out of work and out of school.

Today there is close to a million youngsters, Mr. Chairman, youngsters between 16 and 21, out of school, out of work. A million. Five hundred thousand of these happen to be Negro kids, idle in cities of our country. In cities like Chicago 85 percent of the welfare caseload happens to be Negroes though they certainly don't represent much more than 22 percent of the population.

In Detroit, 60 percent of the unemployed happen to be Negro citizens. We are talking about a group of people who today in this country, one out of every six, lives in a house that is dilapidated and substandard, according to the Census, as compared to one out of thirty-two for white citizens.

We are talking about people whose youngsters receive today 3 and ½ years less schooling than white children.

When you consider that most of that education is received in inferior, some segregated schools, north or south, then the real difference is more like five years. A group of people whose parents still die seven years sooner, a group of people who have a mortality rate of childbirth both for the mother and the child that is on the upgrade, and whose respiratory diseases are now on the upgrade after having gone down for a number of years.

What I am describing to you for the Negro is not a recession, an inconvenience, it is a catastrophe, a disaster, and it is fast becoming a national disgrace for our country where there is no question about its affluence.

It is an indictment of this country. This is where the Poverty program to us takes on real meaning.

Now we have no illusions about the need and the value of passage of the Civil Rights Bill. We are for this 100 percent but we have no illusions that the Civil Rights Bill will in and of itself address itself to this problem that we are talking about.

Today some of the most difficult problems we face are in those cities and states like New York with laws far beyond anything that is presently in the Civil Rights Bill as it now exists. So we are afraid that we might end up here with a mouthful of Civil Rights and an empty stomach, living in a hovel. Let me make it clear. I am not saying either, or. We must have the Civil Rights Bill. This symbolizes dignity, personal worth, something long overdue.

I am saying it must be Civil Rights buttressed by the resources with which people can in fact take advantage of equal opportunity; to provide equal opportunity without providing a deprived, a historically deprived group of citizens with the resources by which they may take advantage of the opportunity is to me to invite upon them disillusionment, frustration, and despair.

Now the alternative to the passage of this kind of legislation is very clear. We will either help Negro citizens become productive, constructive consumers or they will automatically become destructive, disgruntled, dependents.

We will either give the government all resources in much more accelerated fashion and in certain large amounts to responsible Negro organizations and established groups to do this job of self-help, to correct the abuse of the past, or else by indifference we will invite another kind of leadership to take over.

The demonstrations that we are seeing in the streets today are ones fostered by despair and hopelessness and those of us who try to represent responsible Negro leadership in this country desperately need some tangible evidence of the intentions of this country to right a historic wrong.

Now I think Negro citizens in the face of the years have provocation, in the face of the historic abuse, have shown an amazing restraint and an amazing loyalty. I give you only last year as an example. Last year where you saw the March on Washington with its quiet dignity and its fervent pleading. Last year where you saw Negro parents, Negro citizens after their children were bombed in a Sunday school, remain calm and cool and continue to pray. Last year you saw in Jackson, Mississippi, Negro people in a church after their leader had been slain and after the widow of their leader addressed a meeting, a woman who had every right to hate, and she stood there and said, "You mustn't hate, you must love." And to see thousands of people in that audience who had every reason to be incensed, stand up and sing spontaneously without anybody announcing it, "My Country 'tis of Thee, sweet land of Liberty." Now I don't know what more simple element of testimony of faith in a system do you need on the part of the people who have so little reason to have this kind of faith, who have all the provocation, the abuse, the murders, the years of want, poor housing and rats biting their children.

They have said to America, "I believe in you." It seems to me it is time for America through its elected representatives here in Washington, to say to Negro citizens, "We, too, believe in you."

The best way that you can now respond in a responsible way to the responsible kind of leadership we are trying to show is not through vacillation, it is not through talking about methods, but it is actually passage of this kind of legislation.

The Manpower Retraining Bill, what did it do? This said it was going to retrain a hundred thousand people; it retrained 60,000. Of the 60,000 less than a handful were people who were below the eighth grade level. They educated the educable. So that means most of the Negroes were not included at all.

Even though 22 percent of those trained were Negroes—this amounts to less than 15,000 people—and what we have today in this country is one million adult Negroes out of work plus 500,000 Negro youth. It is not a case of which of these approaches we need; we need all of them. We desperately need them passed and sent down to the local level where they can be implemented by coalition of private and public agencies working together.

Finally, let me say that what we are really trying to do here is to ask you to work and provide hope for Negro parents who themselves have no real illusion that they can change overnight from a functional illiterate to a skilled technician, but who desperately are looking for the kind of action that says that this will not be the destiny of your child, that will remove the despair and the hope, that will take the people off the streets and we can get on with the business of retraining and education.

We are asking you to say to those Negro kids and I say this in closing, what was best expressed through a story told by a famous African educator, Dr. Aggrey. He told of a farmer who went out in the woods to hunt and ran across a young eagle which had just been born. He brought the eagle back and put it in with the chickens. Some three or four years later a passing naturalist happened to observe this eagle being raised with the chickens and began to berate the farmer for doing this. The farmer said in all innocence that he had not meant to do anything wrong and that for all intents and purposes, because the eagle had been raised since birth with the chickens, it was now a chicken. The naturalist offered to prove differently.

After many repeated attempts to get the eagle to fly, finally in desperation one morning he took the eagle out and put it on top of a high cliff and he said, "Eagle, thou art an eagle. Thou were meant to fly in the sky and not work on this earth. Lift your wings and fly."

The eagle trembled as if new life had come to it, looked off in the horizon, lifted its mighty wings and flew off into the sun, never to return.

It was an eagle though it had been raised and tamed as a chicken.

This is what we in the Urban League and the other civil rights groups, churches, and hopefully you, will be saying to Negro youth: that though you have faced barriers, discrimination, things that would have suggested that you are a nobody, you are really somebody. And though you have placed in front of you all of the handicaps, the obstacles—though you have been humiliated—and though they would suggest that you are a second class citizen, you are really a first class human citizen.

Stretch your minds and fly. This is what the Poverty Program is all about. You have a great opportunity and it is one that I have confidence that you as decent human beings, sensitive and intelligent, will give us the resources to do the job, that which can be done, but it is up to you.

57. NORMAN HILL: "WE MUST BE CONCERNED WITH THE KIND OF SOCIETY FOR ALL WORKERS"

For Norman Hill, CORE's program director in 1963 and 1964, employment, education and housing were the major problems with which the civil rights organizations would be grappling in the years ahead. He was also one of a growing body of civil rights activists who had become impatient with the fruits of the traditional nonpartisan political stance of civil rights organizations, and who insisted that only through partisan political activity could Negro protest groups achieve real effectiveness. An advocate both of the civil rights organizations becoming more relevant to the needs of the slum dwellers, and of the need to involve the black poor in the activities of these organizations, his vision of the function of the Negro protest movement nevertheless went beyond the goals of civil rights and economic equality for Negroes. In his view, jobs, good schools, and decent housing could not be secured for blacks without guaranteeing them for white people also. Thus, in compelling the nation to eliminate black poverty, the civil rights movement would compel the nation to solve also the problems of poverty among white Americans. A democratic socialist, Hill is a close associate of Bayard Rustin, and at present he works with the A. Philip Randolph Institute.

When one tries to think through the political dimensions of the civil rights movement one is in fact assessing where we are today and what has brought us here, because it is clear and ap-

Norman Hill, Address to the St. Louis Area Conference of the Congress of Racial Equality, April 4, 1964. Reprinted with permission of Norman Hill.

parent that whatever we do in the civil rights movement today is, whether we like it or not, a political act, and has consequences on city, state and federal decision makers in our society. . . . [O]nce we shifted our emphasis from the area of public accommodations in which we have made great strides North and even in the South, and moved into the basic, dirtiest aspects of segregation and discrimination, moved to attack basic problems of housing, education and jobs, which the great mass of Negroes face in cities throughout the country North and South, we were then moving into the area of politics. . . .

Let me spell this out and indicate what I mean precisely. When one takes the question of schools, whether it be in the North or South, to be really concerned about the kind of education that a minority child gets in our present system, it is not just merely the question of whether he is able to sit in the same classroom beside a white child, but what in fact happens to him during the school day. And if this is the real measure of the kind of education that a minority child gets, it is also an equal measure of the kind of education that all children in our society get. So in looking at this question we have become concerned then not just about the mere physical integration of the Negro minority child, but about what really happens inside our public school system. And the whole question of the quality of our school system is being raised as never before by the civil rights movement in its very attempt to foster and encourage integration. In so doing then we are making a political challenge because whether a board of education is appointed or elected the kinds of priorities that are placed upon the educational system and the kind of money that is set aside for it are in fact political decisions. The kinds of priorities that are raised, which will indicate whether or not we have a high quality educational system available for all children, is in fact dependent on the kind of political climate that you and I create in city after city throughout the country.

Secondly, when the civil rights movement, in addition to being concerned about whether or not we broke through in this or that lily-white area in housing, decided to move also to alleviate and change the basic housing conditions which great majorities of Negroes have to live in, in ghetto after ghetto throughout the North, we were again raising a basic decision in terms of the kinds of facilities, the kinds of priorities our society places on the social needs of the great majority of people. In so doing, we were saying that it was not enough just to provide decent housing for minority families, because we could only do that when there was enough housing, at rents all people are able to pay, for all people. And in so doing we were challenging the basic financial entrenched interests which had put a priority on the exploitation of minority peoples in order to maintain their own profits in the area of housing. So therefore we are mounting again a political challenge, because it depends on who really exercises power whether in fact we have enough decent quality housing for all people, black and white.

We can take a third illustration in the area of jobs, and thereby see that in addition to fighting the fight that has been fought at Jefferson Bank here in St. Louis against job bias, against the unwillingness to take necessary steps to make sure that there is substantial visibility of minority employees at all levels of a given firm, we found another problem. We found that increasingly what once had been thought progress for the Negro worker was being eroded. The very basis upon which he had begun to enter into the mainstream of our economy, the industrial sector of our economy which had previously provided new openings, a larger pay check for the average worker to take home, was now undergoing vast changes. During World War II and immediately after when Negro workers came North and began to enter into large industrial plants, where they began to be a part of the mainstream of American labor, it looked as though there might really be substantial increase in employment opportunities for Negro workers. But today we are faced with a problem, whereby those very jobs which had provided this entrance for the Negro worker are being wiped out of our economy, where there is indeed a fast-growing shortage of opportunity for the unskilled or even semi-skilled worker, because of automation, new machines, and consolidation. And so in a very real sense then the

Negro finds his economic base being literally wiped out from under him. In order to begin to attack this problem we find that we must not only be concerned about the elimination of job bias, but have to be concerned about the kind of society which would relegate a substantial segment of its population to the slag heap of almost permanent unemployment. And therefore the civil rights movement is concerned not just with the breaking down of job bias, but with the kind of economy, the kind of society which will provide meaningful economic opportunities for all workers. And this means that therefore we are concerned with the whole problem of jobs and job creation, massive education, and training in a society which is placing increasing premium on skill. But this kind of program, this kind of opportunity can only come to fruition when there is in fact a political decision made on the city, state and federal level, that we will make the kind of sacrifice, make the kind of economic allocation which will make this a reality for all workers in our country. And this only comes about when there is the kind of political climate created which is truly responsible to social needs, to the needs not just of Negroes but of all people, black and white. In a very real sense what are being raised as civil rights demands are truly political demands.

The second aspect of which the Negro plays a particular role politically in our society is in terms of where he lives. For we find that the Negro is not only a particularly crucial minority, but that he is a concentrated minority, a minority which lives in the major political and economic centers of our country. Some sociologists have projected that by 1970, if present population trends continue, seven out of the ten largest cities in this country will be majority Negro. So we're talking about a political force, about a force which is concentrated in large, important, political and economic centers in this country, which is therefore crucial in terms of what kinds of decisions are made, who gets into office, who stays in office and on what terms. And it [is] in this sense that civil rights is indeed politics.

There is a great debate going on now in the Senate of the United States over the civil rights bill. But to understand this debate in its real context, to understand the fundamental, under-lying meaning I think we have to go back to the original setting from which the civil rights bill came to be introduced. And we have to see that the late President Kennedy introduced the bill, not so much because it had been part of his political timetable (since he had hoped to accomplish what he had planned to do in the way of civil rights by executive order), but by his own ad-mission because the civil rights movement created a situation in which the problem of the Negro could no longer be swept under the rug. The problem of the Negro had to be accommodated to, had to be dealt with in very real terms. And so the political timetable in Washington was upset, was upset because of Bir-mingham, because of Cambridge, Md., because of Danville, Va., because of Greensboro, N.C. We saw in this context then that a civil rights bill was introduced into this session of the legislature. Not necessarily because all of a sudden there was a welling up of good will but because it became a political necessity, because of the kind of climate that we in the civil rights movement cre-ated by our own actions in the streets.

. . . [W]e are talking about what in fact is a real challenge to politics-as-usual, the politics as we know it in the United States of the last twenty years. And if this is the case in civil rights, how can we mount this challenge effectively? Because whether or not we do, really depends on whether or not the kinds of program-matic problems that are raised in basic areas like housing, jobs and schools, are solved not just for us but for all people, par-ticularly for the poor in our society. Whether or not there is the kind of priority placed on social needs that is really necessary to begin to meet the problems of the great masses of Negroes de-pends on whether or not we break through the political stalemate that we have [arising from the congressional alliance of southern Dixiecrats and northern Republicans]. Therefore it becomes not enough just to elect people who vote right for measures which may have already been compromised or watered down, but who in fact are willing to fight right from the very beginning to see that we get the kinds of social measures that are really designed to meet the needs of our people. This means that we're not just interested in "responsible liberals" who maybe do the work of the administration when called upon to do it. . . . We're talking about the emergence of the kind of political power, the kind of political climate which will create candidates who are responsive and responsible to the needs of the great masses of American people, particularly Negroes. And this kind of climate will only emerge . . . out of the civil rights movement getting deeper and deeper into the community for which it hopes to be responsible, and to the minority people and to all people of good will, who will begin to take a stand for what counts socially and politically in this country.

This will only emerge if we do more than is done in cities like Chicago where for years the people who were the main opponents of such legislation as fair housing were not necessarily whites because they [the whites] could take their cues from the Negroes who were in office in Chicago, who for their own reasons refused to take a stand on fair housing legislation. We saw the ironic spectacle of [such] legislation being introduced in that city not by the six Negro aldermen but by a white alderman. And if this is the kind of candidates that we in the Negro community are going to stand for then we are in serious trouble because our needs will never be met. And it seems to me that we're looking to build the kind of movement that will not stand for this kind of political shenanigans, which will not stand for this kind of compromise, or this kind of hypocrisy, [but] out of which there will emerge people who are responsive to our basic needs, who respond to us because they know that without doing so they will not maintain their own political positions.

. . . [I]t is no longer enough for us to demonstrate [i.e. engage in direct action]. But we must demonstrate . . . to show in fact why we are being held back politically. . . . Therefore it seems that we have a clear task before us: . . . to begin to build the kind of movement which is a basic grass roots movement, which involves all people, black and white in our struggle . . . and [which] says to people that this is your movement; that you need to be a part of it because you will basically determine the kind of climate that we have in this country; that this is your movement because democracy will only be made real if you come in and be a part of it. Therefore we need to talk not about civil rights for the middle class but we need to talk about civil rights for all people regardless of their economic status. We need to talk about a movement which speaks to the everyday needs of our people, which speaks to why they don't have decent housing, why they don't have enough heat, why they don't have plumbing, why they can't get decent jobs at decent pay, why the children have to go to inferior schools and come out not equipped to participate fully in our society. It is when we build this kind of movement that democracy will clearly be on the agenda not just for Negroes but for all people. It is in this context that the struggle for racial and social justice must be waged. It is then and only then that CORE and in fact all civil rights groups will begin to take on real meaning in our society.

Toward political action

58. BAYARD RUSTIN:
"FROM PROTEST TO POLITICS"

By 1964 there was increasing discussion of the use of politics as a vehicle for achieving the goals of the Negro protest movement. In part this was due to the limitations of direct-action techniques when applied to the solution of the problems of the black poor. In part it was due to the dramatic developments in Mississippi, where the voter-registration campaign sponsored by COFO came to a climax with the formation of the MFDP and the challenge at the Democratic Convention in 1964.

One of the early champions of the shift to political activity was Bayard Rustin. Though Rustin had long been a dedicated direct actionist, he had come to believe that the fundamental structural problems facing the black slum dwellers required a political solution. In contrast to those who, particularly in SNCC, advocated independent all-black political parties, Rustin believed that, given the Negro's minority position in American society, the only viable strategy was to engage in coalition politics. Specifically he urged a coalition of Negro rights organizations with organized labor, middle-class white liberals, and the increasing numbers of sympathetic elements in the white churches.

I

The decade spanned by the 1954 Supreme Court decision on school desegregation and the Civil Rights Act of 1964 will un-

Bayard Rustin, "From Protest to Politics: The Future of the Civil Rights Movement," COMMENTARY, XXXIX, 2 (February 1965), 25–31. Reprinted with permission of Bayard Rustin.

doubtedly be recorded as the period in which the legal foundations of racism in America were destroyed. To be sure, pockets
of resistance remain; but it would be hard to quarrel with the
assertion that the elaborate legal structure of segregation and
discrimination, particularly in relation to public accommodations, has virtually collapsed. On the other hand, without making
light of the human sacrifices involved in the direct-action tactics
(sit-ins, freedom rides, and the rest) that were so instrumental
to this achievement, we must recognize that in desegregating
public accommodations, we affected institutions which are relatively peripheral both to the American socio-economic order and
to the fundamental conditions of life of the Negro people. In a
highly industrialized, 20th-century civilization, we hit Jim Crow
precisely where it was most anachronistic, dispensable, and vulnerable—in hotels, lunch counters, terminals, libraries, swimming pools, and the like. For in these forms, Jim Crow does
impede the flow of commerce in the broadest sense: it is a nui-
sance in a society on the move (and on the make). Not surprisingly, therefore, it was the most mobility-conscious and
relatively liberated groups in the Negro community—lower-
middle-class college students—who launched the attack that
brought down this imposing but hollow structure.

The term "classical" appears especially apt for this phase of
the civil rights movement. But in the few years that have passed
since the first flush of sit-ins, several developments have taken
place that have complicated matters enormously. One is the
shifting focus of the movement in the South, symbolized by
Birmingham; another is the spread of the revolution to the
North; and the third, common to the other two, is the expansion
of the movement's base in the Negro community. To attempt to
disentangle these three strands is to do violence to reality. David
Danzig's perceptive article, "The Meaning of Negro Strategy."[1]
correctly saw in the Birmingham events the victory of the concept of collective struggle over individual achievement as the
road to Negro freedom. And Birmingham remains the un-
matched symbol of grass-roots protest involving all strata of the

[1] *Commentary*, February 1964.

black community. It was also in this most industrialized of Southern cities that the single-issue demands of the movement's classical stage gave way to the "package deal." No longer were Negroes satisfied with integrating lunch counters. They now sought advances in employment, housing, school integration, police protection, and so forth.

Thus, the movement in the South began to attack areas of discrimination which were not so remote from the Northern experience as were Jim Crow lunch counters. At the same time, the interrelationship of these apparently distinct areas became increasingly evident. What is the value of winning access to public accommodations for those who lack money to use them? The minute the movement faced this question, it was compelled to expand its vision beyond race relations to economic relations, including the role of education in modern society. And what also became clear is that all these interrelated problems, by their very nature, are not soluble by private, voluntary efforts but require government action—or politics. Already Southern demonstrators had recognized that the most effective way to strike at the police brutality they suffered from was by getting rid of the local sheriff —and that meant political action, which in turn meant, and still means, political action within the Democratic party where the only meaningful primary contests in the South are fought.

And so, in Mississippi, thanks largely to the leadership of Bob Moses, a turn toward political action has been taken. More than voter registration is involved there. A conscious bid for *political power* is being made, and in the course of that effort a tactical shift is being effected: direct-action techniques are being subordinated to a strategy calling for the building of community institutions or power bases. Clearly, the implications of this shift reach far beyond Mississippi. What began as a protest movement is being challenged to translate itself into a political movement. Is this the right course? And if it is, can the transformation be accomplished?

II

The very decade which has witnessed the decline of legal Jim Crow has also seen the rise of *de facto* segregation in our most

fundamental socio-economic institutions. More Negroes are unemployed today than in 1954, and the unemployment gap between the races is wider. The median income of Negroes has
dropped from 57 per cent to 54 per cent of that of whites. A
higher percentage of Negro workers is now concentrated in jobs
vulnerable to automation than was the case ten years ago. More
Negro attend *de facto* segregated schools today than when the
Supreme Court handed down its famous decision; while school
integration proceeds at a snail's pace in the South, the number
of Northern schools with an excessive proportion of minority
youth proliferates. And behind this is the continuing growth of
racial slums, spreading over our central cities and trapping Negro youth in a milieu which, whatever its legal definition, sows
an unimaginable demoralization. Again, legal niceties aside, a
resident of a racial ghetto lives in segregated housing, and more
Negroes fall into this category than ever before.

These are the facts of life which generate frustration in the
Negro community and challenge the civil rights movement. At
issue, after all, is not *civil rights,* strictly speaking, but social and
economic conditions. Last summer's riots were not race riots;
they were outbursts of class aggression in a society where
class and color definitions are converging disastrously. How can
the (perhaps misnamed) civil rights movement deal with this
problem?

Before trying to answer, let me first insist that the task of the
movement is vastly complicated by the failure of many whites of
good will to understand the nature of our problem. There is a
widespread assumption that the removal of artificial racial barriers should result in the automatic integration of the Negro into
all aspects of American life. This myth is fostered by facile analogies with the experience of various ethnic immigrant groups,
particularly the Jews. But the analogies with the Jews do not
hold for three simple but profound reasons. First, Jews have a
long history as a literate people, a resource which has afforded
them opportunities to advance in the academic and professional
worlds, to achieve intellectual status even in the midst of economic hardship, and to evolve sustaining value systems in the
context of ghetto life. Negroes, for the greater part of their pres-

ence in this country, were forbidden by law to read or write. Second, Jews have a long history of family stability, the importance of which in terms of aspiration and self-image is obvious. The Negro family structure was totally destroyed by slavery and with it the possibility of cultural transmission (the right of Negroes to marry and bear children is barely a century old). Third, Jews are white and have the *option* of relinquishing their cultural-religious identity, intermarrying, passing, etc. Negroes, or at least the overwhelming majority of them, do not have this option. There is also a fourth, vulgar reason. If the Jewish and Negro communities are not comparable in terms of education, family structure, and color, it is also true that their respective economic roles bear little resemblance.

This matter of economic role brings us to the greater problem —the fact that we are moving into an era in which the natural functioning of the market does not by itself ensure every man with will and ambition a place in the productive process. The immigrant who came to this country during the late 19th and 20th centuries entered a society which was expanding territorially and/or economically. It was then possible to start at the bottom, as an unskilled or semi-skilled worker, and move up the ladder, acquiring news skills along the way. Especially was this true when industrial unionism was burgeoning, giving new dignity and higher wages to organized workers. Today the situation has changed. We are not expanding territorially, the western frontier is settled, labor organizing has leveled off, our rate of economic growth has been stagnant for a decade. And we are in the midst of a technological revolution which is altering the fundamental structure of the labor force, destroying unskilled and semi-skilled jobs—jobs in which Negroes are disproportionately concentrated.

Whatever the pace of this technological revolution may be, the *direction* is clear: the lower rungs of the economic ladder are being lopped off. This means that an individual will no longer be able to start at the bottom and work his way up; he will have to start in the middle or on top, and hold on tight. It will not even be enough to have certain specific skills, for many skilled jobs are also vulnerable to automation. A broad educational background, permitting vocational adaptability and flexibility, seems more imperative than ever. We live in a society where, as Secretary of Labor Willard Wirtz puts it, machines have the equivalent of a high school diploma. Yet the average educational attainment of American Negroes is 8.2 years.

Negroes, of course, are not the only people being affected by these developments. It is reported that there are now 50 per cent fewer unskilled and semi-skilled jobs than there are high school dropouts. Almost one-third of the 26 million young people entering the labor market in the 1960's will be dropouts. But the percentage of Negro dropouts nationally is 57 per cent, and in New York City, among Negroes 25 years of age or over, it is 68 per cent. They are without a future.

To what extent can the kind of self-help campaign recently prescribed by Eric Hoffer in the *New York Times Magazine* cope with such a situation? I would advise those who think that self-help is the answer to familiarize themselves with the long history of such efforts in the Negro community, and to consider why so many foundered on the shoals of ghetto life. It goes without saying that any effort to combat demoralization and apathy is desirable, but we must understand that demoralization in the Negro community is largely a common-sense response to an objective reality. Negro youths have no need of statistics to perceive, fairly accurately, what their odds are in American society. Indeed, from the point of view of motivation, some of the healthiest Negro youngsters I know are juvenile delinquents: vigorously pursuing the American Dream of material acquisition and status, yet finding the conventional means of attaining it blocked off, they do not yield to defeatism but resort to illegal (and often ingenious) methods. They are not alien to American culture. They are, in Gunnar Myrdal's phrase, "exaggerated Americans." To want a Cadillac is not unAmerican; to push a cart in the garment center is. If Negroes are to be persuaded that the conventional path (school work, etc.) is superior, we had better provide evidence which is now sorely lacking. It is a double cruelty to harangue Negro youth about education and training when we do not know what jobs will be available for them. When a Negro youth can reasonably foresee a future free of slums, when the prospect of gainful employment is realistic, we will see motivation and self-help in abundant enough quantities.

Meanwhile, there is an ironic similarity between the self-help advocated by many liberals and the doctrines of the Black Muslims. Professional sociologists, psychiatrists, and social workers have expressed amazement at the Muslims' success in transforming prostitutes and dope addicts into respectable citizens. But every prostitute the Muslims convert to a model of Calvinist virtue is replaced by the ghetto with two more. Dedicated as they are to maintenance of the ghetto, the Muslims are powerless to affect substantial moral reform. So too with every other group or program which is not aimed at the destruction of slums, their causes and effects. Self-help efforts, directly or indirectly, must be geared to mobilizing people into power units capable of effecting social change. That is, their goal must be genuine self-help, not merely self-improvement. Obviously, where self-improvement activities succeed in imparting to their participants a feeling of some control over their environment, those involved may find their appetites for change whetted; they may move into the political arena.

III

Let me sum up what I have thus far been trying to say: the civil rights movement is evolving from a protest movement into a full-fledged *social movement*—an evolution calling its very name into question. It is now concerned not merely with removing the barriers to full *opportunity* but with achieving the fact of *equality*. From sit-ins and freedom rides we have gone into rent strikes, boycotts, community organization, and political action. As a consequence of this natural evolution, the Negro today finds himself stymied by obstacles of far greater magnitude than the legal barriers he was attacking before: automation, urban decay, *de facto* school segregation. These are problems which, while conditioned by Jim Crow, do not vanish upon its demise. They are more deeply rooted in our socio-economic order; they are the result of the total society's failure to meet not only the Negro's needs, but human needs generally.

These propositions have won increasing recognition and acceptance, but with a curious twist. They have formed the common premise of two apparently contradictory lines of thought which simultaneously nourish and antagonize each other. On the one hand, there is the reasoning of the New York *Times* moderate who says that the problems are so enormous and complicated that Negro militancy is a futile irritation, and that the need is for "intelligent moderation." Thus, during the first New York school boycott, the *Times* editorialized that Negro demands, while abstractly just, would necessitate massive reforms, the funds for which could not realistically be anticipated, therefore the just demands were also foolish demands and would only antagonize white people. Moderates of this stripe are often correct in perceiving the difficulty or impossibility of racial progress in the context of present social and economic policies. But they accept the context as fixed. They ignore (or perhaps see all too well) the potentialities inherent in linking Negro demands to broader pressures for radical revision of existing policies. They apparently see nothing strange in the fact that in the last twenty-five years we have spent nearly a trillion dollars fighting or preparing for wars, yet throw up their hands before the need for overhauling our schools, clearing the slums, and really abolishing poverty. My quarrel with these moderates is that they do not even envision radical changes; their admonitions of moderation are, for all practical purposes, admonitions to the Negro to adjust to the status quo, and are therefore immoral.

The more effectively the moderates argue their case, the more they convince Negroes that American society will not or cannot be reorganized for full racial equality. Michael Harrington has said that a successful war on poverty might well require the expenditure of a $100 billion. Where, the Negro wonders, are the forces now in motion to compel such a commitment? If the voices of the moderates were raised in an insistence upon a reallocation of national resources at levels that could not be confused with tokenism (that is, if the moderates stopped being moderates), Negroes would have greater grounds for hope.

Meanwhile, the Negro movement cannot escape a sense of isolation.

It is precisely this sense of isolation that gives rise to the second line of thought I want to examine—the tendency within the civil rights movement which, despite its militancy, pursues what I call a "no-win" policy. Sharing with many moderates a recognition of the magnitude of the obstacles to freedom, spokesmen for this tendency survey the American scene and find no forces prepared to move toward radical solutions. From this they conclude that the only viable strategy is shock; above all, the hypocrisy of white liberals must be exposed. These spokesmen are often described as the radicals of the movement, but they are really its moralists. They seek to change white hearts—by traumatizing them. Frequently abetted by white self-flagellants, they may gleefully applaud (though not really agreeing with) Malcolm X because, while they admit he has no program, they think he can frighten white people into doing the right thing. To believe this, of course, you must be convinced, even if unconsciously, that at the core of the white man's heart lies a buried affection for Negroes—a proposition one may be permitted to doubt. But in any case, hearts are not relevant to the issue; neither racial affinities nor racial hostilities are rooted there. It is institutions—social, political, and economic institutions—which are the ultimate molders of collective sentiments. Let these institutions be reconstructed *today*, and let the ineluctable gradualism of history govern the formation of a new psychology.

My quarrel with the "no-win" tendency in the civil rights movement (and the reason I have so designated it) parallels my quarrel with the moderates outside the movement. As the latter lack the vision or will for fundamental change, the former lack a realistic strategy for achieving it. For such a strategy they substitute militancy. But militancy is a matter of posture and volume and not of effect.

I believe that the Negro's struggle for equality in America is essentially revolutionary. While most Negroes—in their hearts

—unquestionably seek only to enjoy the fruits of American society as it now exists, their quest cannot *objectively* be satisfied within the framework of existing political and economic relations. The young Negro who would demonstrate his way into the labor market may be motivated by a thoroughly bourgeois ambition and thoroughly "capitalist" considerations, but he will end up having to favor a great expansion of the public sector of the economy. At any rate, that is the position the movement will be forced to take as it looks at the number of jobs being generated by the private economy, and if it is to remain true to the masses of Negroes.

The revolutionary character of the Negro's struggle is manifest in the fact that this struggle may have done more to democratize life for whites than for Negroes. Clearly, it was the sit-in movement of young Southern Negroes which, as it galvanized white students, banished the ugliest features of McCarthyism from the American campus and resurrected political debate. It was not until Negroes assaulted *de facto* school segregation in the urban centers that the issue of quality education for *all* children stirred into motion. Finally, it seems reasonably clear that the civil rights movement, directly and through the resurgence of social conscience it kindled, did more to initiate the war on poverty than any other single force.

It will be—it has been—argued that these by-products of the Negro struggle are not revolutionary. But the term revolutionary, as I am using it, does not connote violence; it refers to the qualitative transformation of fundamental institutions, more or less rapidly, to the point where the social and economic structure which they comprised can no longer be said to be the same. The Negro struggle has hardly run its course; and it will not stop moving until it has been utterly defeated or won substantial equality. But I fail to see how the movement can be victorious in the absence of radical programs for full employment, abolition of slums, the reconstruction of our educational system, new definitions of work and leisure. Adding up the cost of such programs, we can only conclude that we are talking about a refashioning of our political economy. It has been estimated, for example, that the price of replacing New York City's slums with public housing would be $17 billion. Again, a multi-billion dollar federal public-works program, dwarfing the currently proposed $2 billion program, is required to reabsorb unskilled and semi-skilled workers into the labor market—and this must be done if Negro workers in these categories are to be employed. "Preferential treatment" cannot help them.

I am not trying here to delineate a total program, only to suggest the scope of economic reforms which are most immediately related to the plight of the Negro community. One could speculate on their political implications—whether for example, they do not indicate the obsolescence of state government and the superiority of regional structures as viable units of planning. Such speculations aside, it is clear that Negro needs cannot be satisfied unless we go beyond what has so far been placed on the agenda. How are these radical objectives to be achieved? The answer is simple, deceptively so: *through political power.*

There is a strong moralistic strain in the civil rights movement which would remind us that power corrupts, forgetting that the absence of power also corrupts. But this is not the view I want to debate here, for it is waning. Our problem is posed by those who accept the need for political power but do not understand the nature of the object and therefore lack sound strategies for achieving it; they tend to confuse political institutions with lunch counters.

A handful of Negroes, acting alone, could integrate a lunch counter by strategically locating their bodies so as *directly* to interrupt the operation of the proprietor's will; their numbers were relatively unimportant. In politics, however, such a confrontation is difficult because the interests involved are merely *represented.* In the execution of a political decision a direct confrontation may ensue (as when federal marshals escorted James Meredith into the University of Mississippi—to turn from an example of non-violent coercion to one of force backed up with the threat of violence). But in arriving at a political decision, numbers and organizations are crucial, especially for the economically disenfranchised. (Needless to say, I am assuming that the forms of political democracy exist in America, however imperfectly, that they are valued, and that elitist or putschist conceptions of exercising power are beyond the pale of discussion for the civil rights movement.)

Neither that movement nor the country's twenty million black people can win political power alone. We need allies. The future of the Negro struggle depends on whether the contradictions of this society can be resolved by a coalition of progressive forces which becomes the *effective* political majority in the United States. I speak of the coalition which staged the March on Washington, passed the Civil Rights Act, and laid the basis for the Johnson landslide—Negroes, trade unionists, liberals, and religious groups.

There are those who argue that a coalition strategy would force the Negro to surrender his political independence to white liberals, that he would be neutralized, deprived of his cutting edge, absorbed into the Establishment. Some who take this position urged last year that votes be withheld from the Johnson-Humphrey ticket as a demonstration of the Negro's political power. Curiously enough, these people who sought to demonstrate power through the non-exercise of it, also point to the Negro "swing vote" in crucial urban areas as the source of the Negro's independent political power. But here they are closer to being right: the urban Negro vote will grow in importance in the coming years. If there is anything positive in the spread of the ghetto, it is the potential political power base thus created, and to realize this potential is one of the most challenging and urgent tasks before the civil rights movement. If the movement can wrest leadership of the ghetto vote from the machines, it will have acquired an organized constituency such as other major groups in our society now have.

But we must also remember that the effectiveness of a swing vote depends solely on "other" votes. It derives its power from them. In that sense, it can never be "independent," but must opt for one candidate or the other, even if by default. Thus coalitions are inescapable, however tentative they may be. And this is the case in all but those few situations in which Negroes running on an independent ticket might conceivably win. "Independence," in other words, is not a value in itself. The issue is which coalition to join and how to make it responsive to your program. Necessarily there will be compromise. But the difference between expediency and morality in politics is the difference between selling out a principle and making smaller concessions to win larger ones. The leader who shrinks from this task reveals not his purity but his lack of political sense.

The task of molding a political movement out of the March on Washington coalition is not simple, but no alternatives have been advanced. We need to choose our allies on the basis of common political objectives. It has become fashionable in some no-win Negro circles to decry the white liberal as the main enemy (his hypocrisy is what sustains racism); by virtue of this reverse recitation of the reactionary's litany (liberalism leads to socialism, which leads to Communism) the Negro is left in majestic isolation, except for a tiny band of fervent white initiates. But the objective fact is that *Eastland and Goldwater* are the main enemies—they and the opponents of civil rights, of the war on poverty, of medicare, of social security, of federal aid to education, of unions, and so forth. The labor movement, despite its obvious faults, has been the largest single organized force in this country pushing for progressive social legislation. And where the Negro-labor-liberal axis is weak, as in the farm belt, it was the religious groups that were most influential in rallying support for the Civil Rights Bill.

The durability of the coalition was interestingly tested during the election. I do not believe that the Johnson landslide proved the "white backlash" to be a myth. It proved, rather, that economic interests are more fundamental than prejudice: the backlashers decided that loss of social security was, after all, too high a price to pay for a slap at the Negro. This lesson was a valuable first step in re-educating such people, and it must be kept alive, for the civil rights movement will be advanced only to the degree that social and economic welfare gets to be inextricably entangled with civil rights.

The 1964 elections marked a turning point in American politics. The Democratic landslide was not merely the result of a negative reaction to Goldwaterism; it was also the expression of a majority liberal consensus. The near unanimity with which Negro voters joined in that expression was, I am convinced, a vindication of the July 25th statement by Negro leaders calling for a strategic turn toward political action and a temporary curtailment of mass demonstrations. Despite the controversy surrounding the statement, the instinctive response if met with in the community is suggested by the fact that demonstrations were down 75 per cent as compared with the same period in 1963. But should so high a percentage of Negro voters have gone to Johnson, or should they have held back to narrow his margin of victory and thus give greater visibility to our swing vote? How has our loyalty changed things? Certainly the Negro vote had higher visibility in 1960, when a switch of only 7 per cent from the Republican column of 1956 elected President Kennedy. But the slimness of Kennedy's victory—of his "mandate" —dictated a go-slow approach on civil rights, at least until the Birmingham upheaval.

Although Johnson's popular majority was so large that he could have won without such overwhelming Negro support, that support was important from several angles. Beyond adding to Johnson's total national margin, it was specifically responsible for his victories in Virginia, Florida, Tennessee, and Arkansas. Goldwater took only those states where fewer than 45 per cent of eligible Negroes were registered. That Johnson would have won those states had Negro voting rights been enforced is a lesson not likely to be lost on a man who would have been happy with a unanimous electoral college. In any case, the 1.6 million Southern Negroes who voted have had a shattering impact on the Southern political party structure, as illustrated in the changed composition of the Southern congressional delegation. The "backlash" gave the Republicans five House seats in Alabama, one in Georgia, and one in Mississippi. But on the Democratic side, seven segregationists were defeated while all nine Southerners who voted for the Civil Rights Act were re-elected.

It may be premature to predict a Southern Democratic party of Negroes and white moderates and a Republican Party of refugee racists and economic conservatives, but there certainly is a strong tendency toward such a realignment; and an additional 3.6 million Negroes of voting age in the eleven Southern states are still to be heard from. Even the *tendency* toward disintegration of the Democratic party's racist wing defines a new context for Presidential and liberal strategy in the congressional battles ahead. Thus the Negro vote (North as well as South), while not *decisive* in the Presidential race, was enormously effective. It was a dramatic element of a historic mandate which contains vast possibilities and dangers that will fundamentally affect the future course of the civil rights movement.

The liberal congressional sweep raises hope for an assault on the seniority system, Rule Twenty-two, and other citadels of Dixiecrat-Republican power. The overwhelming of this conservative coalition should also mean progress on much bottlenecked legislation of profound interest to the movement (e.g., bills by Senators Clark and Nelson on planning, manpower, and employment). Moreover, the irrelevance of the South to Johnson's victory gives the President more freedom to act than his predecessors had and more leverage to the movement to pressure for executive action in Mississippi and other racist strongholds.

None of this *guarantees* vigorous executive or legislative action, for the other side of the Johnson landslide is that it has a Gaullist quality. Goldwater's capture of the Republican party forced into the Democratic camp many disparate elements which do not belong there. Big Business being the major example. Johnson, who wants to be President "of all people," may try to keep his new coalition together by sticking close to the political center. But if he decides to do this, it is unlikely that even his political genius will be able to hold together a coalition so inherently unstable and rife with contradictions. It must come apart. Should it do so while Johnson is pursuing a centrist course, then the mandate will have been wastefully dissipated. However, if the mandate is seized upon to set fundamental changes in motion, then the basis can be laid for a new mandate, a new coalition including hitherto inert and dispossessed strata of the population.

Here is where the cutting edge of the civil rights movement can be applied. We must see to it that the reorganization of the "consensus party" proceeds along lines which will make it an effective vehicle for social reconstruction, a role it cannot play so long as it furnishes Southern racism with its national political power. (One of Barry Goldwater's few attractive ideas was that the Dixiecrats belong with him in the same party.) And nowhere has the civil rights movement's political cutting edge been more magnificently demonstrated than at Atlantic City, where the Mississippi Freedom Democratic Party not only secured recognition as a bona fide component of the national party, but in the process routed the representatives of the most rabid racists —the white Mississippi and Alabama delegations. While I still believe that the FDP made a tactical error in spurning the compromise, there is no question that they launched a political revolution whose logic is the displacement of Dixiecrat power. They launched that revolution within a major political institution and as part of a coalitional effort.

The role of the civil rights movement in the reorganization of American political life is programmatic as well as strategic. We are challenged now to broaden our social vision, to develop functional programs with concrete objectives. We need to propose alternatives to technological unemployment, urban decay, and the rest. We need to be calling for public works and training, for national economic planning, for federal aid to education, for attractive public housing—all this on a sufficiently massive scale to make a difference. We need to protest the notion that our integration into American life, so long delayed, must now proceed in an atmosphere of competitive scarcity instead of in the security of abundance which technology makes possible. We cannot claim to have answers to all the complex problems of modern society. That is too much to ask of a movement still battling barbarism in Mississippi. But we can agitate the right questions by probing at the contradictions which still stand in the way of the "Great Society." The questions having been asked, motion must begin in the larger society, for there is a limit to what Negroes can do alone.

59. JAMES FARMER:
"WE MUST BE IN A POSITION OF POWER"

While some, like Bayard Rustin, emphasized the strategy of coalition politics, others, equally concerned with the economic and social problems of the Black Ghetto but disillusioned with the tactics of both organized labor and the political establishment, came to advocate what they described as "independent" political action. In 1964 SNCC paved the way for this strategy when it inspired the formation of the Mississippi Freedom Democratic party.

Subsequently, the thrust for independent political action spread to the North. Here, civil rights organizations were finding direct-action demonstrations against *de facto* segregated schools, poor housing, unemployment, and police brutality relatively ineffective, in large part because of the entrenched position of white-dominated Democratic political machines in Negro slums. In a few northern cities, the tactic of independent political action had been articulated in an extreme form as early as 1963, by a fringe group known as the Freedom Now party. In 1965 CORE rescinded its constitutional prohibition on partisan political action and, like SNCC, prepared to mobilize the political potential of the Black Ghetto.

As CORE meets at its 23rd Annual Convention, we have behind us many successes achieved and victories won. But this report will not be a recounting of past successes, to rest on one's laurels is to atrophy and die. Past victories—in public accommo-

Annual Report to the CORE National Convention, Durham, N.C., July 1, 1965. Printed with permission of James Farmer.

dations, in voting rights, in the support of law and public policy —have been in battles preceding the major encounter.

The major war now confronting us is aimed at harnessing the awesome political potential of the black community in order to effect basic social and economic changes for all Americans, to alter meaningfully the lives of the Black Americans (our plight has not been and will not be changed by past victories), and to bring about a real equality of free men.

This job cannot be done for us by the Government. In the first place, the establishments—Federal, State, and Local— have too much built-in resistance to fundamental change. Any establishment by definition seeks its own perpetuation and rejects that which threatens it. For example, politicians take over and seek to make the anti-poverty programs an adjunct of their political aspirations. They attack community action programs of the anti-poverty war as being anti-city hall. School Boards, which have already lost the drop-outs and other under-privileged youth, reach out greedily to control community education programs and see that they do not shake up the school systems. Powerful lobbies, such as the financial and the real estate interests, exert tremendous pressure to see that programs to relieve poverty do not threaten their interests.

Further, it is impossible for the Government to mount a decisive war against poverty and bigotry in the United States while it is pouring billions down the drain in a war against people in Viet Nam. The billion dollars available to fight poverty is puny compared with the need and insignificant compared with the resources expended in wars.

Thus, we must be constructive critics of the anti-poverty program, using its resources for our fight where we can, insisting that local anti-poverty boards be truly representatives of the deprived communities and the minorities which they are supposed to help, and attacking waste and pork-barreling wherever it occurs.

Yet it would be fatal to think that the anti-poverty program alone can make the necessary changes in the social and economic life of Black Americans. It can be no more a solution to our problems than the Civil Rights Acts of 1957, 1960, 1964 were, or the Voter Rights Act of 1965 will be. Like those laws, the anti-poverty program has to be seen as no more than a tool, useful at times but inadequate at best to do the job.

We can rely upon none but ourselves as a catalyst in the development of the potential power of the black community in its own behalf and in behalf of the nation. CORE alone has the nationwide network of militant chapters required, unshackled by compromising entanglements, political commitments and alliances. CORE alone has the flexibility to move in the new directions demanded by this phase of the war, while it fulfills its commitments to the unfinished tasks of the last phase.

In this new phase of our war to change the life of the Negro in a changed America, there are two aspects: Community organization and Political organization. It must be clearly seen that neither aspect is an end in itself. Community organization, including social services, for its own sake is mere social uplift and has no basic importance in changing the life role of the Negro. Political organization for its own sake is sheer opportunism. While both aspects must be undertaken simultaneously, the first, community organization, may be seen as a step to increase the effectiveness of the second, political organization. Or another way of viewing it, is to see community organization as a tool—a tool to build a vehicle. Political organization, then, is the vehicle to take us to the desired objective. That objective is an open society free of race discrimination and forced segregation, shorn of poverty and unemployment, with decent housing and high-quality education for all. The objective, in a word, is a new society, a free and open society.

Community organizations

The term, community organization, has become almost a cliché. The need now is to put content into that cliché. For two years, community organization has been widely discussed within CORE. For many, the discussion of it has been a substitute for taking concrete steps to achieve it. Many CORE

Chapters, however, have moved their offices into the heart of the black ghetto and have made a serious attempt at ghetto involvement and community organization. If we are honest we will admit that most have failed, though a few have had small successes at organizing their community. Thus the impact of some of our chapters has dwindled.

So now, here we stand, faltering for a necessary transition. If the need for community organization has been great in the past, it is now, I believe, desperate. It is now or never. CORE's survival as a viable and relevant organization depends upon it. . . .

Before a community can be organized in a way that is meaningful to the community, we must engage in a dialogue with that community. The indigenous people of a community know their hurts, their needs and their problems far better than we. We must encourage the community to speak, for it has much to say. And we must be prepared to listen. Yet we must not be afraid to talk to the community, for we, too, have something of importance to say growing out of our experience in the movement. The decisions, however, must rest with the people of a community or a neighborhood, for it is their lives to be fulfilled, their dreams to be realized. . . .

Political organization and action

It is clear that the objectives we seek—in the wiping out of poverty and unemployment, elimination of bad housing, city planning for integration in housing and schools, quality education—are political objectives depending upon responses we can exact from political machinery. We can no longer rely on pressuring and cajoling political units toward desired actions. We must be in a position of power, a position to change those political units when they are not responsive.

The only way to achieve political objectives is through power, political power. Only diminishing returns can be achieved through the pressure of demonstrations not backed up by political muscle.

We have won amazing successes without political muscle.

The New York City CORE chapters came out against Wagner, and the National Director backed them up, and we toppled a Police Commissioner and a Mayor. Now, everyone is a candidate for Mayor and bidding for CORE support. This does not indicate strength. It merely shows what CORE can accomplish in spite of weakness, and thus how much more could be done if we had the political power which can derive from community organization and political organization. . . .

As we organize the community through directed centers, so we must seek to organize the community politically—or, more accurately, to *reorganize* it politically. For the bosses and the machines have already organized it after a fashion with their ward heelers and their petty precinct captains. The greatest tragedy of all would be for the existing black vote to remain in, and the new black vote to be dumped into the general political soup now brewed by the machine bosses—black or white.

What is needed, I believe, is independent political action through indigenous political organizations. This is the Freedom Democratic Party in Mississippi and CORE is supporting it fully, including its challenge. After the Summer CORE Project in Louisiana, if activated communities articulate the desire we will help them organize a Louisiana Freedom Democratic Party.

In the North, independent political voices are needed too. When the black ghetto communities with which CORE chapters have dialogued articulate the desire, we must take the lead in helping them develop Freedom Democratic Movements to serve as a political voice for their awakening self-expression.

Only through such independent action can the growing black vote achieve maximum effectiveness in moving toward the goals we seek. Freedom Democratic Movements must not be racist and should not exclude whites. But their base must be in the black ghetto, else they will be merely another exercise in liberal futility!

We must be prepared to put up candidates for nomination, when necessary, through such political vehicles, and to endorse or oppose candidates for election. A few of our chapters, Brooklyn, for example, are already doing this. Brooklyn CORE took the initiative in helping people in the Bedford-Stuyvesant ghetto in setting up the Brooklyn Freedom Democratic Movement. The CORE Chairman, Major Owens, is a candidate for nomination to the City Council under the BFDM banner (with the backing of the national organization)—challenging an incumbent machine politician. And Owens has a fighting chance to win the nomination [in the Democratic Primary].

This is, of course, a new departure in CORE policy. But the old policy is no longer applicable to the needs of the movement. We may as well admit that the old policy is dead, and move boldly on with the new.

Such ghetto-oriented political movements must avoid, at all costs, becoming an adjunct to, or a tool of, any political party, bloc, or machine. They must be controlled by the interests of the black ghetto alone. They must be in a position to make alliances when called for, and break them when necessary. There should be no binding Grand Alliances where the black ghetto becomes a tail to some other kite, or a dancer to some other political fiddler's tune!

Now, it will be a disservice to the ghetto community if we seek to be its manipulators, to substitute CORE as the boss of a political machine which will, in the very nature of the case, become corrupt and oppressive, as boss-ridden machines always are. CORE bossism may be *benevolent* despotism, but it would be despotism nonetheless, and essentially no different from any other.

What is called for, instead, is *dialogue* and *interaction* between CORE and the community to determine goals. We must listen to them, and have the machinery for doing so, and hope that they will listen to us. But the community must be the boss, not we! . . . And through the ghetto's emerging voice we must speak to the nation—and to the world.

Such new directions are developing in the South and being groped for in the North. In North and South, now, we must get moving with no further delay if the civil rights revolution is to succeed in this enormously difficult and highly complex new phase into which our past successes have thrust us.

In the North our chapters must make quick transitions from the old phase to the new if we are to remain relevant to the needs of the struggle. In the South, except for Klanism and massive police violence, our problems are not vastly different from the North. The South is becoming, and will become, increasingly like the North with *de facto* segregation substituted for *de jure* with the black man confined to a status of built in low-man on the economic, social and political totem pole—able to eat a hamburger, but not to have a rewarding life.

Our direction in the South, therefore, is essentially the same as it should be in the North. And in the South, CORE is doing community organization on a significant scale. In Bogalusa, for example, we do not attempt to be the leaders of the black community. CORE staff members interact with the Bogalusa Voters League, build up its leaders and have their expression through the indigenous voice of the community. It is A. Z. Young and Robert Hicks who speak for Bogalusa, and we are their consultants and advisors. . . .

This convention, then, has one over-riding purpose: to re-tool our organization to meet the changed requirements of the new phase of the war. Any organization which cannot do it does not deserve to survive. We *can* do it. *CORE, the cutting edge of the old battles, will now become the sword's point of the new thrust!*

the
era
of
Black Power

PART FOUR

The varieties of Black Power

60. JULIUS LESTER:
"THE ANGRY CHILDREN OF MALCOLM X"

"The Angry Children of Malcolm X," by Julius Lester, a former
SNCC field secretary, and author of *Look Out Whitey! Black Power's
Gon' Get Your Mama!,** is a moving, personal document capturing
the mood of frustration and disillusionment that characterized many
of the militant activists by 1966. It also illustrates the extent to which
the young black nationalists were indebted to Malcolm X, a sacred
symbol who functioned as a source of both inspiration and ideology.

> This is their message: The days of sing-
> ing freedom songs and the days of com-
> batting bullets and billy clubs with love
> are over. "We Shall Overcome" sounds
> old, out-dated. "Man, the people are too
> busy getting ready to fight to bother
> with singing any more!"

The world of the black American is different from that of the
white American. This difference comes not only from the segregation imposed on the Black, but it also comes from the way
of life he has evolved for himself under these conditions. Yet,

Julius Lester, "The Angry Children of Malcolm X," KEY LIST MAILING:
SELECTED DOCUMENTS OF CURRENT AND LASTING INTEREST IN
THE CIVIL RIGHTS MOVEMENT (San Francisco Regional Office of SNCC,
December 11, 1966).
* New York: Dial Press, 1968.

America has always been uneasy with this separate world in its midst. Feeling most comfortable when the black man emulates the ways and manners of white Americans, America has, at the same time, been stolidly unwilling to let the black man be assimilated into the mainstream.

With its goal of assimilation on the basis of equality, the civil rights movement was once the great hope of black men and liberal whites. In 1960 and 1961 Negroes felt that if only Americans knew the wrongs and sufferings they had to endure, these wrongs would be righted and all would be well. If Americans saw well-dressed, well-mannered, clean Negroes on their television screen not retaliating to being beaten by white Southerners, they would not sit back and do nothing. *Amor vincit omnia!* and the Reverend Dr. Martin Luther King, Jr., was the knight going forth to prove to the father that he was worthy of becoming a member of the family. But there was something wrong with this attitude and young Negroes began to feel uneasy. Was this not another form of the bowing and scraping their grandparents had had to do to get what they wanted? Were they not acting once again as the white man wanted them to? And why should they have to be brutalized, physically and spiritually, for what every other American had at birth? But these were only timid questions in the mind for which no answer was waited. You simply put your body in the struggle and that meant entering the church in Albany, Danville, Birmingham, Greenwood, Nashville, or wherever you were, entering the church and listening to prayers, short sermons on your courage and the cause you were fighting, singing freedom songs—Ain't Gon' Let Nobody Turn Me Round and you would name names, the sheriff's, the Mayor's, the Governor's and whoever else you held responsible for the conditions and—always at the end—We Shall Overcome with arms crossed, holding hands of the person next to you and swaying gently from side to side, We Shall Overcome Someday someday but not today because you knew as you walked out of the church, two abreast, and started marching toward town that no matter how many times you sang about not letting any-

body turn you around red-necks and po' white trash from
four conties and some from across the state line were waiting
with guns, tire chaines, baseball bats, rocks, sticks, clubs and
bottles, waiting as you turned the corner singing about This
Little Light of Mine and how you were going to let it shine as
that cop's billy club went upside your head shine shine shining
as you fell to the pavement with someone's foot into your back
until a cop dragged you away, threw you into the paddy wagon
and off to the jail you and the others went, singing I Ain't
Scared of Your Jail 'Cause I Want My Freedom. Freedom!
Freedom! Was it a place somewhere between Atlanta and
Birmingham and you kept on missing it everytime you drove
that way? It was a street in Itta Bena, Mississippi. Ain't that a
bitch? Freedom Street! Ran right by the railroad tracks in the
Negro part of town and Love Street ran right into it. Freedom
and Love. It would be nice to have a house right on that corner.
Freedom and Love. But from what you'd heard it was just a
street in Itta Bena. Maybe it was a person—Freedom. Somebody sitting on a porch somewhere. You wondered what he
looked like as you sat in the jail cell with ten, twenty, thirty
others and one toilet that wouldn't flush and one useless window stopped up with bars. If it was summer the jailer would
turn the heat on and if it was winter he'd turn it off and take
the mattresses and you'd sing Freedom Songs (your brother sent
you a note and said you looked real good on the six o'clock news
on TV walking down the street singing) until the guard came
and said Shut Up All That Damn Noise and you'd sing louder
and he'd take one of you out at a time and everybody'd get quiet
and listen to the screams and cries from the floor above and then
that one would come back, bleeding, and you'd sing again because if one went to jail, all went; if one got a beating, all got
beatings and then that night or the next day or the day after
the people would've got up enough money to bail you out and
you'd go back to the church and march again and your brother
would see you on the six o'clock news for thirty seconds between
the stock market report and Jackie Kennedy flying to Switzer-
land with her children for skiing lessons.

But a response did begin to come from the nation. All across the North young white kids held sympathy demonstrations and then with the Freedom Rides in 1961 whites came South to go to jail with Negroes—for Freedom. Those who came said integration was their fight, too, because they could never be whole men, either, in a segregated society. Some whites stayed after the Freedom Rides and moved into Negro communities to live and to work.

At that time there was a split between activists in the Movement. Some felt that more and more demonstrations were needed while others felt that the effect of demonstrations was limited. Power was what was needed and power came through having a say in the system. That came through the ballot. Once you had some say in government, you could have some say about jobs. After all, what was the point of desegregating a lunch counter if you didn't have the money to buy a hamburger?

So began the slow tedious work of going into a town, finding someone who wouldn't be afraid to have a civil rights worker living in his house and would help the worker become known in the community. The civil rights worker had to find a minister courageous enough to let his church be used for a mass meeting and then he had to go around the community asking people to come out to the meeting. At the mass meeting there was usually hymn singing and a prayer service first. Then the minister would make a few remarks before introducing the civil rights worker, who by that time, if he were a veteran, would've been through the sit'ins, the Freedom Rides, five or six different jails and a lot of hungry days. He had dropped out of college, or quit his job if he had never been to college to become a full-time organizer for SNCC. His job was simple: organize the community to march down to the courthouse to register to vote. In small Mississippi towns, though, he didn't even think of organizing the community. He would feel good if he could convince five people to go. If five went and if the inevitable happened (violence, arrests), he had a good chance of organizing the community. It was not important at that time if one name was put on the voter registration rolls. The most important thing was to get the people organized.

It was out of Mississippi that one of the most important concepts of "the movement" came. Let the people lead themselves. SNCC field workers provided the impetus to a community, but let the community choose its leaders from its own ranks. To symbolize their new feeling, they began wearing denim work overalls, saying that they, too, were one of the community, that community of the poor. They rejected the idea of the 'talented tenth,' who would come out of the colleges to lead. There would be no 'talented tenth.' Only the community.

There were still demonstrations, but now they were not aimed as much at public accommodations, the most obvious symbols of oppression. The picket line around the courthouse, the symbol of the seat of power, were the new targets. The immediate result was the same. Heads that had been beaten before were beaten again. Heads that had never been beaten were beaten. New bloody heads were on the six o'clock news alongside ones that still had scabs from the last head-whipping session. If you were a civil rights worker in Mississippi you learned many things quickly. Don't sleep by windows if possible. Don't answer a knock at the door in the middle of the night unless your caller showed you nothing less than his birth certificate. If you're on the highway at night, you learned to drive as if you were training to be an astronaut. If a car was following you while you were doing 90 and it didn't sound a siren, it was safe to assume that the people in that car were not delivering a telegram. One SNCC worker, an ex-stock car driver, learned how to make a U-turn while doing ninety. (Take your hands off the wheel and pull the hand-brake. The car will spin around. Release the hand-brake and accelerate.) Each organizer had his own little techniques for staying alive. Non-violence might do something to the moral conscience of a nation, but a bullet didn't have morals and it was beginning to occur to more and more organizers that white folks had plenty more bullets than they did conscience.

How naive, how idealistic they were then. They had honestly believed that once white people knew what segregation did, it would be abolished. But why shouldn't they have believed it? They had been fed the American Dream, too. They believed in Coca Cola and the American Government. "I dreamed I got my

Freedom in a Maidenform Bra." They were in the Pepsi Generation, believing that the F.B.I. was God's personal emissary to uphold truth and punish evil.

That was before the countless demonstrations where the F.B.I. took notes standing next to cracker cops while they were wiping the nigger blood off their bill-clubs, and checking the batteries in their cattle-prods. That was before the promises of the Justice Department began to sound like the teasing of a virgin who never gets down to where its at. Sure, it was nice to see that picture of Bobby Kennedy up all night at his desk during the Freedom Rides. He looked almost like a civil rights worker, drinking coffee with his shoes off, but it took those Freedom Rides to make the ICC rule out segregated seating on interstate bus travel. It was Birmingham, '63 that finally forced the Image of Youth and Liberty, Jack Kennedy, into proposing a Civil Rights Bill, which was then almost immediately comprised into ineffectiveness when the Brother of the Image, Bobby, the K. appeared before the Senate Judiciary Committee. They didn't like the idea of the march on Washington, but managed to turn it into a Kennedy victory and finally endorsing it as being in the American tradition, whatever that means. After the March, the American Monarch had the Big Six Negro Leaders over to the White House for tea and cookies and to chat with Jackie about the Riviera in the winter (it's a whole lot better than the Delta I hear). The Monarch, his face rugged from the spray of the wind-swept Atlantic, as thousands of eulogies have proclaimed since his swift demise, stood there smiling, feeling pretty good because all the liquor stores and bars in Washington had been closed for the day so there was no danger of a bunch of niggers getting ahold of some fire-water, forgetting that they weren't in Harlem, Buttermilk Bottom and all those other weird-named places niggers picked to live in. (The order forbidding the sale of alcoholic beverages is one of the biggest insults Negroes have ever had hurled at them. It would have been much easier to take if it had simply been said The Great White Father can't trust his pickaninnies if the bars and liquor stores are left open.) Jack could also stand there and smile because John Lewis of SNCC had had his speech censored by the more 'responsible' leaders, who threatened to withdraw from the march. Even censored, Lewis' speech raised pertinent questions—questions that had been on the mind of many, those not leaders, those not responsible. "The party of Kennedy is also the party of Eastland. The party of Javits is also the party of Goldwater. *Where is our party?*" But Jack could smile, because John Lewis had deleted from his speech the most pertinent question of all, "I want to know—which side is the Federal Government on?"

A lot of people wanted to know that, particularly after Lyndon Baines Johnson became President of the United States in a split second one Friday afternoon. When he asked for the nation's help and God's in that cracker drawl, Negroes began pulling out road maps, train schedules and brushing up on their Spanish. A lot of them had always wanted to see what Mexico was like anyway, and it looked as if the time to do that thing was near.

But Big Lyndon, despite his beagle hounds and daughters, fooled everybody. Not only did he strengthen the civil rights bill and support it fully, he started giving Martin Luther King competition as to who was going to lead "the movement." King lost.

With the push for the civil rights bill in Congress, there began talk of a white backlash in the '64 elections. It seemed that whites were getting a little tired of picking up the papers and seeing niggers all over the front page. Even if they were getting their heads kicked in half the time, four years of seeing that was about enough. The average white person didn't know what niggers wanted and didn't much care. By now they should have gotten whatever the hell it was they said they didn't have and if they hadn't gotten it by now, they either didn't deserve it or didn't need it.

What was really bothering Northern whites, however, was the fact that the Movement had come North. De Facto Segregation and De Facto Housing were new phrases meaning No Niggers Allowed in This School and You Damn Well Better Believe No

Niggers Allowed in This Neighborhood. If you believed the liberal press, though, it wasn't as serious a problem as the one down South, because in the North segregation wasn't deliberate, it just sort of happened that way. Many Negroes never found out what De Facto meant, but they assumed it was the De Facto and not segregation they ran up against when they couldn't find an apartment to rent outside of Harlem. Soon, though, the mask fell from the North's face. In New York it happened when CORE threatened a stall-in on all of the city's express-ways the morning of the World's Fair opening. The threat alone was enough to make over three-fourths of the people who drove to work leave their cars in the garage and take the train or simply call in sick. The threat alone was enough to make New York liberal newspapers read as if they had acquired Southern accents over night. A few months later, an organization of whites arose in New York which called itself SPONGE—Society for the Prevention of Negroes Getting Everything. It was difficult to speak any longer of a North and a South. As Malcolm X once said, that everything south of the Canadian border was South. There was only up South and down South now, and you found "cracker" both places.

While the North was being shocked into realizing that there were Negroes in its midst, the South was sympathizing with the assault that Mississippi was about to suffer. Almost a thousand white students were going into the State in June, 1964, to work in Freedom Schools, community centers and to register people in the Mississippi Freedom Democratic Party, a political party organized that winter which was going to challenge the state Democratic organization at the Democratic Convention in August.

The Mississippi Summer Project was the apex of white participation. Within SNCC, there had been widespread opposition to the idea. Many felt that it would be admitting that Negroes couldn't do the job alone. Others thought that it would destroy everything which they had accomplished. Whites, no matter how well-meaning, could not relate to the Negro community. A Negro would follow a white person to the courthouse, not because he'd been convinced he should register and vote, but simply because he had been trained to say Yes to whatever a white person wanted. Others felt, however, that if they were ever to expose Mississippi racism to America, it would only be through using whites. After all, SNCC had repeatedly informed the press of the five Negroes killed that year in Mississippi, because of their involvement with The Movement. The press had refused to print or investigate the information. Put a thousand white kids in Mississippi and the press would watch everything and print it. And who could tell? Maybe one of the white boys would get himself killed and really make some publicity. A few said it. Most thought it. It happened.

The murders of Goodman, Schwerner and Chaney stuned the nation. Whites were shocked. Negroes were hurt and angry. Rita Schwerner, wife of one of the murdered men, reflected the feelings of the Negroes as she commented that if James Chaney had been killed alone, no one would have cared. This was made even more evident the following year when Jimmie Lee Jackson's murder in Alabama evoked little reaction from whites but the murder of Rev. James Reeb brought thousands of whites to Harlem on a march protesting the slaying.

The Mississippi Summer Project had accomplished its purpose; the press came to Mississippi. The feature stories it wrote usually went something like, "Blop-blop is a blue-eyed blonde from Diamond Junction-on-the-Hudson, New York. She is a twenty-year-old junior at Radcliffe majoring in Oriental mataphysics and its relationship to the quantum theory, when the sun is in Saggitarius. This summer she's living with a Negro family in Fatback, Mississippi who has never heard of the quantum theory, etc., etc., etc." All summer the articles came about white boys and white girls living with poor Negroes in Mississippi. It didn't escape the attention of Negroes that seemingly no one cared about the Negro civil rights workers who have been living and working in Mississippi for the previous three years. Didn't anyone care about Willie Peacock, born and raised on a Mississippi plantation, who couldn't go back to his home town because he was an organizer for SNCC and the white people would kill him if he went to see his mother? Apparently not.

Mississippi was taken out of the headlines in July, however, when Harlem held its own summer project, to protest the murder of a thirteen-year-old boy by a policeman. Summer projects, northern style, usually involve southern coke bottle with gasoline, stuffing a rag down the neck and lighting it. *Things go better with coke.*—Harlem, Bedford-Stuyvesant, Rochester and Chicago sent coke after coke after coke that summer but the granddaddy of them all, Watts to come the following summer.

If the press had ever screamed as loudly for an end to segregation and discrimination as it screamed for law and order, segregation would be a vague memory today. Somehow, though, law and order becomes all important only when Negroes take to the streets and burn or wipe out a few of the white man's stores. Law and order is never so important to the press when the police is whuppin niggers' heads on the week-ends. It slowly began to dawn on Negroes that whites didn't care quite as much about helping them get their freedom as they did about law and order. "Law and order must prevail" has become the cliche of the '60's. Law and order have always prevailed— upside the Black man's head at every available opportunity.

The system was breaking down, but it was breaking in ways few had foreseen and fewer understood. The walls of segregation and discrimination were not crumbling and giving way to flowers of love and brotherhood. The walls were crumbling, but only to reveal a gigantic castle with walls ten times thicker than the walls of segregation. The castle was painted a brilliant white and lettered in bright red were the words Racism. What it meant to the Negro was simple. The white man only wanted you to have what he wanted you to have and you couldn't get it any other way except the way he said you could get it. Racism. It was the attitude that closed the bars and liquor stores on the day of the March. It was the attitude which made newspapers and government officials, even Big Lyndon Himself, say, "that if Negroes went about things in the wrong way, they would lose the friends they already had." It was the attitude that made the press continue to call Muhammad Ali, Cassius Clay even though that was no longer his name. But the movement was moving. It was no longer a Friendship Contest. It was becoming a War of Liberation.

More than any other person Malcolm X was responsible for the new militancy that entered The Movement in 1965. Malcolm X said aloud those things which Negroes had been saying among themselves. He even said those things Negroes had been afraid to say to each other. His clear uncomplicated words cut through the chains on black minds like a giant blowtourch. His words were not spoken for the benefit of the press. He was not concerned with stirring the moral conscience of America, because he knew—America had no moral conscience. He spoke directly and eloquently to black men, analyzing their situation, their predicament, events as they happened, explaining what it all meant for a black man in America.

America's reaction to what the Negro considered just demands was a disillusioning experience. Where whites could try to attain the American Dream, Negroes always had had to dream themselves attaining The Dream. But The Dream was beginning to look like a nightmare and Negroes didn't have to dream themselves a nightmare. They had been living one a long time. They had hoped that America would respond to their needs and America had equivocated. Integration had once been an unquestioned goal that would be the proudest moment for Negro America. Now it was beginning to be questioned.

The New York school boycotts of 1964 pointed this up. Integration to the New York City Board of Education meant busing Negro children to white schools. This merely said to Negroes that whites were saying Negroes had nothing to offer. Integration has always been presented as a Godsend for Negroes and something to be endured for whites. When the Board of Education decided to bus white children to Negro schools the following year, the reaction was strangely similar to that of New Orleans and Little Rock. Today, whites in Chicago and New York chant at Negro demonstrators, "I wish I was an Alabama deputy, so I could kill a nigger legally."

When it became more and more apparent that integration was only designed to uplift Negroes and improve their lot, Negroes began wondering whose lot actually needed improving. Maybe the white folks weren't as well-educated and cultured as they thought they were. Thus, Negroes began cutting a path toward learning who they were.

Of the minority groups in this country, the Negro is the only one lacking a language of his own. This is significant in that this has made it difficult for him to have a clear concept of himself as a Negro. It has made him more susceptible to the American lie of assimilation than the Puerto Rican, Italian or Jew who can remove himself from America with one sentence in his native language. Despite the assimilation lie, America is not a melting pot. It is a nation of national minorities, each living in a well-defined geographical area and retaining enough of the customs of the native land to maintain an identity other than that of an American. The Negro has two native lands: America and Africa. Both have been denied him.

Identity has always been the key problem for Negroes. Many avoid their blackness as much as possible by trying to become assimilated. They remove all traces of blackness from their lives. Their gestures, speech, habits, cuisine, walk, everything becomes as American Dream as possible. Generally, they are the 'responsible leaders,' the middle class, the undercover, button-down collar Uncle Toms, who front for the white man at a time of racial crisis, reassuring the nation that "responsible Negroes deplore the violence and looting and we ask that law and order be allowed to prevail." A small minority avoid the crux of their blackness by going to another extreme. They identify completely with Africa. Some go to the extent of wearing African clothes and speaking Swahili. They, however, are only unconsciously admitting that the white man is right when he says, Negroes don't have a thing of their own.

For other Negroes the question of identity is only now being solved by the realization of those things that are their's. Negroes do have a language of their own. The words may be English, but the way a Negro puts them together and the meaning that he gives them creates a new language. He has another language, too, and that language is rhythm. It is obvious in music, but it is also expressed in the way he walks and the way he talks. There is a music and rhythm to the way he dresses and the way he cooks. This has been recognized by Negroes for some time now. "Soul" is how these things peculiarly black are recognized by black men in America. In Africa they speak Negritude. It is the same. The recognition of those things uniquely theirs which separate them from the white man. "Soul" and Negritude become even more precious when it is remembered that the white man in America systematically tried to destroy every vestige of racial identity through slavery and slavery's little brother, segregation. It is a testament to the power of "Soul" that it not only survived but thrived.

Now the Negro is beginning to study his past, to learn those things that have been lost, to recreate what the white man destroyed in him and to destroy that which the white man put in its stead. He has stopped being a Negro and has become a black man in recognition of his new identity, his real identity. 'Negro' is an American invention which shut him off from those of the same color in Africa. He recognizes now that part of himself is in Africa. Some feel this in a deeply personal way, as did Mrs. Fannie Lou Hamer who cried when she was in Africa, because she knew she had relatives there and she would never be able to know them. Her past would always be partially closed.

Many things that have happened in the past six years have had little or no meaning for most whites, but have had vital meaning for Negroes. Wasn't it only a month after the March on Washington that four children were killed in a church bombing in Birmingham? Whites could feel morally outraged, but they couldn't know the futility, despair and anger that swept through the nation within a nation—Black America. There are limits to how much one people could endure and Birmingham Sunday possibly marked that limit. The enemy was not a system. It was an inhuman fiend who never slept, who never rested and no one would stop him. Those Northern protest rallies where Freedom Songs were sung and speeches speeched and applause applauded and afterwards telegrams and letters sent to the President and Congress—they began to look more and more like moral exercises. See, my hands are clean. I do not condone such a foul deed, they said, going back to their magazines, feeling purged because they had made their moral witness.

What was needed that Sunday was ol' John Brown to come riding into Birmingham as he had ridden into Lawrence, Kansas, burning every building that stood and killing every man, woman and child that ran from his onslaught. Killing, killing, killing, turning men into fountains of blood, spouting spouting spouting until Heaven itself drew back before the frothing red ocean.

But the Liberal and his Negro sycophants would've cried, Vengeance accomplishes nothing. You're only acting like your oppressor and such an act makes you no better than him. John Brown, his hand and wrists slick with blood, would have said oh so softly and so quietly, Mere Vengeance is folly. Purgation is necessity.

Now it is over. America has had chance after chance to show that it really meant "that all men are endowed with certain inalienable rights." America has had precious chances in this decade to make it come true. Now it is over. The days of singing freedom songs and the days of combating bullets and billy clubs with love. We Shall Overcome (and we have overcome our blindness) sounds old, out-dated and can enter the pantheon of the greats along with the IWW songs and the union songs. As one SNCC veteran put it after the Mississippi March, "Man, the people are too busy getting ready to fight to bother with singing anymore." And as for Love? That's always been better done in bed than on the picket line and marches. Love is fragile and gentle and seeks a like response. They used to sing "I Love Everybody" as they ducked bricks and bottles. Now they sing:

> Too much love,
> Too much love,
> Nothing kills a nigger like
> Too much love.

They know, because they still get headaches from the beatings they took while love, love, loving. They know, because they died on those highways and in those jail cells, died from trying to change the hearts of men who had none. They know, the ones who have bleeding ulcers when they're twenty'tree and the ones who have to have the eye operations. They know that nothing kills a nigger like too much love.

At one time black people desperately wanted to be American, to communicate with whites, to live in the Beloved Community. Now that is irrelevant. They know that it can't be until whites want it to be and it is obvious now that whites don't want it.

Does all of this mean that every American white is now a potential victim for some young Nat Turner? Does it mean the time is imminent when the red blood of blue-eyed, blonde-haired beauties will glisten on black arms and hands?

For many black people, the time is imminent. For others it simply means the white man no longer exists. He is not to be lived with and he is not to be destroyed. He is simply to be ignored, because the time has come for the black man to control the things which effect his life. Like the Irish control Boston, the black man will control Harlem. For so long the black man lived his life in reaction to whites. Now he will live it only within the framework of his own blackness and his blackness links him with the Indians of Peru, the miner of Bolivia, the African and the freedom fighters of Vietnam. What they fight for is what the American black man fights for—the right to govern his own life. If the white man interprets that to mean hatred, it is only a reflection of his own fears and anxieties and black people leave him to deal with it. There is too much to do to waste time and energy hating white people.

The old order passes away. Like the black riderless horse, boots turned the wrong way in the stirrups, following the coffin down the boulevard, it passes away. But there are no crowds to watch as it passes. There are no crowds, to mourn, to weep. No eulogies to read and no eternal flame is lit over the grave. There is no time for there are streets to be cleaned, houses painted, and clothes washed. Everything must be scoured clean. Trash has to be thrown out. Garbage dumped and everything unfit, burned.

> The new order is coming child,
> The old is passing away.

61. CHICAGO OFFICE OF SNCC: "WE MUST FILL OURSELVES WITH HATE FOR ALL WHITE THINGS"

A year after SNCC first popularized the slogan, Black Power, officials in its Chicago office produced a leaflet, "We Want Black Power," setting forth the cultural and political nationalism of SNCC's extreme left wing. The document, which appeared in the midst of the widespread rioting that engulfed the country's major cities during the summer of 1967, called for black revolutionary action. It urged alliances with the poor peoples' movements of the undeveloped nations and offered specific advice on tactics of sabotage in the United States. The document is also notable for its explicit expression of anti-white sentiment and its excoriation of the black bourgeoisie.

Black men of America are a captive people

The black man in America is in a perpetual state of slavery no matter what the white man's propaganda tells us.

The black man in America is exploited and oppressed the same as his black brothers are all over the face of the earth by the same white man. We will never be free until we are all free and that means all black oppressed people all over the earth.

Chicago Office of SNCC, WE WANT BLACK POWER, leaflet (Chicago: Chicago Office of SNCC, 1967).

We are not alone in this fight, we are a part of the struggle for self-determination of all black men everywhere. We here in America must unite ourselves to be ready to help our brothers elsewhere.

We must first gain BLACK POWER here in America. Living inside the camp of the leaders of the enemy forces, it is our duty to our Brothers to revolt against the system and create our own system so that we can live as MEN.

We must take over the political and economic systems where we are in the majority in the heart of every major city in this country as well as in the rural areas. We must create our own black culture to erase the lies the white man has fed our minds from the day we were born.

The black man in the ghetto
will lead the Black Power Movement

The black Brother in the ghetto will lead the Black Power Movement and make the changes that are necessary for its success.

The black man in the ghetto has one big advantage that the bourgeois Negro does not have despite his 'superior' education. He is already living outside the value system white society imposes on all black Americans.

He has to look at things from another direction in order to survive. He is ready. He received his training in the streets, in the jails, from the ADC check his mother did not receive in time and the head-beatings he got from the cop on the corner.

Once he makes that first important discovery about the great pride you feel inside as a BLACK MAN and the great heritage of the mother country, Africa, there is no stopping him from dedicating himself to fight the white man's system.

This is why the Black Power Movement is a true revolutionary movement with the power to change men's minds and unmask the tricks the white man has used to keep black men enslaved in modern society.

The bourgeois Negro cannot be a part
of the Black Power Movement

The bourgeois Negro has been force-fed the white man's propaganda and has lived too long in the half-world between white and phony black bourgeois society. He cannot think for himself because he is a shell of a man full of contradictions he cannot resolve. He is not to be trusted under any circumstances until he has proved himself to be 'cured.' There are a minute handful of these 'cured' bourgeois Negroes in the Black Power Movement and they are most valuable but they must not be allowed to take control. They are aware intellectually but under stress will react emotionally to the pressures of white society in the same way a white 'liberal' will expose an unconscious prejudice that he did not even realize he possessed.

What Brother Malcolm X taught us
about ourselves

Malcolm X was the first black man from the ghetto in America to make a real attempt to get the white man's fist off the black man. He recognized the true dignity of man—without the white society prejudices about status, education and background that we all must purge from our minds.

Even today, in the Black Power Movement itself we find Brothers who look down on another Brother because of the conditions that life has imposed upon him. The most beautiful thing that Malcolm X taught us is that once a black man discovers for himself a pride of his blackness, he can throw off the shackles of mental slavery and become a MAN in the truest sense of the word. We must move on from the point our Great Black Prince had reached.

We must become leaders for ourselves

We must not get hung-up in the bag of having one great leader who we depend upon to make decisions. This makes the

Movement too vulnerable to those forces the white man uses to keep us enslaved, such as the draft, murder, prison or character assassination.

We have to all learn to become leaders for ourselves and re-move all white values from our minds. When we see a Brother using a white value through error it is our duty to the Movement to point it out to him. We must thank our Brothers who show us our own errors. We must discipline ourselves so that if necessary we can leave family and friends at a moment's notice, maybe forever, and know our Brothers have pledged themselves to protect the family we have left behind.

As a part of our education, we must travel to other cities and make contracts with the Brothers in all the ghettos in America so that when the time is right we can unite as one under the banner of BLACK POWER.

Learning to think Black and remove white things from our minds

We have got to begin to say and understand with complete assuredness what black is. Black is an inner pride that the white man's language hampers us from expressing. Black is being a complete fanatic, who white society considers insane.

We have to learn that black is so much better than belonging to the white race with the blood of millions dripping from their hands that it goes far beyond any prejudice or resentment. We must fill ourselves with hate for all white things. This is not vengeance or trying to take the white oppressors' place to be-come new black oppressors but is a oneness with a worldwide black brotherhood.

We must regain respect for the lost religion of our fathers, the spirits of the black earth of Africa. The white man has so poisoned our minds that if a Brother told you he practiced Voodoo you would roll around on the floor laughing at how stupid and superstitious he was.

We have to learn to roll around on the floor laughing at the black man who says he worships the white Jesus. He is truly sick.

We must create our own language for these things that the white man will not understand because a Black Culture exists and it is not the wood-carvings or native dancing it is the black strength inside of true men.

Ideas on planning
for the future of Black Power

We must infiltrate all government agencies. This will not be hard because black clerks work in all agencies in poor paying jobs and have a natural resentment of the white men who run these jobs.

People must be assigned to seek out these dissatisfied black men and women and put pressure on them to give us the information we need. Any man in overalls, carrying a tool box, can enter a building if he looks like he knows what he is doing.

Modern America depends on many complex systems such as electricity, water, gas, sewerage and transportation and all are vulnerable. Much of the government is run by computers that must operate in air conditioning. Cut off the air conditioning and they cannot function.

We must begin to investigate and learn all of these things so that we can use them if it becomes necessary. We cannot train an army in the local park but we can be ready for the final confrontation with the white man's system.

Remember your Brothers in South Africa and do not delude yourselves that it could not happen here. We must copy the white man's biggest trick, diversion, (Hitler taught them that) and infiltrate all civil rights groups, keep them in confusion so they will be neutralized and cannot be used as a tool of the white power structure.

The civil rights, integrationist movement says to the white man, "If you please, Sir, let us, the 10 percent minority of American have our rights. See how nice and nonviolent we are?"

This is why SNCC calls itself a Human Rights Organization. We believe that we belong to the 90 percent majority of the people on earth that the white man oppresses and that we

should not beg the white man for anything. We want what belongs to us as human beings and we intend to get it through
BLACK POWER.

How to deal with black traitors

Uncle Tom is too kind of a word. What we have are black
traitors, quisslings, collaborators, sell-outs, white Negroes.

We have to expose these people for once and for all for what
they are and place them on the side of the oppressor where they
belong. Their black skin is a lie and their guilt the shame of
all black men. We must ostracize them and if necessary exterminate them.

We must stop fighting a "fair game." We must do whatever is
necessary to win BLACK POWER. We have to hate and disrupt and destroy and blackmail and lie and steal and become
blood-brothers like the Mau-Mau.

We must eliminate or render ineffective all traitors. We must
make them fear to stand up like puppets for the white men,
and we must make the world understand that these so-called
men do not represent us or even belong to the same black race
because they sold out their birthright for a mess of white society
pottage. Let them choke on it.

Pitfalls to avoid
on the path to Black Power

We must learn how close America and Russia are politically.
The biggest lie in the world is the cold-war. Money runs the
world and it is controlled completely by the white man.

Russia and America run the two biggest money systems in the
world and they intend to keep it under their control under any
circumstances. Thus, we cannot except any help from Communism or any other "ism."

We must seek out poor peoples movements in South America,
Africa and Asia and make our alliances with them. We must

not be fooled into thinking that there is a ready-made doctrine that will solve all our problems.

There are only white man's doctrines and they will never work for us. We have to work out our own systems and doctrines and culture.

Why propaganda is our most important tool

The one thing that the white man's system cannot stand is the TRUTH because his system is all based on lies.

There is no such thing as "justice" for a black man in America. The white man controls everything that is said in every book, newspaper, magazine, TV and radio broadcast.

Even the textbooks used in the schools and the bible that is read in the churches are designed to maintain the system for the white man. Each and every one of us is forced to listen to the white man's propaganda every day of our lives.

The political system, economic system, military system, educational system, religious system and anything else you name is used to preserve the status quo of white America getting fatter and fatter while the black man gets more and more hungry.

We must spend our time telling our Brothers the truth.

We must tell them that any black woman who wears a diamond on her finger is wearing the blood of her Brothers and Sisters in slavery in South Africa where one out of every three black babies die before the age of one, from starvation, to make the white man rich.

We must stop wearing the symbols of slavery on our fingers.

We must stop going to other countries to exterminate our Brothers and Sisters for the white man's greed.

We must ask our Brothers which side they are on.

Once you know the truth for yourself it is your duty to dedicate your life to recruiting your Brothers and to counteract the white man's propaganda.

We must disrupt the white man's system to create our own. We must publish newspapers and get radio stations. Black Unity is strength—let's use it now to get BLACK POWER.

62. THE BLACK PANTHER PARTY:
"WE MUST DESTROY
BOTH RACISM AND CAPITALISM"

In 1966 the Black Panther party was formed in Oakland, California. With SNCC in decline, it emerged as the leading nationalist organization among black youth. Excoriating the American capitalist system, the Black Panthers preached a doctrine of self-defense and revolutionary nationalism. By 1969, however, they were soft-pedaling their nationalist ideology and formed an alliance with a group of Communists and New Left radicals.

The first document printed here is the official program of the organization formulated at the time of its founding in 1966. The second is an interview with Huey Newton, the party's Minister of Defense, held in 1968. At the time, he was on trial for the slaying of an Oakland policeman. Shortly after the interview Newton was convicted of "voluntary manslaughter" and sentenced to a two-to-fifteen year prison term.

A. The Black Panther program

BLACK PANTHER
PARTY
FOR SELF DEFENSE

WHAT WE WANT   WHAT WE BELIEVE

What we want now!:

1. We want freedom. We want power to determine the destiny of our black community.

Black Panther Party Program, KEY LIST MAILING: SELECTED DOCUMENTS OF CURRENT AND LASTING INTEREST IN THE CIVIL RIGHTS MOVEMENT (San Francisco Office of SNCC, March 19, 1967).

2. We want full employment for our people.

3. We want an end to the robbery by the white man of our black community.

4. We want decent housing fit for shelter of human beings.

5. We want education for our people that exposes the true nature of this decadent American society. We want education that teaches us our true history and our role in the present day society.

6. We want all black men to be exempt from military service.

7. We want an immediate end to *police brutality* and *murder* of black people.

8. We want freedom for all black men and women held in federal, state, county, and city prisons and jails.

9. We want all black people when brought to trial, to be tried in court by a jury of their peer group or people from their black communities, as defined by the Constitution of the United States.

10. We want land, bread, housing, education, clothing, justice and peace.

What we believe:

1. We believe that black people will not be free until we are able to determine our destiny.

2. We believe that the federal government is responsible and obligated to give every man employment or a guaranteed income.

   We believe that if the white American business men will not give full employment, then the means of production should be taken from the business men and placed in the community so that the people of the community can organize and employ all of its people and give a high standards of living.

3. We believe that this racist government has robbed us and now we are demanding the overdue debt of forty acres and two mules. Forty acres and two mules was promised 100 years ago as retribution for slave labor and mass murder of black people. We will accept the payment in currency which will be distributed to our many communities. The Germans are now aiding the Jews in Israel for the genocide of the Jewish people. The Germans murdered 6,000,000 million Jews. The American racist has taken part in the slaughter of over 50,000,000 million black people; therefore, we feel that this is a modest demand that we make.

4. We believe that if the white landlords will not give decent housing to our black community then the housing and the land should be made into cooperatives so that our community, with government aide, can build and make decent housing for its people.

5. We believe in an educational system that will give to our people a knowledge of self. If a man does not have knowledge of himself and his position in society and the world, then he has little chance to relate to anything else.

6. We believe that black people should not be forced to fight in the military service to defend a racist government that does not protect us. We will not fight and kill other people of color in the world who, like black people, are being victimized by the white racist government of America. We will protect ourselves from the force and violence of the racist police and the racist military, by whatever means necessary.

7. We believe we can end police brutality in our black community by organizing black *self defense* groups that are dedicated to defending our black community from racist police oppression and brutality. The Second Amendment of the Constitution of the United States gives us a right to bear arms. We therefore believe that all black people should arm themselves for *self defense*.

8. We believe that all black people should be released from the many jails and prisons because they have not received a fair and impartial trial.

9. We believe that the courts should follow the United States Constitution so that black people will receive fair trials. The 14th Amendment of the U. S. Constitution gives a man a right to be tried by his peer group. A peer is a person from a similar economical, social, religious, geographical, environmental, historical and racial background. To do this the court will be forced to select a jury from the black community from which the black defendant came. We have been, and are being tried by all white juries that have no understanding of the "average reasoning man" of the black community.

10. When in the course of human events, it becomes necessary for one people to dissolve the political bonds which have connected them with another, and to assume among the powers of the earth, the separate and equal station to which the laws of nature and nature's God entitle them, a decent respect to the opinions of mankind requires that they should declare the causes which impel them to the separation.

We hold these truths to be self-evident, that all men are created equal, that they are endowed by their Creator with certain unalienable rights, that among these are life, liberty and the pursuit of happiness. That to secure these rights, governments are instituted among men, deriving their just powers from the consent of the governed,—*that whenever any form of government becomes destructive of these ends, it is the right of people to alter or to abolish it, and to institute new government, laying its foundation on such principles and organizing its powers in such form, as to them shall seem most likely to effect their safety and happiness.*

Prudence, indeed, will dictate that governments long established should not be changed for light and transient causes; and accordingly all experience hath shewn, that mankind are more disposed to suffer, while evils are sufferable, than to right themselves by abolishing the forms to which they are accustomed. *But when a long train of abuses and usurpations, pursuing invariably the same object, evinces a design to reduce them under absolute despotism, it is their right, it is their duty, to throw off such government, and to provide new guards for their future security.*

B. Interview with Huey Newton

THE MOVEMENT: The question of nationalism is a vital one in the black movement today. Some have made a distinction between cultural nationalism and revolutionary nationalism. Would you comment on the differences and give us your views?

HUEY P. NEWTON: There are two kinds of nationalism, revolutionary nationalism and reactionary nationalism. Revolutionary nationalism is first dependent upon a people's revolution with the end goal being the people in power. Therefore to be a revolutionary nationalist you would by necessity have to be a socialist. If you are a reactionary nationalist you are not a socialist and your end goal is the oppression of the people.

Cultural nationalism, or pork chop nationalism, as I sometimes call it, is basically a problem of having the wrong political perspective. It seems to be a reaction instead of responding to political oppression. The cultural nationalists are concerned with returning to the old African culture and thereby regaining their identity and freedom. In other words, they feel that the African culture will automatically bring political freedom. Many times cultural nationalists fall into line as reactionary nationalists.

Papa Doc in Haiti is an excellent example of reactionary nationalism. He oppresses the people but he does promote the

HUEY NEWTON TALKS TO THE MOVEMENT (Chicago: Students for a Democratic Society, 1968).

African culture. He's against anything other then black, which on the surface seems very good, but for him it is only to mislead the people. He merely kicked out the racists and replaced them with himself as the oppressor. Many of the nationalists in this country seem to desire the same ends.

The Black Panther Party, which is a revolutionary group of black people, realizes that we have to have an identity. We have to realize our black heritage in order to give us strength to move on and progress. But as far as returning to the old African culture, it's unnecessary and it's not advantageous in many respects. We believe that culture itself will not liberate us. We're going to need some stronger stuff.

Revolutionary nationalism

A good example of revolutionary nationalism was the revolution in Algeria when Ben Bella took over. The French were kicked out but it was a people's revolution because the people ended up in power. The leaders that took over were not interested in the profit motive where they could exploit the people and keep them in a state of slavery. They nationalized the industry and plowed the would-be profits into the community. That's what socialism is all about in a nutshell. The people's representatives are in office strictly on the leave of the people. The wealth of the country is controlled by the people and they are considered whenever modifications in the industries are made.

The Black Panther Party is a revolutionary Nationalist group and we see a major contradiction between capitalism in this country and our interests. We realize that this country became very rich upon slavery and that slavery is capitalism in the extreme. We have two evils to fight, capitalism and racism. We must destroy both racism and capitalism.

MOVEMENT: Directly related to the question of nationalism is the question of unity within the black community. There has been some question about this since the Black Panther Party has run candidates against other black candidates in recent California elections. What is your position on this matter?

HUEY: Well a very peculiar thing has happened. Historically you got what Malcolm X calls the field nigger and the house nigger. The house nigger had some privileges, a little more. He got the worn-out clothes of the master and he didn't have to work as hard as the field black. He came to respect the master to such an extent until he identified with the master because he got a few of the leftovers that the field blacks did not get. And through this identity with him, he saw the slavemaster's interest as being his interest. Sometimes he would even protect the slavemaster more than the slavemaster would protect himself. Malcolm makes the point that if the master's house happened to catch on fire the house Negro will work harder than the master to put the fire out and save the master's house. While the field Negro, the field blacks was praying that the house burned down. The house black identified with the master so much that when the master would get sick the house Negro would say, "Master, we's sick!"

Black bourgeoisie

The Black Panther Party are the field blacks, we're hoping the master dies if he gets sick. The Black bourgeoisie seem to be acting in the role of the house Negro. They are pro-administration. They would like a few concessions made, but as far as the overall setup, they have a little more material goods, a little more advantage, a few more privileges than the black have-nots; the lower class. And so they identify with the power structure and they see their interests as the power structure's interest. In fact, it's against their interest.

The Black Panther Party was forced to draw a line of demarcation. We are for all of those who are for the promotion of the interests of the black have-nots, which represents about 98% of blacks here in America. We're not controlled by the white mother country radicals nor are we controlled by the black bourgeoisie. We have a mind of our own and if the black bourgeoisie cannot align itself with our complete program, then the black bourgeoisie sets itself up as our enemy. And they will be attacked and treated as such.

MOVEMENT: The Black Panther Party has had considerable contact with white radicals since its earliest days. What do you see as the role of these white radicals?

HUEY: The white mother country radical is the off-spring of the children of the beast that has plundered the world exploiting all people, concentrating on the people of color. These are children of the beast that seek now to be redeemed because they realize that their former heroes, who were slave masters and murderers, put forth ideas that were only facades to hide the treachery they inflicted upon the world. They are turning their backs on their fathers.

The white mother country radical, in resisting the system, becomes somewhat of an abstract thing because he's not oppressed as much as black people are. As a matter of fact his oppression is somewhat abstract simply because he doesn't have to live in a reality of oppression.

Black people in America and colored people throughout the world suffer not only from exploitation, but they suffer from racism. Black people here in America, in the black colony, are oppressed because we're black and we're exploited. The whites are rebels, many of them from the middle class and as far as any overt oppression this is not the case. So therefore I call their rejection of the system somewhat of an abstract thing. They're looking for new heroes. They're looking to wash away the hypocrisy that their fathers have presented to the world. In doing this they see the people who are really fighting for freedom. They see the people who are really standing for justice and equality and peace throughout the world. They are the people of Vietnam, the people of Latin America, the people of Asia, the people of Africa, and the black people in the black colony here in America.

White revolutionaries

This presents somewhat of a problem in many ways to the black revolutionary, especially to the cultural nationalist. The cultural nationalist doesn't understand the white revolutionaries because he can't see why anyone white would turn on the system. So they think that maybe this is some more hypocrisy being planted by white people.

I personally think that there are many young white revolutionaries who are sincere in attempting to realign themselves with mankind, and to make a reality out of the high moral standards that their fathers and forefathers only expressed. In pressing for new heroes the young white revolutionaries found the heroes in the black colony at home and in the colonies throughout the world.

The young white revolutionaries raised the cry for the troops to withdraw from Vietnam, hands off Latin America, withdraw from the Dominican Republic and also to withdraw from the black community or the black colony. So you have a situation in which the young white revolutionaries are attempting to identify with the oppressed people of the colonies and against the exploiter.

The problem arises then in what part they can play. How can they aid the colony? How can they aid the Black Panther Party or any other black revolutionary group? They can aid the black revolutionaries first by simply turning away from the establishment, and secondly by choosing their friends. For instance, they have a choice between whether they will be a friend of Lyndon Baines Johnson or a friend of Fidel Castro. A friend of Robert Kennedy or a friend of Ho Chi Minh. And these are direct opposites. A friend of mine or a friend of Johnsons. After they make this choice then the white revolutionaries have a duty and a responsibility to act.

The imperialistic or capitalistic system occupies areas. It occupies Vietnam now. They occupy them by sending soldiers there, by sending policemen there. The policemen or soldiers are only a gun in the establishment's hand. They make the racist secure in his racism. The gun in the establishment's hand makes the establishment secure in its exploitation. The first problem it seems is to remove the gun from the establishment's hand. Until lately the white radical has seen no reason to come into conflict with the policemen in his own community. The reason I said until recently is because there is friction now in the mother country between the young white revolutionaries and the police. Because now the white revolutionaries are attempting to put some of their ideas into action, and there's the rub. We say that it should be a permanent thing.

Black people are being oppressed in the colony by white policemen, by white racists. We are saying they must withdraw. We realize that it is not only the Oakland police department but rather the security forces in general. On April 6 it wasn't just the Oakland police department who ambushed the Panthers. It was the Oakland police department, the Emeryville police department and I wouldn't be surprised if there were others. When the white revolutionaries went down to close up the Army terminal in October 1965 it wasn't the Oakland police by themselves who tried to stop them. It was the Oakland police, the Berkeley police, the Highway Patrol, the Sherriff's Department and the national guard was standing by. So we see that they're all part of one organization. They're all a part of the security force to protect the status quo; to make sure that the institutions carry out their goals. They're here to protect the system.

As far as I'm concerned the only reasonable conclusion would be to first realize the enemy, realize the plan, and then when something happens in the black colony—when we're attacked and ambushed in the black colony—then the white revolutionary students and intellectuals and all the other whites who support the colony should respond by defending us, by attacking the enemy in their community. Every time that we're attacked in our community there should be a reaction by the white revolutionaries, they should respond by defending us, by attacking part of the security force. Part of that security force that is determined to carry out the racist ends of the American institutions.

As far as our party is concerned, the Black Panther Party is an all black party, because we feel as Malcolm X felt that there can be no black-white unity until there first is black unity. We have a problem in the black colony that is particular to the colony, but we're willing to accept aid from the mother country as long as the mother country radicals realize that we have, as Eldridge Cleaver says in SOUL ON ICE, a mind of our own. We've regained our mind that was taken away from us and we will decide the political as well as the practical stand that we'll take. We'll make the theory and we'll carry out the practice. It's the duty of the white revolutionary to aid us in this.

So the role of the mother country radical, and he does have a role, is to first choose his friend and his enemy and after doing this, which it seems he's already done, then to not only articulate his desires to regain his moral standard and align himself with humanity, but also to put this into practice by attacking the protectors of the institutions.

MOVEMENT: You have spoken a lot about dealing with the protectors of the system, the armed forces. Would you like to elaborate on why you place so much emphasis on this?

HUEY: The reasons that I feel very strongly about dealing with the protectors of the system is simply because without this protection from the army, the police and the military, the institutions could not go on in their racism and exploitation. For instance, as the Vietnamese are driving the American imperialist troops out of Vietnam, it automatically stops the racist imperialist institutions of America from oppressing that particular country. The country cannot implement its racist program without the guns. And the guns are the military and the police. If the military were disarmed in Vietnam, then the Vietnamese would be victorious.

We are in the same situation here in America. Whenever we attack the system the first thing the administrators do is to send out their strongarm men. If it's a rent strike, because of the indecent housing we have, they will send out the police to throw the furniture out the window. They don't come themselves. They send their protectors. So to deal with the corrupt exploiter you are going to have to deal with his protector, which is the police who take orders from him. This is a must.

MOVEMENT: Would you like to be more specific on the conditions which must exist before an alliance or coalition can be formed with predominantly white groups? Would you comment specifically on your alliance with the California Peace and Freedom Party?

HUEY: We have an alliance with the Peace and Freedom Party. The Peace and Freedom Party has supported our program in full and this is the criterion for a coalition with the black revolutionary group. If they had not supported our program in full, then we would not have seen any reason to make an alliance with them, because we are the reality of the oppression. They are not. They are only oppressed in an abstract way; we are oppressed in the real way. We are the real slaves! So it's a problem that we suffer from more than anyone else and it's our problem of liberation. Therefore we should decide what measures and what tools and what programs to use to become liberated. Many of the young white revolutionaries realize this and I see no reason not to have a coalition with them.

MOVEMENT: Other black groups seem to feel that from past experience it is impossible for them to work with whites and impossible for them to form alliances. What do you see as the reasons for this and do you think that the history of the Black Panther Party makes this less of a problem?

SNCC and liberals

HUEY: There was somewhat of an unhealthy relationship in the past with the white liberals supporting the black people who were trying to gain their freedom. I think that a good example of this would be the relationship that SNCC had with its white liberals. I call them white liberals because they differ strictly from the white radicals. The relationship was that the whites controlled SNCC for a very long time. From the very start of SNCC until here recently whites were the mind of SNCC. They controlled the program of SNCC with money and they controlled the ideology, or the stands SNCC would take. The blacks in SNCC were completely controlled program-wise; they couldn't do any more than these white liberals wanted them to do, which wasn't very much. So the white liberals were not working for self-determination for the black community. They were interested in a few concessions from the power structure. They undermined SNCC's program.

Stokely Carmichael came along and realizing this started to follow Malcolm X's program of Black Power. This frightened many of the white liberals who were supporting SNCC. Whites were afraid when Stokely came along with Black Power and said that black people have a mind of their own and that SNCC would be an all-black organization and that SNCC would seek self-determination for the black community. The white liberals withdrew their support leaving the organization financially bankrupt. The blacks who were in the organization, Stokely and H. Rap Brown, were left very angry with the white liberals who had been aiding them under the disguise of being sincere. They weren't sincere.

The result was that the leadership of SNCC turned away from the white liberal, which was very good. I don't think they distinguished between the white liberal and the white revolutionary, because the white revolutionary is white also and they are very much afraid to have any contact whatsoever with white people. Even to the point of denying that the white revolutionaries could give support, by supporting the programs of SNCC in the mother country. Not by making any programs, not by being a member of the organization, but simply by resisting. Just as the Vietnamese people realize that they are supported whenever other oppressed people throughout the world resist. Because it helps divide the troops. It drains the country militarily and economically. If the mother country radicals are sincere then this will definitely add to the attack that we are making on the power structure. The Black Panther Party's program is a program where we recognize that the revolution in the mother country will definitely aid us in our freedom and has everything to do with our struggle!

Hate the oppressor

I think that one of SNCC's great problems is that they were controlled by the traditional administrator: the omnipotent administrator, the white person. He was the mind of SNCC. And so SNCC regained its mind, but I believe that it lost its political perspective. I think that this was a reaction rather than a response. The Black Panther Party has NEVER been controlled by white people. The Black Panther Party has always been a black group. We have always had an integration of mind and body. We have never been controlled by whites and therefore we don't fear the white mother country radicals. Our alliance is one of organized black groups with organized white groups. As soon as the organized white groups do not do things that would benefit us in our struggle for liberation, that will be our departure point. So we don't suffer in the hangup of a skin color. We don't hate white people; we hate the oppressor. And if the oppressor happens to be white then we hate him. When he stops oppressing us then we no longer hate him. And right now in America you have the slave-master being a white group. We are pushing him out of office through revolution in this country. I think the responsibility of the white revolutionary will be to aid us in this. And when we are attacked by the police or by the military then it will be up to the white mother country radicals to attack the murderers and to respond as we respond, to follow our program.

Slave masters

MOVEMENT: You indicate that there is a psychological process that has historically existed in white-black relations in the U. S. that much change in the course of revolutionary struggle. Would you like to comment on this?

HUEY: Yes. The historical relationship between black and white here in America has been the relationship between the slave and the master, the master being the mind and the slave the body. The slave would carry out the orders that the mind demanded him to carry out. By doing this the master took the manhood from the slave because he stripped him of a mind. He stripped black people of their mind. In the process the slave-master stripped himself of a body. As Eldridge puts it the slave master became the omnipotent administrator and the slave became the supermasculine menial. This puts the omnipotent administrator into the controlling position or the front office and the supermasculine menial into the field.

The whole relationship developed so that the omnipotent administrator and the supermasculine menial became opposites. The slave being a very strong body doing all the practical things, all of the work becomes very masculine. The omnipotent administrator in the process of removing himself from all body functions realizes later that he has emasculated himself. So the slave lost his mind and the slave-master his body.

Penis envy

This caused the slave-master to become very envious of the slave because he pictured the slave as being more of a man, being superior sexually, because the penis is part of the body. The omnipotent administrator laid down a decree when he realized that his plan to enslave the black man had a flaw, when he discovered that he had emasculated himself. He attempted to bind the penis of the slave. He attempted to show that his penis could reach further than the supermasculine menial's penis. He said "I, the omnipotent administrator can have access to the black woman." The supermasculine menial then had a psychological attraction to the white woman (the ultra feminine freak) for the simple reason that it was forbidden fruit. The omnipotent administrator decreed that this kind of contact would be punished by death. At the same time in order to reinforce his sexual desire, to confirm, to assert his manhood, he would go into the slave quarters and have sexual relations with the black women (the self-reliant Amazon). Not to be satisfied but simply to confirm his manhood. Because if he can only satisfy the self-reliant Amazon then he would be sure that he was a man. Because he doesn't have a body, he doesn't have a penis, he psychologically wants to castrate the black man. The slave was constantly seeking unity within himself; a mind and a body. He always wanted to be able to decide, to gain respect from his woman.(Because women want one who can control.) I give this outline to fit into a framework of what is happening now. The white power structure today in America defines itself as the mind. They want to control the world. They go off and plunder the world. They are the policemen of the world exercising control especially over people of color.

Re-capture the mind

The white man cannot gain his manhood, cannot unite with the body because the body is black. The body is symbolic of slavery and strength. It's a bioligical thing as he views it. The slave is in a much better situation because his not being a full man has always been viewed psychologically. And it's always easier to make a psychological transition than a biological one. If he can only recapture his mind, recapture his balls, then he will lose all fear and will be free to determine his destiny. This is what is happening at this time with the rebellion of the world's oppressed people against the controller. They are regaining their mind and they're saying that we have a mind of our own. They're saying that we want freedom to determine the destiny of our people, thereby uniting the mind with their bodies. They are taking the mind back from the omnipotent administrator, the controller, the exploiter.

In America black people are also chanting that we have a mind of our own. We must have freedom to determine our destiny. It's almost a spiritual thing, this unity, this harmony. This unity of the mind and of the body, this unity of man within himself. Certain slogans of Chairman Mao I think demonstrate this theory of uniting the mind with the body within the man. An example is his call to the intellectuals to go to the countryside. The peasants in the countryside are all bodies; they're the workers. And he sent the intellectuals there because the dictatorship of the proletariat has no room for the omnipotent administrator; there's no room for the exploiter. So therefore he must go to the countryside to regain his body; he must work. He is really done a favor, because the people force him to unite his mind with his body by putting them both to work. At the same time the intellectual teaches the people political ideology, he educates them, thus uniting the mind and the body in the peasant. Their minds and bodies are united and they control their country. I think this is a very good example of this unity and it is my idea of the perfect man.

The guerrilla

MOVEMENT: You mentioned at another point that the guerrilla was the perfect man and this kind of formulation seems to fit in directly with the guerrilla as a political man. Would you like to comment on this?

HUEY: Yes. The guerrilla is a very unique man. This is in contrast to Marxist-Leninist orthodox theories where the party controls the military. The guerrilla is not only the warrior, the military fighter; he is also the military commander as well as the political theoretician. Debray says "poor the pen without the guns, poor the gun without the pen". The pen being just an extension of the mind, a tool to write down concepts, ideas. The gun is only an extension of the body, the extension of our fanged teeth that we lost through evolution. It's the weapon, it's the claws that we lost, it's the body. The guerrilla is the military commander and the political theoretician all in one.

In Bolivia Che said that he got very little help from the Communist Party there. The Communist Party wanted to be the mind, the Communist Party wanted to have full control of the guerrilla activity. But yet weren't taking part in the practical work of the guerrillas. The guerrilla on the other hand is not only united within himself, but he also attempts to spread this to the people by educating the villagers, giving them political perspective, pointing out things, educating them politically, and arming the people. Therefore the guerrilla is giving the peasants and workers a mind. Because they've already got the body you get a unity of the mind and the body. Black people here in America, who have long been the workers, have regained our minds and we now have a unity of mind and body.

MOVEMENT: Would you be willing to extend this formula in terms of white radicals; to say that one of their struggles today is to get back their bodies.

HUEY: Yes. I thought I made that clear. The white mother country radical by becoming an activist is attempting to regain his body. By being an activist and not the traditional theoretician who outlines the plan, as the Communist Party has been trying to do for ever so long, the white mother country radical is regaining his body. The resistance by white radicals in Berkeley during the past three nights is a good indication that the white radicals are on the way home. They have identified their enemies. The white radicals have integrated theory with practice. They realize the American system is the real enemy but in order to attack the American system they must attack the ordinary cop. In order to attack the educational system they must attack the ordinary teacher. Just as the Vietnamese people to attack the American system must attack the ordinary soldier. The white mother country radicals now are regaining their bodies and they're also recognizing that the black man has a mind and that he is a man.

MOVEMENT: Would you comment on how this psychological understanding aids in the revolutionary struggle?

HUEY: You can see that in statements until recently black people who haven't been enlightened have defined the white man by calling him "the MAN". "The Man" is making this decision, "The Man" this and "The Man" that. The black woman found it difficult to respect the black man because he didn't even define himself as a man! Because he didn't have a mind, because the decision maker was outside of himself. But the vanguard group, the Black Panther Party along with all revolutionary black groups have regained our mind and our manhood. Therefore we no longer define the omnipotent administrator as "the Man" . . . or the authority as "the MAN". Matter of fact the omnipotent administrator along with his security agents are less than a man because WE define them as pigs! I think that this is a revolutionary thing in itself. That's political power. That's power itself. Matter of fact what is power other than the ability to define phenomenon and then make it act in a desired manner? When black people start defining things and making it act in a desired manner, then we call this Black Power!

MOVEMENT: Would you comment further on what you mean by Black Power?

HUEY: Black Power is really people's power. The Black Panther Program, Panther Power as we call it, will implement this people's power. We have respect for all of humanity and we realize that the people should rule and determine their destiny. Wipe out the controller. To have Black Power doesn't humble or subjugate anyone to slavery or oppression. Black Power is giving power to people who have not had power to determine their destiny. We advocate and we aid any people who are struggling to determine their destiny. This is regardless of color. The Vietnamese say Vietnam should be able to determine its own destiny. Power of the Vietnamese people. We also chant power of the Vietnamese people. The Latins are talking about Latin America for the Latin Americans. Cuba, Si and Yanqui, Non. It's not that they don't want the Yankees to have any power they just don't want them to have power over them. They can have power over themselves. We in the black colony of America want to be able to have power over our destiny and that's black power.

MOVEMENT: A lot of white radicals are romantic about what Che said: "In a revolution one wins or dies . . ." For most of us it is really an abstract or theoretical question. It's a real question for you and we'd like you to rap about how you feel about it.

HUEY: Yes. The revolutionary sees no compromise. We will not compromise because the issue is so basic. If we compromise one iota we will be selling our freedom out. We will be selling the revolution out. And we refuse to remain slaves. As Eldridge says in SOUL ON ICE "a slave who dies of natural causes will not balance two dead flies on the scales of eternity." As far as we're concerned we would rather be dead than to go on with the slavery that we're in. Once we compromise we will be compromising not only our freedom, but also our manhood. We realize that we're going up against a highly technical country, and we realize that they are not only paper tigers, as Mao says, but real tigers too because they have the ability to slaughter many people. But in the long run, they will prove themselves paper tigers because they're not in line with humanity; they are divorced from the people. We know that the enemy is very powerful and that our manhood is at stake, but we feel it necessary to be victorious in regaining ourselves, regaining our manhood. And this is the basic point. So either we will do this or we won't have any freedom. Either we will win or we will die trying to win.

Mood of black people

MOVEMENT: How would you characterize the mood of black people in America today? Are they disenchanted, wanting a larger slice of the pie, or alienated, not wanting to integrate into a burning house, not wanting to integrate into Babylon? What do you think it will take for them to become alienated and revolutionary?

HUEY: I was going to say disillusioned, but I don't think we were ever under the illusion that we had freedom in this country. This society is definitely a decadent one and we realize it. Black people are realizing it more and more. We cannot gain our freedom under the present system; the system that is carrying out its plans of institutionalized racism. Your question is what will have to be done to stimulate them to revolution. I think it's already being done. It's a matter of time now for us to educate them to a program and show them the way to liberation. The Black Panther Party is the beacon light to show black people the way to liberation.

You notice the insurrections that have been going on throughout the country, in Watts, in Newark, in Detroit. They were all responses of the people demanding that they have freedom to determine their destiny, rejecting exploitation. Now the Black Panther Party does not think that the traditional riots, or insurrections that have taken place are the answer. It is true they have been against the Establishment, they have been against authority and oppression within their community, but they have been unorganized. However, black people learned from each of these insurrections.

They learned from Watts. I'm sure the people in Detroit were educated by what happened in Watts. Perhaps this was wrong education. It sort of missed the mark. It wasn't quite the correct activity, but the people were educated through the activity. The people of Detroit followed the example of the people in Watts, only they added a little scrutiny to it. The people in Detroit learned that the way to put a hurt on the administration is to make Molotov cocktails and to go into the street in mass numbers. So this was a matter of learning. The slogan went up "Burn, baby, burn". People were educated through the activity and it spread throughout the country. The people were educated on how to resist, but perhaps incorrectly.

Educate through activity

What we have to do as a vanguard of the revolution is to correct this through activity. The large majority of black people are either illiterate or semi-literate. They don't read. They need activity to follow. This is true of any colonized people. The same thing happened in Cuba where it was necessary for twelve men with a leadership of Che and Fidel to take to the hills and then attack the corrupt administration, to attack the army who were the protectors of the exploiters in Cuba. They could have leafleted the community and they could have written books, but the people would not respond. They had to act and the people could see and hear about it and therefore become educated on how to respond to oppression.

In this country black revolutionaries have to set an example. We can't do the same things that were done in Cuba because Cuba is Cuba and the U.S. is the U.S. Cuba has many terrains to protect the guerrilla. This country is mainly urban. We have to work out new solutions to offset the power of the country's technology and communication; its ability to communicate very rapidly by telephone and teletype and so forth. We do have solutions to these problems and they will be put into effect. I wouldn't want to go into the ways and means of this, but we will educate through action. We have to engage in action to make the people want to read our literature. Because they are not attracted to all the writing in this country; there's too much writing. Many books make one weary.

Threat from reformers

MOVEMENT: Kennedy before his death, and to a lesser extent Rockefeller and Lindsay and other established liberals have been talking about making reforms to give black people a greater share in the pie and thus stop any developing revolutionary movement. Would you comment on this?

HUEY: I would say this: If a Kennedy or Lindsay or anyone else can give decent housing to all of our people; if they can give full employment to our people with a high standard; if they can give full control to black people to determine the destiny of their community; if they can give fair trials in the court system by turning over the structure to the community; if they can end their exploitation of people throughout the world; if they can do all of these things they would have solved the problems. But I don't believe that under this present system, under capitalism, that they will be able to solve these problems.

People must control

I don't think black people should be fooled by their come-ons because every one who gets in office promises the same thing. They promise full employment and decent housing; the Great Society, the New Frontier. All of these names, but no real benefits. No effects are felt in the black community, and black people are tired of being deceived and duped. The people must have full control of the means of production. Small black businesses cannot compete with General Motors. That's just out of the question. General Motors robbed us and worked us for nothing for a couple hundred years and took our money and set up factories and became fat and rich and then talks about giving us some of the crumbs. We want full control. We're not interested in anyone promising that the private owners are going to all of a sudden become human beings and give these things to our community. It hasn't ever happened yet and, based on empirical evidence, we don't expect them to become Buddhists over night.

MOVEMENT: We raised this question not because we feel that these reforms are possible, but rather to get your ideas on what effects such attempted reforms might have on the development of a revolutionary struggle.

HUEY: I think that reforms pose no real threat. The revolution has always been in the hands of the young. The young always inherit the revolution. The young population is growing at a very rapid rate and they are very displeased with the authorities. They want control. I doubt that under the present system any kind of program can be launched that will be able to buy off all these young people. They have not been able to do it with the poverty program, the great society, etc. This country has never been able to employ all of its people simply because it's too interested in private property and the profit motive. A bigger poverty program is just what it says it is, a program to keep people in poverty. So I don't think that there is any real threat from the reforms.

MOVEMENT: Would you like to say something about the Panthers' organizing especially in terms of the youth?

HUEY: The Panthers represent a cross section of the black community. We have older people as well as younger people. The younger people of course are the ones who are seen on the streets. They are the activists. They are the real vanguard of change because they haven't been indoctrinated and they haven't submitted. They haven't been beaten into line as some of the older people have. But many of the older people realize that we're waging a just fight against the oppressor. They are aiding us and they are taking a part in the program.

Jail

MOVEMENT: Tell us something about your relations with the prisoners in the jail.

HUEY: The black prisoners as well as many of the white prisoners identify with the program of the Panthers. Of course by the very nature of their being prisoners they can see the oppression and they've suffered at the hands of the Gestapo. They have reacted to it. The black prisoners have all joined the Panthers, about 95% of them. Now the jail is all Panther and the police are very worried about this. The white prisoners can identify with us because they realize that they are not in control. They realize there's someone controlling them and the rest of the world with guns. They want some control over their lives also. The Panthers in jail have been educating them and so we are going along with the revolution inside of the jail.

MOVEMENT: What has been the effect of the demonstrations outside the jail calling for "Free Huey"?

HUEY: Very positive reactions. One demonstration, I don't remember which one, a couple of trustees, white trustees, held a cardboard sign out the laundry window reading "Free Huey". They say people saw it and responded to it. They were very enthusiastic about the demonstrators because they too suffer from being treated unfairly by the parole authorities and by the police here in the jail.

Open or underground

MOVEMENT: The Panthers' organizing efforts have been very open up until this point. Would you like to comment about the question of an underground political organization versus an open organization at this point in the struggle?

HUEY: Yeah. Some of the black nationalist groups feel that they have to be underground because they'll be attacked. But we don't feel that you can romanticize being underground. They say we're romantic because we're trying to live revolutionary lives, and we are not taking precautions. But we say that the only way we would go underground is if we're driven underground. All real revolutionary movements are driven underground. Take the revolution in Cuba. The agitation that was going on while Fidel was in law school was very much above ground. Even his existence in the hills was, so to speak, an above the ground affair because he was letting it be known who was doing the damage and why he was doing the damage. To catch him was a different story. The only way we can educate the people is by setting an example for them. We feel that this is very necessary.

This is a pre-revolutionary period and we feel it is very necessary to educate the people while we can. So we're very open about this education. We have been attacked and we will be attacked even more in the future but we're not going to go underground until we get ready to go underground because we have a mind of our own. We're not going to let anyone force us to do anything. We're going to go underground after we educate all of the black people and not before that time. Then it won't really be necessary for us to go underground because you can see black anywhere. We will just have the stuff to protect ourselves and the strategy to offset the great power that the strong-arm men of the establishment have and are planning to use against us.

White organizing

MOVEMENT: Your comments about the white prisoners seemed encouraging. Do you see the possibility of organizing a white Panther Party in oppr 'ion to the establishment possibly among poor and working whites?

HUEY: Well as I put it before Black Power is people's power and as far as organizing white people we give white people the privilege of having a mind and we want them to get a body. They can organize themselves. We can tell them what they should do, what their responsibility is if they're going to claim to be white revolutionaries or white mother country radicals, and that is to arm themselves and support the colonies around the world in their just struggle against imperialism. But anything more than that they will have to do on their own.

63. ROBERT S. BROWNE
URGES "A FORMAL PARTITIONING
OF THE UNITED STATES
INTO TWO TOTALLY SEPARATE
AND INDEPENDENT NATIONS"

One of the most reasoned arguments for racial separatism is that made in a series of papers and speeches by Robert S. Browne, an economics professor at Fairleigh-Dickinson University. A firm believer in black consciousness and the cultural distinctiveness of the black community, Browne advocates partitioning the United States and assigning a substantial area in the Deep South to the Negro people. This proposal for complete political separatism is a central doctrine in the platform of the Republic of New Africa, a revolutionary nationalist organization, founded by the Detroit attorney Milton Henry in 1967, for which Browne serves as an advisor. It is a secular version of the Black Muslim call for "a land of our own," and is the most recent of a long succession of similar recommendations going back to the ante-bellum period.

There is a growing ambivalence in the Negro community which is creating a great deal of confusion both within the black community itself, and within those segments of the white community that are attempting to relate to the blacks. It arises from the question of whether the American Negro is a cultural group, significantly distinct from the majority culture in ways that are ethnically rather than socio-economically based.

If one believes the answer to this is yes, then one is likely to favor emphasizing the cultural distinctiveness and to be vigorously opposed to any efforts to minimize or to submerge the

Robert S. Browne, "A Case for Separation," in Robert S. Browne and Bayard Rustin, SEPARATISM OR INTEGRATION: WHICH WAY FOR AMERICA?—A DIALOGUE (New York: A. Philip Randolph Educational Fund, 1968), pp. 7–15.

differences. If, on the other hand, one believes that there are no cultural differences between the blacks and the whites or that the differences are minimal and transitory, then one is likely to resist the placing of great emphasis on the differences and to favor accentuating the similarities.

These two currents in the black community are symbolized, and perhaps over-simplified, by the factional labels of separatists and integrationists.

The separatist would argue that the Negro's foremost grievance is not solvable by giving him access to more gadgets, although this is certainly a part of the solution, but that his greatest thirst is in the realm of the spirit—that he must be provided an opportunity to reclaim his own group individuality and to have that individuality recognized as having equal validity with the other major cultural groups of the world.

The integrationist would argue that what the Negro wants, principally, is exactly what the whites want—that is, that the Negro wants "in" American society, and that operationally this means providing the Negro with employment, income, housing, and education comparable to that of the whites. This having been achieved, the other aspects of the Negro's problem of inferiority will disappear.

The origins of this ideological dichotomy are easily identified. The physical characteristics that distinguish blacks from whites are obvious enough; and the long history of slavery, supplemented by the post-emancipation pattern of exclusion of the blacks from so many facets of American society, are equally undeniable. Whether observable behavioral differences between the mass of the blacks and the white majority are more properly attributable to this special history of the black man in America or are better viewed as expressions of racial differences in life style is an arguable proposition.

What is not arguable, however, is the fact that at the time of the slave trade the blacks arrived in America with a cultural background and a life style that was quite distinct from that of the whites. Although there was perhaps as much diversity amongst those Africans from widely scattered portions of the continent as there was amongst the European settlers, the differences between the two racial groups was unquestionably far greater, as attested by the different roles which they were to play in the society.

Integrationist and separatist viewpoints

Over this history there seems to be little disagreement. The dispute arises from how one views what happened during the subsequent 350 years.

The integrationist would focus on the transformation of the blacks into imitators of the European civilization. European clothing was imposed on the slaves; eventually their languages were forgotten; the African homeland receded ever further into the background. Certainly after 1808, when the slave trade was officially terminated, thus cutting off the supply of fresh injections of African culture, the Europeanization of the blacks proceeded apace. With emancipation, the national constitution recognized the legal manhood of the blacks, United States citizenship was unilaterally conferred upon the ex-slave, and the Negro began his arduous struggle for social, economic, and political acceptance into the American mainstream.

The separatist, however, takes the position that the cultural transformation of the black man was not complete. Whereas the integrationist is more or less content to accept the destruction of the original culture of the African slaves as a *fait accompli*, irrespective of whether he feels it to have been morally reprehensible or not, the separatist is likely to harbor a vague sense of resentment toward the whites for having perpetrated this cultural genocide and he is concerned to nurture whatever vestiges may have survived the North American experience and to encourage a renaissance of these lost characteristics. In effect, he is sensitive to an identity crisis which presumably does not exist in the mind of the integrationist.

To many observers, the separatist appears to be romantic and even reactionary. On the other hand, his viewpoint strikes an harmonious chord with mankind's most fundamental instinct—

the instinct for survival. With so powerful a stimulus and with the oppressive tendencies congenitally present in the larger white society, one almost could have predicted the emergence of the burgeoning movement toward black separatism. Millions of black parents have been confronted with the poignant agony of raising black, kinky-haired children in a society where the standard of beauty is a milk-white skin and long, straight hair. To convince a black child that she is beautiful when every channel of value formation in the society is telling her the opposite is a heart-rending and well-nigh impossible task. It is a challenge that confronts all Negroes, irrespective of their social and economic class, but the difficulty of dealing with it is likely to vary directly with the degree to which the family leads an integrated existence. A black child in a predominantly black school may realize that she doesn't look like the pictures in the books, magazines, and TV advertisements, but at least she looks like her schoolmates and neighbors. The black child in a predominantly white school and neighborhood lacks even this basis for identification.

The problem of identity

This identity problem is not peculiar to the Negro, of course, nor is it limited to questions of physical appearance. Minorities of all sorts encounter it in one form or another—the immigrant who speaks with an accent; the Jewish child who doesn't celebrate Christmas; the vegetarian who shuns meat. But for the Negro the problem has a special dimension, for in the American ethos a black man is not only "different," he is classed as ugly and inferior.

This is not an easy situation to deal with, and the manner in which a Negro chooses to handle it will be both determined by and a determinant of his larger political outlook. He can deal with it as an integrationist, accepting his child as being ugly by prevailing standards and urging him to excel in other ways to prove his worth; or he can deal with it as a black nationalist, telling the child that he is not a freak but rather part of a larger international community of black-skinned, kinky-haired people who have a beauty of their own, a glorious history, and a great future. In short, he can replace shame with pride, inferiority with dignity, by imbuing the child with what is coming to be known as black nationalism. The growing popularity of this latter viewpoint is evidenced by the appearance of "natural" hair styles among Negro youth and by the surge of interest in African and Negro culture and history.

Black Power, black consciousness and American society

Black Power may not be the ideal slogan to describe this new self-image that the black American is developing, for to guilt-ridden whites the slogan conjures up violence, anarchy, and revenge. To frustrated blacks, however, it symbolizes unity and a newly found pride in the blackness with which the Creator endowed us and which we realize must always be our mark of identification. Heretofore this blackness has been a stigma, a curse with which we were born. Black Power means that henceforth this curse will be a badge of pride rather than of scorn. It marks the end of an era in which black men devoted themselves to pathetic attempts to be white men and inaugurates an era in which black people will set their own standards of beauty, conduct, and accomplishment.

Is this new black consciousness in irreconcilable conflict with the larger American society?

In a sense, the heart of the American cultural problem always has been the need to harmonize the inherent contradiction between racial (or national) identity and integration into the melting pot which was America. In the century since the Civil War, the society has made little effort to find a measure to afford the black minority a sense of racial pride and independence while at the same time accepting it as a full participant in the larger society.

Now that the implications of that failure are becoming apparent, the black community seems to be saying "Forget it! We'll solve our own problems." Integration, which never had a high priority among the black masses, now is being written off by them as not only unattainable but as actually harmful—driving a wedge between those black masses and the so-called Negro elite.

To these developments has been added the momentous realization by many of the "integrated" Negroes that, in the United States, full integration can only mean full assimilation—a loss of racial identity. This sobering prospect has caused many a black integrationist to pause and reflect, even as have his similarly challenged Jewish counterparts.

Integration—a painless genocide?

Thus, within the black community there are two separate challenges to the traditional integration policy which long has constituted the major objective of established Negro leadership. There is the general skepticism that the Negro, even after having transformed himself into a white black-man, will enjoy full acceptance into American society; and there is the longer-range doubt that even should complete integration somehow be achieved, it would prove to be really desirable, for its price may be the total absorption and disappearance of the race—a sort of painless genocide.

Understandably, it is the black masses who have most vociferously articulated these dangers of assimilation, for they have watched with alarm as the more fortunate among their ranks have gradually risen to the top only to be promptly "integrated" off into the white community—absorbed into another culture, often with undisguised contempt for all that had previously constituted their racial and cultural heritage. Also, it was the black masses who first perceived that integration actually increases the white community's control over the black one by destroying black institutions, and by absorbing black leadership and coinciding its interests with those of the white community.

The international "brain drain" has its counterpart in the black community, which is constantly being denuded of its best trained people and many of its natural leaders. Black institutions of all sorts—colleges, newspapers, banks, even community organizations—are experiencing the loss of their better people to the newly available openings in white establishments, thereby lowering the quality of the Negro organizations and in some cases causing their demise or increasing their dependence on whites for survival. Such injurious, if unintended, side effects of integration have been felt in almost every layer of the black community.

Negro distrust of white America

If the foregoing analysis of the integrationist *vs.* separatist conflict exhausted the case, we might conclude that all the problems have been dealt with before, by other immigrant groups in America. (It would be an erroneous conclusion, for while other groups may have encountered similar problems, their solutions do not work for us, alas.) But there remains yet another factor which is cooling the Negro's enthusiasm for the integrationist path: he is becoming distrustful of his fellow Americans.

The American culture is one of the youngest in the world. Furthermore, as has been pointed out repeatedly in recent years, it is essentially a culture that approves of violence, indeed enjoys it. Military expenditures absorb roughly half the national budget. Violence predominates on the TV screen and the toys of violence are best-selling items during the annual rites for the much praised but little imitated Prince of Peace. In Vietnam, the zeal with which America has pursued its effort to destroy a poor and illiterate peasantry has astonished civilized people around the globe.

In such an atmosphere the Negro is understandably restive about the fate his white compatriots may have in store for him. The veiled threat by President Johnson at the time of the 1966 riots, suggesting that riots might beget pogroms and pointing out that Negroes are only 10 percent of the population was not lost on most blacks. It enraged them, but it was a sobering thought. The manner in which Germany herded the Jews into concentration camps and ultimately into ovens was a solemn warning to minority peoples everywhere. The casualness with which America exterminated the Indians and later interned the Japanese suggests that there is no cause for the Negro to feel complacent about his security in the United States. He finds little consolation in the assurance that if it does become necessary to place him in concentration camps it will only be as a means of protecting him from uncontrollable whites. "Protective incarceration" to use governmental jargonese.

The very fact that such alternatives are becoming serious topics of discussion has exposed the Negro's already raw and sensitive psyche to yet another heretofore unfelt vulnerability— the insecurity he suffers as a result of having no homeland which he can honestly feel is his own. Among the major ethno-cultural groups in the world he is unique in this respect.

Need for nationhood

As the Jewish drama during and following World War II painfully demonstrated, a national homeland is a primordial and urgent need for a people, even though its benefits do not always lend themselves to ready measurement. For some, the homeland constitutes a vital place of refuge from the strains of a life led too long within a foreign environment. For others, the need to reside in the homeland is considerably less intense than the need merely for knowing that such a homeland exists. The benefit to the expatriate is psychological, a sense of security in knowing that he belongs to a culturally and politically identifiable community. No doubt this phenomenon largely accounts for the fact that both the West Indian Negro and the Puerto Rican exhibit considerably more self-assurance than does the American Negro, for both of the former groups have ties to an identifiable homeland which honors and preserves their cultural heritage.

It has been marvelled that we American Negroes, almost alone among the cultural groups of the world, exhibit no sense of nationhood. Perhaps it is true that we do lack this sense, but there seems to be little doubt that the absence of a homeland exacts a severe if unconscious price from our psyche. Theoretically, our homeland is the U. S. A. We pledge allegience to the stars and stripes and sing the national anthem. But from the age when we first begin to sense that we are somehow "different," that we are victimized, these rituals begin to mean less to us than to our white compatriots. For many of us they become form without substance; for others they become a cruel and bitter mockery of our dignity and good sense; for relatively few of us do they retain a significance in any way comparable to their hold on our white brethren.

The recent coming into independence of many African states stimulated some interest among Negroes that independent Africa might become the homeland which they so desperately needed. A few made the journey and experienced a newly-found sense of community and racial dignity. For many who went, however, the gratifying racial fraternity which they experienced was insufficient to compensate for the cultural estrangement that accompanied it. They had been away from Africa for too long and the differences in language, food, and custom barred them from experiencing that "at home" sensation they were eagerly seeking. Symbolically, independent Africa could serve them as a homeland; practically, it could not. Their search continues—a search for a place where they can experience the security that comes from being a part of the majority culture, free at last from the inhibiting effects of cultural repression and induced cultural timidity and shame.

"This land is our rightful home"

If we have been separated from Africa for so long that we are no longer quite at ease there, then we are left with only one place to make our home, and that is in this land to which we were brought in chains. Justice would indicate such a solution in any case, for it is North America, not Africa, into which our toil and effort have been poured. This land is our rightful home and we are well within our rights in demanding an opportunity to enjoy it on the same terms as the other immigrants who have helped to develop it.

Since few whites will deny the justice of this claim, it is paradoxical that we are offered the option of exercising this birthright only on the condition that we abandon our culture, deny our race, and integrate ourselves into the white community. The "accepted" Negro, the "integrated" Negro, are mere euphemisms, hiding a cruel and relentless cultural destruction which is sometimes agonizing to the middle class Negro but which is becoming intolerable to the black masses. A Negro who refuses to yield his identity and to ape the white model finds he can survive in dignity only by rejecting the entire white society, which ultimately must mean challenging the law and the law enforcement mechanisms. On the other hand, if he abandons his cultural heritage and succumbs to the lure of integration he risks certain rejection and humiliation along the way, with absolutely no guarantee of ever achieving complete acceptance.

That such unsatisfactory options are leading to almost continuous disruption and dislocation of our society should hardly be cause for surprise.

Partition as a solution

A formal partitioning of the United States into two totally separate and independent nations, one white and one black, offers one way out of this tragic situation. Many will condemn it as a defeatist solution, but what they see as defeatism may better be described as a frank facing up to the realities of American society. A society is stable only to the extent that there exists a basic core of value judgments that are unthinkingly accepted by the great bulk of its members. Increasingly, Negroes are demonstrating that they do not accept the common core of values that underlies America—whether because they had little to do with drafting it or because they feel it is weighted against their interests.

The alleged disproportionately large number of Negro law violators, of unwed mothers, of illegitimate children, of nonworking adults *may* be indicators that there is no community of values such as has been supposed, although I am not unaware of racial socio-economic reasons for these statistics also. But whatever the reasons for observed behavioral differences, there clearly is no reason *why* the Negro should not have his own ideas about what the societal organization should be. The Anglo-Saxon system of organizing human relationships certainly has not proved itself to be superior to all other systems and the Negro is likely to be more acutely aware of this fact than are most Americans.

This unprecedented challenging of the "conventional wisdom" on the racial question is causing considerable consternation within the white community, especially the white liberal community, which has long felt itself to be the sponsor and guardian of the blacks. The situation is further confused because the challenges to the orthodox integrationist views are being projected by persons whose roots are authentically within the black community—whereas the integrationist spokesmen of the past often have been persons whose credentials were partly white-bestowed. This situation is further aggravated by the classical inter-generational problem—with black youth seizing the lead and speaking out for nationalism and separatism whereas their elders look on askance, a development which has at least a partial parallel within the contemporary white community, where youth is increasingly strident in its demands for thoroughgoing revision of our social institutions.

The black nationalists

If one were to inquire as to who the principal spokesmen for the new black nationalism or for separatism are, one would discover that the movement is essentially locally based rather than nationally organized. In the San Francisco Bay area, the Black Panther party is well known as a leader in the tactics of winning recognition for the black community. Their tactic is *via* a separate political party for black people, a format which I suspect we will hear a great deal more of in the future. The work of the Black Muslims is well known, and perhaps more national in scope than that of any other black nationalist group. Out of Detroit there is the Malcolm X Society, led by attorney

Milton Henry, whose members reject their United States citizenship and are claiming five southern states for the creation of a new Black Republic. Another major leader in Detroit is the Rev. Albert Cleage, who is developing a considerable following for his preachings of black dignity and who has also experimented with a black political party, thus far without success.

The black students at white colleges are one highly articulate group seeking for some national organizational form. A growing number of black educators are also groping toward some sort of nationally coordinated body to lend strength to their local efforts for developing educational systems better tailored to the needs of the black child. Under the name of Association of Afro-American Educators, they recently held a national conference in Chicago which was attended by several hundred public school teachers and college and community workers.

This is not to say that every black teacher or parent-teacher group that favors community control of schools is necessarily sympathetic to black separatism. Nevertheless, the general thrust of the move toward decentralized control over public schools, at least in the larger urban areas, derives from an abandoning of the idea of integration in the schools and a decision to bring to the ghetto the best and most suitable education that can be obtained.

Ghetto improvement efforts

Similarly, a growing number of community-based organizations are being formed for the purpose of facilitating the economic development of the ghetto, for replacement of absentee business proprietors and landlords by black entrepreneurs and resident owners. Again, these efforts are not totally separatist in that they operate within the framework of the present national society, but they build on the separatism that already exists in the society rather than attempting to eliminate it. To a black who sees salvation for the black man only in a complete divorce of the two races, these efforts at ghetto improvement appear futile—perhaps even harmful. To others, convinced that coexistence with white America is possible within the national framework if only the white will permit the Negro to develop as he wishes and by his own hand rather than in accordance with a white-conceived and white-administered pattern, such physically and economically upgraded black enclaves will be viewed as desirable steps forward.

Finally, those blacks who still feel that integration is in some sense both acceptable and possible will continue to strive for the color-blind society. When, if ever, these three strands of thought will converge toward a common outlook I cannot predict. In the meanwhile, however, concerned whites wishing to work with the black community should be prepared to encounter many rebuffs. They should keep ever in mind that the black community does not have a homogeneous vision of its own predicament at this crucial juncture.

64. SAN FRANCISCO STATE COLLEGE BLACK STUDENTS UNION: "IT IS DETRIMENTAL TO US AS BLACK HUMAN BEINGS TO BE CONTROLLED BY RACISTS"

Beginning in the spring of 1968 a movement for black consciousness and black separatism swept Negro students on northern and western colleges campuses. Their principal demand was for black studies programs. At some institutions they wanted separate departments and even separate schools within the university. Often there was an insistence that the black students autonomously operate these programs. Other demands included aggressive recruitment of Negro faculty, separate dormitories for students wishing them, separate Afro-American cultural and recreational centers, and special efforts

Demands of San Francisco State College Black Students Union. Leaflet, 1969.

to enroll minority group students unable to meet the usual entrance requirements. Among the most famous of the protests were those of the Black Students Union and Third World Liberation Front (a coalition of non-white students) at San Francisco State College, precipitated by the dismissal of a black instructor who advocated carrying guns on campus. These demands epitomize the nationalist sentiment of the most militant of the student separatists.

Demand #1

All Black Studies courses being taught through various departments be immediately part of the Black Studies department and that all the instructors in this department receive full time pay.

At the present time, the so-called black studies courses are being taught from the established departments which also control the function of the courses. We, the Black Students at San Francisco State College, feel that it is detrimental to us as Black human beings to be controlled by racists, who have absolute powers over determining what we should learn.

Take for example the School of Behavioral and Social Sciences controlling the social welfare classes. The School of Humanities control over the English classes. In our social welfare classes our first downfall is that our instructors are completely ignorant of the ethnic backgrounds of black people. They are in some cases people who have never been married and have no children. They tell us, or try to tell us, the best way to raise our children when they have never in their lives raised one. As a matter of fact our mothers raised most of theirs. In our English classes we are taught to dig on writers such as Chaucer and Arthur Miller. These writers do not deal in any realistic manner with Black people. Black people should be aware of our own writers such as Dr. Hare, LeRoi, Baldwin, Williams, Wright, etc. We are taught in our English classes to speak differently, so that when we return to our communities we are not able to communicate with our people. Therefore a diversity among the race results. If there was a real black studies department there would only be qualified instructors who would receive full-time pay since they would be full-time instructors.

Demand #2

That Dr. [Nathan] Hare, Chairman of the Black Studies Department, receive a full professorship and a comparable salary according to his qualifications.

Dr. Hare is the only black administrator at SF State who was selected and hired by the black students. And his loyalty is to the blacks on the campus and not to the white racist administration.

His salary bears witness to that well-known governmental fact that a black person with a Ph.D. earns, on the average, the same as a white person with a high school diploma.

He is a noted Ph.D. who has been published in the leading black magazines, sociological journals, as well as the so-called "slick" magazines, and has authored a book about the black middle class, "Black Anglo-Saxons."

Because he is a revolutionary and not an Uncle Tom, the administration has thrown him a few crumbs, in spite of the fact that he is responsible for coordinating and administering the department, which has 33 courses scattered throughout various "sympathetic" schools and departments on campus.

Therefore it is immediately incumbent to pay Dr. Hare for his work and his qualifications.

Demand #3

That there be a Department of Black Studies which will grant a Bachelor's degree in Black Studies; that the Black Studies Department, chairman, faculty and staff have the sole power to hire faculty and control and determine the destiny of its department.

The Black Studies Department should have the power to grant a Bachelor degree to anyone who wishes to major in the field, and that Black Studies Department, chairman, faculty and staff have the sole power to hire and fire without the interference of the administration and the chancellor. Past experiences with the racist dogs have taught blacks to "do their own thing."

The present Black Studies consist of thirty-three scattered courses throughout different school departments. It is most important that a credited department for the works of Black People be formed on this college campus, to feed the needs of its Black Student Body. The now Black Studies program does not allow a strong department of studies. The Blacks recognize the urgent need for Black Studies that would tell the true nature of this decadent American society.

The Black Students of SFSC have long struggled for three years to obtain a Black Studies Program with little or no support from the faculty and administration. If our demands are not soon met, we will have to use force.

Demand #4

That all unused slots for Black Students from Fall 1968 under the Special Admissions program be filled in Spring 1969.

Many Black Students are unable to be accepted in a college because of low grade points received by taking the A.C.T. or S.A.T. test, for middle-class suburban honkies. But through the demands, hard work and study of the BSU, Black Students are in this college.

There were more than enough Black Students to be accepted into SFSC under the Black Studies Institute, OMFE, STEP, Upward Bound and College Commitment Program (which is the so-called "Educational Opportunity Program"). But because of the hassle with the administration (that is, the administrators told many Black Students that their transcripts were late and the students who were receiving Grants or Loans were told that they hadn't come in) many of these students were accepted in other colleges where they were given their Grants and Loans— so that left 128 unused slots open.

We have demanded and demonstrated to get the unused 128 slots filled by Black Students and Third World Students who wish to be admitted in SFSC in the Spring 1969.

Demand #5

That all Black Students wishing so be admitted in Fall 1969.

By admitting all black students who apply, the state can make up for years of neglecting Black people trying to get a college education. The current racist quota system must be abolished— not ten years from now, but by September 1969. Entrances based on high school grades are also unjust to Third World students; these grades were originally based on knowledge of a white culture that denied the existence of any relevant Third World cultures. We have hassled too long with racist administrators and their systematic exclusion of Third World Students; we must change this now.

Demand #6

That 20 full-time teaching positions be allocated to the Department of Black Studies.

No department on any college campus can function unless it has instructors. A department such as Black Studies, which offers 33 courses, needs 20 faculty members to adequately teach these and more courses. The positions are there and all the administration needs to do is allocate them to the Black Studies Department.

At the end of the summer of 1968, there were 47 open teaching positions. Donald Garrity, the racist top pig on the campus, declared that these positions would go into other areas where he felt they were needed. He felt the money should go to other administrators' pockets rather than into the Black Studies Department.

The racist Garrity gave away positions that could have been filled by qualified, nationally known Black men and women such as Harold Cruse, Sarah Fabio and Alvin Poussant. The administration had the positions and refused to give them to us, and we are again demanding that the Black Studies Department be given 20 positions.

Demand #7

That Dr. Helen Bedesom be replaced from the position of Financial Aid Officer and that a Black person be hired to direct it; that Third World people have the power to determine how it will be administered.

Dr. Helen Bedesom has consistently ignored the needs of Third World students, particularly black students. Money which has been given to the college for Black students has been sent back by this power-mad woman with the explanation that she could not accept earmarked money or the outright lie that no qualified students applied. Yet this slavemistress has allowed similarly "earmarked" funds to be used by Chinese students.

Dr. Bedesom, who it is rumored achieved her position not by the normal process of appointment, but by successfully staging a vicious power play when the position was vacated, has brought young black sisters to tears with her verbal attacks on their personal lives. She has told black students that there was no money available just prior to her sending back of funds allocated to poor students by the federal government.

Demand #8

That no disciplinary action will be administered in any way to any student workers, teachers, or administrators during and after the strike as a consequence of their participation in the strike.

We are striking because it is a necessity, a necessity for our education, for black people, and especially black youth and black children, throughout the Bay Area, this state, and all over the country.

Already eleven students, black and white, have suffered disciplinary measures; because of their devotion to this necessity. One white teacher has been fired because of his radical position.

If the school chooses to use this as one of their methods of retaliation, we have no choice but to further escalate our struggle.

The more students suspended and teachers fired, the more committed our efforts become, and the deeper our struggle.

If any discipline is needed, run it on Pig Ronnie and Fuehrer Dumke.

Demand #9

That the California State College Trustees not be allowed to dissolve any Black programs on or off San Francisco State College campus.

The Tutorial Program, and Black Students Union, the Third World Liberation Front, the Bookstore, the Commons; all these and anything else which the students now control are due to be co-opted and controlled by Reagan and his lackeys—the Trustees.

Title five if revised would eliminate student self-government, would give the Trustees total authority to decide what activities are allowable and which ones aren't, and the Chancellor would have to approve in writing any and all activities before they are implemented.

They plan to control all the auxiliary organizations which are defined as (1) associated student organizations, (2) any organization using the name of the state or that state college, (3) any organization which represents an official relationship with the college, (4) any organization in which college officials participate as directors as part of their official position, (5) any organization which provides services to the campus.

Black people and other Third World students who need financial aid will be directly at the mercy of the Trustees and the President. In short, the need that Black people feel to determine their own destiny would be completely and utterly wiped out.

Specifically, the Trustees would have the power to:
1. Eliminate the Experimental College and activities they don't like, such as the Tutorial Program;
2. Censor any student paper, play, or film they wish;
3. Raise the price of books and food without consultation and use the profits any way they desire;

4. Use student money to finance any college program—whether it relates to students or not;

5. Prevent students from working in the community.

Demand #10

That George Murray maintain his teaching position on campus for the 1968–69 academic year.

George Murray, who is a graduate of S.F. State, is a well-qualified English instructor. He is able to relate to the needs of his Black students, while most white instructors ignore the unique problems of Black students on a white campus such as S.F. State. Black students on this campus need an instructor like George who teaches students about Black authors and their works, for these Black authors talk to the student about his own experiences in the Black community.

George Murray's presence on this campus should not be determined by white people and their standards. Black people on this campus need to defend themselves against a power structure of which S.F. State is a part because Black brothers and sisters are killed every day, whether in Viet Nam or in San Francisco, by racist policemen who lay siege to our community. George's statement about students defending themselves is not grounds for dismissal as an instructor. White administrators know little about needs of Black people and therefore should have no power to fire a man such as George Murray, who speaks truthfully about our needs as Black people in a white America.

65. JAMES FORMAN: "WE HAVE A CHANCE TO HELP BRING THIS GOVERNMENT DOWN"

An example of the combination of militant black nationalism and revolutionary Marxism, which was to be found at the extreme left wing of the black protest movement, was the call for armed revolution and monetary reparations made by James Forman at the Black Economic Development Conference held in Detroit in April 1969. The conclave was sponsored by Interreligious Foundation for Community Organizations (IFCO), an interfaith coalition created by major Protestant and Jewish organizations in 1967 to fund militant local community action groups. The conference adopted a manifesto demanding five hundred million dollars from the Protestant and Jewish churches as a partial reparation for past racial discrimination. This money would be used for economic development within the black community free from any control of the donors.

This manifesto had been proposed by James Forman, Executive Secretary of SNCC during its most active period, 1961–1966. In presenting it Forman made clear that he viewed it as part of a broad revolutionary strategy. This revolutionary thrust is also illustrated by the second document, a leaflet distributed to radical delegates at the conference, containing the arguments they were to marshal for maximum impact during the discussions. In his speech Forman threatened to cripple the American economy by sabotage and advocated armed revolution and guerrilla warfare "to help bring this government down."

A. Manifesto of the National Black Economic Development Conference

MANIFESTO TO THE WHITE CHRISTIAN CHURCHES AND THE JEWISH SYNAGOGUES IN THE UNITED STATES OF AMERICA AND ALL OTHER RACIST INSTITUTIONS

Introduction

TOTAL CONTROL AS THE ONLY SOLUTION TO THE ECONOMIC PROBLEMS OF BLACK PEOPLE

Brothers and Sisters:

We have come from all over the country, burning with anger

"Manifesto to the White Christian Churches and the Jewish Synagogues of America and all other Racist Institutions. Presentation by James Forman Delivered and Adopted by the National Black Economic Development Conference in Detroit, Michigan on April 26, 1969," leaflet.

and despair not only with the miserable economic plight of our people, but fully aware that the racism on which the Western World was built dominates our lives. There can be no separation of the problems of racism from the problems of our economic, political, and cultural degradation. To any black man, this is clear.

But there are still some of our people who are clinging to the rhetoric of the Negro and we must separate ourselves from those Negroes who go around the country promoting all types of schemes for Black Capitalism.

Ironically, some of the most militant Black Nationalists, as they call themselves, have been the first to jump on the bandwagon of black capitalism. They are pimps; Black Power Pimps and fraudulent leaders and the people must be educated to understand that any black man or Negro who is advocating a perpetuation of capitalism inside the United States is in fact seeking not only his ultimate destruction and death, but is contributing to the continuous exploitation of black people all around the world. For it is the power of the United States Government, this racist, imperialistic government that is choking the life out of all people around the world.

We are an African people. We sit back and watch the Jews in this country make Israel a powerful conservative state in the Middle East, but we are not concerned actively about the plight of our brothers in Africa. We are the most advanced technological group of black people in the world, and there are many skills that could be offered to Africa. At the same time, it must be publicly stated that many African leaders are in disarray themselves, having been duped into following the lines as laid out by the Western Imperialist governments.

Africans themselves succumbed to and are victims of the power of the United States. For instance, during the summer of 1967, as the representatives of SNCC, Howard Moore and I traveled extensively in Tanzania and Zambia. We talked to high, very high, governmental officials. We told them there were many black people in the United States who were willing to come and work in Africa. All these government officials who were part of the leadership in their respective governments, said they wanted us to send as many skilled people that we could contact. But this program never came into fruition and we do not know the exact reasons, for I assure you that we talked and were committed to making this a successful program. It is our guess that the United States put the squeeze on these countries, for such a program directed by SNCC would have been too dangerous to the international prestige of the U. S. It is also possible that some of the wild statements by some black leader frightened the Africans.

In Africa today, there is a great suspicion of black people in this country. This is a correct suspicion since most of the Negroes who have left the States for work in Africa usually work for the Central Intelligence Agency (CIA) or the State Department. But the respect for us as a people continues to mount and the day will come when we can return to our homeland as brothers and sisters. But we should not think of going back to Africa today, for we are located in a strategic position. We live inside the U. S. which is the most barbaric country in the world and we have a chance to help bring this government down.

Time is short and we do not have much time and it is time we stop mincing words. Caution is fine, but no oppressed people ever gained their liberation until they were ready to fight, to use whatever means necessary, including the use of force and power of the gun to bring down the colonizer.

We have heard the rhetoric, but we have not heard the rhetoric which says that black people in this country must understand that we are the Vanguard Force. We shall liberate all the people in the U. S. and we will be instrumental in the liberation of colored people the world around. We must understand this point very clearly so that we are not trapped into diversionary and reactionary movements. Any class analysis of the U. S. shows very clearly that black people are the most oppressed group of people inside the United States. We have suffered the most from racism and exploitation, cultural degradation and lack of political power. It follows from the laws of revolution that the most oppressed will make the revolution, but we are not talking about just making the revolution. All the parties on the left who consider themselves revolutionary will say that blacks are the Vanguard, but we are saying that not only are we the Vanguard, but we must assume leadership, total control and we must exercise the humanity which is inherent in us. We are the most humane people within the U. S. We have suffered and we understand suffering. Our hearts go out to the Vietnamese for we know what it is to suffer under the domination of racist America. Our hearts, our soul and all the compassion we can mount goes out to our brothers in Africa, Santa Domingo, Latin America and Asia who are being tricked by the power structure of the U. S. which is dominating the world today. These ruthless, barbaric men have systematically tried to kill all people and organizations opposed to its imperialism. We no longer can just get by with the use of the word capitalism to describe the U. S., for it is an imperial power, sending money, missionaries and the army throughout the world to protect this government and the few rich whites who control it. General Motors and all the major auto industries are operating in South Africa, yet the white dominated leadership of the United Auto Workers sees no relationship to the exploitation of black people in South Africa and the exploitation of black people in the U. S. If they understand it, they certainly do not put it into practice which is the actual test. We as black people must be concerned with the total conditions of all black people in the world.

But while we talk of revolution which will be an armed confrontation and long years of sustained guerrilla warfare inside this country, we must also talk of the type of world we want to live in. We must commit ourselves to a society where the total means of production are taken from the rich and placed into the hands of the state for the welfare of all the people. This is what we mean when we say total control. And we mean that black people who have suffered the most from exploitation and racism must move to protect their black interest by assuming leadership inside of the United States of everything that exists. The time has passed when we are second in command and the white boy stands on top. This is especially true of the Welfare Agencies in this country, but it is not enough to say that a black man is on top. He must be committed to building the new society, to taking the wealth away from the rich people such as General Motors, Ford, Chrysler, the DuPonts, the Rockefellers, the Mellons, and all the other rich white exploiters and racists who run this world.

Where do we begin? We have already started. We started the moment we were brought to this country. In fact, we started on the shores of Africa, for we have always resisted attempts to make us slaves and now we must resist the attempts to make us capitalists. It is the financial interest of the U. S. to make us capitalist, for this will be the same line as that of integration into the mainstream of American life. Therefore, brothers and sisters, there is no need to fall into the trap that we have to get an ideology. We HAVE an ideology. Our fight is against racism, capitalism and imperialism and we are dedicated to building a socialist society inside the United States where the total means of production and distribution are in the hands of the State and that must be led by black people, by revolutionary blacks who are concerned about the total humanity of this world. And therefore, we obviously are different from some of those who seek a black nation in the United States, for there is no way for that nation to be viable if in fact the United States remains in the hands of white racists. Then too, let us deal with some arguments that we should share power with whites. We say that there must be a revolutionary black Vanguard and that white people in this country must be willing to accept black leadership, for that is the only protection that black people have to protect ourselves from racism arising again in this country.

Racism in the U. S. is so pervasive in the mentality of whites that only an armed, well-disciplined, black-controlled government can insure the stamping out of racism in this country. And that is why we plead with black people not to be talking about a few crumbs, a few thousand dollars for this cooperative, or a thousand dollars which splits black people into fighting over the dollar. That is the intention of the government. We say . . . think in terms of total control of the U. S. Prepare ourselves to seize state power. Do not hedge, for time is short and all around the world, the forces of liberation are directing their attacks against the U. S. It is a powerful country, but that power is not greater than that of black people. We work the chief industries of the country and we could cripple the economy while the brothers fought guerrilla warfare in the streets. This will take some long range planning, but whether it happens in a thousand years is of no consequence. It cannot happen unless we start. How then is all of this related to this conference?

First of all, this conference is called by a set of religious people, Christians, who have been involved in the exploitation and rape of black people since the country was founded. The missionary goes hand in hand with the power of the states. We must begin seizing power wherever we are and we must say to the planners of this conference that you are no longer in charge. We the people who have assembled here thank you for getting us here, but we are going to assume power over the conference and determine from this moment on the direction in which we want it to go. We are not saying that the conference was planned badly. The staff of the conference has worked hard and have done a magnificent job in bringing all of us together and we must include them in the new membership which must surface from this point on. The conference is now the property of the people who are assembled here. This we proclaim as fact and not rhetoric and there are demands that we are going to make and we insist that the planners of this conference help us implement them.

We maintain we have the revolutionary right to do this. We have the same rights, if you will, as the Christians had in going into Africa and raping our Motherland and bringing us away from our continent of peace and into this hostile and alien environment where we have been living in perpetual warfare since 1619.

Our seizure of power at this conference is based on a program and our program is contained in the following MANIFESTO:

Black Manifesto

We the black people assembled in Detroit, Michigan for the National Black Economic Development Conference are fully aware that we have been forced to come together because racist white America has exploited our resources, our minds, our bodies, our labors. For centuries we have been forced to live as colonized people inside the United States, victimized by the most vicious, racist system in the world. We have helped to build the most industrial country in the world.

We are therefore demanding of the white Christian churches and Jewish synagogues which are part and parcel of the system of capitalism, that they begin to pay reparations to black people of this country. We are demanding $500,000,000 from the Christian white churches and the Jewish synagogues. This total comes to 15 dollars per nigger. This is a low estimate for we maintain there are probably more than 30,000,000 black people in this country. $15 a nigger is not a large sum of money and we know that the churches and synagogues have a tremendous wealth and its membership, white America, has profited and still exploits black people. We are also not unaware that the exploitation of colored peoples around the world is aided and abetted by the white Christian churches and synagogues. This demand for $500,000,000 is not an idle resolution or empty words. Fifteen dollars for every black brother and sister in the United States is only a beginning of the reparations due us as people who have been exploited and degraded, brutalized, killed and persecuted. Underneath all of this exploitation, the racism of this country has produced a psychological effect upon us that we are beginning to shake off. We are no longer afraid to demand our full rights as a people in this decadent society.

We are demanding $500,000,000 to be spent in the following way:

1. We call for the establishment of a Southern land bank to

help our brothers and sisters who have to leave their land because of racist pressure for people who want to establish cooperative farms, but who have no funds. We have seen too many farmers evicted from their homes because they have dared to defy the white racism of this country. We need money for land. We must fight for massive sums of money for this Southern Land Bank. We call for $200,000,000 to implement this program.

2. We call for the establishment of four major publishing and printing industries in the United States to be funded with ten million dollars each. These publishing houses are to be located in Detroit, Atlanta, Los Angeles, and New York. They will help to generate capital for further cooperative investments in the black community, provide jobs and an alternative to the white-dominated and controlled printing field.

3. We call for the establishment of four of the most advanced scientific and futuristic audio-visual network to be located in Detroit, Chicago, Cleveland and Washington, D. C. These TV networks will provide an alternative to the racist propaganda that fills the current television networks. Each of these TV networks will be funded by ten million dollars each.

4. We call for a research skills center which will provide research on the problems of black people. This center must be funded with no less than 30 million dollars.

5. We call for the establishment of a training center for the teaching of skills in community organization, photography, movie making, television making and repair, radio building and repair and all other skills needed in communication. This training center shall be funded with no less than ten million dollars.

6. We recognize the role of the National Welfare Rights Organization and we intend to work with them. We call for ten million dollars to assist in the organization of welfare recipients. We want to organize the welfare workers in this country so that they may demand more money from the government and better administration of the welfare system of this country.

7. We call for $20,000,000 to establish a National Black Labor

Strike and Defense Fund. This is necessary for the protection of black workers and their families who are fighting racist working conditions in this country.

*8. We call for the establishment of the International Black Appeal. (IBA) This International Black Appeal will be funded with no less than $20,000,000. The IBA is charged with producing more capital for the establishment of cooperative businesses in the United States and in Africa, our Motherland. The International Black Appeal is one of the most important demands that we are making for we know that it can generate and raise funds throughout the United States and help our African brothers. The IBA is charged with three functions and shall be headed by James Forman:

(a) Raising money for the program of the National Black Economic Development Conference.

(b) The development of cooperatives in African countries and support of African Liberation movements.

(c) Establishment of a Black Anti-Defamation League which will protect our African image.

9. We call for the establishment of a Black University to be funded with $130,000,000 to be located in the South. Negotiations are presently under way with a Southern University.

10. We demand that IFCO allocate all unused funds in the planning budget to implement the demands of this conference.

In order to win our demands we are aware that we will have to have massive support, therefore:

(1) We call upon all black people throughout the United States to consider themselves as members of the National Black Economic Development Conference and to act in unity to help force the racist white Christian churches and Jewish synagogues to implement these demands.

(2) We call upon all the concerned black people across the country to contact black workers, black women, black students

* (Revised and approved by Steering Committee)

and the black unemployed, community groups, welfare organizations, teachers organizations, church leaders and organizations explaining how these demands are vital to the black community of the U. S. Pressure by whatever means necessary
should be applied to the white power structure of the racist
white Christian churches and Jewish synagogues. All black
people should act boldly in confronting our white oppressors
and demanding this modest reparation of 15 dollars per black
man.

(3) Delegates and members of the National Black Economic
Development Conference are urged to call press conferences in
the cities and to attempt to get as many black organizations as
possible to support the demands of the conference. The quick
use of the press in the local areas will heighten the tension and
these demands must be attempted to be won in a short period
of time, although we are prepared for protracted and long
range struggle.

(4) We call for the total disruption of selected church sponsored agencies operating anywhere in the U. S. and the world.
Black workers, black women, black students and the black unemployed are encouraged to seize the offices, telephones, and
printing apparatus of all church sponsored agencies and to hold
these in trusteeship until our demands are met.

(5) We call upon all delegates and members of the National
Black Economic Development Conference to stage sit-in demonstrations at selected black and white churches. This is not to
be interpreted as a continuation of the sit-in movement of the
early sixties but we know that active confrontation inside white
churches is possible and will strengthen the possibility of meeting our demands. Such confrontation can take the form of reading the Black Manifesto instead of a sermon or passing it out to
church members. The principle of self-defense should be applied if attacked.

(6) On May 4, 1969 or a date thereafter, depending upon
local conditions, we call upon black people to commence the disruption of the racist churches and synagogues throughout the
United States.

(7) We call upon IFCO to serve as a central staff to co-ordinate the mandate of the conference and to reproduce and distribute en mass literature, leaflets, news items, press releases and other material.

(8) We call upon all delegates to find within the white community those forces which will work under the leadership of blacks to implement these demands by whatever means necessary. By taking such actions, white Americans will demonstrate concretely that they are willing to fight the white skin privilege and the white supremacy and racism which has forced us as black people to make these demands.

(9) We call upon all white Christians and Jews to practice patience, tolerance, understanding and nonviolence as they have encouraged, advised and demanded that we as black people should do throughout our entire enforced slavery in the United States. The true test of their faith and belief in the Cross and the words of the prophets will certainly be put to a test as we seek legitimate and extremely modest reparations for our role in developing the industrial base of the Western world through our slave labor. But we are no longer slaves, we are men and women, proud of our African heritage, determined to have our dignity.

(10) We are so proud of our African heritage and realize concretely that our struggle is not only to make revolution in the United States, but to protect our brothers and sisters in Africa and to help them rid themselves of racism, capitalism, and imperialism by whatever means necessary, including armed struggle. We are and must be willing to fight the defamation of our African image wherever it rears its ugly head. We are therefore charging the Steering Committee to create a Black Anti-Defamation League to be funded by money raised from the International Black Appeal.

(11) We fully recognize that revolution in the United States and Africa, our Motherland, is more than a one dimensional operation. It will require the total integration of the political, economic, and military components and therefore, we call upon all our brothers and sisters who have acquired

training and expertise in the fields of engineering, electronics, research, community organization, physics, biology, chemistry, mathematics, medicine, military science and warfare to assist the National Black Economic Development Conference in the implementation of its program.

(12) To implement these demands we must have a fearless leadership. We must have a leadership which is willing to battle the church establishment to implement these demands. To win our demands we will have to declare war on the white Christian churches and synagogues and this means we may have to fight the total government structure of this country. Let no one here think that these demands will be met by our mere stating them. For the sake of the churches and synagogues, we hope that they have the wisdom to understand that these demands are modest and reasonable. But if the white Christians and Jews are not willing to meet our demands through peace and good will, then we declare war and we are prepared to fight by whatever means necessary. We are, therefore, proposing the election of the following Steering Committee:

Lucious Walker	Mark Comfort
Renny Freeman	Earl Allen
Luke Tripp	Robert Browne
Howard Fuller	Vincent Harding
James Forman	Mike Hamlin
John Watson	Len Holt
Dan Aldridge	Peter Bernard
John Williams	Michael Wright
Ken Cockrel	Muhammed Kenyatta
Chuck Wooten	Mel Jackson
Fannie Lou Hamer	Howard Moore
Julian Bond	Harold Holmes

Brothers and sisters, we no longer are shuffling our feet and scratching our heads. We are tall, black and proud.

And we say to the white Christian churches and Jewish synagogues, to the government of this country and to all the white racist imperialists who compose it, there is only one thing left that you can do to further degrade black people and that is to kill us. But we have been dying too long for this country. We have died in every war. We are dying in Vietnam today fighting the wrong enemy.

The new black man wants to live and to live means that we must not become static or merely believe in self-defense. We must boldly go out and attack the white Western world at its power centers. The white Christian churches are another form of government in this country and they are used by the government of this country to exploit the people of Latin America, Asia and Africa, but the day is soon coming to an end. Therefore, brothers and sisters, the demands we make upon the whole Christian churches and the Jewish synagogues are small demands. They represent 15 dollars per black person in these United States. We can legitimately demand this from the church power structure. We must demand more from the United States Government.

But to win our demands from the church which is linked up with the United States Government, we must not forget that it will ultimately be by force and power that we will win.

We are not threatening the churches. We are saying that we know the churches came with the military might of the colonizers and have been sustained by the military might of the colonizers. Hence, if the churches in colonial territories were established by military might, we know deep within our hearts that we must be prepared to use force to get our demands. We are not saying that this is the road we want to take. It is not, but let us be very clear that we are not opposed to force and we are not opposed to violence. We were captured in Africa by violence. We were kept in bondage and political servitude and forced to work as slaves by the military machinery and the Christian church working hand in hand.

We recognize that in issuing this manifesto we must prepare for a long range educational campaign in all communities of this country, but we know that the Christian churches have contributed to our oppression in white America. We do not intend to abuse our black brothers and sisters in black churches who have uncritically accepted Christianity. We want them to understand how the racist white Christian church with its hypocritical declarations and doctrines of brotherhood has abused our trust and faith. An attack on the religious beliefs of black people is not our major objective, even though we know that we were not Christians when we were brought to this country, but that Christianity was used to help enslave us. Our objective in issuing this Manifesto is to force the racist white Christian Church to begin the payment of reparations which are due to all black people, not only by the Church but also by private business and the U. S. government. We see this focus on the Christian Church as an effort around which all black people can unite.

Our demands are negotiable, but they cannot be minimized, they can only be increased and the Church is asked to come up with larger sums of money than we are asking. Our slogans are:

ALL ROADS MUST LEAD TO REVOLUTION
UNITE WITH WHOMEVER YOU CAN UNITE
NEUTRALIZE WHEREVER POSSIBLE
FIGHT OUR ENEMIES RELENTLESSLY
VICTORY TO THE PEOPLE
LIFE AND GOOD HEALTH TO MANKIND
RESISTANCE TO DOMINATION BY THE WHITE
    CHRISTIAN CHURCHES AND THE JEWISH
    SYNAGOGUES
REVOLUTIONARY BLACK POWER
WE SHALL WIN WITHOUT A DOUBT

B. Instructions for radical delegates at the conference

The Revolutionary line for the National Black Economic Development Conference

1. Anti-Black capitalism.
2. Push concepts of cooperatives and community socialism.

"The New Revolutionary Line for the National Black Economic Development Conference" [1969], leaflet.

3. Avoid intense ideological squabbles. Push need for concrete programs for the Black community.
4. Push for publishing houses.
5. Push for television stations and especially cable TV.
6. Push for some money for organizers to work with welfare recipients who will carry forth the fight to obtain more funds from the state.
7. Push for national Labor Defense and Strike Fund for Black workers.
8. Push for United Black Appeal to raise money for cooperatives.
9. Push for Black university to be located in the South.
10. Push for the central staff of the conference to follow up on our demands. Demand an accounting from conference committees of funds spent for the conference and allocated for this conference.
11. Push the line that church and capitalism and imperialism are interrelated and that the church must give up some bread in massive forms as well as the government.
12. Demand that we get a breakdown of the functions of the church and its agencies. This cannot be obtained at the conference, but we need to know what the church is in to, especially the World Council.
13. Criticize the funding of conservative groups in the Black community by the Church and control the church is trying to exercise in the Black community through its money channeled through white administrators.
14. All control of church money should be placed in the hands of those opposed to capitalism and dedicated to building a socialist society, a cooperative society, a communal society.

The details and the specifics of all these programs have been worked out and will be revealed at the proper moment, but we as revolutionaries are concerned that the workers generate a feeling around all the demands we are making or rather listed above. Specific ways to implement these demands have been worked out and will also be revealed at the right time.

People are not to criticize the conference as phony. It is an objective fact, and it will move to the right or left depending upon our following the lines which have been set forth in this paper.

Victory to the people

Do not reveal this paper to any suspicious cat, but spread the word among your friends that there is a revolutionary line for this conference which cannot be stopped.

66. CHARLES V. HAMILTON: BUILDING "A NEW SENSE OF COMMUNITY AMONG BLACK PEOPLE"

Black Power has been a slogan meaning different things to different people as Professor Charles V. Hamilton of Columbia University points out in this article. Although he is the co-author, with former SNCC Chairman Stokely Carmichael, of *Black Power: The Politics of Liberation in America,** Hamilton must actually be classed as an advocate not of revolutionary black power, but of what can best be described as a reformist version of black power. He advocates black community organization along the lines of cooperative economic endeavor, bloc voting, and community control of public schools. Thus his program is one of uniting Negroes to act together for the achievement of equality in American society. In fact, Hamilton's views bear remarkable similarities to the militant (as opposed to accommodationist) advocates of race solidarity and self-help at the turn of the century. This article in the *New York Times Magazine,* written when Hamilton was teaching at Roosevelt University, is an especially lucid expression of this reformist version of black power.

Charles V. Hamilton, "An Advocate of Black Power Defines It," NEW YORK TIMES MAGAZINE, April 14, 1968, pp. 22–23, 79–83. Reprinted by permission of the NEW YORK TIMES COMPANY © 1968 and Charles V. Hamilton.

* (New York: Random House, 1967)

Black Power has many definitions and connotations in the rhetoric of race relations today. To some people, it is synonymous with premeditated acts of violence to destroy the political and economic institutions of this country. Others equate Black Power with plans to rid the civil-rights movement of whites who have been in it for years. The concept is understood by many to mean hatred of and separation from whites; it is associated with calling whites "honkies" and with shouts of "Burn, baby, burn!" Some understand it to be the use of pressure-group tactics in the accepted tradition of the American political process. And still others say that Black Power must be seen first of all as an attempt to instill a sense of identity and pride in black people.

Ultimately, I suspect, we have to accept the fact that, in this highly charged atmosphere, it is virtually impossible to come up with a single definition satisfactory to all.

Even as some of us try to articulate our idea of Black Power and the way we relate to it and advocate it, we are categorized as "moderate" or "militant" or "reasonable" or "extremist." "I can accept your definition of Black Power," a listener will say to me. "But how does your position compare with what Stokely Carmichael said in Cuba or with what H. Rap Brown said in Cambridge, Md.?" Or, just as frequently, some young white New Left advocate will come up to me and proudly announce: "You're not radical enough. Watts, Newark, Detroit—that's what's happening, man! You're nothing but a reformist. We've got to blow up this society. Read Ché or Debray or Mao." All I can do is shrug and conclude that some people believe that making a revolution in this country involves rhetoric, Molotov cocktails and being under 30.

To have Black Power equated with calculated acts of violence would be very unfortunate. First, if black people have learned anything over the years, it is that he who shouts revolution the loudest is one of the first to run when the action starts. Second, open calls to violence are a sure way to have one's ranks immediately infiltrated. Third—and this is as important as any reason—violent revolution in this country would fail; it would be met with the kind of repression used in Sharpeville,

South Africa, in 1960, when 67 Africans were killed and 186 wounded during a demonstration against apartheid. It is clear that America is not above this. There are many white bigots who would like nothing better than to embark on a program of black genocide, even though the imposition of such repressive measures would destroy civil liberties for whites as well as for blacks. Some whites are so panicky, irrational and filled with racial hatred that they would welcome the opportunity to annihilate the black community. This was clearly shown in the senseless murder of Dr. Martin Luther King Jr., which understandably—but nonetheless irrationally—prompted some black militants to advocate violent retaliation. Such cries for revenge intensify racial fear and animosity when the need—now more than ever—is to establish solid, stable organizations and action programs.

Many whites will take comfort in these words of caution against violence. But they should not. The truth is that the black ghettos are going to continue to blow up out of sheer frustration and rage, and no amount of rhetoric from professors writing articles in magazines (which most black people in the ghettos do not read anyway) will affect that. There comes a point beyond which people cannot be expected to endure prejudice, oppression and deprivation, and they *will* explode.

Some of us can protect our positions by calling for "law and order" during a riot, or by urging "peaceful" approaches, but we should not be confident that we are being listened to by black people legitimately fed up with intolerable conditions. If white America wants a solution to the violence in the ghettos by blacks, then let white America end the violence done to the ghettos by whites. We simply must come to understand that there can be no social order without social justice. "How long will the violence in the summers last?" another listener may ask. "How intransigent is white America?" is my answer. And the answer to that could be a sincere response to legitimate demands.

Black Power must not be naive about the intentions of white decision-makers to yield anything without a struggle and a confrontation by organized power. Black people will gain only as much as they can win through their ability to organize independent bases of economic and political power—through boycotts, electoral activity, rent strikes, work stoppages, pressure-group bargaining. And it must be clear that whites will have to bargain with blacks or continue to fight them in the streets of the Detroits and the Newarks. Rather than being a call to violence, this is a clear recognition that the ghetto rebellions, in addition to producing the possibility of apartheid-type repression, have been functional in moving *some* whites to see that viable solutions must be sought.

Black Power is concerned with organizing the rage of black people and with putting new, hard questions and demands to white America. As we do this, white America's responses will be crucial to the questions of violence and viability. Black Power must (1) deal with the obviously growing alienation of black people and their distrust of the institutions of this society; (2) work to create new values and to build a new sense of community and of belonging, and (3) work to establish legitimate new institutions that make participants, not recipients, out of a people traditionally excluded from the fundamentally racist processes of this country. There is nothing glamorous about this; it involves persistence and hard, tedious, day-to-day work.

Black Power rejects the lessons of slavery and segregation that caused black people to look upon themselves with hatred and disdain. To be "integrated" it was necessary to deny one's heritage, one's own culture, to be ashamed of one's black skin, thick lips and kinky hair. In their book, "Racial Crisis in America," two Florida State University sociologists, Lewis M. Killian and Charles M. Grigg, wrote: "At the present time, integration as a solution to the race problem demands that the Negro forswear his identity as a Negro. But for a lasting solution, the meaning of 'American' must lose its implicit racial modifier, 'white.'" The black man must change his demeaning conception of himself; he must develop a sense of pride and self-respect. Then, if integration comes, it will deal with people who are psychologically and mentally healthy, with people who have a sense of their history and of themselves as whole human beings.

In the process of creating these new values, Black Power will, its advocates hope, build a new sense of community among black people. It will try to forge a bond in the black community between those who have "made it" and those "on the bottom." It will bring an end to the internal back-biting and suspicious bickering, the squabbling over tactics and personalities so characteristic of the black community. If Black Power can produce this unity, that in itself will be revolutionary, for the black community and for the country.

Black Power recognizes that new forms of decision-making must be implemented in the black community. One purpose, clearly is to overcome the alienation and distrust.

Let me deal with this specifically by looking at the situation in terms of "internal" and "external" ghetto problems and approaches. When I speak of internal problems, I refer to such things as exploitative merchants who invade the black communities, to absentee slumlords, to inferior schools and arbitrary law enforcement, to black people unable to develop their own independent economic and political bases. There are, of course, many problems facing black people which must be dealt with outside the ghettos: jobs, open occupancy, medical care, higher education.

The solution of the internal problems does not require the presence of massive numbers of whites marching arm in arm with blacks. Local all-black groups can organize boycotts of disreputable merchants and of those employers in the black communities who fail to hire and promote black people. Already, we see this approach spreading across the country with Operation Breadbasket, initiated by Dr. King's Southern Christian Leadership Conference. The national director of the program, the Rev. Jesse Jackson, who was with Dr. King when he was murdered in Memphis, has established several such projects from Los Angeles to Raleigh, N. C.

In Chicago alone, in 15 months, approximately 2,000 jobs

worth more than $15 million in annual income were obtained for black people. Negotiations are conducted on hiring and up-grading black people, marketing the products of black manu-facturers and suppliers and providing contracts to black com-panies. The operation relies heavily on the support of black businessmen, who are willing to work with Operation Bread-basket because it is mutually beneficial. They derive a profit and in turn contribute to the economic development of the black community.

This is Black Power in operation. But there is not nearly enough of this kind of work going on. In some instances, there is a lack of technical know-how coupled with a lack of ade-quate funds. These two defects constantly plague constructive pressure-group activity in the black communities.

CORE (Congress of Racial Equality) has developed a num-ber of cooperatives around the country. In Opelousas, La., it has organized over 300 black farmers, growers of sweet pota-toes, cabbages and okra, in the Grand-Marie Co-op. They sell their produce and some of the income goes back into the co-op as dues. Initially, 20 percent of the cooperative's members were white farmers, but most of the whites dropped out as a result of social and economic pressures from the white community. An offshoot of the Grand-Marie group is the Southern Con-sumers' Cooperative in Lafayette, La., which makes and sells fruit cakes and candy. It has been in existence for more than a year, employs approximately 150 black people and has led to the formation of several credit unions and buying clubs.

The major effort of Black Power-oriented CORE is in the direction of economic development. Antoine Perot, program director of CORE, says: "One big need in the black commu-nity is to develop capital-producing instruments which create jobs. Otherwise, we are stuck with the one-crop commodity—labor—which does not produce wealth. Mere jobs are not enough. These will simply perpetuate black dependency."

Thus, small and medium-sized businesses are being devel-oped in the black communities of Chicago, San Francisco, De-troit, Cleveland, New York and several other urban centers.

CORE hopes to call on some successful black businessmen around the country as consultants, and it is optimistic that they will respond favorably with their know-how and, in some instances, their money. The goal is to free as many black people as possible from economic dependency on the white man. It has been this dependency in many places that has hampered effective independent political organizing.

In New York, Black Power, in the way we see it, operates through a group called N.E.G.R.O. (National Economic Growth and Reconstruction Organization). Its acronym does not sit too well with some advocates of black consciousness who see in the use of the term "Negro" an indication of less than sufficient racial pride. Started in 1964, the group deals with economic self-help for the black community: a hospital in Queens, a chemical corporation, a textile company and a construction company. N.E.G.R.O., with an annual payroll of $1 million and assets of $3 million, is headed by Dr. Thomas W. Matthew, a neurosurgeon who has been accused of failing to file Federal income tax returns for 1961, 1962 and 1963. He has asserted that he will pay all the Government says he owes, but not until "my patient is cured or one of us dies." His patient is the black community, and the emphasis of his group is on aiding blacks and reducing reliance on the white man. The organization creates a sense of identity and cohesiveness that is painfully lacking in much of the black community.

In helping oneself and one's race through hard work, N.E.-G.R.O. would appear to be following the Puritan ethic of work and achievement: if you work hard, you will succeed. One gets the impression that the organization is not necessarily idealistic about this. It believes that black people will never develop in this country as long as they must depend on handouts from the white man. This is realism, whatever ethic it is identified with. And this, too, is Black Power in operation.

More frequently than not, projects will not use the term "Black Power," but that is hardly necessary. There is, for instance, the Poor People's Corporation, formed by a former S.N.C.C. (Student Nonviolent Coordinating Committee) worker, Jessie Norris, in August, 1965. It has set up 15 cooperatives in Mississippi, employing about 200 black people. The employees, all shareholders, make handbags, hats, dresses, quilts, dolls and other hand-craft items that are marketed through Liberty House in Jackson, Miss. Always sensitive to the development of the black community, the Poor People's Corporation passed a rule that only registered voters could work in the co-ops.

These enterprises are small; they do not threaten the economic structure of this society, but their members look upon them as vital for the development of the black people. Their purpose is to establish a modicum of economic self-sufficiency without focusing too much attention on the impact they will have on the American economic system.

Absolutely crucial to the development of Black Power is the black middle class. These are people with sorely needed skills. There has been a lot of discussion about where the black middle class stands in relation to Black Power. Some people adopt the view that most members of the class opt out of the race (or at least try to do so); they get good jobs, a nice home, two cars, and forget about the masses of blacks who have not "made it." This has been largely true. Many middle-class blacks simply do not feel an obligation to help the less fortunate members of their race.

There is, however, a growing awareness among black middle-class people of their role in the black revolution. On Jan. 20, a small group of them (known, appropriately enough, as the Catalysts) called an all-day conference in a South Side Chicago church to discuss ways of linking black middle-class professionals with black people in the lower class. Present were about 370 people of all sorts: teachers, social workers, lawyers, accountants, three physicians, housewives, writers. They met in workshops to discuss ways of making their skills and positions relevant to the black society, and they held no press conferences. Though programs of action developed, the truth is that they remain the exception, not the rule, in the black middle class.

Another group has been formed by black teachers in Chicago, Detroit and New York, and plans are being made to expand. In Chicago, the organization is called the Association of Afro-American Educators. These are people who have traditionally been the strongest supporters of the status quo. Education is intended to develop people who will support the existing values of the society, and "Negro" teachers have been helping this process over the years. But now some of them (more than 250 met on Feb. 12 in Chicago) are organizing and beginning to redefine, first, their role as black educators vis-à-vis the black revolution, and, second, the issues as they see them. Their motivation is outlined in the following statement:

"By tapping our vast resources of black intellectual expertise, we shall generate new ideas for *meaningful* educational programs, curricula and instructional materials which will contribute substantially toward raising the educational achievement of black children.

"Our purpose is to extricate ourselves momentarily from the dominant society in order to realign our priorities, to mobilize and to 'get ourselves together' to do what must be done by those best equipped to do it."

This is what they *say;* whether they can pull it off will depend initially on their ability to bring along their black colleagues, many of whom, admittedly, do not see the efficacy of such an attitude. Unless the link is made between the black middle-class professionals and the black masses, Black Power will probably die on the speaker's platform.

Another important phenomenon in the development of Black Power is the burgeoning of black students' groups on college campuses across the country. I have visited 17 such campuses—from Harvard to Virginia to Wisconsin to U.C.L.A.—since October. The students are discussing problems of identity, of relevant curricula at their universities, of ways of helping their people when they graduate. Clearly, one sees in these hundreds (the figure could be in the thousands) of black students a little bit of Booker T. Washington (self-help and the dignity of common labor) and a lot of W. E. B. DuBois (vigorous insistence on equality and the liberal education of the most talented black men).

These are the people who are planning to implement social, political and economic Black Power in their home towns. They will run for public office, aware that Richard Hatcher started from a political base in the black community. He would not be Mayor of Gary, Ind., today if he had not first mobilized the black voters. Some people point out that he had to have white support. This is true; in many instances such support is necessary, but internal unity is necessary first.

This brings us to a consideration of the external problems of the black community. It is clear that black people will need the help of whites at many places along the line. There simply are not sufficient economic resources—actual or potential—in the black community for a total, unilateral, boot-strap operation. Why should there be? Black people have been the target of deliberate denial for centuries, and racist America has done its job well. This is a serious problem that must be faced by Black Power advocates. On the one hand, they recognize the need to be independent of "the white power structure." And on the other, they must frequently turn to that structure for help—technical and financial. Thus, the rhetoric and the reality often clash.

Resolution probably lies in the realization by white America that it is in her interest not to have a weak, dependent, alienated black community inhabiting the inner cities and blowing them up periodically. Society needs stability, and as long as there is a sizable powerless, restless group within it which considers the society illegitimate, stability is not possible. However it is calculated, the situation calls for a black-white rapprochement, which may well come only through additional confrontations and crises. More frequently than not, the self-interest of the dominant society is not clearly perceived until the brink is reached.

There are many ways whites can relate to this phenomenon. First, they must recognize that blacks are going to insist on an equitable distribution of *decision-making power*. Anything less will simply be perpetuating a welfare mentality among blacks. And if the society thinks only in terms of *giving* more jobs, better schools and more housing, the result will be the creation of more black recipients still dependent on whites.

The equitable distribution of power must result from a conviction that it is a matter of mutual self-interest, not from the feelings of guilt and altruism that were evident at the National Conference of New Politics convention in Chicago in August. An equitable distribution means that black men will have to occupy positions of political power in precincts, counties, Congressional districts and cities where their numbers and organization warrant. It means the end of absentee white ward committeemen and precinct captains in Chicago's black precincts.

But this situation is much easier described than achieved. Black Americans generally are no more likely to vote independently than other Americans. In many Northern urban areas, especially, the job of wooing the black vote away from the Democratic party is gigantic. The established machine has the resources: patronage, tradition, apathy. In some instances the change will take a catalytic event—a major racial incident, a dramatic black candidate, a serious boner by the white establishment (such as splitting the white vote). The mere call to "blackness" simply is not enough, even where the numbers are right.

In addition, many of the problems facing black people can be solved only to the extent that whites are willing to see such imperatives as an open housing market and an expanding job market. White groups must continue to bring as much pressure as possible on local and national decision-makers to adopt sound policy in these fields. These enlightened whites *will* be able to work with Black Power groups.

There are many things which flow from this orientation to Black Power. It is not necessary that blacks create parallel agencies—political or economic—in all fields and places. In some areas, it is possible to work within, say, the two-party system. Richard Hatcher did so in Gary, but he first had to organize black voters to fight the Democratic machine in the primary. The same is true of Mayor Carl Stokes in Cleveland. At some point it may be wise to work with the existing agencies, but this must be done only from a base of independent, not subordinated, power.

On the other hand, dealing with a racist organization like George Wallace's Democratic party in Alabama would require forming an independent group. The same is true with some labor unions, especially in the South, which still practice discrimination despite the condemnation of such a policy by their parent unions. Many union locals are willing to work with their black members on such matters as wages and working conditions, but refuse to join the fight for open housing laws.

The point is that black people must become much more pragmatic in their approach. Whether we try to work within or outside a particular agency should depend entirely on a hard-nosed, calculated examination of potential success in each situation—a careful analysis of cost and benefit. Thus, when we negotiate the test will be: How will black people, not some political machine downtown or some labor union boss across town, benefit from this?

Black Power must insist that the institutions in the black community be led by and, wherever possible, staffed by blacks. This is advisable psychologically, and it is necessary as a challenge to the myth that black people are incapable of leadership. Admittedly, this violates the principle of egalitarianism ("We hire on the basis of merit alone, not color"). What black and white America must understand is that egalitarianism is just a *principle* and it implies a notion of "color-blindness" which is deceptive. It must be clear by now that any society which has been color-conscious all its life to the detriment of a particular group cannot simply become color-blind and expect that group to compete on equal terms.

Black Power clearly recognizes the need to perpetuate color

consciousness, but in a positive way—to improve a group, not to subject it. When principles like egalitarianism have been so flagrantly violated for so long, it does not make sense to think that the victim of that violation can be equipped to benefit from opportunities simply upon their pronouncement. Obviously, some positive form of special treatment must be used to overcome centuries of negative special treatment.

This has been the argument of the Nation of Islam (the so-called Black Muslims) for years; it has also been the position of the National Urban League since its proposal for preferential treatment (the Domestic Marshall Plan, which urged a "special effort to overcome serious disabilities resulting from historic handicaps") was issued at its 1963 Denver convention. This is not racism. It is not intended to penalize or subordinate another group; its goal is the positive uplift of a deliberately repressed group. Thus, when some Black Power advocates call for the appointment of black people to head community-action poverty programs and to serve as school principals, they have in mind the deliberate projection of blacks into positions of leadership. This is important to give other black people a feeling of ability to achieve, if nothing else. And it is especially important for young black children.

An example of concentrated special treatment is the plan some of us are proposing for a new approach to education in some of the black ghettos. It goes beyond the decentralization plans in the Bundy Report; it goes beyond the community involvement at I.S. 201 in Harlem. It attempts to build on the idea proposed by Harlem CORE last year for an independent Board of Education for Harlem.

Harlem CORE and the New York Urban League saw the Bundy Report as a "step toward creating a structure which would bring meaningful education to the children of New York." CORE, led by Roy Innis, suggested an autonomous Harlem school system, chartered by the State Legislature and responsible to the state. "It will be run by an elected school board and an appointed administrator, as most school boards are,"

CORE said. "The elected members will be Harlem residents. It is important that much of the detailed planning and structure be the work of the Harlem community." Funds would come from city, state and Federal governments and from private sources. In describing the long-range goal of the proposal, CORE says: "Some have felt it is to create a permanently separate educational system. Others have felt it is a necessary step toward eventual integration. In any case, the ultimate outcome of this plan will be to make it possible for Harlem to choose."

Some of us propose that education in the black community should be family-oriented, not simply child-oriented. In many of the vast urban black ghettos (which will not be desegregated in the foreseeable future) the school should become the focal point of the community. This we call the Family-Community-School-Comprehensive Plan. School would cease to be a 9-to-3, September-to-June, time-off-for-good-behavior institution. It would involve education and training for the entire family—all year round, day and evening. Black parents would be intimately involved as students, decision-makers, teachers. This is much more than a revised notion of adult education courses in the evening or the use of mothers as teachers' aides.

This plan would make the educational system the center of community life. We could have community health clinics and recreational programs built into the educational system. Above all, we could reorient the demeaning public welfare system, which sends caseworkers to "investigate" families. Why could we not funnel public assistance through the community educational program?

One major advantage would be the elimination of some of the bureaucratic chaos in which five to ten governmental agencies zero in on the black family on welfare, seldom if ever coordinating their programs. The welfare department, for one, while it would not need to be altered in other parts of the state, would have to work jointly with the educational system in the black community. This would obviously require administrative reorganization, which would not necessarily reduce bureaucracy but would consolidate and centralize it. In addition to being "investigators," for example, some caseworkers (with substantially reduced case loads) could become teachers of budgetary management, and family health consultants could report the economic needs of the family.

The teachers for such a system would be specially trained in a program similar to the National Teacher Corps, and recruits could include professionals as well as mothers who could teach classes in child-rearing, home economics, art, music or any number of skills they obviously possess. Unemployed fathers could learn new skills or teach the ones they know. The curriculum would be both academic and vocational, and it would contain courses in the culture and history of black people. The school would belong to the community. It would be a union of children, parents, teachers, social workers, psychologists, urban planners, doctors, community organizers. It would become a major vehicle for fashioning a sense of pride and group identity.

I see no reason why the local law-enforcement agency could not be integrated into this system. Perhaps this could take the form of training "community service officers," or junior policemen, as suggested in the report of the President's Commission on Civil Disorders. Or the local police precinct could be based in the school, working with the people on such things as crime prevention, first aid and the training of police officers. In this way, mutual trust could be developed between the black community and the police.

Coordinating these programs would present problems to be worked out on the basis of the community involved, the agencies involved and the size of the system. It seems quite obvious that in innovations of this sort there will be a tremendous amount of chaos and uncertainty and there will be mistakes. This is understandable; it is the price to be paid for social change under circumstances of widespread alienation and deprivation. The recent furor about the Malcolm X memorial program at I.S. 201 in Harlem offers an example of the kind of problem to be anticipated. Rather than worrying about what one person said from a stage at a particular meeting, the authorities should be concerned about how the Board of Education will cooperate to transfer power to the community school board. When the transfer is made, confusion regarding lines of authority and program and curriculum content can be reduced.

The longer the delay in making the transfer, however, the greater the likelihood of disruption. One can expect misunderstanding, great differences of opinion and a relatively low return on efforts at the beginning of such new programs. New standards of evaluation are being set, and the experimental concept developed at I.S. 201 should not be jeopardized by isolated incidents. It would be surprising if everything went smoothly from the outset.

Some programs *will* flounder, some will collapse out of sheer incompetence and faulty conception, but this presents an opportunity to build on mistakes. The precise details of the Comprehensive Plan would have to be worked out in conjunction with each community and agency involved. But the *idea* is seriously proposed. We must begin to think in entirely new terms of citizen involvement and decision-making.

Black Power has been accused of emphasizing decentralization, of overlooking the obvious trend toward consolidation. This is not true with the kind of Black Power described here, which is ultimately not separatist or isolationist. Some Black Power advocates are aware that this country is simultaneously experiencing centralization and decentralization. As the Federal Government becomes more involved (and it must) in the lives of people, it is imperative that we broaden the base of citizen participation. It will be the new forms, new agencies and structures developed by Black Power that will link these centralizing and decentralizing trends.

Black Power structures at the local level will activate people, instill faith (not alienation) and provide a habit of organization and a consciousness of ability. Alienation will be overcome and trust in society restored. It will be through these local agencies that the centralized forces will operate, not through insensitive, unresponsive city halls. Billions of dollars will be needed each year, and these funds must be provided through a more direct route from their sources to the people.

Black Power is a developmental process; it cannot be an end in itself. To the extent that black Americans can organize, and to the extent that white Americans can keep from panicking and begin to respond rationally to the demands of that organization—to that extent can we get on with the protracted business of creating not just law and order but a free and open society.

67. JAMES FARMER:
"DEVELOP GROUP PRIDE"
AND THEN "CULTURAL PLURALISM"

James Farmer, as one of the founders of the Congress of Racial Equality, had articulated a philosophy of color-blind interracialism, and had been sharply critical of nationalist movements (see Document 33). The rapidly changing landscape of the 1960s, however, led him to see greater validity in a nationalist perspective. Though disagreeing with Malcolm X (see Document 53), he was frankly impressed by him. As black participation in CORE burgeoned, Farmer was among those who perceived black leadership of the movement as a necessity. As he said about the time he resigned as CORE's national director in 1966, "We have found the cult of color-blindness not only quaintly irrelevant but serious flawed . . . [because] we would have to give up our identities . . . at the very moment when the movement was teaching us to love ourselves. . . ."*

Subsequently, after two years of lecturing, and an unsuccessful campaign for a seat in Congress in 1968, Farmer accepted a position

Transcript of address by James Farmer at Syracuse University, 1968. Printed with permission of James Farmer.

* James Farmer, *Freedom—When?* (New York: Random House, 1966), p. 87.

as assistant secretary in the Department of Health, Education, and Welfare—the highest post occupied by a black man in the Nixon administration. By then his ideology had become one that can best be described as "ethnic pluralism." Typical of Farmer's statements in the period since he resigned from CORE was a series of lectures given at Syracuse University in 1968. In these talks he embraced a reformist version of Black Power and Black Consciousness that explicitly avowed a hope for the eventual full integration of Negroes into American society. He advocated black community organization for the elevation of the race along all lines: black capitalism and black economic cooperatives; black control of neighborhood schools; Negro bloc voting and the development of black political power through unified action on the part of the masses; and above all a cultural nationalism and a sense of black identity. At the same time he disavowed the concept of a parallel separate economy and the ideal of a separate state, and viewed the task of the black protest movement as reforming American society to the point where it will provide for full inclusion of Negroes within it.

We print here the first of the Syracuse University lectures, an example of cultural nationalism that today, as in the 1920s, occupies such a prominent place in the thinking of black people of all classes and of widely varying points of view.

. . . I am pleased these days to meet with any group of thinking Americans who are discussing the most crucial issue confronting the nation—the issue of the black struggle or the relations between the races or whatever terminology one wishes to use. As Dr. Du Bois put it in 1903, *"The* problem of the twentieth century will be the problem of the color line, or the relations between the lighter and darker peoples of the earth, in Asia and Africa, in America and the islands of the sea."

Those words clearly were prophetic. We have lived to see them come true. We have also lived to see much confusion and misunderstanding. Today more than ever before there is a seething torrent of debate and discussion within the black community. Much of this discussion has created confusion in the ranks of the rest of the national community. Words are being used to mean totally different things and sometimes opposing things, indeed. The agenda has changed. Answers to questions which used to seem obvious and adequate now seem obsolete and archaic.

I had a phone call from a friend of mine some months ago in which he said, "Jim, I am baffled and puzzled and confused." Now this is a black man and I had not seen him for some years. I asked him what the trouble was. He said, "Well now, a few years ago you so-called civil rights leaders told us that the most militant and progressive and meaningful thing that we could do was to integrate a lily white suburb. Well, we took you at your word. My wife and I took the bull by the horns and we moved out into Lovely Lane next door to Gorgeous Garden. We bought a split level house and we mowed the lawn. We faced all the gaff, all of the rocks and the garbage and the burning crosses and the isolation. Now," he said, "we have overcome. We are accepted by our neighbors. They invite us over for cocktails and we have them over for tea. But now," he added, "we're called Uncle Toms for living out there with all those white folks."

This is indicative of the kind of change that is taking place in the agenda and in the answers to questions. More recently I was in Los Angeles conducting a series of seminars for the Board of Education of that sprawling metropolis. In the course of the discussion some of the officials of the Board informed me that very shortly the Board of Education of Los Angeles was coming out with a total desegregation plan.

In order to understand how interesting this was you will have to remember that it was only ten or twelve years ago when the civil rights movement started its battle in Los Angeles and other cities to end *de facto* school segregation. The Los Angeles Board then did not even acknowledge that it had a problem. It said, in effect, "This must be a case of mistaken identity. This is not Mississippi, this is Los Angeles; there is no segregation in Los Angeles." Well, a few years later the Los Angeles Board woke up to the fact that there was segregation there, but they said, "It's different here, because it's *de facto* and not *de jure* and that renders it outside of our field of competence and beyond our jurisdiction, because after all it's tied in with housing and we are not the housing authority, we're the education authority." Well, a short while later they acknowledged that it was their responsibility to do something about it, but they didn't know what to do.

Now they told me they are coming out with a plan that in one fell swoop will eliminate *de facto* school segregation. I had to tell the gentlemen that even if their plan is all that they say it's going to be, when they come out with it they must expect that it will meet with a lukewarm reception in the black community, and from large segments of that community, outright hostility. Because the agenda has changed in just that manner. The old shibboleths, the old cliches have to be reevaluated.

I don't think that the tabloid headline formulation of the issues has helped at all. It is not a question of militancy versus moderation. What is Whitney Young? Is he a militant now that he has endorsed black power? I don't think Whitney Young is any more militant than he was before. He is a moderate. There are militants and moderates on both sides of the issue.

Nor is it a question of integration versus separation. Because look for a moment at the black student who voluntarily elects to go to a predominantly white institution and once there joins a black students association. What is he, a separationist or an integrationist? It is not a question of integration versus separation. The issues go much deeper than that and I suggest to you this evening that they are the most critical and meaningful debates that are taking place in American society today. I believe that we are in a period that will be seen by historians as a period of the black renaissance. A period when the black man is seeking to find himself; when critical discussion and debate in the black community will reach its height; when there will be a flourishing of art and creative writing; when the black man will suddenly come alive. He will find an identity, not merely an answer to that age old question, "Who am I?" but more significantly, an answer to the question, "What is my relationship to society and to the people round about me?"

Those are the kinds of questions which are now plaguing the black community. In essence, the black American is wrestling with what the Kerner Commission report referred to as white racism. I do not believe that the Kerner Commission report was saying that all white Americans are bigots. I think that would be nonsense. It was not saying that all Americans are Bull Connor —that would be ludicrous. What it was saying, in fact, was that all of us, white and black—and since it is a predominantly white society; then predominantly it is true of white Americans—have been programmed by all of the cultural instruments in our society to think to some extent in a racist manner. I suggest to you that this has affected the black American as well as the white American—that we all have been programmed and it is the worst victim of this programming, the black man, who is now seeking somehow to pull himself up by his own bootstraps and so to find the death knell of the very racism which has persecuted and intimidated him.

It began very early with all of us. We were not born with any racism, obviously, but at the point of consciousness it began to be poured into our minds in pre-school books. I looked through a series of pre-school books several years ago to find out how the little black child would view himself, and I found what many of you will suspect, that in most of them he wouldn't see himself at all, unless he was cleaning somebody else's house or carrying someone else's bag or in some ridiculous position with a string tied around his toe and other kids poking fun at him and laughing—clearly not an acceptable self-image. But an image which has in myriad ways been pounded into the consciousness of the black American, and that is what he has been told he is. Just as important that is what the white child has been told that the black child is too.

And up through the school, elementary and high school, the same programming is taking place. In Washington, D. C. for example, EBONY magazine tells us that they are still using the old textbooks—and this is not unique, by and large the old stereotyping textbooks are used all over the country and we are all victimized by them, black and white. But the one in Washington says quite bluntly that Negroes made ideal slaves; they fitted admirably into the slave system; they thrived upon the paternalistic love and care of their owners; they enjoyed nothing more than sitting under the magnolia tree strumming their guitars and singing sweetly of the hereafter. That kind of nonsense is still being poured into children's minds.

Ninety-three percent of the school population in Washington happens to be black, and that is what those kids are told they are. And it is what the white kids, who are seven percent, are told that the black kids are. And believe it or not, EBONY magazine informs us that in this textbook there is a full page illustration, a picture to show these kids what a Negro is. The picture is of a cotton field with slaves—banjo eyes, wide tooth grins, bandanas around their heads—chopping cotton and having a wonderful time. The caption says, in effect, these are the Negroes to whom we referred on a previous page. In other words, they were in their element; they were naturally cut out to be slaves. This is the message that is put across. This is what the black youngsters are told that they are and the white youngsters are told that the black kids are.

And why did this idyllic picture ever come to an end? Indeed, there is no mention of the slave revolts which rocked the southland for two generations before emancipation, because that would contradict that image, the stereotype, the picture. Now in fairness it must be pointed out that some of the publishers have in the past several years been putting out improved textbooks and pre-school books, but those are only a drop in the bucket compared with the mass of stereotype nonsense that is being perpetrated upon our youngsters throughout the land— and in colleges too. One might do well to check out the history textbooks at the University of Syracuse.

I was out at Reid College in Oregon several years ago—that, as you know, has a very high academic rating—and I met with history majors who were seniors, about to graduate—young historians. I discovered to my chagrin that not a single one of them was aware that there were hundreds of thousands of black troops fighting on the Union side in the Civil War. They had never heard of that. They had the magnolia myth image, that they were happy and content, that they sat under the magnolia tree strumming guitars, singing of the hereafter. Not a single one of those young historians had ever heard of Nat Turner, Denmark Vesey, Gabriel Prosser or a couple of dozen other slave revolt leaders. This may seem fantastic to you, but it is true.

I believe that all of the media for the dissemination of culture within our land have to some extent been partners in the perpetration of this crime. The crime has caused the black man to reject himself and even to hate himself. He has been taught that what he is is bad and that he should try to be something else. He has been taught that his skin is a deformity. Imagine for instance a man whose skin is black and whose hair is kinky, referring to kinky hair as "bad hair" and to straight hair as "good hair"—a very common occurrence within the black community. Less common, it is true, within the past two or three years, but common nevertheless. It is indicative of the kind of programming that has taken place, and thus the kind of rejection.

We had rejected Africa, and that had been part of the self-rejection too. For we had, as most Americans had, the Hollywood image of Africa. And we are all familiar with that image —a few half naked black savages dancing around a boiling pot with a missionary in it. That was the way we saw Africa, and a common saying in the black community was, "Man, I ain't lost nothing in Africa; I ain't no African." We would go to the movies to watch the Tarzan pictures and with whom did we identify? With Tarzan, of course. We'd say, "Kill that savage, Tarzan, kill him" . . . Kill me, Tarzan. I remember as a child in Austin, Texas, after we left Marshall—we later returned to Marshall—as a child in Austin, about ten years of age, my buddy and I would go down to the movie every Saturday to watch the half hour Tarzan serial. We had to see our hero; we couldn't miss a single week. We would watch the missionary in the pot with the sweat dripping from his brow as the heat built up underneath and he awaited the inevitable and timely arrival of Tarzan. They would show the Africans dancing round the pot to the tom-tom beat; then would flash on the screen a close-up of the face of one of the Africans, all painted and fierce. Then I'd elbow my buddy

and say, "Irving, that's you." Well, you can imagine Irving's reaction. It was quite negative: "No, man, that ain't me; I didn't
come from no Africa."

Irving and millions of Irvings were similarly rejecting themselves. They had been told and had come to believe that they
had come from nowhere and thus were nobody and were going
no place. We were the only Americans who had no roots which
they acknowledged, who had no umbilical cords into the past,
as though we had sprung alive full grown out of the Reconstruction period. Naturally self-esteem and self-respect suffered.

Of course, as the new nations of Africa began to emerge,
a new identity and pride came to the surface and many black
Americans, especially the young ones, saw a proud black image.
They looked, for instance, at a Chief Adebo debating some fine
point of international law in the councils of the U. N. and said,
"Why, wait a minute, that man is me, and if that's Africa, then
what happened to the boiling pot?"

The new image proliferated and tended to eclipse the old, and
black Americans began asserting their blackness as never before, saying, "I am a black man." Ten years ago, fifteen years
ago, if you called a man black it would have been a fighting
word, because he thought black was evil and he would have
insisted he was not black, he was brown, bronze, he was tan,
but he was not black. Now he would assert, "I am a black man."

Many black Americans began calling themselves Afro-
Americans, becoming hyphenated Americans. This had not
happened before on any mass scale whatever. It was a part of
the new bursting identity, the new drive toward self-esteem and
respect, toward, I might call it an ethnic cohesiveness that was
coming about in the black community. People began walking
ten feet tall. This is the renaissance. They began studying African art and culture and history, emphasizing too Afro-American
art, culture and history. Many women began wearing their hair
au naturel, unstraightened, emphasizing those characteristics
which had heretofore been rejected. I observe with some interest that one of the firms that manufactures wigs is now putting out a natural hair wig for white women. That'll be the day,

when we see white women wearing negroid hair, as a wig. But then perhaps we will have arrived. We find now young black men wearing their hair long and emphasizing those qualities that once they sought to derogate. This new pride and the new self-esteem among black Americans is a positive, not a negative thing.

Africa isn't a place to go home to; I reject the notion that it's a place to go home to. Instead I love Africa, but I love it as the source of my roots, my heritage, my ancestry. When I first visited Africa in 1958 it was almost a religious experience. A friend of mine before I left, a young man, handed me an empty bottle and said, "Jim, when you get to Africa fill this with water from the river Nile and bring it home to me." A woman handed me an empty box and said, "Fill this with soil from mother Africa, bring it to me and I will plant a flower in it." My father who was a scholar and not given to much show of emotion, said, "Son, when you get to West Africa look up my relatives and tell them that I'm doing well." Now, of course, he had no notion where his relatives were or what nation or tribe his ancestors had come from, but he wanted to show his feeling. And when my plane touched ground for the first time there I felt an almost overpowering compulsion to fall on my knees and kiss the earth. I resisted that compulsion, but I felt it nonetheless.

Now as I look back on it, it occurs to me that the feeling that I had on that occasion was not essentially different from the feeling that a third generation Irish-American might have visiting the old sod. Jack Kennedy going to the village from which his ancestors had come, looking for different relatives, walking through the graveyards, examining the tombstones for names of families that he would remember from childhood conversations with his grandfather. And not much different, perhaps, from the feeling an American Jew might have going to Israel for the first time. So, it is not a place to go home to, but a source of roots in that way.

The black American, then, is trying to find himself and find an identity and to give back to the black skin color its lost dignity. What in essence he is finding an answer to is that question, "What does it mean to be a black American?" This is not a new question in America. Every ethnic group has asked that question in its own context—"What does it mean to be Italian and American?", "What does it mean to be Irish and American?", "What does it mean to be Jewish and American?", "What does it mean to be Polish and American?", and so on. The immigrant groups have been plagued with that question, especially during their first generation and often well into the second generation. They usually answered it with a hyphen, they became hyphenated Americans. They became both; a kind of dual identity.

The emphasis during the first generation as the external pressure was great upon them tended to be toward an ethnic cohesiveness rather than dispersal or assimilation. The Irish, for instance, in the 1860's as their great wave of immigration came to the land and they faced all sorts of obstacles—signs in windows, "Man wanted—no Irishman need apply," "man wanted—NINA," everyone knew what it meant—sang songs, one of which I heard sung recently by Joe Glaser, in which they shouted, "It's an honor to be born an Irishman." That's good—it is an honor to be born an Irishman. Black is beautiful, it's wonderful to be black. What's the difference? It is the same idea, the same context, but very different people. It is an honor to be born an Irishman. It's an honor to be born whatever one is born, so long as it's not a dishonor to be born what one is not. And when a people are pushed around, stepped upon and told that they are nothing but dirt, then it is all the more important that they assert loudly, "We are something of infinite importance and worth." It's not a dishonor to be born what one is not; it is not necessary to hate someone else in order to love oneself. Self love is essential, and if one does love himself then he does not find it necessary to hate those who are not like him. Black is beautiful. That does not mean that not to be black is vile or ugly.

The black American is trying to answer that question of what it means to be black and American in a similar way to the way that the immigrant groups from Europe answered it. He is American too, even though there are those who deny it. The late

Malcolm X—who, by the way, I respected very highly—the last year of his life used to insist that the black man is not an American and should not call himself an American. He is just a black man and should call himself that. I heard him debating another black fellow in Chicago and Malcolm followed his line and his opponent insisted, "I *am* an American." "Why do you call yourself an American?", Malcolm asked. The answer was, "Because I was born here in this country." Malcolm smiled and said, "Now look, if a cat has kittens in the oven, does that make them bisquits?"

Obviously it doesn't and if the black man is an American his Americanism cannot rest solely on the accident of birth. It must rest instead upon the fact that his subculture, which determines what a people is, grew out of his experiences here in this land. And perhaps that culture—his life style, his art, his music, his dance, his songs—perhaps that subculture is the only indigenous American culture, except for the American Indian. He is an American, but he is also black and that kind of sets him apart. Will he find the same answer that other Americans have found? Will he become a hyphenated American? My answer to that is yes. If I read the scribblings that are on the walls of our cities, the black man is seeking to become a hyphenated American, a black American or an Afro-American. Seeking, one may hope, to discover the hyphen in order eventually to lose it as others have done.

What we must never forget is that the process of losing the hyphen will be infinitely more difficult for him than it was for others, because when the white persons came to this country they looked very much like the people who lived outside the slums and the ghettoes. It was easy for them to be absorbed by the outside world, be assimilated into it, dissolved into it, but it's not that easy for the black man because of his high visibility. You can see him; in fact, it doesn't help him much even to change his name. Elijah Muhammad is still called boy.

It will be much more difficult for him also because of the history of slavery. As I read history I see no parallel to the black man's situation where he is the descendent of former slaves, is seeking rapprochement with the descendents of former slave owners, and in the land where that slavery took place. That makes a very difficult situation, with its historical roots. Added difficulties will be the racism in American culture. But I think it will be possible for him.

His first generation, however, will be much, much longer. You say, "First generation, what are you talking about, the black man has been here for some time." And you are absolutely right. He didn't come over on the Mayflower but he sort of met that boat. In a way, however, it is our first generation. It is the black man's first generation as an urban dweller. More than 70 percent of black Americans now live in the cities. That was not true up until this generation. And living in the cities we have grown close together helped by the ease of communication and facility of cohesiveness, rather than being dispersed on miles and miles of plantation in the South where transportation is by mule train and communication by grapevine.

It is his first generation as a people with a sense of "groupness," because up until a few years ago the aspiration that had been held out to the black American was an aspiration of self-abnegation—to forget himself. What the nation said to the black man—and the civil rights organizations similarly said to him —was, "Forget that you are a member of a group. Think of yourself as an individual, and if as an individual you can gain a little education, a little money, then you will be acculturated and as an individual can be assimilated and will become in effect a white man with an invisible black skin."

That was the color blind dream that was held out to the black American. One saw it in crystal clear fashion after the Supreme Court decision of 1954, when it was generally assumed that integration would take place very quickly and the black ghettoes would soon disappear and that the black man would be dispersed, roughly in a one to ten ratio around the country. You would have to have a countdown in reverse to find one of us, it was assumed. You know, "6, 7, 8, 9, 10—there you are, the black man, the tenth man."

No responsible black leader in those days would dared have

proposed improving any of the facilities of the ghetto—housing,
schools, jobs. That would have been seen as perpetuating the
evil of segregation, which was, it was thought, to be short lived.
I recall in the late 'fifties visiting white campuses, and very
frequently white students would come to me and say, "Mr.
Farmer, we don't understand the Negro students. They seem a
little clannish—they stick together." "What do you mean?", I
asked. "Well, when two of them walk into the dining hall for
dinner, they stick together." I asked, "What would you expect?"
and incredible as it may seem, the answer was, "One should
sit over there and one should sit over there, so that they would
be fully integrated." Well, you see what nonsense it was.

The black man was taught to abnegate himself, to reject himself. Now he is rejecting that notion and seeking to develop a
pride, a dignity, a self-esteem and an identity. But the big question is, "What has he developed his pride for, toward what end?"
And that is where the debate now rages. The debate about
developing pride and identity is almost over. Very rarely in the
black community can one get a debate on that any more. Three
years ago there were frenzied debates on that issue. Many
argued, "Don't try to develop pride as a black man, develop
pride as an American, but not as a black man." Now it is pretty
generally accepted that one has to find that hyphen before he
can lose it. One has to develop pride in himself as a group before
he can lose that groupness by merging it with a larger groupness.

Now the debates are, "Do we want separation, or what?" We
have already discussed the return to Africa which I consider
to be nonsense. There has been no period of the black man's
history when there have not been some who have taught a
colonization notion—a re-colonization, a return to Africa. And
in the twenties Marcus Garvey proceeded apace, he even bought
the ships that were standing in the harbor—the Black Star Line
—to begin the trek back to Africa, before the federal gov'-
ment cracked down on him and sent him away to Atlanta federal penitentiary for using the mails to defraud—allegedly. But
I see no hope of returning to Africa. Before a thousand got over
there, two thousand would be born here. And furthermore, what

country has an economy that can absorb such a mass migration of black Americans? No, the black man is an American and his destiny will be in this country; this we might as well face.

Will that destiny then be in a separate state, as some would argue? These are debates that one hears almost daily. Well, I think not. I once had a debate with Malcolm X—several times, in fact. In the last year of his life we declined to debate each other because we felt that we were merely conducting circuses for the amusement of white audiences, and we decided that when he disagreed with me, he'd come by my house and tell me about it and when I disagreed with him I'd go by his house and tell him about it. This is the way we operated. But prior to this agreement we did debate and he talked about a black state and I told him that if I had the power I would gladly give him not one state, but two—Mississippi and Alabama. His answer was, "No, brother James, we want California." He did have a sense of humour.

I think that there is no feasibility at all to a black state or separate states. First of all, it would make us far too much of a target. One controlled atom bomb could eliminate us if someone chose to do it. And economically we could so easily be strangled.

The idea of a separate state is not a new notion either. Back in the 'thirties it became a political issue. Some people proposed it as a solution to the race problem even then. It was dropped in the 'forties and picked up again by Elijah Muhammad and the Muslims and now has been picked up by some others. But the voices that speak for a separate state are comparatively few, though not muted. Others speak of the black man as being a nation and say therefore, as a nation, he must have land some place, if not in the South and not in Africa, then some place else, but he must have land.

I do not object to the notion of the black man being a nation. If by a nation we mean a people with a common past and hopefully a common future. I consider the Jews a nation; I consider many other people a nation who happen to be dispersed around the world or within nations. But I do not consider the black American to be a nation state, which has to be tied to land or to some specific geographical area. I would see the concept of a nation as helping the development of pride, but it should be a cultural and mystical concept rather than a geographical concept to make any sense today. I would see him, then, developing his pride and his cohesiveness within his own community in order that the cultural unit that he has developed may then join forces with other similar cultural entities in a cultural pluralism, which is after all what the nation is.

This nation has not been a melting pot in the usual sense of the word, where we have poured nationalities into a pot, mixed them up and come out with a polyglot. No, instead it has been a pluralistic culture where various nationalities have maintained certain ethnic traits and cultural identities, and yet they have learned to accept and respect the cultural traits and identities of others. So I would see the black man tending in this direction as thoroughly American. Not as American as cherry pie as H. Rap Brown put it in another context, because that kind of means "follow the WASP." I would see it instead as American as gefilte fish, pizza pie, all the rest of the ethnic cultures which have existed within our land.

Those are the arguments—that is the pride. But how, then, does the black man deal with racism? Hardly a week goes by but that some of my colleagues in the young, militant ranks (so-called) do not say to me that it is impossible for us to develop ourselves within this land and for us to have a rapprochement, certainly no detente, within the American context, because we are black and there is that fact of racism. How does one deal with racism? While I think it is theoretically possible to eliminate racism from a nation's culture, that would be quite a trick. It would require a generation or two of de-programming, using all of the instruments for the dissemination of culture which have created and perpetuated that racism up to the present— using them now to seek to destroy racism and to put a different image into the cultus of the people. I am not certain that that would work. A better psychologist than I would have to wrestle with that problem and a better tactician. But in the meantime I think that it is possible and it is feasible for us to checkmate racism. I have not given up on the dream of my good friend the late Dr. King, of a day when the nation will be colorblind and when all men will love one another as brothers. But that day is not now; it will not come within my lifetime. It will not come within my children's lifetime. It will come possibly at the millenium. In the meantime, we must live in the real world of the here and now. Men may not love us, but relationships can be arranged so that men will be bound to respect us as equals and deal with us. That then is the meaning of power.

In the past the civil rights movement had suggested that all we need do was appeal to the conscience of the nation, and this became the raison d'etre of the movement. An appeal to conscience—beautiful, poignant, artistic, profound, moving. But the consciences were not moved sufficiently. What we said to the nation was, "We will assail your ears, America, with the stories of the wrongs done to us; we will reveal our bloody heads as we have fallen beneath the bludgeonings of southern sheriffs, northern policemen. We will show you our prison sentences as we have filled the jails to bursting. We will parade before you the corpses of our martyrs, and we hope, O Nation, that your conscience will be so moved that you will right the old wrongs and correct the injustices."

But the consciences were not moved sufficiently. Oh, yes, as people watched the television screens and saw the police dogs biting little children in Birmingham and firehoses rolling women in the streets and heads being cracked of black and white civil rights workers, some movement of conscience took place. But I suspect that what happened is that most people said, "Isn't that terrible, that awful Bull Connor, if only something were done about him. Why do there have to be such people as that in the world?" Which did not get at the depth of racism, which totally ignored the fact that the nation itself was racist and that Bull Connor was an overt need—exaggerated, caricatured, but (black and white) me. The conscience wasn't moved enough.

What we found was that consciences are moved most frequently by other factors. When we deal with an employer, for instance, on discrimination in jobs, his conscience becomes more mobile when he discovers that we can hurt him in his pocket-book, that we can withhold patronage and stop purchasing his goods and services. We can talk until we are blue in the face, but until we get to that point there is not great motion on the part of his conscience. But at that point he becomes very conscientious. We find when we deal with a politician we can talk until we fall flat, but his conscience becomes most active when he finds that we have the votes that can take him out of office or put him in office—then he becomes conscientious.

So now, in power, what we seek to do is wield those levers of power which effect social change so that we can sit at the negotiations table and bargain from a position of strength and not weakness. Even those who hate us will negotiate with those who can wield some power. Sanction, that is what I mean by power, the capacity to impose sanctions. Many of the vilest anti-semites will negotiate with Jews and deal and barter because power will deal with power.

That has become the new raison d'etre of the Movement and I am pleased that Whitney Young, head of the National Urban League has endorsed that view. We will never give up seeking to eliminate racism, but in the meantime we will seek to checkmate it. Humanity does transcend color, but one cannot really love humanity until he first learns to love himself. If he hates himself, then how can he love mankind of which he is a part? But on the other hand, he cannot really love himself unless at the same time he learns to love mankind, for that is an extension of himself. In the words of the great rabbi Hillel, "If I am not for myself who will be for me? If I am for myself alone, what am I? And if not now, when?"

68. MARTIN LUTHER KING, JR.
"WE STILL BELIEVE
IN BLACK AND WHITE TOGETHER"

In the last two years of Martin Luther King's life, before he was assassinated in 1968, the Southern Christian Leadership Conference modified its program to include work in the northern cities as well as in the South, and shifted its emphasis from constitutional rights to economic problems. In other respects, however, King and SCLC, unlike CORE and SNCC, remained committed to their basic philosophy of attaining full participation in an integrated society through mass direct nonviolent action.

King's last project, the Poor People's Campaign, a mass demonstration lasting several weeks in Washington in the spring of 1968, after he had been assassinated, was an effort to prove the viability of his method and philosophy as applied to the problems of the urban and rural poor. In the article reprinted here, written shortly before his assassination on April 4, King articulated his continuing faith in nonviolence and racial integration, and his desire to dramatize the whole problem of poverty.

The policy of the Federal Government is to play Russian roulette with riots; it is prepared to gamble with another summer of disaster. Despite two consecutive summers of violence, not a

Martin Luther King, Jr., "Showdown for Non-Violence," LOOK, XXXII (April 16, 1968), pp. 23–25. Reprinted by permission of Joan Daves. Copyright © 1968 by the Estate of Martin Luther King, Jr.

single basic cause of riots has been corrected. All of the misery
that stoked the flames of rage and rebellion remains undimin-
ished. With unemployment, intolerable housing and discriminatory education a scourge in Negro ghettos, Congress and the
Administration still tinker with trivial, halfhearted measures.

Yet only a few years ago, there was discernible, if limited,
progress through non-violence. Each year, a wholesome, vibrant
Negro self-confidence was taking shape. The fact is inescapable
that the tactic of non-violence, which had then dominated the
thinking of the civil-rights movement, has in the last two years
not been playing its transforming role. Non-violence was a
creative doctrine in the South because it checkmated the rabid
segregationists who were thirsting for an opportunity to physically crush Negroes. Non-violent direct action enabled the Negro to take to the streets in active protest, but it muzzled the
guns of the oppressor because even he could not shoot down in
daylight unarmed men, women and children. This is the reason
there was less loss of life in ten years of Southern protest than
in ten days of Northern riots.

Today, the Northern cities have taken on the conditions we
faced in the South. Police, national guard and other armed
bodies are feverishly preparing for repression. They can be
curbed not by unorganized resort to force by desperate Negroes
but only by a massive wave of militant non-violence. Non-
violence was never more relevant as an effective tactic than
today for the North. It also may be the instrument of our national salvation.

I agree with the President's National Advisory Commission
on Civil Disorders that our nation is splitting into two hostile
societies and that the chief destructive cutting edge is white
racism. We need, above all, effective means to force Congress
to act resolutely—but means that do not involve the use of violence. For us in the Southern Christian Leadership Conference,
violence is not only morally repugnant, it is pragmatically barren. We feel there is an alternative both to violence and to useless timid supplications for justice. We cannot condone either
riots or the equivalent evil of passivity. And we know that non-

violent militant action in Selma and Birmingham awakened the conscience of white America and brought a moribund, insensitive Congress to life.

The time has come for a return to mass non-violent protest. Accordingly, we are planning a series of such demonstrations this spring and summer, to begin in Washington, D. C. They will have Negro and white participation, and they will seek to benefit the poor of both races.

We will call on the Government to adopt the measures recommended by its own commission. To avoid, in the Commission's words, the tragedy of "continued polarization of the American community and ultimately the destruction of basic democratic values," we must have "national action—compassionate, massive and sustained, backed by the resources of the most powerful and the richest nation on earth."

The demonstrations we have planned are of deep concern to me, and I want to spell out at length what we will do, try to do, and believe in. My staff and I have worked three months on the planning. We believe that if this campaign succeeds, non-violence will once again be the dominant instrument for social change—and jobs and income will be put in the hands of the tormented poor. If it fails, non-violence will be discredited, and the country may be plunged into holocaust—a tragedy deepened by the awareness that it was avoidable.

We are taking action after sober reflection. We have learned from bitter experience that our Government does not correct a race problem until it is confronted directly and dramatically. We also know, as official Washington may not, that the flash point of Negro rage is close at hand.

Our Washington demonstration will resemble Birmingham and Selma in duration. It will be more than a one-day protest—it can persist for two or three months. In the earlier Alabama actions, we set no time limits. We simply said we were going to struggle there until we got a response from the nation on the issues involved. We are saying the same thing about Washington. This will be an attempt to bring a kind of Selma-like movement, Birmingham-like movement, into being, substantially around the economic issues. Just as we dealt with the social problem of segregation through massive demonstrations, and we dealt with the political problem—the denial of the right to vote—through massive demonstrations, we are now trying to deal with the economic problems—the right to live, to have a job and income—through massive protest. It will be a Selma-like movement on economic issues.

We remember that when we began direct action in Birmingham and Selma, there was a thunderous chorus that sought to discourage us. Yet today, our achievements in these cities and the reforms that radiated from them are hailed with pride by all.

We've selected 15 areas—ten cities and five rural districts—from which we have recruited our initial cadre. We will have 200 poor people from each area. That would be about 3,000 to get the protests going and set the pattern. They are important, particularly in terms of maintaining non-violence. They are being trained in this discipline now.

In areas where we are recruiting, we are also stimulating activities in conjunction with the Washington protest. We are planning to have some of these people march to Washington. We may have half the group from Mississippi, for example, go to Washington and begin the protest there, while the other half begins walking. They would flow across the South, joining the Alabama group, the Georgia group, right on up through South and North Carolina and Virginia. We hope that the sound and sight of a growing mass of poor people walking slowly toward Washington will have a positive, dramatic effect on Congress.

Once demonstrations start, we feel, there will be spontaneous supporting activity taking place across the country. This has usually happened in campaigns like this, and I think it will again. I think people will start moving. The reasons we didn't choose California and other areas out West are distance and the problem of transporting marchers that far. But part of our strategy is to have spontaneous demonstrations take place on the West Coast.

A nation-wide non-violent movement is very important. We

know from past experience that Congress and the President won't do anything until you develop a movement around which people of good-will can find a way to put pressure on them, because it really means breaking that coalition in Congress. It's still a coalition-dominated, rural-dominated, basically Southern Congress. There are Southerners there with committee chairmanships, and they are going to stand in the way of progress as long as they can. They get enough right-wing Midwestern or Northern Republicans to go along with them.

This really means making the movement powerful enough, dramatic enough, morally appealing enough, so that people of goodwill, the churches, labor, liberals, intellectuals, students, poor people themselves begin to put pressure on congressmen to the point that they can no longer elude our demands.

Our idea is to dramatize the whole economic problem of the poor. We feel there's a great deal that we need to do to appeal to Congress itself. The early demonstrations will be more geared toward educational purposes—to educate the nation on the nature of the problem and the crucial aspects of it, the tragic conditions that we confront in the ghettos.

After that, if we haven't gotten a response from Congress, we will branch out. And we are honest enough to feel that we aren't going to get any instantaneous results from Congress, knowing its recalcitrant nature on this issue, and knowing that so many resources and energies are being used in Vietnam rather than on the domestic situation. So we don't have any illusions about moving Congress in two or three weeks. But we do feel that, by starting in Washington, centering on Congress and departments of the Government, we will be able to do a real educational job.

We call our demonstration a campaign for jobs and income because we feel that the economic question is the most crucial that black people, and poor people generally, are confronting. There is a literal depression in the Negro community. When you have mass unemployment in the Negro community, it's called a social problem; when you have mass unemployment in the white community, it's called a depression. The fact is, there is a major depression in the Negro community. The unemployment rate is extremely high, and among Negro youth, it goes as high as 40 percent in some cities.

We need an Economic Bill of Rights. This would guarantee a job to all people who want to work and are able to work. It would also guarantee an income for all who are not able to work. Some people are too young, some are too old, some are physically disabled, and yet in order to live, they need income. It would mean creating certain public-service jobs, but that could be done in a few weeks. A program that would really deal with jobs could minimize—I don't say stop—the number of riots that could take place this summer.

Our whole campaign, therefore, will center on the job question, with other demands, like housing, that are closely tied to it. We feel that much more building of housing for the low-income people should be done. On the educational front, the ghetto schools are in bad shape in terms of quality, and we feel that a program should be developed to spend at least a thousand dollars per pupil. Often, they are so far behind that they need more and special attention, the best quality education that can be given.

These problems, of course, are overshadowed by the Vietnam war. We'll focus on the domestic problems, but it's inevitable that we've got to bring out the question of the tragic mix-up in priorities. We are spending all of this money for death and destruction, and not nearly enough money for life and constructive development. It's inevitable that the question of the war will come up in this campaign. We hear all this talk about our ability to afford guns and butter, but we have come to see that this is a myth, that when a nation becomes involved in this kind of war, when the guns of war become a national obsession, social needs inevitably suffer. And we hope that as a result of our trying to dramatize this and getting thousands and thousands of people moving around this issue, that our Government will be forced to reevaluate its policy abroad in order to deal with the domestic situation.

The American people are more sensitive than Congress. A

Louis Harris poll has revealed that 56 percent of the people feel that some kind of program should come into being to provide jobs to all who want to work. We had the WPA when the nation was on the verge of bankruptcy; we should be able to do something when we're sick with wealth. That poll also showed that 57 percent of the people felt the slums should be eradicated and the communities rebuilt by those who live in them, which would be a massive job program.

We need to put pressure on Congress to get things done. We will do this with First Amendment activity. If Congress is unresponsive, we'll have to escalate in order to keep the issue alive and before it. This action may take on disruptive dimensions, but not violent in the sense of destroying life or property; it will be militant non-violence.

We really feel that riots tend to intensify the fears of the white majority while relieving its guilt, and so open the door to greater repression. We've seen no changes in Watts, no structural changes have taken place as the result of riots. We are trying to find an alternative that will force people to confront issues without destroying life or property. We plan to build a shantytown in Washington, patterned after the bonus marches of the thirties, to dramatize how many people have to live in slums in our nation. But essentially, this will be just like our other non-violent demonstrations. We are not going to tolerate violence. And we are making it very clear that the demonstrators who are not prepared to be non-violent should not participate in this. For the past six weeks, we've had workshops on non-violence with the people who will be going to Washington. They will continue through the spring. These people will form a core of the demonstration and will later be the marshals in the protests. They will be participating themselves in the early stages, but after two or three weeks, when we will begin to call larger numbers in, they will be the marshals, the ones who will control and discipline all of the demonstrations.

We plan to have a march, for those who can spend only a day or two in Washington, and that will be toward the culminating point of the campaign. I hope this will be a time when white people will rejoin the ranks of the movement.

Demonstrations have served as unifying forces in the movement; they have brought blacks and whites together in very practical situations, where philosophically they may have been arguing about Black Power. It's a strange thing how demonstrations tend to solve problems. The other thing is that it's little known that crime rates go down in almost every community where you have demonstrations. In Montgomery, Ala., when we had a bus boycott, the crime rate in the Negro community went down 65 percent for a whole year. Anytime we've had demonstrations in a community, people have found a way to slough off their self-hatred, and they have had a channel to express their longings and a way to fight non-violently—to get at the power structure, to know you're doing something, so you don't have to be violent to do it.

We need this movement. We need it to bring about a new kind of togetherness between blacks and whites. We need it to bring allies together and to bring the coalition of conscience together.

A good number of white people have given up on integration too. There are a lot of "White Power" advocates, and I find that people do tend to despair and engage in debates when nothing is going on. But when action is taking place, when there are demonstrations, they have a quality about them that leads to a unity you don't achieve at other times.

I think we have come to the point where there is no longer a choice now between non-violence and riots. It must be militant, massive non-violence, or riots. The discontent is so deep, the anger so ingrained, the despair, the restlessness so wide, that something has to be brought into being to serve as a channel through which these deep emotional feelings, these deep angry feelings, can be funneled. There has to be an outlet, and I see this campaign as a way to transmute the inchoate rage of the ghetto into a constructive and creative channel. It becomes an outlet for anger.

Even if I didn't deal with the moral dimensions and questions of violence versus non-violence, from a practical point of view, I don't see riots working. But I am convinced that if rioting continues, it will strengthen the right wing of the country, and we'll end up with a kind of right-wing take-over in the cities and a Fascist development, which will be terribly injurious to the whole nation. I don't think America can stand another summer of Detroit-like riots without a development that could destroy the soul of the nation, and even the democratic possibilities of the nation.

I'm committed to non-violence absolutely. I'm just not going to kill anybody, whether it's in Vietnam or here. I'm not going to burn down any buildings. If non-violent protest fails this summer, I will continue to preach it and teach it, and we at the Southern Christian Leadership Conference will still do this. I plan to stand by non-violence because I have found it to be a philosophy of life that regulates not only my dealings in the struggle for racial justice but also my dealings with people, with my own self. I will still be faithful to non-violence.

But I'm frank enough to admit that if our non-violent campaign doesn't generate some progress, people are just going to engage in more violent activity, and the discussion of guerrilla warfare will be more extensive.

In any event, we will not have been the ones who will have failed. We will place the problems of the poor at the seat of government of the wealthiest nation in the history of mankind. If that power refuses to acknowledge its debt to the poor, it will have failed to live up to its promise to insure "life, liberty and the pursuit of happiness" to its citizens.

If this society fails, I fear that we will learn very shortly that racism is a sickness unto death.

We welcome help from all civil-rights organizations. There must be a diversified approach to the problem, and I think both the NAACP and the Urban League play a significant role. I also feel that CORE and SNCC have played a very significant roles. I think SNCC's recent conclusions are unfortunate. We have not given up on integration. We still believe in black and white together. Some of the Black Power groups have temporarily given up on integration. We have not. So maybe we are the bridge in the middle, reaching across and connecting both sides.

The fact is, we have not had any insurrection in the United States because an insurrection is planned, organized, violent rebellion. What we have had is a kind of spontaneous explosion of anger. The fact is, people who riot don't want to riot. A study was made recently by some professors at Wayne State University. They interviewed several hundred people who participated in the riot last summer in Detroit, and a majority of these people said they felt that my approach to the problem—non-violence —was the best and most effective.

I don't believe there has been a massive turn to violence. Even the riots have had an element of non-violence to persons. But for a rare exception, they haven't killed any white people, and Negroes could, if they wished, kill by the hundreds. That would be insurrection. But the amazing thing is that the Negro has vented his anger on property, not persons, even in the emotional turbulence of riots.

But I'm convinced that if something isn't done to deal with the very harsh and real economic problems of the ghetto, the talk of guerrilla warfare is going to become much more real. The nation has not yet recognized the seriousness of it. Congress hasn't been willing to do anything about it, and this is what we're trying to face this spring. As committed as I am to non-violence, I have to face this fact: if we do not get a positive response in Washington, many more Negroes will begin to think and act in violent terms.

I hope, instead, that what comes out of these non-violent demonstrations will be an Economic Bill of Rights for the Disadvantaged, requiring about ten or twelve billion dollars. I hope that a specific number of jobs is set forth, that a program will emerge to abolish unemployment, and that there will be another program to supplement the income of those whose earnings are below the poverty level. These would be measures of success in our campaign.

It may well be that all we'll get out of Washington is to keep Congress from getting worse. The problem is to stop it from moving backward. We started out with a poverty bill at 2.4 billion dollars, and now it's back to 1.8 billion. We have a welfare program that's dehumanizing, and then Congress adds a Social Security amendment that will bar literally thousands of children from any welfare. Model cities started out; it's been cut back. Rent subsidy, an excellent program for the poor, cut down to nothing. It may be that because of these demonstrations, we will at least be able to hold on to some of the things we have.

There is an Old Testament prophecy of the "sins of the Fathers being visited upon the third and fourth generations." Nothing could be more applicable to our situation. America is reaping the harvest of hate and shame planted through the generations of educational denial, political dis-franchisement and economic exploitation of its black population. Now, almost a century removed from slavery, we find the heritage of oppression and racism erupting in our cities, with volcanic lava of bitterness and frustration pouring down our avenues.

Black Americans have been patient people, and perhaps they could continue patient with but a modicum of hope; but everywhere, "time is winding up," in the words of one of our spirituals, "corruption in the land, people take your stand; time is winding up." In spite of years of national progress, the plight of the poor is worsening. Jobs are on the decline as a result of technological change, schools North and South are proving themselves more and more inadequate to the task of providing adequate education and thereby entrance into the mainstream of the society. Medical care is virtually out of reach of millions of black and white poor. They are aware of the great advances of medical science—heart transplants, miracle drugs—but their children still die of preventable diseases, and even suffer brain damage due to protein deficiency.

In Mississippi, children are actually starving, while large landowners have placed their land in the soil bank and receive millions of dollars annually not to plant food and cotton. No provision is made for the life and survival of the hundreds of thousands of sharecroppers who now have no work and no food. Driven off the land, they are forced into tent cities and ghettos of the North, for our Congress is determined not to stifle the initiative of the poor (though they clamor for jobs) through welfare handouts. Handouts to the rich are given more sophisticated nomenclature such as parity, subsidies and incentives to industry.

White America has allowed itself to be indifferent to race prejudice and economic denial. It has treated them as superficial blemishes, but now awakes to the horrifying reality of a potentially fatal disease. The urban outbreaks are "a fire bell in the night," clamorously warning that the seams of our entire social order are weakening under the strains of neglect.

The American people are infected with racism—that is the peril. Paradoxically, they are also infected with democratic ideals—that is the hope. While doing wrong, they have the potential to do right. But they do not have a millennium to make changes. Nor have they a choice of continuing in the old way. The future they are asked to inaugurate is not so unpalatable that it justifies the evils that beset the nation. To end poverty, to extirpate prejudice, to free a tormented conscience, to make a tomorrow of justice, fair play and creativity—all these are worthy of the American ideal.

We have, through massive non-violent action, an opportunity to avoid a national disaster and create a new spirit of class and racial harmony. We can write another luminous moral chapter in American history. All of us are on trial in this troubled hour, but time still permits us to meet the future with a clear conscience.

69. THE NAACP: "WE SEEK . . . THE INCLUSION OF NEGRO AMERICANS IN THE NATION'S LIFE, NOT THEIR EXCLUSION"

In the face of the rise of separatist tendencies, the NAACP reaffirmed its traditional integrationist position. The NAACP believes that the press has greatly exaggerated the extent of nationalist tendencies among black Americans, contending that the overwhelming majority have not modified their goals. Though the Association has taken steps to give concrete assistance to black business, has given more attention to the encouragement of Negro history, and has become involved in local ghetto community organization, its basic thrust toward the principle of full participation in an integrated society remains unchanged. The selections reprinted below make clear the NAACP's continuing commitment to its traditional ideology.

A. Roy Wilkins, address to NAACP convention, 1966

All about us are alarums and confusions as well as great and challenging developments. Differences of opinion are sharper. For the first time since several organizations began to function where only two had functioned before, there emerges what seems to be a difference in goals.

Heretofore there were some differences in methods and emphasis but none in ultimate goals. The end was always to be the inclusion of the American Negro, without racial discrimination, as a full-fledged equal in all phases of American citizenship.

There has now emerged, first a strident and threatening challenge to a strategy widely employed by civil rights groups, namely non-violence. One organization which has been meeting in Baltimore has passed a resolution declaring for defense of themselves by Negro citizens if they are attacked.

This position is not new as far as the NAACP is concerned. Historically, our Association has defended in court those persons who have defended themselves and their homes with firearms.

But neither have we couched a policy of manly resistance in such a way that our members and supporters felt compelled to maintain themselves in an armed state, ready to retaliate instantly and in kind whenever attacked.

Roy Wilkins, "Whither Black Power." Excerpts from keynote address delivered at NAACP 57th Annual Convention, Los Angeles, July 5, 1966. CRISIS (August–September 1966), pp. 353–354.

We venture the observation that such a published posture could serve to stir counterplanning, counteraction and possible conflict. If carried out literally as instant retaliation, in cases adjudged by aggrieved persons to have been grossly unjust, this policy could produce—in extreme situations—lynchings, or, in better-sounding phraseology, private vigilante vengeance.

Moreover, in attempting to substitute for derelict enforcement machinery, the policy entails the risk of a broader, more indiscriminate crack-down by law officers under the ready-made excuse of restoring law and order.

It seems reasonable to assume that proclaimed protective violence is as likely to encourage counterviolence as it is to discourage violent persecution.

But the more serious division in the civil rights movement is the one posed by a word formulation that implies clearly a difference in goals.

No matter how endlessly they try to explain it, the term "black power" means anti-white power. In a racially pluralistic society, the concept, the formation and the exercise of an ethnically tagged power means opposition to other ethnic powers, just as the term "white supremacy" means subjection of all non-white peoples. In the black-white relationship, it has to mean that every other ethnic power is the rival and the antagonist of "black power." It has to mean "going it alone." It has to mean separatism.

Now, separatism, whether on the rarefied debate level of "black power" or on the wishful level of a secessionist Freedom City in Watts, offers a disadvantaged minority little except to shrivel and die.

The only possible dividend of "black power" is embodied in its offer to millions of frustrated and deprived and persecuted black people of a solace, a tremendous psychological lift, quite apart from its political and economic implications.

Ideologically it dictates "up with black and down with white" in precisely the same manner that South Africa reverses that slogan.

It is a reverse Mississippi, a reverse Hitler, a reverse Ku Klux Klan.

If these were evil in our judgment, what virtue can we claim for black over white? If, as some proponents claim, this concept instills pride of race, cannot this pride be taught without preaching hatred or supremacy based on race?

Though it be clarified and clarified again, "black power" in the quick, uncritical and highly emotional adoption it has received from segments of a beleaguered people can mean in the end only black death. Even if, through some miracle, it should be enthroned briefly, the human spirit, which knows no color or geography or time, would die a little, leaving for wiser and stronger and more compassionate men the painful beating back to the upper trail.

We of the NAACP will have none of this. We have fought it too long. It is the ranging of race against race on the irrelevant basis of skin color. It is the father of hatred and the mother of violence.

It is the wicked fanaticism which has swelled our tears, broken our bodies, squeezed our hearts and taken the blood of our black and white loved ones. It shall not now poison our forward march.

We seek, therefore, as we have sought these many years, for the inclusion of Negro Americans in the nation's life, not their exclusion. This is our land, as much as it is any American's— every square foot of every city and town and village. The task of winning our share is not the easy one of disengagement and flight, but the hard one of work, of short as well as long jumps, of disappointments and of sweet success.

B. CRISIS editorials

The black neo-segregationists

The strident cry for racial separation emanating from the extremist black camp is, in essence, a wail of defeat. These mis-

Editorials, CRISIS, LXXIV (November 1967), pp. 439–441.

guided black advocates of apartheid have been convinced of their inability to compete in the open market with other Americans and, accordingly, are seeking refuge in a protective cocoon of racialism, fearful of facing the harsh realities of the competitive society in which we live.

Traditionally the vast majority of Negro Americans have rejected segregation, which they early recognized as a repressive instrument for maintaining the racial inequities of American life. Even before the Civil War the majority of free Negroes steadfastly resisted efforts of the white-sponsored American Colonization Society to ship them off to Africa. They asserted their right to remain in the land of their nativity which they helped to explore, build and defend with their sweat, blood and tears.

We Negroes have had to endure certain forms of segregation imposed upon us by law and custom. But, by and large, we have rejected segregation in principle and have seldom advocated it. The historic Supreme Court decision of May 17, 1954, sounded the death knell of statutory segregation and undermined Jim Crow morés. It did not, of course, end all segregation. But it did demolish the constitutional sanction of this hateful and pernicious system.

We in the NAACP, as well as others, fought segregation because we had faith in our ability, given equal opportunity and fair ground rules, to compete with and achieve, on a man-to-man basis, with any other Americans of whatever origin. We have demonstrated this capacity in education, in the arts and sciences, in public service, and, most notably, in sports and entertainment.

And now come the black neo-segregationists who, in their despair and weakness, confess to their inability to compete and call upon their fellow blacks to join them in retreat; to ignore opportunities never before available to them; and to abandon the fight to share equally in the nation's power and affluence—all this in futile pursuit of the fantasy of isolated racial self-sufficiency in a period of increasing inter-dependency of all the peoples of the world.

Racial pride, yes—racial hatred, no!

The National Association for the Advancement of Colored People and *The Crisis* have, for nearly 60 years, preached racial pride. This magazine has, since its founding by W. E. B. Du Bois, published articles and editorials on Negroes of achievement, both African and American as well as black people in other parts of the world. The NAACP has published booklets on America's black heroes. All of this was designed to implant racial pride in Negroes, particularly among the young people who even today, receive precious little of such teaching in their schools.

But we have never fostered xenophobia. We have not wanted our people to hate or disdain other people who do not share our ancestry. To be proud of one's self or of one's race does not require or justify hatred of other peoples.

It is among defeated peoples that the merger of racial pride and racial hatred is most commonly found. The South, smouldering with resentment from the Civil War defeat became the principal fount of racial pride and hate in America. This obsession has been a vital factor retarding cultural and economic development in the South and keeping it the most backward region in the nation. It has been remarked that the white persons most proud of their race are seldom the ones of which their race is most proud.

History was repeated following defeat in the first World War. The Germans were a depressed, spiritless people feeling put upon by the rest of the world. Then, in the early Thirties, along came Adolf Hitler preaching the doctrine of the *herrenvolk*. He succeeded in making the Germans believe they were a superior people. He achieved this goal by downgrading not only the Jews but all non-Germans including his allies, the Italians and Japanese. The fearful price the world had to pay for this madness is written in the blood of millions of people, German and non-German alike.

In light of this tragic history it is disturbing to hear certain black "militants" blending their race pride exhortations with race hate excoriation. Race hatred is the easiest emotion to arouse. It provides a scapegoat for one's own failings. Historically it has proved costly not only to its targets but also to its advocates.

Teach race pride, to be sure, but never race hatred.

Role of white liberals

In the present racial crisis the role of white liberals has come increasingly under fire. There are bitter black spokesmen who maintain that, being white, these liberals can have no role to play. Obviously flustered by these rebuffs, certain masochistic liberals have sought to placate the angry voices by endorsing whatever outlandish proposals they advance, including hate "whitey" slogans and archaic segregation nostrums, as did the so-called National Conference for New Politics, the National Student Association, and a Catholic organization.

Had these same proposals been advanced by any group other than Negroes, these liberals would have disdained to consider them. In ratifying the black extremists' proposals these particular white liberals revealed themselves for what they really are —patronizers of black folk. They do not expect or demand of Negroes what they do of other people. They make allowance for what they consider the "immaturity" of Negroes. There is nothing Negroes need less of than such patronizing whites.

There is a legitimate role for white liberals in the Fight for Freedom. They cannot, and should not attempt to, silence the angry black voices. They cannot, and should not try to, compel them to accept integration or to seize opportunities to enter the mainstream of American life. What they can do and, if they are genuine liberals, will do, is to keep the doors open to those Negroes who now want to enter and for those misguided ones who, as they grow in age and wisdom, will abandon racism and seek to take advantage of the new opportunities. They will also continue the struggle to eliminate all racial discrimination and to open additional doors to help speed equality in fact as well as in law. This is a rational and productive role for the white liberal who wishes to retain his self-respect and the respect of his Negro fellow citizens.

Time to speak up

The deepening schism within the Negro community over tactics and goals, gleefully fostered and distorted by insensitive and irresponsible news media, is headed toward a major internal crisis requiring each of us to stand up and be counted. Differences among black folk in this country are not new, but a new ingredient has been added—the attempt by a small minority of black extremists to force compliance with its views and tactics. This nihilistic minority professes disdain for all "white" values while at the same time invoking and utilizing, as instruments of controversy, the worst practices of the most benighted stratum of white society, to wit, obscene name-calling, threats, intimidation, suppression of opposing views and violence.

The emergence of this swaggering band of black extremists demanding abandonment of democratic methods and goals and a reversal of the trend toward integration must be met head-on by the vast majority of Negroes who reject the minority's tactics and goals. To be sure, the new mood has been generated by white America's historic racism. In turn, the new black mood nurtures further white racism.

Campaigning in New York City last month, Senator Edmund S. Muskie, the Democratic nominee for Vice President, challenged responsible people of both races to speak up. "We must break through the terrible cycle of action and reaction, assault and counter-assault, hatred and response to hatred," he said.

"The only way to break this vicious cycle," Senator Muskie continued, "is for the moderates in both communities to cope with the merchants of hate and violence within their own ranks. To date, the moderates—both black and white—have been too silent."

On our part, as on the part of white folk, there is urgent need for strong and unequivocal re-affirmation of our commitment to the democratic processes as a means of attaining, here in our homeland, full, equal and unfettered rights for America's

Editorial, CRISIS, LXXV (November 1968), pp. 310–312.

22,000,000 black folk. This means a repudiation of the nihilism of the extremists who are shrilly and insistently espousing apartheid; racism, including anti-Semitism; intimidation and violence.

Most fatuous of the extremists' exhortations is the call for "black revolution"—the seizure of power by the Negro minority. Any revolution remotely possible in this country at this time would not be one that advances the position and cause of Negroes. Rather it would be a revolution of the Right suppressing not only the black community but also curtailing the basic liberties of the total society.

Repeated surveys and polls by reputable and impartial opinion testers show that this minority misrepresents the true views and aspirations of the majority of the nation's Negro population. A September, 1968, survey by the Columbia Broadcasting System found that the "great majority" of Negroes still want integration and want to achieve equality through legal means. Only a very small minority of Negroes approve of violent tactics, nine out of ten in the survey expressing disapproval of violence to achieve equality."

Notwithstanding the evidence that the Negro masses remain committed to the program and tactics which have brought substantial gains in the struggle for equality, the voices within the Negro community which publicly express this majority view have been few and, often, lonely. Partly this has been because of a tendency on the part of the news media to by-pass spokesmen for the majority and to project the minority spokesmen as the authentic voices of the Negro community. There is the additional factor that responsible leaders who speak out against the extremists have been subjected to threats of violence. Moreover, Negro leaders have traditionally been reluctant to speak out publicly in opposition to other black spokesmen.

But the time has come for speaking out loud and clear lest the entire race be branded as hate-mongers, segregationists, advocates of violence, and worse. The silent majority must let its views be known not merely in polls but also in print, on the rostrum, and via radio and television. The time for silence or muted voices is past. The extremists must be answered promptly and forthrightly in the name of the majority. Their racism and anti-Semitism condemned and repudiated. The infantilism of their "governments-in-exile" exposed and scorned. Their advocacy of Jim Crowism rejected as retrogressive. Their suicidal call for violence disavowed.

In a message to the founding conference of the National Association for the Advancement of Colored People in 1909, William Lloyd Garrison expressed the hope "that the Conference will utter no uncertain sound on any point affecting the vital subject. No part of it is too delicate for plain speech."

So it is today. Let there be "no uncertain sound" on the issue confronting us. To make the record clear, let us repeat again and again so that none need be unaware of the Truth: Black America rejects and condemns separation, racism, intimidation, suppression of free speech, and violence. Let it be known that the preachers of hate, the defeatists afraid to compete in the open market, the name callers who substitute epithets and slogans for reason, the exhorters who summon Negro youth to death in futile shoot-outs with the police and the military— let it be known that these media-created "leaders" are not our spokesmen.

Dissent, protest and militancy, yes. Intimidation, disruption, suppression of free speech, extremism and violence, no!

The time to speak up in no uncertain terms, to rally the silent black majority to a constructive program of responsible militancy and resistance to extremism, is now. Tomorrow may be too late.

C. Roy Wilkins: The case against "black academic separatism"

In the 1920s in Kansas City, Mo., I learned a lesson that I never forgot. It has come home to me forcibly these past twelve

Roy Wilkins, "The Case Against Separatism: 'Black Jim Crow,'" from NAACP pamphlet, COMMON SENSE ANYONE? (New York: NAACP, 1969), pp. 11–13.

months in the demands of 1968–69 Negro college students for autonomous black units on some of their campuses. A Kansas City school-bond issue for the then racially segregated town provided $985,000 to build an athletic plant and field for a junior high school for white students—and $27,500 to convert a factory building into an elementary school for black children.

This was the ugly face of segregated education. The system must not be revived. It must not be invited back at the request, nay, the ultimatum of black students themselves.

No person who has watched the halting march of Negro civil rights through the years can fail to sympathize with the frustrations and anger of today's black students. In their hurt pride in themselves and in their outrage, they have called retreat from the tough and trying battle of a minority for dignity and equality. They don't call it a retreat, of course. They have all sorts of fancy rationalizations for their course. They renounce 'white middle-class values' so they can refuse logically to be judged by the standards of the times and of the place they live in. Every black dissenter is an Uncle Tom and every white one a racist. Vituperation, not reason, is invoked.

Racial breast-beating

They say they need to get together in their own dormitories to build a common strength. After they are strong and sure of themselves they will be able to meet other groups as true equals.

Who can declare them completely wrong? Certainly they are right about the strength that comes from being with their brothers. Certainly they are right about the usefulness of a study of Afro-American history and culture. They are right, also, in calling for increased enrollment of Negro students and in requesting more black faculty members. But in demanding a black Jim Crow studies building within a campus and exclusively black dormitories or wings of dormitories, they are opening the door to a dungeon. They do not see that no black history becomes significant and meaningful unless it is taught in the context of world and national history. In its sealed-off, black-studies centers, it will be simply another exercise in racial breast-beating.

Abdication

To oppose black academic separatism is not to ignore black youth or to be unmindful of the spirit displayed by so many of them. They must be heard and they are heard; I have talked on numerous occasions with student groups, some members of which were not Wilkins cheerleaders. But it would be an abdication of responsibility, to them and to those who will follow us both, to acquiesce in a course which we know to be wrong, solely to avoid their criticism.

The keyword in the current spate of similarly worded demands of black students is 'autonomous.' No university administration faithful to its trust can grant this. There is substantial informed opinion that tax money cannot be used to set up racial enclaves within campuses. I am sure that sooner or later a court test would arise. And all this is apart from the practical difficulty that it costs more money to establish real studies centers than most colleges can afford and that the qualified personnel—black or white—is simply not available at this time.

The demanding students might well find themselves saddled with a poor substitute for a center, foisted on them by an administration ready to buy peace at any price. Thus would segregated education once more run true to form.

An alternative with good chances of success would be to concentrate as a beginning on two centers of genuine stature, one on the East Coast and one on the West. The financing and staffing of two such university-based institutes would not be an impossible task, and they would draw not only on their own resident scholars but on exchange and visiting personnel as well. Meanwhile, valid courses in Afro-American history and culture should be established at all good colleges and universities to the extent that qualified faculty, black or white, can be found. Also, it should be the immediate task of every school claiming to be a school to provide an extensive library on the Negro past and present, in Africa, and in the New World.

Incidentally, the familiar 'reading course' should not be disdained; after all, my generation had no 'black studies' curriculum—but we found ways to learn about ourselves and our past.

February 10, 1969

D. Roy Wilkins, annual report for 1968

. . . . The campaign for the vote for Negro citizens is vital. It is the way to execute a peaceful revolution. Vote power is the stepping stone to economic power. If we believe in moving into the American mainstream, voting offers a sure and powerful way.

And power talk brings us to that unfortunate term, Black Power. I insist today, as I did in 1966, that, while it may make a rousing rallying cry, the hanging of an ethnic tag to the power that every man and group seeks is bad strategy, and a provocation that manufactures additional trouble for a people having more than their share of that commodity.

The Black Power people sense this because they have advanced scores of definitions of the term. They have wrestled with the problems which erupted when emotional and opportunity-starved rank-and-filers took up the slogan, applying it to any and all situations that arose between the races.

The desire to develop group power is perfectly understandable and perfectly legitimate. The three basic ingredients— political power, economic power and race pride—have long been goals of the Negro American community. Its banks and savings and loan associations and its scattered businesses all testify to the recognition of the need.

Pride of race was a part of the discipline in every organized Negro family. It was one of the reasons for the founding and flourishing of the black press. It could very well be that the back of the contemptuous conception of Negroes was broken when a drama critic remarked on Rose McClendon's grace as she

From Roy Wilkins, THE STATE OF THE NAACP, 1968. Report of NAACP Executive Director to the Association's Annual Corporation Meeting, New York City, January 13, 1969 (New York: NAACP, 1969), unpaged.

descended a staircase; or when an honest newspaper writer dared to break the taboo and called Lena Horne beautiful in print.

The minute these things were done, the Black is Beautiful campaign was won. It was just a question of mopping up and informing the late thinkers, including, unfortunately, some of our own people.

As for political power, we have long been privy to its usefulness, but, even now, we are not using it to its maximum potential. Like many another American we neglect to register and then to vote.

I was in Augusta, Georgia, about a month ago and they told me about an election they had there in which a committee was going around in an automobile offering to take people to the polls. So they got a telephone call to a certain address and they drove up to the house and the man had a station wagon and a sedan sitting in his driveway. So they said, "Did you call up and ask for a car to take you to the polls?" He said, "Yes." They said, "Why don't you use your own car?" He said, "You think I'm going to use my car to go and vote and help you fellows out?"

So then the man who was driving the car got angry and drove away. And he said. "Let him stew in his own juice." And he said to me, "I got about three blocks away and I said, 'well, he doesn't know any better and we do want the people to vote,' so I turned around and went back to the house and put him in the car and took him to the polls."

Now that kind of man would be the first one down to the NAACP office complaining about some law that the city council had passed that he didn't like and that was hurting his purse and he would say to us as so many people say, "What are you folks doing about this?" Not what are *we* doing about it, but what are *you* folks doing about it.

In the new administration in Washington our political acumen will be tested. It is us and our cause (which is also America's cause) against the powerful forces that helped to elect Mr. Nixon, and that's the contest. If we are wise, we will fashion a big stick out of our votes, watching carefully and talking softly—just in case.

What we need to do, both we and the Black Power boys, is to stop talking and start working. When you have power you don't need to shout about it. Let's build group power, not in a contest with another racial group, but in an effort to strengthen ourselves. The whole NAACP program is about building group power.

We must be for change, yes. Reform, yes. Sharp alteration in methods, yes. Acceleration, most certainly so. But separatism, no.

Sentiment has little to do with this conclusion. Pure practicality is the dominant reason. It is simple suicide—either literal or figurative—for a minority as small and as circumscribed as ours to talk seriously of separatism, apartheid and "going it alone."

We have suffered too many heartaches and shed too many tears and too much blood in fighting the evil of racial segregation to return in 1969 to the lonely and disspiriting confines of its demeaning prison. No matter how impassioned the plea or how beguiling the persuasion, we cannot go back.

And if some white Americans, torn and confused by today's clamor of some black students, should accede officially to the call for separate dormitories and autonomous racial schools within colleges and universities, there will be court action to determine anyone's right to the use of public tax funds to set up what are, in effect, Jim Crow schools.

We of the NAACP cannot permit a minority of less than 3 per cent, regardless of how vocal, to plunge 22 millions of black Americans into the valley of proscription and deprivation. This report today, for example, does not chronicle unalloyed success; the spiritual and material needs remain great; but we are not so utterly cast down as to run away from a fight for our rights as men among men.

We want these young people with us. We need them, their brains, their skills and their belief in themselves. They belong to us and we to them. When their emotion is spent and when they learn more than catch phrases about their race's struggles and history here on these shores the best of them will join the ranks of Freedom's Army. Men and women of all colors, nationalities and religions will be there.

In the tiny sixty years of the NAACP's life, some small darknesses have been pushed back, but much darkness remains. In a minute, a day or a year we cannot overcome, but with each one doing his dedicated bit in his lifetime, men one wondrous day will be able to sing "We have overcome."

For our part, we pledge every energy, every strategy and every sacrifice to bring that day to reality.

70. KENNETH CLARK:
"BLACK POWER
IS A SOUR GRAPES PHENOMENON"

One of the most trenchant critiques of Black Power was made by the noted psychologist, Kenneth Clark, in an address before the convention of the Association for the Study of Negro Life and History in October 1967. Clark, a professor at the College of the City of New York, was a student activist at Howard University in the 1930s and was one of the most important contributors to the NAACP brief which led to the 1954 U.S. Supreme Court desegregation decision, *Brown vs. Board of Education*. In his judgment, Black Power is an "anguished cry" born of desperation and fear. Clark warns that the hopes for a completely polarized society which white segregationists had failed to achieve may now be realized through the black separatists. Central in his explanation is the recognition that the doctrine of Black Power flourishes only because white America has failed, and continues to fail, to permit racial justice. Clark believes that a non-

Kenneth Clark, "The Present Dilemma of the Negro," JOURNAL OF NEGRO HISTORY, LIII (January 1968), pp. 1–11. Reprinted with permission of the publisher.

segregated society can still be attained by thoughtful Negroes joining
with concerned whites to attack the long-standing urban and racial
problems.

The "nuclear" irony of American history and the American
social, political, and economic system is that the destiny of the
enslaved and disadvantaged Negro determines the destiny of
the nation. The fundamental fact around which all questions
of national survival pivot is the fact of inherent racial inter-
relatedness—or integration, if you please—in spite of the persistent demands and attempts to impose racial separatism. The
problems of the American Negro are problems of America. The
conflicts, aspirations, confusions, and doubts of Negro Americans are not merely similar but are identical to those of white
Americans. The Negro need not yearn to be assimilated into
American culture—he is and determines American culture. In
the face of rapid and at times frightening historical, economic,
political, technological, social, and intellectual changes, the
Negro remains the constant, and at times irritating reality that
is America. He remains the essential psychological reality with
which America must continuously seek to come to terms—and
in so doing is formed by.

The moral and ethical aspirations of America have been
accepted totally by Negroes. The moral schizophrenia of America is reflected most clearly in the status of Negroes, starting
with slavery and continuing to the contemporary ghettoes
which blight the powerful and affluent cities of our nation.

The dilemmas of America are the dilemmas of Negro Americans. One cannot, therefore, discuss the dilemmas of the contemporary American Negro without at the same time becoming
involved in an analysis of the historical and psychological fab-
ric of American life. This is the thesis reflecting the bias of a
social psychologist—a bias which might be rejected by more
sophisticated historians, political and economic theorists, or
tougher minded social critics. I nonetheless base my thesis on
the psychological premise that the values, attitudes, and be-

havior of individual human beings and groups of human beings are determined by the complex socialization process—that normal human beings are modifiable and are determined by their environment and culture—and not by any inherent, genetic or racial determinants.

Let us now be specific:

A basic dilemma of America is whether the Negro should be accepted and taken seriously as a human being and permitted the rights and privileges accorded other human beings in our political system. America has endured slave rebellions, developed an underground railroad, fought one of the most bloody wars in human history and is now undergoing a series of urban ghetto implosions in the attempt to resolve this persistent bedeviling question.

The Negro's form of this basic dilemma is whether to persist in his insistence upon his unqualified rights as a human being without regard to the risks or consequences—or whether to accommodate to the resistances by subtle or flagrant forms of withdrawal from the fray. The general acceptance of slavery, the many psychological adjustments and deflection of aggressive reactions to subjugation, the varieties of back-to-Africa movements, the cults, fads, and the recent series of riots in our ghettos are among the many ways in which American Negroes have sought to deal with this basic American dilemma.

The gnawing doubts of white Americans as to their status and worth as human beings—the deep feelings of inferiority coming out of the actual inferior status in the land of their origin in Europe—impelled American whites to develop and enforce social and institutional arrangements designed to inflict upon Negroes an inferior status in American life. This was necessary to bolster the demanding status needs of whites. These needs were powerful enough to counteract the logic, the morality and the powerful political ethics of the egalitarian and democratic rhetoric which is also an important American reality. I differ with early Myrdal only in my belief that the American democratic creed and ideals are not psychologically contradictory to American racism. In terms of dynamics and motivation of the insecure, they are compatible.

This critical American dilemma is reflected in Negroes not only in terms of acceptance of the creeds and its promises literally, but also in terms of deep doubts concerning the worth of self. The former aspect of the dilemma stems from the fact of general indoctrination which transcends even the barriers of racially segregated schools and is reinforced by the development of the mass media in the 20th century. The latter component of the Negro's dilemma arises out of the reality of the inferior status to which he has been subjugated. The walls of segregation are not only humiliating—but given this type of chronic humiliation there develops self doubt, subtle and flagrant forms of self hatred, personal and group frustrations, internalized hostility, aggressions, self denial or bombast. Under these conditions the walls of segregation become pathetically protective. Within them the subjugated individuals need not meet the tests of free and open competition—need not expose vulnerable egos to single standards of competence.

The anguish and resistance of anxious, self-doubting white segregationists and the cautious timidity of striving middle class whites with the psyche of affluent peasants are matched only by the anxieties, doubts, and vacillation of vast numbers of Negroes—working and middle class—as they stand at the threshold of non-segregated society and are confronted by the tremendous psychological challenges for which American history not only did not prepare them but erected seemingly insurmountable barriers. The demand for racial justice on the part of the American Negroes is balanced by an almost equal psychological reality of the fear of the removal of racial barriers.

Within this context—disturbing and painful, but I believe psychologically valid—one can now attempt an analysis of the contemporary manifestations of the dilemma of America and the dilemma of Negro Americans. The value of such an analysis will be determined by whether it provides a basis for constructive, realistic, democratic, and humane resolutions of some of the racial and social problems which afflict America and threaten its survival.

In many disturbing ways the problems of race relations in America today are similar to those of the post-Reconstruction period of the late 19th century which continued and intensified through World War I. This period, which Rayford Logan and John Hope Franklin have described as the "nadir" of the Negro in American life, came as a seemingly abrupt and certainly cruel repudiation of the promises of Reconstruction for inclusion of the Negro into the political and economic life of the nation. This was a period:

> —when the white crusaders for racial justice and democracy became weary as the newly freed Negroes could no longer be considered a purely Southern problem;
>
> —when the aspirations for and movement of Negroes toward justice and equality were curtailed and reversed by organized violence and barbarity perpetrated against them;
>
> —when, as a result of their abandonment and powerlessness, the frustrations, bitterness and despair of Negroes increased and displaced optimism and hope.

This period culminated in the institutionalization of rigid forms of racism—the enactment and enforcement of laws requiring or permitting racial discrimination and segregation in all aspects of American life. This retrogression in racial democracy in America was imposed by white segregationists with the apathy, indifference, or quiet acceptance of white liberals and moderates as necessary accessories.

The parallel with the state of race relations in America today is stark and frightening. The promises and optimism of the Second Reconstruction, initiated by the pattern of litigation which resulted in the *Brown* decision of 1954—which precipitated the high morale mark of the successful boycotts and sit-ins, and which reached its climax in the emotional catharsis of the 1963 March on Washington—were also cruelly aborted by stepped-up violence against Negro and white civil rights workers in the resistant Southern states and the related weariness, racial anxieties, and latent racism of Northern whites which emerged under the guise of "white backlash."

The hopes and beliefs of the Negro that racial equality and democracy could be obtained through litigation, legislation, executive action, and negotiation, and though strong alliances with various white liberal groups, were supplanted by disillusionment, bitterness, and anger which erupted under the anguished cry of "Black Power" which pathetically sought to disguise the understandable desperation and impotence with bombast and rhetoric.

A critical danger—and probably a difference without a pragmatic distinction—between the determinants of retrogression in the first post-Reconstruction period and the present is that whereas the promises of racial progress were reversed in the 19th century by the fanaticism, irrationality, and cruel strength of white segregationists—the impending racial retrogression of today might come about largely through self-hatred leading to the fanaticism, dogmatism, rigidity, and self-destructive cruelty of black separatists. If this comes about, it will not be enough to excuse this monstrous perpetuation of the lie of racism and postponement of the goals of democracy and humanity by asserting that the frustrations and bitterness of the victimized Negro account for his present irrationality and rigidity. A similar and equally valid psychological explanation could be offered to explain the racial cruelties of desperate and miserable poor whites of the past and present. Understanding is not acceptance.

White segregationists were able to inflict and perpetuate racial injustices upon Negroes because rational, sophisticated, and moderate whites were silent in the face of barbarities. They permitted themselves to be intimidated and bullied by white extremists until they were morally and almost functionally indistinguishable from their worst and most ignorant elements. A similar threat and dilemma face the rational, thoughtful Negro today. If he permits himself to be cowed into silence by unrealistic Negro racists, he will be an active partner in fastening the yoke of impossible racial separatism more tightly around the neck of America. He—you, through your silence, will permit the difficult goals of a racially non-segregated society to be lost by default. You would have given to black racists what you, your fathers and grandfathers fought and died to prevent giving to white racists. The victories which white segregationists, in spite of all their material and political power, could not have won for themselves, black separatists would have won for them—and we through our silence would make this possible.

To prevent the repetition of the tragedy of racial retrogression and a return to the "nadir" of race relations in America, we must be realistic in our appraisal of the present state of race relations in America. . . . We must analyze as tough-mindedly as possible the dynamics and symptoms of our times if we are to develop effective and realistic remedies.

During the past few years it became excruciatingly clear for the Negro that the more things changed the more they remained the same—or worsened. The promises and hope for progress became a relentless quagmire of words.

The drama of direct action, non-violent confrontation of the more obvious signs of Southern racial injustice became trite, and was not particularly relevant or effective in dealing with the persistent, pervasive, and subtle problems of racism which afflicted the Northern Negro. More appropriate and effective methods have not yet been found to deal with Northern racism.

The guilt and indignation of some Northern whites against Southern forms of racism turned into white backlash or mutism when the Northern Negro began to take seriously the claims of civil rights progress and sought some observable signs of them in Northern cities.

The anguish and desperation of the Northern Negro have been expressed in the latest series of ghetto eruptions which started in the Harlem riot of the summer of 1964, reached a crescendo in the Watts riot of 1965 and continued through the current series of riots in Newark and Detroit of this past summer. Another significant expression of the Northern Negro's "no-win" fatalism is found in the rise of the "Black Power" slogan and momentum which skyrocketed at the time of the Meredith shooting in Mississippi in June of 1966 and continues as an obbligato to the sounds of ghetto violence and futility.

It is important to keep in mind the date (June, 1966) when the "Black Power" slogan became nationally advertised—in order not to be confused about the cause and effect relationship between "Black Power" and "white backlash."

Whatever may be its tactical, strategic, and rational short-comings and its ambiguity, "Black Power" did not cause "white backlash" . . . The existence of "white backlash," the unwilling-ness of whites to be serious in meeting the demands of Negroes for the same rights and responsibilities granted as a matter of course to all other Americans—including the newest refugee from European, Latin American, or Asiatic oppression—caused the outbursts of hysterical bitterness and random hostility in-herent in the cry of "Black Power."

"Black Power" emerged as a response to the following facts:

—a recognition of the fact that the center of gravity of the civil rights movement had moved to the Northern urban racial ghettos where it was now immobilized by ambiguous intensified white resistance to any meaning-ful change in the predicament of Negroes;

—the recognition of the fact that successful litigation, strong legislation, free access to public accommodations, open housing laws, strong pronouncements on the part of the President, governors or mayors, and even the right to vote or to hold office were not relevant to the overriding fact that the masses of Negroes were still confined to poverty and to the dehumanizing conditions of the ghetto;

—and that in spite of the promises of a Great Society and the activity of the war on poverty, the Negro's children were still doomed to criminally inferior schools and his youth and males the victims of unemployment, under-employment and stagnation.

"Black Power" is the cry of defiance of what its advocates have come to see as the hoax of racial progress—of the cynicism of the appeals to the Negro to be patient and to be lawful as his needs are continually subordinated to more important na-tional and international issues and to the needs, desires, and conveniences of more privileged groups.

Whites, by virtue of their numerical, military, and economic superiority, reinforced by historical American racism which grants higher status to whites by virtues of skin color alone, do have the power to decide whether the future of Negroes— the Negro masses, the Negro middle class, or the Negro elected official—will be positive, negative, or stagnant.

This core reality of the dynamics of power is not likely to be influenced by sentimental and idealistic appeals for justice, by smiles or promises or by emotional sloganeering.

"Black Power," in spite of its ambiguity, its "no-win" premise, its programmatic emptiness and its pragmatic futility does have tremendous psychological appeal for the masses of Negroes who have "nothing to lose" and some middle class Negroes who are revolted by the empty promises and the moral dry-rot of affluent America.

"Black Power" is a bitter retreat from the possibility of the attainment of the goals of any serious racial integration in America. . . .

It is an attempt to make a verbal virtue of involuntary racial segregation. . . .

It is the sour grapes phenomenon on the American racial scene. . . .

"Black Power" is the contemporary form of the Booker T. Washington accommodation to white America's resistance to making democracy real for Negro Americans. While Booker T. made his adjustment to and acceptance of white racism under the guise of conservatism, many if not all of the "Black Power" advocates are seeking to sell the same shoddy moral product in the gaudy package of racial militance.

Nonetheless, today "Black Power" is a reality in the Negro ghettos of America—increasing in emotional intensity, if not in rational clarity. And we, if we are to be realistic, cannot afford to pretend that it does not exist. Even in its most irrational and illusory formulations—and particularly when it is presented as a vague and incoherent basis upon which the deprived Negro can project his own pathetic wishes for a pride and an assertiveness which white America continues mockingly or piously to deny him—"Black Power" is a powerful political reality which cannot be ignored by realistic Negro or white political officials.

It is all too clear that among the casualties of the present phase of American race relations are reason, clarity, consistency and realism. Some "Black Power" spokesmen, like their white segregationist counterparts, demand the subjugation of rational and realistic thought and planning to dogmaticism and fanaticism. By their threats and name calling, they seek to intimidate others into silence or a mindless mouthing of their slogans.

To be effective and to increase his chances of survival in the face of name-calling verbal racial militants, the trained Negro must demonstrate that he is concerned and can bring about some positive changes in the following intolerable areas of ghetto life:

1. criminally inefficient and racially segregated public schools;
2. dehumanizingly poor housing;
3. pervasive job discrimination and joblessness;
4. shoddy quality of goods and high prices in local stores;
5. the dirt, filth, and stultifying drabness of ghetto streets and neighborhoods;
6. the adversary relationship between police and the residents of the ghettos.

This requires the mobilization and use of human intelligence to define the problems, to study and analyze them and to develop practical and implementable solutions to them. This cannot be done on the basis of race—whites and Negroes must join together in an experiment to determine whether systematic and emphatic use of human intelligence and training can be a form of power which can be used constructively in the quest for solutions of long standing urban and racial problems. This is the rationale of The Metropolitan Applied Research Center. We are under no illusions that this will be easy. . . . We know that power confrontation brings risks not found in the cloistered halls of academia. We know that we cannot expect the protections and safety of the detached isolated scholars. But we believe that human intelligence is a social trust and that the stakes are worth the risks.

Another dilemma, not related to the dilemmas and inconsistencies of "Black Power," is the fact that in the present doldrums of the civil rights movement the cleavage between the masses of Negroes and the middle class has become more clear and exacerbating. The masses of Negroes are now starkly aware of the fact that recent civil rights victories benefited primarily a very small percentage of middle class Negroes while their predicament remained the same or worsened. Added to Ralph Bunche and our traditional civil rights leaders who are invited to Washington, we now have Thurgood Marshall, Robert Weaver, Walter Washington as the appointed Mayor of Washington, D. C., a few vice presidents in private industry, a few more Negroes in New England prep schools and Ivy League colleges, and more white colleges and universities are looking for one or two "qualified Negroes" for their faculties. These and other tokens of "racial progress" are not only rejected by the masses of Negroes but seem to have resulted in their increased and more openly expressed hostility toward middle class Negroes. They see the advances of the middle class Negroes as being at their expense, at worst, or obscuring their plight or, at best, not being in any way relevant to their being condemned indefinitely to their dehumanizing predicament. There are some clues which suggest that the recent ghetto implosions were not only anti-white, but also involved vague stirrings of anti-Negro middle class sentiment among the rioters.

The present dilemma of the Negro is focused for the trained Negro intellectual. He must now choose sides. He must now clarify the nature of the enemy. He must dare to say that the enemy was never to be understood in terms of color . . . but in the more difficult and abstract terms of human irrationality, ignorance, superstition, rigidity, and arbitrary cruelty.

These are the common enemies which underlie all forms of tyranny—racism, authoritarianism, McCarthyism. . . .

They are no less enemies when being sold or offered as truth or salvation by blacks, yellows or whites. . . .

If Negroes and whites who can understand this can make it clear, we can help to save America. We will use the power of disciplined intelligence combined with respect for moral values and humanity to save Negroes from the destructive possibilities of white and black dilemmas and thereby contribute to the survival of America. . . . For America cannot survive if Negroes do not. . . . And Negroes and no other group of human beings are likely to survive if America does not.

71. BAYARD RUSTIN: "SOME BLACK YOUTH TODAY HAVE BEGUN TO ACCEPT THE VERY WORST IDEAS . . . EMPLOYED BY SOUTHERN WHITE RACISTS"

An articulate representative of the anti-separatist, anti-black nationalist point of view is Bayard Rustin. An important leader in the nonviolent direct-action wing of the civil rights movement for over two decades, Rustin had achieved national recognition as the architect of the 1963 March on Washington. Through the years he maintained his faith in the ideology of Negro alliance with the labor movement, and his vision of an integrated society. In the selections from his weekly newspaper column released by the A. Philip Randolph Institute, Rustin, director of the institute, criticizes the ideology of black separatism.

A. "Separate is Not Equal"

There is a great irony in the demands now being made by black college students for separate black studies departments, for in essence these students are seeking to impose upon themselves the very conditions of separatism and inequality against which black Americans have struggled since the era of Reconstruction.

Bayard Rustin, "Separate is Not Equal," news release of the A. Philip Randolph Institute, February 13, 1969.

The argument can of course be made that separate need not be unequal. But black people have heard this argument before —from Southern racists justifying Jim Crow and from Northern bigots rationalizing *de facto* segregation. They have heard it long enough to know that "separate but equal" shall always be a form of exploitation and degradation. And it shall continue to be such, whether it is demanded by whites out of malicious intent, or by blacks out of the poignant need, born of fear and insecurity, to withdraw from competition with the larger society.

For if we are to face the truth, however painful this may be, we must recognize that black people have been brutalized in the past by inferior segregated education and economic deprivation to the point where they have been put at a disadvantage with whites. Consequently, when they are placed in a difficult competitive situation, such as obtains at predominantly white universities, their immediate impulse is to retreat into themselves and establish a black curriculum with separate—and lower—standards by which their performance shall be judged.

There are three great dangers here.

First, if history and present circumstances are any indicators, as I think they are, separate black programs will be poorly financed, under-staffed and generally neglected.

Second, rather than demanding a separate (and inferior) program of study, black students should be insisting on the best education that is possible to compensate for their brutalization in the past. They should be demanding access to the best professors, smaller classes, extra work during summer sessions, and more scholarships for other black students. And third, they must have these things because after graduation they will have to engage in free and open competition for jobs in a market place where standards are universal, and black people must get the best jobs available if they are to substantially increase their economic and social power.

In this regard, I reserve my most severe criticism for those white students and faculty members who are aiding and abetting the separatist demands of black students, and for those frightened administrators who do not have the courage to reject these demands. They are not only telling young Negroes what is not true in real life—that a minority can influence social change through violent confrontationism—but they are urging these blacks to do something which they themselves, discontented though they may be, don't have the courage to do—which is to make a head-on attack on our social institutions. And while these whites enjoy their revolution by proxy, they are studying for the degrees that will give them soft jobs in universities and beautiful homes in the suburbs. It is only the blacks who will suffer.

So that I will not be misunderstood, I want to emphasize that I am wholeheartedly in support of black studies. The history of the Negro in America is an extraordinarily significant area of study for *all* Americans which has been mostly neglected or distorted in the past. It is a history that is both magnificent and tragic, and one can only become wiser from studying it. In this regard, I fully commend the proposal of the Harvard faculty committee to offer a degree in Afro-American studies that will be open to all students.

What I fear is that black studies shall be made a pretext for separatism, in which case it will become a means of escaping from reality, not of discovering it. And if this comes to pass, I think that a great injustice will have been committed against black Americans.

B. "What About Black Capitalism?"

There has been much talk recently about black capitalism as the new approach to solving the economic and social problems of Negro Americans. As this approach is gaining considerable support within the Nixon Administration and in certain segments of the black community, I think that we must closely analyze whether or not it can make a contribution to the Negro struggle for equality.

Bayard Rustin, "What About Black Capitalism?" News Release of the A. Philip Randolph Institute, February 27, 1969.

I favor the notion of black people owning and operating businesses, and I should add in this regard that I find particularly creative the efforts that some Negroes have made to form co-operatives. Yet I think that these enterprises have had more of a psychological than an economic effect on black Americans. They have helped destroy the brutal stereotype that black people are not capable of engaging in entrepreneurial activity. But the economic impact of black capitalism has been—and can only be—marginal at best, and if we are not careful, this approach may actually compound the injustices from which Negroes suffer.

We must not forget that businesses are "in business" not to attack social injustice but to make a profit, and that the ghetto represents a poor market to invest in because of its poverty and deprivation. Businesses must, therefore, be attracted into the ghetto through tax incentives which guarantee them a high profit and which also insure that they themselves, and not the poor, will be the prime benefactors of their investments.

Of course some of these benefactors will be black capitalists, but the individuals are a very small and affluent section of the Negro community. It is the black working poor and the unemployed who constitute the mass of Negroes in need of economic uplift, and I think it is both foolish and misleading to speak to these people about becoming capitalists. Rather, our central objective must be to enable them to join their two million brothers and sisters who are part of the American trade union movement which is the institution most responsible for the integration of the black poor into the economic life of our society.

I am also distressed by the separatist framework within which black capitalism is so often discussed. Many of its advocates employ black nationalist rhetoric in proposing the economic development of the ghetto, assuming, therefore, that the ghetto is a separate entity in American life which must be nurtured and made viable. I understand that the ghetto will not disappear tomorrow, but we must not fall into the dangerous and divisive trap of abandoning the goals of integration and the elimination of a separatist social structure which has imposed such degradation and hardship upon black people and which today threatens to divide our nation.

And finally, I am most deeply concerned that black capitalism is projected by some of its proponents not as a marginal and supplementary program, but as an alternative to massive public expenditures for full employment and the reconstruction of our cities. I can think of nothing more potentially harmful to black people than the substitution of the delusion of black capitalism for the absolute necessity of Federal programs to provide all Negroes with dignified employment, decent housing, and superior schools. Black people cannot ignore these objectives without forsaking the ultimate goal of economic liberation.

C. "No More Guns"

Black people have known violence in America. They have known the Ku Klux Klan and the White Citizens Councils. They have seen the white mobs in Mississippi and in Cicero, Illinois. They have understood that violence is synonymous with oppression and destruction. And, therefore, the use of guns on the Cornell University campus by a group of black students should come as a great shock—and a great sorrow—to all black Americans struggling for freedom and social justice.

Those black students who paraded so arrogantly with their guns will not bring progress to the black community or reform to the universities by imitating the tactics of the Klan. Nothing creative can emerge from their mindless use of force. Rifles will not enhance their education; nor will bullets enlighten their minds. And guns will not provide them with the knowledge and skills they need to help uplift their black brothers who are still suffering in the ghetto.

Those black students were not interested in reforming the university. Otherwise they would not have acted in such a way as to destroy the university.

Bayard Rustin, "No More Guns." News Release of the A. Philip Randolph Institute, April 24, 1969.

The fundamental cause for their actions lies not in the failure of the university to provide them with the means of obtaining an adequate education. I say this in full knowledge of the tremendous changes which must be made in policy and curriculum if universities are to meet the profound needs of black students —and white students—in our urban and technological society. And I should add in this regard that Cornell was far ahead of most universities in responding to this challenge.

These students acted as they did because they are under severe psychological stress. They have entered a predominantly white university from predominantly black high schools. In those high schools they were brutalized by inferior segregated education. Therefore, they now not only find themselves in an alien social environment, but they are being asked to perform academically at a level for which they were not prepared. On top of this, they are undergoing a difficult quest for a black identity which is being aggravated by feelings of guilt at having deserted the ghetto.

Caught in a strange and pressured environment and deprived of the psychological security they had in the ghetto, their impulse is to withdraw from the challenge of the university and establish a separate world for themselves. Once a situation of racial separatism has been established, racial hostility becomes inevitable. Mutual misunderstandings, rhetoric, and fear predominate. A psychology of warfare develops, guns are procured, and the university is transformed into an armed camp.

The black students at Cornell only displayed their arms. They used them to intimidate the administration. But built into the situation is the logic of escalation. Violence threatened with bravado will become violence used with viciousness, and the main victims will not be the administration but the black students—and the university.

I, therefore, find those guilt-ridden and nihilistic white students who encouraged them in this madness to be equally as culpable. So too is the indecisive and flaccid administration which has abdicated its authority to insure that reason prevails in our institutions of higher learning. Cheap accommodationism will only bring greater violence in the future.

Moreover, by their irresponsible actions, these black students have strengthened the reactionary forces in the society which will obstruct any progress for black Americans. The fear in the white community which produced George Wallace has also been the source of resistance to programs to rebuild our cities, educate our youth, and employ all of our adults. These students have increased that fear and have thus further obstructed efforts for real social progress. They have not done a service to their black brothers in the ghetto.

Finally, the central and most profound difficulty was well articulated by Dr. Kenneth Clark who perceived in the confrontation tactics of these students "the destruction of the institutions and the total rejection of the rational and democratic process as a basis for redress of grievances." It is thus not only the university which is being threatened by these students, but all of our democratic institutions. And if democracy is destroyed and violence prevails, those who will suffer most will be black Americans. This has been true in the past, and it remains true today. We must repudiate such violence if we are to achieve our liberation.

D. "The Disease of Racism"

Mahatma Gandhi, the great revolutionary of this century, who led India to independence often said, "One becomes the thing he hates." And there is disturbing evidence that some black youth today have begun to accept the very worst ideas and concepts that were employed by Southern white racists to brutalize and emasculate black people.

The racist argues that their culture is threatened by blacks and that segregation is the only policy to insure racial purity. Now, we find black extremists arguing that separation is the only course to be followed if black identity is to be nurtured and maintained.

Bayard Rustin, "The Disease of Racism." News Release of the A. Philip Randolph Institute, n.d. [spring 1969].

The racist contends that whiteness is in itself a value that supersedes all other values. Love, affection, truth and justice are to be sacrificed on the altar of whiteness when white culture is "endangered." Now we find some black people contending that blackness is a value that supersedes all others and that the old fashioned notions of fair play, consideration and honesty will occasionally need to be abandoned if the black community is to be preserved.

The racist violates the democratic process. They use fear, economic pressure and threats. Their slogan is, "Keep the black from the polls." Given the fact that scores of black men and women have been lynched in seeking the right to vote, it is ironic today to hear so many black people argue that the vote is useless. The expression of such sentiments in the black community must bring much solace to the hearts of Eastland, Wallace and Thurmond.

The racists have always argued that the Jews and the "Niggers" are primarily responsible for all that is wrong in the United States and that they should go back where they came from. Today, there are black people who have borrowed these attitudes toward the Jews, and who now argue that the Jews are primarily responsible for all that is wrong in the ghetto.

The racist, in his insecurity, bolsters his sagging ego by calling black men "boys"; by calling black women "Negresses," and by calling black people, in general, "boots," "spooks," "niggers," etc. Now we find young black people calling all white people (good, bad, and indifferent) "honky," "whitey," "blue-eyed devils," and "pigs."

The racist uses economic pressure, brutality and threats of death not only to suppress black people, but also to suppress white people who support the civil rights struggle. Their aim is to contain "the nigger lover," and to act as a veto power over men of good will. Now we find some black extremists using threats, insults and intimidation against those forces in the black community who seek the cooperation of white in our struggle for justice.

This whole process raises for the black community some very serious questions: Do we believe that we can make progress adopting the very values and concepts that have brutalized us? Do we believe that we can make progress by abandoning the very values and concepts that have undergirded the all too limited progress we have made to date? Are we to become the thing we hate?

Index